To b

HOW TO KILL A DRAGON

HOW TO KILL A DRAGON

ASPECTS OF INDO-EUROPEAN POETICS

Calvert Watkins

New York Oxford
OXFORD UNIVERSITY PRESS

1995

Oxford University Press

Oxford New York
Athens Auckland Bangkok Bombay
Calcutta Cape Town Dar es Salaam Delhi
Florence Hong Kong Istanbul Karachi
Kuala Lumpur Madras Madrid Melbourne
Taipei Tokyo Toronto

and associated companies in
Berlin Ibadan

Published by Oxford University Press, Inc.,
200 Madison Avenue, New York, New York 10016

Library of Congress Cataloging-in-Publication Data
Watkins, Calvert.
How to kill a dragon : aspects of Indo-European poetics / Calvert Watkins.
p. cm.
Includes bibliographical references and index.
ISBN 0-19-508595-7
1. Indo-European philology. 2. Poetics. 3. Comparative linguistics. I. Title.
P569.W38 1995
809—dc20 95-20945

1 3 5 7 9 8 6 4 2

Printed in the United States of America
on acid-free paper

For Stephanie

sociai karai

ϝιοστεφανοι αφροδιται

PREFACE

This book is conceived as both an introduction to, and an original contribution to, *comparative Indo-European poetics.* Comparative Indo-European poetics may be defined as a linguistic approach—both historical and theoretical, both genetic and typological, both diachronic and synchronic—to the form, nature, and function of poetic language and archaic literature among a variety of ancient Indo-European peoples. These societies spoke related languages, derived from a common ancestral tongue, and occupied then and now most of the territory from the western isles of Europe to the northern half of the Indian subcontinent.

"Philology is the art of reading slowly." My methodology throughout has been a combination of extremely close reading of text passages in the original—all text passages are translated as well—with the traditional Comparative Method. It is my claim that what may be legitimately if tendentiously termed the "genetic intertextuality" of all the versions of certain particular formulas and themes, varying in time, place and language, constitutes a background without which one cannot fully apprehend, understand and appreciate the traditional elements in a given poetic text in an early Indo-European language. In this sense we may speak of a genetic Indo-European comparative literature.

The work consists of seven parts and 59 chapters. These develop first the subtitle (Aspects of Indo-European Poetics) and then the title (How to kill a dragon) of the whole work. Chapters 1-4 of part I set the stage and background for the approach, the comparative method, explore the Saussurian notions of synchrony and diachrony, and locate the various Indo-European traditions in time and space as well as genre. Chapters 5-6 develop the reconstructible ideology of the spoken word in Indo-European society, its perceived ability to produce an effect on the real world (the "truth formulation"), its perseveration across time, and its extraordinary specificity.

Chapters 7-11 of part II present case studies and selected text analyses from Greek, Indic, Celtic, Italic, and Anatolian: their form of verbal art. Chapters 12-16 then present analyses of inherited phrasal formulas (in the sense of contemporary theory of oral literature), whole noun and verb phrases which are preserved in more than one tradition, inherited stylistic figures, and common traditions of obscurantism and hidden meaning in Vedic and other languages.

Part III (chapters 17-26) explores and argues for the Indo-European antiquity of a liturgical style intermediate between prose and the quantitative Indo-European metrical verse of the Greek and Indic type. I examine this strophic style in some of our oldest monuments of verbal art in liturgy and prayer from Ireland to India, including the central Indo-European royal consecration rite which is the *Aśvamedha* or Horse-sacrifice.

Parts IV-VII, the remainder of the book, set forth the evidence for a Common Indo-European formula expressing the central act of an inherited theme, the serpent or dragon-slaying myth. The 'signature' formula for the myth of the divine hero who slays the serpent recurs *in the same linguistic form* (derivatives of the IE root *g^{w}*hen-*, from Greek φόνος to English *bane*) in texts from the Rig Veda (*áhann áhim* 'he slew the serpent') through Old and Middle Iranian holy books, Hittite myth, Greek epic and lyric, Celtic and Germanic epic and saga down to Armenian oral folk epic of the last century. This formula shapes the narration of 'heroic' killing or overcoming of adversaries over the Indo-European world for millennia. The formula is the vehicle for the central theme of a proto-text, a central part of the symbolic culture of the speakers of Proto-Indo-European itself. The variations rung on this formula constitute a virtually limitless repository of literary expression in archaic and preliterate Indo-European societies, and their careful study can cast light in unexpected places, and bring together under a single explanation a variety of seemingly unrelated, unconnected text passages in a number of different but related languages. The formula is a precious and precise tool for genetic as well as typological investigation in the study of literature and literary theory. The fact is perhaps well-known to Indo-Europeanists; it is clearly less so to philologists, historians of literature, and literary critics.

Part IV treats the Basic Formula (as I term it, after Renou) and its variants in the narration of the serpent slaying myth, in Indic, Iranian and Hittite (chapters 27-35), Greek (36-42), and Germanic (43-44). Part V (44-48) explores some dragons and dragon-slayers of probable Indo-European antiquity, involving comparison of Old Irish, Hittite, Greek, Indic, and Iranian. Some similarities of Greek and other monsters are genetic in nature, while others are due to contact and diffusion.

Part VI (49-55) is entitled From Myth to Epic, and is concerned primarily with the interpretation of Greek text passages from Homer to Lysias in which the hero's adversary is not a mythical monster but another hero. The final part VII (56-59), entitled From Myth to Charm, deals with the application of the Basic Formula to the medicine of incantation in a variety of Indo-European traditions (including Hittite), and by adducing new data and different methodology is able to vindicate the controversial claims asserted already in the mid-19th century by Adalbert Kuhn, the "founder" of Indo-European poetics.

Poetics is the study of what makes a verbal message a work of art, in Jakobson's phrase, and Indo-European poetics, both diachronic and synchronic, is a window onto ancient verbal art. My goal has been to shed some new and different light on just what it is that makes the reading of these ancient texts worthwhile.

* * *

It is a pleasant duty to acknowledge my debt and express my profound thanks to the many individuals and corporate bodies which have given me intellectual, material, and spiritual support during the long preparation of this book.

First, to the National Endowment for the Humanities and the John Simon Guggenheim Memorial Foundation for fellowships during two sabbatical years, and to the Loeb Classical Library Foundation, the Department of the Classics and the Clark

Fund of Harvard University for grants toward the preparation of the manuscript;

Then to the many students or former students who typed the successive versions: Mark Hale, Brian Krostenko, Elizabeth Baer; to Bert Vaux for font composition; to John O'Neil for expert technical advice and support; and primarily to Steve Peter, who did the lion's share of typing, font composition and word processing, and who carried to completion the daunting task of preparation of the entire final camera-ready copy;

To the outside reader for Oxford University Press for his keen eye, and to Joshua Katz and Ben Fortson, who copy-edited the entire manuscript, and whose stylistic sense and philological acumen saved me from many blunders; to Ben Fortson for indispensable aid in typing indexes and bibliography; and to Nancy Hoagland of Oxford University Press for her gracious and sympathetic professionalism;

To several colleagues at Harvard and elsewhere who read the manuscript for their particular areas of competence: Joseph Harris for Germanic, Kim McCone for Irish, James Russell for Armenian, Richard Thomas for Latin and Italic, Gregory Nagy and Emily Vermeule for Greek. To four scholars, all sometime associate professors at Harvard, I am particularly indebted for their contributions: Hayden Pelliccia and Ian Rutherford in Greek, John Carey in Celtic, and Mark Hale in Linguistics. They will know what I mean. Finally, I am most grateful to P. Oktor Skjærvø, and not only for his Iranian expertise, from which I of course profited greatly; for he read and copy-edited the entire manuscript, and whatever clarity the reader finds will often have to be attributed to him.

One name still remains to be mentioned, that of my wife Stephanie Jamison. The book would simply not exist without her inspiration, her knowledge, and her judgment, over these many years. I dedicate this book to her in the hope that she will receive it as a *Bone-house*, with Seamus Heaney, and *Come back past / philology and kennings, / re-enter memory / where the bone's lair / is a love-nest / in the grass.*

CONTENTS

ASPECTS OF INDO-EUROPEAN POETICS

I. The Field of Comparative Poetics: Introduction and Background

II. Case Studies

III. The Strophic Style: An Indo-European Poetic Form

HOW TO KILL A DRAGON IN INDO-EUROPEAN: A CONTRIBUTION TO THE THEORY OF THE FORMULA

IV.   The Basic Formula and Its Variants in the Narration of the Myth

V. Some Indo-European Dragons and Dragon-Slayers

VI. From Myth to Epic

VII. From Myth to Charm

ASPECTS OF
INDO-EUROPEAN POETICS

I

The field of comparative poetics: Introduction and background

1

The comparative method in linguistics and poetics

1. Synchrony and diachrony, typological and genetic comparison

INDO-EUROPEAN is the name that has been given since the early 19th century to the large and well-defined genetic family which includes most of the languages of Europe, past and present, and which extended geographically, before the colonization of the New World, from Iceland and Ireland in the west across Europe and Asia Minor—where Hittite was spoken—through Iran to the northern half of the Indian subcontinent.

A curious byproduct of the age of colonialism and mercantilism was the introduction of Sanskrit in the 18th century to European intellectuals long familiar with Latin, Greek, and the European languages of culture at the time: Romance, Germanic, and Slavic. The comparison of Sanskrit with the two classical languages revolutionized the perception of linguistic relationships.

In the year 1812 a young German named Franz Bopp (1791-1867) traveled to Paris to read Oriental languages. He stayed for four years, serenely unconcerned with the Napoleonic Wars, and in 1816 was published his book *On the Conjugation System of Sanskrit in Comparison with that of the Greek, Latin, Persian, and Germanic Languages*. Bopp was only 25 when the work appeared, but it marks the birth of the Comparative Method. Bopp was not the first to discover that Sanskrit was related to these other languages, the family we now term Indo-European, but he was the first to establish comparison on a systematic basis as an autonomous science to explain the forms of one language by those of another.

As emphasized in the classical description (1925) of the Comparative Method by the greatest Indo-Europeanist of his age, the French scholar Antoine Meillet (1866-1936), there are two kinds of linguistic comparison, equally legitimate but with two distinct goals. The first is TYPOLOGICAL comparison, and its goal is the establishment of universal characteristics or universal laws; this is the ordinary sense of the term 'comparative' in comparative literature, comparative anatomy, or comparative law. But the other type is GENETIC comparison, and its goal is history; that is the ordinary sense of the term comparative linguistics. The same method is in principle perfectly applicable to other disciplines as well. Genetic comparative anatomy is a part of evolutionary—historical—biology. There exists a genetic comparative law, however rudimentary, associated with particular related peoples and cultures. The present work as a whole can be taken as an argument for the existence of a real genetic comparative literature. In all cases it is the genetic model that I will refer to as the Comparative Method in historical linguistics.

The Comparative Method is not very complicated, yet it is one of the most powerful theories of human language put forth so far and the theory that has stood the test of time the longest. Put simply, the comparatist has one fact and one hypothesis. The one fact is that certain languages show similarities which are so numerous and so precise that they cannot be attributed to chance, and which are such that they cannot be explained as borrowings from one language into another or as universal or quasi-universal features of many or all human languages. The comparatist's one hypothesis, then, is that these resemblances among certain languages must be the result of their development from a common original language.

Certain similarities may be accidental, like Latin *deu-s*, Greek *theó-s*, both 'god', and Nahuatl (Aztec) *teo-tl* 'sacred' (the hyphen separates the case marker at the end of each). They may reflect elemental similarities: the Greek stem *pneu-* 'breathe, blow' is virtually identical to the verb *pniw-* 'breathe' of the Klamath of Oregon, and the imitative phrase I learned from my father for the call of the 'hoot owl' (actually the great horned owl, *Bubo virginianus*), *I-cook-for-myself-who-cooks-for-you-all*, is nearly the same in its last five syllables as the Swampy (Woodland) Cree word for the same bird, *ko·hko·hkaho·w* (Siebert 1967:18). Both pairs imitate the physiological gesture (blowing [*pu-*] through the nose [*-n-*]) or the sound of the bird. Finally, languages commonly borrow words and their features from each other in a whole gamut of ways ranging from casual contact to systematic learned coinages of the kind that English makes from Latin and Greek. But where all these possibilities to account for the similarities must be excluded, we have a historical conclusion: the similarities are said to be *genetic* in character, and the languages are spoken of as *related* or *cognate*. The comparatist assumes *genetic filiation* of the languages, in other words, descent from a *common ancestor*, often termed a *proto-language*, which no longer exists. The standard model to display this relation remains the *family tree* diagram.

Wherever the comparative method is carried to a successful conclusion it leads to the restoration of an "original", arbitrarily "initial", language, i.e. the proto-language. We speak of this as *reconstruction.* Reconstructed, and thus not directly attested linguistic features—sounds, forms, words and the like—are conventionally preceded by an asterisk in historical linguistic usage, e.g. the Proto-Indo-European verb form *g^{wh}*en-ti* 'slays, smites' and the Proto-Algonquian noun form **ko·hko·hkaho·wa* 'great horned owl'. The systematic investigation of the resemblances among these languages by the comparative method enables us to reconstruct the principal features of the grammar and the lexicon of this proto-language. The reconstruction, in turn, provides a starting point for describing the history of the individually attested daughter languages—which is the ultimate goal of historical linguistics.

The technique by which reconstruction works consists of *equations* of linguistic forms between languages, from which we may deduce rules of correspondence. These operate on all levels of grammar, the meaningless as well as the meaningful, sound as well as form. The key word is *systematicity* or regularity.

We can, for example, state it as a rule that the *p* and the *d* of the Greek stem *pod-* 'foot' will correspond to the *f* and *t* of English *foot*. That these rules work is demonstrated by the comparison and equation of Greek *pezd-(is)* (πέζις) with its English translation and cognate *(bull)fist*, a kind of puffball, and the comparison and equation of Greek *pord-(ē)* (πορδή) with its English translation and cognate *fart*. The reconstructed Proto-Indo-European roots for these three words, **ped-/*pod-*, **pezd-/*pozd-* and **perd-/*pord-* can be viewed as just a shorthand for the sets of rules of correspondence among the Greek, English, and all other cognates. But the stronger claim, in spite of all the cautionary hedges we may put up, is that these reconstructions are a real model, constructed to the best of our ability, of how we think certain people talked at a remote period before recorded history—before the human race had invented the art of writing.

Let us take as our starting point the simplest possible model of comparative historical linguistics, of genetic filiation as determined by the application of the Comparative Method. Two languages, A and B, exhibit systematic similarities which cannot be attributed to borrowing nor to universals nor to chance. The systematic similarities can be accounted for only by the postulation of an original common language O, the ancestor of A and B, as modeled in Figure 1:

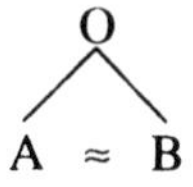

Figure 1

The description of O is its grammar and lexicon, i.e. its 'dictionary'. The task of the historical linguist is both to describe O (by reconstruction) and, more importantly, to show how it is possible to get from O to A and from O to B.

Now, in favorable circumstances the use of languages A and B for artistic purposes, which we will designate POETIC LANGUAGES A′ and B′, may also exhibit systematic similarities which are not attributable to borrowing, universality, or chance. The only explanation of the Comparative Method is again a common "original": the use of O itself for artistic purposes, POETIC LANGUAGE O′, as in Figure 2:

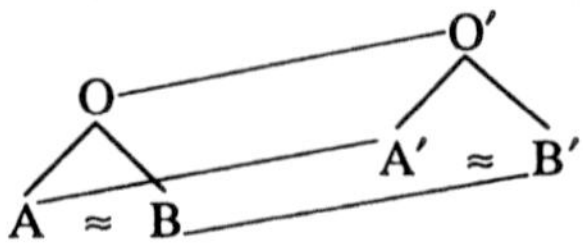

Figure 2

The description of O′ is its poetic grammar and its poetic repertory.

Put as simply as possible, linguistics is the scientific study of language, and poetics is the scientific study of "artistic" language. In a famous and influential phrase of Roman Jakobson (1896-1982), 'poetics deals primarily with the question, *what makes a verbal message a work of art?*' (1981:18, originally published 1960).

Linguistics (and epistemology) owes to Ferdinand de Saussure (1857-1913) the distinction between synchrony and diachrony, between the synchronic study of phenomena (such as linguistic structures) at a particular point in time without reference to history and the diachronic study of phenomena (such as linguistic structures) as they move across or through time. It can be seen that it is synchronic comparison which leads to the perception of universals, the properties of all human languages, at any time and place, whereas diachronic comparison leads to history. Yet the "opposition" of the synchronic to the diachronic plane or axis resolves itself in the nature of the object, language. Synchrony is concerned with how all languages are the same, whereas diachrony is concerned with how all languages are different; every human language combines both properties, universal and particular.

Let us return to our model in Figure 2, the reconstruction of a poetic language. The task of the linguist in this model is much more complex than in Figure 1. It is twofold: first to describe O and O′, the reconstructed proto-language and the reconstructed poetic proto-language, and second to show how it is possible to get from O to A and O to B, and from O′ to A′ and O′ to B′. These are diachronic concerns. But the linguist's task is also to show the relation of language A to poetic language A′, B to B′, and O to O′. These are synchronic concerns.

Poetic language, poetic grammar, and poetic inventory may be approached purely synchronically (typologically), with the goal of discovering universals; but they may also be studied with an eye to history, not just social but genetic, evolutionary history. The two are combined in the field of COMPARATIVE INDO-EUROPEAN POETICS, which is the concern of the present work. Comparative Indo-European poetics may be defined as a linguistic approach to the form, nature, and function of poetic language and archaic literature among a variety of ancient Indo-European peoples. This linguistic approach can and must be both diachronic and synchronic, both historical and descriptive-theoretical, both genetic and typological. Comparative Indo-European historical linguistics in practice combines the diachronic and the synchronic approach, and great comparatists like Ferdinand de Saussure, Berthold Delbrück (1842-1922), Jacob Wackernagel (1852-1938), and Emile Benveniste (1902-1976) moved freely and effortlessly between synchrony and diachrony. In my own way I have tried to follow their model.

2. Culture history and linguistic reconstruction

A language necessarily implies a society, a speech community, and a culture, and a proto-language equally necessarily implies a 'proto-culture', that is, the culture of the users of the proto-language. In terms of our model we can also reinterpret O′, A′, B′ as representing *any* linguistically relevant aspect of the proto-culture, as for example law: A′ and B′ would be cognate legal insitutions in two societies speaking cognate languages A and B, and O′ would be the legal system reconstructible for the society speaking proto-language O. The methods of historical linguistics provide critically important tools for the culture historian concerned with the reconstruction of ancient ways of life as well as ancient forms of speech. Poetic language is of course only one of many registers available to the members of a given society.

Language is linked to culture in a complex fashion: it is at once the expression of culture and a part of it. And it is in the first instance the lexicon of the language or proto-language which affords an effective way—though not the only one—to approach or access the culture of its speakers. Indo-Europeanists saw very early that the agreements in vocabulary among the various ancient languages attest significant features of a common ancestral culture. The same technique of reconstructing culture from the lexicon has been applied successfully to other, non-Indo-European, families as well.

To take a simple example, the word for 'dog' shows systematic similarities in many Indo-European languages:

	OIrish	Hittite	Greek	Vedic	Lith.	PIE
nominative	*cú*	*kuwaš*	*kuṓn*	*ś(u)vā́*	*šuõ*	* *ḱu̯ṓ*
accusative	*coin*	*kuwanan*	*kúna*	*śvā́nam*	*šùnį*	* *ḱu̯ónm̥*
genitive	*con*	*kunaš*	*kunós*	*śúnas*	*šuñs*	* *ḱunós*

From the cognate set we can reconstruct not only the Proto-Indo-European word for 'dog' but also the precise details of its declension. Yet note that we have not only reconstructed a word for 'dog', but we have postulated an item of the material culture of the speakers of Proto-Indo-European as well. The inference that the Indo-Europeans had dogs is obviously trivial, given the remote antiquity of the animal's domestication. A more telling example, however, is an old technical term for an item of chariot harness, the 'reins' held by the charioteer. We find the word in only two traditions, Old Irish and Greek; but in both the one term is specifically linked to charioteering in the earliest texts. We find in Homeric Greek of the 8th century *hēníai* (ἡνίαι) 'reins' and *hēníokhos* (ἡνίοχος) 'charioteer', literally 'reins-holder', which faithfully continue the forms of the same words 500 years earlier in the Bronze Age, Mycenean Greek *anija* 'reins' and *anijoko* 'charioteer, reins-holder'. Their only cognate is in Old Irish of the 8th century A.D., the plural *éisi* or *éise* 'reins', held in the hand of the charioteer in the epic *Táin Bó Cúailnge*. We can reconstruct an Indo-European preform **ansii̯o/ā-*, earlier **$h_2$ans-ii̯o/ah_2-*.[1] As a technical term in chariotry

1. Thus correct the reconstruction given in Liddell-Scott-Jones, Greek-English Lexicon. The attested Mycenean instrumental plural *anijapi* 'with the reins' can even be equated with the attested Old Irish

and the harnessing of the horse it is certainly a non-trivial reconstruction for the material culture of the Proto-Indo-Europeans.

Non-material culture, what anthropologists now term symbolic culture, is equally amenable to reconstruction. We can reconstruct with certainty an Indo-European word for 'god', *_deiu̯ós_, from Irish _dé_, Latin _deus_, Sanskrit _devás_, etc.; it is a derivative of an older root noun *_di̯eu-_ (Hittite _šiu-n-_ 'god'). This form figures as well in the two-part reconstructible name of the chief deity of the Indo-European pantheon, *_di̯eu- ph_$_2$_ter-_. The second element is the general Indo-European word for 'father', not in the sense of 'parent' or 'sire', but with the meaning of the adult male who is head of the household, Latin _pater familias_. He is the 'father god': for the Indo-Europeans the society of the gods was conceived in the image of their own society. The reconstruction *_di̯eu- ph_$_2$_ter-_ recurs not only in Latin _Iuppiter_, Greek _Zeũ páter_, and Vedic _Díauṣ pítar_, but also in Luvian _Tatiš Tiwaz_ 'father _Diw-at-_' and Hittite _Attaš Šiuš_ 'father _Sius_' (written with Sumerograms as ᴰUTU-_uš_). Old Irish has its special contribution to make here as well: the pagan deity known as the _Dagdae_ (_in Dagdae_, literally 'the good-god', always with the article) has the epithet _Oll-athair_ 'great-father', 'super-father'. We can reconstruct a whole Celtic phrase, *_sindos dago-_ **_deiwos_** _ollo-_[**_p_**]**_atīr_**. The Indo-European semantics "father god" (in boldface) is actually better preserved in Old Irish and in Hittite than it is in Greek or Latin with their personalized "father Zeus/Jove". The definite article (older demonstrative) of Irish _in Dagdae_ adds its own archaic modality, like the Hittite god _Šiuš-šummiš_ 'our own God'.

Now another lexical set relating to an aspect of symbolic culture in the semantic realm of power or authority is the group of words including Vedic _ásura-_ and Avestan _ahura-_ 'lord' (usually divinized), Hittite _ḫaššu-_ 'king', and the group of Germanic deities known in Old Norse as the _Æsir_, Germanic *_ansuz_. These are respectively reconstructed as *_h_$_2$_n̥s-u-ró-_, *_h_$_2$_n̥s-ú-_, and *_h_$_2$_ó/áns-u-_.[2]

Most scholars today assume these words for 'king, lord, god' are related to the Hittite verb _ḫāš-/ḫašš-_ 'beget, engender, produce', from *_h_$_2$_o/ans-_. Ferdinand Sommer as early as 1922 noted the parallelism of Hittite _ḫāš-/ḫašš-_ 'engender' beside _ḫaššu-_ 'king' from a single root, and the family of English _kin_ etc. beside the family of English _king_ (Germanic *_kuningaz_) from another single IE root *_ĝenh_$_1$_-_, also meaning 'engender'. The ruler was looked upon as the symbolic generator of his subjects; the notion is still with us in the metaphor 'father of his country', translating the even clearer Latin figure _pater patriae_.

Other Indo-European words for 'king' make reference to other semantic aspects of royalty and kingship. The old root noun *_h_$_3$_rēĝ-_ is found only in the extreme west (Latin _rēx_, Irish _rí_) and extreme east (Vedic _rā́j-_, Avestan _bərəzi-rāz-_ 'ruling on high').[3] The noun clearly belongs with Greek ὀρέγω 'stretch out', Latin _regō_ 'rule', Vedic _raj-_ 'stretch out straight', and a whole set of forms built on the metaphor 'straight, right' and 'rule, ruler, regulate'. The Old Avestan derivative _rāzarə̄_ is

---

dative plural _ésib_, down to the very case ending. We can reconstruct *_ansii̯ābhi_, earlier *_h_$_2$_ans-ii̯ah_$_2$ _-bhi-_, with the same precision as in the word for 'dog'.

2. For the nasal and other details see most recently the dictionaries of Puhvel, Tischler, Mayrhofer, and Lehmann, with references.

3. Or 'commanding aloud' (Kellens 1974).

variously translated as 'ordinance' (Bartholomae), 'order' (Kellens), even 'prayer' (Humbach-Elfenbein-Skjærvø). We may observe yet another metaphor for guidance or governance in Y. 50.6 *raiϑīm stōi mahiiā rāzə̄ṇg* '(we should instruct Zarathustra) to serve as charioteer of my ordinance/prayer'. The metaphor of the ruler as driver, charioteer recurs in the Old Irish text *Audacht Morainn* §22 and frequently in the Rigveda.

This metaphor permits us to return to our words for 'ruler', 'lord', 'king' in Vedic *ásura-*, Germanic **ansuz*, Hittite *ḫaššu-*, and to propose they may be related to the technical term for the chariot driver's means of guiding and controlling his horses: the 'reins', Greek and Irish **ans-io-* from the same Indo-European root *h_2*n̥s-* or *h_2*ans-*, which we discussed above. The designation of the reins rests squarely on a metaphor: the "reins" are the "rulers". It is just the inverse of the metaphor which calls the ruler "charioteer", "helmsman".

In our model of the reconstruction of a poetic language (Figure 2), two cognate poetic languages, A′ and B′, form the base of the triangle, and its apex is the reconstructed poetic proto-language O′. As we stated, the description of this poetic language O′ is its poetic grammar and repertory. The notion of poetic grammar and its analogues to the different components of ordinary grammar such as phonology and syntax will be examined in greater detail in chap. 3. Let us here only note that on a higher level of grammar, where meaning is pertinent, we find the syntactic, semantic, and pragmatic components. This is the domain of FORMULAS, set phrases which are the vehicles of THEMES. The totality of themes may be thought of as the culture of the given society.

The comparison of characteristic formulas in various Indo-European languages and societies permits their reconstruction, sometimes as far back as the original common language and society. The formulas tend to make reference to culturally significant features—'something that matters'—and it is this which accounts for their repetition and long-term preservation. The phrase *goods and chattels* is an example of a formula in English today, fixed in the order of its constituents and pragmatically restricted in deployment and distribution. A glance at The New English Dictionary shows the phrase attested in that form and in that fixed order since the early 16th century and a good century earlier in the form *good(e)s and cattel(s)*. The earliest citation is 1418, but we may safely presume the phrase is much older. It appears to be a translation into English of an Anglo-Latin legal phrase (NED s.v. *cattle*) designating non-moveable and moveable wealth which is attested as *bonorum aliorum sive cattalorum* in the pre-Norman, 11th-century Laws of Edward the Confessor. The coinage *cattala* is from Late Latin *cap(i)tale*, presumably transmitted through Northern or Norman French, but before the Conquest.

This formula is a MERISM, a two-part figure which makes reference to the totality of a single higher concept, as will be shown in chap. 3: *goods* and *chattels*, non-moveable and moveable wealth, together designate all wealth. In its present form this formula is nearly a thousand years old in English. Yet its history may be projected even further back, with the aid of the comparative method. We find a semantically identical formula in Homeric Greek nearlytwo thousand years earlier: the phrase κειμήλιά τε πρόβασίν τε (*Od.* 2.75), where Telemachus complains of the suitors devouring his 'riches which lie and riches which move', the totality of his wealth. For other parallels see Watkins 1979a and 1992a.

In its semantics and as the expression of a cultural theme the formula *goods and chattels* goes all the way back to Indo-European, even if the particular verbal expression, the wording of the phrase itself, does not. Lexical renewal of one or more components of a formula does not affect its semantic integrity nor its historical continuity. We have a renewal of the *signifiant*, the "signifier", while the *signifié*, the "thing signified", remains intact. In cases where we can know, as here, language is almost incredibly persistent, and in this work as a whole it is my goal to emphasize the longevity and specificity of verbal tradition and the persistence of specific verbal traditions, whether in structures of the lexicon, of syntax, or of style.

The collection of such utterances, such formulaic phrases, is part of the poetic repertory of the individual daughter languages, and, where reconstructible, of the proto-language itself. Individual lexical items or sets of these which constitute formulaic phrases are not the only entities amenable to reconstruction. On the basis of similarities—samenesses—we reconstruct language. But it happens that certain texts themselves in some of these cognate languages, or text fragments, exhibit the sort of similarity to suggest that they are genetically related. These texts are in some sense the same. Exploration of what might be termed the "genetic intertextuality" of these variants casts much light on the meaning of the ancient texts themselves; on the basis of the samenesses we may in privileged cases reconstruct proto-texts or text fragments. These too are part of the poetic repertory of the poetic proto-language O′.

Formulas may also function to encapsulate entire myths and other narratives, and the whole of Part Two of the present work is devoted to the 'signature' formula of the Indo-European dragon-slaying myth, the endlessly repeated, varied or invariant narration of the hero slaying the serpent. We will begin in the Rigveda, with the phonetically and syntactically marked phrase *áhann áhim* 'he/you SLEW the SERPENT'. Following the French Indologist Louis Renou (1896-1966) we will term this phrase the BASIC FORMULA. As we shall see, it recurs in texts from the Vedas in India through Old and Middle Iranian holy books, Hittite myth, Greek epic and lyric, Celtic and Germanic epic and saga, down to Armenian oral folk epic of the last century. This formula, typically with a reflex of the same Indo-European verb root **g^{w}hen-* (Vedic *han-*, Avestan *jan-*, Hittite *kuen-*, Greek πεφν-/ φον-, Old Irish *gon-*, English *bane*), shapes the narration of 'heroic' killing or overcoming of adversaries over the Indo-European world for millennia. There can be no doubt that the formula is the vehicle of the central theme of a proto-text, a central part of the symbolic culture of the speakers of Proto-Indo-European.

The formula appears in texts of a variety of genres from cultic hymn and mythological narrative, epic and heroic legend, to spells and incantations of black and white magic. The variations rung on this basic formula constitute a virtually limitless repository of artistic verbal expression in archaic and preliterate Indo-European societies. Their careful study can cast light in unexpected places and bring together under a single linguistic explanation a variety of seemingly unrelated, unconnected text passages in a number of different but related languages. Things that do not make sense synchronically often do make sense diachronically, and, just as in language, the key may lie in a "singular detail" (Meillet 1925:3), like the use of a derivative of the root *g^{w}hen-*. This linguistic approach to the poetics of these ancient texts in related ancient languages I have, I believe legitimately if somewhat tendentiously, termed genetic intertextuality. The method as a whole I have called elsewhere (1989)—rehabilitating an old-fashioned term by insisting on its literal meaning—the new comparative philology.

It should be unnecessary to point out explicitly that the approach to these ancient Indo-European texts I am advocating here is intended only as a supplement or complement to, not a substitute for, the ordinary standard approaches to literary texts in these same languages through literary history, philology, or criticism. The Greek poet Pindar was a historical personage, who practiced his craft and earned his livelihood commemorating in song the accomplishments and virtues of other contemporary personages of a specific historical time and place, Greece and Sicily of the 5th century B.C. Pindar was a product of his own times. But it can only increase our awe before his genius to know that in some of his formulas and themes, some of his genres and subgenres, some of his training and his role in society, he was still part of a cultural tradition, verbally expressed, which reached back thousands of years. It can by the same token only enhance our wonder at Pindar's art to hear his elemental words of water, gold, and fire echoing and reverberating from Celtic ringforts to Indic ritual enclosures:

> ἄριστον μὲν ὕδωρ, ὁ δὲ χρυσὸς αἰθόμενον πῦρ
> ἅτε διαπρέπει νυκτὶ μεγάνορος ἔξοχα πλούτου
>
> Best is water, but gold like burning fire
> by night shines out beyond all lordly wealth.

2

Sketch for a history of Indo-European poetics

The study of what we now term Indo-European poetics has hitherto proceeded in three distinct streams, each with its own historical sequence and sometimes greater, sometimes lesser independence from the other two. These may be termed (1) *formulaics*, (2) *metrics*, and (3) *stylistics*. Formulaics—the oldest—examines and compares lexically and semantically cognate or closely similar phrases in cognate languages, like Homeric Greek ὠκέες ἵπποι 'swift horses', Young Avestan *aspåŋhō* . . . *āsauuō* 'id.', and Vedic *áśvās* . . . *āśávaḥ* 'id.', securely reconstructible in root, suffix, and ending as **h₁ōḱ-éu̯-es h₁éḱu̯-ōs*, in either order. Metrics examines and compares similar versification systems, like the mostly isosyllabic, quantitative, bi- or tricolic verse line grouped into strophes in both Vedic and Greek lyric poetry. Stylistics examines and compares all the other linguistic devices, figures, and other recurrent phonological, morphological, and syntactic variables which may be in play in verbal art in cognate languages.

I treat these three topics separately and in the order given, since their histories are largely independent. A very detailed study of the history of Indo-European poetics, with the emphasis on formulaic comparisons, may be found in Schmitt 1967, the author's dissertation under Paul Thieme. Schmitt's impulse for producing this magnum opus was evidently his discovery six years before of the formula *mṛtyúm tar-* 'overcome death' in the Atharvaveda (quoted in chap. 40), which provided a Vedic phrasal counterpart to the Greek compound νέκ-ταρ, the 'nẹctar' which 'overcomes death', in Thieme's etymology to the root of Latin *nex* 'death' and Vedic *tar-* 'overcome'. See Thieme 1952 and Schmitt 1961 (reprinted in 1968:324) and 1967:190. Many of the classic studies are reprinted in Schmitt 1968; these will be so signaled where mentioned. Other general discussions of the issue may be found in Meid 1978 and Campanile 1987.

1. Formulaics

Rigvedic *ákṣiti śrávaḥ* (1.40.4b, 8.103.5b, 9.66.7c), *śrávaḥ* . . . *ákṣitam* (1.9.7bc) and

Homeric κλέος ἄφθιτον (*Il.* 9.413) all mean 'imperishable fame'. The two phrases, Vedic and Greek, were equated by Adalbert Kuhn as early as 1853, almost *en passant*, in an article dealing with the nasal presents in the same two languages.[1] Kuhn's innovation was a simple one, but one destined to have far-reaching consequences. Instead of making an etymological equation of two words from cognate languages, he equated two bipartite noun phrases of noun plus adjective, both meaning 'imperishable fame'. The comparability extended beyond the simple words to their suffixal constituents *śrav-as- a-kṣi-ta-m*, κλεϝ-εσ- ἀ-φθι-το-ν.[2] What Kuhn had done was to equate two set or fixed phrases between two languages, which later theory would term *formulas*. Thus in M. L. West's somewhat lyrical words (1988a:152), 'With that famous equation of a Rig-Vedic with a Homeric formula . . . Kuhn in 1853 opened the door to a new path in the comparative philologist's garden of delights.' The equation has itself given given rise to a considerable literature, notably Schmitt 1967:1-102 and Nagy 1974; it is discussed at length with further references and the equation vindicated in chap. 15.

Kuhn made further investigations directly concerned with proving a common inherited Indo-European poetics and poetry, basing himself on comparison of the charms and incantations of Atharvavedic white and black magic with those of Medieval and contemporary Germanic folklore. While he was only moderately successful at demonstrating these to posterity, and some of his comparisons rest only on elementary parallels and are therefore to be rejected, a more sophisticated methodology can and has justified the essential correctness of his instincts and many of his insights. They are examined in detail in part VII below. In particular, Kuhn's attention and sensitivity to the comparability of genre was a notable step forward, even if later work has shown that comparable structural sets may also sometimes occur in radically different genres.

In another article in the same year 1853 Kuhn had, again in passing, noted the similarity of the Vedic phrase *iṣiréṇa mánasā*, more or less 'with eager mind' (RV 8.48.7), and its exact Homeric cognate ἱερὸν μένος in the set tag phrase ἱερὸν μένος (Ἀλκινόοιο etc.) 'holy spirit/strength (of Alkinoos)', narratologically equivalent to the proper name alone. The Belgian Iranist Jacques Duchesne-Guillemin renewed the discussion of this still-enigmatic pair in 1937, as did Antonino Pagliaro in an essay first published in 1947/48 and subsequently reprinted (see Schmitt 1967:28, n. 176). The relevance of the formula to the semantic notion of the 'sacred' was touched on by Benveniste 1969:196, perhaps over-hastily. We must recognize that the semantics and pragmatics of the original inherited phrase antedate its attested use in both the Rigveda and Homer. Cf. also Schmitt 1973.

With the contributions of Kuhn, 'the concept of an Indo-European poetic lan-

1. KZ 2.467. The journal, *Zeitschrift für Vergleichende Sprachforschung*, was founded by Kuhn only the previous year, and for the first hundred volumes of its existence was so abbreviated, for "Kuhns Zeitschrift". With volume 101 (1988) it became *Historische Sprachforschung* (HS).

2. The identity of the equation could be captured by a reconstruction reducing each of the two to the same common prototype. Historically the first reconstruction in Indo-European studies, with precisely the declared aim of capturing the common prototype underlying the feminine participles Greek -ουσα and Indic *-antī*, had been made by August Schleicher only the year before Kuhn's article, in the preface to Schleicher 1852.

guage was beginning to emerge' (West 1988a:152). Other scholars added to the corpus of phraseological equations among cognate Indo-European languages, which might with some confidence be attributed to the repertoire of the proto-language itself. A metaphorical expression for the Indo-European poet and his craft was early identified by the French Iranist James Darmesteter (1878) in an article significantly entitled 'A grammatical metaphor in Indo-European'. He compared the Avestan compound *vacas-tašti-* 'hymn, strophe', literally 'utterance-crafting', with Vedic *vácāṁsi āsā́ . . . takṣam* 'with my mouth I have crafted these words' and the Pindaric phrase ἐπέων . . . τέκτονες (*Pyth.* 3.113) 'crafters of words'. Methodologically, note that while the collocation has been claimed to be the 'central Indo-European poetic figure' (Schmitt 1967, 1968), and in all probability is of Indo-European date, it is not confined to Indo-European, for the same metaphor and a similar expression are found in contemporary Egyptian Arabic folk poetry, 'craftsman/fabricator of words' (Dwight Reynolds, p.c.). Virtually any technology can be exploited for such metaphorical purpose, such as weaving: archaic Old Irish *fáig ferb* 'he wove words' (*Amrae Choluimb Chille*), embellished by the borrowing of Latin *uerbum.*

A large number of these common formulaic figures, like κλέος ἄφθιτον and *śrávas . . . ákṣitam*, rest on equations between Vedic and Early Greek. Such is for example the expression of an apparent Indo-European tabu reported by the early Greek epic and gnomic poet Hesiod in his *Works and Days* 727, ὀρθὸς ὀμείχειν 'to urinate standing up', which C. R. Lanman in his additions to W. D. Whitney's translations of the Atharvaveda compared to Vedic *ūrdhvó mekṣyāmi* 'I will urinate standing up' (AV 7.10.2). Both pairs are identical in root, morphology, and syntax.[3]

Vedic represents only the Indic fork of the Indo-Iranian branch of the Indo-European family tree, with Greek another branch; schematically,

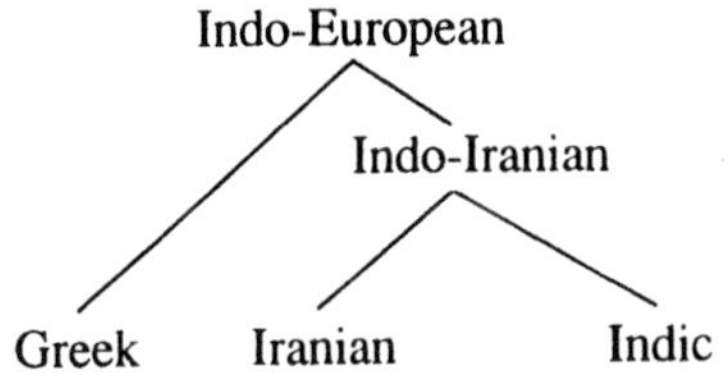

The closeness of the relation is marked by the shared node, the intermediary common language. There are far more lexical correspondences, words shared between Indic and Iranian than between either or both of these and Greek. It should therefore come as no surprise that Indic and Iranian as well share more formulaic phrases than either or both with Greek. Scholars were in fact slow to recognize and exploit this simple fact and principle, viz., the closer to the common proto-language, the greater the frequency of common phrasal retentions. The reason is probably the recentness (relative to Vedic and Greek) of the establishment of a soundly-based Older Iranian philology by Christian Bartholomae and the relative scarceness of the cultivation of Iranian studies relative to that of Sanskrit or the Classics.

3. One of the benefits of the comparison and reconstruction of formulas involving the phrasal combination of two or more words is their contribution to the study of Indo-European syntax, despite the pessimism of Schlerath 1992.

A small but well-chosen and ably commented selection of common Indo-Iranian phrases, the fruit of a lifetime's sporadic gleanings, was published by Emile Benveniste (1968) in the volume honoring his friend and collaborator Louis Renou. A much fuller and systematic collection, without comment or discussion, was presented in the same year by Bernfried Schlerath, in Konkordanz C of his *Vorarbeiten II* to an unfinished Avesta dictionary (1968:148-64; with valuable index of keywords 189-99). His findings are now systematically incorporated into Manfred Mayrhofer's etymological dictionaries of Old Indic (1956-1980, 1986-).

Schlerath's useful introduction (1968:viii-xv) specifically states as a methodological principle that only expressions or formulas with at least two etymologically related words in each language qualified for inclusion. This restriction is not valid, as we saw in the preceding section. Renewal of one, two, or more members of a formulaic syntagma, of one or more *signifiants*, under semantic identity—preservation of the *signifié*—is a perfectly normal and commonplace way for formulaic sequences to change over time, as I and Enrico Campanile and others have long insisted.[4] (See chap. 17 for examples and discussion.)

The most detailed collection of Indo-Iranian phrasal collocations is due to L. G. Gercenberg [Hertzenberg] 1972. He assembled nearly 350 two- or three-member phrasal collocations of cognates in Vedic (almost all Rigveda) and Avestan; his collections include comparisons outside Indo-Iranian where relevant. Each is provided with a syntactic and lexical reconstruction; only collocations involving pairs (or more) of etymologically related words are admitted. His sets are presented laconically, without comment or context, and could well be re-examined with profit. For a single example see chap. 12.

Other languages and traditions have made important contributions to the collection. A famous example first compared by Jacob Wackernagel in 1910 (reprinted in Schmitt 1968:30-33) is that of Avestan *pasu.vīra*, a dual dvandva compound 'cattle [and] men' and Umbrian *ueiro pequo* 'men [and] cattle', possibly showing the same archaic syntax. Comparable expressions from the other traditions like the Roman poet Ovid's *pecudesque virosque* (*Met.* 1.286) were subsequently added by others (see Schmitt 1967:16, 213 and chap. 17, this vol.). Note that this formula like *goods and chattels* is another *merism*, a two-part figure which makes reference to the totality of a single higher concept. *Cattle and men* together designate the totality of moveable wealth, wealth 'on the hoof', chattels. The same semantics underlies another paral phrase first noted by Albrecht Weber in 1873 (see Schmitt 1967:12) in Vedic *dvipáde* (*ca*) *cátuṣpade* (*ca*) '(both) two-footed (and) four-footed', Umbrian *dupursus peturpursus* 'two-footed, four-footed'. See on these Watkins 1979a.

A good example of the unfortunate consequences of Schlerath's restriction is his treatment of the Avestan pair *pasu-* 'cattle' and *nar-* 'man' as against *pasu-* and *vīra-* in the same meaning. His restriction leads him to ignore the Old Avestan *kamnānar-* 'having few men' and *kamnafšuua-* 'few cattle' (Y.46.2), astutely discussed by Benveniste 1968, 1969:1.49.

The collection of formulaic phrases common to two or more Indo-European poetic traditions has proceeded at a slow but steady pace for nearly a century and a

4. See most recently Campanile 1993 for a reaffirmation of our principle, with many examples.

half. See for example Kurke 1989, on the pouring (IE **ĝheu-*) of a poem or prayer like a libation in Vedic (*imā́ gíro . . . juhomi* 'I pour these songs' RV), Greek (εὐκταῖα . . . χέουσα 'pouring votive prayers' Aeschylus), and Latin (*fundere preces* Horace, Vergil). If the Latin examples of the Augustan age might reflect Greek influence, as she acknowledges (124, n. 24), one could also point to the Old Irish idiom *feraid fáilte* 'pours welcome' where Greek influence is not possible.

The collection is still ongoing. Recent acquisitions include the equation in 1992 by a graduate student in Classics at Harvard, Fred Porta, of Vedic *mahó ájmasya* '(Savitṛ the sun rules) the great path, way (of the horses of the sun's chariot)' (RV 4.53.4) with Greek μέγας ὄγμος 'the great path, way (of the horses of the moon's chariot)' (*Homeric Hymn to Selene* 32.11).[5] In the following year, 1993, Michael Weiss in his Cornell dissertation[6] argued convincingly that Latin *iūgis* 'everflowing', Greek ὑγιής 'healthy', Cypriote *uwais*(*e*) *zan* 'forever and ever', Gothic *ajuk-duþs* 'eternity', and Old Avestan *yauuaējī-* 'living forever' are all direct or indirect reflexes of an Indo-European collocation of *h_2*oi̯u-* 'lifetime, eternity' and *$g^{u}ih_3$- 'to live', manifested in a compound *h_2*i̯u*-$g^{u}ih_3$-. Continued study of all the Indo-European traditions can safely be expected to yield still more such equations. Thus the new Simonides fragments (IEG II^2 11.12) bring in the phrase ἅρμα δίκης 'chariot of Justice' the first cognate of Rigvedic *ṛtásya rátha* 'chariot of Truth' with its Old Irish thematic congeners (Watkins 1979b). Yet the concern of Indo-European poetics extends much further than just the accumulation of cognate phrases, whether formulaic or not in the technical sense (see immediately below) in the given tradition.

Formula and theme

The study of these inherited phrases in the various Indo-European traditions was fundamentally affected by the epoch-making work of Milman Parry in his Paris dissertations (1928a and 1928b).[7] Parry's work on Homeric phraseology and the technique of oral composition, largely influenced by his field work on the living epic tradition of Yugoslavia, showed that *formulas* functioned as the 'building blocks' of Homeric verse. His subsequent famous and influential, if now outdated, definition of the formula was 'a group of words which is regularly employed, under the same metrical conditions, to express a given essential idea' (Parry 1930 = A. Parry 1971:266-324). Parry's great contribution was the founding of a new genre in literary theory, termed by him 'oral poetry', even if neither 'orality' in the sense of non-literacy, nor 'poetry' in the sense of 'metrical', is a necessary condition. Later writers, notably Parry's

5. The equation is linguistically noteworthy in further anchoring the residual o-grade of a root in (post laryngeal) *a-*: *h_2*eĝ-* > *h_2*aĝ-* of ἄγω, *ájati* beside *h_2*oĝ-mo-* of ὄγμος, *ájma-*. Contrast Vedic *ájman-* : Latin *agmen*, which show either original e-grade, or more likely generalization of the root-form *ag-*. The equation of ὄγμος and *ájma-* is at least as old as Saussure's *Mémoire* of 1878. The Celtic divine name *Ogmios*, Old Irish *Ogma*, and the name of the writing system *ogam* are probably to be related. See McManus 1991.

6. Refined and developed as 'Life Everlasting', presented to the Twelfth East Coast Indo-European Conference, Cornell University, June 1993.

7. English translations in Parry 1971.

student and successor Albert Bates Lord with his influential 1960 work *The Singer of Tales*, and in selected papers reprinted in *Epic Song and Oral Tradition* (1991), have tended to replace 'oral' by 'oral-traditional', while others, like Gregory Nagy, prefer just 'traditional'.

Parry's theory as developed by Lord has been further significantly modified by the work of others on different traditions around the world, such as Finnegan 1970, 1977, Ivanov and Toporov 1974, Nagy 1974, Kiparsky 1976, and Opland 1983, to name only a few. See the several collections, introduction and bibliography of Foley 1981, 1985, 1986, 1987, 1988. One should mention also the work of J. Latacz (e.g., 1979) and his school, for example E. Visser 1988, with references.

The primary modifications of the notion of the formula were to de-emphasize the purely metrical as a condition *sine qua non*, and to place greater emphasis on the notion of theme (Parry's 'essential idea'). At the Ann Arbor Conference of 1974,[8] bringing to the question the insights of contemporary syntactic theory in a pioneering fashion, Paul Kiparsky felicitously termed the formula a 'ready-made surface structure'. At the same conference I termed the formula in traditional oral literature 'the verbal and grammatical device for encoding and transmitting a given theme or interaction of themes,' and five years later added 'That is to say that *theme* is the deep structure of formula'.[9] The point can stand today even if for some time I have been inclined to think that "deep" theme is not so very far from "surface" formula.

Another modification to Parry's definition has been to remove its restriction to 'a group of words', by recognizing that a single word may have true formulaic status. I argued this at length for Greek μῆνις 'wrath'—the very first word in the *Iliad*—for not just metrical but more important for thematic reasons (Watkins 1977). A similar view is expressed by G.S. Kirk in the preface to his Homer commentary (1985:xxiii): 'single words, even,' may evince 'formular status', 'because they can sometimes have an inherited tendency, not solely dictated by their length and metrical value, to a particular position in the verse.' Here the operative phrase, I would suggest, is 'inherited tendency'. The 'particular position in the verse' is subject to the caution expressed already by Nagy 1974:8 n. 24, that Parry's definition of the formula 'is suitable for a working definition, provided that the phrase "under the same metrical conditions" is not understood to mean "in the same position within the line".' The whole of Part Two of this work shows that the formulaic (or 'formular') status of derivatives of the root **g^{w}hen-* 'smite, slay' is precisely an 'inherited tendency' in all the ancient Indo-European language contextual nexuses—mythic, epic, or apotropaic charms—which continue it, regardless of language or verse-line.

Nowhere is the notion of the formula so important today as in its original locus, the Homeric poems. G.S. Kirk in the preface to his Homer commentary (1985:xxiii) writes further,

> the whole question of the formular, conventional or traditional component in the Homeric language is extremely important for the exact appreciation of any particular passage, and of course of the whole poem. Something of a reaction is detectable

8. Stolz and Shannon.
9. Collitz Lecture published in Watkins 1982; see further below.

> at present from the extreme claims and inconclusive statistics that proliferated after the *Milman Parry revolution* [emphasis mine - C.W.], but it remains true, nevertheless, that the deployment of a partly fixed phraseology is a fundamental aspect of Homer's style and technique—one that shaped his view of life, almost. One can as well ignore Homer's 'use of phrases' as an ordinary poet's 'use of words'.

The same recognition—if somewhat tardy, as he himself acknowledged—of the 'Milman Parry revolution' was well expressed by Ernst Risch in the preface to the second edition of his *Wortbildung der homerischen Sprache* (1974:v): 'Since the studies of Milman Parry (1928), which did not become known until far too late, even the phenomenon of epic poetry looks different.' Risch's first edition had appeared in 1937, 9 years after the publication of Parry 1928, but made no mention of it despite the review articles of such distinguished Homerists and linguists as Chantraine (1929) and Meillet (1929). Parry's work was duly signalled in the bibliography of Meillet's great *Aperçu d'une histoire de la langue grecque* from the 3rd edition of 1930 on.

If scholars have been slow to appreciate the 'Milman Parry revolution' in Homeric studies, they have been even slower to acknowledge its significance and implications for the study of most of the other ancient languages of the family. A notable exception is Kiparsky 1976, who was able to bring the hymns of the Rigveda into the Parry-Lord universe of discourse by showing the artificiality of the latter's insistence on composition in performance as a condition *sine qua non* for 'oral poetry'. The poetry and prose alike of the entire thousand-year Vedic period in India, roughly 1500-500 B.C., was composed orally, memorized, and transmitted orally; only afterwards did the art of writing spread from the West to the Indian subcontinent.

The 'formular, conventional or traditional component' (Kirk, supra) of the language of the Vedic hymns is just as marked and just as important as for the Homeric language, and the same observation is equally valid for early Iranian verse, for the prose—n.b.—narrative of Hittite and Anatolian myth, and to a lesser degree for the early poetic monuments of many, perhaps most later Indo-European traditions.

When in favorable circumstances we can assert that a given phrase or even word, is or was once formulaic (or 'formular') in its own tradition in the technical Parry sense, and when we can also assert that a phrase, or even word, cognate to the first in another tradition is also or was once formulaic in that tradition, then the inference from the comparative method is clear. Both formulas are descended from a common original formula in the technical Parry sense, a building block in the construction of 'literary', 'artistic', or otherwise non-ordinary verbal messages or TEXTS in the—necessarily oral, pre-literate—society of the speakers of the proto-language common to the two traditions. If the two traditions are, for example, Homer and the Vedas, then an Indo-European comparative literature becomes no longer just an antiquarian frill but an interpretative necessity for literary theory. It is the obligation of the student of these literatures, singly or together, to give an account of what Kirk termed, perhaps unwittingly, the real 'inherited tendency'. It is that inherited tendency toward the deployment of parallel partly fixed phraseology which is a fundamental aspect of the style and technique of not only a Homer but a Vasiṣṭha[10]—and one that shaped both

10. I take here only as emblematic the name of one legendary Vedic rishi and his family—with a bow to Heine, Die Heimkehr 45 (*Der König Wiswamitra, / Den treibt's ohne Rast und Ruh', / Er will durch*

poets' views of life, almost. The responsibility is clear; the present work is my own attempt to answer it.

2. Metrics

The middle of the 19th century, not long after Kuhn's 1853 equation of Greek κλέος ἄφθιτον with Vedic *ákṣiti śrávas*, also saw the halting beginnings of a comparative Indo-European metrics, with Westphal 1860. Westphal's attempt lacked—understandably for the time—the requisite sophistication both in the comparative method and in the phonological and prosodic foundation of metrical systems. The defect would be remedied in altogether masterly fashion by Antoine Meillet, with a systematic equation of the meters of the Vedic hymns with those of Greek lyric, based on the quantitative rhythm and prosodic system which is common to both. First announced in an article on Vedic metrics of 1897, then more amply argued in the chapter entitled 'Les origines de la métrique grecque' of his *Aperçu d'une histoire de la langue grecque* (1913),[11] his analysis was finally presented in monograph form in *Les origines indo-européennes des mètres grecs* (1923).

Meillet had proved his case, and it is now generally accepted by competent authorities, e.g. West 1982, even if still largely ignored by most Hellenists. Meillet's own judgment is worth quoting, as expressed in the 3rd edition (1930:xvi) of the *Aperçu*, where the 1923 monograph is the final item in the bibliography: 'Doubtless Hellenists have for the most part remained sceptical as regards the conclusions of this work; but I believe I have there correctly applied the methods of comparative grammar and the principles of rhythmics.'

In the system of the (dialectal) proto-language ancestral to Greek and Indo-Iranian the rhythm was quantitative, based on the alternation of long or heavy ('strong time') and short or light ('weak time') syllables. Long syllables contain a long vocalic nucleus (long vowel or diphthong) followed or not by one or more consonants, or a short vowel followed by at least two consonants; short syllables contain a short vowel followed by no more than one consonant. The basic rhythmic alternation consisted of strong times (–) separated by weak times of one (⏑) or two (⏑ ⏑) shorts. The verse line tended to be isosyllabic, i.e. with a fixed syllable count, sometimes varied by suppression of the final (catalexis) or initial (acephaly) syllable. The arrangement of lines was stichic (line-by-line), typically grouped into three- or four-line strophes which could themselves be grouped in units of three (the Vedic *tṛcas* and the strophe, antistrophe, and epode of Greek choral lyric). The longer line of 10-12 syllables contained an obligatory word boundary (caesura) adjoining the 5th syllable, i.e. 1234 ‖ 5 or 12345 ‖. It contained three cola: the initial, up to the caesura, with free alternation of long and short syllable, a partially regulated internal colon, and a rhythmically fixed final colon or cadence. The shorter line of 7-8 syllables usually lacked a fixed caesura and contained only two cola, the free initial and the fixed cadence. The quantitative opposition of long and short was neutralized in the verse-final syllable (anceps).

Kampf und Büssung / Erwerben Wasischtas Kuh.), which I owe to J. Schindler.

11. On this remarkably innovative work see the penetrating appreciation of A. Morpurgo Davies 1988a.

In Indo-Iranian and Early Greek poetry the convention is that a verse line equals a sentence, whether a longer or a shorter line. In practice verse boundaries are often the boundaries of syntactic constituents of (longer) sentences, and syntactic phenomena sensitive to sentence boundary are frequently found adjoining metrical boundary, both external (e.g. line boundary) and internal (e.g. caesura). Metrical boundaries frequently coincide with formula boundaries. The resultant interplay or counterpoint between syntax and meter is a very distinctive characteristic of the earliest Indo-European poetry, and presumably of the poetic grammar of the proto-language as well.

Paul Thieme 1953:8 could justly claim that 'We may state with certainty that they [the Indo-European community] possessed a poetic art whose metrical form can be reconstructed from the comparison of Indic, Iranian, and Ancient Greek data with an exactitude whose precision excludes any possibility of doubt.'[12]

Other scholars since Meillet have adduced the evidence of many other metrical traditions around the Indo-European world. Roman Jakobson (1952) argued for the Indo-European origin of the South Slavic epic 10-syllable line (*epski deseterac*) with obligatory caesura and a statistical tendency to a rhythmic cadence of an anapest followed by an anceps, ⏑ ⏑ – ⏑. He compared the identical Greek cadence known as the paroemiac or 'proverb' verse, from its frequency as proverbial utterance occupying the second half line or hemistich of a dactylic hexameter, and proposed as Indo-European metrical prototype a 'gnomic-epic decasyllable'.

In the beginning of the 60's (1961 [presented 1960], 1963; more cautiously 1982) I argued for the Indo-European origin of a Celtic meter, the archaic Old Irish heptasyllabic [4 ‖ 3] line with fixed caesura and trisyllabic stress cadence 'o o o or 'o o 'o. It shows as well the variants [5 ‖ 2], [4 ‖ 1], [5 ‖ 3], and others, but the word boundary as caesura is mandatory. While I still believe this archaic Irish verse form is inherited, I would now rather associate it with the other manifestations of the Irish *rosc*, discussed in chap. 24. That is to say it should be compared with other examples of what I term 'strophic structures' or the 'strophic style', an Indo-European poetic form distinct from, and perhaps of earlier date than, the quantitative meter ancestral to that of Greek and Vedic.[13] This poetic form is examined in part III. The 1963 paper (reprinted in Watkins 1994) retains its utility both for the analysis of the different Early Irish *rosc* meters, and for the presentation and derivation of the different Greek and Indic verse forms.

Other traditions as well have been invoked in support of an Indo-European

---

12. Some doubt in fact inheres in the inclusion of Old and Young Avestan here, since the old quantitative opposition of long and short syllable has evidently been given up in Iranian. But it is well-nigh impossible not to compare the [4 ‖ 7] 11-syllable line of the Gathas with fixed caesura after the 4th syllable with the Vedic 11-syllable *triṣṭubh* (or 12-syllable *jagatī*) with caesura after 4, and similarly the typical 8-syllable Younger Avestan stichic line with the Vedic 8-syllable *gāyatrī*. Both the Old and the Younger Avestan lines are likewise arranged in strophes.

13. And doubtless prehistoric Iranian. Old Iranian preserves most clearly the two verse forms, one isosyllabic, with two hemistichs separated by a fixed caesura (the Gathas or Songs), and the other strophic, with lines of variable length corresponding to syntactic groups (the Yasna Haptaŋhāiti liturgy). (See chap. 21.)

metrics. See West 1973, with references to his own work on Lydian, and the introduction to West 1982. The most recent contributions have been by Heiner Eichner, writing on Italic (1988-90) and Anatolian (1993). While characteristically rich in learning, literature, and individual observations, these studies involve many seemingly arbitrary assumptions, and the case for each family remains *sub judice.* I discuss some of the same evidence in chapters 9, 11, and 23.

The orgins of the Greek epic meter, the dactylic hexameter, are particularly challenging. The earlier view set forth by Meillet 1923 and K. Meister 1921 that this meter is an 'Aegean' borrowing is quite unlikely. The general consensus now is that the line must somehow reflect the combination of two hemistichs. I argued in passing in 1969 for a historical relation of the metrical contexts of the formula 'imperishable fame' in Greek and Vedic, and this topic was pursued in considerable detail in Nagy 1974, attacking the metrical problem via formulaics and formula boundary (typically corresponding to metrical boundary). A crucial discovery was the Lille Stesichorus (ca. 620-550 B.C.) papyrus (Parsons 1977), containing some 125 lines of a lengthy choral lyric strophic composition estimated to have contained 2000 lines. The hitherto unique metrical system was first analyzed by Haslam 1978, assuming it was a development of the hexameter; but later West 1982:29-56 showed that the hexameter could be derived from the Stesichorean line, and that this poet provided the critical link between choral lyric and epic.

The precise details of the origin of the hexameter still remain a matter of debate. Other scholars who have treated the question from a different standpoint include N. Berg 1978 and E. Tichy 1981. The quantitative metrics of Greek and Vedic, quite possibly reflecting a late dialectal protolanguage, will receive no further discussion in the present work. My concern in part III is for the more widespread and probably more ancient strophic style, and elsewhere for the synchronic analysis of various metrical or otherwise poetic texts.

3. Stylistics

By this term I refer globally to all the other formal features of language, all the linguistic devices which in Jakobson's phrase are 'what makes a verbal message a work of art' (1981:18, 1987:63). Thus stylistics is in a sense a virtual equivalent of poetics, and in the discussion to come I will tend to use the two indiscriminately.

The notion of Indo-European stylistics in all likelihood arose first as the natural response of literarily sensitive scholars philologically trained in the Classical languages to the reading of poetic texts in a third member of the comparison, typically Vedic Sanskrit. It is thus just as "natural" as the notion of Indo-European comparative linguistics itself, and for the same reasons. Anyone who knows by heart the couplet of the Greek soldier-poet Archilochus (2 IEG):

> **ἐν δορὶ** μέν μοι μᾶζα μεμαγμένη· **ἐν δορὶ** δ' οἶνος
> Ἰσμαρικός· πίνω δ' **ἐν δορὶ** κεκλιμένος

> **In my spear** is my kneaded bread; **in my spear**
> Ismarian wine; I drink leaning **on my spear**,

with its triple figure of anaphora of the weapon, will surely recognize and respond to the same figure of anaphora, this time five-fold, of another weapon in Rigveda 6.75.2:

> **dhánvanā** gā́ **dhánvanā**jíṃ jayema
> **dhánvanā** tīvrā́ḥ samádo jayema
> **dhánuḥ** śátror apakāmáṃ kṛṇoti
> **dhánvanā** sárvāḥ pradíśo jayema

> **With the bow** may we win cattle, **with the bow** the fight;
> **with the bow** may we win fierce battles.
> **The bow** takes away the enemy's zeal;
> **with the bow** may we win all the regions.

The observer will also note that the Vedic anaphora is more complex, encompassing the repeated verb *jayema*, and that the Vedic anaphora includes a figure of polyptoton or variation in case, instrumental ~ nominative.[14]

So James Darmesteter in 1878 entitled his paper on the formulaic nexus 'crafting of words' (above, 1) 'a grammatical metaphor of Indo-European', with full consciousness of its stylistic and poetic nature. Text-linguistic giants like Wilhelm Schulze and Jacob Wackernagel made countless stylistic observations over their lifetimes, but the most influential was a lecture delivered by Wackernagel at Munich on 29 November 1932, called 'Indogermanische Dichtersprache', with the German word, literally "poet-language", that I have paraphrased (1992b:4.86) as 'style and poetic language'. Wackernagel's lecture was published posthumously during the Second World War, and reprinted in his *Kleine Schriften* (1953) and in Schmitt 1968.

The paper is historically significant enough and of such extraordinary richness in its implications—often inadequately recognized—that it requires the detailed examination given below. Here for the first time Wackernagel presented a sketch for a whole Indo-European stylistic and poetic language, centered around four characteristic features: (omission of) the augment, the metrical form, word order, and word selection.

The first is morphological, the absence of the augment (verbal prefix ἐ-, *a*-) in past indicative tense forms (those with 'secondary' endings) in early Greek and Indo-Iranian poetic texts. Wackernagel suggested that the omission of the augment was an archaism of poetic practice, the remnant of a time when there was still no augment.[15] The question is complicated now by the data of Mycenean Greek, which show almost no augmented forms. These are non-poetic texts some 500 years before Homer, so Wackernagel's view is probably to be rejected. For discussion see Morpurgo Davies 1988b:78.

---

14. Saussure noticed the same thing when he referred to Rigveda 1.1 as a 'versified paradigm' of the name of the god Agni.

15. The augment is found only in the dialect area including Greek, Armenian, Indo-Iranian, and the fragmentarily attested Phrygian.

Wackernagel's very brief treatment of metrical form simply spoke favorably of Meillet's work, and disallowed alliteration as a property of Indo-European poetic language in the way that it functioned in later Celtic, Italic, or Germanic, all of which show or showed a fixed 'demarcative', word-initial stress accent (word-final in British).

In my view alliteration was one of a number of phonetic figures available to the Indo-European poet, used widely as an embellishment and not 'bloss ganz vereinzelt und spielerisch' (with Wackernagel of the Indians and Greeks). As such, alliteration was an 'equivalence' token, capable of being promoted to the 'constitutive device of the sequence' (Jakobson 1981:27) any time the appropriate phonological and prosodic conditions were met. This appears to have occurred in different branches at very divergent times.

In Insular Celtic the development of the initial mutations, which presuppose identical treatment of consonants between vowels in syntactic groups both word-internally and across word boundary, is incompatible with a demarcative stress (which would serve to differentiate the two positions). Once the morphophonemic system of mutations was in place, however, it would be natural for the languages to develop demarcative stress, to signal the grammatical information now carried by the initial consonant of the initial syllable. The development of the mutations is generally dated to shortly before 400 A.D.

The system of alliterative verse in Germanic must be considerably older, on the evidence of a crucial feature. Finite verb forms do not regularly participate in the alliterative scheme, unless they are verse- or sentence-initial. This convention must be related to the accentuation of the finite verb in Indic and indirectly in Greek: the finite verb in main clauses was unaccented[16] except in verse- or sentence-initial position. This scheme is found already in our earliest documentation of Germanic (Gallehus runic inscription) *ek hlewagastiʀ **h**oltijaʀ **h**orna tawido* 'I, Hlewagastiz of Holt, made the horn' and must reflect very ancient Germanic prosodic practice.

Wackernagel's most acute observations are found in his final two topics, word order and word selection ('diction'). The parallelism between the two is clearer in the German *Wortstellung* and *Wortwahl*, as is their striking similarity to Jakobson's model of the intersecting axes of *combination* and *selection* (1981:27), on which more below.

Wackernagel begins by pointing out the well-known contrast in early Indo-European between the highly regulated word order of Vedic prose or the Old Persian inscriptions and the highly variable, apparently 'free' or non-configurational word order observable in the Vedic hymns or the Songs of Zarathustra. He notes in Ancient Greek poetry three stages of non-prosaic order of increasing 'irrationality': Homer, the least complex; then the choral lyric of Pindar, Bacchylides, and Stesichorus;[17] and finally the quite artificial perturbations of word order found in the

16. Whence the recessive accent in Greek.

17. He points out that Stesichorus 65 (= PMG 242) αὐτόν σε πυλαιμάχε πρῶτον 'yourself first, o fighter at the gate' shows a word order impossible in Homer, who has only σ' αὐτόν (*Il.* 10.389, 22.351). One would like to know the full verbal and metrical context of this hemistich, and the position of the verb governing the accusative. See note 20 below.

recherché versification of the Hellenistic period (and its Roman imitators). Wackernagel regards the latter as 'manifestations of overripeness', and compares the artifices of Old Norse skaldic poetry. As we will see in chap. 9, the same degree of perturbation of normal word order is found in Ireland, in the late sixth and seventh centuries, long before the language of the skalds.

Wackernagel then turns to Homer, to examine clearly inherited features of poetic word order. Some of these are in fact rules of ordinary grammar. Wackernagel first signals three: sentence-second position of enclitics and other weakly stressed particles ('Wackernagel's law'),[18] Behaghel's 'law of increasing members', and the disjunction (German *Sperrung*) of constituents of syntactic groups.

Recent work of considerable syntactic sophistication has shown that there are in fact at least three 'Wackernagel's laws' governing the positioning of enclitics, particularly in strings, which account for superficially variable or contradictory orders. See in detail Hale 1987 and to appear.

Behaghel's 'law of increasing members' rests on a plethora of examples from Germanic, Greek, and the other Indo-European languages which show the stylistic figure of enumerations of entities whereby only the last receives an epithet: "X and Y and snaggle-toothed Z". The Catalogue of Ships in *Iliad* 2 offers in its lists of names of persons, peoples, and places examples practically without exception. The fact gains interest with the recognition today that the Catalogue is in some—though hardly all—respects a 'Bronze Age' text, accurately reflecting the geography and settlements of middle to late second-millennium Greece.[19]

The poetic disjunction of the constituents or syntactic groups has received considerable light from the study of formula and its relation to meter. In particular there is a marked tendency for separated constituents to themselves adjoin metrical boundaries. Thus in Wackernagel's example from Tibullus (I.9.4):

> **sera** tamen *tacitis* **poena** uenit *pedibus*
>
> yet **tardy justice** comes on *silent feet*,

where *sera* and *poena* follow line-initial and hemistich boundary, and *tacitis* and *pedibus* precede hemistich and line-final boundary.

Wackernagel goes on to point to two cases at the beginning of each epic where contrary to received opinion Homer violates his own word-order practice. One is *Od.* 1.7 αὐτῶν γὰρ σφετέρῃσιν ἀτασθαλίῃσιν ὄλοντο 'they perished because of their own folly', where the genitive αὐτῶν quite abnormally precedes the pronominal possessive adjective.[20] 'Presumably this reflects the modification of a formulaic prototype like *Il.* 4.409' writes S. West in the *Odyssey* commentary, citing the same model

18. Wackernagel illustrates his famous law with *Il.* 1.8 τίς τάρ σφωε θεῶν . . . 'who of the gods (brought) these two . . .' The correctness of his reading of the particle ταρ, rather than the τ' ἄρ of the vulgate, will be discussed in chap. 11.2, on the language and poetry of the Trojans.

19. Cf. Page 1959, Huxley 1960, and Hope Simpson and Lazenby 1970. For a more cautious treatment see Kirk 1985:158-250.

20. It is striking that the Stesichorean innovation αὐτόν σε noticed by Wackernagel (note 17 above) involves the same elements, αὐτός and a pronominal form.

as Wackernagel had. The other is the more common licence, beginning with *Il.*1.1, to reverse the natural "iconic" order of name and patronymic ('from the oldest Indians to the Russians of today'): Πηληϊάδεω 'Αχιλῆος. A comparable poetic licence is to depart from the historical order in the enumeration of public offices held, the *cursus honorum*, for metrical reasons: the Roman saturnian in a Scipionic inscription *consol censor aidilis hic fuet apud uos*. Such licences probably belong to the domain of poetic universals.

Under 'word selection' ('diction') Wackernagel includes formulaic noun phrases like 'imperishable fame', noting that their locus is precisely the language of poetic eulogy—the business of the Indo-European poet. He likewise links Germanic and Indo-European two-part personal names to poetic phraseology, as later defended by R. Schmitt 1973, and links the poetic and the hieratic in the language of cult, as exemplified by Greek Ζεῦ πάτερ, Latin *Iuppiter*, Vedic *díauṣ pítar*. As we saw in chap. 1.2, the last can now be extended by Anatolian and Celtic facts.

Wackernagel then turned his attention from phrasal and lexical phenomena to the non-meaningful level of phonology and morphology: deformations like metrical lengthening and shortenings, and the special doubly marked poetic *o*-stem nominative plural ending *-āsas* (for *-ās*) of Vedic and Avestan, which after going "underground" in Classical Sanskrit resurfaced in Middle Indic early Buddhist poetry and whose hieratic value was transparent in the unique Old Persian example, the formula *Auramazdā . . . utā aniyāha bagāha tayaiy ha*^{n}*tiy* 'Ahuramazda and the other gods there are.'

His final example was a widespread stylistic feature of (typically prose) folktales, a text-initial, existential form of the verb 'to be' introducing the typical person or place: in Homer ἔστι πόλις 'Εφύρη (*Il.* 6.152) 'There is a city Ephyre . . .', ἦν δέ τις ἐν Τρώεσσι Δάρης (*Il.* 5.9) 'There was among the Trojans a certain Dares . . .' One need only compare the numerous Indo-European texts beginning 'There was a king . . .', Sanskrit *āsīd rājā*, Old Irish *boí rí*, Lithuanian *bùvo karãlius*, Russian *žil-byl korol'* (*car'*). Greek preserves a remarkable morphological and semantic archaism in Alcman (PMG 74) ἦσκε τις Καφεὺς ϝανάσσων 'There was a certain Cepheus ruling . . .', where the existential value of the suffixed form in -σκε corresponds exactly to the same value of Old Latin *escit* 'there is', demonstrated by Fränkel 1925:442. The verb can undergo ellipsis, as in the description of Calypso's island (*Od.* 1.51), beginning νῆσος δενδρήεσσα, θεὰ δ' ἐν δώματα ναίει 'An island full of trees, a goddess dwells within'. This syntactic and stylistic feature must be itself inherited; it recurs at the very beginning of the narrative part of the Hittite Appu-folktale StBoT 14, I 7ff (following the moralistic proem) URU-*aš ŠUM-an=šet* ^{URU}*Šudul* ^{URU}*Lulluwa=ya=ššan* KUR-*e aruni* ZAG-*ši ēšzi* 'A city—Šudul its name—and the Lulluwa-land is on the edge of the sea.'

With this programmatic lecture, delivered in 1932 at the crowning point of Wackernagel's long career, the study of Indo-European stylistics and poetic language had found itself.

For the work of the last two generations we can be brief. In the postwar period the German Indologist Paul Thieme made a number of contributions, reprinted in

Schmitt 1968. One in particular is discussed in chap. 42 below. The same decade saw the publication of seminal works on the general theory of stylistics, linguistics, and poetics by Roman Jakobson, reprinted in 1981. The Italian classicist and Indo-Europeanist Marcello Durante in 1958, 1960, and 1962 published three very imaginative and learned treatises, part of an ongoing project of research into the prehistory of Greek poetic language. They deal with metaphor, the terminology of poetic creation, and the epithet, resting primarily on original observations of verbal and thematic parallels to Greek texts in Vedic and other languages. They too are reprinted in German translation in Schmitt 1968, and revised and somewhat streamlined versions were later published in Durante 1970 and 1976. The latter is particularly rich in Indo-European comparanda.

Schmitt 1967, already cited at the outset, is important also for stylistics, approaches to genre in Indo-European, and a host of individual correspondences, not to mention the virtually exhaustive bibliography up to that date.

The Italian Indo-Europeanist and Celticist Enrico Campanile published in 1977 an important monograph with the intriguing title *Studies in Indo-European poetic culture*. The great innovation of this work was to emphasize the cultural and societal position and function of poet and poetry, based largely on the study of the traditional poet in Celtic and Indic society. Campanile makes valuable observations on stylistics, on the poet as professional, and on the "total"—all-embracing—character of Indo-European poetic culture, and makes very precise our notion of the functional meaning of some Indo-European stylistic figures. Later works of this author, most recently 1990, develop some of the same themes, with the notions of societal and culture history predominating.

Indo-European 'poetic culture' is also the domain of a number of lengthy recent contributions of Françoise Bader, with the accent on myth. These include Bader 1989, 1991, and 1993.

In 1981 there appeared in German translation an article of fundamental importance by the Russian Indo-Europeanist Vladimir Nikolaevič Toporov. This lengthy, learned, and literarily sophisticated essay in fact offers no less than a theoretical foundation for the study of Indo-European poetics. It is marked by the thought of Roman Jakobson, as well as Saussure and Starobinsky, but most firmly and clearly by the two traditions with which it is concerned, the language and literatures of Vedic and Classical India on the one hand, and the European critical aesthetic and intellectual tradition of the last century or so on the other. Striking is his juxtaposition (p. 194 with n. 8) of the definition of Bhāmaha (7/8th century A.D.) in his *Poetics* (*Kāvyālaṃkāra*) I 16: *śabdārthau sahitau kāvyam* 'poetry is sound and meaning put together' with the statement of Paul Valéry, writing in 1938: "L'opération du poète s'exerce au moyen de la valeur complexe des mots, c'est-à-dire en composant à la fois *son* et *sens* . . . comme l'algèbre opérant sur des nombres complexes" (*Oeuvres* 1.1414). Toporov's work appears to be widely unknown to Sanskritists, Indo-Europeanists, and students of literary theory alike, but it amply repays serious study.

In 1988, there appeared an important article by M.L. West, 'The Rise of the Greek Epic', with extensive reference to the Indo-European poetic literary and cultural background. We may look forward to the promised—or at least envisaged—

book developing the ideas there presented, and detailing the genesis of the Homeric poems.

For completeness's sake, let me merely record that in 1979 I gave the Collitz lecture to the Linguistic Institute in Salzburg, with the title 'Aspects of Indo-European Poetics' (published 1982), in which I tried to sketch in a few lines a total picture of the essentials of Indo-European poetic language, its function, and its techniques. At the University of Texas at Austin in 1981, at the Session de linguistique et de littérature at Aussois (Savoie) in 1983, at St. Johns College, Annapolis, and Yale University in 1984, I presented variations on a lecture entitled 'How to Kill a Dragon in Indo-European', subsequently published in Watkins 1987c. As the titles would indicate, these two articles (reprinted in Watkins 1994) together furnish the nucleus from which the present work has grown.

I conclude this brief history with a paragraph from Meillet 1930:144 (compare 1913:159), to reiterate what we have known now for 80 years:

> Greeks and Indo-Aryans received from the Indo-European period a literary tradition . . .This literary tradition made no use of writing . . . But there was an oral tradition of Indo-European poetry, as shown by the original identity of the two metrics, which one must take account of in order to explain the beginnings both of Greek poetry and of Greek thought.

That is to say that the comparative method in linguistics and poetics can illuminate not only ancient ways of speech but ancient modes of thought.

3

Poetics as grammar: Typology of poetic devices and some rules of poetic grammar

We noted in the preceding chapter the coincidence of the Indian theorist Bhāmaha and the French poet Valéry's formulation of poetry as the 'putting together' (*sahita-*, *sam-dhā-*; *composition*, *com-ponere*) of sound and meaning, *śabda* and *artha*, *son* and *sens*. *Sound and Meaning* was the title already in the 1950's of Roman Jakobson's never-finished opus, his 'quest for the essence of language'.

We may consider poetic language as a sort of grammar, in our case an Indo-European grammar, which distinguishes levels of sound and levels of meaning. On the level of sound alone, where meaning per se and meaningful units are not in play, we have the domains of METRICS and other rhythmic features and of the various sound devices which we can refer to globally as PHONETIC FIGURES, such as alliteration and rhyme. On a higher level, this poetic grammar has a morphological component, where sound and grammatical meaning alone are in play: we have the domain of GRAMMATICAL FIGURES. Figures of grammar may also—but do not necessarily—involve meaning per se, i.e. lexical meaning. On a still higher level, lexical meaning is pertinent and obligatory, both in vocabulary, i.e. DICTION, and in the syntactic and semantic components of the grammar. Vocabulary and syntax are the domain of FORMULAS, which are the vehicles of semantic THEMES. These themes are collectively the verbal expression of the culture of the Indo-Europeans.[1]

The essential characteristic of verse for Jakobson (1979:241; 1987:71) is that 'equivalence is promoted to the constitutive device of the sequence.' This profound but stylistically somewhat enigmatic observation can be easily explained and illus-

1. A PRAGMATIC component of the poetic grammar—involving the study of poetic signs in the context in which they occur—would be the domain of poet-performer/audience interaction. In practice we are largely ignorant of most aspects of performance in the historical languages until very recent times. Hence inferential conclusions about the pragmatics of performance of Indo-European poetry are neither possible nor legitimate and will not be made here.

trated in the domain of metrics and other rhythmic features, where the equivalence TOKENS are syllables or syllable types. As Jakobson continues, 'If a syllable is treated as a pertinent constituent of a verseline, then one syllable is equated with any other syllable of the same sequence, whereas speakers do not measure the number of syllables in their ordinary speech.' In ISOSYLLABIC verse all syllables are equivalent; in QUANTITATIVE verse all long syllables are equivalent, as are all short syllables; in accentual (stress-timed) verse all accented syllables are equivalent, and so forth.

With phonetic figures like alliteration, rhyme, assonance, but also commonly just repetitions or echoes of sequences with or without variations, the equivalence tokens are speech sounds, sound sequences, or distinctive features (phonetic components of speech sounds, e.g. voiced, continuant, sonorant, etc.).

In the case of grammatical figures and formulas the equivalence tokens are grammatical categories, morphemes, syntagmas, and words or phrase groups. In all instances the fundamental organizing principle is RECURRENCE (repetition) or SEQUENCING (counting) of these equivalence tokens: they have no inherent semantic content.

We may illustrate these notions with an English "cliché", a remarkably complex figure, in which at once sound, grammatical form, grammatical meaning, and lexical meaning are in play, and which, paradoxically perhaps, represents a prototypical Indo-European sequence or poetic formula:

last but not **least**.

This is a phonetic figure in both its mirror-image "choriambic" rhythm ⏒́ ⏑ ⏑ ⏒́ and its alliteration **l**- **l**-; it is a grammatical figure in the repeated monosyllabic superlatives. Semantically the figure is one of antithesis, Argument plus Negated Counter-Argument (see below), but the real force of the semantic contrast lies in the phonetic and grammatical near-identity of the opposing members, **l** - **st** . . . **l** - **st**. Small wonder that this cliché, as modern stylistics would view it, is embarrassingly and enduringly popular (especially to non-native speakers of English); it appeals to a far older aesthetic, for it is cast in an Indo-European mold.

The function of such figures of sound and grammar is INDEXICAL: they serve to point to the message, the poetic text, and call attention to it. Phonetic and grammatical figures may also have an ICONIC function,[2] and serve as a verbal "picture" of the notion, as does the expressive doubling (lengthening) of consonants in Greek *aprosórāton **okkhéonti** pónon* 'they endure toil that none can look upon' (Pindar, *Ol.* 2.67), *hèx ámata **sunnekhéōs*** 'for six days continuously' (Bacchylides 5.113 et passim), *aiólon **ópphin*** 'wriggling snake' (Homer, *Il.* 12.208). The deformation of the consonant mimics the semantics of the word which contains it.

The possibility of such deformations may be extended beyond the expressive domain to generate "artificially" appropriate metrical or rhythmic sequences. Thus Homer has λύτο (*ŭ*) 'was loosed' in a common formula, but λῦτο (*ū*) in *Il.* 24.1, in line-initial position, where the first syllable must be long. So in the same position always κλῦθι 'hear!' with *ū*. In Vedic the favored initial sequence is ⏑ –, as in

2. The terms *iconic*, *indexical*, and *symbolic* (of signs, functions) are taken and developed by Jakobson from the writings of C. S. Peirce.

śrudhí tvám 'hear thou!', but where only a single consonant follows, *śrudhī́ naḥ* 'hear us!' etc. Such poetically generated variants can be generalized in ordinary language; beside the short *u* of Greek κλυτός, Vedic *śrutás*, Old Irish *ro-cloth* 'was heard' (**k̑lu-tó-*), the Germanic family of *loud*, Old English *hlūd* etc., presupposes **k̑lū-tó-* with lengthened vowel. There are other sources as well for such "licenses", which cannot be detailed here. The basic principle is that the poetic grammar may exploit variants generated in ordinary grammar and extend their use.

Particularly frequent in several archaic Indo-European traditions is the deployment of pairs of words, linked by a strong phonetic figure, which express not an antithesis proper but an indexical linkage, a calling attention to the connection. Such, for example is the marking of reciprocal notions in the archaic social system of gift-exchange relation between poet and patron, in which the poet by his art gives fame and honor to the patron, who rewards him richly for thus providing a necessity for maintaining the patron in his prerogative.[3] Examples of such phonetically indexed pairs are Classical Modern Irish (Bardic poetry)

clú 'fame' : ***cnú*** 'nut; jewel' (metaphor for reward),

with alliteration and rhyme; Old Irish

dúan 'poem' : ***dúas*** 'reward for a poem',

with alliteration and shared nucleus; and the most frequent, Classical Greek (5th century encomiastic choral lyric, etc.)

nī́kā 'victory' : ***tīmā́*** 'recompense of honor'.

The phonetic figure in the last is based on distinctive features: the vowels are identical, and the sequence nasal sonorant consonant plus oral unvoiced stop consonant of the one (***n*** - ***k***) is reversed in the other (***t*** - ***m***).[4]

We find three instances of indexical linking by phonetic figure in a proverb quoted by Hesiod, *Works and Days* 25-6:

καὶ **κ**εραμεὺς **κ**εραμεῖ **κ**οτέει καὶ **τέκτ**ονι **τέκτ**ων
καὶ **πτ**ωχὸς **πτ**ωχῶι **φθ**ονέει καὶ ἀοιδὸς ἀοιδῶι

Potter begrudges potter, and carpenter carpenter;
and beggar is jealous of beggar, and poet of poet.

The first set is alliterative, ***k***- ***k***- ***k***-, the second more complex, ***k*** - ***t***- ***t*** - ***kt***- ***t*** - ***kt***-, while the third shows alliteration with variation in the distinctive feature of aspiration: ***pt***-

3. For fuller discussion see chap. 5.

4. The *tīmā́* : *nī́kā* figure (Pindar throughout and in Bacchylides) is to be examined in detail in a forthcoming study by Abby Westervelt.

pt- p^h t^h-. The two lines are themselves linked by metrical and grammatical parallelism, the identically placed and identically derived verbs κοτέει (from κότος 'rancor') and φθονέει (from φθόνος 'envy'), with their identical vowels and semantic equivalence. The many vowels of the poet (ἀοιδός) beside the harsh stop consonants of the others is iconic to his special and privileged status.

The same complex double linkage as in the second set above unites the first and last words of an Umbrian prayer (quoted in full in chap. 18), *nerf . . . frif*: both ***-rf fr-*** and ***-rf -r*** . *f*.

Not all phonetic figures are as precisely functional in this manner, however. What we may describe as ECHOIC repetition is widespread in verse in many languages from all periods, down to the present. In the Partheneion or Girls' Chorus (PMG 1.75-6) of the 7th-century Spartan poet Alcman three girls are mentioned, with the last alone receiving an epithet, by Behaghel's law of increasing members, A + B + epithet C:

Φίλυλλα
Δαμαρ[έ]τα τ' ἐρατά τε Ϝιανθεμίς

Philulla
and Damareta and lovely Wianthemis.

The effect of the echo,

damARETA T' ERATA TE wianthemis,

is to spread the epithet over both girls.

Such an echo has the force of a refrain in the repeated phrase of one of the earliest and finest poetic monuments in Old Welsh, the *Gododdin*:

gwyr a AETH gatrAETH

The men who went to Catraeth . . .

While not an obligatory feature, such echoes are occasionally in this poem 'promoted to the constitutive device of the sequence':

glasved eu hANcWYN, a gwENWYN vu

Bright mead their refreshment, but it was poison,

a gwedi ELWCH tawELWCH vu

But after rejoicing there was silence.

Echoes may frequently show metathesis or be otherwise phonetically varied. The Old Russian *Laurentian Chronicle* of 1377 records a metrical saying in Rus' after the lifting of the Tatar yoke:

> poGIBOše aKI OBrě
>
> They perished like Avars.

Such echoes continue to delight the ear, just as do the recurrent sequences of sounds in Seamus Heaney's line

> turns cursive, unscarfing,

which I deliberately take out of its context.[5]

The echoic function plays a critical role in the formulaics of oral poetry, whether or not the poet composer-performer is conscious of it. Kirk 1985:57 calls attention to 'an interesting formular system that is aurally generated':

ἀπάνευθε θεῶν	'apart from the gods' (*Il.* 3x)
ἀπάνευθε νεῶν	'apart from the ships' (*Il.* 4x)
ἀπάνευθε κιών	'going apart' (*Il.* 1x, *Od.* 2x),

always in the internal colon before the hephthemimeral caesura. The words following ἀπάνευθε have no link but phonetic similarity.

The 3sg. imperfect ἤην 'was' of the vulgate (for which Chantraine (1973:289) suggests reading and scanning ἤεν before consonants and ἤεν(ν) before vowel)[6] is attested only four times in Homer (*Il.* 1x, *Od.* 3x). In three of these, ἤην is enjambed from the previous line, which ends with a cluster of *s* plus dental stop before vowel:

5. Viking Dublin: Trial Pieces. From *North* (1975), reprinted in Heaney 1980:

> (III . . .)
> and for this trial piece
> incised by a child,
> a longship, a bouyant
> migrant line.
>
> IV
> That enters my longhand,
> turns cursive, unscarfing
> a zoomorphic wake,
> a worm of thought
>
> I follow into the mud.

Virtually every stressed syllable in the two quatrains echoes or is echoed by another.

6. This account is to be preferred over that adopted by Hainsworth 1993:309.

Il. 11.807-8

ἶξε θέων Πάτροκλος, ἵνα σφ' ἀγορή τε θέμι**ς τε**[7]
ἤην (v.l. ἦεν), τῆι δὴ καί σφι θεῶν ἐτετεύχατο βωμοί

Patroklos came running to where their place of assembly was, and where the altars of the gods had been made.

The "jingle" is even more striking in the two other passages:

Od. 23.315-6

καὶ πέμπ', οὐδέ πω αἶσα φίλην ἐς πατρίδ' **ἱκέσθαι**
ἤην, ἀλλά μιν αὖτις ἀναρπάξασα θύελλα

. . . and sent him on; nor was it yet his fate to come to his dear native land, rather a storm wind picked him up again . . .

Od. 24.342-3

δώσειν πεντήκοντα, διατρύγιος δὲ **ἕκαστος**
ἤην· ἔνθα δ' ἀνὰ σταφυλαὶ παντοῖαι ἔασιν

. . . would give fifty, and each was everbearing;
on them were all kinds of bunches of grapes . . .

An equally striking phonetic echo is the following:

Od. 17.119
(≅ 7.214)

Ἀργεῖοι Τρῶές τε θεῶν **ἰότητι** μόγησαν

Argives and Trojans labored by the will of the gods

Od. 19.266

τῶι τέκνα τέκηι φιλ**ότητι μ**ιγεῖσα

to whom she might bear children, mingling in love.

The last is a common formula with many variants.

Such resonances and echoes must have frequently influenced the direction of oral composition and oral performance. The use of the echo as a compositional device to enhance the perception of both performer and audience is characteristic of choral lyric, notably of its master, Pindar.[8] This poetry makes serious demands on listener and performer alike. Each individual composition, with its unique metrical form, is penetrated by the responsion of the lines of strophe, identical antistrophe, and epode, repeated ad libitum. The philologist F. Metzger set forth in his Pindar commentary of 1880:33-41 his echo theory of Pindaric composition. As described—not kindly—by Gildersleeve 1885:l-li:

---

7. Line-final ἀγορή τε θέμι**ς τε** is itself formulaically linked to *Od.* 9.112 τοῖσιν δ' οὔτ' ἀγοραὶ βουληφόροι οὔτε θέμι**στ**ες.

8. On choral lyric see the views of Meillet 1930:199-206.

> While committing the odes of Pindar to memory he noticed the frequent recurrence of the same word, or close equivalent, in the corresponding parts of strophe and antistrophe, epode and epode. These recurrent words are all significant, . . . and were all intended as cues to aid the memory of the chorus and to guide the thoughts of the hearers. It is a mnemonic device, but more than a mnemonic device, for it lets us into the poet's construction of his own poem, and settles forever the disputed meanings of the odes. If this were true, it would hardly heighten our admiration of antique art, and although the coincidences are interesting and the observation of them a proof of loving study that deserves to be honored, the discovery of the recurrent word is not the end of all controversy—there are too many recurrent words.

The basic rectitude of Metzger's theory was first rediscovered by David C. Young in his brilliant and influential 'Pindaric criticism' of 1964 (reprinted in Calder and Stern 1970), who termed it 'the greatest single aid for an understanding of a Pindaric ode.'[9] At the same time he observed that 'Metzger failed to realize that the repetition of words . . . *etc.*, were not mere word-play, but a real and vital part of the natural tools by which the poet expresses himself fully, . . . and by which ideas are developed and relationships between ideas are expressed.'

On the other hand one cannot agree with the further extension made by C. Carey 1981, who claims that 'the important restriction is that the echoes should be thematic, organic. An echo of sound alone without a connection of thought and context is without value.' To claim such is to misapprehend wholly the indexical function of poetic language.[10]

The function of metrics and other rhythmic features is to organize and, very importantly, to demarcate the poetic message, i.e., the text. A particular form of echo serving a demarcative function is the stylistic device known as *ring-composition*.[11] Ring-composition is the beginning and the ending of a discourse, or complex utterance longer than a sentence, with the same or equivalent word, phrase, or just sound sequence. It is a signal of demarcation: a series of sentences is thereby symbolically transformed into a finite set, a closed text or text segment. This device, sometimes with more complex 'nesting' of recurrences, is an extraordinarily widespread compositional technique in the archaic Indo-European world and is not terribly common outside it.

Ring-composition is of enormous importance in oral literature for isolating unities within a larger discourse, as in the stichic verse of Greek epic. The recognition scene of Odysseus and his dog Argos is introduced by

Od. 17.291-2 ἂν δὲ **κύων** κεφαλήν τε καὶ οὔατα **κείμενος** ἔσχεν,
Ἄργος

9. See now the collections of Schürch 1971.

10. Gildersleeve himself was well aware of this when he wrote (1885:xxxvi) that Pindar 'drains dry the Greek vocabulary of words for light and bright, shine and shimmer, glitter and glisten, ray and radiance, flame and flare and flash, gleam and glow, burn and blaze.' He had learned his lesson well.

11. This device was first so named, and systematically studied in early Greek, by van Otterlo 1944 and 1948. His two studies may still be read with profit.

The **dog lying** there raised up his head and ears,
Argos, . . .

and concluded in the same order with

Od. 17.300 ἔνθα **κύων κεῖτ' Ἄργος** . . .

There **lay** the **dog Argos** . . .

This ring is the only mention of the name of the pathetic beast, who expires a few lines later; but the little ring identifies a topos of Indo-European date. The Vedic compound name *ṛjí-śvan-* 'having swift/white dogs' gives the 'Caland-form', like Greek ἀργι-, of the adjective in the Homeric formula κύνες ἀργοί 'swift/white dogs'. See further chap. 14.

Hesiod, *Works and Days* 202ff., says 'now I will tell a fable for princes . . .' which begins

ὧδ' ἴρηξ προσέειπεν ἀηδόνα

Thus the **hawk said** to the nightingale . . .

and ends

ὣς ἔφατ' ὠκυπέτης **ἴρηξ**, τανυσίπτερος ὄρνις

Thus said the swift-flying **hawk**, the long-winged bird.

Here the fable is framed by the phonetic identities *hōd'* and *hōs*, and by the two phrases with reversed word order, 'hawk said' and 'said hawk', the last expanded by further epithets.

The second stasimon of Aeschylus' *Agamemnon* also contains a short beast fable. Like the Hesiodic one, the passage is an admonitory instruction for princes[12] and is interlaced with Indo-European thematic elements and poetic figures. The strophe begins (717-19) with the verb,

ἔθρεψεν δὲ λέοντος ἶνιν **δόμοις** . . . / . . . ἀνήρ

There **reared** a lion's cub in his **house** . . . a man,

and the antistrophe ends (735-6) with the same verb:

ἐκ θεοῦ δ' ἱερεύς τις Ἄτας **δόμοις προσεθρέφθη**.

12. The genre is itself inherited, though not confined to the Indo-European world. In Greek we cannot exclude the influence of the Ancient Near East.

By divine will a priest of destruction for the **house had been reared**.

In this Aeschylean example ring-composition is combined with the typical Indo-European figure of poetic syntax of sentence initial verb at the beginning of tales or other texts, discussed in the preceding chapter, in *cataphoric* function ('referring forward' as opposed to *anaphoric* 'referring back'). See Dressler 1969. We saw examples with the verb of existence, 'There was . . .', 'There is . . .'; note from the Rigveda with other verbs,

5.1.1a **ábodhy** agníḥ

Awakened is Agni . . .

7.9.1a **ábodhi** jārá uṣásām

Awakened is the suitor of the dawn's rays (Agni) . . .

8.103.1a **ádarśi** gātuvíttamo

The best pathfinder (Agni) **appeared** . . .

1.144.1a **éti prá** hótā vratám asya māyáyā

The hotṛ (Agni) **goes forth** to his duty, cloaked in magic . . .

7.73.1a **átāriṣma** támasas pārám asyá

We have crossed over to the other shore of this darkness . . .

From early Greek note *Od.* 18.1, the beginning of the Iros-episode (which shows the mock-heroic to be as old as the epic itself),[13]

ἦλθε δ' **ἐπὶ** πτωχὸς πανδήμιος

There **approached** a public beggar . . .

and the *Margites* I,

13. Homer clearly knew both the synchronic etymology to the name of the goddess Iris, οὕνεκ' ἀπαγγέλλεσκε κιών (7) 'because he used to go delivering messages', and the diachronic etymology to the word for 'strength', οὐδέ οἱ ἦν ἶς / οὐδὲ βίη (3-4) 'he had no strength or force', the last reinforced by the play Ἶρος Ἄϊρος (73) 'Iros un-Iros'. The etymology was demonstrated by Françoise Bader 1976: it is the only attestation in Greek of one of the Indo-European words for 'man, male', **u̯ih$_x$-ró-* in Vedic *vīrás*, Lithuanian *výras*, Umbrian *ueiro*, Latin *uir*, Old Irish *fer*, Old English *wer*.

> **ἦλθέ** τις εἰς Κολοφῶνα
>
> A certain (poet) **came** to Colophon . . .

and the only other Homeric book to begin with a verb, *Il.* 24.1

> **λῦτο** δ' ἀγών
>
> The assembly **was dissolved** . . .

In the poetic grammar the indexical, demarcative function of a discourse-initial verb is thus quite different from the emphasizing function—topicalization, fronting, or focus—of sentence-initial verbs.

Examples of ring-composition could be multiplied from many early Indo-European traditions. In Ireland it became a fixed requirement of many types of versification to end a poem with its first word, phrase, or syllable. The choice of word is indifferent; only the echo matters, and that echo can even be of a meaningless first syllable (see chap. 9). Compare from well-known Old Irish poems (EIL 1, 53):

> **Messe** ocus Pangur bán
>
> **I** and white Pangur
> . . .
> **messe.**
>
> **scél** lim dúib
>
> I have **tidings** for you
>
> . . .
>
> é mo **scél**.
>
> These my **tidings**.

The Irish technical term is *dúnad*, literally 'closing', and the image is that of closing a ring-fort, a circular stone structure of the Iron Age, Irish *dún*. The metaphor could have been created millennia ago (Watkins 1991).

In all these poetic realms of sound and echo considered hitherto, meaning per se has not been relevant or pertinent. Even resolutely "synchronic" stylistic features and non-meaningful poetic devices such as rhythm and meter, alliteration and rhyme, deformation and metrical lengthening, sound echoes and ring-composition are amenable in principle to the comparative method. But it is the meaningful level of poetic language, the domains of POETIC DICTION and POETIC SYNTAX—what Jakobson referred to as the intersecting axes of selection and combination—where meaning is in play,[14] that affords the greatest opportunities for comparison, historical analysis, and reconstruction.

To attempt an overview of poetic diction in any early Indo-European tradition, much less all of them, is obviously out of the question; it would amount to a discussion of the dictionary of each language. I point out here only that within many of these languages there can be found indications of a tradition of recognizing different kinds of language, and different levels of language within the lexicon. One metaphor for this is that of 'language of gods' and 'language of men', to refer to a hierarchy of aesthetically marked versus aesthetically unmarked appellations of the same entity. I have treated the question in Watkins 1970a, and see as well Toporov 1981, both with references. The traditions include Homeric Greek, with scattered examples like the river in *Il.* 20.74,

> ὃν Ξάνθον καλέουσι θεοί, ἄνδρες δὲ Σκάμανδρον
>
> which the gods call Xanthos, but men Skamandros;

Old Hittite texts translated from non-Indo-European Hattic originals, giving formulas for divine names like

> tandukešni ^{D}Tašimetti DINGIR^{MEŠ}-naš=a ištarna
> ^{D}Ištar SAL.LUGAL
>
> to mankind you are Tasimettis, but among the gods
> Ishtar the queen;

a single Indic example repeated in Yajurvedic and Brāhmaṇa passages, which we know to be archaic since it figures in the Aśvamedha ritual (see chap. 25),

> hayo bhūtvā devān avahad vājī gandharvān
> arvāsurān aśvo manuṣyān
>
> as steed he carried the gods, as charger the Gandharvas,
> as courser the Asuras, as horse men;

a complete poem—a 'versified synonymy'—in the Old Norse Poetic Edda, the *Alvíssmál*, with strophes of the pattern

9 [Thor] segðu mér þat, Alvíss . . .[15]
hvé sú iǫrð heitir . . .

---

14. Selection and combination of course operate on the meaningless level as well, for example in the case of individual speech sounds.

15. Compare the repeated Old Avestan phrase in Y.44.1-19, *tat̰ ϑβā pərəsā ərəš mōi vaocā ahurā* 'This I ask you. Tell me truly, Lord'.

10 [Alvíss] iǫrð heitir með mǫnnum enn með ásom fold
kalla vega vanir
ígrœn iǫtnar álfar gróandi
kalla aur uppregin

[Thor] Tell me that, Alvíss . . .
how the earth is called . . .
[Alvíss] earth it is called by men and by the Æsir *land*
the Vanir call it way
green the giants the elves growing
the Uppregin call it sandy soil;

and finally the set of Early Irish appellations like *bérla na filed* 'language of the poets', of which the Medieval Irish glossatorial tradition preserved hundreds of lexical examples.

The other side of these hierarchies, focusing on poetic versus ordinary language, poetic versus "human" language, is the specific avoidance of certain words in the lexicon as 'unpoetic', well documented by Axelson 1945. In Homer the word for 'merchant' ἔμπορος is never found—despite the existence of a thriving mercantile commerce since the early Bronze Age. As etymological 'im-porter', ἔμπορος could be a calque of Old Hittite *unnattallaš* 'id.', attested already in the Laws. Hesiod, whose lexicon in *Works and Days* is more humble, does have ἐμπορίη 'commerce' at 646.[16]

A widespread Indo-European convention or rule of poetic grammar, which surely goes back to the proto-language, is the convention 'verse line = sentence'. It is found in traditions outside Indo-European as well and may be a universal in languages where the equation of the two is not automatic or by definition. Grammatical phenomena sensitive to sentence or clause boundary (initial, final, second, pre-final) will occur also at verse or hemistich boundary. Such are for example the accent of the finite verb in initial position in main clauses in Vedic, 'second' position of enclitics in most of the Indo-European languages, and many others.

The prominence and emphasis accorded to sentence-inital position may be repeated in successive verses, such that the initial elements of each may be "read"—i.e. heard and processed—"vertically", as a syntactic constituent. The subject of the single sentence which runs for three lines of the gāyatrī strophe RV 9.54.3 is the noun phrase *ayám punānáḥ sómaḥ* 'this pressed soma', each word of which is initial in the three lines:

ayám̐ víśvāni tiṣṭhati
punānó bhúvanopári
sómo devó ná sū́ryaḥ

This pressed soma stands

16. Compare the chapter title in Benveniste 1969:1.139, 'Un métier sans nom: le commerce.'

over all creation
like god Sūrya.

Of the other constituents, the verb *tiṣṭhati* 'stands' (whose unmarked position is sentence-final) is verse-final to the first line; the sentence- and verse-internal postpositional clause *víśvāni bhúvanopári* 'over all creation' must be read "vertically" as well as horizontally. The *sóma* is soma the plant, not (*ná*) soma the god (*devó*); the tension of the juxtaposition *sómo devó* is not resolved until the last word establishes the syntactic constituency *devó ná sū́ryaḥ* 'like god Sūrya' and at the same time re-establishes "horizontal" linearity as the proper organizing principle of the linguistic sign.

That such "vertical" constituents recur in other old traditions is shown by an early ode of Pindar's, *Pyth.* 12.9ff. (490 B.C.). The three main syntactic constituents of lines 9-11 are the three line-initial words τὸν . . . ἄιε . . . Περσεύς 'which Perseus heard', in the order Object-Verb-Subject:

τὸν παρθενίοις ὑπό τ' ἀπλάτοις ὀφίων κεφαλαῖς
ἄιε λειβόμενον δυσπενθέιε̂ σὺν καμάτωι
Περσεύς, ὁπότε . . .

Which Perseus heard being poured with grievous toil from
the maidenly, unapproachable heads of snakes, when . . .

Once again it is the final 'when' clause of lines 11-12 which re-establishes the proper "horizontal" linear sequence.

Constituents of syntagmas, such as noun phrases consisting of Noun and Adjective or Noun and Genitive, commonly adjoin one another in the entire Indo-European family from the earliest prose texts on. But the separation or disjunction of the two is widespread in many early Indo-European poetic texts. This characteristic feature of poetic language in these traditions has sometimes been labeled 'freedom of word order', in the sense of true 'non-configurational' word order as it is found, for example, in many Australian languages. While the variations and perturbations of word order in some cases may seem aleatory at first blush, much of this freedom is in fact governed by rules of poetic grammar. Thus the disjoined constituents of noun phrases typically adjoin metrical colon boundaries, which are particularly liable to syntactic disjunction. We may leave unspecified just how the disjunction is effectuated (e.g. by a movement rule which shifts the verb to the left so that it splits the noun phrase, or by one which moves one constituent of the noun phrase to the right to straddle the verb).[17] But adjoining caesura (|) and verse (||) boundary we find numberless examples like the following:

17. Other parts of speech can of course be so 'straddled', but the phenomenon is particularly frequent with verbs.

Vedic	gávām I adadād usríyānām II
	gave some of the dawn cows,
Old Avestan	I vāzišto aŋhaitī astiš II
	shall be your strongest guest,
Greek	νηυσὶ I παρήμενος ὠκυπόροισι II
	sitting in swift ships,
Luvian	alati I awinta Wilušati II
	came from steep Wilusa,
South Picene	mefiín I veiat vepetí II
	lies in the middle of the tomb,
Faliscan	sociai I porded karai II
	gave to his dear girlfriend.

Such a syntactic device in poetic language can safely be assumed for the proto-language.

One of the characteristics of poetic or other elevated styles of language in many traditional societies is the extensive use of FORMULAS, whole phrases which are repeated with little or no variation, rather than recreated. Formulas play an important role in certain styles of oral composition in various traditions, notably South Slavic and other languages of the Balkans (Lord 1960, 1991); but their usage is far more widespread and more nuanced than just these traditions and reaches back into prehistory. The issue has been discussed with some examples in the preceding chapter, under Formulaics and Formula and Theme, in connection with the theory of 'Oral Poetry'. As we noted there, neither 'poetry' nor 'orality' in the sense of 'non-literacy' are conditions *sine qua non*. The prose of the saṁhitās, brāhmaṇas, and sūtras of Vedic India is every bit as formulaic as the poetry of a Homer or an Avdo Međedović. Exactly the same is true of the prose rituals, state and domestic, which form the bulk of our documentation of second-millennium Hittite and Cuneiform Luvian, and which continue only trivially altered verbal tradition and verbal style over more than 500 years. Vedic prose, like Vedic hymnic poetry and mantras, was composed orally (but probably not in performance) and the fixed text then preserved and transmitted by collective rote memory. Hittite rituals, notably the ^{SAL}ŠU.GI 'old woman' rituals in the first person ("then I take the following ..."), were presumably dictated to scribes who wrote them down on clay tablets. These could then be read out and re-performed verbatim for hundreds of years, to judge from the many ritual tablets in the cuneiform paleography or 'ductus' of the Old Kingdom (17th-16th centuries B.C.) still preserved in the Palace Archives of the New Kingdom (to 1200 B.C.) in Boğazköy, and from then to the 20th century A.D. and doubtless beyond. (The clay tablet remains demonstrably the most permanent way of preserving written records yet devised by man.)

The comparison of characteristic formulas in various traditional Indo-European languages and societies permits their reconstruction as far back as the original common language and society. These formulas are whole noun phrases or verb phrases, with wholly or partially reconstructible semantics, syntax, lexical expression, morphology, and phonology; their complexity is a remarkable testimony to the power of the comparative method in historical linguistics. An example from the inherently conservative language of prayer is

PROTECT MEN (and) LIVESTOCK.

I here introduce the convention of using English upper case (and normal English word order) to identify the semantics and lexical constituents of a reconstructed formula. The upper case thus makes an asterisk redundant. Parentheses enclose optional elements; parentheses enclosing asterisked Indo-European roots represent the lexical specification of the reconstructed "semanteme", e.g.,

PROTECT (**pah*$_2$-) MEN (**u̯ih*$_x$*ro*-) (and) LIVESTOCK (**pek̑u*-).

This formula, discussed in greater detail in chap. 17, is attested in four separate Indo-European languages in two branches of the family. Each has undergone certain historical changes but preserves the essential unity intact. Umbrian and Avestan both attest the object noun phrase MEN (and) LIVESTOCK, *ueiro pequo* and *pasu vīra* respectively; Latin and Vedic have independently introduced other, alliterative words for MEN: *pastores* and *púruṣam*. The Italic branch, Umbrian and Latin, has replaced PROTECT by a two-part phrase 'keep safe': *ueiro pequo . . . salua seritu* 'keep safe men (and) livestock', *pastores pecuaque salua seruassis* 'may you keep safe shepherds and livestock'. The Indo-Iranian branch, Avestan and Vedic, has substituted the verb *trā*- for **pah*$_2$- in the same meaning PROTECT: *ϑrāϑrāi pasuuå vīraiiå* 'for the protection of livestock (and) men', *trāyantām . . . púruṣaṃ páśum* 'let them protect man (and) livestock'. For Indo-Iranian *pā*- PROTECT in other formulas see chap. 17, as well.

From the comparison of these four semantically equivalent formulas we can draw valuable inferences about the poetic grammar of the proto-language, about such questions as word order and its variation, government, case and number agreement, modal usage and equivalences, and conjunction or its absence (asyndeton)—as well as about alliteration and sound play. The collection and study of such formulas yields not only grammatical and lexical information about the proto-language but also opens a window onto how phrases and formulas change across time. And finally, their study can provide insight into the cognitive processes and conceptualizations of a prehistoric society and culture.

We saw in the preceding chapter that Indo-European poetics has from the beginning been concerned with formulaic phraseology. Yet the narrowly restricted search for possible cognate verbal formulas has led most researchers—notable exceptions are Benveniste, Thieme, and on the synchronic Greek plane the interesting and ambitious work of Pavese 1968—to neglect their semantics. As I put it (1982:112, 1979:269),

> More broadly, what is neglected in the study of formulas—and this applies not only to linguists but to students of oral literature as well—is the function of these formulas as expressions of an underlying semiotic system. These poetic formulas in archaic societies are not repeated and remembered just because they delight the ear; they are *signals*, in poetic elaboration and as verbal art, of the relations of things: of the traditional conceptualizations, the perception of man and the universe, and the values and aspirations of the society.

We saw in chap. 2.1 that the formula MEN (and) LIVESTOCK, first identified as an inheritance by Wackernagel, was a type of two-part noun-phrase figure known as a merism (see below). These figures exhibit characteristic Indo-European stylistic properties, over and above the ordinary grammatical relations of such formulas as IMPERISHABLE FAME. If we examine these Indo-European bipartite noun-phrase formulaic figures as a group from a more formal point of view certain interesting properties emerge. In describing them I make use of some of the terminology developed by Jakobson in his classic paper 'Shifters' (1971:130-47; originally published 1957).

We may distinguish *simple* figures and *complex* figures. Simple figures, or *designators*, are symbolic signs. Designators may be either *quantifiers* or *qualifiers*.

Indo-European quantifier formulas are of two types. One has the structure Argument + Negated Argument, as in:

gods spoken (and) unspoken	(Hittite DINGIR^{MEŠ} *tarantes̆* DINGIR^{MEŠ} *ŪL tarantes̆*)
diseases seen and unseen	(Latin *morbos uisos inuisosque*)
seen (or) unseen ritual flaw	(Umbrian *uirseto auirseto uas*)
the seen (and) the unseen	(Vedic *dr̥ṣṭā́n adŕ̥ṣṭān*)
magistrates girt (and) ungirt	(Umbrian *nerf śihitu anśihitu*).

The other has the semantically equivalent structure Argument + Counter Argument under shared semantic features, as in:

both here and elsewhere	(Old Avestan *iiadacā aniiadacā*)

gods above and below	(Greek τῶν ἄνω τε καὶ κάτω)
be you god or goddess	(Latin *si deus si dea es*).

Both types of quantifier formulas have as their function to designate the *totality* of the notion: 'gods spoken and unspoken, above and below, god or goddess' are alike equivalent to 'all gods'.

Indo-European *qualifier* formulas have two structures, litotic and non-litotic. The litotic has the structure Argument + Negated Counter-Argument, *Aussage plus negierte Gegenaussage*, in the words of its formulator Helmut Humbach (1959):

girt and not ungirt	(Avestan *aiβiiāsta nōiṯ anaiβiiāsta*)
true and not false	(Old Pers. *hašiyam naiy duruxtam*)
Achaean women, not men	(Greek Ἀχαιΐδες, οὐκέτ' Ἀχαιοί).

The non-litotic has the structure Argument + Synonymous Argument:

safe and sound	(the English, and L. *sane sarteque*)
whole and roofed	(Latin *sarcta tecta*)
prayers and incantations	(Greek λιτάς τ' ἐπαοιδάς).

Qualifier formulas have as their function to intensify the Argument. Both litotic 'safe and undisturbed' and non-litotic 'safe and sound' are equivalent to 'very safe', though the two are not necessarily stylistic equivalents.

Note that most of these *designators* are at the same time *grammatical figures*, since they either share (*sarc**ta** tec**ta***) or oppose (*si de**us** si de**a***) a morphological sign. Synonyms lacking a shared morphological sign are commonly linked by a phonetic figure (***s**ane **s**arteque*, *with **m**ight and **m**ain*), as in countless Germanic examples.

To these *simple* figures, or *designators*, we may oppose the *complex* figures, or *connectors*. Both have the ordinary symbolic function of linguistic signs, but the connectors have as well an *indexical* function: they point to, or make reference to, another entity.

The connector formulas in Indo-European are of two types: the *kenning* and the *merism*. The *kenning* is a bipartite figure of two nouns in a non-copulative, typically genitival grammatical relation (A of B) or in composition (B-A) which together make reference to, 'signify', a third notion C:

horses of the sea (ships) sea-horse (ship)	(Greek ἁλὸς ἵπποι) (Old Norse *vág-marr*)
milk of grain (ale)	(Old Irish *melg n-etha*)

whales' sanctuary (sea)	(Old Irish *nemed mbled*)
whales' road (sea)	(Old English *hron-rād*)
dog of the river (fish)	(Hittite ÍD-*aš* UR.ZÍR)
house carrier (snail)	(Greek φερέοικος)
whose shoulders are apart (cobra)	(Vedic *vyàṁsa*, Schmidt 1964)

Probably of Indo-European antiquity are:

shepherd of the people (king)	(Greek ποιμένα λαῶν, Vedic *gopā́ jánasya*, Old English *folces hyrde*, Old Irish *tír dianad buachail* 'land of which he is the shepherd', [and Psalm 23])
descendent of the waters (fire)	(Vedic *ápām nápāt*, Avestan *apąm napå*, Old Norse *sævar niðr*).

The ancient Indo-European collocation for 'master', **déms pótis*, may be in origin a frozen kenning, a "dead metaphor", something like 'himself of the house'.[18]

The second connector figure is the *merism*: a bipartite noun phrase consisting of two nouns in a copulative relation (A and B), two nouns which share most of their semantic features, and together serve to designate globally a higher concept C, i.e. to index the whole of a higher taxon C. Thus we find

barley (and) spelt	(Hittite *ḫalkiš* ZÍZ-*tar*)[19]

as a global indication of all cereals, and

grains (and) grapes	(Hittite *ḫalkieš* GIŠGEŠTINḪI.A)
grain (bread) and wine	(Greek σῖτος καὶ οἶνος / μέθυ)

for all agricultural products and alimentation. We have seen MEN (and) LIVESTOCK, TWO-FOOTED (and) FOUR-FOOTED; the same semantics is conveyed in another way in the following two sets of contiguous compounds:

18. See on the kenning Krause 1930, Marquardt 1938, and Campanile 1977.

19. If ZÍZ-*tar* is to be read *ḫātar* (Latin *ador* 'spelt') we have the phonetic figure of alliteration.

horse-devouring, man-devouring (Avestan *aspō.garəm nərə.garəm*)

ox-slaying, man-slaying (Vedic *gohā́ nr̥hā́*).

The *kenning*, as long recognized, is a metaphorical figure, based on a relation of similarity. The *merism* on the other hand is a metonymic figure, based on a relation of contiguity. Both refer indexically to an external notion. The Argument of the kenning and the merism, the metaphor and the metonym alike, is precisely that indexical reference.

We may summarize this partial typology of Indo-European bipartite noun-phrase formulaic figures in the following scheme:

I. Simple (Designators): symbolic signs
  1. Quantifiers
    a. Argument + Negated Argument
    b. Argument + Counter-Argument
      (under shared semantic features)
  function: totality of notion
  2. Qualifiers
    a. Argument + Negated Counter-Argument
    b. Argument + Synonymous Argument
  function: intensive

II. Complex (Connectors): both symbolic and indexical signs
  1. Kenning (relational)
    (A + B) = C
  2. Merism (copulative)
    C
    /\
    (A + B)
  function: metonymic, index of totality of higher taxon C.

In the chapters to follow we will see many more examples of such figures in the texts.

A particular variant of the bipartite merism is the indexical list, which typically functions as an overt or implied totality of the entity listed. Such lists abound in early Indo-European literatures, from India through Anatolia and the Classical world to Ireland. They may be arranged according to very concrete 'natural' contiguity relations like the lists of the body-parts in the '12 members' of Hittite rituals (Gurney 1979), or the '12 doors of the soul' in the Archaic Old Irish *Judgements of Dían Cécht* (Binchy 1966), or the make-up of the 'canonical creature' discussed (after Jamison 1986) in part VII below. They may be developed into a special genre, like the Celtic Triads and Heptads. But the important thing is that these lists are *formulaic* in the technical sense. They are memorized and transmitted as accurately as circumstances permit, and they may preserve strikingly archaic linguistic features, like the reflex of

IE *-$k^{u}e$ 'and' at the end of the Hittite list of 'all the seeds' (Watkins 1985a:495), or equally ancient cultural features like those examined in part VII.

What seem at first sight to be simple lists or enumerations may turn out to be artistically elaborated merisms, where phonetic figures of arrangement are all deployed. The notion of solid (opposed to liquid) agricultural produce, as a higher taxon, may be expressed by the merism of the subcategories *cereals* and *legumes*. And each of these may in turn be represented by a merism of subcategories of each. Consider the traditional English round

Oats, peas, beans, and barley grow.

It is a masterpiece of the Indo-European poet's formulaic verbal art. Consider the order of the elements, which is anything but random. The two cereals *oats* and *barley* are distracted, positioned to frame the two legumes *peas* and *beans*. The latter are linked by the indexical labial stop and identical vowel /pi-/, /bi-/. *Beans* must follow *peas* in order to alliterate with *barley*. *Barley* as the only disyllable comes last in the list, in conformity with Behaghel's law of increasing members. The verb *grow* still surfaces in the underlying sentence-final position which it has occupied since Indo-European times. And *oats* must come first, to form a perfect phonetic ring-composition; the whole utterance, the seven-syllable poetic verse-line sentence begins and ends with the vowel /o/: *oats*, *grow*.

This particular formulaic utterance now functions only to amuse children; its surface linguistic expression is of no great antiquity, though doubtless many generations, perhaps some centuries older than the present day. But in its essential semantics, formulaics, and poetics it could perfectly well have been periodically and continuously re-created on the same model, over the course of the past six or seven thousand years. We could have in this round ringing in our ears the transformation of the central merism of an Indo-European agricultural prayer, harvest song, or the like.[20]

That my adducing *oats, peas, beans, and barley grow* is not altogether fanciful appears from the consideration of some far earlier Indo-European traditions. We began the discussion of the merism with the Hittite phrase

ḫalkiš ZÍZ-tar

barley (and) spelt.

This particular Hittite formulaic merism is an Indo-European inheritance in its principal semantic features and their functional deployment. Compare the recurrent Homeric formula

20. The transposition of an old ritual utterance to the contemporary function of a child's pastime has parallels. All and only the Indo-European elements of an inherited image symbolizing the sexual act of fecundation survive in the verbal behavior, the playing song of a late 19th-century North Russian children's game, and the name of the game itself, *ërga*, continues intact an Indo-European lexeme for the sexual act (Watkins 1975e).

πυροὶ καὶ κριθαί

wheat and barley.

The formula is expanded to a full hexameter line by the splitting of wheat into another merism and the addition of a traditional epithet to the final member (again, Behaghel's law of increasing members), in *Od.* 4.604:

πυροί τε ζειαί τε, ἰδ' εὐρυφυὲς κρῖ λευκόν

Wheat and emmer, and broad-growing white barley.

The hiatus at the caesura and the difference in conjunction indicates that we have a juncture of two formulas, each occuping a hemistich. Thus a merism with ζειαί in second position,

πυροί τε ζειαί τε.

Even if ζειαί probably designated in Homer's time a kind of emmer, it is certain that it is a derivative of the traditional Indo-European word for 'barley', **i̯éu̯o-*. The same lexeme is found, in the same position in the merism, in Old Hittite

šeppit euwann=a

wheat and barley,

and in the Atharvaveda, with substitution of a wholly new grain for the first member:

vrīhír yávaś ca

rice and barley.

It is not unlikely that the word **i̯éu̯o-* 'barley' can be reconstructed in this second, unmarked position in the merism for the Proto-Indo-European formula itself. The word **i̯éu̯o-* apparently designated the unmarked grain, like English *corn* ('wheat' in England, 'barley' in Scotland, 'oats' in Ireland, and 'maize' in the U.S.). In Avestan *yauua-* is just generic 'grain, cereal'; note the plural, and the archaic absence of a formal superlative in Avestan (N. 28)

yauuanąm gaṇtumō ratu.friš

of the cereals wheat is dear(est) to the Ratus.

What is important is the semantic and thematic structure of the Indo-European merismatic formula

GRAIN$_{sp.}$ and BARLEY (**i̯éu̯o-*),

where the word order is iconic, and the "nobler", more highly marked cereal precedes. The formula is an indexical figure, designating globally the higher taxon, all cereals, and their hierarchy.

Cognate formulas, like cognate cultural institutions, may but need not be accompanied by cognate linguistic expressions. Lexical substitution and cultural change in the course of millennia may leave only the semantic features of the original expression present. But this must not mask the fundamental fact of the preservation of an inherited unitary formulaic and thematic "deep structure". In the Hittite, Greek, and Vedic examples above and, I submit, in the English expression *oats, peas, beans, and barley grow*, we have six versions, six "performances" in the language of oral literature, of the same Indo-European merism, of the same Indo-European text.

4

Poetics as repertory: The poetic traditions of the Indo-European world—Sources and texts

Historical linguists, and Indo-Europeanists in particular, pursue their study in two opposite but complementary directions. On the one hand they proceed back from the data of the languages compared to restore a common prototype. On the other hand they proceed from the established forms of the proto-language to follow their development in the individual languages—the emergent new and independent structures which result from the transformations of elements of the earlier system.[1] So it is with Indo-European poetics as well. On the one hand we reconstruct a system of poetic elements and features from the individual poetic traditions, like Anatolian, Indic, Iranian, Greek, Germanic, etc., which we term "Common Indo-European". On the other hand we investigate the manifestation of this "Common Indo-European" poetics in the works of art of the individual traditions, like the Luvian Songs of Istanuwa, the Vedas, the Avesta, Greek Epic and Lyric, *Beowulf*, the *Edda*, etc. These two approaches to the study of the field are not only mutually dependent but illuminate each other: innovations in the one enable us to recognize archaisms in the other, and vice-versa.[2]

We may here survey in brief compass the attested branches of the Indo-European family and the character of their documentation: what each has to contribute to the determination or establishment of a poetic tradition, what genres are represented in each—in short, what are the literary rather than simply linguistic remains of these early Indo-European-speaking peoples.

The principal branches of the family will be detailed in the order of their earliest historical attestation with the focus on their documentation in the earlier periods. In comparative poetics just as in comparative linguistics we may take it as given a priori

1. Benveniste 1969:8.
2. Toporov 1981:189.

that the older the documentation, and thus the nearer in time to the proto-language, the greater will be the *concentration* of inherited features. This principle does not preclude or prejudice the potential preservation or attestation of *isolated* archaic features at any point down to the present time. But the very fact of the isolation of such features, rather than their being components of a coherent system, reduces their inherent interest; cultural inheritance from Indo-European becomes simply a curious fact rather than an explanatory device. So *goods and chattels* in English today is in a real sense, as we have seen, the semantic continuation of an Indo-European formula, albeit accidentally; but it is rather because of the manifestation of semantically cognate formulas in Ancient Greek (e.g., κειμήλιά τε πρόβασίν τε), Vedic, and Hittite, where they are integrated into a total taxonomy of wealth, that the comparative method, the "Indo-European approach", can make a real contribution to the interpretation of the historical texts themselves. For these reasons we concentrate on the older and earlier attested traditions.

Three branches of the family are attested in the second millennium B.C.: Anatolian, Indo-Iranian, and Greek. Of these Anatolian was probably the earliest to branch off from the Proto-Indo-European common language and is set apart by a number of features both linguistic and poetic. Indo-Iranian and Greek clearly belong closely together in a central dialect area and have traditionally—not always justifiably—served as the principal model for the reconstruction of the proto-language both in linguistics and poetics.

Anatolian

Excavations in Central Turkey at Hattusas, the capital city of the Hittite Empire (near the village of Boğazköy, now Boğazkale), have unearthed extensive documents in **Hittite** written on clay tablets in a cuneiform script. Philologically we can distinguish **Old Hittite** (ca. 1700-1500 B.C.), **Middle Hittite** (1500-1350 B.C.), and **Neo-Hittite** (1350-1200 B.C.). Fragmentary remains of two other related languages are found in the same cuneiform Hittite sources: **Palaic**, in texts contemporary with Old Hittite and spoken to the northwest of Hattusas, and **Cuneiform Luvian**, in texts contemporary with Old and Middle Hittite and spoken over much of southern and western Anatolia (a form of Luvian in the northwest may have been the language of the Trojans). The preponderance of Luvian personal names and the loanwords in Neo-Hittite texts would indicate a widespread use of the Luvian language in Hittite context as well. A very closely related dialect is **Hieroglyphic Luvian** (formerly called Hieroglyphic Hittite), written in an autochthonous pictographic syllabary, known from seals and isolated rock inscriptions from Middle and Neo-Hittite times and a number of monumental and other inscriptions from the region of northern Syria, 1000-750 B.C. In classical times in southwestern Anatolia we have sepulchral and administrative inscriptions (some quite extensive) in **Lycian** (5th-4th cent. B.C.) and, further north in the west, short inscriptions in **Lydian** (6th-4th cent. B.C.), both written in epichoric alphabets. Lycian is clearly developed from a variety of Luvian; the other Anatolian languages cannot yet be organized into subgroups.

Most of the Hittite texts are catalogued in Laroche 1971, with supplements 1972, 1975.[3] The great majority of our texts are religious in character, public and private. The texts comprise great seasonal festivals lasting many days, cultic temple rituals to particular divinities, and royal funerary rites. They include prayers of various sorts, conjurations, and private rituals. All these ceremonies, meticulously recorded on clay tablets, are devoted to a generally concrete and immediate goal, whether appeasing perceived divine wrath, or rectifying by verbal magic and the manipulation of symbolic objects—by word and deed—any abnormal or unwanted situation or condition. Their function is thereby to assure the health and welfare of the participants and the community. The performance of these festivals and rituals involves many embedded utterances and recitations which are stylistically and artistically elaborated and may be considered poetry; they are also frequently obscure. We find also stichomythic and quasi-choral passages, which may function as poetic and dramatic 'interludes' in the rituals; some are examined in chap. 11.1. These short texts have scarcely been studied heretofore, much less systematically collected. This remains an important task for future students of Hittite and Anatolian literature and poetics.[4] The authors of many of our Hittite rituals are from Southern or Western Anatolia, Kizzuwatna and Arzawa, like those of the women Mastiggas and Pissuwattis translated by A. Goetze in Pritchard 1955:349-51. They almost certainly were originally Luvian-speaking and reflect Luvian cultic and poetic traditions.

Old Hittite texts of legendary history may contain embedded songs, like the dirge cited in chap. 23.1, recognized already in 1929 by the decipherer of Hittite, B. Hrozný, as 'le plus vieux chant indo-européen'. One of the very oldest Hittite historical compositions, the Siege of Uršu, is written in Akkadian but contains a (nearly unintelligible) song in Hittite.

Hittite mythological texts, sometimes free-standing compositions and sometimes recitations embedded in rituals, are mostly in prose but contain portions that are clearly to be chanted or sung; cf. the 'Voyage of the Human Soul' quoted in chap. 26. For other Hittite myths in translation see Hoffner 1990.

In addition to these native Hittite compositions there exists a body of Sumero-Akkadian translation literature in Hittite, for example the several Sun Hymns, a fragment of *Gilgamesh*, legends of Sargon of Akkad the King of Battle, and others. Even where heavily influenced by Mesopotamian literature they may show some native and possibly inherited features. The Hittites were from the earliest times exposed to the influence of other languages each of which had a literary tradition. As indicated by the form of the cuneiform writing, the Hittites were profoundly influenced by Mesopotamian culture as mediated through the Peripheral Akkadian of Northern Syria, and before that by the contact with the Assyrian merchant colonies of the 19th and 18th centuries, which did not lead to writing Hittite but left a mark on

3. Archaeological excavations in Turkey are ongoing and continue to yield new texts and fragments of texts in Hittite and in the other Anatolian languages as well; we have the pleasant paradox of a dead language whose corpus is not closed.

4. An example of such a collection is the very useful catalogue of Hittite similes (of the type 'as the back wheel never catches up to the front wheel, so may evil not catch up to the celebrant') collected by Ahmet Ünal in Mikasa 1988.

Hittite literature when it was still only oral (Hoffner 1968, Watkins 1979a).

The autochthonous language of central Anatolia when the Hittites "arrived" was Hattic, which was preserved as a language of cult, and one in which we have a fairly large body of clearly poetic liturgical texts, albeit virtually unintelligible. Some Hattic mythological texts are preserved in bilingual tablets, like *The Moon that fell from Heaven* (translated in Pritchard 1955) and the 'language of gods and men' texts (one example in the preceding chapter).

The major cultural influence, at least in religion and cult, came from Hurrian, the language of the kingdom of Mittanni or Hanikalbat in Southeastern Anatolia and Northern Mesopotamia. With the Hurrianization of the Hittite pantheon came a number of epic tales and songs (Sumerogram SÌR, Hittite *išḫamai-*) which were in part directly translated into (Middle) Hittite on the evidence of bilingual tablets (the newly discovered and as yet unedited *Song of Emancipation*, with both mythological and wisdom literature texts) and in part (possibly) composed in Hittite on Hurrian models, like the *Song of Ullikummi*, the Kumarbi-cycle, the myths of the monster Ḫedammu, the hunter Keššì, and others. These texts exhibit a high degree of literary sophistication and value, particularly the new bilinguals.[5] They evidence a very fruitful cultural and literary symbiosis, one which vitalized Hittite civilization.

In the earlier period of the Old Kingdom Hittite contacts with Hurrian had been hostile; the dirge referred to above comes from an account of the Hurrian wars. From this early, culturally less sophisticated period comes the origin legend known as the *Zalpa Tale* (Hoffner 1990:62-3). This extraordinary prose text of prodigious multiple birth and incest as an origin tale may very well lay claim to Indo-European antiquity. Compare the beginning (KBo 22.2 obv. 1),

> [SAL.LUGA]L ^{URU}Kaniš 30 DUMU^{MEŠ} 1^{EN} MU-anti ḫāsta
>
> The queen of Kaniš (= Nesas) gave birth to 30 sons in a single year,

with Rigveda 10.86.23ab

> párśur ha nā́ma mānavī́ sākáṃ sasūva viṁśatím
>
> The daughter of Manu, Parśu by name, gave birth to 20 at once.

Manu is the first *man*; *Parśu* ('rib') has been related to the name of the *Persians*; and the same mythological themes as origin tale, of prodigious multiple births and incest as in the Hittite, recur exactly in the Greek legend of the 50 daughters of *Danaos* ('Greek') fleeing an incestuous marriage with their parallel cousins, the 50 sons of *Aigyptos* ('Egyptian'), which is the subject of Aeschylus' play *The Suppliants*. We have here clear thematic reflexes, in the three oldest Indo-European traditions, of a single proto-text (Watkins 1989:796-7).

The other second-millennium Anatolian languages are Luvian and Palaic.

5. Available in cuneiform edition, *K[eilschrifttexte aus] Bo[ghazköi]* 32 (Berlin 1990).

Cuneiform Luvian is represented by a number of rituals containing spells and incantations, similar in kind to those we find in Hittite. The entire corpus of the language is edited (without translation) in Starke 1985 and the most recent interpretation is in Melchert 1993b. Most promising for the student of Anatolian and Indo-European poetics are the *Songs of Istanuwa*, ritual texts from that cult city. They are described in detail in chap. 11.2. For the (obscure) Hieroglyphic Luvian inscriptions of the 2nd millennium the possibility of verse or song has been raised (Hawkins and Eichner, apud Eichner 1993:113-14), but nothing concrete has been demonstrated.

For Palaic we have a mere handful of texts, analyzed in Carruba 1972 and Melchert 1984b. These include a Palaic version of the Anatolian Myth of the Vanishing God, with the formula familiar from several Hittite mythological texts 'the gods ate and did not satisfy their hunger; they drank and did not satisfy their thirst' (cf. chap. 11.1), a ritual of sandwich-like bread offerings, and a ritual to the god Zaparwa which contains rhythmic or strophic utterances. See on the last chap. 23.1.

The most recent and extensive contribution to Anatolian poetics and metrics is Eichner 1993, to which global reference is made for textual and bibliographical references. It begins with a perceptive discussion of Hittite and Luvian, while the major part of this work (pp. 114-59) is devoted to the 1st-millennium Anatolian languages Lydian and Lycian. Some Lydian inscriptions have since 1916 been known to be in (isosyllabic) verse lines organized into strophes and to exhibit the feature of *rhyme*—perhaps its earliest systematic attestation in the Indo-European world (Littmann, Miller, West, and others apud Eichner 1993). The rhyme schemes involve identical vowel nuclei and sometimes systematic and sequential, sometimes random consonantal codas of sonorant (liquid or nasal), continuant (usually sibilant), and stop. For the "Lycian B", Milyan "poetic dialect" of Lycian already recognized in Kalinka's *Tituli Lyciae* (1901), in nos. 44 (Xanthos stele) and 55 (Lion sarcophagus), see the analysis of Frei and Eichner in Eichner 1993. Their ingenious analysis is not self-evident and remains *sub iudice*. But that we have to do with poetry is proved epigraphically beyond question by the recurrent marker ")" of strophe end every three lines, for a total of 36 strophes. It remains clear that in Lydian and Lycian we have two continuations of an Anatolian metrical tradition, developed over more than a thousand years since the attestation of Anatolian verse in Hittite, Luvian, and Palaic in the 2nd millennium B.C. The actual interpretation and understanding of these texts remains a challenging task for the future. Melchert 1993a gives an alphabetical word list of Milyan (Lycian B).

Indic

Extended Indic texts in **Vedic Sanskrit** begin with the Rigveda, whose earliest parts were probably composed in the Punjab in the second half of the second millennium B.C., and continue through the other Vedas, Brāhmaṇas, Sūtras, etc. By ca. 500 B.C. the language was codified in the grammar of Pāṇini as **Classical Sanskrit**, used to the present day as a learned literary language. From the 5th century B.C. on we have extensive **Middle Indic** documents (Pāli, Prakrits); the very numerous **Modern Indo-Aryan** languages begin to be attested around 1000 A.D.

Vedic literature (from *veda* 'knowledge; sacred knowledge') begins with the greatest and oldest of the *saṁhitās* or 'collections', the Rigveda (*ṛgvedasaṁhitā*, RV).[6] The Rigveda (Rig- = *ṛg*- is a form of *ṛc* 'verse') is arranged in 10 books or *maṇḍalas* ('circles'), and contains 1028 hymns or *sūktas* addressed for the most part to particular deities. The whole contains over 10,000 lines, just under 154,000 words, and 432,000 syllables; it was preserved and transmitted entirely orally for the first millennium and a half of its existence, and largely orally even after the introduction of writing down to the present day. The oldest maṇḍalas 2-7 are known as the Family Books, being composed by poets of six individual families (enumerated in chap. 5). Book 8, hymns 1-66 are by the Kaṇva family, the remainder from other families. Book 9 contains only hymns to Soma, the deified intoxicating or hallucinogenic plant of uncertain and controversial nature, which was pressed for its juice and ingested for ritual purposes since Common Indo-Iranian times. Compare the formula Vedic *sómaḥ sutáḥ* = Avestan *haomō hutō* 'pressed soma'. The collection of soma hymns was doubtless excerpted from other books at some time. Books 1 and especially 10 belong to the youngest layer of the Rigveda. While absolute dates in India are subject to caution, the oldest parts of the Rigveda probably belong around the middle of the second millennium B.C. as the Indians moved eastward through Afghanistan into the Punjab and thence to the region of Delhi. RV 1.131.5 preserves a clear memory of the migration across the Punjab, 'Five-rivers' land:

> ā́d ít te asyá vīryàsya carkiran
> mádeṣu vṛṣann uśíjo yád ā́vitha
> sakhīyató yád ā́vitha
> cakártha kārám ebhyáḥ
> pṛ́tanāsu právantave
> té anyā́m-anyāṃ nadyàṃ saniṣṇata
> śravasyántaḥ saniṣṇata
>
> Indeed they praise this manly deed of yours in their intoxication,
> o Bull (Indra), when you came to the aid of the Uśij priests,[7]
> when you came to the aid of the comrades.
> You made victory for them,
> to win in the battles.
> They won for themselves one river after another;
> they won for themselves, seeking glory.[8]

---

6. For a virtually complete guide to Vedic literature, including texts and translations see Santucci 1976 and for an elegantly compact and literate summary Jamison 1991:5-16.

7. Vedic *uśíj*- = Old Avestan *usig*- is an Indo-Iranian word for a kind of priest. Here it is used metonymically for those of the old Aryan (Indo-Iranian) religion.

8. The meter is the uncommon atyaṣṭi (Arnold 1967:237). Note the repetitions at the end of *bc* and *fg*, which run through all seven stanzas of the hymn. It is termed *punaḥpadam* in Aitareya-Brāhmaṇa 5.11.1 (Geldner ad RV 1.127). The intensive *saniṣ(a)ṇ*- is attested only here in the Rigveda. In ***pṛ́tanāsu právantave*** we have both alliteration and a phonetic figure.

The standard translation of the Rigveda is the German of K. F. Geldner; no complete English translation exists. The other Saṁhitās are the Atharvaveda, the Sāmaveda, and the Yajurveda. The Atharvaveda (AV), from *atharvan-* 'fire-priest', is an extensive collection of hymns not used in the worship but to appease, bless, and curse. They are the formulations of priestly families of both "white" and "black" magic, for matrimonial happiness, protection, love, luck in gambling, etc., or against diseases, enemies, rivals in love, sorcerers, noxious animals, etc. It is younger than the older parts of the Rigveda, and contains the first mention of the tiger (*vyāghra*) and of rice (*vrīhi*), indicating deeper penetration into the Indian subcontinent. It exists in two recensions, the Śaunaka (translated by W. D. Whitney) and the Paippalāda, of which new manuscripts have only recently come to light.

The Sāmaveda (*sắman-* 'chant', probably related to Hittite *išḫamiya-* 'sing') is largely identical with the Rigveda with some new mantras; it is associated with the performance of the soma worship. The Yajurveda (*yájuṣ-* 'sacrificial formula') includes two parts, the White (*śukla*) YV, the Vājasaneyi-saṁhitā (VS), which consists of liturgical formulas (*mantras*) alone, and the Black (*kṛṣṇa*) YV which adds to the verse mantras prose explanation and commentary, ritual exegesis. The last comprises four saṁhitās, the Kāṭhaka-, Kapiṣṭhala-Kaṭha-, Maitrāyaṇi-, and Taittirīya-saṁhitā. Only the last has been translated. The VS and mantra portions of the YV are chronologically only a little younger than the Atharvaveda; the YV saṁhitā prose portions are a little later and represent our earliest Vedic prose.

This whole vast body of textual material is still almost wholly unexplored for comparative poetic purposes. An example (which I only noticed in Jamison [to appear]) is the mantra accompanying the girding of the wife (*patnīsamnahana*) with a cord around her waist before she can undertake any sacral duties in the performance of a ritual. KS 1.10 (5:6):

saṃnahye sukṛtāya kam

I gird myself for good action.[9]

Compare the beginning and ending of the Old Irish *Lorica* or breastplate of St. Patrick:

atom-riug indiu
niurt tríun . . .

I gird myself today
with a great strength . . .

See Greene and O'Connor 1967:27.

To each of the Saṁhitās are further attached exegetical Brāhmaṇas, collections of utterances of brahmans, the priestly class who are the repositories and communi-

9. The mantra is a variant of one first found in a wedding hymn of the Atharvaveda (14.1.42) spoken to the bride: *sáṃ nahyasvāmṛ́tāya kám* 'gird yourself for the immortal one', as Jamison shows. The shift in pronominalization is probably part of a spoken ritual interchange.

cators of sacred knowledge. These may date from 1000 to 650 B.C. Representative Brāhmaṇas are the Aitareya- and Kauṣītaki-br. to the Rigveda, the Jaiminīya-br. to the Sāmaveda, rich in myth and legendary material, and the Taittirīya- and Śatapatha-br. to the Black and White YV respectively. Still later, toward the end of the Vedic period, come the Sūtras, which are meticulous descriptions of rituals, public and private: the numerous Śrauta and Gṛhya-sūtras.

The end of the Vedic period, and the beginning of Classical Sanskrit, is the codification of that language in the grammar of Pāṇini, ca 500 B.C. The composition of the great epics Mahābhārata and Rāmāyaṇa probably belong to this time or a little later. While the language is post-Vedic, the nucleus of the Mahābhārata is a vast repository of mythological and other themes of Indo-European antiquity.

Iranian

Iranian,[10] once spoken over vast stretches of southeastern Eurasia, is attested in **Old Avestan** and **Young Avestan** and **Old Persian**. Old Persian is the language of the monumental inscriptions of the Achaemenid kings of the 6th-4th centuries B.C. Several Middle Iranian languages are known. From western Iran **Parthian** is known from the Arsacid period, from the 1st century B.C. onward, and **Middle Persian** (or **Pahlavi**), the descendant of Old Persian and ancestor of **Modern Persian**, from the 3rd century A.D. onward. From eastern Iran we know, among others, **Bactrian**, from circa 100 B.C. onward, written in Greek script, **Sogdian**, from the 4th century A.D. onward, and **Chorasmian**, which survived well into Islamic times. There are numerous **Modern Iranian** languages, some of them with old literatures (**Modern Persian** in several dialects, **Kurdish**, **Pashto**, **Balochi**).

The grammatical structure of Old Avestan is more or less identical with that of Rigvedic, which points to a comparable date: second half of the second millennium B.C. The term Young Avestan is used indiscriminately to refer to the language of a wide variety of texts, from texts written in a grammatically consistent and correct language to texts compiled by authors who no longer knew the grammar of the language. The grammatical structure of "correct" Young Avestan is comparable to, but more archaic than, that of Old Persian of the 6th century, while that of the latest texts is comparable to the "incorrect" Old Persian of the 4th century. As no Western Iranian (either Median or Achaemenid) geographical names are mentioned in the texts we may place the oldest Young Avestan texts in the period antedating the Median expansion around 700 B.C. and the latest texts in the late Achaemenid period (some possibly even later), that is, the oldest Young Avestan texts were probably composed and compiled during the 9th/8th centuries B.C.

The Old Avestan hymns, the *gāϑās* (Gathas) are traditionally attributed to Zarathustra, who is frequently mentioned in them.[11] Inserted into the corpus of Gathas

10. This presentation is largely due to P.O. Skjærvø, for which I am profoundly in his debt.

11. It is no derogation of Zarathustra's stature as the founder of one of the world's great religions to observe with Skjærvø that there is no evidence in the Gathas that they were composed by Zarathustra. On the contrary, the complete and sovereign mastery of a variety of meters and the techniques of versification

is the liturgical text the Yasna Haptaŋhāiti, in which Zarathustra's name is not mentioned. It is discussed and illustrated in chap. 21. The Young Avestan texts are religious and mythological; representative texts are the Hōm Yašt (*Yasna* [Y.] 9) hymning Haoma = Vedic Soma, the Mihr Yašt (*Yašt* [Yt.] 10) celebrating the god Mithra, the Tištr Yašt (Yt. 8) celebrating the star Sirius. They contain much verse, typically octosyllabic. The titles of these texts are in Pahlavi, the language of the native exegesis. Both *yasna* and *yašt* are derivatives of the root *yaz-* 'worship', cognate with Vedic *yaj-* and Greek ἅζομαι 'worship', ἅγιος 'holy'. The Vidēvdāt 'law against the daevas' is collection of instructional (purification rituals, legal issues) and mythological texts.

Some of the texts in Middle Iranian languages continue Old Iranian traditions, both thematic and formulaic, especially the 'Pahlavi Books', written down in the 9th century but incorporating material from the religious writings of the 3rd century A.D. and before. They include the *Bundahišn* 'primal creation', a cosmological text based upon the Pahlavi translation of lost Avestan texts; the *Dēnkard*, a Zoroastrian encyclopaedia that includes, among other things, a summary of the Avesta as it was known in the Sasanian period (ca. 5th century A.D.) and several Pahlavi commentaries on the Gathas; and the late *Kārnāmag ī Ardaxšīr ī Pābagān*, the deeds of Ardaxšīr, the founder of the Sasanian dynasty. The Modern Persian epic the *Šāhnāme* of Firdawsi contains much traditional Iranian lore.

Greek

First attested in documents is **Mycenean** Greek, on the mainland and in Crete from the 13th century B.C., written in the Linear B syllabary and deciphered only in 1952. Greek was written on the island of Cyprus in the Cypriot syllabary, clearly of common origin with the Linear B syllabary. The oldest inscription is a single name from the 11th century B.C.; the rest date from the 8th century B.C. to Hellenistic times. Alphabetic Greek is attested continuously from ca. 800 B.C., beginning with the Homeric poems and continuing through the **Classical** and **Hellenistic** (*koinē*) periods, to **medieval** (Byzantine) and **modern** times.

---

and composition shows that the author of the Gathas must have been a trained professional, a member of the class of poets, a *kauui* = Vedic *kaví*. The only *kauui* who figures prominently in the Gathas is Kauui Vištāspa. It would be far more in accord with what we know of the Indo-Iranian and Indo-European poet's role in society (on which see the next chapter) if Zarathustra were the patron and Vištāspa one of his poets. This hypothesis would accord also with those passages in the Gathas where the name of Kauui Vištāspa is linked to the Indo-Iranian vocabulary and formulary of the *dānastuti* or 'praise of the gift' of patron to poet (chap. 5). Compare Y.46.14 and 19, 51.16, and probably 29.11 if *mā* 'me' refers to the poet rather than the soul of the cow: *mazōi magāi* 'for the great offering', *magahiiā xšaϑrā* 'power over the offering', *mazōi magāi.ā . . . rātōiš* . . . 'for the great offering . . . in accordance with the munificence . . .' beside RV 1.122.7-8, a *dānastuti*, *stuṣé . . . rātír . . . asyá stuṣe máhimaghasya rā́dhaḥ* 'the gift is praised . . . the bounty of the offerer of the great offerings is praised.' Humbach-Elfenbein-Skjærvø 1991:2.44 ad Y. 29.11 and Schlerath 1968:157 both cite the critical Vedic parallel. Note also that 29.11 is the final strophe of the hymn, the usual place for a *dānastuti* in the Rigveda, as Y. 46.19 as well. But this question of authorship, due to Kellens, as Skjærvø points out, must be left to other specialists to debate. See Kellens-Pirart 1988:17-20 and especially Kellens 1991a:59ff. with arguments independent of those offered here.

Anatolian Hittite, Vedic Indic, and Old Iranian poetic literatures are by and large religious and cultic in character and purpose and represent the work and the art of a priestly class and of a ruling class whose duties included the administration of public worship and cult. The Hittite prose of the Laws, of annalistic history, of the treaties is indeed secular in character and purpose, and while the prose style follows clear formulaic patterns, it is not consciously composed with a view to "art". In Early India and Iran none of our materials, hymns, mantras, and prose alike, are secular either in composition or audience.

The situation is entirely the reverse in Early Greek, where virtually all our monuments of verbal art are secular; their composers were either themselves of, or employed by, a secular, warrior, or ruling class and, with the evolution of social institutions in Early Greece, by the city-state itself, by the *polis*. The values and aesthetics of this literature are those of this secular class; we have in the early period little direct evidence of religion and cult viewed from the eyes and spoken from the lips of the priestly class itself. One can in fact discern more than a hint of tension and antagonism between the warrior class and the priestly class in the first book of the *Iliad*, in the legend of the sacrifice of Iphigenia, and elsewhere.

Ancient Greek literature is so widely known and cultivated that it is not necessary to dilate upon it to any extent here. For a sympathetic and admirably brief treatment by experts see Dover 1980, as well as the perennially satisfying work of Meillet 1948.

The documents in Mycenean Greek include no literature per se, though some scholars have heard metrical lines, specifically the second hemistich of a dactylic hexameter, the paroemiac or 'proverb' line, in phrases like *toikhodomoi demeontes* 'masons who are to build' (PY An 35); syntactically the phrase recalls *Od.* 17.299 δμῶες . . . κοπρήσοντες 'slaves who are to spread manure'.

Our poetic monuments begin in the 8th century with the two great Homeric epics the *Iliad* and the *Odyssey*, together with the *Theogony* and the *Works and Days* of Hesiod. Their language and style clearly attest the cultivation of a long period of oral literary elaboration and the development of an Ionic epic literary dialect, with features from other dialects as well. The association of genre with dialect is a characteristic feature of Greek literary language throughout the classical period. The epic dactylic hexameter tradition includes the somewhat later *Homeric Hymns* and other fragmentarily preserved rhapsodic texts.

From the 7th century we have extended fragments of choral lyric and mythological compositions of Stesichorus and Alcman in a literary Doric dialect, elegiac and iambic verse of Archilochus in Ionic, and elegiacs of the Spartans Tyrtaeus and Mimnermus, and a half-century later, of the Athenian Solon. In the 6th century we find a flourishing of lyric (melic) poetry on the island of Lesbos in the poems of Sappho and Alcaeus in syllable-counting strophic meters inherited directly from Indo-European. The 5th century marks the high point of epinician praise-poetry in the person of Pindar and Bacchylides composing in a mixed literary Doric and Aeolic, and the great age of the tragedians Aeschylus, Sophocles, and Euripides, and the comic poet Aristophanes. The dramatists write iambic trimeters in the Attic dialect for the main spoken text, with choral passages in various lyric meters in literary Doric.

We may illustrate what we referred to above, the secular character of Greek poetic art, and what Nagy 1990b:2 referred to as 'the Hellenization of Indo-European poetics' by three passages, reflecting three stages in that process. The first is an inscription from Selinous. As Thucydides 6.4 recounts, colonists from Doric Megara under Lamis founded Megara Hyblaia in eastern Sicily in the 8th century, ca. 727 B.C. A hundred years later, in the 7th century, colonists from Megara Hyblaia under Pamillus (from the mother city Megara), venturing further west than any Greek colony before, founded Selinous on the coast of the southwestern corner of Sicily. We have a large votive inscription from there referring to an otherwise unknown war. The inscription is mid-5th century, dated 460-450, but the conservative Doric tradition of this isolated colony is, as commonly, much more archaic. Their simple Doric faith comes through in the enumerative litany:[12]

> δια τον Δια νικομες και δια τον Φοβον
> και δια Ηερακλεα και δι' Απολλονα
> και δια Ποτειδανα και δια Τυνδαριδας
> και δι' Αϑαναυαν και δια Μαλοφορον
> και δια Πασικρατειαν και δια τος αλλος ϑεος
> δια δε Δια μαλιστα
>
> By Zeus we are victorious, and by Terror (Ares),
> and by Heracles, and by Apollo,
> and by Poseidon, and by the Dioscuri,
> and by Athena, and by (Demeter) Fruit-bearer,
> and by Universal-Queen, and by the other gods,
> but mostly by Zeus.

The antiquity of the verbal formula διὰ GOD νικᾶν appears from *Od.* 8.520: the Phaeacian bard Demodocus sings of Odysseus at the sack of Troy, who braved the most terrible fight,

> **νικῆσαι** καὶ ἔπειτα **διὰ** μεγάϑυμον **'Αϑήνην**
>
> and in the end **was victorious by** great-hearted **Athena**.

Zeus comes in second place to the City in the proud lines of admonition to her citizens by Solon the Athenian (4.1-2 West), composed perhaps in the early 6th century:

> ἡμετέρη δὲ πόλις κατὰ μὲν Διὸς οὔποτ' ὀλεῖται
> αἶσαν καὶ μακάρων ϑεῶν φρένας ἀϑανάτων

12. It is not necessary to see these lines as metrical verse, as some have done (Calder 1963); their power lies in their relentless grammatical parallelism.

Our city will never perish by the destiny of Zeus
or the will of the blessed immortal gods.

Finally we may point to Pindar's famous dithyramb in praise of Athens for her role in the Persian wars (*fr.* 76, 474 B.C.). Here the city is all:

ὦ ταὶ λιπαραὶ καὶ ἰοστέφανοι καὶ ἀοίδιμοι
Ἑλλάδος ἔρεισμα, κλειναὶ Ἀθᾶναι, δαιμόνιον πτολίεθρον.

Oh, the shining and the violet-crowned and the storied
in song, pillar of Greece, glorious Athens, citadel divine.

For this single verse of praise, according to Isocrates, Pindar was rewarded by the Athenians with 10,000 drachmas. The sum is perhaps a rhetorical exaggeration (for 1000), with Race 1987, but the important point is that the City herself has become the patron.

Alongside the literary poetic tradition of Greek preserved in manuscript we have, from the earliest times of alphabetic writing in Greek, epigraphic attestation of poetry, some of exceptional literary quality, written on vases and other artifacts or carved in stone, and unearthed by archaeologists. Our oldest document in Attic Greek is the 8th-century Dipylon prize jug, a rather plain vessel with a text inscribed retrograde with childish-looking letters of increasing size, but in its use of metrics, formula, and diction clearly the work of an accomplished *aoidos*, or 'singer':

hος νυν ορχεστον παντον αταλοτατα παιζει το τοδε [garbled]

Whoever of the dancers sports most gaily, his is this [ ].

For an illustration of this object and its text see Jeffery 1990: plate I. These epigraphic poetic texts are a valuable supplement to our literary evidence; see Hansen 1983.

Italic

Two substantial branches and several fragmentary languages are attested in the 1st millennium B.C. **Old Latin** and the closely related **Faliscan** are attested in short inscriptions from the 6th to the 3rd century B.C.; from then on we have extensive documentation of **Classical Latin**. The main other Italic dialects **South Picene**, **Oscan**, and **Umbrian** (together constituting the **Sabellic** group) are attested in inscriptions from the 7th or 6th to the 1st century B.C.

The Italic languages provide us much material in their earliest attested stages, particularly the ancient prayers preserved in Archaic Latin and Umbrian (chapters 17-19) and the poetry inscribed on stones, pots, and other artifacts in the period ca. 600-300 B.C. in Faliscan, South Picene, and other dialects (chap. 10). The Roman and the native Italic culture was a traditional one, in which it is legitimate to look for archaism and Indo-European inheritance. But we tend in Italy to find these in the language of religion and cult and the language of law—the greatest legacy of Rome to Western civilization—rather than in literature per se. The rich literature of Classical Latin has had rather less to contribute to Indo-European poetics, in that the Latin literary language of the Republic and the Empire is not conservative but innovative and is in many respects an artificial construct.[13] The Latin literary language began as a language of translation from Greek in the 3rd century B.C. (Livius Andronicus, *Odissea*, in the saturnian meter of disputed origin and character). In the same century Cn. Naevius composed the *Bellum Punicum* in saturnians, beginning with the flight of Aeneas from Troy, with copious references to a divine pantheon already completely hellenized (the *interpretatio graeca*) whether in native name (*summi deum regis fratrem Neptunum* 'Neptune the brother of the highest king of the gods') or already in Greek form (*Pythius Apollo*, who is however *inclutus arquitenens / sanctus Ioue prognatus* 'the glorious archer / holy offspring of Jove', combining Greek themes and native inherited Latin lexicon). This developing vigorous literature soon gave up its native Italic (?) versification entirely for Greek meters. Latin metrics was at first still profoundly influenced by the phonological structure of Early Latin, as seen in the comedies of Plautus, but Greek meters later were perfectly transferred to Latin epic, elegiac, and lyric. The literature from the early Republic on was fundamentally permeated by Hellenistic Greek aesthetic[14] and a learned cultivation and valuation of allusion and imitation.

Yet even in this rarified and exquisitely hellenized Roman verbal art some of the inherited Italic and Indo-European tradition still seeps through in the language associated with religion and cult, as in Horace's epithet of *far* in *Carmina* 3.23.20: the countrywoman's hand, touching the altar but bearing no sumptuous offering but grain and salt:

> molliuit auersos Penatis
> **farre pio** et saliente mica
>
> softens the indifferent household gods
> with **holy barley** and the leaping spark.

The Alcaic strophic meter and the gnomic perfectum of the verb are Greek, but the 'holy' barley and the sparking salt are the terms of an ancient Italic ritual.

The justly famous lines of the ghost of Anchises to his son Aeneas in Vergil, *Aen.* 6.847ff., envision and define the Roman genius: *excudent alii* . . . 'Others will hammer out bronzes that breathe, draw living faces from marble . . .'

---

13. The prolongation of Latin throughout the Middle Ages, Renaissance, Reformation, and Baroque is in this respect more comparable to the Classical Sanskrit literary language, which was cultivated in its post-Pāṇinean form only trivially altered down to the present.

14. The rhetoric is observable already in public monuments of the end of the 3rd and beginning of the 2nd century B.C., like the tombs of the Scipios on the Appian Way.

tu regere imperio populos, Romane, memento
(hae tibi erunt artes) . . .

Do you, Roman, remember you will rule over peoples in dominion.
(These will be your arts) . . .

Yet Vergil lets Anchises follow these stirring yet innovative lines of a New Order with a prophetic vision of an ancient Roman ritual, cast in an Indo-European mold, the *spolia opima* which Marcellus would offer, having stripped them from a Gaulish chieftain (859),

tertiaque arma patri suspendet capta Quirino

and will hang up the third spoils, the captured arms, to father Quirinus.

For the ritual see Festus 202-4 L. and the discussion in Latte 1960:204-5 and Dumézil 1966:172-4—a rare agreement. The balanced line with its double distracted noun and adjective straddling the verb is as ancient in poetic form as the apposition *pater Quirinus* 'Father Quirinus' (like Father Jove and Father Mars who receive the *prima* and *secunda spolia* respectively) is in religious theme.

Celtic

Celtic languages were in the first millennium B.C. spoken over large areas of Europe, from the Iberian peninsula through southern Germany, the Po valley, and Austria to the Danube plains, and as far as Galatia in central Anatolia. In our documentation we distinguish geographically between **Continental Celtic** (3rd cent. B.C. - 3rd cent. A.D., extinct; inscriptions in **Gaulish, Celtiberian, Lepontic**, and others) and **Insular Celtic**, the languages spoken now or formerly in the British Isles. These form two groups, **Goidelic** (Gaelic) in Ireland and **Brittonic** (British) in Britain. The former comprise **Irish (Primitive** or **Ogam** 400-600 A.D., **Old Irish** 600-900 A.D., **Middle** 900-1200 A.D., and **Modern** 1200+); **Scottish Gaelic** (1200+) and the extinct **Manx**. Brittonic includes **Welsh (Old** 8th-12th cent. A.D., **Middle** 12th-15th cent., **Modern**), **Breton (Old** and **Modern**), and the extinct **Cornish**.

Our scattered inscriptions from Classical times in Continental Celtic would not be expected to yield much for Indo-European poetics. It is the more surprising that two or our longer inscriptions, Chamalières and Larzac, have yielded one parallel and one exact equivalent of an Old Irish formulaic phrase 'spells of women' (cited in chap. 12). The Chamalières inscription contains as well two rhetorically crafted phrases in succession which have clear affinities to Indo-European poetico-legal and mantic traditions:

reguc cambion exsops pissiumi

I straighten the crooked; blind, I will see.

For the former compare the proem to Hesiod, *Works and Days* 7, ἰθύνει σκολιόν 'he straightens the crooked', discussed in chap. 7.[15]

Both branches of Insular Celtic have a rich literary tradition going back to their earliest attestation. Ireland was christianized in the 5th century. By the end of the next century we have a flourishing poetical literature of both secular and monastic inspiration, including lyrics, praise poetry, versified law, aphoristic literature, hagiographic and devotional works, and genealogies. Prose texts are found from the 7th century on, notably the vast body of legal texts, the saga tales (*scéla*) with their characteristic telescoped, *sūtra*-like prose style, often alternating with dithyrambic portions in archaic or archaizing verse (*roscada*).

The earliest Welsh literary monuments are the poetry of the *Gododdin* (*Canu Aneurin*), a 9th-century recension of an oral composition going back perhaps to the 6th century. A large body of prose literature is attested in Middle Welsh, notably the Four Branches of the Mabinogi. The Welsh word *ceinc* (Modern *cainc*) 'branch' is a cognate of Vedic *śākhā* in the same meaning, used as a designation for the different Vedic 'schools'; this 'literary' use of the word may be an ancient metaphor, though it is natural enough to have been created independently.

The remaining five branches of the Indo-European family are first attested in the Christian era, three of them from Bible translations emanating from the Eastern Church.

Germanic

The earliest extensive representative is **Gothic** (extinct), known from the Bible translation of the 4th century, which together with the other language remnants (Vandalic, Burgundian, etc.) form **East Germanic**. **North Germanic** is attested from a few Runic inscriptions (3rd cent. A.D.+) and principally from **Old Norse** (9th-16th cent.) and the later West (Norwegian, Icelandic) and East (Danish, Swedish) Scandinavian languages. The principal earliest **West Germanic** monuments are in **Old English** (ca. 700 A.D.+), **Old High German** (ca. 750+), and **Old Saxon** (ca. 850+), with the later medieval and modern forms of English, Frisian, Dutch, Low German, and High German.

Our richest poetic documentation is in Old English and Old Norse. The standard edition of the former corpus, the *Anglo-Saxon Poetic Records* [Krapp et al. 1931-42], numbers six volumes and includes the great epic *Beowulf* as well as religious poems, lyrics, wisdom literature, riddles, and spells. In Old Norse we have the *Poetic Edda* and other poems, as well as a body of the obscure and obscurantist Skaldic verse; see

15. The 1sg. verb *reguc* in sentence-initial position corresponds to an Old Irish 1sg. absolute **rigu* (conjunct *-riug*) from **regū* (< **regō*) + some element *x*; *x* assimilates to the following consonant, here the *c* of *cambion*. The 1sg. *pissiumi* in sentence-final position corresponds to an Old Irish conjunct, as in the cognate *-ciu* < **kʷis-i̯ū*. If the *-ss-* is real we must have a future morpheme *-si̯e/o-*. The 1sg. ending *-ūmi* is from **-ō* > **-ū* plus later *-mi*, like Vedic *-āmi*. It corresponds to Welsh *-if* (historically conjunct), e.g. *kenif* < **kanū* + *mi* 'I sing'. For *exsops* see Watkins 1983.

respectively J. Harris and R. Frank in Clover and Lindow 1985:68-156, 157-197. The *Prose Edda* of Snorri Sturluson (1179-1241), Iceland's most famous man of letters, is an invaluable guide to Norse poetics and mythology. Old Saxon shows two devotional poems, *Heliand* ('Savior') and the fragmentary *Genesis*. The latter comes from a 9th-century text which was translated into Old English and interpolated into an earlier Old English *Genesis* as "Genesis B". Lastly we have the poetic monuments of Old High German, mostly Christian in character, most extensively the rhyming *Liber evangeliorum* of Otfrid (9th century), but also including diverse hymns, songs, and the non-rhyming alliterative *Muspilli* fragment of just over 100 lines. Of heroic poetry in Old High German we have only the all too brief fragment (68 lines) of the *Hildebrandslied*, as well as some short spells discussed in chapters 56.2 and 58.1. The similarities and often identities in poetic form and thematic and mythological substance among all four of the early medieval Germanic languages are such that something like a genetic Common Germanic comparative literature was envisioned already in the 19th century. See the rich discussion in Harris 1985.

Armenian

Known from the Bible translation of the 5th century and subsequent literature is **Classical Armenian**, with its medieval and modern descendants spoken in several dialects, notably the Eastern (Russian) and the Western (Turkish and post-Diaspora).

Armenian literature of the early Classical period is almost entirely prose, religious and historical. Some pre-Christian oral poetry was recorded by the historian Moses of Chorene (Movsēs Xorenac'i), the *Songs of Gołt'n* (a toponym). See on these chap. 23.2.

Tocharian

Two languages, now extinct, found in documents (mostly Buddhist translation literature) from the eastern (**Toch. A**) and western (**Toch. B**) parts of the Tarim Basin in Chinese Turkestan (Xinjiang), dating from the 6th-8th centuries.

Even Tocharian shows a lingering trace of Indo-European phraseology in the word for 'fame', A. *ñom-klyu*, literally 'name-fame', compare the Greek formula ὄνομα κλυτός 'famed for his name', compound name Ὀνομάκλυτος, and Vedic *nā́ma śrútyam* (RV 8.46.14) 'famous name'. That the compound 'name-fame' is of Common Tocharian date is clear from the title A *ñom-kälywāts*, B *ñem-klawis(s)u*, translating Sanskrit *bhagavat* 'Eminence'. A *klyu* = B *kälywe* reflect precisely IE **k̂leu̯os*, Vedic *śrávas* = Greek κλέ(ϝ)ος. On the curious rhyming form *tsekeṣi pekeṣi pat* 'of a figure or of a picture' and its cognate Latin equivalent (in the reverse order) *pictus fictus* etc. (Cicero, *De natura deorum* 2.145) see Schulze 1933:257-61, reprinted in Schmitt 1968:34-9.

That Tocharian even in a translation literature with apparently borrowed meters deployed poetic features in a characteristically "Indo-European" way may be shown by the thoroughgoing grammatical parallelism, the figure of anaphora, and the metrical line positioning of the anaphors (boldface) in the following 7-syllable lines or hemistichs from the beginning of the Puṇyavantajātaka in A, the tale of the mechanical maiden (for parallels see the Greek and Vedic verses cited at the beginning of chap. 2.3):

tsraşiśśi māk nişpalntu
tsraşiśśi māk śkaṃ şñaşşeñ
nämseñc yäsluş **tsraşisac**
kumseñc yärkant **tsraşisac** I
tsraşiñ waste wrasaśśi
tsraşiśśi mā praski naş
tämyo kāsu **tsraşşune**
pūkaṃ pruccamo ñi pälskam II

The strong have great riches; **the strong** have also many relatives.
Enemies bow down to **the strong**; honors come to **the strong**.
The strong (are) the protection of creatures; **the strong** have no fear.
Therefore **strength** (is) good; best of all in my opinion.

Balto-Slavic

The Slavic and Baltic languages appear to form a single subgroup within Indo-European, though some scholars would keep them apart. **Slavic** is first attested in the Bible translation of the 9th century in **Old Church Slavonic**. The dialect division into **East Slavic** (Russian, Ukrainian, Byelorussian), **West Slavic** (Polish, Czech, Slovak, etc.), and **South Slavic** (Slovene, Serbo-Croatian, Macedonian, Bulgarian) is probably not much older than the middle of the first millennium A.D. Of the **Baltic** languages, the earliest attested is the extinct Old Prussian (14th-17th century), followed by the two flourishing East Baltic languages Lithuanian and Latvian (16th century +).

Both the older attested Slavic and the much more recently attested Baltic languages have a vast tradition of oral folk poetry and, in the case of Slavic, of oral epic poetry, heroic tales, songs, and the like, with traditional, sometimes pre-Christian themes. Lithuanian and Latvian folk poetry was collected and examined from the middle of the 19th century on, particularly the *dainos* 'songs' and *raudos* 'laments'. Other folk-genres like riddles and spells are also well represented. See Ivanov and Toporov 1974 and later works of both scholars noted in Gamkrelidze and Ivanov 1984 and Toporov 1975-.

Albanian

Albanian is known only from the 15th century on, in two dialects, a northern (Geg) and a southern (Tosk). Albanian has as well a rich folk tradition and an oral epic tradition comparable to that of South Slavic. Its potential contribution to Indo-European poetics probably resides more in theme, as reflected in customs. Such are for example the legal institutions of the Northern Albanians reflected in the *Kanun* of Lek Dukagjini, preserved orally since the Middle Ages. See Fox 1989.

I conclude this survey of the Indo-European speaking peoples and their poetic traditions with the resumé of a lecture by Emile Benveniste on 'The Indo-Europeans and the peopling of Europe', delivered at the Journées de synthèse historique of 1938:[16]

> In their diversity these invasions have traits in common. They never involved vast movements of warriors. They are rather hardy little groups, strongly organized, founding their order on the ruin of established structures. They clearly knew neither the sea, nor cities. They have neither writing, nor a complicated religion, nor any sort of refinement. They will all preserve, along their individual destiny, the distinctive features of their first community: the patriarchal structure of the "extended family", united in the cult of its ancestors, living from farming and animal husbandry; aristocratic style of a society of priests, warriors, and farmers; "naturalistic" worship and kingship sacrifice (of which the most significant was that of the horse, the Vedic *aśvamedha*); a conquering instinct and a taste for open spaces; a sense of authority and attachment to worldly goods. At the beginning they seem to be absorbed into the mass of often more civilized peoples which they have overwhelmed. A long silence follows their conquest. But by and by, from the new order which they found, there springs up a culture at first full of local elements, then developing in forms ever newer and bolder. An inventive power marks these creations, on which the language of masters confers the most perfect expression. The taking over of the land by ever newer invaders, but sprung from the same stock, thus creates the conditions for a supple and assimilative political organization, the home for a civilization vigorous enough to survive its founders, and original enough to influence permanently even what opposes it.

16. Revue de synthèse, Synthèse historique 1939, p. 18, cited after Haudry 1985:125.

5

The Indo-European poet: His social function and his art

In chap. 3 we considered one of the two aspects of the study of Indo-European poetics, the formal question of the poet's *technique*. The second, to which we now come, concerns the social function of poetry and the poet in Indo-European times: his *purpose*. Both must be looked at together, complementarily. For the art of the Indo-European poet is to say something wholly traditional in a new and interesting, but therefore *more effective* way. It is verbal activity, artistically elaborated, but directed toward a more or less immediate, concrete goal.

We noted earlier in connection with the verbal formula (chap. 1.2) that formulas are the vehicles of themes, and that in the totality of these we find the doctrine, ideology, and culture of the Indo-Europeans. These formulas are collectively the verbal expression of the whole traditional culture of the Indo-Europeans.

The *function* of the Indo-European poet was to be the custodian and the transmitter of this tradition. The totality of themes as expressed in formulas was in these preliterate societies entrusted precisely to the PROFESSIONALS OF THE WORD, the poets.

The lexical expression of this function of custodianship and transmittal in the Proto-Indo-European language was **mnah₂*- (**mnā*-), a root derivative suffixed form (Benveniste's thème II) of the simple root **men*- expressing 'mental force'. The root **mnah₂*- exhibits a significant range of meanings in the languages which attest it:

> 'look at, see, experience' in Anatolian (Melchert 1993b:135), Cuneiform and Hieroglyphic Luvian *ma-na-a-du* (3 pl. ipv.) = Hittite *aušdu* 'let him see';
>
> 'be mindful of; remember' in Greek μέμνημαι, μνάομαι;
>
> 'commit to memory and hand down' in Vedic, Brāhmaṇas and Sūtras *ā-mnā-*.

The functional orientation is apparent in the figure of the Cretan law-court official *mnāmōn*, μναμονευεν, 'act as *mnāmōn*', the 'Remembrancer', as it is translated by Jeffery and Morpurgo Davies 1970:150. A passage with this verb in the Kauṣītaki-Brāhmaṇa 8.7 can well stand as a guiding principle of traditional Indo-European poetic culture:

> viparyasya dāśatayībhyaṃ vaṣaṭ kuryād iti haika āhur
> **yathāmnātam** iti tv eva sthitam
>
> Inverting the two verses from the Saṁhitā he should utter
> the call of *vaṣaṭ*, some say, but
> **'as it is remembranced'** is the established rule.[1]

The Italian school of students of Indo-European poetics, notably Durante and Campanile, has given considerable attention to the figure of the Indo-European poet, working in particular from the evidence of traditions of India and the Celtic British Isles, as well as Archaic Greece, and to some extent the Germanic world. Campanile 1977:27ff. presents a detailed survey of the figure and function of the traditional poet in Celtic and Indic society and defines him as 'the preserver and the professional of the spoken word. It is he who is by definition competent in all the areas where the word is, or is considered, operative.' This must be understood as a very concrete, practical notion. Those areas where the traditional spoken word is operative, and its control mandatory, impinge upon virtually the totality of the culture. Campanile 1987:26 noted that

> What we term Indo-European poetry was rather a society's sum of knowledge, which was orally transmitted. The features which our western tradition ascribes to poetry (feeling, inspiration, individualism, participation, etc.), and which the aesthetics of romanticism has particularly underscored, were for Indo-European poetry only a side issue, although they were present. The main thing was to preserve and increase cultural elements which presented something essential to the well-being, collectivity, and stability of the society. We are speaking of the magic spells which heal the sick, the legal formulas which settle disputes, the prayers which extort worldly goods from the gods, the genealogies which give to people consciousness of their past and pride in it, the eulogies which legitimize rulers by the celebration of their greatness. He who fulfilled such important functions held a position of the first rank in his society, but his traffic with the Muses was neither particularly frequent nor particularly necessary. For this kind of poetry one could prepare oneself only by years of study; what the Middle Irish Metrics texts tell us about the training of the Early Irish poet is basically valid for the Indo-European one as well.

B. Schlerath 1974 emphasizes the particular link between the activity of the poet and the priest: a religious poem, invocation, or hymn of praise to the gods is inextricably linked with the worship and all the paraphernalia of cult. The principal goal of the poem is the expression of that active, cosmic truth which is Indo-Iranian

1. Keith translates with periphrasis: 'but the rule is to follow the traditional text.'

ṛtá*-. Toporov 1981:200 puts the parallel function of poet and priest more loftily: 'Both combat Chaos, both strengthen Cosmic Order, its Law (ṛtá*) and the safe, lasting place where the gods dwell . . . For society, the poet like the priest is indispensable. It is they who subdue the entropic tendencies of the universe, suppress or rework the elements of chaos, continually renew the world as cosmos, and assure increase, wealth, and continuity of offspring.'

Whether we choose to follow Toporov in this ideological assessment—cf. his further likening the poet, ancient and modern, to the first culture-hero, the Demiurge (1981:200 and 219-27)—is perhaps a question of taste. But one simple socioeconomic fact is clear: the Indo-European poet was the highest-paid professional in his society.

The concept and nature of the Indo-European poet cannot be separated from that of the society in which he operated. Indo-European tribal society was dominated by the Maussian principle of reciprocity and exchange or potlatch, of the gift entailing the counter-gift.[2] The *poet* did not function in that society in isolation; he had a *patron*. The two were precisely in an exchange or reciprocity relation: the poet gave poems of praise to the patron, who in turn bestowed largesse upon the poet. To the aristocracy of Indo-European society this reciprocal relation was a moral and ideological necessity. For only the poet could confer on the patron what he and his culture valued more highly than life itself: precisely what is expressed by the 'imperishable fame' formula.

Perhaps the clearest expression of this relation is the conclusion of a poem addressed by the 6th-century Greek poet Ibycus to the tyrant of Samos Polycrates (PMG 282 = SLG 151.47-8 = PMGF p. 243):

> καὶ σύ, Πολύκρατες, **κλέος ἄφθιτον** ἕξεις
> ὡς κατ' ἀοιδὰν καὶ ἐμὸν **κλέος**
>
> You too, Polycrates, will have **undying fame (kleos)**
> in accordance with my song and my **kleos**.

The two uses of *kléos* (IE **k̂léu̯os*) are the poet's pledge-token of reciprocity: the poet's *kléos* is the vehicle of the patron's. In this way we can understand the development of IE **k̂léu̯os* to the meaning 'word' in Old Iranian and Slavic (diffusion from Iranian?) and 'epic lay' already in Old Russian *slovo*.

The same reciprocity relation as between poet and patron existed between poet and the gods. We have the same eulogistic model: a good hymn of praise, saying something wholly traditional in a new and interesting way, is the gift of the poet to the god. This gift then *obligates* that deity to bestow as counter-gift that which is prayed for: prosperity, fecundity, long life. Poetry and poets were not a "frill" in Indo-European society but a necessity of life, a necessary condition for existence. The spoken word could produce a physical effect on the world, but only if properly formulated by the poet.

Typically the patron would commission a hymn by the poet to a god, to benefit

2. As demonstrated at length by Benveniste 1949 and 1969:1.65ff., cf. also Watkins 1976b.

the patron (in Vedic the *yajamāna*, 'he for whom the worship is performed'), for which the poet would be rewarded, i.e. paid. Most of the hymns of the Rigveda are so occasioned. It is a mark of the permansiveness of this system throughout the Indo-European world that 'a king without poets' was proverbial in Ireland for 'nothing', and that Aeschylus (*Ag.* 979) could call, wholly negatively, an unwanted fear

ἀκέλευστος ἄμισθος ἀοιδά

an uncommissioned, unrewarded song.

Greek μισθός, the base of negative ἄμισθος 'unrewarded', has already in Homer the sense of 'wages, hire'. Yet one of the self-designations of Greek and Indo-European poets is ἐπέων τέκτονες 'craftsmen of words', and like the journeyman the poet is worthy of his hire. Pindar freely uses μισθός for his compensation (*Pyth.* 1.75-77 ἀρέομαι . . . μισθόν 'I will earn as recompense') in a positive sense.[3] The word is a clear Indo-European inheritance, **misdhó-*, and its meaning 'honorific compensation for deed performed', as established by Benveniste 1969:1.163-9 on the basis of its Iranian (*mīždəm*) and Germanic (English *meed*) cognates. The word has a clear 'exchange value' in the Maussian system of reciprocity; note the related Avestan *miiazda-*, Vedic *miyedha-* 'offering, oblation'.

In Vedic the word for the poet's reward (or fee) was *dákṣinā-* (scil. *gáuḥ*, *dhenúḥ*), the *dákṣinā*-cow. The original force of the adjective is still a matter of dispute. For the aetiology see below.

Our knowledge of the socio-economic position of the Indo-European poet is inferential, from the daughter societies, especially India, Ireland, and Greece. The evidence from these three in turn will be considered in the following sections. The first two offer abundant evidence that poets belonged to a hereditary class or caste in an aristocratic society. Books 2 through 7 of the Rigveda are called the Family books because they are composed respectively by members of six families: Gṛtsamada, Viśvāmitra, Vāmadeva, Atri, Bharadvāja, and Vasiṣṭha. In these books self-references by the poets are not uncommon.[4] In RV 4.4.10-11 we find a complex intertwining of the themes of the poet's genealogy, the power of the word, and the reciprocal gift-exchange relationship (Vedic *ātithyá*, Greek *xenía* 'guest-friendship', from *átithi*, *xénos* 'guest') of both poet with patron and patron (mediated by the poet) with god. The Vāmadevas of Book 4 were poets of the line of King Trasadasyu, one of whom is figured here returning from war laden with booty. The god Agni is addressed:

yás tvā sváśvaḥ suhiraṇyó agna
upayā́ti vásumatā ráthena
tásya trātā́ bhavasi tásya sákhā

3. See the discussion in Nagy 1990b:188-90 for the 'Hellenization' of this Indo-European function.
4. For a detailed analysis of one such see Dandekar 1974.

yás ta ātithyám ānuṣág júj oṣat
mahó rujāmi bandhútā vácobhis
tán mā pitúr gótamād ánv iyāya
tvám̐ no asyá vácasaś cikiddhi
hótar yaviṣṭha sukrato dámūnāḥ

He of good horses, good gold, who approaches you,
Agni, with wealth-laden chariot,
you become his protector, his friend,
he who duly enjoys your guest-friendship.

By my family, by the words of (my) great (father)
I smash (obstacles); that has come to me from my father Gotama.
Heed you this word of ours,
Hotṛ, o youngest, o wise one, as householder.

Note that *ātithyám* 'guest-friendship' is applied equally to the reciprocity relation between host and guest, poet and patron, and god and worshiper.

The reference of *rujāmi* 'I smash' is to the Vala-myth, a cosmogonic variant of the dragon-slaying myth (Vala and Vṛtra are from the same root *vṛ-*), which is narrated allusively in the preceding and difficult hymn 4.1, verses 13-17. Here the poet-priests (*náraḥ . . . uśíjaḥ*) by remembering (*manvata*, root **men-*) the thrice-seven highest secret names of the cows (a "skaldic" expression for the poetic language of the Rigveda: Geldner ad loc.) with their divine word (*vácasā dáivyena*) smash open the cave to release the captive cows, the light, the dawn's rays, the glorious milk of the dawn cows (*aruṇī́r yaśásā góḥ*). Geldner adds that the deeper meaning of the passage is that the act of remembering the cow's names is at the same time the birth of poetic inspiration, the 'divine word'. And from the released cows, the dawn's rays, the milk of the dawn cows came the first *dákṣinā*, the reward and recompense of the poet.

The "Mercenary Muse" who sings for hire (Pindar, *Isth.* 2.6, see below) is thus as old as creation, in the Indic view. That this myth in some form may go back to the proto-language is indicated on the one hand by the Irish myth of the *teora ferba fíra* 'three milk cows', with *fír* 'milk' cognate with Vedic *vā́r* in *usríyānām vā́r* (RV 4.5.8) 'milk of the dawn cows' (Watkins 1987d:402), and on the other by the isolated and much-discussed Greek expression νυκτὸς ἀμολγός, quasi 'milk of the night' (Lazzeroni 1971, cf. Campanile 1977:24).

The image of thrice-seven secret names of the cows as Vedic poetic language recurs in a hymn of a Vasiṣṭhid to Varuṇa, RV 7.87.4:

uvā́ca me váruṇo médhirāya
trī́ḥ saptá nā́mā ághnyā bibharti
vidvā́n padásya gúhyā ná vocad
yugā́ya vípra úparāya śíkṣān

Varuṇa said to me, the wise one:

"The cow bears thrice seven names.
He who knows the track should tell them like secrets,
if he would serve as inspired poet to the later generation."

The metaphor of the track (*padám*), which comes to mean 'word', is repeated in RV 4.5.2-3, a Vāmadevid hymn like those cited earlier:

mā́ nindata yá imā́m máhyaṃ rātíṃ
devó dadáu mártyāya svadhā́vān
. . .
padáṃ ná gór ápagūḷhaṃ vividvā́n
agnír máhyam préd u vocan manīṣā́m

Do not blame him who gave me this gift,
the self-powerful god to a mortal . . .
Agni, having found the hidden word like the track of the cow,
made known to me the understanding.

For all that the poet attributes his knowledge to divine inspiration, he knows in practice that it had to be acquired by decades of laborious study. The same hymn continues (RV 4.5.6):

idám me agne . . . gurúm bhāráṃ ná mánma . . . dadhātha

You have placed on me this knowledge, o Agni, like a heavy burden.

Though it confers privileged status the poet's wisdom is a heavy responsibility to bear.

Note that the words for the poet's understanding (*manīṣā́*) and wisdom (*mánma* = Old Irish *menmae* 'mind'), and the remembering (*manvata*) the 3x7 secret names of the cow which is Vedic poetics itself, are all derivatives of the root **men-* expressing active mental force, thinking, perceiving, remembering. So too is Greek Μοῦσα (Aeolic Μοῖσα) 'Muse', daughter of Zeus and Mnemosyne 'Memory': Proto-Greek **montwa* from **mon-tu-*h_2, cf. Vedic *mántu-*, *amantú-* '(un)caring, (un)mindful'. The inspiration of the divine Muse is thus only a personification of the trained mind of the poet.

Perhaps the single most telling indication of the common Indo-European origin of the reciprocal poet-patron relation as we have described it is the existence of a special literary genre in Vedic, Greek, Celtic, and Germanic, which we can call by its Sanskrit name *dānastuti* or 'praise of the gift'. The *dānastuti* is a short coda of one or more verses of thanks to the patron who commissioned the poem, praising his generosity and enumerating his gifts, which is incorporated into many Vedic hymns. These *dānastuti*s regularly record such rewards (or fees) as 200 cows, 4 horses, and 2 wagons, like RV 7.18.22-25. The word for gift-chattels, masculine *dā́nās* (beside normally neuter *dā́nam* 'gift') is here and elsewhere linked by contiguity to the *śrávas* 'fame' of the generous patron. RV 8.46.23-24 records '10 chestnuts . . . the gift-chattels of Pṛthuśravas ('Broad-fame')', and the poet plays there with his patron's name in another dimension: *várṣiṣṭham akṛta śrávas* 'he got for himself loftiest fame'.

RV 6.63.9-10, to the Aśvins, makes clear the nature of the process. The poet itemizes to the gods hymned the generosity of the patron(s): 'and for me two swift mares of Puraya's, a hundred (cows) with Sumīḷha, and cooked food with Peruka . . .'[5]

sáṃ vāṃ śatā́ nāsatyā sahásrā
áśvānām purupánthā giré dāt
bharádvājāya vīra nū́ giré dāt

Purupanthā gave together hundreds, thousands
of horses for your song of praise, o Nāsatyas,
To Bharadvāja he gave (them) for the song of praise, o heroes.

The poet of RV 5.61.17-19 dedicates his composition to a distant benefactor, the message—the hope of future reward—to be delivered by the goddess of Night, with an exact address. The *envoi* has a slightly Pindaric ring:

etám me stómam ūrmye
dārbhyā́ya párā vaha
gíro devi rathī́r iva

utá me vocatād íti
sutásome ráthavītau
ná kā́mo ápa veti me

eṣá kṣeti ráthavītir
maghávā gómatīr ánu
párvateṣv ápaśritaḥ

Carry this my song of praise, o Night,
to the descendant of Darbha,
my songs, o Goddess, like a charioteer.

And say for me thus
to Rathavīti who has pressed soma,
"My desire does not abate."

This generous Rathavīti
dwells along the Gomatī rivers,
hidden away in the mountains.

5. The phonetic linkage with the names, ***sumīḷhé śatám peruké ca pakvā́***, is doubtless intentional, and the name *Sumīḷha* probably still carried a trace of its etymological meaning of 'reward, prize', IE **misdho-*, like Avestan *humižda-* 'bringing good reward'.

Examples of *dānastutis* from other Indo-European traditions are given below.

The reciprocal situation of poet and patron may have a negative side as well. Generosity leads to praise, but ungenerous payment can provoke blame, invective, and satire, the 'formidable weapon' (Binchy 1940:69) of poets from India and Greece to Ireland. A Vedic example with a thematically close parallel in Old Irish is given in chap. 16.

We pass now from the allusive and fleeting world of ancient Vedic India in the second millennium B.C. to the comparative clarity of Christian Ireland from the seventh to the seventeenth centuries. Despite the enormous differences in tone and cultural outlook the system, the structural position of the poet in each society, is remarkably similar in India and Ireland, and the Irish system remained basically static over the 1000 years from the beginning of our documentation to the collapse of the Gaelic world. For the early period compare the *Mittelirische Verslehren* (ed. Thurneysen, *Irische Texte* 3.1-182)[6] and the other legal texts edited and analyzed in Breatnach 1987 and for the Bardic poet of the Classical Modern Irish period Bergin 1970. For the Continental Celtic evidence from Gaul, as seen through Greek and Roman eyes, cf. the clear summary in MacCana 1970:14ff.

From the earliest times in Ireland the poet (Old Irish *fili*, Middle and Modern Irish *file*, plural *filid*) belongs to a poetic family for at least three generations. Compare *Uraicecht na Ríar* §§4 and 7 *amail as-beir fénechus: Ní tét acht lethdíre do ṡuidib, manip do chlaind genetar . . . Ceist, cuin as cland filed in chland? Ní hansae, fili a n-athair 7 a senathair* 'as Irish law says: "Only half honor-price goes to sages if it is not to a family (of sages) that they are born" . . . Question, when is the family a family of poets? Not difficult; their father is a poet and their grandfather.' The ideal combination, as Breatnach shows (1987:96ff.), was family background, ability in poetry (*airchetal*, the actual poetic product, which the text speaks of having or not having), and study (*frithgnum*). With ability and study alone it was possible to become a poet, an *ánroth* 'splendid stream', second only to the *ollam* 'supreme', but it took again three generations, like most advancement to nobility or professions in medieval Ireland. The seven grades of *fili* in the eighth century are modeled on those of the 7th-century Irish church, as Breatnach notes. And the distinction between *fili* and *bard* (Welsh *bardd*), which is not found in Wales, seems also to be an innovation.

The patrons of the poets were the kings and nobles or the Church (Breatnach 1987:89). He cites there *Ériu* 13.17.20: *ní saora, ní sloinde acht righ no airigh, as doibh dligidh mormhainbhthe dia moaighid maoin* 'ennoble only, make known only a king or a noble, for it is from them that is due great wealth through which prosperity increases.'

Early Irish has a word *cerd* meaning both 'craft' and 'poetry', both 'craftsman' and 'poet'. Early Welsh has the same word *cerdd* meaning both 'craft' and 'poetry, poem'. In their synchronic semantics the two meanings of these Celtic words exhibit a *metaphor*, a *similarity* relation: poetry is like a craft, and the poet like a craftsman.

6. The text is in the process of being edited by D. Ó hAodha.

But we have a *metonymy*, a *contiguity* relation projected back on the diachronic plane—reconstructed if you will—in the semantics of the Celtic words *cerd*, *cerdd* 'craft, poetry' and their unique cognate, Greek κέρδος, which means 'profit, gain'. The etymology is sure, but it rests on a metonymic figure: *craft—and poetry—is profit*. We can prove the etymology only by making explicit the cultural and pragmatic context in which such a metonymy was meaningful.

We see by this etymology just how arch Pindar was being in setting up as a foil[7] (one might think rather 'smokescreen') his "Mercenary Muse"—the word is φιλο**κερδής** 'profit-loving', from our κέρδος—in *Isth*. 2.6:

ἁ Μοῖσα γὰρ οὐ φιλο**κερδής** πω τότ' ἦν οὐδ' ἐργάτις

For the Muse then did not yet love **gain** nor work for hire.

For an analysis of the whole poem as *dānastuti* see below.

In Ireland right down to the collapse of the Gaelic world in the 17th century (and in Scotland in the 18th) the Gaelic poet, in Bergin's apt phrase, had to be *both born and made*. In his justly famous 1912 lecture on Bardic Poetry, Bergin (1970:3ff.) gives this description:

> For we must remember that the Irish *file* or *bard* was not necessarily an inspired poet. That he could not help. He was, in fact, a professor of literature and a man of letters, highly trained in the use of a polished literary medium, belonging to a hereditary caste in an aristocratic society, holding an official position therein by virtue of his training, his learning, his knowledge of the history and traditions of his country and his clan . . . At an earlier period he had been regarded as a dealer in magic, a weaver of spells and incantations, who could blast his enemies by the venom of his verse, and . . . a well-turned malediction.[8] He might be a poet, too, if in addition to his training he was gifted with the indefinable power, the true magic, of poetry. But whether he was a poet in this higher sense or not, he always composed in verse.

These sentences could be applied virtually without alteration to the Vedic *kavi* and to the mostly nameless composers, over hundreds of years, of the more than a thousand collected and preserved hymns, some good and some indifferent, which make up the Rigveda.

As illustration Bergin quotes from the description of a Bardic School by one who attended it in the early 17th century, in the *Memoirs of the Marquis of Clanricarde* (apparently the work of one Thomas O'Sullevane, see R. Flower, *British Museum Catalogue of Irish Manuscripts* 3.16 [editors' note]) which I excerpt:

---

7. For the notion here of 'foil for the positive value of a transcendent reciprocity' see Nagy 1990:188, with references.

8. For a description of the fearsome satire called *glám dícenn*, which involves poets chanting the satire on the top of a hill before sunrise while piercing with a thorn of the whitethorn a clay image of the man against whom the satire is made, see Breatnach 1987:114-15,140. See also Watkins 1993.

> The poetical Seminary or School... was open only to such as were descended of Poets and reputed within their Tribes...
> The Structure was a snug low Hut, and beds in it at convenient Distances, each with a small Apartment without much Furniture of any kind, save only a Table, some Seats, and a Conveniency for Cloaths to hang upon. No Windows to let in the Day, nor any Light at all us'd but that of Candles, and these brought in at a proper Season only...
> The Professors (one or more as there was occasion) gave a Subject suitable to the Capacity of each Class, determining the number of Rhimes, and clearing what was to be chiefly observed therein as to Syllables, Quartans, Concord, Correspondence, Termination and Union[9], each of which were restrained by peculiar Rules. The said Subject (either one or more as aforesaid) having been given over Night, they worked it apart each by himself upon his own Bed, the whole next Day in the Dark, till at a certain Hour in the Night, Lights being brought in, they committed it to writing. Being afterwards dress'd and come together in a large Room, where the Masters waited, each Scholar gave in his Performance, which being corrected or approved of (according as it requir'd) either the same or fresh subjects were given against the next Day...
> Every *Saturday* and on the Eves of Festival Days they broke up and dispers'd themselves among the Gentleman and rich Farmers of the Country, by whom they were very well entertain'd and much made of... Nor was the People satisfied with affording this Hospitality alone; they sent in by turns every Week from far and near Liquors and all manner of Provision toward the Subsistence of the Academy...
> Yet the course was long and tedious, as we find, and it was six or seven years before a Mastery or the last Degree was conferred...
> As every Professor, or chief Poet, depended on some Prince or great Lord, that had endowed his Tribe, he was under strict ties to him and Family, as to record in good Metre his Marriages, Births, Deaths, Acquisitions made in war and Peace, Exploits, and other remarkable things relating to the Same...
> The last Part to be done, which was the *Action* and *Pronunciation* of the Poem in the Presence of the Maecenas, or the principal Person it related to, was performed with a great deal of Ceremony in a Consort of Vocal and Instrumental Musick. The Poet himself said nothing, but directed and took care that everybody else did his Part right. The Bard having first had the composition from him, got it well by Heart, and now pronounced it orderly, keeping even pace with a Harp, touch'd upon that Occasion; no other musical Instrumental being allowed for the said purpose than this alone, as being Masculin, much sweeter and fuller than any other.

This remarkable document probably comes as close as we will ever get to an eyewitness account of the formation of an Indo-European poet.

Another window on the Irish Bardic Poet's art and its mode of acquisition is furnished by the *Irish Grammatical Tracts*, edited by Bergin 1955, which contains myriads of quatrains cited as examples and described by such terms as *lochtach* 'faulty'. Whether these are 'detritus' from the schools or deliberately composed as such, it is clear that their assiduous study was part of the Bardic education. On these texts as a whole, and a beginning to the assessment of their place in the history of

9. These all translate precise Irish technical terms; see chap. 9.

linguistics, see Bergin 1939 and Armstrong 1985 (rich bibliography p. 266). For they respond to the same sort of poetic challenge as did the nameless Hindu grammarians of the long tradition that culminated in the 'perfection' of the grammar of Pāṇini. Compare the words of Saussure cited from Starobinsky 1971:35 by Toporov 1981:216: "Le poète se livrait, et avait pour ordinaire métier de se livrer à l'analyse phonique des mots: que c'est cette science de la forme vocale des mots qui faisait probablement, dès les plus anciens temps indo-européens, la superiorité, la qualité particulaire, du *Kavis* des Hindous, du *Vātēs* des Latins, etc."

I close the account of Irish with some lines of Mathghamhain Ó Hifearnáin or Mahon O'Heffernan (Bergin 1970:145, 279), who belonged to the early 17th century, the time of confiscations and plantations, the collapse of the aristocratic Gaelic world, which brought along the ruin of its poets. He was the author of the well-known bitter verses beginning *A mhic, ná meabhraigh éigse* 'My son, cultivate not the poetic art':

1 Ceist! cia do cheinneóchadh dán?
a chiall is ceirteólas suadh:
an ngéabhadh, nó an áil le haon,
dán saor do-bhéaradh go buan?

4 Ceard mar so ní sochar dhún,
. . .
ga bríogh d'éinfhior dul re dán?

Question, who will buy a poem? Its meaning is genuine learning of scholars. Will any take, or does any lack, a noble poem that shall make him immortal? . . . Such an art (*ceard*, Old Irish *cerd*) as this is no profit to me . . . What use is it to anyone to profess poetry?

For the rhyme scheme (end rhyme *b d*, internal rhymes *a b*, *c d*, 'consonance' *a c*) and alliteration see chap. 9. Both the ideology and the vocabulary go back to Indo-European times.

For Germanic we need cite only some lines of the Old English *Widsith* which attest the institution of the mutual dependence, the reciprocity relation of poet and patron, and the genre of the *dānastuti*. Widsith the traveling court-poet of the speaking name ("Wide-journey") unlocked his word-hoard (*wordhord onleac*, 1) and told of meeting many peoples over the earth (*ofer eorþan* 2) and how (3-4)

oft he on flette geþah
mynelicne maþþum

Often did he in hall get desirable treasure.

In lines 64-7 of the first part of the poem, an ancient catalogue of peoples which the poet speaks in the first person, we find

Mid Þyringum ic wæs, ond mid Þrowendum,
ond mid Burgendum, þær ic beag geþah;
me þær Guðhere forgeaf glædlicne maþþum
songes to leane. Næs þæt sæne cyning!

I was with Thuringians and with Throwendians
and with Burgundians, where I received precious rings;
Gunther there gave me brilliant treasure
as reward for the song. That was no slow king!

'Reward for the song', *songes to leane*, shows the same word in the same construction as the expression

sigores to leane

as reward for the victory,

of the sword that Hrothgar son of Healfdene gave to Beowulf (line 1020) for slaying Grendel. The phrase is a Common Germanic formula, recurring in the Gothic compound *sigislaun* 'reward for victory, *Siegeslohn*'.

The victory-song composed by Hrothgar's poet to celebrate Beowulf's victory over Grendel (867ff.) included a narrative of the Common Germanic myth of Sigemund (Sigurðr, Sigfrit) slaying a dragon and gaining great glory. Lines 884-5:

Sigemunde gesprong
æfter deaðdæge **dom unlytel**

To Sigemund came, after his death-day, **no little fame**.

Old English *dōm* is the moral and semantic equivalent of Greek κλέος and the litotic *dom unlytel* that of the Greek formula μέγα κλέος. But the Old English poet also gets *dom*. Widsith ends his moving composition with the lines (142-3)

lof se gewyrceð
hafað under heofonum heahfæstne **dom**.

He who works praise has under heaven enduring **fame**.

The relation is precisely that expressed by Ibycus in the passage cited at the beginning of this chapter: both patron and poet get κλέος, and Widsith's enduring 'high-fast' fame is precisely Ibycus' κλέος ἄφθιτον.[10] Note finally that the poet by ring-composition effects the closure of the poem with the semantic frame *ofer eorþan* 'over earth' (2)—*under heofunum* 'under heaven' (144).

10. For a perceptive appreciation and analysis of *Widsith*, its date, and the position it occupies in Germanic heroic poetry see Harris 1985.

For the social context of the poet and his patron in ancient Greece I examine only a couple of representative passages of Pindar, some hidden formulas expressing themes of far greater antiquity than he.

Isthmian 2, of the famous "Mercenary Muse",[11] commemorates a chariot-victory in the 470's of the late Xenocrates of Akragas and is addressed to his son Thrasuboulos. Pindar had earlier celebrated Xenocrates' victory of 490, as well as Thrasuboulos, in *Pythian* 6, in which the theme of filial piety dominates. The whole poem—three triads and 48 lines—is an elaborate *dānastuti*, a memorial of prior munificence and a clear hint for more.

Pindar accomplishes his purpose by a set of echoes, recurrent words and phrases which serve to index and develop the essential idea. The theme is *xenía*, usually rendered 'guest-friendship', the mutual hospitality which Pindar viewed as the essence of the relation between himself and his patron. This is not merely 'traditional ties of religion, family, and society' (Woodbury 1968), but a reciprocal contractual relation.

The key recurrent words in the three triads which make up the ode are the following:

ἁ Μοῖσα γὰρ οὐ **φιλοκερδής** πω τότ' ἦν οὐδ' **ἐργάτις**

for the Muse then did not **love gain** nor **work for hire**,

taken up again in seemingly artless fashion, in the exact middle line of the ode, in the aside on the Elean hearalds bearing the sacred Olympian truce, who recognized the charioteer Nikomakhos,

παθόντες πού τι **φιλόξενον ἔργον**

having experienced (from him) some **deed of hospitality**.

It is finally set forth again doubly in the praise of the late victor's hospitality:

οὐδέ ποτε **ξενίαν** / οὖρος ἐμπνεύσαις ὑπέστειλ' ἱστίον
ἀμφὶ **τράπεζαν**

nor did a blasting wind strike sail about his **hospitable table**,

which is duly and properly praised by the poet's songs as he shifts to the first person:

οὐκ ἐλινύσοντας αὐτοὺς **ἐργασάμαν**

I did not **make** them to stand idle.

11. Woodbury 1968 and Nagy 1990:188, as above.

The whole is a message for the late victor's son Thrasuboulos, addressee of the poem, in the final line of the ode:

> ταῦτα, Νικάσιππ', ἀπόνειμον, ὅταν
> **ξεῖνον ἐμὸν ἠθαῖον** ἔλθῃς
>
> Give this message, Nikasippos, when
> you come to **my customary guest-friend.**[12]

Even the name of the victor Xenocrates echoes the *xénos*-theme, just as those of the charioteer Nikomakhos and the doubtless fictitious messenger Nikasippos echo the victory theme (*níkā*) and the phrase ἵπποισι νίκαν 'victory with horses'.

Victory requires a song of praise, which conveys the recompense of honor. This nexus is poetically expressed by the iconic phonetic figure in Pindar and other writers discussed in chap. 3: *níkā : tīmā́*. The vowels are identical and the sequence nasal consonant-oral unvoiced stop consonant is reversed. In *Isthmian* 2, where the whole poem is a *dānastuti*, the link binds the three stanzas in balance: νίκα 13, 26, τιμά 29, 34. The *níkā/tīmā́* theme is Pindar's pledge-token of his side of the contractual relation to his patron.

Xenía is a reciprocal notion, with what Benveniste called a 'valeur d'échange' in his programmatic work (1966:315) building on Mauss' *Essai sur le don.* And in *Pythian* 10, the earliest epinician ode of Pindar we possess (498 B.C.), we find a formula nestled between two iconically reciprocal grammatical and phonetic figures:

> **ἑτέροις ἑτέρων ἔρωτ**ες **ἔ**κνιξαν **φρένας**
>
> as the age changes, new loves flutter the heart
>
> **πέποιθα ξενίαι**
>
> I trust in hospitality
>
> φιλέων φιλέοντ' ἄγων ἄγοντα προφρόνως
>
> friend to friend, leader to leader in kindness.

Pindar expresses by the stative perfect of the root **bheidh-* his trust and faith in the fundamental reciprocal social contract between guest/poet and host/patron. He repeats the formula at *Nem.* 7.65, again nesting and embedding it in the middle of a thoroughly traditional passage on his, the poet's, proper function in the traditional order, with such characteristic verbal themes as praise (αἰνέσω) and blame (μέμψομαι, ψόγος), oath (ἀπομνύω), glory (κλέος) for the patron, which is at the same time his

12. For the pregnant meaning of ἠθαῖος (Ionic ἠθεῖος) 'customary' here as 'with whom one shares consecrated usage' (ἦθος, Vedic *svadhā́-*, Archaic Latin *suodālis*) see Watkins 1989:786-9.

reward (μισθός), which the poet brings to him like water to a plant. The formula itself is first indexed by the key word ξεῖνος, then echoed in a following personal name:

> **ξεῖνός** εἰμι
>
> I am a **guest-friend**
>
> **προξενίαι πέποιθα**
>
> **I trust in hospitality**
>
> **Εὐξένιδα** πάτραθε Σώγενες
>
> Sogenes, descended of **Euxenos**.

The formula is embellished by alliteration, ***pro . . . pepoi*** . . . That it means 'I trust in hospitality', just as in *Pyth.* 10.64, rather than 'I trust in proxeny', was seen and amply discussed by Pavese 1966.

Pindar even artfully echoes the lexical sequence of the formula without its semantics at *Ol.* 1.103-104:

> **πέποιθα** δὲ **ξένον** / μή τιν'
>
> **I trust** that no host . . .

Finally we may note the contiguity relation in the marked positioning (clause-initial and clause-final) of the same elements in fragment 94b (*Parth.*)

> **πιστὰ** δ' Ἀγασικλέει
> μάρτυς ἤλυθον ἐς χορόν
> ἐσλοῖς τε γονεῦσιν
> ἀμφὶ **προξενίαισι· τί-**
>
> **μαθεν** γὰρ τὰ πάλαι τὰ νῦν
> τ' ἀμφικτιόνεσσιν
> ἵππων τ' ὠκυπόδων πο[λυ-
> γνώτοις ἐπὶ **νίκαις**
>
> As a **faithful** witness I have come to the dance, in honor of Agasikles and his noble parents, by reason of our **guest-friendship**. For of old as well as now they have been **honored** among their neighbors, both for the famous **victories** of swift-footed horses . . .

The identical placement of τίμαθεν and νίκαις, with the familiar Pindaric linkage, indexes and reinforces the linkage πιστά/προξενίαισι.

The true formulaic status of this Pindaric phrase πέποιθα ξενίαι is shown also by the attestation of the same collocation in the compound personal name Πιστόξενος attested from Mantinea in Arcadia (IG V 2.271.20, Schwyzer 662) and some 18 examples from the islands in vol. 1 of Fraser and Mathews 1987.

The root **bheidh-* recurs in reciprocal context in the Latin formula (Ennius, *Ann.* 32V.)

> accipe daque fidem, foedusque feri bene firmum
>
> give and take trust, and strike a treaty truly firm,

and significantly in the fundamental expression of the social contract among the Northern Albanians up to the 1930's, beside *be* 'oath',

> besë 'pledge, truce, trust'.

In the *Fjalor i gjuhës shqipe* as translated by M.E. Huld (1984) 'A term for the freedom and security that the house of a murdered man used to give to the murderer or the men of his family with an assurance that it would not seek blood [n.b., *kërkoj gjak* = Hitt. *eš̬har šanḫ-* 'seek blood', C.W.] during a certain time'. The term *besë* was analyzed as **bhidh-tā-* by Eric Hamp 1961, who later (1985) proposed **bhidh-ti-* + *ā*, and brilliantly compared the 'Simonidean' (92 D.) epitaph for the Spartan dead at Thermopylae ῥήμασι πειθόμενοι 'obedient to (their) words'. Hamp is surely right in suggesting that πειθόμενοι here is used pregnantly in the contractual sense of the root **bheidh-*, in the Greek middle 'comply with, obey', perfect 'trust in, rely on'. But equally pregnant here is the use of ῥήματα, for it is a phonetic icon and etymological figure for the 'great ῥήτρα' (Dor. ϝρήτρα), the 'covenant', the military as well as social contract of Sparta and of other Doric polities. The social contract of the soldier and that of the poet are two formulas expressing variants of a single theme of Indo-European antiquity, an all-important cultural nexus: Pindar's πέποιθα ξενίαι and 'Simonidean' ῥήμασι πειθόμενοι may be reconstructed as

> TRUST (**bheidh-*) **gh(o)s-*
> TRUST (**bheidh-*) **u̯reh*$_1$-.

The objects of TRUST are respectively HOSPITALITY as the total reciprocity relation between poet and patron, guest and host (**gh(o)s-*) and the covenant of the SPOKEN word (**u̯reh*$_1$-), which is the expression and the reification of the same relation.

Another formula with Indo-European **u̯reh*$_1$- in Greek is apt to reinforce the reciprocal contractual relation of gift exchange between poet and patron. In *Il.* 21.445 the gods Poseidon and Apollo were indentured for a year to King Laomedon of Troy,

> μισθῶι ἔπι ῥητῶι
>
> at a specified wage.

The 'terrible' king (ἔκπαγλος 452) by welshing on the agreement robs them of their wage and thus breaks the covenant. Greek μισθός is also both the recompense of the poet and the reward of the patron in Pindar, as we have seen (*Pyth.* 1.76, *Nem.* 7.63). Nothing stands in the way of reconstructing an ancient, perhaps even Indo-European formula

COVENANTED (**u̯r̥h₁-tó-*) RECOMPENSE (**misdhó-*),

where the covenant is precisely the all-powerful spoken word, **u̯r̥h₁-tó-*, literally 'spoken'.

In the unifying and coherent Indo-European cultural nexus all three formulas, the Pindaric, the Simonidean, and the Homeric, lose their isolation and reveal themselves as deep archaisms. There exists a network of such formulaic contiguity relations, which lies partly below the surface; it is our responsibility to bring them to the light.

I conclude with a brief look at another of the many examples of the iconic phonetic figure linking the two words νίκα 'victory' and τιμά 'honor' in Pindar. It is a phrase in the author's prayer to Father Zeus at the conclusion of *Nemean* 9, lines 54-5: τιμαλφεῖν λόγοις νίκαν 'to do honor to victory by my words'. Honor (τιμ-) to victory (νίκαν) is conferred by the poetic message (λόγοις). The reciprocal gift of honor by the poet and the victory of the patron are linked by the verbal notion -αλφεῖν, from an Indo-European root **algʷh-* which has precisely a Benvenistean 'valeur d'échange'—a semantic component of exchange and reciprocity: it means in Greek 'to fetch a prize in return for', in Indo-Iranian 'to be worth, to deserve'. The syntax, semantics, and derivational history of the Greek and Indo-Iranian forms are complex. Both verbs, Greek ἀλφάνω and Sanskrit *arhati*, select an accusative argument. Greek τιμαλφέω in the first instance is a denominative verb built on the compound adjective τιμαλφής[13] 'fetching a prize'. It is the victory which is worth the honor, and which fetches the prize of honor, but it is the victory (νίκαν) which is the accusative in our passage. The meaning of τιμαλφεῖν λόγοις νίκαν is thus 'make victory fetch the prize of honor by my words'. The phrase is a good illustration of the syntactic complexity of Greek and Indo-European compounds, but it is the pragmatics of reciprocal gift and exchange which makes it intelligible. The phrase remains a valid and powerful icon of the Indo-European poet, his art, and his social function.

13. The *s*-stem *-alph-es-* could well be an inheritance: cf. the Avestan *s*-stem noun *arəjō* 'worth' < **algʷh-es-*.

6

The poet's truth: The power, particularity, and perseveration of the word

The Indo-European poet is the professional of the spoken word, the curator and custodian of the power of the spoken word, and on occasion its unleasher. The power of the spoken word as an Indo-European cultural notion is attested clearly in the equation between the Hindu Act of Truth (Pāli *saccakiriyā* < Sanskrit **satyakriyā*) or Utterance of Truth (*satyóktiḥ* from *satya-ukti-* [**u̯ekʷ-*]) and the Early Irish institution of the *Ruler's Truth* (*fír flathemon*). As defined by Lüders 1951-59 for Indic, the Act of Truth 'consists of the solemn pronunciation of a truth, in order thereby to produce a definite, usually immediate effect on the external world.' See especially Brown 1972. The comparison of the two institutions at the opposite ends of the Indo-European area, first made by Dillon 1947, permits its reconstruction as a feature of Indo-European culture: a simple but powerful ethical and religious notion of the Ruler's Truth (Vedic *ṛtám*, later *satyám*, Avestan *aṣ̌əm*, Greek δίκη, Irish *fír*), as an active intellectual force, verbally expressed, which ensures the society's prosperity, abundance of food, and fertility, and its protection from plague, calamity, and enemy attack. The verbal expression is a formula, articulated and related by the poets of India and Ireland, consisting respectively by the instrumental case of Vedic *ṛtá* and *satyá* followed by a sentence [S], and the 'cleft sentence' with copula and the equivalent prepositional phrase with Irish *fír* (*flathemon*) likewise followed by a sentence [S]:

ṛténa / satyéna [S]	'by Truth [S]'
is tre fír (flathemon) [S]	'it is by (the Ruler's) Truth that [S]'.

For examples and full discussion see Watkins 1979b and chap. 24.

The power of the spoken word as formula and the power of the poet as the custodian of the word and formula both derive from their *truth*. See the rich discussion of this theme in Greek in Detienne 1973 and Nagy 1990:44-61, and for Indo-European itself, the notion of 'la religion de la vérité' in Haudry 1985.

In two odes of the same year 476 to the same patron Theron of Akragas, Pindar praises his patron's generosity in a form very reminiscent of a Truth-formulation. Referring to *Ol.* 1.1-2 of the same year, ἄριστον μὲν ὕδωρ, ὁ δὲ χρυσὸς . . . διαπρέπει . . . ἔξοχα πλούτου 'Best is water, and gold outshines all other wealth', Pindar in *Ol.* 3.42 says:

εἰ δ' ἀριστεύει μὲν ὕδωρ, κτεάνων δὲ
χρυσὸς αἰδοιέστατος

If water is best, and gold the most awesome of possessions,

then Theron in virtue comes to the outermost edge, and reaches from his house to the Pillars of Heracles.

In *Ol.* 2.92 the Truth-formulation is overt:

αὐδάσομαι ἐνόρκιον λόγον ἀλαθεῖ νόωι

I will speak with truthful mind a word under oath,

that the city has not in a hundred years given birth to a man more magnificent in heart and more ungrudging in hand than Theron. In each case it is the 'Poet's Truth' which assures his proper recompense.[1]

We may illustrate the 'Poet's Truth' in Vedic with RV 3.33, which presents in ballad-like strophes with alternating speakers the myth of the poet Viśvāmitra. The tale recounts how the poet persuades the two torrential rivers Vipāś and Śutudrī to allow the host of the Bhārata, who are on a cattle raid, to cross safely. The rivers first refuse but then are finally persuaded by the poet's narrative of Indra's praiseworthy deed, the Indic dragon-slaying myth par excellence, splitting the *ahi* and releasing the waters to flow. The rivers reply (3.33.8):

etád váco jaritar mā́pi mr̥ṣṭhā
ā́ yát te ghóṣān úttarā yugā́ni
ukthéṣu kāro práti no juṣasva
mā́ no ní kaḥ puruṣatrā́ námas te

This word, o singer, do not forget
which future generations would hear from you.
Be kind to us, o poet, in your hymns.
Do not let us down among men. Reverence to you![2]

---

1. See chap. 16 for the poet's pledge-token of his truth, the anagram of his patron's city (*Akragant-*, Agrigento) line 87 **ἄκραντα γα**ρύετον, which is resolved in line 91-2 ἐπί τοι / **'Ακράγαντι** τανύσαις 'bending the bow toward Akragas', a poetic "Truth" immediately preceding, in the same sentence, the line (92) quoted above.

2. One can observe a veritable constellation of inherited words and roots relating to poetry in this passage. For the 'future generations' recall RV 7.87.4 cited above. Note further : *vácas-* 'word' = Gk.

Geldner comments that the vanity of the rivers makes them change their minds, but they are in fact acceding to the power of the poetic formulation, and echoing it. Verse 9 is uttered by Viśvāmitra:

ó ṣú svasāraḥ kāráve śṛṇota
yayáu vo dūrā́d ánasā ráthena
ní ṣū́ namadhvam . . .

Hearken to the poet, o sisters,
he has come to you from afar with wagon and chariot.
Bow well down . . .

They reply in verse 10, first echoing, then rising to the lyrical:

ā́ te kāro śṛṇavāmā vácāmsi
yayā́tha dūrā́d ánasā ráthena
ní te namsai pīpyānéva yóṣā
máryāyeva kanyā̀ śaśvacaí te

We will hearken to your words, o poet;
you have come from afar with wagon and chariot.
I will bow down to you like a milk-swollen woman
(to her child), like a girl to her lover I will yield to you.

Viśvāmitra concludes with a two-verse summation of the turning point of the myth, cast again in balanced responsion, a dramatic narrative which shows his mastery of the poetic art (3.33.11-12):

yád aṅgá tvā bharatā́ḥ **saṃtáreyur**
gavyán grā́maḥ . . .
árṣād áha prasaváḥ . . .
ā́ vo vṛṇe sumatíṃ yajñíyānām

Just when the Bharatas **cross** you **together**,
the cattle-raiding host . . .
then your rush will flow . . .
I ask the favor of you worshipworthy ones.

átāriṣur bharatā́ gavyávaḥ **sám**
ábhakta vípraḥ sumatím nadī́nām
prá pinvadhvam . . .
ā́ vakṣáṇāḥ pṛṇádhvam yātá śī́bham

(ϝ)έπος (*$\underset{\frown}{u}$ek^u-es-); *jaritár-* 'singer' (*g^uerh$_2$-): Celtic **bardo-* 'poet' (*g^uṛh$_2$-dhh$_1$-o-), Lith. *gìrti* 'to praise' (*g^uerh$_2$-); *ukthá-* 'hymn' (uk^u-th$_2$o-): Irish *anocht* 'metrical fault' = Skt. *an-uk-ta-* 'unsaid'; *kāru-* 'poet' : Gk. κᾶρυ-, κῆρυ- 'herald' (**kār-*).

> The cattle-raiding Bharatas **have crossed together**,
> the poet has obtained the favor of the rivers;
> swell forth . . .
> Fill up your underbelly; go quickly!

The grammatical contrast in tense-aspect (present-aorist) and mood (optative-indicative), the emphatic inversion of verb and preverb in *saṃtáreyur* and *átāriṣur . . . sám* call vivid attention to this implementation of a basic mythographic formula.[3] Sentence-initial verbs frame the final strophe: *átāriṣur, ábhakta, yātá.* Form and style recall the Greek paean (chap. 55).

The substance of the myth, however artistically conveyed, is the power of the word of the poet, his recitation, to effect a change in the physical world: here the pacification of the rivers. The myths of Orpheus, Arion, and other Greek poet-singers reflect a similar ideology.

The 'Poet's Truth' has itself a formulaic expression in Vedic, which has all the earmarks of a proverb. RV 1.152.2b:

> **satyó mántraḥ** kaviśastá ŕ̥ghāvān

> **True** is the powerful **formula** pronounced by the poet.

We can observe here an extraordinary nexus of inherited themes, formulas, and illusions. The poetic formula (*mántra*, another derivative of IE *men-) is *satyá-*, veridical; it will come true, since it is fashioned and spoken (*-śastá*) by a true poet (*kaví*). In *kaví* we have an old Indo-European word for the poet-seer and priest, related to German *schauen* 'look', English *show.* Cognates are Old Avestan *kauui* a poet-priest, Greek (Hesychius) κοίης or κόης, a priest of the mysteries of Samothrace, and Lydian *kaveś*, a kind of priest: they suggest a preform *(*s*)*kou̯*h_x*-ē*(*i̯*)- (B. Fortson).[4]

Vedic *satyá* 'true' and Avestan *haiϑiia-* are formally derivatives of the participle of the verb 'to be': *h_1*s-n̥t-i̯ó-*. The meaning is thus 'real, existing'. For the same participle in the confessional formula of Hittite and its Latin cognate *sōns* 'guilty' see chap. 15. The confession of sin, transgression, is another instance of the power of the word; the Brāhmaṇic doctrine is that confession simply wipes out the fault and re-establishes community among people. See Lévi 1898 and Watkins 1978c.

In the verse-final epithet *ŕ̥ghāvān*, literally 'possessing reproductive power', we have a formulaic phonetic echo of, or perhaps a pun on, *r̥tā́vā* 'possessing Truth' in the same verse-final position in RV 7.61.2a and elsewhere; cf. also *ŕ̥ghāvā* in the same position in 4.24.8a, and *svadhā́van* 'self-powerful' in 4.5.2b cited above. Such echoes call attention to the poetic message.

The real extent of the thematic and formulaic nexus and the poetic power behind it becomes clear only if we compare another pair of verses from book 1, 67.4-6. The

3. See chapters 34-35 on the root *$terh_2$-, Vedic *tar*^{i} and its deployment in the narration of the dragon-slaying myth.

4. The suffix may recur in Latin *uāt-ēs* (stem *uāt-i-*), though the root *uāt-* is more likely an early Celtic borrowing: see chap. 9.

meter is the infrequent *dvipadā virāj*, 10-syllable dipodies:

vidántīm átra **náro** dhiyaṃdhā́
hṛdā́ yát **taṣṭā́n mántrāṁ áśaṃsan** ||
ajó ná kṣā́ṃ dādhā́ra pṛthivī́ṃ
tastámbha dyā́m **mántrebhiḥ satyáiḥ** |
priyā́ **p**adā́ni **p**aśvó ní **p**āhi
viśvā́yur a**g**ne **g**uhā́ **g**úhaṃ **g**āḥ ||

Thinking **men** (poets) find him (Agni) there
when they **pronounced** the **formulas fashioned** in the heart.
Like the Unborn (Primal God) he fixed the broad earth,
he supported heaven with **true formulas**.
Protect the dear tracks of the cattle;
having all life, o Agni, you go from hiding place to hiding place.

Here we find *mántrebhiḥ satyáiḥ* 'with true formulas' like *satyó mántraḥ*: the only two attestations of the collocation in the Rigveda. It is a Common Indo-Iranian poetic phrase, found also in Old Avestan (Y. 31.6):

ahmāi aŋhaṯ vahištəm yə̄ mōi vīduuā̊ vaocāṯ **haiϑīm**
mąϑrəm yim hauruuatātō aṣ̌ahiiā amərətātascā
mazdāi auuaṯ xšaϑrəm hiiaṯ hōi vohū vaxšaṯ manaŋhā

To him shall belong the best (power), the Knowing One who
  shall pronounce for me the **true**
formula concerning the integrity and immortality of Truth;
to the Wise One (shall belong) that (best) power which he
  shall make grow with his Good Thought.[5]

Both the Indic and the Iranian go back to **satyá- mántra-*.

The Vedic poet's pledge-token of his formulaic truth is the following subsequent phonetic embellishment of the last two lines, the double four-fold alliteration **p**- **p**- **p**- **p**-, -**g**- **g**- **g**- **g**-. Zarathustra's pledge-tokens of his formulaic truth are the multiple alliterations (*ahmāi aŋhaṯ, viduuā̊ vaocāṯ, aṣ̌ahiiā amərətātascā, vohū vaxšaṯ*), sound echoes (*xšaϑrəm . . . vaxšaṯ* like *xšaϑrā . . . vaxšt* Y.34.11), and above all the phonic linkage of the 'true formula' *HaiϑīmMąϑrəm* to 'integrity and immortality' *Hauruuatātō . . . aMərətātascā*. All these phonetic figures serve to call attention to the poetic message.

The formulas are not only 'true' but also 'crafted, fashioned', *taṣṭā́n mántrān* by the men-poets (*náraḥ*) who pronounced them (*áśaṁsan*). Both these phrases recur in other lexical combinations, and both are again Common Indo-Iranian phrases.

In RV 7.7.6 we find the verb phrase *yé mántram . . . náryā átakṣan* '(the poets)

5. My translation builds on that of Humbach-Elfenbein-Skjærvø 1991.

who crafted the formula in manly fashion'. And in Old Avestan, Y. 29.7, the same verb phrase occurs as *mąϑrəm tašaṯ* '(the Lord) crafted the formula': Common Indo-Iranian **mantram taćs-*.

For Vedic men-poets (*náraḥ*) who pronounced (*áśaṁsan*) these formulas in RV 1.67.4 note first the adjective *nárya-* 'manly' in 7.7.6 above. Both are hymns to Agni. The important comparandum is the phrase *narā́ṃ śáṁsa-* 'praise of men',[6] hypostasized to *nárāśáṁsa-* (n.b. double accent), a frequent epithet of Agni and one of the key words in fixed order (always number 2) prescribed in the *āprī*-hymns, the litany of the old animal sacrifice; see on these chap. 21. Vedic *śáṁsa-* 'praise' is a nominal form of the verb *śaṁs-* 'praise, declare, aver, solemnly state', IE **k̂ens-*.

The phrase *narā́m śáṁsa, nárāśáṁsa* too is at least of Common Indo-Iranian date. It corresponds exactly in form and function to the name of the Iranian Messenger of the Gods, *nairiiō.saŋha-*, who is thus the equivalent of Agni *Nárāśáṁsa*, who is the Messenger (*dūtá*), the mediator between gods and men. The functional correspondence is completed in Avestan with the use of *nairiiō.saŋha* as a name of the god Fire (Avestan *ātar-*), thus semantically identical with Vedic *Agni* 'Fire'. See in detail Schmitt 1967:97-101. The treatment of *nairiiō.saŋha* as a juxtaposition rather than a true compound (separable by enclitic, *nairīmca saŋhəm*, etc.) can be correlated with the Vedic accent on each member in *nárāśáṁsa*. Schmitt further compares the adjectival form *nairiiō* with the Vedic equivalent at RV 1.185.9a (nominative dual, cf. Geldner ad loc.) *śaṁsā náryā*. The adjective *náryāḥ* in RV 7.7.6 is also part of the same nexus of associations.

The *-ti-* abstract noun to the verbal root *śas-* is *śastí-* 'praise' from zero-grade **k̂n̥s-tí-*. In the Rigveda it occurs three times: once in the Agni-verse of a hymn to All-the-Gods (Viśve Devāḥ) 1.186.3, and twice in the same Agni-hymn 4.3, verses 3 and 15. In both of these the word is juxtaposed to a form of *devá-* 'god': 3 *devā́ya śastím . . . śaṁsa* 'sing praise (figura etymologica) to the god' (the poet addresses himself); 15 *śastím devávātā* '(may thy) praise desired by the gods (resound, o Agni)'. In these examples *devá- śastí-*, *śastí-devá-* 'praise of the gods (of the poets)' looks very like the antithesis of *nár(ya)- śáṁsa-* 'praise of men-poets (of the gods)', in the same Agni-context. It is perhaps relevant that the Avestan cognate of Vedic *śastí-*, *sasti-* 'praising; praise; directive', is found in Y. 62.7 *vīspaēibiiō sastīm baraiti ātarš* 'Fire brings a directive to all'.

It is therefore the more interesting that Heubeck 1957, incorporating an idea of Mayrhofer's (see now Mayrhofer 1956-80:285), suggested that the two Greek names Καστιάνειρα (a secondary wife of Priam, *Il.* 8.305) and Κασσάνδρη (daughter of Priam, *Il.* 13.366, 24.699, brought home by Agamemnon as booty and murdered by his wife Klutaimestra, *Od.* 11.422) could contain the Greek cognates of *śasti-* and *nar(ya)-* : **kasti-an(e)r-ya*, **kasty-andrā*.[7] Cassandra's role as seer and prophetess (a function of the poet), whose visions go unheeded, is surely relevant; cf. Janko 1992:94. The etymology remains controversial, cf. Schmitt 1967:101 and the dictionaries of Frisk

6. Probably intentionally ambiguous and to be read both as subjective and objective genitive.

7. Greek *kasti-*, *kasty-* from **k̂n̥sti-*; for the variants cf. προτί, πρός from **proty*. If Mycenean *ke-sa-da-ra*, *ke-sa-do-ro* are to be interpreted as *Kessandrā*, *Kessandros* we would also have a full grade **kesty-* from **k̂ens-ti-*.

and Chantraine. If it is correct we would have a phrase of not only Indo-Iranian but Greco-Aryan date.

The *power of the word*, the poet's formula, his truth, has a simple corollary, which we may call the *particularity of the word.* One must pay attention to it in its specificity, to the precise wording, the verbal expression of the text. We have seen how an entire set of resonances can be found in every single word and morpheme of one single utterance, the formula line *satyó mántraḥ kaviśastá ŕ̥ghāvān.* To alter the expressed word is to deprive it of its power. Compare the Kauṣītaki-Brāhmaṇa passage quoted at the beginning of this chapter: some say he should invert the two verses and call *vaṣaṭ*, but 'as it is remembranced' is the established rule. Similarly Aitareya-Brāhmaṇa 2.53 prescribes the ritual order 'call, *nivid* ['direction'], hymn'; for the hotr̥-priest to insert the *nivid* in the hymn or the hymn in the *nivid* 'deprives the worshiper of his power'.[8] This is the essence of *bráhmaṇ-* 'formula; proper, appropriate form', Old Persian *brazman-* (if related). Without the proper form ritual fails, "prayer" is useless. But the proper form of a hymn, the proper ordering of ritual speech, *compels* the divinity to grant the wishes of the maker or commissioner of the hymn.

The never-ending search for that proper form explains immediately the frequency of the adjectives *náva, návya, návyas-* 'new' with *bráhmaṇ-* (RV 6.50.6, 4.16.21, 10.89.3, etc.) and with the many words for poetic composition, hymn, song, etc. It is not mere novelty which is sought.

From the importance of the particularity and precision of the word follows another corollary: *the perseveration of the word*, which is only another manifestation of formulaic diction. People say the same thing the same way when the same message is repeated and retold. Even the unending variation leading to the 'new formula', the 'new song' just alluded to, cannot mask the continuity and perseveration of the very formulas *návyam bráhma, návayā girā́*, etc., themselves.

Consider from our own culture the tale beginning 'Once upon a time, long, long, ago, there lived in a house upon a hill a pig, a duck, a cat, and a little red hen . . .' The diction is formulaic, invariant, and the rhetoric and poetics of the prose narrative, its division into balanced cola, polished and precise. The genre, wisdom literature cast as beast fable, is far older than Aesop. I do not know how old 'The Little Red Hen' is, nor how long English speakers have been telling a tale to children in this form or something like it. But it is striking that the whole story does not seem to contain a single Romance or even Scandinavian loanword, nor a single Latin loanword with the exception of *mill*, which probably entered the language prior to the Anglo-Saxon migration from the Continent to Britain.

A Vedic example is the short myth of Indra, the Yatis, and the Sālāvr̥keyas, which has been explained for the first time by Jamison 1991 in her pathfinding work. This myth is narrated some 15 times in 6 texts: 4 Brāhmaṇas to the Black Yajurveda (MS, KS =KapS, TS), and 2 Brāhmaṇas to the Sāmaveda (JB, PB). As Jamison states (51f.), 'When all three participants are mentioned, the narrative always begins with the

8. A. B. Keith, *Rigveda Brāhmaṇas* 24 (Harvard Oriental Series 25 [1925]).

same sentence, invariant:

> índro vaí yátīnt sālāvṛkeyébhyaḥ prā́yachat
>
> Indra handed over the Yatis to the Sālāvṛkeyas.

The complete agreement of all versions on this sentence appears to be quite old in Vedic, predating the rigid divisions into śākhās ('branches', the (Black) Yajurveda and the Sāmaveda). The fact that the myth *must* be introduced in this fashion suggests that the precise wording of the sentences is important, that it is a formulaic encapsulation of the entire myth, much as *áhann áhim* ('he/you slew the serpent') encapsulated the Vṛtra-slaying myth.'

These formulas have a history which can be and must be approached by the comparative method. Their perseveration can be demonstrated by the familiar tree-model, with branching nodes starting with a Vedic "original" poetic repertory *O′:

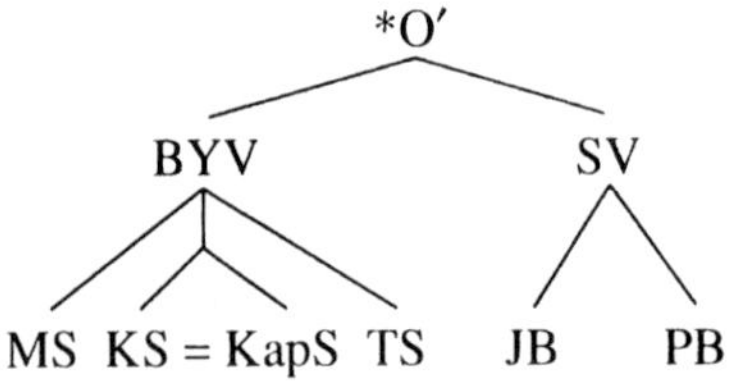

We saw a case in point with deeper perseveration in

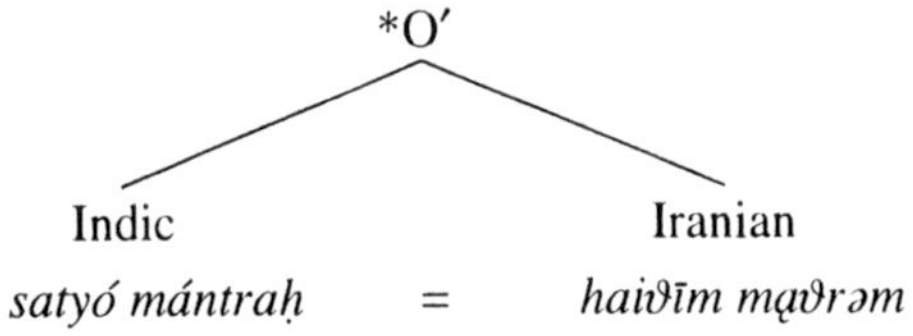

where TRUE FORMULA must be recognized as a formula in a higher, older poetic repertory *O′, the higher Common Indo-Iranian node. In the case of *nárāśáṁsa*, *nairiiō.saŋha* and Κασσάνδρη the node *O′ is yet higher, dominating both Indo-Iranian and Greek, a poetic repertory corresponding to an Indo-European dialect area on other linguistic grounds. And finally we shall see in detail in Part IV of this work that the formulas encapsulating the dragon-slaying myth, beginning with Vedic *áhann áhim*, can be projected all the way back to a pre-dialectal Proto-Indo-European poetic repertory. This "original" node *O′ dominates not only Indo-Iranian and Greek (i.e., Greco-Aryan), but Germanic, Celtic, and Anatolian Hittite as well. This Proto-Indo-European poetic repertory includes a central mythographic formula

> (HERO) SLAY (**g^u̯hen-*) SERPENT

whose verbal history can be traced through nearly every branch of the Indo-European family.

All of these cases, the Sālāvṛkeya-myth, the 'true formula', 'praise-of-men', and 'slew the serpent', combine to show why the present approach to traditional poetics, literature, and narrative is not merely helpful but necessary, indeed indispensable.

II

Case studies

7

Greece and the art of the word

The Greek word προοίμιον 'proem', literally 'fore-song', is first attested in an early (485?) ode of Pindar, *Nem.* 2.1-5:

ὅθεν περ καὶ Ὁμηρίδαι
ῥαπτῶν ἐπέων τὰ πόλλ' ἀοιδοί
ἄρχονται, Διὸς ἐκ προοιμίου, καὶ ὅδ' ἀνήρ
καταβολὰν ἱερῶν ἀγώνων νικαφορίας δέδεκται
          πρῶτον, Νεμεαίου
ἐν πολυυμνήτωι Διὸς ἄλσει

From whence the descendants of Homer,
the singers of woven words, most often
begin, from Zeus as a proem, so this man too
has won an earnest of victory in the sacred games
          for the first time, in the
much-sung grove of Nemean Zeus.

The 5 lines of the first strophe serve as Pindar's own proem. They introduce a set of words which will be echoed in sound or meaning in the final two strophes of this short (25-line), but itself tightly woven ode: Ὁμηρίδαι 1 'descendants of Homer': Τιμοδημίδαι 18 'descendants of Timodemos', Διός 3 'of Zeus': Διός 24, ἄρχονται 3 'begin': ἐξάρχετε 25 'begin the song'. The Pindaric figure indexically linking forms of *nīkā* 'victory' and *tīmā́* 'reward for victory' (chap. 3) is richly deployed in the ode, in the name of the victor and his lineage: **νικα**φορίας 4, **νικᾶν Τιμ**ονόου 9-10, **Τιμ**όδημε 14, **Τιμ**οδημίδαι 18, **νίκας** 19, **Τιμ**οδήμωι 24.

The proem shows an early instance of the poet-as-craftsman metaphor, ῥαπτῶν ἐπέων 'woven words', as noted by Schmitt 1967:300,[1] and the shared suffix in ῥαπτός 2 and πολυύμνητος 5 'much-hymned' makes a grammatical figure. The proem is

1. Schmitt also cites Hesiod *fr.* 357.2 Merkelbach-West ἐν νεαροῖς ὕμνοις ῥάψαντες ἀοιδήν 'weaving a song in new hymns', with the collocation underlying the later compound *rhapsode*.

particularly rich in phonetic figures like alliteration (**ὅ**θεν . . . Ὁ**μ**ηρίδαι, **ἀ**οιδοί **ἄ**ρχονται), which with the repetition Διός 3 . . . Διός 5 serves to call attention precisely to the three words which will be repeated or paralleled at the close of the poem. Finally we have the echo of the complex vowel sequence with hiatus in

> **aoi**doi
> pr**ooi**-
> pol**uu**mn-.

The effect is even more striking if the last two were pronounced *prohoi-*, *poluhu-*.[2]

We find the same richness of rhetorical structure, parallelism, phonic texture and echo in a 'real' Epic proem, lines 1-10 of Hesiod's *Works and Days*:

> Μοῦσαι Πιερίηθεν, ἀοιδῆισι κλείουσαι,
> δεῦτε, Δί' ἐννέπετε σφέτερον πατέρ' ὑμνείουσαι,
> ὅν τε διὰ βροτοὶ ἄνδρες ὁμῶς ἄφατοί τε φατοί τε
> ῥητοί τ' ἄρρητοί τε Διὸς μεγάλοιο ἕκητι.
> ῥέα μὲν γὰρ βριάει, ῥέα δὲ βριάοντα χαλέπτει,
> ῥεῖα δ' ἀρίζηλον μινύθει καὶ ἄδηλον ἀέξει,
> ῥεῖα δέ τ' ἰθύνει σκολιὸν καὶ ἀγήνορα κάρφει
> Ζεὺς ὑψιβρεμέτης ὃς ὑπέρτατα δώματα ναίει.
> κλῦθι ἰδὼν ἀιών τε, δίκηι δ' ἴθυνε θέμιστας
> τύνη· ἐγὼ δέ κε Πέρσηι ἐτήτυμα μυθησαίμην

> Muses from Pieria, who glorify by songs, come to me, tell of Zeus your father in your singing. Because of him mortal men are unmentioned and mentioned, spoken and unspoken of, according to great Zeus' will. For easily he makes strong, and easily he oppresses the strong, easily he diminishes the conspicuous one and magnifies the inconspicuous, and easily he makes the crooked straight and withers the proud—Zeus who thunders on high, who dwells in the highest mansions. O hearken as thou seest and hearest, and make judgment straight with righteousness, Lord; while I should like to tell Perses words of truth.

Martin West, whose 1988 translation I have given here, notes in his 1978 edition and commentary ad loc. that 'the lines are rather stylized, marked by anaphora (5-7), chiasmus (3-4, 7), a balancing of phrases with results in rhyme (1-2, 5-8), and perhaps *figura etymologica* in 2-3.' This is quite correct: anaphora ῥέα . . . ῥέα . . ., ῥεῖα . . .,[3] the chiastic order of the negated member, **ἄ**φατ- . . . φατ- . . . ῥητ- . . . **ἄ**ρρητ- (for

2. Evidence for this pronunciation is the variant φροίμιον employed by the tragedians for *prooímion*, which presumes aspiration 'jump' and deletion of like vowel, *prohoim-* → *phroim-*.

3. And probably a 'hidden' anaphora phonetically linking the first syllable ῥη- of line 4 to the first (monosyllabic) ῥέα of line 5 (in synizesis).

line 7 see below), the rhyming endings **κλείουσαι** : ὑμ**νείουσαι**, and χαλέπτ**ει** : ἀέξ**ει** : κάρφ**ει** : ναί**ει**, the etymological figure or play on the god's name and the (postposed) preposition, in identical phonetic environment and metrical position δεῦ**τε Δί'** (elided Δία) : ὅν **τε διὰ** 'because of whom'.[4] But there is more.

With the postposition as a constituent with the relative in ὅν τε διὰ 'because of whom' compare the beginning of line 507 of the same poem, with the preposition and no such constituency: ὅς τε διὰ Θρῄκης '(the North Wind) who (blows) across Thrace'. Such examples afford a window onto the technique of epic composition.

The figure of Argument plus Negated Argument (usually in that order) in 3-4 ἄφατοί τε φατοί τε / ῥητοί τ' ἄρρητοί τε 'unmentioned and mentioned, spoken and unspoken of' is one of Indo-European antiquity; examples are given in chapters 3 and 17. Here the semantic doubling effects a sort of "magic square", if West is right that φατός and ῥητός are virtually identical in meaning. But ῥητός may have some of the semantic features suggested in chap. 5, 'engaged by the spoken word'.

Another rhetorical pair are βριάει and βριάοντα in line 5, but here the art lies in a grammatical figure: the antithesis of transitivity and intransitivity in what is taken as the same verb, factitive βριάει 'makes strong (βριαρός)', but intransitive, stative participle βριάοντα '(who is) strong'. The verb is not otherwise found in early Greek. Comparison of a parallel passage in another tradition may shed light on this striking rhetorical contrast. The Hittite factitive verb *armaḫḫ-i* means 'makes pregnant, impregnates'; with the reflexive particle *-za* it means 'gets pregnant, conceives'. Beside this verb we have a possessive adjective in *-want-* (: Greek -ϝεντ-, Mycenean also *-wont-*) *armawant-* 'pregnant'.[5] Verb and adjective are collocated in a repeated topos in the Old Hittite myth of the Vanishing God Telepinus (KUB 17.10 i 14-15, cf. also 33.4 i 2-3, 33.24 i 11-13):

> nu=za namma GUD$^{HI.A}$ UDU$^{HI.A}$ DUMU.LÚ.ULÙ.LU^{MEŠ} *ŪL*
> *armaḫḫanzi armawanteš=a* kuieš nu=za apiya
> *ŪL* ḫaššanzi
>
> Cattle, sheep, and humans no longer get pregnant
> but those who (are) pregnant do not then give birth.

The rhetorical similarity of *armaḫḫanzi armawanteš* to Hesiod's unique βριάει . . . βριάοντα is striking, and the morphological similarity even more so. The Hittite verb is a factitive with suffix *-aḫḫ-*, IE **-ah₂-*, with 3sg. pres. *-i* < **-ei*. The Greek adjective is βριαρός < **g^{w}rih$_2$-ró-* or **g^{w}rih$_2$-aró-*. The rules of Indo-European word formation would require deletion of the suffix *-(a)ró-* before factitive suffix **-ah$_2$-*: 3sg. **g^{w}rih$_2$-ah$_2$-ei*, which would yield precisely βριάει. A **g^{w}rih$_2$-ah$_2$-wont-* could yield βρια-(ϝ)οντ-.[6] Alternatively, the Hittite factitive also has a passive participle *armaḫḫ-ant-* 'pregnant', and Hesiod's βριάοντα could just reflect **g^{w}rih$_2$-ah$_2$-ont-*, with the verb not

4. Norden 1966:29 n. 1 suggested the phonetically perfect pun by reading ὅν τε δία, with anastrophe (accent retraction) in the postposition. See West ad loc.

5. See Puhvel, HED svv. *arma-*, *armai-*.

6. Whether with the phonology of ἀπριάτην (*Il.* 1.99) or analogically.

intransitive but the participle in its ancient passive function with transitive verbs, '(made) strong'.[7] In either case Hesiod's βριάει . . . βριάοντα represents a striking and unique archaism[8] and one which both in its morphological form and in its rhetoric and stylistics shows the same links to the Orient, in this case Anatolia, as have been repeatedly noted by West 1988b, 1978, and 1966 passim.

Of the two lines 6 and 7 linked by anaphora of ῥεῖα,

> ῥεῖα δ' ἀρίζηλον μινύθει καὶ ἄδηλον ἀέξει,
> ῥεῖα δέ τ' ἰθύνει σκολιὸν καὶ ἀγήνορα κάρφει
>
> easily he diminishes the conspicuous one and
> magnifies the inconspicuous,
> easily he straightens the crooked and withers the proud,

West had noted a figure of chiasmus in the word order of line 7, Verb Object Verb, 'straightens the crooked and the proud withers.' While perfectly true on the "horizontal" linear level, far more interesting is the same figure of chiasmus on the "vertical" level of lines 6 and 7. Two constituents flank the line break (caesura, obligatory word boundary), with the order of the constituents reversed:

. . . ἀρίζηλον ‖ μινύθει . . .	. . . Object ‖ Verb . . .
. . . ἰθύνει ‖ σκολιὸν . . .	. . . Verb ‖ Object . . .

The transposition of the order of the two pairs—separated by 10 syllables in the stream of speech—is indexed and thus perceptually cued for the listener by a phonetic figure in the two verbs: identical vowels (save for length) and identical but transposed consonants. Thus,

> . . . arizēlon ‖ mINUTHEI . . .
> . . . ITHUNEI ‖ skolion . . .

The metaphorical opposition of 'straight' and 'crooked' and the antithetical metaphor in 'straighten the crooked' probably belong to the realm of human universals. But in this example Hesiod deliberately plays on the contrast of syntax and semantics as 'crooked' versus 'straight'; after the "vertical" sound linkage and play it is the god himself, 'Zeus who thunders on high', who straightens the crooked syntax and reestablishes "horizontal" linearity as the proper organizing principle of the linguistic sign.

The closure of this 10-line proem is effected with no less art. The message is simply 'to Perses'—said to have been the poet's brother, but who may well be a complete fiction—'I would speak true things': ἐτήτυμα μυθησαίμην. The simple

7. Like Greek γέροντ-, Vedic *járant-* '(made) old' (Watkins 1969:144).

8. The inherited factitive function was expressed in Greek already in Mycenean by what comes to be the -όω class: *eleutherōse* 'made free'.

message is in fact *the poet's truth*, and it is cunningly hidden and cunningly unveiled. The poet's truth sees in two directions at once, forward and back;

etĒTUMA MUTHĒsaimēn

is an iconic palindrome of the elements of TRUE and SPEAK. This phonetic inversion finally calls attention to—perceptually cues—the hidden phonetic and semantic ring which frames the entire proem. The first word is Μοῦσαι, the Muses, the personified mind of the poet as we saw in chap. 5. And the last word of the proem contains a Saussurian hypogram of the same word, to form a ring:

MOUSAI

MUthēSAImēn

The Muses—collectively the mind of the poet—are thus literally embodied in the poet's first person singular verb μυθησαίμην (muthēsaimēn) 'I would speak'.

The echoic function clearly played an important role in oral composition. The following passages are found just 18 lines apart in *Iliad* 9; they are entirely distinct in syntactic constituency, but manage to repeat four of the same words in the same order and in the same metrical slots:

(97-9, second line of Nestor's address to Agamemnon)
ἐν σοὶ μὲν λήξω, σέο δ' ἄρξομαι,[9] οὕνεκα **πολλῶν**
λαῶν ἐσσι ἄναξ καί τοι **Ζεὺς** ἐγγυάλιξε
σκῆπτρόν τ' ἠδὲ θέμιστας

I will end with you and begin with you, since
you **are** king **of many hosts** and to you **Zeus** has vouchsafed
the sceptre and judgments . . .

(116-18, second line of Agamemnon's reply)
ἀντί νυ **πολλῶν**
λαῶν ἐστιν ἀνὴρ ὅν τε **Ζεὺς** κῆρι φιλήσηι

Of the worth
of many hosts is the man whom **Zeus** loves in his heart . . .

Such echoes—repetitions of words in the same sequence but in different and unrelated syntactic constituency—recall the Rigvedic *āprī*-hymns, the liturgy of the old animal sacrifice, in which successive verses must contain, in fixed order, one of eleven lexical key words, beginning with *sámiddha* 'kindled' and ending with

9. The counter-intuitive, unnatural hysteron proteron order of the verbs 'end' (λήξω) - 'begin' (ἄρξομαι) may be iconic to the context.

vanaspáti 'tree, sacrificial post' followed by *svā́hā* (ritual cry) 'hail!'. They are enumerated in chap. 21. To use again Jakobson's felicitous expression, in the *āprī*-hymn genre the repetition of a series of key words as equivalences has been promoted to the constitutive device of the sequence, while in the Homeric passages above the same equivalences have only the status of nonce echoes. It is possible diachronically in any poetics for such features to pass from the one status to the other, as in the case of alliteration in Greek and Indo-Iranian beside alliteration in Italic, Celtic and Germanic, or the case of rhyme ('*homoioteleuton*') in Greek or Latin beside rhyme in the Latin and vernacular poetry of the Early Middle Ages and beyond.

Pure echoes of sound are very frequent in Archaic Greek poetry. Their function is indexical, to call attention to the poetic message; they have no inherent semantic value. The three-line epigram from 8th century Pithecoussa, now the island of Ischia in the Bay of Naples (SEG 14.604, Hansen CEG 454 with references (reading ε[ιμ]ι); cf. Watkins 1976a and *Il.* 9.63 cited in chap. 8),

> Νεστορος ε[στ]ι : ευποτ[ον] : ποτεριον
> hος δ' αν τοδε πιεσι : ποτερι[ο] : αυτικα κενον
> hιμερος hαιρεσει : καλλιστε[φα]νο : Αφροδιτες
>
> Nestor's cup is good to drink from;
> but he who drinks from *this* cup, forthwith him
> will seize desire of fair-garlanded Aphrodite,

presents in its first line a double phonetic figure,

> nESToros ESTi euPOTon POTerion,

followed by an alliteration in each of the succeeding lines, *p*- *p*- and *h*- *h*-, both of which adjoin metrical boundaries: *p*- | *p*-, || *h*- *h*- |.

Stesichorus in the 7th century presents many examples within a small corpus. In PMG 211,

> ὄκα ϝῆρος
> ὥραι κελαδῆι χελιδών
>
> when in springtime the swallow sings,

we find the type of internal rhyme called 'consonance' (Irish *uaitne*, chap. 9), in which vowels agree in length but not quality, *wēr* . . . *hōr*-, and the sequence of consonants is identical but for the feature of aspiration, *KeLaDēi KHeLīDōn* (Stesichorus possibly still had χελιδϝών). The Lille papyrus Stesichorus (PMG 222A) furnishes many examples of alliteration and other sound figures or repetitions, such as 285-7, restored by Page and Parsons:

τεύξ[ηι μεγάλαν ἀυά]ταν **πόλει** τε **πάσαι**
ματ[ρί τ' ἀ**μαχ**ανί]**αν**
ἀεὶ **πο**[ταίνιόν τ]ε **πένθος**

may fashion (great disaster) for the whole city
and for his mother (perplexity and fresh) grief always.
(tr. Campbell 1991, also below).

We find internal rhyme in 295 (restored e.g. by Parsons),

ἐρχόμεν[ος δ' ἀν' ὁδ]ὸν **στεῖχ**εν, μέγα **τεῖχ**[ος ἀμείψας

Making his way he began his journey along the road,
passing the great wall . . .,

and what could be described as 'Irish rhyme' (v. chap. 9) in 299-300 (restored by Barrett, Parsons, and West)

πομπα[ῖσι θεῶν· ταχέω]ς δ' ἵ**κοντο** 'Ισθμόν
ποντίου ['Εννοσίδα]

under the escort (of the gods); and (soon) they reached the Isthmus
of the sea-god, (the earth-shaker).

All of these occur within 15 lines of Stesichorus; the restorations do not affect the figures themselves, which are certain.

The Spartan poet Alcman in the Louvre partheneion or girls' chorus (PMG 1), cited for a phonetic figure in chap. 3 (lines 75-6), uses an internal rhyme in the same line as the link between two syntactically complex clauses. Lines 40-45:

ὁρῶ
ϝ' ὥτ' ἅλιον, ὅνπερ ἇμιν
'Αγιδὼ μαρτύρεται
φαίνην· ἐμὲ δ' οὔτ' **ἐπαινῆν**
οὔτε μωμήσθαι νιν ἁ κλεννὰ χοραγὸς
οὐδ' ἁμῶς ἐῆι

I see
her like the sun, which Agido summons
to shine on us as our witness; but our illustrious
choir-leader by no means allows me either to **praise**
her or to fault her.

Alcman in the same poem (line 36) quotes what looks like a much older proverb from the 'Geometric' age:

ἔστι τις θεῶν[10] τίσις

There is such a thing as the vengeance of the gods.

The phonetic form begins with an existential predication, followed by a quasi-palindrome flanking 'the gods' (in the relational, genitive case), an icon of the reciprocal nature of 'the vengeance':

es TITIS theōn TISIS,

continuing an earlier Doric form

es TITIS theōn TITIS,

and perhaps an even earlier Common Greek form

es TIK^{W}IS theōn K^{W}ITIS.

The proverbial line is surely far older than Alcman.

The same poet begins a poem with an existential predication[11] in the style of a folktale (PMG 74),

ἦσκε τις Καφεὺς ϝανάσσων

There was a certain Cepheus ruling,

with a double phonetic figure like the Nestor's cup epigram:

ēSKe tiS KapheuS wanaSSōn.

It is not only in the archaic period that such figures are found. Sophocles in the identical metrical lines of the second strophe and antistrophe of the famous choral ode to man in the *Antigone* 332ff. furnishes at once a metrical responsion and a 'horizontal' grammatical figure ('Argument plus Negated Argument', chap. 3):

360 παντοπόρος· ἄπορος . . .

all inventive; helpless . . .

370 ὑψίπολις· ἄπολις . . .

of proud city; without city . . .

10. The papyrus has the later Spartan form σιῶν for θεῶν, but this would be anachronistic for Alcman's time, at least 200 years before these sound changes show up in epigraphic or literary texts.

11. And a morphological archaism, the suffix *-sk-* in existential function with the verb 'to be' as in Old Latin, Palaic and Tocharian.

The two are at the same time a "vertical" phonetic figure: *por-* : *pol-*. The figure in 360 is followed by another in line 362, with Dawe's 1979 Teubner text, following a conjecture of Meinecke and Heinsdorf (ἐπάξεται codd.):

> **φ**ε**ῦξ**ιν οὐκ **ἐπ**ε**ύξ**εται
>
> He will not give thanks for escaping (death).

Like Alcman's partheneion line above it opposes phonetic "sameness" and morphological "otherness": *pheuks-* : *(e)p-euks-* like *phain-ēn* : *(e)p-ain-ēn*. We shall see this pattern recurring in many Indo-European poetic traditions.

We cited in chap. 3 examples of iconic sound features in Bacchylides and Pindar, the doubling or prolongation of internal stop consonants in words expressing continuous or incessant action, συ(ν)νεχέως 'continuously' and ὀ(κ)χέοντι 'they endure', much like the iconic doubling or prolongation of *-m-* in colloquial German *immer wieder* 'over and over'. Let us re-examine the first of these passages to illustrate the interweaving of iconic and indexical figures of sound in Bacchylides.

Bacchylides 5.111-113 recounts the Aetolians' fight with the ravaging boar of Calydon:

> τῶι δὲ στυγερὰν δῆριν Ἑλλάνων ἄριστοι
> στασάμεθ' ἐνδυκέως
> ἓξ ἄματα συ(ν)νεχέως
>
> We, the best of the Hellenes, waged baneful battle
> with him, steadfastly
> for six days on end.

We have no less than three sets of phonetic recurrences of vowel sequences in the 28 syllables of these lines. The vowel sequence **u** - **e** of στυγε(ρὰν) is reversed in ἐνδυ(κέως), then reestablished in the final συ(ν)νε(χέως), where the two vowels straddle the iconically doubled -νν-. Line final ἐνδυκέως and the iconic συ(ν)νεχέως 'rhyme', i.e. show homoioteleuton. And the vowel sequence **e** - **ā** - **a** of Ἑλλ**ά**νων **ἄ**ριστοι is permuted in the following στ**ᾱ**σάμεθ', then reestablished in **ἓ**ξ **ἄ**μα(τα). The purpose of these figures is indexical; their effect is to focus the listener's attention precisely on the steadfast and continuous heroic striving of the BEST OF THE HELLENES (chap. 50).

As examples of grammatical figures, where meaning is also in play, we may offer the measured responsion in the dialogue of Antigone and Ismene keening their brothers who have killed each other in Aeschylus' *Seven against Thebes* 961ff., as elucidated by Lloyd-Jones 1959. Thematically the passage belongs to 'the slayer slain' motif (chap. 31) within the genre of lament or keening (Medieval and Modern Irish *coíniud*, *caoineadh*):

Αντ. παισθεὶς ἔπαισας.	Ισμ. σὺ δ᾽ ἔθανες κατακτανών.
Αντ. δορὶ δ᾽ ἔκανες.	Ισμ. δορὶ δ᾽ ἔθανες.
Αντ. μελεοπόνος.	Ισμ. μελεοπαθής.
<Αντ.> πρόκεισαι.	<Ισμ.> κατέκτας.
Αντ. ἴτω γόος.	Ισμ. ἴτω δάκρυα . . .

Ant. You struck and were stricken.	Ism. You slew and were slain.
Ant. By the spear you killed.	Ism. By the spear you were killed.
Ant. Wretched in action,	Ism. Wretched in suffering,
Ant. you lie there—	Ism. you killed—
Ant. Let the keening go forth.	Ism. Let the tears go forth . . .

Such passages afford a window onto the probable antecedents of drama in ritual. The themes are precisely those inherited from Indo-European discussed in chap. 53.

The *Seven against Thebes* provides an example of another and quite complex set of responsion or repetition figures, this time involving both sound alone (rhyme or homoioteleuton) and both grammatical and lexical meaning as well, all within 6 lines. The lyric passage occurs not long before that just quoted; Antigone and Ismene learn that their brothers have just slain each other. Lines 900-905, the beginning of the second antistrophe:

διήκει δὲ καὶ πόλιν στόν**ος**·
στένουσι πύργοι, στέν**ει**
    πέδον φίλανδρον· μέν**ει**
κτέανα τοῖς ἐπιγόν**οις**,
δι᾽ ὧν αἰνομόρ**οις**,
δι᾽ ὧν νεῖκος ἔβα θανάτου τέλ**ος**

Groaning pervades the city;
the ramparts groan, the plain
    that loves men groans; there remain
for their descendants the possessions
for which they came to a dreadful fate,
for which their strife arose—death's end.

We can observe first the final syllable rhyme, linking 901-2, 903-4, and framing the whole 900-5. The repeated δι᾽ ὧν . . . δι᾽ ὧν 'for which . . . for which' echoes the repeated αἰαῖ . . . αἰαῖ 'alas . . . alas' in the corresponding lines (893-4) of the preceding strophe, as does νεῖκος ἔβα θανάτου 'strife arose—death's' of 905 the ἀντιφόνων θανάτων 'of deaths by mutual slaughter'. Iconically and indexically τέλος 'end' is the last word. These are all purely synchronic poetic features of the passage; but others may have a diachronic intertextual dimension as well. The interplay of verb and verb phrase with related noun in διήκει . . . στόνος, . . . στένουσι, . . . στένει 'groaning pervades . . .', '. . . groan', '. . . groans' is not only Greek but an Indo-European stylistic figure; examples from Greek, Latin, Umbrian, Old Armenian and Hittite are given in chap. 13.

Thematically as well we can point to a striking parallel in another tradition, far enough removed in time and space to exclude borrowing or diffusion. European vernacular literature begins with the Irish lament for St. Columba, the *Amrae Choluimb Chille*, composed just after the saint's death in 597. Its first two lines (after the rhymed strophic prologue) are

> Ní dísceil duae Néill,
> Ní huchtot oenmaige.

> Not newsless is the rampart of Níall,
> It is not the groan of a single plain.

Coincidence and universality cannot of course be excluded. But given that rampart and plain are features of Indo-European architecture and landscape it is not altogether fanciful to suggest that the 'lamentation of the rampart and the plain' might be an Indo-European literary topos, a part of the poetic repertory of the proto-language.

For a glimpse of purely synchronic Greek poetics, consider just a single line of Sappho, 49.1 L-P:

> ἠράμαν μὲν ἔγω σέθεν, Ἄτθι, πάλαι πότα

> I loved you once, Atthis, long ago.

The line is formed of two hemistichs of 6 syllables (bounded by long vowels) and 8 syllables, contrasting the pronominalization I-you by consonant symbolism: the first ('I') with 5 sonorants and 1 obstruent, the second ('you') with 7 obstruents and only 2 sonorants. The line begins with the verb in marked position, sentence- and discourse-initial, and a subject pronoun which is emphatic in a pro-drop language. Then, after the object pronoun and name, the line trails off with distancing and indefinite adverbs, mirrored metrically by the unbounded series of dactyls. The bridge between the hemistichs is the iconic juxtaposition of the subject and object pronouns.[12] But the real grammatical figure is the semantics of the genitive case of the object; the genitive focuses on the extent of the participation of the entity in the message, implying it is not total. The result is a powerful tension of the physical juxtaposition of the pronouns I-you where 'you' is marked for 'unattainability'. The whole message takes 14 syllables; such is the art of the syllable in ancient Greece.

I conclude this brief survey with another feature of Indo-European poetry in Greek, which is discussed at length (for Vedic) by Toporov in his seminal 1981 paper (see chap. 2.3). Following and developing the anagram or hypogram theory of Ferdinand de Saussure, for which he cites extensive references (p. 239 n. 131), he points out the two-fold character of Indo-European poetry and poetics: that a given content might be encoded at least twice, first explicitly and then on the anagrammatic plane. Examples of this poetic feature from Greek and Vedic are given in chap. 16,

12. An identical if blatant iconicity in Catullus 16.1 *pedicabo ego uos et irrumabo*. The accusative marks the object as governed and attainable.

on 'the hidden track of the cow'. One may suffice here, a hidden word encoded twice at the beginning and end of the first strophe of Sappho's hymn to Aphrodite, 1 L-P:

ποικιλόϑρον' ἀϑανάτ' 'Αφρόδιτα,
παῖ Δίος δολόπλοκε, λίσσομαί σε,
μή μ' ἄσαισι μηδ' ὀνίαισι δάμνα,
πότνια, ϑῦμον

Throned in splendor, deathless, O Aphrodite,
child of Zeus, charm-fashioner, I entreat you
not with griefs and bitternesses to break my
spirit, O goddess.
(tr. R. Lattimore 1960).

The hidden frame of the first word and the last adonic clausula is

POikiloTHrON, ↘
POtnia THumON.

The phonetic frame is POTHON (πόϑον), the word for 'desire' in the accusative, the governed case par excellence. In the poetic message, 'desire' is the direct object of an unspecified—and unknowable—transitive verb.

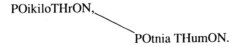

8

Vedic India and the art of the word

The language of India from its earliest documentation in the Rigveda has raised the art of the phonetic figure to what many would consider its highest form. Let us look at some examples; above all they impress us with their sheer exuberance. Compare the fourfold figura etymologica in RV 5.48.2:

> **áp**o **áp**ācīr **áp**arā **áp**ejate
>
> (The pious one) drives the later (dawns) far back,

or the iconic onomatopoeia of repeated RV 6.53.7=8, where the kavi is enjoined to 'tear up, rip apart' the hearts of the Paṇis:

> **á ri**kha **kikirá kṛ**ṇu.

RV 8.103.11a praises Agni, 'dearest of the dear' *préṣṭham u priyā́nām*, itself a grammatical figure. J. Schindler called my attention some years ago to its remarkable contrapuntal figure—noted also by Geldner—opposing phonetic "sameness" and grammatical "otherness":

> ú**ditā** yó ní**ditā** vé**ditā** vásu
>
> (Agni) who at sunrise (*úd-itā*) procures (*védi-tā*) the
> tethered (*ní-ditā*) wealth.

The grammatical and morphological analyses are completely different in each case: *úd-itā* loc. sg., *ní-ditā* nt. pl., *védi-tā* *tṛ*-agent noun. Such figures, which we saw also in Greek in the preceding chapter, have an indexical function. They point to the message and call attention to it. The poet praises the god Agni by calling attention to his own cleverness.

We had occasion in chap. 2.3 to cite the 'Blessing of the Weapons', RV 6.75, for the anaphora in verse 3 *dhánvanā . . . dhánvanā . . .* 'by the bow . . . by the bow . . .', recalling as it does Archilochus' ἐν δορί . . . ἐν δορί . . . 'in my spear . . . in my spear . . .' Verse 13 of the same hymn plays phonetically with two forms of the verb 'to strike, smite', *jaṅghan-* and *jighna-*, a similar but unrelated word *jaghána-*, and the word for the apostrophized 'horsewhip' of the battle charioteer:

> **ā́ jaṅghanti** sā́nv eṣāṃ **jaghánā̃m̐** úpa **jighnate**
> áśv**ājani**
>
> It strikes their back, it smites their croup,
> o horsewhip . . .

The effect is a purely phonetic, non-semantic anaphora Ā JANghanti . . . aśvĀJANi . . . iconic to the whip itself.

Karl Hoffmann in a 1987 article (reprinted 1992:858-863) devoted to Vedic *próṣṭha-* 'night quarters, field bed', used metonymically for the war chariot fitted out with a field bed (*ráthaproṣṭha-* 'having the chariot as night quarters', RV 10.60.5), cites a martial mantra addressed to the king in the Paippalāda Atharvaveda Saṁhitā 2.52.5 and elsewhere in Vedic Brāhmaṇa and Sūtra literature (TB 2.7.17.1, ĀpŚS 22.28.4, BauŚS 18.19, HirŚS 23.4.44). The double phonetic figures produce a brisk and vivid military tattoo:

> **ā́ ro**ha **pro**ṣṭha ví **ṣa**hasva **śa**trūn
>
> Mount the chariot field bed, defeat the foes!

In chap. 5 we suggested an etymology of the name of the Muses in Greek, μοῦσα < **monsa* < **montwa* < **mon-tu-h₂*. The *-tu-* stem to the root expressing mental activity recurs in the Vedic nominal forms *mantú-* 'guide, counsel; mindful, caring' (Old Avestan *mąntu-* 'counsel') and negated *amantú-* 'unmindful, uncaring'. For the first note RV 10.63.8, with its several figures of grammar:

> yá ī́śire bhúvanasya prácetaso
> víśvasya sthātúr jágataś ca **mántavaḥ**
> té naḥ kṛtā́d ákṛtād énasas páry
> adyā́ devāsaḥ pipṛtā svastáye
>
> O ye gods who rule over the whole world, fore-thinking
> over all that stands and goes, **mindful**,
> protect us today from done and undone sin
> for well-being.

The form *amantú-* recurs in the famous hymn to Vāc 'Speech', who unveils her power to the poet, RV 10.125.4:

máyā só ánnam atti yó vipáśyati
yáḥ prā́ṇiti yá īm śṛṇóti uktám
amantávo mā́m tá úpa kṣiyanti
śrudhí śruta śraddhiváṃ te vadāmi

Through me [Speech] he eats food; he who sees,
who breathes, who hears the uttered word (does so only through me);
unmindful, they depend on me. [To the poet:]
Listen, o famous one, something worthy of trust I say to you.

These lines of course strikingly recall the words of the Muses in their epiphany to the Greek poet Hesiod tending his sheep in the slopes of Mt. Helicon, *Th.* 26-8:

ποιμένες ἄγραυλοι, κακ' ἐλέγχεα, γαστέρες οἶον,
ἴδμεν ψεύδεα πολλὰ λέγειν ἐτύμοισιν ὁμοῖα,
ἴδμεν δ' εὖτ' ἐθέλωμεν ἀληθέα γηρύσασθαι

Shepherds that camp in the wild, disgraces, merest bellies;
we know to tell many lies that sound like truth,
but we know to sing reality when we will.
(tr. West 1988b)

Yet most striking of all is the character of Speech's poetic message in the last pāda (verse line of *ṛc* 'strophe'). It is indexed by an insistent 3-2 phonetic figure, tripling and doubling sibilant, liquid, dental, and glide:

ŚRuDHi ŚRuTa ŚRaDdhiVAṃ Te VADāmi

But the hidden message of the goddess Speech to the poet, the extreme phonetic figure, is an exhaustive classification of the speech sounds of the Vedic language, with one example of each class: the vowels *a i u* and a single icon each of the oppositions of quantity (*a* : *ā*) and nasalization (*a* : *aṃ*); a single sibilant *ś*; a single liquid *r*; a single semi-vowel (glide) *v*; a single nasal *m*; and a single order of stops, the dentals *t d dh* as tokens of the oppositions of voicing (*t* : *d*) and aspiration or murmur (*d* : *dh*). As I said in 1983 (published in 1987), by this spoken act of inventory, this hidden iconic performative, the goddess Speech 'se donne totalement à l'auditeur'.

B. van Nooten has called attention (Amer. Orient. Soc. meeting, Atlanta, March 1990) to the phonic echo in the Soma hymn RV 9.74.3 between *gávyūti* 'pasture' and the bizarre form *itáūti* 'having aid from here out'. The distortion of the grammar is here, as often in these texts, correlated with and in the service of phonological patterns and a figure of sound:

máhi psáraḥ súkṛtaṃ somyám mádhu
urvī́ **gávyūtir** áditer ṛtáṃ yaté
íśe yó vṛṣṭér itá usríyo vṛ́ṣā
apā́ṃ netā́ yá **itáūtir** ṛgmíyaḥ

A great pleasure is the well made somic sweet
the broad pasture of Aditi for him who goes the way of Truth,
(Soma) who rules the rain from here out as the dawn bull,
who is leader of the waters, having aid from here out, praiseworthy.

Here *itáūtir* picks up the identically placed *itáḥ* 'from here out' (following the break) of the preceding line. Note that the phrase *urvī́ gávyūti* 'broad pasture' and the equivalent possessive compound *urúgavyūti* 'having broad pasture', occurring here as always in the Rigveda (6x) in the opening (up to the break), is a formula of Common Indo-Iranian date. Its equivalent in Avestan is the compound epithet of Mithra *vouru.gaoiiaoiti* 'having broad pasture', Yt. 10 passim. Other interesting features of this mantra are the fronting of the verb around the relative pronoun in *ī́śe yó* 'who rules', creating a 'Pindaric' (ἔπαθον αἵ 'who suffered' *Ol.* 2.23) or Celtic relative clause structure (Gaulish *dugiiontiio* 'who serve', Old Irish *bertae* 'who bear' < **bheronti yo-*, Middle Welsh *yssyd* 'who is' < **esti yo-*). Placing the relative pronoun there produces a string *yó vŕ̥ṣ-(ṭér)* which is then echoed at the end of the line in *(usrí)-yo vŕ̥ṣ-(ā)*, reinforcing the etymological figure. These 'horizontal' echoes in pāda *c* are in counterpoint to the 'vertical' echoes between pādas *b* and *d gávyūti* : *itáūti* and *r̥taṃ ya-* : *r̥gmiya-*.

Whether the etymological connection between *vr̥ṣṭí-* 'rain' and *vŕ̥ṣā* 'bull' was perceived as such by the kavis is uncertain; the two may have been seen only as a purely phonetic echo. But both a sure etymological figure and a type of polyptoton (repetition of a word in a different case or suffixed form)[1] occur in RV 6.32.3cd:

púraḥ purohā́ sákhibhiḥ sakhīyán
dr̥ḷhā́ ruroja kavíbhiḥ kavíḥ sán

The citadel-smiter, associating with the friends,
has smashed the strong citadels, with the seers himself a seer.

The 'vertical' sound correspondences like *purohā́* : *ruroja*, *sákhibhiḥ* : *kavíbhiḥ*, *sakhīyán* : *kavíḥ sán* provide a striking counterpoint.

Polyptoton links the first two pādas of RV 1.53.7,

yudhā́ yúdham úpa ghéd eṣi dhr̥ṣṇuyā́
purā́ púraṃ sám idáṃ haṁsy ójasā

Fight after fight you approach in boldness,
citadel after citadel there you smash (root **gʷhen-*) together with
your strength.

1. Doubtless the best known figure of polyptoton in the Rigveda is 1.1, described by Saussure as 'a versified paradigm of Agni', which begins *agním īḷe* 'I worship Agni' (accusative) and continues with the god's name in different cases (nominative, instrumental, dative, nominative) in the first pāda of each of the (next four) verses, followed by the vocative in three of the succeeding and final four verses.

The second two pādas present another variant of the basic demon-slaying formula (chap. 27.3), already indexed by the root *g^{w}hen- (*haṁsi*), framed and sewn together by the beginning, recurrent, and ending syllable *nam*:

> **nám**yā yád indra sákhyā parāváti
> nibarháyo **námu**ciṃ **nā́m**a māyí**nam**
>
> When afar, o Indra, with your companion Namī
> you laid low the trickster, Namuci by name.

In the basic formula here the syllable *nam* is the indexical link between the MONSTER and the HERO's COMPANION. The verb *haṁsi* of the preceding pāda spreads its formular semantic overtones onto the verb *nibarháyas* (on which see Jamison 1983:97) in a way we will see often in parts IV and VI, particularly in Greek.

The figure of anaphora, repetition of a sound, word, or phrase at the beginning of successive verses or other units is very common in Vedic. RV 8.70.11 combines a phonetic anaphora in *a*(*nya*-) 'other-' and *a*(*va*) 'off' with a semantic one in *a*- 'un-', and concludes with the repetition of the same word at the end of pādas *c* and *d*, a sort of 'cataphora' known as *punaḥpadam* (chap. 4 n.8), which runs through 6 verses of the hymn. The strophe is bṛhatī, 8/8/12/8 syllables:

> anyávratam **á**mānuṣam
> **á**yajvānam **á**devayum
> **á**va sváḥ sákhā dudhuvīta **párvataḥ**
> sughnā́ya dásyum **párvataḥ**
>
> Him who follows another commandment, the non-man,
> non-worshipping godless one,
> may his (your?) friend the mountain shake down,
> the mountain the barbarian, the easier to slay.

For the anaphora of privative compounds of similar semantics compare *Il*. 9.63-4:

> ἀφρήτωρ ἀθέμιστος ἀνέστιός ἐστιν ἐκεῖνος
> ὃς πολέμοι' ἔραται ἐπιδημίοο κρυόεντος
>
> Clanless, lawless, hearthless is he
> that lusts for chilling war among his own people.

This figure can be securely posited for the poetic grammar of the protolanguage. The whole of RV 8.70 is examined in chap. 16.

V. N. Toporov 1981:244-5 has noted several striking synchronic poetic features of RV 2.23, notable the complementary distribution of the two names of the god hymned, the patron god of hymns and the protector of poets: Bráhmaṇas páti in the odd strophes 1, 5, 9, 11, 17, 19, and Bṛ́haspáti in strophes 2-4, 6-8, 10, 12-16, 18. Toporov calls attention to the anagrammatic indexing of the one god Bṛ́haspáti in 9 (*suv**ṛdhā** bráhmaṇas páte **spā́rhá***) and of the other god Bráhmaṇas páti in 12 (***mán**asā* . . . ***mán**yamāno . . . bṛ́haspate . . . **manyú***). The author of this hymn, as of all those in book 2 of the Rigveda, belongs to the Gṛtsamadas. He closes the hymn (19d) with the signature line of his family, identical in hymns 2.1, 23, 35, 39-40, 42-3. The line with its complex figures of rhyme, consonance, and alliteration is

bṛ**hád vad**ema **vid**áthe suvī́rāḥ

We would like to speak the great word as masters in the ceremony.

The word *vadema* is an anagrammatic link between the poet's name (Gṛtsa*mada*) and the god (*deva*) he hymns:

vadema : **deva** (ma)

va**dema** : (va) **made**

The two names of the god (*deva* = *vade*-ma), Bṛ́haspáti and Bráhmaṇas páti, are both anagrammatically indexed in the signature line of the family as well:

bṛh(ád) vad**ema** . . .

Such poetic family signature lines are frequent in the family books of the Rigveda and amply repay close examination. For more on this particular hymn 2.23 see chap. 22.

We find an interesting grammatical figure in another Gṛtsamada hymn, RV 2.39. It is addressed to the two Aśvins, the divine twins whose equation with the Greek *Dioskouroi* 'Zeus's boys' Castor and Pollux is one of the surer comparisons in Indo-European mythology (Puhvel 1987: passim). The trope is a series of comparisons of the Aśvins addressed (in the dual of nouns and verbs), comparisons always to objects in the dual. The comparisons run through verses 1-7, from the first word of the hymn *grā́vāṇeva* 'like 2 millstones' (the English cognate is *quern*) through some 28 duals to *hásteva* 'like 2 hands'. The poets concludes, 'these edifications, the formula (and) the praise the Gṛtsamada's have made, enjoy them and come. We would like to speak the great word as masters in the ceremony.' His family signature is a touch of Pindaric pride in his craft.

RV 2.31 presents an elaborate metaphor, the hymn or song of praise itself as 'chariot' (the inherited word *rátha*), repeated and carried through verses 1-4. In 5 and 7 respectively we find the inherited topos discussed above of the poem as 'new utterance' (*návyasā vácā*) as offerings which the poets 'fashioned' (the inherited topos *átakṣan*) for a 'new occasion' (*návyase*). Verse 6 uses another inherited term for the poem: *utá vaḥ śáṁsam uśíjām iva 'śmasi* 'we want for you two a song of praise like that of the Uśij priests', with a reference to the old Indo-Iranian traditional designation noted for RV 1.131.5 in chap. 4 n. 7. This whole tightly organized poem of 7 verses is finally indexed and demarcated by the likewise inherited stylistic feature of ring composition: lines 1d and 7c begin alike with the epithet *śravasyávaḥ* 'eager for glory', expressing the Indo-European theme of **k̂leu̯os*. Recall the strophe-final *śravasyántaḥ* 'seeking glory' of RV 1.131.5 just referred to (cited in chap. 4), as well as the last word of *Beowulf* (3182), *lofgeornost* 'most eager for glory', of the dead hero himself (chap. 50). Our hymn 2.31 is in theme, style, and vocabulary a remarkable poetic and artistic archaism.

RV 8.3.24 is the last of a four-verse *dānastuti* praising the poet's patron Pākasthāman for his gift of a horse. The inherited genre of the *dānastuti* has been examined in chap. 5. This concluding verse combines a topos of the Ancient Near East, the triad of food, raiment, and unguent, presumably diffused to Ancient India, with what we should probably recognize as an Indo-European stylistic device, albeit known principally from Greece: the priamel. This stylistic figure is defined by Elroy Bundy in his seminal 1962 work (reprinted 1986:5) as 'a focusing or selecting device in which one or more terms serve as foil for the point of particular interest.' He illustrates the priamel by the 'straightforward example' of Sappho 16.1-4 L-P:

οἰ μὲν ἰππήων στρότον οἰ δὲ πέσδων
οἰ δὲ νάων φαῖσ' ἐπὶ γᾶν μέλαιναν
ἔμμεναι κάλλιστον, ἔγω δὲ κῆν' ὄτ-
τω τις ἔραται

Some there are who say that the fairest thing seen
on the black earth is an array of horsemen;
some, men marching; some would say ships; but I say
she whom one loves best.
(tr. Lattimore)

The priamel (*praeambulum*) is, as Bundy insists (*ibid.*), 'a frequent manifestation of perhaps the most important structural principle known to choral poetry, in particular to those forms devoted to praise.' See also Race 1982. We should therefore look for the priamel in the praise literature of other, cognate traditions, and indeed we find a clear example in RV 8.3.24, down to the 1sg. pronominalization 'cap' (Bundy) of the laudator and the 'name cap' of the laudandus:

ātmā́ pitús tanū́r vā́sā
ojodā́ abhiyáñjanam
turī́yam íd róhitasya pā́kasthāmānam
bhojáṃ dātā́ram abravam

The soul is food, the body clothing,
unguent gives strength;
as the fourth I have named Pākasthāman,
generous giver of the bay.

It is well to remember at all times when interpreting these ancient poetic texts in Vedic, just as in Old Avestan hymns and Classical Greek lyric, that they are rhetorically driven. What Bundy says in his *Studia Pindarica* may, indeed must, be applied verbatim to the hymnic poetry of the Vedas and the Gathas of Zarathustra: 'What is required . . . is a thorough study of conventional themes, motives, and sequences . . . in short, a grammar of choral style . . . [reflecting] systems of shared symbols . . .' (32). These poems are 'the products of poetic and rhetorical conventions whose meaning . . . is recoverable from comparative study' (35). And in conclusion, 'in this genre the choice involved in composition is mainly a choice of formulae, motives, themes, topics, and set sequences of these that have, by convention, meanings not always easily perceived from the surface denotations of the words themselves . . . we must . . . seek through careful analysis of individual odes the thematic and motivational grammar of choral composition' (92). No clearer program for the task of an Indo-European comparative literature has yet been offered.

9

Ireland and the art of the syllable

Our knowledge of Early Irish metrics rests on the four texts published by R. Thurneysen as *Mittelirische Verslehren* in *Irische Texte* 3 (1891) 1-182, begun with ninth- century examples and worked successively in the tenth and eleventh century.[1] This wealth of material has been organized and presented in concise and exemplary fashion in G. Murphy's fundamental 1961 work, from which most of the present account is taken.

The terminology of poetry and poetics in Irish is native and old.[2] The ordinary word for a learned poet was *fili* (plural *filid*), etymologically 'seer': Medieval Welsh *gwelet* (Mod. *gwel(e)d*) 'to see', IE **u̯el-*. Compare *fel-mac* 'pupil, apprentice', glossed (O'Davoren) *mac uad* 'son of poetic art'. His craft was *filedacht*. Another word for poet was *bard* (Welsh *bardd* 'poet'), functionally and etymologically 'eulogist, praise-maker', from a Celtic compound **bar-do-* from IE *g^{u}r̥h$_2$-dhh$_1$-o-* related to the Indo-Iranian verb phrase in Vedic *giró dhā-*, Avestan *garō dā-* 'make praises' (Campanile 1980). Armenian *kardam* 'I raise my voice, call, recite out loud' appears to be built on a similar form.

'Poetry, poetic art' was variously termed. We have *aí* < **aui*, gen. *uad*, *uath* < **aueth*, IE **au̯-et-* from a root **au̯-* 'see' which we have in Hittite *au(š)-* 'see', and Welsh *awen* 'poetic inspiration'.[3]

The old glossary word *creth* 'poetry' is remade from *cretho*, gen. sg. of *cruth* 'form' < *k^{u}r̥-tu-* (McManus 1983). The form recurs in Welsh *prydydd* 'poet' < *k^{u}r̥-t-i̯i̯o-*. It is further related to Vedic *kr̥ṇóti* 'makes'; for the semantics cf. Greek ποίησις, ποιήτης : ποιέω 'make'.

Irish *cerd* and Welsh *cerdd* mean both 'craft' and 'poetry', the Irish noun also 'craftsman' and 'poet'. The unique cognate is Greek κέρδος 'gain, profit'; the etymology has been discussed in chap. 5.

---

1. See now Ó hAodha 1991.

2. This treatment is confined to Irish, but the metrical system of Welsh is comparable in complexity and the terminology of equal antiquity, sometimes unique and sometimes shared with Irish or other Celtic languages as well.

3. Thus correct what I said at Watkins 1963b:215-16.

Old Irish *fáth* 'prophecy, prophetic wisdom' and Welsh *gwawd* 'poetry' (**u̯ōt-u-*) as well as the agentive *fáith* 'prophet, seer' (**u̯ōt-i-*), Gaulish οὐάτεις (nom. pl.) borrowed early into Latin as *uātēs* 'seer' are old derivatives of the root **u̯et-* seen in Old Irish *fethid* 'sees, watches, observes, pays attention to' (secondarily a weak *i*-verb) and the compound *ar-feith* 'tends' (a regular thematic strong verb).[4] Irish *fethid, -feith* makes an exact equation with Vedic *ápi vatati* 'is familiar with, aware of, cognizant of', causative *ápi vātaya-*, Avestan *apiuuataite* 'id.', Old Avestan causative *fra* *⁺vātaiia-* 'make (others) acquainted with', the meanings shown by Tichy 1980.[5] The meaning is basically the pre-Thieme one of 'mentally perceive' (Grassmann) and 'understand, comprehend' (Monier-Williams), a verb of cognition.

The root **u̯et-* has lengthened *o*-grade cognates not only in Celtic but in Germanic, Pokorny IEW 1113.[6] These may be grouped as a noun **u̯ṓt-o-* (perhaps earlier a root noun) with a range of meanings like 'cognizance, knowledge, shamanic wisdom, tradition, poetry' appearing as Germanic **wōþa-* in Old English *wōþ* 'song, poetry', Old Norse *ōðr* 'poetry', as well as Old Irish *fáth* 'prophetic wisdom', Welsh *gwawd* 'poetry'. From this noun we have a derived adjective with possessive accented thematic vowel suffix **u̯ōt-ó-* 'having **u̯ṓt(o)-*, shamanic wisdom' appearing as Germanic **wōða-* in Old English *wōd*, Old Norse *ōðr* 'furious, frenzied', Old High German *wuot* 'insanitus', Gothic **woþs*, acc. *wodan* 'possessed'. Finally, with the suffix *-e/onó-* as in Gothic *þiudans* 'king' ('who incarnates the tribe [*þiud*]'), *kindins* 'governor' ('who incarnates the kin-group [*kind*]'), Latin *dominus* 'master' ('who incarnates the household [*dom-*]'), we have **u̯ōt-e/onó-*, Germanic **wōði/ana-* ('who incarnates shamanic wisdom, poetry') in the divine name of Old Norse *Oðinn*, Old English *Wōden*, Old High German *Wuotan*.[7]

The technical term for a meter is *aiste* (pl. *aisti*), of disputed origin. The meters of the (inferior) bards are called *brosnacha suad* 'experts' faggots', probably playing on the more lofty and ancient metaphor of the *fili*'s 'crafting of words'. A poem is called variously *dúan* (**dap-nā*) or *laíd* (**loidā* : Latin *lūdus* 'play'??). Later *dán* is so used, with semantic shift 'gift' (: Latin *dōnum*) > 'craft' > 'poetry' > 'poem'. The strophe, typically a quatrain, is called *rann* (probably **pr̥h₃-sno-*, related to *rann* 'part, division' < **pr̥h₃-snā-* : Latin *pars*). The first and second two lines of a quatrain are known as *lethrann* ('half-stanza') *toísech* ('leading') and *lethrann dédenach* ('second') respectively; the same terms *toísech* and *dédenach* are used of the first two divisions of the poetico-legal tract *Bretha Nemed*, chap. 24.

Meters were distinguished by their syllable count (*tomus* 'assessment'). In counting syllables in verse the term is *dëach* (probably a derivative of 'two'), which can refer to a single syllable or any set of syllables envisaged as a unit to be counted

4. Cf. the attestation cited at chap. 24 with n. 13 below. For others see Kelly's note to that text ad loc., and the RIA Dict. under (incorrectly) *ar-feid*. The equation with the Indo-Iranian forms was first correctly seen by G. Klingenschmitt apud Tichy 1980.

5. Against the meaning 'inspire, blow' argued for by Thieme 1954 = 1984: 139-49, and wrongly accepted by me in Watkins 1963:215-16 = 1994:370-71 and 1985 s.v. *wet-*[1].

6. Compare **pōd-* 'foot' in Germanic *fōt-* and Celtic **ād-* in the Hesychian gloss ἄδες· πόδες, probably a Galatian word (J. Schindler, pers. comm.).

7. On this family cf. also the views of M. Schwartz, to appear (paper presented to the Amer. Orient. Soc., Cambridge, MA, 29 March 1992).

for the purpose of metrical analysis. These were labeled and ranged from *dialt* = 1 syllable ('jointless') to *bricht* = 8 syllables ('spell, incantation').[8]

A possibly very old term is the word for a kind of metrical fault *anocht*, which corresponds exactly to Vedic *anukta-* 'unuttered' (Kauṣītaki-Brāhmaṇa 16.6). The Indo-European root **u̯ekʷ-* 'speak', zero-grade in **n̥-ukʷ-to-* 'not (to be) spoken', survived in Celtic only in isolated lexical items like *foccal* 'word' < **u̯okʷ-tlo-*. The word *anocht* could not have been freely formed for a long time prior to its attestation.

The principal relevant phonetic features are the many varieties of rhyme and alliteration. The final 'foot' of the line is termed *rind* 'point, edge', and the word is used for 'end rhyme' as well. The term *cuibdius* 'harmony' and *cubaid* 'harmony' is sometimes used of 'rhyme', from *com* + *fid* 'of like stave', *fid* 'wood' also '(Ogam) letter name'. Rhyme of a line-final word with an initial or internal word of the next line is called *aicill*. The two principal quatrains are the *rannaigecht* type (*rann* 'stanza') with end rhyme *b d*, and the *deibide* type (*de-bíthe* 'cut in two') with end rhyme *a b* and *c d*. In *deibide* meters there is commonly rhyme of a stressed final syllable (*rind*) with the unstressed final of a polysyllable (*airdrind*), e.g. *'**súain*** : *'ad**úair***.

Rhyme in Irish requires that vowels or diphthongs be identical in quality and quantity and that consonants must agree in 'quality', i.e. palatalized or non-palatalized. Irish is unusual in that consonants involved in a rhyme need not be identical but must belong to the same class, of which the system recognizes six:

> voiced stops: b d g
> unvoiced stops: p t k
> unvoiced continuants: f ϑ x
> tense sonorants: m N L R
> voiced continuants and lax sonorants: β δ γ w̃ n l r
> sibilant: s (can rhyme only with itself).

While some exceptions do occur, and the restrictions can be slightly eased for consonant clusters, this system of rhyme remained basically unchanged from the first attested poetry of the sixth century through the end of the Early Modern period in the seventeenth century. The prologue of the *Amrae Choluimb Chille* (ca. 598) rhymes both *néit* : *méit* [-e:d′] and *ndér* : *nél* [-e:r] : [-e:l], and before that Colmán mac Lé néni (†604, active in the second half of the sixth century) has such rhymes as *dírnaib* : *rígnaib* [-i:rnaβ′] : [-i:γnaβ′], *aidbse* : *cailgse* [aδ′β′s′e] : [-al′g′s′e], *crapscuil* : *apstail* [-abskal′] : [abstal′], *indlis* : *bindris* [iN′d′l′is′] : [-iN′d′r′is′], *ndíchmaircc* : *rígmaicc* [-i:xw̃ar′k′] : [-i:γw̃ak′]. The last attests already before 600 two of the exceptions noted by Murphy (p. 33) from later times, unvoiced and voiced continuant (and lax sonorant) [x] : [γ] (here in a cluster) and cluster with the same simple consonant [r′k′] : [k′].

A further adornment used concurrently with rhyme is 'consonance'. Irish *úaitne* 'prop, pillar', in which stressed vowels agree in quantity (length) but not in quality (timbre), final consonants as in rhyme agree in class and quality (palatalization), and

8. For other uses of the words *alt* 'joint' and *bricht* 'spell' and their antiquity see chapters 58.2 and 12 respectively.

interior consonants need not agree in quality. An early example of *úaitne* in the final strophe (24) of *Fo réir Choluimb* is *ro-n-**ain*** : *do-n-**foir***, where its substitution for end rhyme in *b d* permits a perfect *dúnad* or closure (discussed further below).

The native term for alliteration seems to have been *úaimm* 'stitching', judging from later sources. The metaphor is at least as old as the phrase *suainem filidechta*, the 'seam of poetry', 'thread of poetry' put round the Senchus Már (CIH 1654.33). The term *fidrad freccomail* 'staves of counter-joining' refers to binding or concatenating alliteration which links the last word of a stanza or line with the first word of the next.

Stress in Early Irish falls normally on the first syllable of the word, but there are large classes of words and morphemes which are proclitic, enclitic, or unstressed, such as prepositions, some adverbs, the first preverb in compound verbs. Alliteration in the classical Old and Middle Irish verse is normally between stressed words in the same line. Unlike Germanic usage unstressed words may come between stressed alliterating words. In *fidrad freccomail*, and more generally elsewhere in the earlier period (for example across the caesura), stressed and unstressed words may also alliterate.

Irish is unusual in that alliteration is by underlying morphophonemes, not by surface phonemes. The grammar has rules according to which the initial of a word may undergo certain mutations to express a variety of morphosyntactic functions in the sentence. These are presented in the following chart. The basic morphophonemes, as they would appear for example in word initial of citation forms, are given in the first horizontal row. Under this are the corresponding forms of the three consonant mutations: lenition (which has no effect on an initial vowel), nasalization (which prefixes *n-* to an initial vowel), and "gemination", the significant absence of mutation of a consonant, which prefixes *h-* to an initial vowel.[9] Consonant quality (palatalization) plays no role in Irish alliteration.

	p	t	k	b	d	g	f	s	m	N	L	R	V-
lenited:	(f)[10]	ϑ	x	β	δ	γ	-[11]	h	w̃	n	l	r	V-
nasalized:	(b)	d	g	m(b)[12]	N(d)	ŋ(g)	β	s	m	N	L	R	nV-
'geminated':	p	t	k	b	d	g	f	s	m	N	L	R	hV-[13]

The mutations are not systematically noted in Early Irish orthography. Typically all the surface consonant phonemes in a single vertical column could alliterate with each other, but identical surface phonemes from different underlying morphophonemes, like [β] from lenited *b* and [β] from nasalized *f*, could not alliterate.[14] As in Germanic any Irish initial vowel or vocalic nucleus could alliterate with any other, but could in Irish also alliterate with a vowel prefixed by *n* (nasalization) or by *h* ('gemination').

The first strophe of *Fo réir Choluimb*, to be examined in detail presently,

9. Historically these are the effects in phrasal groups of a lost preceding word-final vowel for lenition, a lost preceding word-final vowel plus *n* for nasalization, and a lost preceding word-final vowel plus obstruent for "gemination".

10. The mutations of initial *p* are probably analogical.

11. Zero, sometimes noted *ḟ* with punctum delens.

12. The final stop of *m(b)*, *N(d)*, *ŋ(g)* was lost during the Old Irish period.

13. The *h-* is not noted in Early Irish orthography.

14. See also Bergin 1970 for a discussion of the interplay of 'phonetic and psychological factors'.

contains such alliterative pairs as ***Ch**oluimb* : ***c**éin* [x : k′], *ad-**f**ías* : ***f**ind* [β′ : f′], *fri **hú**athu* : ***úa**ir* [húa : úa], *no-**t**ías* : *ni cen **t**oísech* [d′ : t].

Now let us as illustration look briefly at the mastery of verse technique shown by the Archaic Irish poet Bécán mac Luigdech, author of the magnificent poem *Fo réir Choluimb céin ad-fías*, edited by Fergus Kelly.[15]

As argued by Kelly, surely rightly, Bécán was two generations later than Columb Cille (c. 522-597), and thus is likely to have lived in the 7th century. The poem belongs to a critical turning point in the development of Early Irish poetry.

Stylistically the poem shares certain features with the *Amra Choluimb Chille* (ACC), the eulogy or threnody written shortly after St. Columba's death and which marks the beginning of vernacular literature in Europe. *Fo réir Choluimb* is in fact closely modeled on ACC.[16] A notable shared feature is the conscious perturbation of normal Irish word order tolerated for the ends of versification. This appears to function as a renvoi or recollection of the sort of "non-configurational" word order characteristic of the elevated poetry of most early Indo-European languages; but the 6th and 7th-century Irish poets more likely knew it from Vergil or Ovid.

The poem contains some of the finest lines in Irish, as in the recurrent images of Columb's voyage over the sea to found the monastery on the island of Iona off the west coast of Scotland:

> cechaing noïb nemeth mbled
>
> He crossed in ships the whales' sanctuary,

with the kenning for 'sea' (like the later Old English *hronrád* 'whale's road') showing the semantically charged Celtic word for 'hallowed place, object, or being', first attested on an Old Etruscan grave marker from near Genoa in the first half of the 5th century B.C.[17] The verse concludes with four constituents in the reverse of prose order:

> fairrge al druim dánae fer
>
> A bold man over the sea's ridge.

Compare the later-attested Old English formula *ofer sæs hrycg* (*Leechdoms* 3.34.16) 'over the sea's ridge', *ofer wæteres hrycg* (*Beowulf* 471). And again with scrambled order and an otherwise unattested verb form,[18]

---

15. Kelly 1973, from which my citations are mostly taken. I have at times preferred the version in Greene and O'Connor 1967.

16. A systematic comparison of the two is the only lacuna of Kelly's admirable edition, but it would considerably further our understanding of both poems. The shared vocabulary alone is striking.

17. The text reads *mi nemetieś* 'I (am the tomb) of Nemetie'. See Watkins 1981:241-3 = 1994:666-668.

18. Cf. *rodom-sibsea sech riaga* ACC §141.

curchaib tar sál sephtus cló

a whirlwind swept them over the sea in curraghs.

The poem is described in the manuscript as a *laíd imrind* 'poem with rhymes all around'. Each verse has four lines of seven syllables, with end-rhyme *a c*, *b d*. Each line of each verse typically has a fixed caesura (break, word boundary), normally after the fourth syllable (for the exceptions see immediately below). There is concatenating or chain alliteration between the last word of each verse and the first (stressed) word of the next (6d-7a being the only exception); concatenating or chain alliteration between the last word of every line and the first (stressed) word of the next; and bridging alliteration between the words on either side of the caesura. Absence of the latter two types is compensated for by linkage of grammatical figures (parallelism) or by alliteration elsewhere in the line. Using G. Murphy's notational conventions (1961: vi) of boldface italic or roman for end-rhyme and italic for chain alliteration, plus boldface italic for bridging alliteration, | for caesura, and capitals for *dúnad* or closure ("ring composition"), the first quatrain is

FO Réir ***Ch***oluimb | ***c***éin ad-***fías***
*f*ind for ***n***imib | ***sn***áidsium *s***echt**
*s*ét fri ***húa***thu | ***úa***ir no-***tías***
*n*í cen ***t***oísech | ***t***áthum *n***ert**

Obedient to Columb, as long as I speak,
may the fair one in the seven heavens protect me;
when I walk the path to terrors,
It is not without a leader, I have strength.

The initial syllable is repeated for a perfect *dúnad* by the last syllable of verse 24:

*R*ígdae ***b***ráthair | ***b***úadach *r***íg**
*r*athmar ***f***íado | ***f***eib ron-***ain***
*g*était *g*oiste | *nd*emnae *d***ím**
*d*úbart a ***b***ard | ***b***és don-**FOIR**

May the royal victorious kinsman of kings,
the gracious lord protect us with goodness.
I will remove (?) the snare of demons from me;
the supplication of his poets may perhaps help us.

Here the stressed FOIR /for′/ repeats the pretonic first syllable of the poem FO R /fo r′/, 24 verses, 96 lines, and 671 syllables later.[19]

19. Verse 25 is with Kelly almost certainly a later addition, since it is unglossed and shows a different rhyme and alliteration scheme. The motivation for its addition must have been precisely to provide a more salient (and less sophisticated) *dúnad*, repetition of the whole first line.

In 24c the double alliteration ***gétait goiste* | *ndemnae dím*** compensates for the lack of alliteration across the caesura and between the end of 24b and the beginning of 24c. Similarly in 1b the alliteration ***snáidsium secht*** compensates for its absence across the caesura, as Kelly notes, though we may probably see a secondary bridging alliteration in ***nimid* | *snáidsium*** and in 14a *línmar* | *sláin* beside *lessach línmar.*

It is evident that Bécán is a master of his art. The very first verse establishes the metrical scheme, the patterns of alliteration, and boldly stretches the limits of word order deviation. Now Kelly states (p. 4) that 'In all verses but 2, 3, 4, 5 and 25 there is a regular caesura between the 4th and 5th syllable of each line.' We may ignore 25 which is a later addition (n. 19 above). Are we then to conclude that Bécán presented his metrical scheme in the great quatrain 1, then floundered until he found it again in 6, from which point he maintained it through 24? Surely not.

A second look at verses 2 through 6 shows that Bécán is systematically playing with several of the parameters of the verse scheme he presented so forcefully in 1, while holding others constant. The parameters of isosyllabism and rhyme remain constant, as does the chain alliteration binding both verses and lines, which is always present save in 4b-c and c-d. But the line-internal alliteration can be either present, as throughout 3 and 5, or absent, as throughout 2 and 4ab, and it may either bridge the caesura or flank it. Furthermore the position of the caesura can be varied from quatrain to quatrain, but not within the quatrain. Using the notation [4 || 3] (as in Watkins 1963: 220 = 1994:375) for the 7-syllable line with caesura after the 4th syllable, [5 || 2] after the 5th, etc., and assigning a + or - feature for presence or absence of internal alliteration, quatrains 1 through 6 show the clearly intentionally varied pattern

1	[4 || 3 +]
2	[5 || 2 -]
3	[6 || 1 +]
4	[6 || 1 -]
5	[5 || 2 +]
6	[4 || 3 +],

which systematically illustrates each variable before returning to the "default setting" [4 || 3 +].

Stanzas 2-6 follow, with metrical commentary in the notes:

*N*íbu fri coilcthi | ***tincha*** [5 || 2 -]
*t*indscan ernaigdi | ***c*assa**
*c*rochais—níbu i | ***cinta***
a *ch*orp for tonna | ***g*lassa.**[20]

It was not on soft beds
he undertook elaborate prayers;
he crucified—it was not for crimes—
his body on the green waves.

20. The absence of the adornment of internal alliteration may be iconic to the content of this quatrain.

*G*abais a n-**adamrae** | n-***aí*** [6 || 1 +]
*i*s **coïr** Mo **Chummae** i | n-**Í**
*i*s mó **imbrádud** cach | ***aí***
a ndo-**rigni** airi in | ***rí***.[21]

He made the marvel of a claim,
it is right that Mo Chummae should be in Iona;
greater than anyone could think
what the King did for him.

*R*o-fes i n-ocus i | ***céin*** [6 || 1 -]
*C*olumb coich boí acht ba | **oín**
tindis a **ainm amail** | **gr*éin***
ba lés i **comair cach** | ***o*ín**.[22]

It was known near and far
whose Columb was, but he belonged to the One;
his name shone like the sun,
he was a light before everyone.

A n-*óe*n as **dech di** | ***rétaib*** [5 || 2 +]
*r*o-*sóe*r a **manchu** | ***moínib***
*m*ár thendál **íarna** | ***éccaib***
a n-***ai***mn as **úaisliu** | ***d*oínib**.[23]

The one (thing) which is best of things:
he has freed his monks of riches;
a great blaze after his death,
is the name which is nobler than (other) people('s).

Is *d*ín[24] **úathaid** | is dín *slúaig* [4 || 3 +]
*sl*án cach **eslán** | asa ***d*ún**
is *d*ún n-inill | is caín *mbúaid*
*b*uith ía r **Coluimb** | **Chille cúl**.

---

21. In *acd* we have alliteration bridging the caesura, so final monosyllables with vowel initial alliterate "twice", both within the line and with the initial of the next line. In *b* the alliterative pair is to the left of the caesura. Note that unstressed words may be fully integrated into the system of alliteration, unlike later Irish (and Germanic) practice.

22. The initials of lines *cd* lack chain alliteration. The lack is compensated for by the internal alliteration, which is non-bridging. On account of this I class the whole quatrain as structurally [6 || 1 -]. In *i n-ocus i céin, coich boí - ba oín* we may have grammatical figures. Cf. *coich boí coich bia* ACC §65.

23. Lines *b* and *c* have bridging alliteration, *a* and *d* non-bridging: *moínib, éccaib* and *ainm* therefore each count twice, for linking and internal alliteration.

24. Cf. *Ba dín do nochtaib* ACC §85, and perhaps read *Ba dīn do bochtaib* with LH for the continuation in view of the double figure in our poem here.

He is the protector of few, he is the protector of many,
safe is every unsafe one whose fort he is;
it is a safe fort, it is a fair advantage
to be under the protection of Columb Cille.

With quatrain 6 we are back in the original verse scheme [4 || 3 +], still with some ambiguities since in *a* and *c* it is not clear whether the grammatical parallelism *is dín úa.* | *is dín sl.*, *is dún n-i.* | *is caín mb.* should take precedence over the weak bridging alliteration.

There is no alliteration linking the end of quatrain 6 *cúl* with the beginning of 7 *Ní séim n-atach* 'He is no slight refuge'. The latter topos serves as a discourse initial figure in one of the poems of Colmán mac Lénéni, also of the 7th century: *Ní séim anim* 'It is no slight blemish ...' (Thurneysen 1932). It is therefore at least possible that quatrain 7 begins a new sub-section of *Fo réir Choluimb*, and that 6d *buith íar Coluimb* forms a little ring closing the first sub-section 1-6, with the saint's name in the same syllable slot before the caesura in both lines, 1a and 6d.

In any case the first six quatrains of this poem in their handling of meter, syllabism, rhyme, and alliteration must be regarded not as an irregularity but as an artistic tour de force, a paradigm of the art of the syllable in early medieval Ireland.

10

Saxa loquuntur: The first age of poetry in Italy— Faliscan and South Picene

Historians speak of 'the flowering of Italy' in the Archaic Period (8th to 5th centuries B.C.)[1] as a response to the waves of colonization spreading over the coastal areas, then penetrating slowly into the interior of the Mezzogiorno and Sicily. The single most important cultural manifestation was the spread of alphabetic writing. In the south it was direct, and local languages are written in the varieties of Greek alphabet their users were in contact with: Sikel, Messapic, the dialect of Bruttium, and a little later the Oscan of Lucania. In the North, presumably due to their role in maritime commerce, it is the Etruscans who first took up a western Greek alphabet (earliest texts 7th century), and it is through Etruscan that writing came to the Faliscans, located just on the southeastern edge of Etruria. Faliscan is linguistically as well as geographically close to Latin and forms with Latin a separate branch of Italic.

The city of Falerii in the Ager Faliscus some 50 km. north of Rome flourished from the sixth century to the third, when it was destroyed by the Romans in 241 B.C. The Faliscans had among their more severe southern neighbors the reputation of living entirely for pleasure. Varro could speak of the *Falisci uentres* 'Faliscan bellies' (*L.L.* 5.22, 111), cf. also Martial 4.54.8. The same spirit is reflected more solemnly in the Latin inscription on a leaf of bronze recording the dedication of a collegium of the Faliscan cooks in Sardinia in the 2nd century BC (CIL I^2 364, XI 3087, Ernout 62). The orthography of the text is archaizing and uncertain. The text on the verso appears to consist of six faulty saturnian lines (Ernout). Note 3-4 (alliterations boldface):

> Quei soveis **a**[**a**st]utieis **o**pidque Volgani
> **g**ondecorant sai[pi]sume   **c**omvivia loidosque

> Who by their own cunning   and the aid of Vulcan
> embellish frequently   banquets and entertainments.

---

1. See Pallottino 1991:59.

The Faliscan *Fescennini versus* 'Fescennine verses' were characterized by obscenity and by verbal play. The expression was ancient in Latin; Paulus in his epitome of the dictionary of Festus (P. F. 76 Lindsay) cites the form *fescemnoe* which is to be read *fescen<n>inoe* with the nominative plural (*-oi*, later *-ī*) characteristic of the 6th century B.C., albeit in later orthography.

Just such a picture can be inferred from some of the early Faliscan documents themselves. One such, well known, is the inscription on an apparently mass-produced vase

> foied . uino . pipafo . cra . çarefo
>
> Today I shall drink wine, tomorrow I shall do without,

(also attested with the variant *pafo*[2]) with an unambiguously erotic scene of revelry (Vetter 244, Giacomelli 5, Morandi 10, second half of 4th century B.C.).

Most striking, however, is our oldest Faliscan text, known as the Ceres inscription, Vetter 241, Giacomelli 1, Morandi 8, from ca. 600 B.C. The fragmentary text is inscribed around the neck of a larger vessel, as illustrated in Morandi.

Reading and interpretation of the inscription have received a good deal of attention in the last quarter-century. Probably the most dramatic improvements were those made in a joint study by Joseph and Klein 1981, building in part on the insight of Lejeune 1953 that the first line of the text contained quoted older gnomic material, a blessing formula, to which the text of 600 B.C. was making epigrammatic reference. The key to the restoration and interpretation of this inscription is understanding it as verbal art and appreciating all the poetic conventions and devices which it deploys.

I present the text first, without translation, as a unit of five long lines. These are in all likelihood further divisible into two hemistichs. A word divider (:) is present, and correctly but not consistently distributed; fewer than half of the word boundaries or metrical boundaries are so marked:

> ceres : farme[ ]tom : louf[ ]rui[ ]m : [ ]ṛad
> euios : mamazextosmedf[ ]iqod :
> prauiosurnam : sociaipordedkarai :
> eqournela[ ]telafitaidupes :
> arcentelomhuticilom : pe : parai[ ]douiad.

The identity with the name of the Roman goddess of grain *Ceres* was immediately evident. The restoration of a single letter yielded the divine name *Louf[i]r* (Vetter), the expected Faliscan correspondent to Latin *Līber*, god of wine.[3] Restoration of *u[in]om* 'wine' was contextually predictable, with the last word [ ]*ṛad* a 3sg. subjunctive verb with a meaning in the semantic sphere of 'giving' or the like: 'may

2. Cf. unreduplicated Latin *dat*, *dabō* beside reduplicated Paelignian *didet*, *dida*.

3. The identification is certain (immediate preform **loudheros*, Greek ἐλεύθερος), even if the vowel to be restored is not. (It is based on Paelignian *famel. inim. loufir* 'servus et liber', Vetter 209) The identification is contested, wrongly I think, by Radke 1965.

Louf[i]r GIVE wine'. We expect the first clause to be parallel; recognition of the word for 'barley' in *far* (Latin *far*) yielded an elliptic blessing formula 'May Ceres [GIVE] __ barley, may Louf[i]r GIVE wine'. It remained for Lionel Joseph and Jared Klein, independently and simultaneously in the same Harvard classroom, to see in *farme[la]tom* uel sim. the Faliscan reflex of an Indo-European formulaic noun phrase 'ground barley (or other species of grain)' which we have in Latin *far molitum*, Young Avestan *yauua aṣ̌a*, and Hittite ZÍD.DA ZÍZ *mallan*.[4] The line final verb [ ]*rad* of this traditional blessing must still be specified.

The verb at the end of line 2 was restored, on the basis of another inscription with *medfifiked* (Vetter 257, Giacomelli 11) to *f[if]iqod* or *f[i:f]iqod* 'finxerunt', 3pl. perf. in *-o(n)d*. With the words divided the second line reads

euios : mama zextos med f[if]iqod.

The vessel itself is speaking: '. . . made (3 pl.) me'. The verb form presupposes a plurality of subjects. Vetter suggested that *Euios* was a family name in the nominative plural, with the old thematic ending *-ōs* as in Sabellic. But the unambiguous vocative plural feminine with the old pronominal ending *-ai* (not *-ās*) in a contemporary Faliscan inscription (Vetter 243, Giacomelli 3 *saluete sociai* 'greetings, girlfriends') would suggest that the masculine thematic nominative plural was also the pronominal *-oi*, just as in the most closely related Latin at the same time. I will therefore assume a triad of artisans: 'Euios, Mama, (and) Zextos made me'. Whether this line is part of the poem itself is unclear.

Line 3 shifts out of the first person mode and artfully records the donor, the object, and its destination:

prauios urnam : sociai   porded karai

Prauios presented the pot to his dear girlfriend.

In the typical Indo-European figure of poetic word order the two constituents of the dative noun phrase have been distracted to straddle the verb and each adjoins a metrical boundary:

sociai | porded **karai** ||.

Compare also from later Italic dialects, Vetter 213 (Paelignian):

eite . uus . pritrome pacris
puus . *ecic* ***lexe lifar***

4. On which see Watkins 1973, 1975c, 1978b. The variation in cereal names (**bhars-*, **i̯eu̯o-*) and verbs (**melh₂-* [*h₂* due to Luvian *mammalḫ-*, Melchert 1993b], **alh₁-*) should not be allowed to detract from the semantic unity of the phrase, which goes back to the dawn of agriculture among the Indo-Europeans.

Go ye forth in peace
who read this text;

Poccetti 205 (Marrucinian):

sacracrix
cibat . cerria
Licina Saluta

(Here) lies
the priestess of Ceres,
Licina Saluta.

The pattern of straddling word order and alliteration of the verb with the following element is constant. Vetter himself saw that this word order in the Faliscan text proved the author was writing verse.

The fourth line reasserts the first-person style of the speaking object in a mincing, diminutive mode. The solution to the lacuna is given by Giacomelli A1 *eco urna tita uendias*... 'I am the *urna tita* of Vendia': *urna tita* must have a pragmatic meaning not far from our 'piggy bank'. The restoration is secure:

eqo urnela [ti]tela fitaidupes

I'm the little *urna tita* . . .

with double diminutivization. The rest of the line is, however, obscure.[5]

The fifth line continues at first both the first person and the diminutive mode. It empowers a reconstruction for the final verb of the first line and then brings about a highly complex resolution to the poem as an epigrammatic whole. The final line is

arcentelom huticilom : pe : parai[ ]douiad.

The precious verb form *pe:parai* gives the preform for Latin *peperī* 'I have given birth (to)'; the *urnela titela* is the subject, the likewise diminutivized *arcentelom huticilom* the object. The first is clearly 'silver'; the second is less certain, but looks like a derivative of the verbal adjective 'poured', **ĝhu-to-*, Greek χυτός, Old Latin *(ex)futi*, with a meaning comparable to the financial senses of 'ready' and 'liquid'.

The line is not finished; there remains the verb form *douiad*. As Vetter saw, there is probable nothing missing in the small lacuna before it; the space functions as a dash. The verb can scarcely be anything but 3sg. subjunctive of 'give': Vetter paraphrases '*her damit*'; Szemerényi 1987:2.896 is inconclusive. We thus obtain a finish something like

5. I have no explanation for *fitaidupes*. Earlier suggestions are recorded in Vetter and Giacomelli. If it is one word rather than the two usually assumed, note the curious resemblance to South Picene (Penna S. Andrea) *pidaitúpas*, compared to Umbrian *eitipes* by Eichner, 1988-90 [1992]:200.

arcentelom huticilom   peparai — douiad

I've given birth to a little bit of ready silver — let her give!

Pace Vetter the interjected *douiad* is an integral part of the verse line. As the last hemistich it forms both a metrical and a grammatical responsion to the first hemistich of the poem: *Ceres far me[la]tom* and *peparai—douiad* both contain six syllables with stress on the fourth, a cadence '4 5 6, and both have feminine subjects. We have both a phonetic and a grammatical index of closure, a *dúnad* (for the term see chap. 9).

The first line of our poem is a traditional blessing formula, as we have seen: May Ceres (give) ground grain, Liber wine. A similar blessing forms the closing line of a Paelignian inscription, Vetter 213:

dida uus deti   hanustu Herentas

May gracious Venus give you riches.

Here 'give' (3sg. subjunctive) is precisely what we expect and find. In the Faliscan Ceres inscription we expect the same, but we find not 'give' but a verb [ ]*ṛad*. I suggest that the composer of this epigram has altered the traditional blessing, to frustrate our expectation, and in place of 'give' (*douiad*) put [*pa*]*ṛad* 'give birth (to)'.[6] This verb of 'frustrated expectation' makes a lexical verbal responsion, ring-composition with the apparent final verb of the text, *peparai*. The frustrated expectation is then resolved at the very end, by the interjected *douiad*: as the real final verb of the text, it makes real ring-composition with the underlying, expected verb of the blessing, which is *douiad*. Marking the identities by boxing in different lines we have

Ceres far me[la]tom   Louf[i]r ui[no]m p[a]ṛad

arcentelom huticilom   peparai—douiad

The double line boxes the identity of syllable count and feminine subject. The plain line boxes the identity which is ring-composition of frustrated expectation. The broken line boxes the identity which is ring-composition of the real underlying form. We can thus restore and re-establish the true form of the traditional blessing:

*Ceres far melatom   Loufir uinom douiad.

This Faliscan poet has produced an epigram for an occasion. With all the techniques of quotation (poem within a poem), frustrated expectation, traditional epithet, distraction of word order, diminutivization, complex ring-composition, and resolution he has

6. From the thematic **parō* whose participle is Latin *parent-* 'parent' beside the *i̯o*-stem of Latin *pariō* 'give birth'. Cf. Ernout-Meillet DEL s.vv. Vetter states that the first letter could be *p* or *f*, so we may in fact legitimately just transcribe *p*[*a*]*ṛad*.

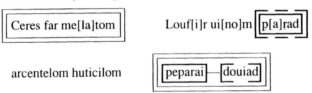

deftly succeeded in four or five lines in incorporating and contextualizing a traditional blessing formula and focusing its message onto the particular occasion itself. The inscription of the poem on the pot transforms the simple gift into a *strena*, as Vetter rightly terms it, a ritual gift which brings good fortune and good luck. The object comes from a necropolis of Old Falerii: small wonder that the recipient took it with her to the grave.

In sixth-century Faliscan we can observe some of the first writing down of what must have been a long oral tradition of poetry. On the other side of the Italian peninsula in the central Adriatic region at about the same time we can observe another flourishing Italic language and culture, South Picene. The language is a dialect of Sabellic, the group that includes Umbrian (occupying the territory between Picenum and Etruria), Oscan, and the several central Italic dialects like Sabine.[7]

In South Picenum we find a number of grave stelae from the sixth and fifth centuries, sometimes adorned with a crude relief figure of a human face or body, with extended texts written vertically, boustrophedon, or in elliptic spirals. These are written in a local alphabet ultimately based on the Etruscan, yet distinct. They defied reading (and a fortiori interpretation) for a long time, but thanks to recent work are now yielding up their secrets.[8] Many of these texts turn out to be poetic; their analysis is currently ongoing and correspondingly controversial.[9] The following examples of poetic interpretation are offered in that spirit.

The stele of Bellante (TE[ramo] 2 Marinetti) is a large ovoid stone, 1.75 meters in height, with a central human figure in relief, around which the inscription runs in a spiral. Beginning on the left at the figure's right foot, it goes up and around his head, then down, turning under the feet and continuing up on the left on the outside of the first line, finishing at the height of the figure's shoulder. The letters are large and clear; as is usual in South Picene each word is separated by a triple interpunct.[10] The text as written on the stone is thus continuous:

postin : viam : videtas : tetis : tokam : alies : esmen : vepses : vepeten

It is possible, though not absolutely certain, that we have a strophe of three heptasyllabic lines each ending in a trisyllable:[11]

---

7. Close or identical to South Picene are several short, non-literary texts from fifth and fourth century Campania, as far south as Capua, written in the South Picene or the Etruscan alphabet. See Meiser 1986.

8. They are very ably edited by Anna Marinetti 1985, superseding all earlier treatments.

9. Eichner 1988-90 [1992] in three recent articles has offered a wealth of commentary, interpretation, and metrical analysis of several archaic Italic texts, South Picene (TE 5, AP 2), Faliscan (Vetter 242), Latin (Duenos inscription, Ernout 3), and the Novilara stele. While he brings much of value to the understanding of these texts, I remain unconvinced by his (quantitative) metrical analyses, despite the certainty with which they are presented.

10. The autonomy of the word in the sentence or poetic utterance may well indicate the presence in the language of a demarcative stress, which functions to signal the presence of a word boundary. Initial stress is the likeliest assumption.

11. As such describable as Early Irish stichic 7^3 lines.

postin **v**iam **v**idetas
tetis **t**okam **a**lies
esmen **v**epses **v**epeten

Along the way you see
. . .[12]
buried in this tomb.

What is clear is that we have a run of sequential, concatenating or chain alliteration, marked in boldface. Equally clear is the figure of poetic grammar in the last line, distracted constituents of a noun phrase straddling the verb. Here the verb (participle?) *vepses* splits *esmen vepeten* 'in this tomb'; verb and noun are also an etymological figure.

These poetic figures are not likely to be borrowed from Greek; they are independent and autonomous developments of an inherited and much more ancient poetics. All three figures of the South Picene strophe (3 x 7 syllables)—concatenating alliteration, distracted constituents, and figura etymologica—coexist in a single Rigvedic *gāyatrī* strophe (3 x 8 syllables), 9.9.8:

nū́ **n**ávyase **n**ávīyase
sūktā́ya **s**ādhayā **p**atháḥ
pratnavád **r**ocayā **r**úcaḥ

Prepare the paths for every new hymn;
as before make your lights shine.

Cf. chap. 16. The Vedic etymological figure *rocayā rúcaḥ* (cf. also RV 9.49.5c, 6.39.4c) has itself an exact "etymological" equivalent in Archaic Latin, Ennius *Ann.* 156 *lumina lucent* '(the slaves) light the lights'. But while the causative stem **loukéi̯e-* is of Indo-European date (Hittite *lukkizzi*), the etymological figures are best regarded as parallel but independent creations since they are capable of being freely formed at any time.

Of the 21 South Picene inscribed stones (including the 'Warrior of Capestrano') at least two and possibly more show the word order figure of distracted constituents straddling a verb, which Vetter considered diagnostic for verse. The other sure example is M(a)C(erata) 1 from Loro Piceno, written boustrophedon in four continuous lines:

apaes : qupat : esmín : púpúnis : nír : mefiín : veiat : vepetí.

---

12. Among the stylistic features of the South Picene inscriptions is a taste for verbal play, ellipsis, and ambivalence, which (as a manifestation of the obscure style [chap. 16]) serves as a barrier protecting the poetic message. Here *Tetis Alies* may be the genitive (read perhaps *Tites*?) of a 'double' name *Titos Allios*, but *alies* may also be 'of another'. The accusative *tokam* [= *togam*?] may be the 'covering' of the defunct (i.e. the stele itself), but may also be something like the 'external form' of 'another', referring to the standing figure carved in relief on the stone. For these reasons I forbear to translate the second line.

The last three words are clearly 'lies (*veiat*) in the middle of the tomb (*mefiín vepetí*)'. Marinetti has discussed very ably (106-7) the stylistic structure of the whole: 'paratactic with a formulary insertion, stylistically intended but of obscure motivation'. In the bipartite message she sees 'a disjunction for stylistic ends of the concept "lie" of the dead, expressed by the two verbs *qupat* and *veiat* (= Faliscan *cupat*, *lecet*, Latin *cubat*, *iacet*), correlated as an expressive choice with the doubling of the deictic reference in *esmín* / *mefiín* 'in this/in the middle (of)' both going with *vepetí* 'tomb'. As she prints it,

apaes qupat esmín	púpúnis nír	
	púpúnis nír	mefiín veiat vepetí

The elder lies (*qupat*) in this (tomb), the Picene chief;
(The Picene chief) lies (*veiat*) in the middle of the tomb.

Depending on which line *púpúnis nír* is counted with we have a strophic couplet of a canonical Indo-European longer line and a shorter line, 7 + 4 = 11 and 8, or the reverse, 7 and 4 + 8 = 12. Alliteration marks the cadence of the last line, *veiat vepetí*.

Another pattern of alliteration may possibly be discerned in the cippus of Castignano, A(scoli) P(iceno) 2.[13] The stone is inscribed vertically on two faces, which for internal reasons are to be read in the order *a*, *b*. One of the common deployments of alliteration in Archaic Irish is concatenating, bridging hemistich or line boundaries. If we so divide and so arrange the lines of this text we obtain the following strophic structure of sides *a* and *b* of sequentially decreasing syllable count (noted on the right):

a	matereíh patereíh qolofítúr	10
	qupíríh arítih ímih puíh	9
b	púpúnum estufk apaiús	8
	adstaíúh súaís manus	7
	meitimúm	3

He who well . . . __s mother (and) father,
(him)[14] here the elders of the Picenes
have set up with their own hands
as memorial (uel sim.)
(tr. after Eichner)

The last lines 7 + 3 = 10 also equal the first in syllable count. The extreme extraposition of the nominative singular (with Eichner) relative pronoun *puíh* to the very end of its clause is a surely conscious poetic figure of "non-configurational" word order. The

13. Divergent colometry and quantitative metrical analysis ("trochaic") in Eichner 1988-90 [1992]: 200-1; a speculative but in many ways convincing interpretation and translation *ibid.* 195.7.

14. The stele itself, topped by a human head in relief, is probably anthropomorphic and represents the defunct.

identical figure with the same relative pronoun (in the dative singular) recurs for a certainty in the contemporary inscription from Penna San Andrea (TE[ramo] 5),[15] in which a lengthy sequence of twenty words and seven or eight alliterative pairs (as in TE 2 cited above) finishes at the very end of the inscription,

praistaklasa posmúi.

Who has (to whom is) this eminence/token of award.

Here *praistakla-sa* makes both an etymological figure and a semantic play on the verb *praistaít* 'furnishes, provides, *praestat*' earlier in the text, as Eichner suggests.

The first age of poetry in Italy is not confined to Faliscan and South Picene, nor are the texts we have examined their only poetic monuments. It is to be hoped that further study will yield more results and that the soil of Italy may yet give up more verbal treasures. The advent of writing in Italy in the seventh and sixth centuries only opened a window onto an extraordinarily thriving world of different but related poetic cultures.

15. Conjectural translation, commentary, and metrical analysis in Eichner 1988-90 [1992]:198-200.

11

Most ancient Indo-Europeans

1. Hittite ritual and the antecedents of drama

Most scholars and thinkers since Aristotle have proceeded on the assumption that the chorus of Greek drama, certainly the chorus of comedy and satyr-play and possibly the chorus of tragedy as well, originated with the cult of Dionysos.[1] Henrichs cites a number of recent treatments, from Pickard-Cambridge and Webster 1962 through Burkert 1966 to Winnington-Ingram 1985. For tragedy this view has been challenged or modified by other scholars 'who prefer to situate tragedy and its chorus more concretely in the contemporary framework of the polis religion and of active Dionysiac cult' (Henrichs),[2] in the social and psychological context of the Greek city-state in the crucial 5th century, which spanned the birth and death of tragedy in Athens. These views were originally expressed and elaborated by the French schools of Henri Jeanmaire, Louis Gernet, and subsequently Jean-Pierre Vernant and Pierre Vidal-Naquet. In a contribution originally presented in 1968, Vernant wrote 'Over the last half century the inquiries of Greek scholars have centered above all on the origins of tragedy . . . thus the problem of origins is, in a sense, a false one. It would be better to speak of antecedents.'[3] Virtually the same was said by Gernet in a 1953 essay[4] (on Jeanmaire's *Dionysos*): 'As a historical problem that of the *origins* of tragedy could well be a pseudo-problem. We can perceive the surroundings; we can just catch a glimpse of some antecedents' (1982:97). It is in their sense that I use the terms antecedents in my title.

It is not my intention in this chapter to address the question of possible ritual antecedents, direct or indirect, of drama in Greece, and still less the question of the position of tragedy or the role of Dionysos, which is the thrust of Henrichs' own work. My aim is much simpler. I find the evolutionist ritual model (tragedy as sacrifice) of

1. Here and in the next lines I follow the historical introduction, with rich bibliography, of an as yet unpublished monograph by my colleague Albert Henrichs (1993).

2. Citing Goldhill 1987 and 1990.

3. Vernant and Vidal-Naquet 1988:23.

4. Collected in Gernet 1982a:81-118.

Burkert 1966 oversimplified and overstated, as in his concluding line 'Human existence face to face with death—that is the kernel of τραγῳδία' (p. 121), but I do find myself in sympathy with the arguments advanced by Seaford 1984, in the introduction to his edition of the only satyr-play we have preserved more or less intact, Euripides' *Cyclops*, particularly his straightforward conclusion (p. 14) that 'the unfashionable view that the performance of tragedy originated in the practice of ritual is thereby confirmed.' I would only substitute 'has its antecedents' for 'originated'.

As we noted in chap. 4, the great majority of our documents in the 2nd-millennium Anatolian languages Hittite, Luvian, and Palaic are rituals. Thanks to the diligence of the Hittite scribes and their supervisors these clay tablets, inscribed and recopied often over centuries, faithfully record, catalogue, and preserve all the details of these rituals: the requisite material objects and their sequential manipulation and deployment in ritual acts, and the verbatim recording of all the ritual utterances and their speakers in their proper sequence. The purpose is to assure the correct and flawless regular *re-performance* of the ritual, on which the well-being of the society was felt to rest. The result for us is that we are far better informed about 2nd-millennium Anatolian ritual than about that of any other Indo-European culture of the period, and indeed better than Greece in the 5th century and earlier.

My aim as a comparatist in this chapter is simply to call to the attention of Hellenists certain manifestations within Hittite and Anatolian rituals which show clear and striking affinities to what we think of as drama. They thus afford a typological comparandum to the possible but unattested antecedents of Greek drama in ritual. The comparison is typological, and the Hittite and Luvian rituals in question are more than a thousand years earlier than 5th-century Athens. Still, it is well to remember that Anatolian-speaking and Greek-speaking cultures were geographically contiguous and certainly in contact at this early period, and that the worship of Dionysos is attested in second-millennium Mycenean Greek documents.

My first example is taken from one of a collection of Old Hittite compositions grouped together by Laroche as CTH 820, Bénédictions pour le tabarna-roi. CTH 820.5 was unearthed in 1933 (excavation no. 406/c) but not published (in cuneiform autograph) until 1973, as *K(eilschrifttexte aus) Bo(ghazköi)* 21.22. The fragmentary text has been transliterated and translated by Kellerman 1978 and (independently) Archi 1979.

The text is a single-column tablet, written continuously on recto and verso. The beginning is broken off, as is the colophon that probably followed verso 57′ in the empty space at the end. The intelligible part contains a series of ritual episodes, graphically demarcated by a double paragraph line. They each conclude with the phrase *AWAT x QATI* 'The word/formula/spell (Hittite *uttar*) of the *x* is finished'. Compare Ro. 18′-21′, which contains the only first person singular of the celebrant:

---

kāša GIŠ.ERÍN karpīemi nu labarnaš taluqauš MU$^{ḪI.A}$-uš
ušneškimi kāša GIŠ.ERÍN karpīemi n=ašta
^{SAL}tawanannaš taluqauš MU$^{ḪI.A}$-uš ušneškimi
AWAT GIŠ.ERÍN araḫza *QATI*

Behold! I lift up the scales, and I put up for sale[5] the long
years of the Labarna-king; behold, I lift up the scales, and
I put up for sale the long years of the Tawananna-queen.
The spell of the scales outside is finished.

If that spell involved pantomime and the manipulation of an object, perhaps with the words being accompanying explanation, another clearly includes question and answer, even if we have no indication of anyone speaking besides the celebrant. Verso 36′-45′:

---

^{D}IM-aš wattaru uit n=at māḫḫ[an iyan
katta=šara=at=kan NA_4-ta uedan iškiy[an]luli[t$^{?}$
n=at paršaneš pāḫšanta wātar=šed=a=kan[
lūliaz arašzi n=an paḫḫašnuandu lab[arn]an
[LUG]AL-un paššileš n=aš ^{D}UTU-wa<š> AN.BAR kišar[u

---

^{D}IM=aš wattaru iyanzi nu=wa wattaru māḫḫan iyan
kunnanit=at uedan arzilit=at ḫaniššān
AN.BAR=at iškiyan n=ašta ^{D}IM-naš tān annaš=šiš
kattanta pait n=at=za ešat ^{D}IM-ni=aš AMA-*ŠU*
labarni=ma=aš išḫiešša=ššit *AWAT* ^{NA_4}paššilaš *QATI*

There came the fountain of the Storm God. How is it made?
From bottom to top it is made of stone, it is coated with [
Panthers protect it. But its water [ ] flows from a pool.
Let them protect him, the pebbles the Labarna-king, and let him
become the iron of the Sun God.

They make the fountain of the Storm God. "How is the fountain made?"
It is made with copper, it is plastered with gypsum, it is
coated with iron. The mother of the Storm God came down
for the second time, and she sat down on it. For the
Storm God she is his mother, but for the Labarna she is
his binding. The spell of the pebbles is finished.

The quotation marks in the question in the second paragraph translate the particle *=wa* of direct, quoted speech. The symbolism of much of this allusive and elliptic, perhaps condensed or abbreviated spell escapes us, but the question and answer is apparent, as is the hymnic, dithyrambic choral character of the benediction. The action of the Storm God's mother sitting on the fountain recalls the epithet *sādádyoni-* of Agni (RV 5.43.12) and the verb phrase *yónim sad-* 'sit on the seat' of Agni, Mitra-Varuṇa, and

5. In the interest of the buyer, i.e. the king and the queen, as shown by Neu 1980:82. The frankly commercial metaphor in the ritual is striking.

other Vedic deities. The 'mandate' (see Melchert 1988) represents a contractual notion of obligation, cf. *išḫiul* 'contract' from the same verbal stem *išḫiya-* 'bind'. It appears to symbolize the divine legitimization of the Labarna-king and his authority.

The most striking in dramatic character of the spells of this text is that contained in Verso 22′-30′, between the two just cited. Here an almost stichomythic riddling dialogue leads directly into a veritable hymnic chorale. The dialogue exchange is formally marked by the particle *=wa* of quoted speech. The text follows:

ḫāš nu kuēz uwaši šuppaz=wa uwami
nu=wa kuēz šuppayaz zaḫanittennaz=wa
nu=wa kuēz zaḫanittennaz ^{D}UTU-waš=wa É-az
nu=wa kuēz ^{D}UTU-az ēšri=šet=wa GIBIL-an GAB-*ŠU* GIBIL
[SAG]-*ZU*=wa GIBIL-an LÚ-tar=šet=wa nēwan

[KA x U]D$^{ḪI.A}$-*ŠU*-wa *ŠA* UR.MAḪ IG[I$^{ḪI.A}$-*ŠU*-wa ḫ]āranaš
[nu=wa ḫ]āranili ša<ku>i[škizzi

]x namma parā[
] *AWAT* [

"Open!"
"Whence comest thou?"
"From the Holy."
"From what Holy?"
"From the *zaḫanittenna*."
"From what *zaḫanittenna*?"
"From the house of the Sun-God."
"From what Sun-God?"
"His form is new, his breast is new,
his head is new, his manhood is new."

"His teeth are those of a lion; his eyes are those of an eagle;
he sees like an eagle."

] moreover forth [
] the spell of the [(is finished)

The initial imperative 'open!'[6] provides a dramatic frame to begin the dialogue,

6. The variant *ḫé-e-eš* of the parallel passage KUB 55.2 (Bo 2226) Vo. 5′ (cited in full below) proves that *ḫa-a-aš* here must be the imperative of *ḫāšš-/ḫēšš-* 'open' (cf. Oettinger 1979:50) rather than the nominative singular *ḫa-a-aš* 'ashes; soda ash; potash; soap', with earlier commentators. So Kellerman's 'Washing powder!' 'formula [of the washing powder]', Archi's '(Questa è) sostanza purificatrice' 'il detto [della sostanza purificatrice]', and Puhvel's lapidary 'Soap, whence comest thou? From clean[sing supply] I come' (1991:210). The error is understandable, if amusing; soap (*ḫāš*) is utilized in other Hittite rituals.

a device that is still with us today from doorkeeper scenes to knock-knock jokes. This is its first appearance in the Indo-European speaking world. For the adjective *šuppi-* 'ritually pure, consecrated, holy' see Watkins 1975d. The word *zaḫanittenna-* is attested only here, and its meaning is unknown. It is probably a Hattic loanword,[7] perhaps a word for a particular house or temple.

We are fortunate in having another version of this same spell, in two fragments which duplicate each other. They make it clear that the dialogue part involves two speakers, a 'chamberlain' (DUMU É.GAL), one of the palace personnel, and the 'Old Woman' (^{SAL}ŠU.GI) familiar from countless Hittite rituals. The "choral" part is separated by a paragraph line, and carries no indication of speakers or singers.[8] The two texts are (A) KUB 20.54 + KBo 13.122 (41/s, unearthed in 1960, published in cuneiform 1967)[9] and (B) KUB 55.2 (Bo. 2226, published in cuneiform 1985). I give a composite based on B, with restorations from A in parentheses. B ro 5′ follows the paragraph line. A 1 is the first line of the verso; the recto is missing.

Ro. 5′ DUMU (É.GAL)] tezzi ḫēš ^{SAL}ŠU.G[(I tezz)i nu kuezza
(uwatte)]eni[10] *UMMA* DUMU É.GAL šu[(ppayaza=wa pē)daza uwaueni
7′ *UMMA* ^{SAL}Š]U.GI nu=wa kuezza šuppay[aza pēda(za *UMMA* DUMU
É.GAL zaḫa<ne>t)tenaza *UMMA* ^{SAL}ŠU.GI
Vo. 1 (nu=wa kuē)]zza zaḫanettennaza *UMMA* DUMU É.GAL [*UM*[*MA*]]?
(^{D}UTU-aš=wa par$^{!}$na)]z[11] *UMMA* ^{SAL}ŠU.GI nu=war=aš GIM-an
^{D}UTU-uš

---

3 (ēšri=ššet=w)]a nēuwan GAB-*ŠU*=wa nēuwan pišna[(tar=šet=wa
(nēuwan SA)]G.DU-*ZU* AN.BAR-aš KA x UD-*ŠU*=wa ŠA UR.MAḪ
š[akuwa=šet=wa
5 (ḫarran)aš nu=wa ḫāranil]i šākuiškizzi uddani=šet=a=w[(a nēuwan)

The chamberlain says,[12] "Open!"
The Old Woman says, "Whence come ye?"
As follows the chamberlain: "We come from the Holy Place."
As follows the Old Woman: "From what Holy Place?"

---

7. The audience of these benedictions for the labarna-king is clearly Hattic; the Hattic divinities ^{D}T]eneraiuš ^{D}Tetepiriš[in the fragmentary following section, Vo. 34′, recur in the same order in a Hattic recitation in KUB 28.74 Ro. 7. The same Hattic text (Vo. 1,3) contains both the words *tabarna* 'king' and *ḫapalkian* 'of iron', recalling the second of our Hittite spells cited above.

8. The "choral" parts of both (one was still unpublished) were first treated by Neu and Otten in 1972, in their classic paper equating the Sumerogram LÚ-*natar* 'manhood' with the new versions' *pišnatar*, thus demonstrating the reading *pišna-* for the Hittite word for 'man, male' (Sumerogram LÚ) and its evident etymology **pes-nó-* 'having a **pes-*' (cf. Greek πέος < **pes-os*, Latin *pēnis* < **pes-ni-*).

9. Edited by Kellerman 1978 and Archi 1979.

10. A *ú-wa-at-te-ni*, B]*-e-ni*.

11. So Kellerman. The tablet has *an-na-az*.

12. Dialogue sentences introduced by *tezzi* 'says' lack the quotative particle =*wa*. Those introduced by *UMMA* 'as follows' have it, as do those of the following "chorale", with one probably inadvertent exception. But see n. 15 below.

As follows the chamberlain: "From the *zaḫanettenna*."
As follows the Old Woman: "From what *zaḫanettenna*?"
As follows the chamberlain: "From the house of the Sun-God."
As follows the Old Woman: "How is he, the Sun-God?"

"His form is new, his breast is new, his manhood is new.
His head is of iron, his teeth are those of a lion, his eyes
are those of an eagle, and he sees like an eagle. <All> that of
his[13] in the spell, moreover, is new."

The text clearly describes the performance of a ritual dialogue by the palace personnel. Note that the chamberlain (DUMU É.GAL) is in the singular throughout, despite the plurality ('Whence come ye?' 'We come . . . ') of his role in this version. He is thus by a dramaturgic convention a spokesperson for the group, like the Marut in the dialogue hymn RV 1.165. Note also how the successive questions of the dialogue lead into the hymnic chorale, which is framed by the *nēuwan* '(is) new' clauses. The pregnant notion of 'renewal' is apparent in another Old Hittite ritual with close affinities to the texts we have cited: KUB 29.1 and its duplicates (one in the Old Kingdom ductus), CTH 414, the famous 'Bauritual'. It is most recently edited by Carini 1982 and Marazzi 1982. Note only ii 48-54, with a variant of the same "chorale":

^{D}UTU-uš
^{D}U-ašš=a utnē EGIR-pa LUGAL-i maniaḫ<ḫir>
MU$^{\text{ḪI.A}}$-ašš=a EGIR<-pa> newaḫḫir naḫšarattan
newaḫḫir

ALAM-i=šši[14] NAGGA-aš iēr SAG.DU-*ZU* AN.BAR-aš
iēr šākuwa=šši Á^{MUŠEN}-aš iēr
KA x UD$^{\text{ḪI.A}}$=ma=šši UR.MAḪ-aš iēr.

The Sun-God and the Storm-God have entrusted the land to the king;
They have renewed his years, they have renewed his awesomeness.

They have made his form of steel (lit. tin), they have made his
head of iron, they have made his eyes those of an eagle,
they have made his teeth those of a lion.

This lengthy ritual involves substantial recitation, as punctuated and italicized in

13. This interpretation of *uddani=šet=a=wa* (the reading is sure) is very uncertain. Neu and Otten omit it.

14. Here and in the following the Old Hittite original probably had *=ššit* 'his' in place of *=šši* 'to him', to judge by the Akkadogram in SAG.DU-*ZU* 'his head' and the variants we have seen: ALAM is the Sumerogram for Hittite *ēšri*.

Carini 1982. Even the freestanding fire altar (GUNNI, Hittite *ḫaššaš* : Latin *āra*) has a small speaking role (iii 47 etc.):

GUNNI tezzi[15] apāt=wa=mu=za āššu

The altar says, "For me that is good." (= "I like that.")

As our final example we may take a text first published in cuneiform only in 1988 (KUB 58.48), which is now edited with other duplicates and parallels identified by van den Hout 1991. This scholar correctly identified the passage as 'a dramatic interlude in the Hittite KI.LAM ritual'; for the latter see Singer 1983-84. As I stated in Watkins 1993:475, cf. 478: '. . . col. iv of the new tablet . . . contains a dialogue in dramatic form—complete with stage directions—between the king and the chief of the men of Tissaruliya, then at the king's behest between the chief of the bodyguards and the man from Tissaruliya. This confirms the suggestion of I. Singer (StBoT 27.49, 61-2) and V.G. Ardzinba and V.V. Ivanov (cited ibid.) that the KI.LAM festival contained episodes of a literary nature, recitations of mythological matter, perhaps in verse (Ivanov), as clearly in 1.b.iii 1′-14′.[16] The passage of 58.48 . . . makes the impression of an "entertainment" in dramatic dialogue form. Like the dramatic stichomythic and choral episodes in other Hittite ritual texts . . . these texts have much to teach us about the possible ritual origins (or "antecedents" . . .) of drama in Early Greece as well.'

In what follows I give a composite text and translation of van den Hout's 1.A = KUB 58.48 Vo. iv 1′-16′ and duplicate 1.B KUB 36.45, 1′-11′. Occasional additions have been made to the translation from his 2. KUB 43.31, left col. 1′-11′, which appears to be in the old ductus, and 3.A. KBo 13.228 Ro. and 3.B. KUB 44.10 Vo. These are enclosed in square brackets. Conjectures or interpretations of mine are enclosed in parentheses.

LUGAL-uš EGIR-pa G]AL *MEŠEDI* pīēzzi
UMMA ŠU]-*MA* mā=wa zaḫḫiya
LUGAL-uš t]ēzzi nu=wa=tta kuit
kāša=tt]a=wa ^{D}U-an atta =man
nu=wa marnuan kitta nu=w]a UZU UDU kitta

ēt nu=z[a išpāi eku nu]=za ninki
UMMA ŠU-MA takkumi=wa *ŪL*=wa=z ētmi

15. Here the dialogue sentences introduced by *tezzi* 'says' do contain the particle =*wa*; see note 12 above.

16. These KI.LAM 'gate-house' ritual passages are now discussed in Eichner 1993:112-113. In the first it is tempting to see a bird's name in the unexplained '*tīešteš larīeš* of the sea (*arunaš*)', namely the abundant blackheaded gull, *Larus ridibundus*, whose present winter range covers almost all of central Anatolia as well as its littoral according to the map in Jonsson 1993:264. If the similarity *larīeš* : Greek λάρος '("sea") gull' is not just coincidental, *tuḫḫandat* 'sobbed, gasped' would refer to this bird's cry, described in Jonsson as 'a nasal melodious 'auhr', near colonies screaming and obtrusive'. The verse (KBo 10.24 iii 11′-14′, Singer 2.18) would then mean something like 'When the *tīešteš* gulls of the sea sobbed, the divine ones above in heaven were shrieking.'

takkumi=wa *ŪL*=wa=z ekumi zaḫḫiya=wa
uwanun LUGAL-š=a tezzi
kuit=a=wa zaḫḫiya=ma uēš nu=wa SIG$_5$-in

GAL LÚ^{MEŠ} ^{URU}Tiššaruliya LUGAL-i
menaḫḫanda SAG.DU-*ZU* ninikzi
tašta paizzi EGIR-pa=ma=aš
namma uizzi n=aš $^{\text{NA4}}$ḫūwašiya
ḫikta LUGAL-uš GAL *MEŠEDI*
pīezi GAL *MEŠEDI* <GAL> LÚ^{MEŠ} ^{URU}Tiššaruliya
punušzi kuit=wa uēš
UMMA ŠUMA kuitma=wa [
pāun ÉRIN^{MEŠ}-az=miš=a
ḫanti šarrattati

[the king sends the chief of the bodyguards (to ask the chief of the men of the city of Tissaruliya)
"Why have you come?"
"I would like to call upon the king."
The chief of the bodyguards brings the message to the king.
The king sends back] the chief of the bodyguards.
As follows (the man of Tissaruliya): "I would like to fight."
The king says, "What to you (have I done?) Behold,
for you (I have invoked?) the Storm-God my father.
[*Marnuan*-drink has been set out,] mutton has been set out.

Eat and satisfy your hunger, drink and satisfy your thirst."
As follows (the man of Tissaruliya): "I will (hold out?) I
will not eat. I will (hold out? I will not drink.)
I have come for a fight."
The king, however, says, "But why have you come for
a fight? (Everything is) fine."

The chief of the men of Tissaruliya shakes his head
at the king, and he departs. But then
he comes back, at the *ḫuwaši* cultic stone he
bows before the king. The king sends the
chief of the bodyguards. The chief of the bodyguards
questions the chief of the men of Tissaruliya:
"Why have you come?"
As follows (the man of Tissaruliya): "While . . . I went
but my army has broken apart."

One can only speculate what is meant or intended by this dramatic interlude, but it is certain that it formed a part of the Old Hittite KI.LAM (gate-house) ritual, a cult ceremony of Hattic origin, involving liturgical recitations in Hattic and lasting for three days. The 'men of Tissaruliya' otherwise figure only as cultic functionaries who get rations in the KI.LAM tablets (Singer 1983-84:1.26 et passim). Another set of texts, CTH 742, mention 'women of Tissaruliya' ($SAL^{MEŠ}$ ^{URU}T.), who sing in Hattic. Clearly the city was at some point real, and Hattic-speaking or in the Hattic sphere. Perhaps our text is a historical playlet, a vignette which is a dramatic re-enactment of the hostilities or tensions between the immigrating Hittites and the autochthonous Hattic speakers. This dramatic vignette might have concluded with a symbolic re-enactment of the resolution of those conflicts, in the cultural symbiosis of Hittite and Hattic which is attested by the continued performance of the ritual itself. Our text unquestionably goes back to the Old Hittite period, as do all the others we have examined in this chapter. The implication is clear: by the 17th century B.C. we have unambiguous evidence for the incorporation of self-contained episodes of dramatic dialogue into the performance of ritual in Hittite Anatolia. The seeds of drama are there.

In just the same way Lévi 1890:301f. could point to the seeds of Indian drama already in the dialogue hymns of the Rigveda.[17] As he noted, the number of speakers is never more than three, and frequently a collective personage, a sort of chorus, functions as a character. Thus the dialogue of Indra, Agastya, and the (spokesman for the) Maruts, Saramā and the (spokesman for the) Paṇis, just as we saw in Hittite the King, the chief of the bodyguards, and the (spokesman for the) men of Tissaruliya. And the different versions of the Hittite question-and-answer series, climaxing in the question 'How is the Sun-God? / What Sun-God?' which elicits the choral hymn of definition of the deity, find an exact counterpart in the dialogue of the divine bitch Saramā and the Paṇis, RV 10.108. I cite just the first one or two pādas of the first four verses:

kím icchántī sarámā prédám ānaṭ

The Paṇi: In search of what did Saramā come here?

índrasya dūtī́r iṣitā́ carāmi
mahá icchántī paṇayo nidhī́n vaḥ

Saramā: Sent as Indra's messenger I come
in search of your great treasures, o Paṇis.

kīdṛ́ṅṅ índraḥ sarame kā́ dṛśīkā́
yásyedáṃ dūtī́r ásaraḥ parākā́t

The Paṇi: What is Indra like, o Saramā, what is his appearance,
as whose messenger you have come from afar?

17 1.165, 170, 179; 3.33; 4.18; 7.33; 8.100; 10.10, 28, 51-53, 86, 95, 108, thus already in the oldest layer, the Family Books.

náhám̩ tám̩ veda dábhyam̩ dábhat sá
yásyedám̩ dūtír ásaram parākā́t

Saramā: I do not know him as one to be deceived; *he* deceives,[18]
as whose messenger I have come from afar.

In India as well as Anatolia dramatic dialogue in ritual hymnic poetry is already fully developed and skillfully deployed by the middle of the 2nd millennium B.C. Had we such texts from Crete, Mycenae, or Athens from the same period it is not unlikely that they would exhibit the same phenomenon.

2. The language and poetry of the Trojans

This section subsumes and brings fresh evidence for the thesis, advocated first in Watkins 1986, that the language of Troy and the Trojans in the northeast corner of Anatolia was a variety of Luvian, close to if probably not identical with the language of our Cuneiform Luvian monuments of the middle of the 2nd millennium.

Among our Cuneiform Luvian texts is the ritual of one Puriyanni, which sets forth in detail directions for performing a private household ritual of sympathetic magic, a conjuration designed to ward off evil and impurity from someone's house. For the whole text and its dating see Starke 1985:55f.; the oldest tablets, from the beginning of the 14th century, are themselves for internal reasons copies of an earlier archetype of at least 15th-century date. The text is bilingual: the directions for the ritual actions are in Hittite while the ritual utterances, what we may call the "spells", are in Luvian. The 'Conjuration of water and salt' in KUB 35.54 Vo. iii 12-21 contains two paragraphs, the first in Hittite and the second in Luvian:

nu=ššan *ANA* GAL GIR_4 kuit wātar lāḫuwan
MUN=ya=kan anda išḫuwān
n=at=kan É-ri anda papparašzi
ANA BEL SISKUR=ya=ššan šarā papparašzi
nu kiššan memai

---

wāarša=tta ÍD-ti [nan]amman
MUN-ša=pa ālāti uwā[niyati] upamman
wāarša=tta zīl[a ÍD-i] anda nāwa iti
MUN-ša=pa=[tta z]ila āli uwāniya nā[wa it]i

(Hittite) The water which is poured into the clay bowl
and the salt which is shaken in it

---

18. The reciprocal figure is a variant of 'the slayer slain' formula defining the hero or the divinity, discussed in chap. 33: RV 8.84.9 *nákir yám ghnánti hánti yáḥ* 'whom none slay, who slays'.

he sprinkles in the house
and sprinkles on the celebrant
and speaks as follows:

(Luvian) "The water is led from the river
and the salt is brought from the steep rock face;
the water to the river nevermore will go back
and the salt to the steep rock face nevermore will go back."[19]

We recognize at once the rhythmic, grammatically parallel, syntactic strophic style of the Luvian spell, which is clearly verbal art.

The adjective *āli-* 'high, lofty, steep' of mountains, rock face, may have been borrowed, perhaps as a toponym, by Mycenean Greek speakers and transformed into ἀλίβατος (πέτρα Pindar, Aeschylus), ἠλίβατος (πέτρη Homer), 'steep (rock)'. The Luvian form *āl-i-*, with lengthened *ā* in open syllable, may be related to the family of Latin *al-tus*.

Now this Luvian adjective has one further attestation, which has serious implications: it is an epithet for the city of Wilusa. The city of *Wiluša* or *Wilušiya* is well attested in Hittite texts, as a city of the Luvian-speaking Arzawa lands of Western Anatolia, with a king *Alakšanduš* whose name immediately recalled *Alexandros*, the other name of the Trojan prince Paris, son of Priam. For this and other reasons the identification of Wilusa with Greek (F)Ἴλιος, *(W)ī́lios*, one of the names for Troy, was made long ago and is today widely, though not universally, accepted (Güterbock 1986; skeptical Bryce 1988).

It is therefore of considerable interest that Wilusa is also found in a very special Luvian-language context and genre: the 'sacred songs' (Hittite *šuppa uddār*) of the rituals of the cultic city of Istanuwa. The location of the city is unknown, but its name must be derived from that of the Anatolian Sun-deity, Hittite *Ištanu-* from Hattic *Eštan*.[20] Among our Luvian texts the rituals from Istanuwa occupy a place apart, as Laroche saw (1959:12). The vocabulary is often unlike that of the usual Luvian magical texts, though morphology and syntax are straightforwardly Luvian. It is possible, though not certain, that they represent a special dialect, but the real difference is that these 'sacred words' 'develop different themes', in Laroche's phrase. The

---

19. The interpretation of Luvian *wāar* (+ neuter *-ša*) as 'water' is confirmed by its cognates Vedic *vā́r*, scanned disyllabic *váar*, and Latin *ūr-īna* '*water'. That of *āli- uwāni-*, the place where salt comes from, as *āli-* 'high, lofty, steep' or the like (an epithet of mountains) and *uwāni(ya)-* 'rock face, cliff, escarpment', is confirmed by a new Hittite text unearthed in 1986 and published in 1988, the Bronze Tablet treaty Bo 86/299 (Otten 1988) ii 5ff., to be translated 'When they drive (livestock) from the Ḫulaya river land to the great saltlick rock face (*šalli lāpani* ⁝ *wāniya*), they should not take the saltlick rights (⁝ *lapanalianza*) away from him. They are given to the king of Tarḫuntašša, and he can take the salt (MUN) at any time.' Luvian ⁝ *lapan-* (with *Glossenkeil* ⁝ in the Hittite texts) is not 'summer pasture' but 'saltlick', a derivative of 'lick' (Hittite *lip-*), IE **leb-* in English *lap*, *lip*. Cuneiform Luvian ⁝*uwāni(ya)-* 'rock face' is the same stem as Hieroglyphic *wani(ya)-* 'dressed stone, stele' confirming the source of salt. Güterbock observed that just such a stratum of white salt on the face of a mountain was visible from the national highway near Delice in Central Anatolia. See Watkins 1986, 1987d, 1987e, and now Melchert 1993b.

20. See the discussion in Puhvel, HED s.v.

language describing the ritual is Hittite; the Luvian parts are incipits ('Liedanfänge' Starke 1985:300) of interspersed choral chants and responsions, which are sung (SÌR^{RU}, *išḫamiškanzi*). In short they are Luvian verbal art, Luvian poetry. Following Starke ibid. there are good linguistic grounds for dating the Istanuwa texts as a group to the Old Hittite period (16th century).

The text to which I called particular attention in Watkins 1986 is KBo 4.11, 45-6 (Starke 1985:339-42):

EGIR-*ŠU* ᴰŠuwašuran ekuzi
aḫḫ=ata=ta alati awienta Wilušati

(Hittite) Then he drinks to the god Suwasuna (and they sing:)
(Luvian) "When they[21] came from steep Wilusa."

As I suggested there, we have the beginning of a Luvian epic lay about the city of Wilusa, which we may equate with (W)ilios or Troy: a "Wilusiad". This view has been accepted by some (Eichner 1993), received with skepticism by others (Bryce 1988). But there can be no disagreement about the poetics of this line of Luvian verse, which is quite clear. We have two half lines which rhyme, and an alliteration bridges the break. The word order has been permuted according to the by now familiar pattern of Indo-European poetic syntax, the adjective (epithet) distracted from its constituent noun to straddle the verb, and both adjective and noun adjoining metrical boundary. All that can scarcely be accidental:

aḫḫ=ata=ta **alati** || **a**WIenta WIluš**ati**.

In this single line of Luvian poetry we can plainly see the same aesthetic and the same poetic devices—phonetic, morphological, and syntactic—which inform the mantras of the Indo-Iranian *kavis* and the epic and lyric verses of the Greek *aoidoi*. As well as signaling the stylistic figure of the distracted noun phrase, the rhyme in ***alati*** || . . . *wiluš**ati***, at the end of successive hemistichs in the privileged poem-initial position of prominence, can be exactly paralleled by the end-rhymes in RV 4.53.7cd, where the lines occupy the privileged poem-final position of prominence:

sá naḥ kṣapā́bhir áhabhiś ca **jinvatu**
prajā́vantaṃ rayím asmé sám **invatu**

Let him **strengthen** us by night and by day,
let him **produce** for us wealth in offspring.

A close variant of our Luvian line occurs in another text, also as a first line. It is found in a fragmentary paragraph in KUB 35.102 (+) 103 iii 11ff., following a colophon and a double paragraph line, indicating the beginning of a new text, as discussed in Watkins 1986:60. The paragraph reads:

21. For the subject pronoun =*ata* (with intransitive verb) see Melchert 1993b s.v. *a*-, with reference.

ālati=tta aḫḫa LÚ-iš awita [
GÌR^{MEŠ}-ta=du tarweya īššara=d[u
dūwazan tiyammin dūpit[a
šarra i[ ]x-la taršīta

When the man came from steep [
his feet . . ., his hands [. . .
He beat the . . . earth [
up the . . . he . . .-ed

For suggestions about the last three lines see Watkins 1986:60 and Eichner 1993:110; they will not concern us further. But in the first line it is difficult not to restore [*Wilušati*] in the lacuna on the right, yielding (with Luvian phonetic reading of the Sumerogram for 'man' LÚ-*iš*) two formulaic variants as first lines (whether of the same or of related texts):

ālati=tta aḫḫa zitiš || awita [**Wilušati**]
aḫḫ=ata=ta **alati** || awienta **Wilušati**

When the man[22] came from steep [Wilusa]
When they came from steep Wilusa.

Compare from the initial pāda of the first and third verse of the same Rigvedic hymn, 6.23.1a, 3a:

sutá ít tvám̐ || nímiśla indra **sóme**
pā́tā **sutám** || índro astu **sómam**

You are indulging, o Indra, in the pressed soma
Let Indra be the drinker of the pressed soma.

The positions relative to metrical boundary of the distracted noun-phrase constituents, as well as their order (Adj. + N), are identical in the two languages, Luvian and Vedic. The number and the precision of the similarities in the manipulation of poetic formulas are such that we must assume inheritance from a common poetic grammar O′, just as the morphophonemic precision of the equation Hittite 3sg. *kuen-zi* / 3pl. *kun-anzi* and Vedic 3sg. *hán-ti* / 3pl. *ghn-ánti* is by itself sufficient to require assumption of inheritance from a common grammar O. The relative rarity and isolation of these examples in Anatolian, given their special character among our limited documentation of Luvian, is methodologically no object. For all that the Indo-European languages of 2nd-millennium Anatolia have been in contact with and doubtless culturally influenced by the poetic traditions of Hattic on the one hand and Hurrian on the other, it is clear that there is a significant inherited Indo-European component in their poetics as well.

---

22. With overt subject the pronominal subject clitic is not necessary.

In Watkins 1988 I called attention to the similarity of our two Luvian lines in thematics and poetic devices to the first line (subsequently repeated as a sort of refrain) of the Old Welsh epic lay of the Gododdin,

> gwyr a AETH GatrAETH
>
> The men who went to Catraeth . . .,

and to the first lines of the Cyclic Epic *Aithiopis* (fr. I Allen):

> ὣς οἵ γ' ἀμφίεπον τάφον Ἕκτορος· ἦλθε δ' Ἀμαζὼν
> Ἄρηος θυγάτηρ μεγαλήτορος ἀνδροφόνοιο
>
> Thus they performed the burial of Hector. Then came the Amazon, daughter of great-hearted man-slaying Ares.

Similarly *Il.* 3.189:

> ἤματι τῶι ὅτε τ' ἦλθον Ἀμαζόνες ἀντιάνειραι
>
> on that day when the Amazons came, peers of men.

For the poetic devices of sound texture compare the notation of the Old Welsh line with the same of the Luvian:

> **a**ḫ̮ḫ̮=ata=ta **a**lati ‖ **a**WIenta WIlušati
> **ā**lati=tta **a**ḫ̮ḫ̮a zitiš ‖ **a**WIta [WIlušati].

Another, more striking thematic link is the traditional epithet for the city of (W)Ilios in Homer: αἰπεινή 'steep'. It occurs 6 times, always verse-initial (*Il.* 16.773 etc.). Is the semantic identity of Greek (F)Ιλιος αἰπεινή 'steep Ilios' and Luvian *alati Wilušati* 'steep Wilusa' just coincidence, or just an elementary parallel to describe a walled city? Or is it part of a common poetic tradition, a formulaic convention shared between the two geographically contiguous languages, Luvian and Greek? 'If that were so, it would raise all manner of implications for both history and literature in 2nd-millennium Greece and Anatolia,' as I concluded in Watkins 1986. If the Luvians had a song or epic lay about Wilusa-(W)Ilios—Troy—it does not follow that the inhabitants of Wilusa-(W)Ilios—the Trojans—spoke Luvian. But it is one more link, and a not inconsiderable one.

Another is the following. The name of the Luvian cult city of *Ištanuwa* is derived from that of the Anatolian Sun-God *Ištanu*. *Wiluša* figures in the incipit of the Luvian spell—*šuppa uddār* 'holy words'—which is sung to the god *Šuwašuna*. The name of this deity, otherwise attested only in another Istanuvian ritual as ^{D}*Šuwaššunna* (Bo 2447 = KUB 55.65 iv 30, Starke 1985:314), looks very like a form of the Indo-European word for 'sun' (cf. Gothic *sunno*) with intensive or expressive reduplication,[23] or conceivably an ancient compound with Indo-European **sue̯-* 'own' (cf. Hittite ^{D}*Šiu(š)-summiš* '(our) own (Sun-)God', **di̯eu̯s=suu̯o/i-*).

In the Hittite Alaksandus treaty the gods of the city of Wilusa are called to witness. The only one mentioned by name is ^{D}*]a-ap-pa-li-u-na-aš*, as restored by Forrer and defended by Güterbock 1986:42, and the name was already by Forrer equated with that of the Greek god Apollo, in the Common or Proto-Greek form **apeli̯ōn* securely reconstructible from Doric (Cretan, Laconian, Corinthian, etc.) ᾽Απέλλων, Cypriote *to-i-a-pe-i-lo-ni* ICS 215, b 4 (τῶι ᾽Απείλονι) and especially Mycenean *[a-]pe-ro*$_2$*-ne* KN E 842.3 (Ruijgh 1967:274).[24] As originally proposed by Burkert 1975 the name is derived from a word preserved in Doric ἀπέλλα(ι) 'assembly'; but as Peters shows the original meaning must have been rather the Indo-European institution of the "Männerbund", the 'hunter-warrior society of unmarried and propertiless young aristocrats' (McCone).[25] Apollo (**apeli̯ōn*) in this aspect was the leader of such a band (**apeli̯ā*). One might speculate—it is no more than that—that Alaksandus of Wilusa took Appaliunas as his personal god at the same time and from the same cultural source as his 'international' name, Greek Aleksandros, perhaps from personal experience in an **apeli̯ā*.

Apollo's role in the later Greek pantheon is of course much broader. Whether his later connection with the sun can be projected back to the 2nd millennium is uncertain at best, but it is clear in the *Iliad* that Apollo is the special patron of the city of Troy, Ilios, and the Trojans. The syntagmatic and paradigmatic linking of god and city would seem to form a cultural continuum from Luvian to Greek (the determiner ^{D} marks gods, ^{URU} cities):

^{D}UTU = Istanu ——	^{D}Suwasuna —	^{D}Appaliunas ——	᾽Απόλλων
	|	|	|
^{URU}Istanuwa ——	Wilusa ——	^{URU}Wilusa —	(F)Ιλιος - Τροιή

Another argument may be noted. Stephanus of Byzantium mentions the Asiatic Aeolic city of Elaea ('olive') : ᾽Ελαία πόλις τῆς ᾽Ασίας Αἰολική . . . ἡ κ<α>ὶ Δαινις (text ἡ Κίδαινις) ὠνομάζατο 'Elaea . . . which was also called Dainis'. The emendation is due to G. Neumann apud Gusmani 1986:162, who compared Luvian *dāin-* 'olive oil', *dāini(ya)-* 'of olive oil'. Starke 1990:241, convincingly equating the Luvian word with Greek στέαρ, observes that *dāin-*, *dāini(ya)-* are not Lydian, but Luvian, pace Gusmani, for morphological reasons. He is sympathetic to Neumann's suggestion that Greek ᾽Ελαία translated *Dāini(ya)-*, but skeptical because of the location of the city, on the northwestern coast of Anatolia on the Elaitic Gulf across from the island of Lesbos: 'admittedly a long ways from Luvian-speaking territory'. But if Troy and the Troad just to the north spoke Luvian the local name of the city would make perfect sense, and I consider Neumann's interpretation as cogent as it is ingenious.

23. Compare the South Slavic (*Perperuna*, *Dudula*) and Greek (Δωδώνη, Ζεὺς Δωδωναῖος) parallels.

24. See the fundamental discussion of the name of Apollo in Peters 1989:211-13. (He does not mention the Anatolian form.)

25. See Bremmer 1982 and Bremmer and Horsfall 1987 for Rome, J.F. Nagy 1985, McCone 1986 and 1990 for Ireland, Falk 1986 for India.

I conclude by pointing out a curious phrasal coincidence between Luvian and Homeric Greek, which is shared to my knowledge with no other Indo-European language. As we noted in chap. 2, Wackernagel in his famous lecture on Indo-European poetic language chose to illustrate the "law" of clitic placement which bears his name with a conjectural reading at *Il.* 1.8: τίς τάρ σφωε θεῶν 'Who of the gods (brought) these two . . .', with the enclitic particle ταρ (so explicitly Herodian at *Il.* 1.65 and 93) of the Teubner and Budé texts, not τ' ἄρ with the Vulgate as printed in the Oxford text. For the particle ταρ, attested by the Venetus A, see LSJ and Chantraine, DELG *s.v.* despite Neumann 1987. The sentence- and frequently episode-initial combination τίς ταρ recurs at *Il.* 2.761, 3.226, 18.182 and doubtless elsewhere; with other interrogatives we find at least τίπτε ταρ, πῶς ταρ, τί ταρ, πῇ ταρ. That 'τε after interrogative is always followed by ἄρ(α)', i.e. τ' ἄρ, with Denniston 1966:533, strains credulity; Munro's view that 'the ancient grammarian's ταρ is probably right' is surely preferable. Wackernagel's insight on τίς ταρ is vindicated, I would suggest, by later evidence of which he could have had no knowledge, the Luvian 'locatival' enclitic sentential particle *tar* precisely in the combination with the indefinite relative pronoun *kuiš=tar*,[26] the sequence identical to the Greek combination with the interrogative pronoun τίς ταρ, both from earlier *k^{u}*is tar*. The 'coincidental' similarity is the more striking when we realize that in the 2nd millennium, long before the elimination of labiovelars in Greek, the phonetic sequence k^{u}*ís tar* in both languages would have been for practical purposes substantively identical.

The locative force of the Luvian particle is clear in another of the sacred songs of Istanuwa, found in the paragraph immediately following that with the incipit 'When they came from steep Wilusa', KBo 4.11 Vo. 47-9 (to the god ^{D}Wandu):

tappaši=tar tapala
tappaši=tar tapala
lammaur titiyāla
alinan ḫaltittari maššaninzi

There in heaven . . .
There in heaven . . .
. . .
"Gods of . . ." is called out.

The interpretation is largely uncertain, but the particle in the repeated line, which reinforces the alliteration, is sure. Note that we have three rhyming 7-syllable lines followed by an 11-syllable, with a genitival noun phrase distracted to straddle the verb. The last line, as I stated (1986:61), 'even scans mechanically as a tolerably good Sapphic.' For other suggestions and differing rhythmical analysis see Eichner 1993:111.

Now the Luvian particle *tar* is also found enclitic to clause-initial finite verb: *mammanna=tar* 'regard with favor!' (2x). Compare the Iliadic formulas in verse-initial position ῥίγησέν ταρ ἔπειτα 11.254, ὤιμωξέν ταρ ἔπειτα 15.397 etc., κώκυσέν

26. The text in which it occurs (attested in three passages) is quoted in full in chap. 33.

ταρ ἔπειτα 18.37 etc., θάμβησέν ταρ ἔπειτα 3.398, for all of which the vulgate reads τ' ἄρ'. The semantic unity of all these verbs, 'shuddered', 'wailed', 'shrieked', 'was awestruck', as well as their morphological and phrasal rigidity, would suggest that they are ultimately all variants or developments of a single formula. Only in the Odyssey with γήθησέν ταρ ἔπειτα (13.353 etc.) 'rejoiced' do we find the [+ horror] overtones replaced by [+ joy].[27]

The particles Luvian *-tar* and the all but moribund Homeric Greek ταρ share both the same physical shape and the same syntactic deployment; the distribution is unique among the Indo-European languages.[28] It is tempting to see in this an areal feature common to both languages at the geographical point of their contact, Western Anatolia. That in Homer ταρ is confined to fixed formulas raises again the possibility of a component of a shared poetic tradition in Anatolian Luvian and Greek in the 2nd millennium. The presence of the personal name *Aswios* (*a-si-wi-jo*) in Mycenean Greek texts, clearly derived from the Western Anatolian ('Arzawan') territorial name *Aššuwa* in Hittite sources, is ample evidence for possible channels for the connection. For other close verbal links between 2nd-millennium Anatolian and Greek see chapters 26 and 46.

27. These V ταρ ἔπειτα formulas are obviously related to the much more common formulas αὐτὰρ ἔπειτα and αὐτὰρ ἐπεί and suggest that αὐτάρ should be analyzed as αὐ + ταρ rather than αὐτ' + ἄρ. The whole question is examined in Katz 1994, to whom I am indebted for references and examples.

28. Etymologically the particle, 'locatival' in Luvian, reflects IE **tr̥*, the pronominal stem with adverbial ending as in Vedic *tar-hi*, Gothic *þar* (**tor*), English *there* (**tēr*). Parallel is the particle IE **kʷr̥* in Palaic *-kuar*, beside Vedic *kar-hi*, Gothic *ƕar* (**kʷor*), English *where* (**kʷēr*), for which see Melchert 1984b.

12

The comparison of formulaic sequences

We saw in chap. 3 that the syntactic component of the grammar of Indo-European poetics is the domain of "formulaics", and the semantic component the domain of "thematics". Formulas are the vehicles, the carriers of themes; they are collectively the verbal expression of the traditional culture of the Indo-Europeans themselves. The formula can be something big like a myth (Vedic *áhann áhim* 'he slew the serpent'], or transposed to a charm (Old Irish *gono míl* 'I slay the beast'); a component of a myth (OIr. *teora ferba fíra* 'three milk cows'); a value (OIr. *milsem cotalta coiblige* 'copulation is the sweetest part of sleep'); a tabu (Greek ὀρθὸς ὀμείχειν = *mekṣyāmi ūrdhváḥ* 'to urinate upright'); a kenning or other indexical figure (OIr. *melg n-etha* 'milk of grain' = *cuirm* 'ale'); or simply a marked designation of things, like a merism (OIr. *beodil 7 marbdil* 'goods and chattels') or paired words linked by phonetic figures (OIr. *brechtaib ban* 'by spells of women') or by a figure of grammar (OIr. *gonas génta(i)r* 'he who kills will be killed'). The list is merely illustrative, hardly exhaustive.

In formulaics especially, as elsewhere in the study of poetics, the investigator must distinguish the diachronic, historical from the synchronic, descriptive, but at the same time move from the one to the other. Formulaic examples like those given just above from Vedic, Greek, and Old Irish are synchronic formulas. Cases like these just alluded to in Early Irish are synchronic formulas which are also diachronically viable. That is to say that in favorable cases this can be demonstrated by comparanda and motivated. We have for example a real phrasal equation between 7th- or 8th-century Irish *brechtaib ban mberar* 'he is taken by spells of women' (Watkins 1963a:34 = 1994:36), *fri brichtu ban* 'against spells of women' (Lorica I), and two independent attestations in Gaulish from the centuries surrounding the beginning of our era—in our tiny text corpus—of first *brixtia anderon* 'spell of underworld deities' (Chamalières) and now *brictom bnanom* 'spell of women' (Larzac). Again we have the expression of an evidently important cultural nexus, as the pattern and nature of the attestations and other information about the culture would clearly suggest.

The internal dynamics of the relations of synchrony and diachrony in the study of formula may be quite complex. Formulas may make reference to other formulas and derive their full meaning only by comparison with the other formula indexically referred to: a form of "intertextuality". Thus the bold metaphor *fyrena hyrde* 'shepherd of crimes', which is a kenning for Grendel at *Beowulf* 750b, indexes by both lexicon and alliteration the common formula *folces hyrde* 'shepherd of the people' (e.g., of Beowulf 5x), which is widespread in other languages, both Indo-European (ποιμένα λαῶν 'shepherd of the hosts') and non-Indo-European (Psalm 23). Even if *fyrena hyrde* were a nonce creation—which it may be—synchronically, the reference it makes to the diachronic formula *folces hyrde* gives it formulaic status as part of the 'dossier', in a sense a part of the *Rezeptionsgeschichte* of the latter phrase.

In some cases, synchronic formulas might be diachronically viable, but the individual instances escape demonstration: this is commonly the case of kennings, where one cannot exclude the possibility and even likelihood of independent creation of such elemental figures as OIr. *melg n-etha* 'the milk of grain (ale)', Greek ἁλὸς ἵπποι 'horses of the sea (ships)', Hittite KU_6 *arunaš* GUD.MAḪ 'the fish is the ox of the sea' (Otten, RLA III 68), $KU_6^{HI.A}$-*uš* ÍD-*aš* UR.ZÍR 'fish, the dogs of the river'. The *genre* of the kenning (akin to but distinct from riddles) is however likely to be inherited, and given instances are quite possibly genetically related: this is I think certain for Vedic *apām napāt* and Avestan *apąm napå* 'descendent of the waters', and probable for Old Norse *sævar niðr* 'descendent of the sea (fire)' as well (Mayrhofer 1956-80:2.132 with references). But the opposite is arguable, and the case is finally moot. In the realm of formulaic comparisons, of formulaic 'etymologies', we recognize the equivalent of merely possible equations like Greek γόνος : Ved. *jánaḥ* (which could well have been created independently), or pseudo-equations like OIr. *-breth* : Ved. *bhṛtáḥ*.[1]

There are finally synchronic formulas which are not diachronically viable, or only trivially so. In Homeric Greek, strings like αὐτὰρ ἐπεί or ἀλλ' ὅτε δή (both more or less 'but when') are certainly part of a synchronic formulaic system, as appears from their invariance and fixed metrical patterning. But we would not expect them to have cognates *qua formulas*. Similarly the 'flexible formula' of Luvian (chap. 11):

aḫḫa-ta (*-ta*) (*alati*) || 'when (they) (from steep) . . .'

beside

(*ālati*)*-**ta aḫḫa*** (*zitiš*) || 'when (the man) (from steep) . . .'

is semantically comparable to the Greek expressions, but only trivially so, even if the *-te* of Greek ὅτε (Mycenean *o-te*) and the Luvian particle *-ta* should turn out to be cognate. For cognates of Greek -ταρ see chap. 11.2. These are the formulaic equivalent of Meillet's principle that not every word is entitled to an etymology.

The fact of the long-term preservation of formulaic sequences makes possible the application to them of the Comparative Method. Long-term preservation is

1. For the methodology compare Meillet 1926, and his dictum that we reconstruct on the basis of the exceptions, not of the rules.

assured by repetition; thematic continuity—the preservation of an "essential idea"—implies semantic continuity, which in turn may allow lexical renewal. That is to say, we can have the preservation of formulaic status under partial or even total lexical replacement. We will see numerous cases in the pages which follow.

Lexical equations typically lead to reconstructions. Indo-European formulaic equations in a few optimal cases can be expressed by reconstruction with full lexical, morphological, and syntactic specification (**még̑h₂ k̑léu̯os* 'great fame',[2] **égʷhent ógʷhim* 'slew the serpent'[3]) but more frequently are at best only incompletely specifiable, usually just in terms of root semantics. In such cases I use English capitals to express the semantics and an optional Indo-European root form in parenthesis where that may be reasonably suggested, e.g.

GRAIN$_{\text{sp.}}$ and BARLEY (**i̯eu̯o-*)

as discussed in chap. 3.

Consider only that it is in some sense the SAME Indo-European formula which surfaces in Old Hittite as *iyata dameta*, in Homeric Greek as κειμήλιά τε πρόβασίν τε, and in English *goods and chattels*.[4] The underlying semantic opposition—riches which move (Hittite and Greek) versus riches which do not move but 'store' (?, Hittite) or 'lie' (Greek)—is no longer overt in contemporary English. Here even English capitals are of little avail, and the 'reconstructed' Indo-European formula is best simply paraphrased.

It is naturally not always possible to demonstrate whether semantically identical or equivalent formulas in two or more traditions are cognate when they share no lexical correspondence. For example, in the Hittite New Year's ritual in which the myth of the killing of the Illuyanka-serpent is narrated, the priest begins by intoning

udne=wa **māu šešdu**

May the land **grow** (and) **prosper**.

This is resumed as *nu mān māi šešzi nu* EZEN *purulliyaš iyanzi* 'in order that the land grow (and) prosper, they perform the Purulli festival'. The phrase is clearly formulaic and recurs in the likewise Old Hittite prayer to the Sun Goddess of the Earth (CTH 370), KBo 7.28 + ro. 14′-15′:

nu utniyanti **miya[tar** ēšdu . . .
nu **māu šišdu**

Let the land have **grow[th** . . .
Let it **grow** [and] **prosper**.

2. Vedic *máhi śrávas* : Greek μέγα κλέος.
3. Vedic *áhann áhim* : Greek ἔπεφνεν (. . .) ὄφιν.
4. Cf. Watkins 1979a = 1994:644-62.

If correctly restored we would also have an instance of the Indo-European syntactic and stylistic figure treated in chap. 13. The Hittite asyndetic phrase *māu šešdu* 'grow (and) prosper' recalls line 8 of the Old English *Beowulf*:

weox under wolcnum weorðmyndum **þáh**

He **grew** under heaven, **prospered** in honors.

The formulaic character of the two verbs in Old English appears from *Genesis* 2301 (*sunu*) *weox and þah*, 2772 (*cniht*) *weax and þag* 'grew and prospered'. Though none of the verbs are related, the hieratic context of the Hittite passage recalls also the Old Hittite ritual for the erection of a new palace (translated by Goetze, in Pritchard 1955), in which the king addresses an evocation (*talliya-*) to the trees on the mountain to be cut to make the roof. KUB 29.3 = StBoT 25,1, restored after the Neo-Hittite copy 29.1, 8′ff.: *ḫēawe(š)=šmaš ša[llanuškir* 'the rains have made you tall' . . . *nēpišaš ka[tta uliliškiddumat* 'You grew under heaven'. The latter phrase again recalls the Old English, but independent creation of all of these is certainly natural enough. Compare also *Widsith* 144 cited in chap. 5.

It is worthwhile pausing a moment to consider the diachronic dynamics of formulas, for they are by no means always "frozen", or static. I take an example offering an instance of formal lexical renewal and replacement under semantic identity. We can reconstruct an alliterative merism of at least Common Italic date:

STRENGTH (and) LIFE

$*g^{u}i\bar{a}$-$_{\mathrm{pl.}}$ $g^{u}\bar{\imath}ta$-.

The alliteration, a Common Italic poetic property, was continued intact through the regular sound change g^{u} > *b* in Oscan, which preserves both lexemes in the formula (Vetter 3):

biass biítam.

The alliteration was equally intact in Latin, with its regular sound change of initial g^{u}- > *u*-. But here the lexical item **uiā-* pl. 'strength' was threatened by (near-) homonymy with the ancestor of *uia* 'way', and the alliterative formula was renewed in Latin (Ennius, *Ann.* 38) as

uires uitaque,

with a new word for 'strength', significantly also plural. The sound change g^{u}- > *u*- is the terminus *a quo* for the renewal, since *uires* has an original **u̯*-.

It is at least noteworthy that the semantic link which made possible the diachronic replacement of $*g^{u}i\bar{a}$- by *uīrēs* (**u̯ī*-) in Latin along the paradigmatic axis of similarity (both STRENGTH) existed in Homeric Greek synchronically, along the syntagmatic axis of contiguity: the enjambed collocation (*Od.* 18.3-4) giving the real (=diachronic) etymology of the name of the beggar (W)iros, IE **u̯ih$_x$-ro-s* 'man' (Ved. *vīrás*, Lithuanian *výras*, etc):

οὐδέ οἱ ἦν (ϝ)ίς
οὐδὲ βίη

He had no strength
or force.

Synoptically we have the two linkages on the two axes:

biass (**g^{w}ih$_2$-ah$_2$-*)

(**u̯ih-*) (ϝ)ίς —— | —— βίη (**g^{w}ih$_2$-ah$_2$-*)

uīrēs (**u̯ih$_x$-r-*)

No better example could be found to illustrate the interdependence of diachrony and synchrony, of the historical and the descriptive, in Indo-European poetics.

Another syntactically more complex case, involving a much greater time depth, is the formula

PROTECT MEN (and) LIVESTOCK,

whose history is examined in detail in chap. 17.

Yet another pattern of the dynamics of change in formula is the transferred epithet, which plays an important role in etymology. In essence it projects a synchronic contiguity relation onto the diachronic, historical semantic plane. To explain a number of lexical items in various Indo-European languages we must assume the prior existence—perhaps as far back as Indo-European—of fixed formulas of noun and epithet:

DRY (**ters-*) land	→	LAND (Latin *terra*)
MORTAL (**mór-to-*) man		MAN (Vedic *márta-* etc.)
EARTHLY (**dhĝhom-i̯o-*) man		MAN (Irish *duine*)
WHITE (**albho-*) barley		BARLEY (Greek ἄλφιτ-).

In the last case, the lost word for a cereal which ἄλφιτ- replaced was clearly the cognate—unknown to Greek—of Hittite *šeppit-* 'a cereal, wheat sp.', for the epithet **albho-* copied the suffix **-it-* of the noun it replaced, **sepit-*, which shared that suffix with only one noun in all of Indo-European, the word for 'honey':

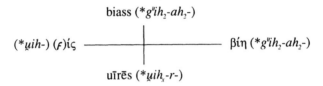

```
*melit-
   |
   |
*sepit-     ⇒     ἄλφιτ-
```

The suffix of the original pair is a morphological index of the opposition *nature* vs. *culture*, and the shared suffix **-it-* an Indo-European indexical sign. Here the study of formula leads to the reconstruction of a total semiotic model for a prehistoric culture.[5]

Not surprisingly a greater number of shared formulas or other collocations is found between closely related languages or dialects. Those of the oldest stages of Indic and Iranian have received particular attention, notably in Benveniste 1968 and Schlerath 1968:148-164.

Such lexical collocations between closely related languages are sometimes not to be termed formulas in the strict sense, where they escape any syntactic constraints. But they are nonetheless valuable indications of diachronic contiguity relations, relations which point to an inherited theme or interaction of themes which can be realized as a formula at any one point. The variations rung on the dragon-slaying formula discussed in part IV below are an obvious case in point.

Perhaps the most extensive collection of reconstructed collocations for any Indo-European tradition is the very valuable one for Common Indo-Iranian made by Hertzenberg (L. Gercenberg) 1972:90-127. He assembles nearly 350 two- and three-member phrasal collocations of cognates in Vedic and Old Iranian, some of which recur in other Indo-European languages as well. The items amply repay further investigation. Thus he lists the Indo-Iranian reconstruction **dhar- sthū-na-* 'hold firm the house post', citing the two cognates at RV 10.18.13 and Yt. 10.28. Examination of the passages yields even closer affinity, with interesting implications.

In the Avestan hymn to Mithra (Yt. 10.28), the divinized Contract is worshipped,

yō **stunå vīδāraiieiti**
bərəzi.**mitahe** nmānahe

who **holds apart** the **posts**
of the high-**built** house.

Elsewhere the house has a thousand posts, in the formulaic epithet (Y. 57.21, Yt. 5.101)

nmānəm . . . **hazaŋrō.stunəm**

the **thousand-posted** house,

5. Cf. Watkins 1978b = 1994:593-601.

which recurs in *sahásra-sthūna-*, of the seat (*sádas-*) of Mitra and Varuṇa, RV 2.41.5.

RV 10.18 is 'a collection of verses for the dead' (Caland apud Geldner ad loc.), an assemblage of obviously traditional material. Verses 12b and 13cd read

> **sahásram mŕta** úpa hí śráyantām
> etā́ṃ **sthū́ṇām** pitáro **dhārayantu** te
> átrā yamáḥ sā́danā te **minotu**
>
> Let a **thousand houseposts** be set up . . .
> Let the Fathers **hold firm** this **housepost** for you;
> Let Yama **build** you a dwelling there.

Avestan in two passages and Vedic in contiguous verses of a single hymn collocate no less than four common Indo-Iranian roots (boldface) as part of the formulaic system describing the HOUSE.

In India this system is preserved in a metaphor of the TOMB as house. The metaphor may be millennia old, and to some extent it belongs to the realm of universals, in a culture which practices inhumation. But the particulars are by no means universal.

It is instructive to compare the Avestan and Vedic passages with an archeologist's description (Gimbutas 1974:293-4):

> [The] burial rites are of exceptional value for an insight into the social and religious structure. Burial practices are not loaned to other cultures; nor are they abruptly abandoned even though they are subject to gradual change. Because graves of Kurgan tradition constitute the overwhelming majority of cultural remains, they are a primary source of information. The characteristic features of grave structure and burial custom are as follows: 1) the presence of a mortuary house built of either stone slabs or timber inside the shaft, roofed with timber or stones or by a tent supported by three or four wooden poles or stakes . . . 2) the grave was covered with a round earthen or stone mound frequently surrounded by a cromlech, i.e., a ring of stones or timber uprights . . . The belief in an afterlife replete with the same earthly social structure is one of the most conservative features of I.E. societies. Kurgan burial rites can be easily distinguished from those of northern Eurasian, Comb- and Pit-marked pottery hunting and fishing peoples and from those of southeast, Mediterranean and western European agriculturalists.

The similarity is striking. I do not mean to imply that an ancestral version of these Vedic verses was recited at some neolithic or chalcolithic graveside; it is only that the formulaic system could make possible the long-term conservation of such verbal collocations when combined with the real conservatism of a cultural nexus. The comparison of formulaic sequences is another and a very special window onto prehistoric material and non-material culture.

To take a second example, this time involving both formula and meter, we cited in chap. 4 a Rigvedic verse recalling the prehistoric crossing of the Punjab, the Five-Rivers-Land. It showed the repeated verb form *saniṣṇata*:

té anyā́m-anyāṃ nadyàṃ saniṣṇata
śravasyántaḥ saniṣṇata

They won for themselves one river after another;
they won for themselves, seeking glory.

A form of the same verb figures in a frequent and variable formulaic phrase with the object *vā́ja-* 'prize, booty', as in verb phrases like *sanóti vā́jam* 'wins the prize' (RV 3.25.2 et passim) and nominalized in the compound *vā́jasāti* 'winning the prize'. The latter is particularly frequent in the dative case *vā́jasātaye* 'to win the prize' in verse-final position (RV 2.31.3 et passim).

Now the Vedic Āryas who had crossed the Punjab eastwards by the middle of the 2nd millennium B.C. were the same stock of people, with the same gods and the same language, as the horse-breeding Āryas who appeared as the dynasty ruling over the Hurrian kingdom of Mittanni (Ḫanikalbat) in Eastern Asia Minor by the upper Euphrates at about the same time (Mayrhofer 1966, 1974). A "poetic" link between the two Indo-Aryan peoples is the name of the Mittanni king *Šattiwaza*, as now read, which contains the same elements *sāti-* 'winning' and *vāja-* 'prize' as the Rigvedic poetic formula in the compound *vā́jasāti* in the reverse order, as frequently in Indo-European onomastics.

One of the many Vedic examples of line-final *vā́jasātaye* occurs in the interesting RV 10.101.12ab, which appears to assimilate the soma-preparation to a form of phallus-worship. The lines are

kápṛn naraḥ kapṛthám úd dadhātana
codáyata khudáta vā́jasātaye

Raise high the penis, o men, the phallus;
drive (it), thrust (it) in, to win the prize.

The verses scan

⏑ – ⏑ – ⏑ ⏑ ⏑ – ⏑ – ⏑ ⏑̄
– ⏑ ⏑ ⏑ ⏑ ⏑ ⏑ – ⏑ – ⏑ ⏑̄.

The sequence of short syllables in the last is uncommon in Vedic metrical practice, and in view of the meaning of the line may be regarded as sexually iconic, climaxing in the cadence – ⏑ – ⏑ ⏑̄. The emotional iconicity of sequences of shorts will be even further developed in some of the lyric meters of Greek drama, as well as in Classical Sanskrit kāvya.

The 'climactic' cadence of the 12-syllable jagatī, here *vā́jasātaye* of *b* echoed in the rhyming and grammatically parallel cadences *cyāvayotáye* and *sómapītaye* of *c* and *d*, with which the hymn ends, has an analogue in Greek metrics as well. The 5-syllable

– ⏑ – ⏑ ⏑̄

may be thought of as a catalectic variant of a 6-syllable

– ⏑ – ⏑ – ⏓.

Given the particular thematic and pragmatic context of this Vedic example (*kápṛn naraḥ kapṛthám* . . . 'the penis, o men, the phallus . . .') it is at least curious that the Greek metrical term since antiquity for this particular 6-syllable line is the *ithyphallic* (Hephaestion 15.2 ἰθυφαλλικόν). The verse line is so called because of its use in the verse accompanying the Dionysiac φαλλαγωγία procession, 'the ritual from which Aristotle derives comedy' (West 1982:97). We have in fact preserved by Athenaeus the very song of the φαλλοφόροι, the phallus-bearers, after they enter the theater (Carmina Popularia, PMG 851a):

ἀνάγετ', εὐρυχωρίαν
τῶι θεῶι ποιεῖτε·
θέλει γὰρ ὁ θεὸς ὀρθὸς ἐσφυδωμένος
διὰ μέσου βαδίζειν

Stand back, make plenty of room for the god!
For the god, erect and at bursting-point,
wishes to pass through your midst.
(tr. D.A. Campbell, Greek Lyric V)

Lines 2 and 4 are ithyphallics,

⏖ ⏑ – ⏑ – ⏓,

and 3 an iambic trimeter, like the continuation of the song κατὰ στίχον (PMG 851b). And line 1 is a dimeter metrically identical with RV 10.101.12a just cited, in the cola, break, and cadence following the caesura:

ἀνάγετ', εὐρυχωρίαν

⏑ ⏑ ⏑ – ⏑ – ⏑ ⏓

kapṛthám úd dadhātana

Raise high the phallus.

The virtual identity of the passages in theme, in pragmatics, in grammar (2 pl. imperative), and in metrics is certainly striking. It is also noteworthy that in its deployment in Greek lyric the *ithyphallic* nearly always comes last, as the final element or refrain in a metrical strophe. The 'climactic' cadence *vā́jasātaye* of RV 10.101.12 may well continue a late Indo-European (Greco-Āryan) metrical icon.

For yet another window opened by the comparison of formulaic sequences consider the following. Ancient metaphors can be expressed in formulas which have become more or less opaque in the tradition where they occur. But where the existence of a cognate formula from another tradition can be demonstrated, the darkness of the first is at least diminished, if not dispelled.

Early Greek knows a phrase, in Homer ἀπὸ δρυὸς οὐδ' ἀπὸ πέτρης, whose meaning and interpretation has been controversial since ancient times. West 1966 at Hesiod, *Th.* 35, gives the textual evidence and a survey of ancient and modern interpretations, concluding that 'the truth is lost in antiquity'. The literal meaning in the absence of further context is 'from oak or from rock', as it is frequently rendered. But West correctly saw that in a phrase of such antiquity and generality the earlier, inherited meaning 'tree' was more appropriate for δρυ-. The following are representative attestations of the phrase. *Il.* 22.122 and 126-8:

> ἀλλὰ τίη μοι ταῦτα φίλος διελέξατο θυμός
> . . .
> οὐ μέν πως νῦν ἔστιν ἀπὸ δρυὸς οὐδ' ἀπὸ πέτρης
> τῶι ὀαριζέμεναι
>
> But why does my heart speak such things to me . . .
> There is no way now from tree or from rock
> to hold converse with him.

Od. 19.163 (Penelope asks the disguised Odysseus for his lineage):

> οὐ γὰρ ἀπὸ δρυός ἐσσι παλαιφάτου[6] οὐδ' ἀπὸ πέτρης
>
> For you are not from the proverbial tree or from rock.

The adjective παλαίφατος identifies the whole phrase as already proverbial in Homer's time, or Penelope's. Hesiod, *Th.* 35:

> ἀλλὰ τίη μοι ταῦτα περὶ δρῦν ἢ περὶ πέτρην
>
> But what are such things to me, round tree and round rock.

West points out that περὶ with the accusative in early epic always has a local sense, 'round', and not 'about, concerning' as it is usually translated.[7] Plato, *Phaedrus* 275 bc:

6. For the contracted thematic genitive παλαιφάτου before οὐδ' we may read elided παλαιφάτο' οὐδ'.

7. But note that Hesiod's ‖ περὶ δρῦν | occupies the same slot between penthemimeral caesura and bucolic dieresis as Homer's ‖ περὶ δρυσὶν | ὑψικόμοισι (*Il.* 14.398), ‖ ἰδὲ δρυσὶν | ὑψικόμοισιν (*Od.* 9.186), ‖ ⏑ ⏑ – δρυὸς | ὑψικόμοιο (*Od.* 12.357), such that the requirement of the singular number in some sense may have entailed the accusative. Note also that περὶ γνυσί 'around the knees' (Forssman 1965) in the same slot in the *h.Merc.* 152 suggests that περὶ δρυσίν was originally the zero-grade dative plural of 'tree'.

ἐν τῶι τοῦ Διὸς τοῦ Δωδωναίου ἱερῶι δρυὸς λόγους
ἔφησαν μαντικοὺς πρώτους γενέσθαι. τοῖς μὲν οὖν τότε . . .
ἀπέχρη δρυὸς καὶ πέτρας ἀκούειν ὑπ' εὐηθείας, εἰ μόνον
ἀληθῆ λέγοιεν

They used to say that the words of the oak in the holy place of Zeus at Dodona were the first prophetic utterances. The people of that time . . . were content in their simplicity to hear an oak or a rock, provided only that it spoke the truth.

Finally a proverb preserved by Macarius (*Paroem. gr.* ii 158) speaks of

δρυὸς καὶ πέτρας λόγοι

words of oak and rock.

used of the 'incredible statements of prattlers and storytellers'. As West notes, this source seems independent of the older epic passages.

The real meaning of the phrase as a whole and its force in context elude us. Some of these examples are concerned with speech (Hesiod), with ancient or traditional genealogy, lore or wisdom (*Odyssey*, Plato), which may have degenerated to mere prattle (Macarius). There are clear overtones of an ethical component as well (*Iliad*, Plato's ἀληθῆ 'truth'), in this ancient formula which we may represent in our notational convention, as

TREE (**dru-*) (and) ROCK.

The first lexeme is a clear Indo-European inheritance, while the second is confined to Greek.

In an important article of 1974 (1975:327) Karl Hoffmann demonstrated the existence of a common Indo-European lexical item **pér-u̯r̥*, **pér-u̯on-/-un- ~ -u̯n̥-* in Vedic *párur, párvan-* 'joint', Greek πεῖραρ, πείρατ(-α γαίης) 'end(s of the earth)', Hittite *peru(r), perun-* 'rock',[8] and Vedic *párvata-* m. 'mountain', Avestan *pauruuatā-* f. 'mountain range' (**per-u̯n̥-to-*). In accord with the root meaning 'come, go' of **per-* (English *fare*), Hoffmann astutely conjectured the basic meaning of Indo-European **per-u̯r̥*, **per-u̯n̥-* to be 'that through or down to which one comes', namely 'bedrock', and of Indo-Iranian **par-u̯n̥-ta* (**par-u̯a-ta-*) as 'having bedrock, rocky'.

It remained for J. Schindler (Harvard class 1986-87) to identify an Avestan reflex of unsuffixed Indo-European **per-u̯(e)n-*, in the suffixless locative *pauruuąn(ca)* Yt. 13.99 = 19.85, interpreting it as '(and) in rock'. The preceding noun with which this is conjoined, Geldner *druca*, was read by Schindler *draoca* with J_{10}, and interpreted by him '(and) in tree'. He thus solved a long-standing crux in Iranian

8. The last with Eichner 1973:98.

philology.[9] The phrase as *druca pauruuą̇nca*, occurring only in this repeated passage, had previously been translated as 'seitlich und vorn' (Bartholomae) or 'from bow and arrow' (Bailey).[10]

Schindler's concern was the restoration and interpretation of the Avestan noun phrase alone. But setting it in its immediate context in Yt. 13.99 = 19.85 (discussed at length by Narten), we have

kauuōiš vīštāspahe ašaonō
frauuašīm yazamaide
. . .
yō draoca pauruuąnca
ašāi rauuō yaēša
yō draoca pauruuąnca
ašāi rauuō vīuuaēδa
yō bāzušca upastaca
vīsata aŋhå daēnaiiå
yat̰ ahurōiš zaraϑuštrōiš

We worship the guardian spirit
of the righteous Kavi Vištāspa,
who searched for space for Truth
in tree and rock,
who found space for Truth
in tree and rock,
who was the arm and support
of this Ahurian, Zarathustrian religion.

Note the metrical contrast of the 6 and 7 syllable lines *yō draoca* . . . with the last three octosyllables.

We thus find in Iranian that the ***locus*** of the highest ethical notion of Active Truth, *Aša* = Vedic *Ṛta* (compare Plato's ἀληθῆ 'truth'), its "space" or free room *rauuō* (= Latin *rūs* 'country', IE **reu̯h-es-*, and cognate with the Germanic family of English *room*), as found and mediated by the highest professional of the word, the poet-priest-seer *kauui* (= Vedic *kaví*, Lydian *kaveś*, Greek [Hesych.] κο(ι)ης [IE **kou̯h-ei̯-*]), is precisely the Iranian formulaic noun phrase *draoca pauruuąnca*, again in our notation,

TREE (**dru-*) and ROCK.

It is difficult not to equate the Iranian and the Greek phrases, in view of the identity

9. As my colleague P. O. Skjærvø notes, the suffixless locative **drau̯* would appear in Young Avestan as **druuō*. But before enclitic *ca* the diphthong would be preserved, cf. **-ai̯* > *-e* but **-ai̯ca* > *-aēca*, **ai̯ai̯* > *-ǝ̄e* but **-ai̯ai̯ca* > *-aiiaēca*. Thus, *draoca* is the expected locative singular of *dru-*. In this instance Hoffmann's three postulates (e.g. 1975:275) all give the same result: the manuscript readings, the philological analysis, and the linguistic reconstruction all support the reading.

10. References (in another context) in Narten 1986:101, who leaves the passage untranslated.

in semantics of the whole, the coincidence in lexical expression of the first members, the same order of the two constituents, and the general similarity of the traditional and ethical overtones of the pragmatics of the two phrases in their context.

That is not to say that our ignorance of the real meaning of the phrase and its force in context has been dispelled. On the contrary the raison d'être of this expression is as elusive as before. But the important result of the linguistic equation of the Greek and Iranian formulas,

> δρυὸς καὶ πέτρας
> draoca pauruuąnca,

is the transformation of the question of the meaning of

> TREE (**dru-*) and ROCK

from a Greek problem to an Indo-European problem. There are now that many more traditions whose evidence may yet provide a real solution.[11]

11. S. Jamison calls my attention to a passage in Durham 1987 [first published 1909]:103 relating the customs of the North Albanians at the beginning of this century: 'The priest of Rechi . . . told us of oaths which, if very solemn ones, are always sworn in Rechi and among all the Pulati tribes on a stone as well as on the cross: "Per guri e per kruch" (By the stone and the cross).' Read perhaps in modern orthography *për guri e për kryqi*. Albanian *gur* 'stone' is the 'heavy' one, IE $*g^{u}\!\!\!\!\!\;_{\circ}rh_2$-*u*-.

The cross is also a 'tree', and recall Achilles' mighty oath in *Il.* 1.234ff., 'by this scepter, (a tree) which nevermore will sprout leaves and branches . . .' Agamemnon's scepter sprouted a mighty shaded bough in Klutaimestra's dream in Sophocles' *El.* 420-423; Pausanias 9.40.11-12 records a cult of Agamemnon's scepter at Khaironeia, where its local name was just δόρυ 'the tree'—IE **dru-*. See on these Nagy 1990b:143, 1979:179, 1974:242. The scepter as symbol of (Greek) authority and dominion is also just called δόρυ (δορὶ Ἑλλενικῶι) in Euripides, *Hec.* 5.

13

An Indo-European stylistic figure

In the preceding chapter we saw that not only words but whole phrases can be equated between or among cognate languages. Such phrases are termed formulas, since their very *repetition* as 'ready-made surface structures' (Kiparsky) over long periods of time is precisely what makes possible the application of the Comparative Method to them. The result is the postulation and reconstruction of a *stylistic* linguistic history.

Not only lexicon and formula, where meaning is relevant, but also more abstract levels of poetic grammar are equally amenable, in favorable circumstances, to treatment by the Comparative Method. This includes the domain of grammatical figures, where only grammatical meaning and sometimes semantic equivalence are in play, not lexical meaning per se. When we can observe the same non-trivial, non-universal, and not obviously borrowed or diffused grammatical or stylistic figure in a number of early Indo-European traditions, we are justified by the exigencies of the Comparative Method in postulating the existence of that figure as a stylistic device in the poetic proto-language.

We may take as exemplum the stylistic figure of the repetition or iteration of a verb form (V_i) by a nominal form from the same root (N_i) in a semantically equivalent verb phrase ($N_i + V$), schematically

$$(V_i) \ldots (N_i + V).$$

Examples follow.

Greek furnishes a number of instances of our stylistic feature. Verb (V_i) and related noun (N_i) occupy the verse-final position of the first and last lines of a Homeric simile in *Il.* 16.823-26:

ὡς δ' ὅτε σῦν ἀκάμαντα λέων **ἐβιήσατο** χάρμηι
. . .
. . . λέων **ἐδάμασσε βίηφιν**

as when a lion **overpowers** in battle-lust an untiring boar

. . .

. . . the lion **overcomes** him by his **power**.

The whole passage, the death of Patroklos, is examined in greater detail in chap. 53. Positioning both Verb and Noun at or near a position of metrical prominence, like verse boundary, points up and indexes the parallelism. Sentence or discourse-initial position are particularly frequent and again call attention to the figure. A striking example is Aeschylus *f.* 44.1-2:

ἐρᾶι μὲν ἁγνὸς οὐρανὸς τρῶσαι χθόνα
ἔρως δὲ γαῖαν **λαμβάνει** γάμου τυχεῖν

Holy heaven **yearns** to wound the earth,
and **yearning seizes** earth to join in mating.

Note that ἐρᾶι (V_i) and ἔρως (N_i) follow the left hand verse boundary, and λαμβάνει, the V of (N_i + V), follows the caesura of the second of these unresolved, powerful isosyllabic trimeter lines, the beginning of Aphrodite's vindication of sex, ending τῶνδ' ἐγὼ παραίτιος 'of all that I am the cause.'

In chap. 18 we will examine in detail an Umbrian prayer in the Iguvine Tables which contains an example of this stylistic figure. Here (V_i) and (N_i + V) frame the intervening text. *Tab. Ig.* VIa 27-28 (lines 21 and 24 of the text in my colometry):

persei tuer perscler **uaseto(m)**[1] **est**

. . .

tuer perscler uirseto auirseto **uas est**

If in thy sacrifice (anything) **has been flawed**,

. . .

(if) in thy sacrifice there **is** a seen or unseen **flaw**.

The intervening text gives four more examples of finite verbs in the same grammatical form as (V_i). The climactic function of (N_i + V) is thus assured and further emphasized by the addition of an adjectival merism *seen or unseen*, itself inherited, to agree with N_i.

An example from Archaic Latin is in Cato's *suouitaurilia* prayer, *De agri cult.* 141.3:

fundi terrae agrique mei
lustrandi lustrique **faciendi** ergo

1. The final *m* is found in the two repetitions of the prayer VIa 37 and 47. The form is an impersonal 3sg. perfect passive, as if Latin *uacatum est*.

to **purify** and **perform the purification**
of my farm, land, and field.

See chap. 17. Here the force is not climactic but iterative: a doubling to yield the figure Argument + Synonymous Argument. The verb phrase (N_i + V) follows (V_i), as always; the grammatically heavier phrase comes last, in accord with Behaghel's law of increasing members.

From the pagan folk-tradition of pre-Classical Armenian we can cite the beginning of the famous song of the birth of Vahagn (< Iranian *Vərəϑraγna*) preserved in Movsēs Xorenacʿi, *Patmutʿiwn Hayocʿ* (History of the Armenians) 1.31. Here the verb is both clause- and discourse-initial, a characteristic position of prominence:

erknēr erkin **erknēr** erkir
erknēr ew covn cirani
erkn i covun **unēr**[2]
zkarmrikn ełegnik

Heaven **was in labor**, earth **was in labor**,
the purple sea too **was in labor**.
Labor pangs in the sea **seized** the little crimson reed.

The concern for alliteration and rhythmic verse patterning as well is unmistakable in this remarkable text, the continuation of which I treat in chap. 23.2.

Compare finally the Hittite confessional formula in the Plague Prayers of King Mursilis II (second half of the 14th cent. B.C.):[3]

ēšziy=at iyawen=at	It **is** (so). We did it.
. . .	
ēšziy=at iyawen=at	It **is** (so). We did it.
. . .	
ašān=at iyanun=at	It (is) **true**. I did it,

with the neuter participle *ašān* of the verb 'be' in the pregnant sense of 'so, real, true', Norwegian *sant*, English *sooth*. Stylistically the climactic figure heightens the pathos of Mursilis' personal (1sg.) confession.

The set verbal formulaic character of the Hittite confessional praxis is shown by a newly published fragment KBo 32.224 Ro 10′-11′]x-*yan=ma* ^{SAL}SUḪUR.LAL

2. I follow Russell 1987:196 in preferring the last line without *ew* after *unēr* (with good manuscript support), against the critical edition of Abełean and Yarutʿunean (Tiflis 1913), now readily available in the reprint with introduction by Thomson 1981. In the first two lines the critical edition so modified, as printed here, gives a better poem, n.b., than the earlier printed version used for example by Benveniste, Dumézil, Gamkrelidze-Ivanov, Jakobson, and myself.

3. §§ 6, 9,10 of the second prayer (KUB 14.8 etc., CTH 378), ed. Götze 1929:212-17.

punuššuen/] . . . *ēšzi=at peḫutenun=an* 'We questioned [ ]yas the hierodule/ . . . [she said] "It is (so). I brought him."' The text is Middle Hittite, at least 15th century B.C. (Otten, Vorwort). It shows as well that there is no necessary link between the participle *ašān=at* and the first person singular *iyanun=at* in the previous example.

But the optional use of the participle of the verb 'to be' in the confessional formula is itself inherited. This is proven both by Latin *sōns* 'guilty', from delocutive 'he who says "*sōns*" (= Hitt. *ašān*)', and by the Germanic family of English *sin*, German *Sünde*, an abstract built on the same utterance.[4]

Methodologically observe the equation of Lat. *sōns* and Hittite *ašān* in the same pragmatic slot (confessional formula), the status of *ašān(=at)* as the climax of a stylistic figure with *ēšzi(=at)*, and the presence of *ēšzi(=at)* alone in the same pragmatic slot (confessional formula), schematically

confessional *ēšzi*

confessional *ašān* = *sōns*.

These equations of style and pragmatics suggest on the one hand the postulation of a Latin confessional *est* = *ēšzi*, for which we need only compare Classical Latin *est* 'yes'. On the other hand the same equations require the reconstruction of this stylistic figure (V_i) . . . (N_i + V) for the proto-language, with the lexical entries **h₁esti* for (V_i) and **h₁sont* for (N_i), with gapped V in the nominal sentence (N_i [+ V]).

The rhetoric of climax and the formulaic style of Mursilis' confession are clearly an Indo-European inheritance, even if the verbal context preceding the confessional formulas themselves (§ 9 'people are sinful' *waššeškanzi*, 'the sin of the father comes to the son' *ŠA ABU-ŠU=kan waštul ANA* DUMU-*ŠU ari*) belongs to the general intellectual and cultural ambience of the Ancient Near East. The Plague Prayers are a good example of the symbiosis of the two traditions, Indo-European and Mesopotamian, in Hittite culture.

The examples of this stylistic figure cited have been drawn from texts in Greek, Umbrian, Latin, Old Armenian, and Hittite. We will see in chap. 43.1 evidence that the same figure must have existed in Proto-Germanic in the prehistoric period, to account for the Common Germanic formulaic phrase 'become the bane of' = SLAY. The texts are spread over some 2200 years, from the 14th century B.C. to the 8th century A.D.; with the exception of Italic none of the cultures involved was significantly or heavily influenced by any of the others at the times of the respective texts.[5] We may there confidently reconstruct the same figure for the poetic proto-language, O′ of figure 2 in chap. 1.1.

The diachronic renewal of verbs wholly or in parts of the tense/aspect system by nominalizations with various portmanteau verbs, which is grouped under the general

4. See Watkins 1967.

5. Greek influence on Classical Armenian belongs to a later period of the Greek language and is a stylistic phenomenon of the learned Christian tradition, not of the popular, oral, pre-Christian tradition from which Movsēs took his materials.

rubric of auxiliation, is cross-linguistically widespread. So is the progression of narrative by iterated phrases with partial variation, as in the *parallelismus membrorum* of Semitic and Uralic poetry. And the use of figura etymologica (like English *sing a song*, Latin *uoce uocabat*) is also widespread outside the Indo-European world as well as in it. Each of these may have something in common with our stylistic figure, but clearly none is in any way comparable in grammar, style, or tone of the whole.

The specificity and the complexity of the iteration figure

$(V_i) \ldots (N_i + V)$

includes such features as the order of the two elements, which is almost always $V_i \ldots N_i$. Within the parentheses N_i and V may be reversed, or disjoined, but they almost always follow (V_i). Stylistically the progression is climactic, which accounts for the preservation of only N_i or $N_i + V$ in Latin *sōns* and Germanic 'become the bane of' (chap. 43.1). And both (V_i) and $(N_i + V)$ in each tradition are placed in parallel positions of prominence in the discourse, verse line, or sentence, making reference to metrical and phrase boundaries.

We can reconstruct the lexical specification of both V_i and N_i for the proto-language in at least two cases:

*$h_1$és-ti . . . h_1s-ónt-
*g^{w}hén-ti . . . g^{w}hón-o-.

Just as Hans Krahe called the *kenning* a typical stylistic figure of Germanic poetics, so we are fully justified in terming ours a typical stylistic figure of Indo-European poetics. It is yet another 'Indo-European touch'.

In chap. 3 I claimed the traditional English round

Oats, peas, beans, and barley grow

as an ideal illustration of the Indo-European poet's formulaic verbal art. I can point in the same language to another ideal illustration, closely related to the second reconstruction above, of this typical stylistic figure of the Indo-European poet, from Michael Innes, *The Daffodil Affair*:

"He didn't die," said Hudspith. "He perished."
"He did a perish," said Appleby corroboratively and idiomatically.

14

A late Indo-European traditional epithet

In one of the few fragments of pre-Christian Armenian oral epic poetry (the text is quoted in chap. 23.2) we find in a simile the phrase *arcui srat'ew* 'sharp-winged eagle'. In this group of noun and adjectival epithet, both in its form and in its semantics, we have a probable inheritance from the common poetic language of Indo-Iranian, Greek, and Armenian.[1]

The Armenian word for 'eagle', *arcui* (from **arciui*), gen. *arcuoy*, goes back to **h₂̥r̥ĝi-pi̯o-*, identical to Vedic *r̥jipyá-*, an epithet of both the eagle (*śyená-*) and the mythological stallion Dadhikrā (RV 4.39.2, 7; 27.4). The Vedic word is substantivized as 'eagle' in 2.34.4, of the bird who robbed the soma and brought it to man. Its Avestan cognate is *ərəzifiia-* 'eagle' in *ərəzifiiō.parəna-* 'having eagle feathers' (epithet of the arrow) and alone as the name of a mountain range. Greek αἰγυπιός 'vulture' has been reasonably explained as a folk-etymology (after γύψ 'vulture' and Αἰγύπτιος 'Egyptian'?) from original *ἀργιπιός.

Greek αἰγυπιός is 'an older word chiefly found in poetry' (LSJ s.v.). The most memorable example is surely Aeschylus, *Ag.* 49ff. αἰγυπιῶν οἵτ' . . . στροφοδινοῦνται πτερύγων ἐρετμοῖσιν ἐρεσσόμενοι 'vultures who wheel eddying round, rowing with oars of wings . . .', lamenting their lost brood and shrieking for the tardy justice of Zeus.

The first element of all these forms is clearly **h₂̥r̥ĝ-i-*, Caland composition form of **h₂̥r̥ĝ-ró-* 'swift, bright'. The second element is uncertain; both **pti̯o-* and a **phₓ-i̯o-* have been proposed, see Mayrhofer EWA s.v. with references.

Charles de Lamberterie, to whom we owe the most thorough and informed study (1978) of the Armenian word and its congeners, comes to the conclusion that both Greek αἰγυπιός and Armenian *arcui* are (independent) borrowings from Iranian. For the first, he argues that folk-etymological deformations are more appropriate to borrowings than native words. But folk-etymology is always a possibility when words are wholly or partially opaque, as the second half of an *ἀργι-πιός surely was (in contrast to, e.g., ἀργι-κέραυνος) from the earliest times. Alteration to *ἀργυπιός after

1. So Schmidt 1985, but without actual argumentation. See note 2 below. Otherwise Greppin 1991. I do not understand the latter's objection to the phonological derivation from **h₂̥r̥ĝipi̯ó-*, and Vedic *r̥jipya-* does not mean 'moving straight upward'. See n. 5 below.

γύψ was a clear possibility, and the similarity to Αἰγύπτιος too strong to resist.[2] The restriction to early and poetic texts and the well-developed system of epithets in Homer also speak against an Iranian borrowing of αἰγυπιός, the more so since the Iranian word was known to the Greeks (Hesychius ἄρξιφος : αἰετός, παρὰ Πέρσαις). The phonology finally speaks against an Iranian source for the Greek word (-πιός [oxytone, n.b.[3]] vs. *-fiia-*), as it does for the Armenian word (*arc-* vs. *ərəzi-*, **r̥zi-*). Similarly the system of epithets (*srat'ew*, below) suggests the Armenian word is native and genuine. Since Indo-Iranian, Greek, and Armenian constitute a dialect area on independent grounds (augment, prohibitive negation, stem formation of denominative verbs) I see no good reason not to regard *r̥jipyá-*, *ərəzifiia-*, αἰγυπιός, and *arcui* with their epithets and collocations as an inheritance from the poetic proto-language of the same dialect area.

In view of the archaic Caland morphology and the Indic mythological connections, which point to a genuine Indo-European form, it is likely that the name of the Urartean king Menua's horse *arṣibi(ni)*, presumed to mean 'eagle', reflects rather a Hurrian borrowing from an Old Indic horse-cult of Dadhikrā (vel sim.) *r̥jipyá-*, as suggested by de Lamberterie 1978:259-61.[4] It would thus join the other elements of horse terminology borrowed from Mittanni Indic into Hurrian (and thence into Hittite) in the middle of the second millennium B.C.

The epithet *srat'ew* 'sharp-winged' is from **sur-a-t'ew*; *sur* 'sharp' < **k̂ōro-* < **k̂oh$_3$-ro-* (Latin *cōs* 'whetstone', Vedic *śiśāti* 'whets') and *t'ew*, *-oy* 'wing', probably from **pte*... It is semantically identical to Latin *acci-piter* 'hawk' < **h$_2$ak̂u-petr-*, with first member more clearly seen in the old word *acupedius* 'sharp-footed' (Paul. Fest. 9.25 L.) In both of these the 'sharp' word **h$_2$ak̂u-* shares some of the semantic range and distribution of the 'swift' word **h$_1$ōk̂u-*. Just as *r̥jipyá-* in Vedic is an epithet of both large birds of prey and horses, so in Greek the adjective ὠκυπέτης 'swift-flying' is used both of horses (*Iliad*) and hawks (Hesiod), as well as ὠκύπτερος 'swift-winged' of the latter and ὠκύπους 'swift-footed' of the former. The hawk is also in Homer ὤκιστος πετεηνῶν 'swiftest of flying creatures'.

Vedic shows the hapax *āśupátvā* 'swift-flying' as epithet of *śyenáḥ* 'eagle' in the same hymn complex (RV 4.26.4-27.5, to the eagle who robbed the soma) which shows *r̥jīpī́ śyenáḥ* (26.6), *r̥jipyá . . śyenáḥ* (27.4a), and *antáḥ patat patatrí asya parṇám* (27.4c) 'his wing feather flew between (heaven and earth, after having been shot by the soma-watcher)'.

With Vedic *parṇám* here compare also Avestan *ərəzifiiō.**parəna**-* 'eagle-feathered (arrow)'. Rigvedic *r̥jipyá-* is itself used substantively as an epithet for 'arrow' in the kenning-like line 6.67.11c *ánu yád gā́va 'sphurā́n r̥jipyám* 'When the cow(gut bowstring)s send whizzing the swift-flying (arrow)'.[5] In Homeric Greek arrows (ἰοί, ὀιστοί) are 'swift' (ταχύς, ὠκύς) and 'feathered' (πτεροείς).

---

2. It is perhaps relevant that there is an *Egyptian vulture* (*Neophron percnopterus*, French *percnoptère d' Egypte*), whose range extends to Greece: Petersen et. al. 1983:70, map 69; Jonsson 1993:124.

3. For the (inherited) suffix **-i̯o-* see Peters 1980:73.

4. Diakonoff 1985:602 envisages the possibilty of a borrowing from Proto-Armenian into Hurro-Urartean, though he prefers the other way around, as also argued 1986:45 (but written before the previous article).

5. Related to AV 1.2.3 *vr̥kṣáṃ yád gā́vaḥ pariṣasvajānā́ anusphurám śarám árcanty r̥bhúm*

We may recall finally the old comparison for Indo-European poetic language made first by Schulze 1933:124: the Vedic name *ṛjíśvan-* 'having swift dogs' beside ἀργίποδας κύνας 'swift-footed dogs' (*Il.* 24.211), uncompounded κύνας ἀργούς (*Il.* 1.50), κύνες πόδας ἀργοί (*Il.* 18.578).[6] The younger compound type Πόδαργος either in the sense 'swiftfoot' or 'whitefoot' is the name of both Hector's and Menelaus' horse; it is there already in Mycenean times as *podako* /podargos/, probably in the latter sense, as the name of an ox at Knossus.[7] Note also Odysseus' dog Ἄργος (with regularly retracted accent) *Od.* 17.292.

We find thus a nexus in poetic language of semantically similar and partially overlapping epithet systems for horses, dogs, large birds of prey, and arrows, all compounds or noun phrases with phonetically similar and partially overlapping lexemes as first member:

> *h_2ṛĝi-
> *h_1ōk̂u-
> *$h_2$ak̂u-,

and likewise phonetically similar and partially overlapping lexemes as second member:

> *pet(h_2)-
> *ped-
> *pet-r-/*pt-er-/*per-.

Indo-European **h_2ṛĝi-p-i̯ó-* in a sense stands for all three second members, and might be built (with adjectival *-i̯ó-*) on a hypocoristic or otherwise truncated epithet **h_2ṛĝi-p* . . . As such it could well belong to a layer of Indo-European (or Greco-Armeno-Indo-Iranian) poetic language characterized by what in Irish is termed *díchned* 'beheading': an artificial deformation of the word for poetic purposes, as I have described it.[8] The phenomenon is again familiar in onomastics but not confined to it; compare Greek ἥδυμος : *ἡδυ-μενής,[9] κύδιμος : Κυδί-μαχος, ἄλκιμος : Ἀλκι-μέδων.[10]

'When the cows, embracing the tree, sing the whizzing reed' = 'When the gut string on the wooden bow makes the reed arrow whistle' (Whitney).

6. The constant epithet ἀργυρόπεζα 'silver-footed' of the goddess Thetis may be a metrical substitute for *ἀργί-πεζα (*-ped-i̯a*) 'swift-footed' or 'white-footed' with Bader 1971:206-7, but this is at best uncertain.

7. Durante in Schmitt 1968:301 (Italian original 1962). Note that the connection of Indo-European poetic language and name-giving extends to domestic animals as well.

8. Watkins 1970a:13. The archaic Irish (pre-syncope) term refers to apheresis/apocope of initial/final consonant. See for discussion of this and similar phenomena and their theoretical foundation Toporov 1981:214-19.

9. Leumann 1950:44.

10. Schwyzer 1968:1.494-5.

15

An Indo-European theme and formula: Imperishable fame

The middle of the 19th century saw the first extensions of the purlieu of linguistic comparison beyond the word level to that of the phrase: the remark of Adalbert Kuhn 1853b:467 equating Homeric Greek (*Il.* 9.413) κλέος ἄφθιτον and Rigvedic (1.9.7bc) *śrávas . . . ákṣitam,* both meaning 'imperishable, unfailing fame'.

Kuhn's innovation lay in the fact that instead of equating two words in two languages he equated two phrases in the two languages, two syntagmas of noun and adjective which have, as we shall see, every right to be termed formulas.

Despite the intense study of the Greek traditions by classicists and theoreticians we lack a principled account of what can constitute a formula, and there is in practice wide disagreement over whether a given textual nexus—including the famous κλέος ἄφθιτον—is or is not "formulaic". Gregory Nagy in numerous publications (1974, 1979, 1990b) has rightly focused on the importance of distinguishing the synchronic and the diachronic in the study of formulas. The diachronic may be within a single tradition, without recourse to comparison. It is circular to claim that κλέος ἄφθιτον is a Homeric formula simply because of its agreement with Vedic *śrávas . . . ákṣitam,* as Margalit Finkelberg 1986 rightly points out in a recent study. She objects to and rejects the formulaic status of κλέος ἄφθιτον in its unique Homeric attestation (*Il.* 9.413). Her remarks have merit synchronically: the adjective is predicate, not attributive, '[my] fame will be imperishable', and it could perfectly well be generated ad hoc. But diachronically within Greek this line must be a transformation of an earlier real formula. The same process of internal reconstruction must be applied to the equally unique Rigvedic example of *śrávas . . . ákṣitam* (1.9.7bc) beside *ákṣiti śrávas* of RV 1.40.4b, 8.103.5b, 9.66.7c. The diachronic analysis has been set forth basically by Nagy 1974 and the material earlier by Schmitt 1967. But since I differ from Nagy in certain crucial respects, and since his analysis apparently did not convince Finkelberg, I set forth briefly here my own apologia for κλέος ἄφθιτον.

After writing these lines in 1986 I was pleased to read the decisive paper of Ernst

Risch (1987). As he shows, the Mycenean woman's name *a-qi-ti-ta* (dative, MY Oe 103) was identified as *Akʷhthitā* by both Heubeck and Schmeja. Its formation either presupposes a full compound name **Akʷhthitoklewejja* or is built directly on the 'feste Verbindung' **akʷhthiton klewos*. 'So oder so ist dieser mykenische Frauenname ohne das Vorbild der dichtersprachlichen Wendung kaum denkbar' (p. 11). For other more recent perspectives on κλέος ἄφθιτον one may note Edwards 1988 and Floyd 1980, as well as Nagy 1990b passim.

Finkelberg 1986:4, citing Nagy 1974:105, asserts that 'combinations of κλέος with forms of the verb εἶναι at the end of the hexameter . . . may with every right be identified as a Homeric formula.' I disagree entirely. While we lack a study of what are the possible syntactic and semantic constraints on formulas, I submit that

FAME (κλέος) BE (εἶναι / ἐστί / εἴη)

is not a complete formula, because it is not meaningful. It is only a formulaic constituent. The 'essential idea' (in Parry's phrase) to be complete requires further specification: the presence of a pronominal reference and predication. Compare the examples (with the formula and metrical breaks marked):

Il. 10.212 **μέγα** κέν **οἱ** ὑπουράνιον **κλέος εἴη** #

his fame would be great under heaven,

Od. 9.264 # **τοῦ** . . . **μέγιστον** || ὑπουράνιον **κλέος ἐστί** #

whose fame is the greatest under heaven,

Od. 4.584 # χεῦ' 'Αγαμέμνονι τύμβον, ἵν' **ἄσβεστον κλέος εἴη** #

I heaped up a tomb to Agamemnon, that his **fame might be unquenchable**,

Od. 7.332-3 | **τοῦ**
ἄσβεστον κλέος εἴη ||

his would be unquenchable fame,

Il. 17.232 | τὸ δέ **οἱ κλέος ἔσσεται** ὅσσον **ἐμοί** περ #

his fame shall be even as **my own**,

Il. 22.513-14 οὐδέν **σοί** γ' ὄφελος, ἐπεὶ οὐκ ἐγκείσεαι αὐτοῖς
ἀλλὰ πρὸς Τρώων καὶ Τρωϊάδων **κλέος εἶναι**

> (all these clothes I will burn)—no use **to you**, since you will not be laid out in them—but **to be an honor** to you from the men and women of Troy.

The formulaic unit, as a thematic, semantic, and syntactic whole, is both larger and more flexible. Within this larger unit we find formulaic constituents which are themselves formulas: thus we can safely assert that *Il.* 10.212 is a transformation of the formula μέγα κλέος regularly occurring between the trochaic caesura and the bucolic diaeresis (*Il.* 6.446 et passim).

The situation is the same for the larger formulaic unit of which κλέος ἄφθιτον (ἔσται) is a constituent. Consider the following, as part of the formulaic background of Achilles' speech setting forth his choice in book 9:

Il. 10.212-13 **μέγα** κεν **οἱ** ὑπουράνιον **κλέος εἴη**
πάντας ἐπ' ἀνθρώπους, καί οἱ δόσις ἔσσεται ἐσθλή

his fame would be great under heaven
among all men, and a goodly gift will be his,

Od. 24.93-4 ὣς σὺ μὲν οὐδὲ θανὼν ὄνομ' ὤλεσας, ἀλλά **τοι αἰεί**
πάντας ἐπ' ἀνθρώπους **κλέος ἔσσεται ἐσθλόν**, 'Αχιλλεῦ

not even in death did you lose your name, but **forever**
among all men **you will have good reknown**, Achilles.

Here κλέος . . . ἐσθλόν can be translated predicatively ('your fame will be great', Lattimore), but it is in either case only a transformation of the clearly formulaic κλέος ἐσθλόν (ἄροιτο) of *Il.* 5.3 et passim. The important fact is that κλέος + adjective is part of a larger verb phrase whose semantics we may model (in normal English word order) as

PRO + BE /	HAVE	IMPERISHABLE	FAME	(FOREVER).
	GET	UNQUENCHABLE		
	WIN	GOOD		
	GRANT	GREAT		

This verb phrase underlies two names in the *Iliad*, as noted by Schmitt 1967:63: the noble Myrmidon 'Εχεκλῆς (*Il.* 16.189) and the two Trojans Ἔχεκλος slain by Patroklos (*Il.* 16.694) and Achilles (*Il.* 20.474). Yet the clearest expression of it is in the archaic metrical votive inscription from the 7th century in Krisa (Schw. 316):

ταсδε γ Αθαναιαι δραϝεος [. . .]αριστος εθεκε
Ηεραι τε hος και κενος **εχοι κλεϝος απθιτον αιϝει**

> [ ]aristos dedicated these *draweoi* to Athena and
> to Hera, that he too **might have imperishable fame forever**.

That there is a metrical and formulaic seam at the bucolic diaeresis (following κλεϝος) does not affect the syntactic structure where noun and attribute are dominated by a single node.

One should not forget that κλέος ἄφθιτον shows up precisely at Achilles' great expression of his choice—perhaps *the* central Indo-European theme—in a context which is that of the verb phrase:

> LOSE return—GAIN imperishable fame
>
> LOSE good fame—GAIN long life:

Il. 9.413-16 ὤλετο μέν **μοι** νόστος, ἀτὰρ **κλέος ἄφθιτον ἔσται**
. . .
ὤλετο **μοι κλέος ἐσθλόν**, ἐπὶ δηρὸν δέ μοι **αἰὼν** ἔσσεται

Then lost is **my** return, but my **fame will be imperishable** . . .
then lost is **my noble fame**, but my life will long endure . . .

It is part of the dramatic uniqueness of the language of Achilles in Homer's presentation that we find a unique formulaic constituent in just this nexus, just as the adverbial phrase ἐπὶ δηρόν 'for a long time' is also unique to this passage in Homer. But κλέος ἄφθιτον is a formula, as well as a constituent of a larger formulaic unit, including the verb phrase with BE and a pronoun (dative of 'interest' and dative of possession are ultimately the same), and an expression of FOREVER, here αἰών, echoing αἰεί in the same slot.

In Achilles' speech the noun phrase κλέος ἄφθιτον has been transformed; but it is syntactically and metrically intact in line-final position in Sappho 44.4 L-P, which provides metrical and formulaic testimony independent of Homer, pace Finkelberg, as conclusively demonstrated by Nagy 1974. The situation is comparable to that of the formula ταχὺς ἄγγελος, 'swift messenger'. In

Il. 18.2 Ἀντίλοχος δ' Ἀχιλῆϊ ‖ **πόδας ταχὺς** | **ἄγγελος** ἦλθε

Antilokhos, **swift of foot**, came as **messenger** to Achilles,

we have a clear formulaic, syntactic, and metrical boundary or seam between ταχὺς and ἄγγελος. Each constituent occurs elsewhere without the other:

Il. 17.676 ὅν τε καὶ ὑψόϑ' ἐόντα ‖ **πόδας ταχὺς** | οὐκ ἔλαϑε πτώξ

(the eagle) to whom though on high the **swift-footed** hare is not unseen,

Il. 3.121 etc. Ἶρις δ' αὖϑ' Ἑλένηι λευκωλένωι | **ἄγγελος ἦλϑεν**

Iris **went as a messenger** to white-armed Helen.

But the two words are clearly a formulaic unit in the only other Homeric occurrence of the collocation:

Od. 15.526 κίρκος, Ἀπόλλωνος ‖ **ταχὺς ἄγγελος**· | ἐν δὲ πόδεσσι

a hawk, the **swift messenger** of Apollo; in his feet . . .

And again we have the confirmation of Sappho 44.3 L-P, where ταχὺς ἄγγελος is once more line-final in the same metrical slot as κλέος ἄφϑιτον in the following line.

We may conclude that ταχὺς ἄγγελος like κλέος ἄφϑιτον is a true Homeric formula. Just as ταχὺς ἄγγελος can be compared for the semantics with the Vedic formula *dūtá- ajirá-* 'swift messenger' (RV 3.9.8, 10.98.2), so the comparison of κλέος ἄφϑιτον with Vedic *śrávas . . . ákṣitam* and *áksiti śrávas* can stand as the first in our discipline. But in concluding I would like to suggest that the real comparison is syntactically deeper—i.e., higher—than just the noun phrase and that it is an all the more remarkable formulaic, syntactic, and thematic equation. We may state the following rules:

Where a man is the subject, the notion HAVE (IMPERISHABLE FAME) is expressed either by the verb BE (*$*h_1es$-*) and a dative pronoun (PRO), or by a true verb (e.g.,**seĝh-*, *$*dheh_1$-* middle) and a subject pronoun, together with an optional form of the word for EVER(LASTING), ETERNITY, LIFETIME.

Thus in Indo-European lexical shape:

PRO_{dat}	$*h_1$es-	*k̂leu̯os	*n̥dg^{u}hitom	$*h_2$ai̯u-
PRO_{nom}	*seĝh- $*dheh_1$-	*k̂leu̯os	*n̥dg^{u}hitom	$*h_2$ai̯u-

as in Greek

μοι . . . κλέος ἄφϑιτον ἔσται . . . αἰὼν
κενος εχοι κλεϝος απϑιτον αιϝει
ἵνα οἱ κλέος ἄφϑιτον εἴη,

and Vedic

sá dhatte ákṣiti śrávaḥ

he gets imperishable fame.

Where a god is the subject the verb is GRANT (e.g. **dheh₁-* active) and the indirect object (man) is expressed in the dative pronoun (PRO):

PRO_{dat} *dheh₁- *k̂leu̯os *n̥dgʷhitom *h₂ai̯u-

asmé pr̥thú **śrávo** br̥hát / viśv**āyur dhehy ákṣitam**

As **everlasting** one, **grant us wide, lofty, imperishable fame**.

The seemingly redundant **h₂ai̯u-* (EVER) comes into its own in such variants as

PRO_{gen} *k̂leu̯os NEVER PERISH
poss

Il. 7.91 ἐμὸν κλέος οὔ ποτ' ὀλεῖται

Od. 16.241 ὦ πάτερ, ἦ τοι σεῖο μέγα κλέος αἰὲν ἄκουον.

The formula takes on an added dimension in view of Cowgill's (1960) etymology of Greek οὐ as **h₂oi̯u*, o-grade of **h₂ai̯u-*. Cf. also Old Norse *Hávamál* 77 *ek veit einn* ***at aldri deyr / dómr*** *um dauðan hvern* 'I know one thing that never dies: a dead man's fame' and Early Welsh (VKG 2.338) *trengid golud, ni threing molud* 'wealth perishes, fame does not perish'. But treatment of this and other variants must be left to the future.

16

The hidden track of the cow: Obscure styles in Indo-European

In the poetic traditions of most or all of the early Indo-European languages we find texts, often in large numbers, which for one reason or another present, or seem to present, some sort of obstacle between the hearer—the "reader"—and the message. And it often seems that that "obstacle" is in some sense what that society considers art. *paró 'kṣakāmā hí devā́ḥ* 'For the gods love the obscure', as we read in the Śatapatha-brāhmaṇa 6.1.1.2 and many places elsewhere in Vedic literature.

It should be emphasized that in the early Indo-European world the primary form of artistic expression is precisely *verbal*. Visual art typically plays a distinctly limited role until relatively late in the tradition. In Indo-European-speaking areas from the British Isles, the Celtic, Germanic, Baltic, and Slavic continent, Italy and Hellas, to Anatolia, Iranian Asia, and Western India the discrepancy in sophistication between plastic and verbal art at the dawn of our documentation is striking. Contrast the blackened, rather pedestrian Athenian pot from the 8th century B.C. hidden away in a dark corner of the museum in Athens, the Dipylon jug, and the childish lettering of its inscription, with the unchallenged mastery of meter, formulaic technique, and poetic creativity (on which see Watkins 1976d) which the crafter of its text exhibits. The text is cited in chap. 4. Or to take a less well-known example, there is a world of difference between the crudely carved human figure and external appearance of the South Picene inscribed grave stele of Bellante from ca. 500 B.C. (TE[ramo] 2 Marinetti), and the artistry of its message, with its colometric isosyllabism, fixed caesura, chain alliteration, and conventionalized speaker-hearer discourse relation. The text is cited in chap. 10 and illustrated with a photograph in Marinetti 1985.

For the Indo-European world, the further back we go the greater the emphasis on purely verbal art, the art of the spoken word. For the spoken word is a force, a creative power that can have a physical effect on the external world, when it is 'worked' or 'crafted' by the poet: compare the ideology of Truth in the Vedic maxim discussed in chap. 6:

satyó mántraḥ kaviśastá ŕ̥ghāvān (RV 1.152.2b)

True is the powerful formula pronounced by the poet.

The verbal figure is a formula of common Indo-Iranian date, as shown by the exactly cognate Old Avestan phrase *haiϑīm mąϑrəm* 'true formula'. We find the same ideology in archaic Greece (on which see Detienne 1973), as in the Muses' epiphany to Hesiod, *Th.* 26-8:

ποιμένες ἄγραυλοι, κάκ' ἐλέγχεα, γαστέρες οἶον,
ἴδμεν ψεύδεα πολλὰ λέγειν ἐτύμοισιν ὁμοῖα,
ἴδμεν δ', εὖτ' ἐθέλωμεν, ἀληθέα γηρύσασθαι

Shepherds of the wilderness, wretched things of shame, mere
bellies, we know how to speak many false things as though they
were true; but we know, when we will, to utter true things.

These lines strikingly recall the message of Vāc, divinized Speech, to the poet in the famous hymn RV 10.125.4:

máyā só ánnam atti yó vipáśyati
yáḥ prā́ṇiti yá īṃ śr̥ṇóti uktám
amantávo mā́ṃ tá úpa kṣiyanti
śrudhí śruta śraddhiváṃ te vadāmi

Through me he (merely) eats food, he who (just) sees,
breathes, and hears what is spoken—
(Even) these uncomprehending ones depend upon me.
(But) listen, o famed one: I say to you something worthy of trust.

As Toporov 1981 has shown in detail, the message is that those who see and hear still do not properly comprehend: RV 10.71.4 *utá tvaḥ páśyan ná dadarśa vā́cam utá tvaḥ śr̥ṇván ná śr̥ṇoty enām / utó tvasmai tanvàṃ ví sasre jāyéva pátya uśatī́ suvā́sāḥ* 'The one, looking, does not see Speech; the one, listening, does not hear her; to the one she reveals her body as a desiring wife, well-dressed, to her husband.'

We have already noted in chap. 8 the hidden meaning of Vāc's message to the poet in 10.125.4d *śrudhí śruta śraddhiváṃ te vadāmi*. It is an extreme phonetic figure, an exhaustive classification of the speech sounds of the language with a single example for each class. Recall also Hesiod's invocation of the Muses in the proem to the Works and Days (1-10), analyzed in chap. 7. Like the poet of the hymn to Vāc, Hesiod frames and closes the invocation with a complex phonetic figure. The proem begins with the word *Mousai* 'Muses' and ends (9-10) with the palindrome *et***ETUMA MUTHE**-, which itself calls our attention to the hidden phonetic echo closing the ring **MOUSAI** . . . **MU***thē***SAI***mēn*, as we saw in chap. 7. There can be little doubt that these Vedic and Greek examples reflect a common ideology of the theory and practice of poetics.

It is as much a common inheritance from the proto-poetic language as the verb forms κλῦθι and *śrudhí* 'listen!' are a common inheritance from the proto-language.

The Indo-European poet is the 'professional of the word' (Campanile 1977:32), and like any professional he must guard the secrets of his trade. In Indo-European poetry, that is to say in the poetry of many early Indo-European-speaking societies—and naturally many other language families one could name—there existed a conscious tradition of obscurantism, of secrecy, which serves like a cipher to protect the poetic message. To take only one of countless examples furnished by the Vedic Brāhmaṇas consider the mantras in the Soma worship spoken at the stirring of the Soma in the water, together with their 'explanation' (TS 3.3.3.1d-p):

> mā́ndāsu te śukra śukrám ā́ dhūnomi, bhandánāsu, kótanāsu, nū́tanāsu,
> réśīṣu, méṣīṣu, vā́śīṣu, viśvabhŕ̥tsu, mā́dhvīṣu, kakuhā́su, śákvrīṣu;
> śukrā́su te śukra śukrám ā́ dhūnomi . . .
>
> In the gladdening (waters) the pure for thee, o pure one, I stir,
> in the joyous, in the kotanās, in the new, in the reśīs, in the meṣīs,
> in the roaring, in the all-supporting, in the sweet, in the lofty, in
> the strong; in the pure I stir the pure for thee, o pure one.

3.3.4.1 etád vā́ apā́ṃ nāmadhéyam gúhyaṃ yád ādhāvā́; mā́ndāsu te śukra śukrám ā́ dhūnomī́ty āhā 'pā́m evá nāmadhéyena gúhyena divó vŕ̥ṣṭim áva runddhe

> The stirrings are the secret names of the waters; 'In the gladdening (waters) the pure for thee, o pure one, I stir,' he says; verily with the secret names of the waters he wins the rain from the sky.

The feminine gender of all the names (several of which are still obscure to us) serves to index the understood *apsú* 'in the waters', of feminine gender.

In what follows we will explore and illustrate some of the manifestations of this tradition in a number of different early Indo-European literatures.

There is a metalinguistic doctrine in many Indo-European traditions that there are different kinds of language. On the level of the lexicon this "diglossia" or "polyglossia" often finds its metaphorical expression in the opposition "language of men" versus "language of gods", in Homer, in Vedic, in Old Norse, and in Irish. Compare the detailed examples given in chap. 3.

These examples reflect a hierarchy in the lexicon: in terms of markedness the semantically unmarked member is identified with men (Greek Σκάμανδρος, Vedic *áśva* 'horse', Old Norse *iǫrð* 'earth'), but the marked member or members with gods or other superhuman beings (Gk Ξάνθος; Vedic *háya* 'steed' etc.). In all cases the fundamental opposition can in terms of markedness be reduced to one of

(-)		(+)
ordinary language	:	poetic language
human language	:	poetic language.

In Petronius' *Satyricon* (chap. 90) Encolpius says to the poet Eumolpus, *minus quam duabus horis mecum moraris, et saepius poetice quam humane locutus es*: 'you have been in my company less than two hours, and you have talked more often like a poet than like a human being.'

We have an excellent illustration in the Old Irish kennings for the letter names of the Ogam alphabet, as they appear in texts edited by Damian McManus 1988, amplified and modified in McManus 1991. The two-theme structure of the kenning and the concatenating alliteration of one set of these particular kennings prove that they were to be recited in alphabetical order as a poetic commentary on the alphabet itself. As McManus notes (1991:42), 'The opposition between *kenning* and *letter name* is that of a semantically marked synonym to an unmarked norm, or of poetic to ordinary language.' Thus the letter GG, named *gétal*, has the kennings *lúth lego* 'sustenance of a leech', *étiud midach* 'raiment of physicians', and *tosach n-échto* 'beginning of slaying'. McManus showed that *gétal* must be the old verbal noun of *gonid* 'slays, wounds', from IE **g^{u}hen-*, and this explanation establishes the Primitive Irish value /g^{w}/ for this letter.

The Irish doctrine as set forth in the *Auraicept na n-Éces*, The Poets' Primer, is a threefold oppposition of 'language' (*bérla*) in an ascending order of complexity and markedness:

			(-)		(+)
(-)	gnáthbérla:	senbérla	ordinary	:	old
	bérla Féine:	bérla na filed	professional	:	poetic
(+)	bérla tóbaide:	bérla fortchuide	selected	:	concealed

Thus the most highly marked form of discourse in Irish is that which is archaic, uniquely poetic, and obscure. How is this implicit goal—'saepius poetice quam humane'—attained in these traditions?

"Language" is in Indo-European languages most readily accessible in the lexicon; hence the attention to hierachization of vocabulary into aesthetically marked and unmarked forms (language of gods / language of men). The obscure style may favor a special vocabulary, like the names of things in Irish *bérla na filed* 'language of the poets' or the Vedic *devā́nam gúhyā nā́māni* 'secret names of the gods' (RV 5.5.10b). The obscure style, poetic language for short, may also favor the systematic avoidance of part of the lexicon as 'unpoetic': this is a characteristic feature of Latin literary language, well described in Axelson 1945.

Not only lexicon but also grammar may be so stigmatized. In the Latin literary language the 3rd pl. ending of the perfect was e.g. *uēn-ērunt* (unmarked) and *uēn-ēre* (marked). But the Romance languages show that what the man in the street actually said was *uēn-erunt* (French *ils vinrent*).

It is well to remember that the total effect of all forms of poetic technique is going to be a *distancing* of the poetic message from ordinary human language. And this distancing is itself a powerful contributing factor to the obscure style. The techniques include sound features like phonetic figures on the one hand and metrics on the other, grammatical figures, morphological and syntactic, and a variety of perturbations and deformations of natural language at every level, from word order to style of delivery. None of these, be it noted, involves a level of meaning higher than grammatical meaning. Thus in each of the messages cited above for the language of men/gods, the doctrine is vehicled by phonetic figures which function indexically to call attention to the opposition, as noted by Toporov:

ὃν Ξάνθον καλέουσι θεοί, ἄνδρες δὲ Σκάμανδρον

ks th th andr sk andr

GODS || MEN

In the Old Norse *Alvíssmál* the distribution of the men's words and the gods' words is governed by two simple phonological rules of poetic grammar, as I showed elsewhere (Watkins 1970a): (1) if the men's word begins with a vowel, the gods are called *Æsir* for alliteration and the choice of the gods' word is free; (2) if the men's word does not begin with a vowel, the gods are called *goð* and the gods' word must alliterate with the men's word:

'earth'	(men)	*iǫrð*	(*Æsir*)	*fold*
'heaven'	(men)	*himinn*	(*goð*)	*hlyrnir*.

We must recognize however that there are in fact two levels to the obscure style, just as there are for language itself: the meaningless and the meaningful. Note that 'meaningless' does not mean 'contentless'; it is just a level where ordinary meaning, typically lexical meaning, is simply not in play. It is characteristic that "meaningful obscurity" is the kind immediately thought of. But there is meaningful obscurity and meaningless obscurity, and we will have to consider—and the linguist will have an opinion—which is the more insidious.

Consider the case of isosyllabism, syllable-counting verse. In ordinary discourse speakers do not count the syllables of their utterances. But in *Astérix et Cléopatre*, one of the series of comic cartoon creations of A. Uderzo and R. Goscinny, when the Gauls arrive by ship in Alexandria, the druid Panoramix is greeted by his colleague, an Egyptian priest, with the words

Je suis, mon cher ami, très heureux de te voir.

The Gaul Astérix explains,

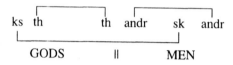

C'est un Alexandrin.

As is often the case, verbal play sheds light on verbal art.

We are amused but not moved by the blatant iconicity of Ennius'

saxo **cere**- comminuit -**brum** (*Ann.* 609)

Smashed his brain with a stone,

where the verb cleaves the noun in twain. But in Early Irish poetic doctrine there is a recognized figure of word-deformation, the deletion of a word-initial or word-final consonant, termed *díchned* 'beheading'. And we are moved by the iconic distraction of the two constituents of the noun phrase 'Æschere's head', separated by a whole hemistich, in *Beowulf* 1420-1

syðþan **Æscheres**
on þám holmclife **hafelan** métton

When they met **Æschere's head** on that sea-cliff.

In what follows I will examine from the point of view of phonetic and grammatical features an entire text, RV 8.70, to observe the poetic structure of a whole hymn in Vedic. RV 8.70 is metrically complex, consisting of six pragātha strophes (1-6) alternating bṛhatī/satobṛhatī lines, six bṛhatī verses (7-12), and concluding with the sequence uṣṇih/anuṣṭubh/uṣṇih (13-15). The text and a rough-and-ready translation are given in the Appendix to this chapter. What is of particular interest is the different deployment of grammatical, phonetic, and lexical figures in the three metrically demarcated subunits: 1-6, 7-12, 13-15.

Verse 1 begins with a relative clause, whose antecedent, the god Indra whom the hymn celebrates, is not identified until verse 2: 1a *yó rā́jā* . . . 2a *índram tám śumbha* '(He) who is king . . . Glorify that Indra'. The grammatical figure is a device familiar in both Vedic and Greek poetry.

Verse 3 introduces two phonetic figures, whose nature will be apparent only with their repetition in the same slot in subsequent verses: line 3a ends *kármaṇā* ***naśad***, and line 3d, the mantra-final, ends *dhṛṣṇv****ojas****am*. The first sets a pattern of quasi-, i.e. either apparent or real, 'intensive reduplication' with long vocalism in the 'reduplicator', short in the 'root' syllable:

3a kármaṇ**ā naśad**
4a **sāsahím**
4c **anonavur**
4d **anonavur**
5c sū́ry**ā ánu**
9b ś**ūra rā́dhase** (quantities 'reversed')
10c **ūruór**.

The second sets a pattern of mantra-final (C)**oCaCV**(-):

3d dhṛṣṇv**ò**ja**s**am
4d an**ona**vur
5d r**ód**asī
7d yuy**ó**ja**te**.

Both figures predominate in the first metrical section (1-6), and are only faintly echoed in the second (7-12). In return, however, the repetition of the same word at the end of lines 4c and 4d of the first section deftly prefigures the same repetition throughout section two:

4c,d **anonavur**
7c,d **yuyójate**
8c,d **hávyo, hávyaḥ**
9a,d **vaso mahé**, śravase **mahé**
11c,d **párvataḥ**
12c,d **sáṃ gṛbhāya asmayúr**.

Such consistent patterning can scarcely be accidental.

Verse 6 of this hymn stands outside these particular patterns. But lines 6ab provide a veritable symphony of sound figures, including alliteration, repetition, concatenation, and phonetic framing:

ā́ paprātha mahinā́ **vṛ́ṣṇ**yā **vṛṣan**
víśvā **śav**iṣṭha **śáv**asā

You have filled with your greatness, with your bull-strength, o bull,
all (space), o mightiest with your might.

The two etymological figures in succession (*vṛṣ- vṛṣ-*, *śav- śav-*) are linked by a word combining both *v-* and *-śv-*. The resulting sequence

vṛṣṇ . . . vṛṣ-n v-śv. ś-v . . . ś-v

could be described syntactically in terms of the resultant word order as "heavy poetic noun phrase extraposition." Lines cd continue the pattern with alliteration *a- a-*, repetition *ava . . . -ava-*, and a concatenating phonic echo:

*a*smā́ṁ ***ava*** maghavan gómati **vrajé**
vájriñ citrā́bhir ūtíbhiḥ

Help us, o generous one, to a stall rich in cattle,
o cudgel-bearer, with your wondrous help.

Verse 9 of the second metrical section of the hymn shows only an allusive repetition, but in return it provides rich examples of alliteration, rhyme, and consonant play, combined with a curious pattern of anaphora. I give first the sound figures in boldface:

> **úd ū ṣú** ṇo **vaso mahé**
> **m**ṛśásva śūra rā́dhase
> **úd ū ṣú m**ahyaí **ma**ghavan **ma**ghā́ttaya
> **úd** indra śrá**vase mahé**
>
> Stretch out well (your hand) for us, o Good One,
> for great generosity, o Hero;
> (stretch) out well for great giving, o Generous one,
> (stretch) out (well) for great fame, o Indra.

The anaphora is in greater part elliptic, such that we have a sort of "dwindle gapping":

> **úd ū ṣú** . . . **mṛśásva** . . .
> **úd ū ṣú** . . .
> **úd** . . .

Observe that the constituents of the verb phrase in lines ab must be read, so to speak, "vertically".

A widespread Indo-European convention or rule of poetic grammar which surely goes back to the proto-language is the convention of verse line = sentence. Grammatical phenomena sensitive to sentence or clause boundary (initial, final, second, pre-final) will occur also at verse or hemistich boundary, as the accented *mṛśásva* in this example. The metrical constituents of this bṛhatī quatrain are 8-8-12-8, but the clauses are in fact three, of 16-12-8 syllables, corresponding iconically to the "dwindle gapping".

After the virtuoso display of phonetic and grammatical figures of the metrically complex pragātha (1-6) and bṛhatī (7-12) verses, climaxing in the poetically exuberant and syntactically intricate praise of the generosity of the god Indra, the hymn concludes in 13-15 with the traditional *dānastuti*, the 'praise of the gift' of his patron to the poet for his poem. But the patron has been stingy, and that violation of the contract between poet and patron leaves the latter open to another form of the obscure style: the "inverse *dānastuti*". The *dānastuti* or praise of the gift is a familiar genre in other early Indo-European literatures from the Pindaric ode of ancient Greece to the Germanic and Celtic Middle Ages and beyond, from *Beowulf* to Classical Modern Irish Bardic Poetry. Less familiar, but still well-attested, is its inverse, the poetic blame of niggardliness which counter-balances the poetic praise of generosity. This we may term "inverse *dānastuti*"; the Irish called it 'false praise which was equivalent to satire,' *molad ngoa fris-suid air* (CIH 2192.20).

Our Rigvedic hymn provides an example of inverse *dānastuti* from the Indian tradition (an example from Old Irish is quoted below). The three verses (13-15) of the *dānastuti*, in stark contrast to the preceding sections, is devoid of phonic ornamentation. The poetic device is lexical and semantic and the message brief, ironic, and anticlimactic. It names the princely (**sūri**) patron (descendent of **Śūra**deva) and his generosity (**maghavan**) with flashbacks to Indra (**śūra**) and *his* generosity (**maghavan**, verse 6), but ends with a sorry prize indeed: one calf to be divided among three (**vatsa**) and a she-goat (**ajā**)!

> Friends, look for inspiration! How shall we achieve the praise of Śara, the generous noble prince, who is not to be ashamed of?
>
> You will be praised, somehow, by many worshipful *ṛṣis* when you hand out calves this way, Śara, one at a time.
>
> Grabbing it by the ear, the generous son of Śūradeva led a calf to the three of us like a prince: a she-goat to suck on.

A famous Early Irish inverse *dānastuti* is the quatrain preserved in the *Mittelirische Verslehren* III, *Irishe Texte* 3.67, Murphy, EIL 38. Its unique metrical form [$3^2\ 7^2\ 7^1 1^1$] is called *deibide baise fri tóin* 'slap on the arse deibide':

ro-cúala	I have heard
ní tabair eochu ar dúana	he gives no horses for poems;
do-beir a n-í as dúthaig dó	he gives what is his nature,
bó	a cow.

Here the framing device *ro-cúala* 'I have heard . . .' can be paralleled in Vedic praise of generosity, e.g. RV 1.109.2,5:

> **áśravaṃ** hí bhūridā́vattarā vām . . .
>
> For **I have heard** you two give more plentifully . . .
>
> yuvā́m indrāgnī vásuno vibhāgé
> távastamā **śuśrava**
>
> **I heard**, o Indra and Agni, that you are the stoutest
> in distributing goods ...

Vedic *śuśrava* and Old Irish (*ro-*)*cúala* are exact cognates, IE **k̑uk̑lou̯h₂a*. For 'I have heard' as an introductory framing device in Germanic literatures compare the first line of the *Hildebrandslied* and the commentary of Lühr 1982.

Following are some further Vedic examples of this obscure style. RV 9.91.5ab contains two sequential noun phrases, *návyase sūktā́ya* and *patháḥ prā́caḥ*, with distraction of constituents to positions adjacent to metrical boundary, as discussed in chap. 3:

sá pratnaván I **návyase** viśvavāra
suktā́ya patháḥ I kṛṇuhi **prā́caḥ**

Make **ready** as before, o all-desired one, the **paths** for the **new hymn**.

Now formulas can undergo change in transmission across time while maintaining their essential identity; they may also remain intact but their deployment change. RV 9.91 above in the triṣṭubh meter is attributed by the Anukramaṇī to the sage Kaśyapa. RV 9.9 in gāyatrī meter is attributed to the sage Asita, descendant of Kaśyapa; both names are familiar in later Saṁhitā and Brāhmaṇa literature. RV 9.9.8 contains the same formula *návyase sūktā́ya* as 9.91.5 ab (*patháḥ*, *pratnavát*), and is obviously related:

nū́ **n**ávyase **n**ávīyase
sūktā́ya **s**ādhaya **p**atháḥ
pratnavád **r**ocayā **r**úcaḥ

Prepare the paths for every new hymn;
as before make your lights shine.

We have a new poetic figure in this verse, however: a clear run of sequential, concatenating or chain alliterations: *n n n s s p p r r*. In other Indo-European traditions (with fixed initial stress) this feature will become the 'constitutive device of the sequence', as discussed earlier. The oldest example known to me outside India is precisely that mentioned above from 6th-century B.C. South Picene in Italy, analyzed in chap. 10:

postin **v**iam **v**idetas
tetis **t**okam **a**lies
esmen **v**epses **v**epeten.

The pattern of chain alliteration is very common in Early Irish, as in the seventh-century Leinster genealogical poems.

On the level of phonology, finally, the obscure style may be manifested by anagrams or hypograms concealing or artfully disclosing the name of the poet or of the god, or of a key notion. RV 10.20-26 are attributed by the Anukramaṇī to the poet Vimada, who mentions himself by name in 10.20.10, linked to the verb form *vakṣat*:

. . . **vimadó** manīṣā́m . . .
gíra **ā́** **vakṣat**

Vimada will bring you a hymn . . . songs of praise.

But his real signature is the recurrent refrain in 10.21.1-8, 10.24.1-3, and 10.25.1-11:

ví vo **máde** . . . vi**vakṣ**ase

In intoxication I wish to tell you . . .,

with an anagrammatic or hypogrammatic display of both elements. In 10.23 he mentions his people (6a *vimadā́*) and himself (7b *vimadásya ca ŕ̥ṣeḥ*) and follows both with an anagram of his name in the c line beginning *vidmā́* (6c, 7c); the last (7c) closes with another anagram, thus creating a frame:

vidmā́ . . . jāmi**vád**.

Finally in 10.24 after the signature refrain above he weaves in an eponymous mythical Vimada (4c *vi**madé**na yád īlitā́*), then concludes the hymn with repeated phonetic indexes of his own name with *madhumat* 'rich in sweet (of honey, mead, and the intoxicationg soma)':

mádhuman me . . .
mádhumat . . .
. . . **mádhumat**as kr̥tám.

In the Homeric *h.Ap.* 362, **PHOI**-*non* **APO**-*pneiousa* 'breathing out gore' prefigures the god's name at the end of the line **PHOI**-*bos* **APO**-*llōn*:

φοινὸν **ἀπο**πνείουσ'· ὁ δ' ἐπηύξατο **Φοῖ**βος **Ἀπό**λλων

. . . breathing out gore; then Phoebus Apollo boasted over her.

We have seen above the ring composition of the proem to Hesiod's *Works and Days*, beginning with the name of the Muses **MOUSAI** (1. 1), echoed at the end of this and the next line by . . . **OUSAI**, . . . **OUSAI**, and ending with the hypogrammatic hidden echo **MU***thē***SAI***mēn*. We find a similar echo of the same word in the first strophe of Pindar's *Ol.* 3.4:

MOISA . . . pOI . . . **MOI** neoSigAlon.

The first word of the first strophe of Sappho 1, the hymn to Aphrodite, **PO***ikilo***TH***r***ON**' is echoed in the adonic closure **PO***tnia* **TH***um***ON**.

Perhaps the most famous Greek example is Pindar's anagram of the name of his patron and hymnee Theron of Akragas in *Ol.* 2.2:

tina **TH**eon, tin' h**ĒRŌ**a, tina d' a**N**dra keladēsomen

What god, what hero, what man shall we hymn?

Further on in the same ode (87) Pindar ventures to pun on the name of his patron's city, speaking of his rival poets

> korakes hōs **akranta gar**ueton[1]
>
> Chattering in vain like a pair of crows,

boldly asserting the solution four lines later (91):

> **Akraganti** tanusais
> audasomai enorkion logon
>
> Toward Akragas I will bend the bow
> and speak a word under oath.

See also chap. 6.

An extreme case of the obscure style is the Old Avestan Ahuna Vairiia prayer (Y. 27.13), the Zoroastrian Paternoster as it is sometimes termed. Like the Paternoster the Zoroastrian prayer takes its name from its *incipit*, *yaϑā* ***ahū vairiiō***. This text consists of just three lines or 6 hemistichs of 16 syllables [7 + 9] each. The resulting 48-syllable utterance encapsulates the Mazdayasnian religion; its recitation by Zarathustra had the power to drive out demons (Yt. 19.81). Yet its 'syntactic density' (Russell 1993) renders it remarkably opaque, and the translations offered by specialists from Bartholomae on differ radically.[2] I give the text and a translation based on the version in Humbach-Elfenbein-Skjærvø, but I suspect the last word has not been said on either translation or exegesis.

> yaϑā ahū vairiiō   aϑā ratuš aṣ̌āṯcīṯ hacā
> vəŋhə̄uš dazdā manaŋhō   ś̌iiaoϑənanąm aŋhə̄uš mazdāi
> xšaϑrəmcā ahurāi.ā   yim drigubiiō dadaṯ vāstārəm
>
> As it (judgment) is to be chosen by the world,
>   so the judgment (which is) in accord with truth,
> (which is to be passed) on the actions of good thought of the world,
>   is assigned to the Wise (Lord) [*Mazdāi*],
> and the power (is assigned) to the (Wise) Lord [*Ahurāi.ā*],
>   whom they established as shepherd to the needy.

Humbach has shown that much of the syntactic complexity is additive; thus to the (doubtless Indo-Iranian[3]) formulaic and nominal sentence *aϑā ratuš* 'so (is) the

1. For the reading see H. Lloyd-Jones 1985.
2. They are enumerated in Humbach-Elfenbein-Skjærvø 1991:2.4-6. Russell's 1993 translation is again different.
3. They rightly compare RV 1.162.19 *táthā r̥túḥ* 'so is the regulation' in the *aśvamedha* hymn to

judgment' is added the verbal predicate *dazdā*, totally altering the structure in a fashion reminiscent of 'garden path' sentences.[4] Line 2 apparently conflates two Old Avestan formulas, *vəŋhəuš šiiaoϑana- manaŋhō* 'actions of good thought' (Y. 50.9:2) and *aŋhəuš . . . šiiaoϑana-* 'actions of the world' (Y. 31.8:6). The resulting opacity is surely intentional.

Contributing to the general density are the intersecting syntactic figures: correlation *yaϑā . . . aϑā . . .*, delayed conjunction *ratuš . . . xšaϑrəmcā*, multiple gapping, the doubling in *Mazdāi . . . Ahurāi.ā*, and the distracted noun phrase straddling a syntactically very distant verb in *vəŋhəuš dazdā manaŋhō*.

But most striking of all is the linkage by phonetic figures, which inextricably bind together the three lines. The lines and hemistichs are linked by whole word repetitions (*ahū* 1 : *aŋhəuš* 2, *dazdā* 2 : *dadaṯ* 3), by rhyme (*vəŋhəuš* : *aŋhəuš*), and triply by alliteration (***v**airiiō . . . **v**əŋhəuš . . . **v**āstārəm*, ***d**rigubiiō **d**a**d**aṯ*) and more subtle phonetic responsion (***R**a**T**u**Š** . . . x**Š**a**ΘR**əm . . . vā**ST**ā**R**əm*). Both names of the deity are preceded by their phonetic echo: alliterative in ***a**ŋhəuš **a**hurāi.ā*, anagrammatic in *da**ZDĀ MA**naŋhō . . . **MAZDĀ**i*. One could seek no better illustration of the power and the beauty of the hidden, obscure style in the performative language of religion in the Indo-European tradition.

A Vedic poet contemplating his own art could boast of 'having found the hidden word like the track of the cow' (RV 4.5.3c *padám ná gór ápagūḷhaṃ vividvā́n*). For as one poet tells us (RV 8.41.5):

> yá usrā́ṇām apīcyā̀ véda nā́māni gúhyā
> sá kavíḥ kā́vyā purú rūpáṃ dyáur iva puṣyati
>
> He who knows the secret hidden names of the dawn cows,
> he the kavi brings to flower his many poetic arts, as heaven its beauty.

Appendix: RV 8.70

1	**yó** rā́jā carṣaṇīnā́m	(He) who is king of the people,
	yā́tā ráthebhir ádhriguḥ	chariot-rider, the grand-one,
	víśvāsāṃ tarutā́ pŕ̥tanānāṃ	victor of all battles,
	jyéṣṭho **yó** vr̥trahā́ gr̥ṇé	who is sung as the mightiest Vr̥tra-slayer,
2	**índraṃ táṃ** śumbha puruhanmann ávase	glorify that Indra, o Puruhanman, for favor
	yásya dvitā́ vidhartári	in whose hand to hold it indeed
	hástāya vájraḥ práti dhāyi darśató	the weapon was placed, fair to see
	mahó divé ná sū́ryaḥ	like the great sun in heaven.

the sacrificial horse. For such sententious, proverb-like correlative sentences as Avestan *yaϑā* X, *aϑā* Y (*ratuš*), Vedic (*yáthā*) X, *táthā* Y (*r̥túḥ*), compare also Kauṣītaki-Brāhmaṇa 8.7 *yathāmnātam iti tv eva sthitam* '"as it is remembered," so is the established rule', of the form *yathā* X, (*tathā*) Y. My translation tries to capture this correlation.

4. For example, "The horse raced past the barn fell".

3 nákiṣ ṭáṃ kármaṇā **naśad** yáś cakā́ra sadā́vṛdham índraṃ ná yajñáir viśvágūrtam ṛ́bhvasam ádhṛṣṭaṃ dhṛṣṇvòjasam	None could approach him in deed who produced an ever-invigorating one like Indra all-praised with worship, masterful, unassailable, of daring strength;
4 áṣāḷham ugrám pṛ́tanāsu **sāsahíṃ** yásmin mahī́r urujráyaḥ sáṃ dhenávo jā́yamāne **anonavur** dyā́vaḥ kṣā́mo **anonavuḥ**	unconquered, powerful, victorious in battle at whose birthing the broad-streaming rivers (and) the cows bellowed together, heaven (and) earth bellowed.
5 yád dyā́va indra te śatáṃ śatám bhū́mīr utá syúḥ ná tvā vajrin sahásraṃ sū́ryā **ánu** ná jātám aṣṭa **ródasī**	If you had a hundred heavens, o Indra, and a hundred earths, a thousand suns would not equal you, o cudgel-bearer, nor the two worlds, once born.
6 ā́ paprātha mahinā́ **vṛ́ṣṇyā vṛṣan** **víśvā śaviṣṭha śávasā**	You have filled with your greatness, with your bull-strength, o bull, all (space), o mightiest, with your might.
asmā́n ava magh**avan** gómati **vrajé** **vájriñ** citrā́bhir ūtíbhiḥ	Help us, o generous one, to a cow-filled pen, o cudgel-bearer, with your wonderous help.
7 ná sīm ádeva āpad íṣam dīrghāyo mártyaḥ étagvā cid yá étaśā **yuyójate** hárī índro **yuyójate**	Let not the godless mortal obtain refreshment, o long-lived one; whichever (Indra) yokes the two brindled, (whichever) Indra yokes the two bays,
8 táṃ vo mahó mahā́yyam índraṃ dānā́ya sakṣáṇim yó gādhéṣu yá ā́raṇeṣu **hávyo**	that Indra should you glorify, victorious, forgiving; he who (is) to be invoked in the shallows (and) the depths,
vā́jeṣu ásti hávya**ḥ**	(who) is to be invoked in the competitions.
9 **úd ū ṣú** no vaso **mahé** **mṛ**śásva **śūra rā́dhase** **úd ū ṣú m**ahyaí maghavan magháttaya **úd** indra śrá**vase mahé**	Stretch out well (your hand) for us, o good one, for a great gift, o hero; (stretch) out well, o generous one, for great generosity, (stretch) out (well), o Indra, for great fame.
10 tváṃ na indra ṛtayús tvānído ní tṛmpasi mádhye vasiṣva tuvinṛmṇa **ūruór**	You are true to us, o Indra, you devour those who revile you; cover yourself, o manly one, in the middle of your two thighs
ní dāsáṃ śiśnatho háthaiḥ	strike down the Dāsa with your blows.
11 anyávratum ámānuṣam áyajvānam ádevayum áva sváḥ sákhā dudhuvīta **párvataḥ** sughnā́ya dásyum **párvataḥ**	Him who follows another commandment, the non-man, non-worshipping godless one, may his friend the mountain shake down, the mountain the barbarian, the easier to slay.
12 tváṃ na indrāsāṃ háste śaviṣṭha dāváne dhānā́nāṃ ná **sáṃ gṛbhāya asmayúḥ** dvíḥ **sáṃ gṛbhāya asmayúr**	Do you, o Indra, take of these (cows) in your hand, o powerful one, to give us; take as of grains to please us, take double to please us.

13	sákhāyaḥ krátum ichata kathā́ rādhāma **śarásya** úpastutim bhojáḥ **sūrír** yó áhrayaḥ	Friends, look for inspiration! How shall we achieve the praise of Śara, the generous noble prince, who is not to be ashamed of?
14	bhū́ribhiḥ samaha ṛ́ṣibhir barhíṣmadbhi staviṣyase yád itthám ékamekam ṛ́c **chára vatsā́n** parādádaḥ	You will be praised somehow, by many worshipful *ṛṣis* when you hand out calves this way, o Śara, one at a time.
15	karṇagṛ́hyā maghávā śauradevyó **vatsáṃ** nas tribhyá ā́nayat **ajā́ṃ sūrír** ná dhā́tave	Grabbing it by the ear, the generous son of Śūradeva led a calf to the three of us like a prince: a she-goat to suck on.

III

The strophic style: An Indo-European poetic form

17

Some Indo-European prayers: Cato's lustration of the fields

The ancient Roman ritual of lustration or 'purification' of the fields is described in a passage in Cato, *De agri cultura* 141.1ff. It is prescribed to the landowner to order the set of three animals which constitute the *suouitaurilia*—pig, sheep, and bull-calf—to be driven around the circumference of the fields with the words

> cum diuis uolentibus quodque bene eueniat,
> mando tibi, Mani, uti illace suouitaurilia
> fundum agrum terramque meam
> quota ex parte siue circumagi siue circumferenda censeas
> uti cures lustrare
>
> That with the gods favorable everything will turn out well,
> I order you, NN,[1] to take care of the lustration of my
> farm, field, and land, from whatever side you deem these
> *suouitaurilia* should be driven or carried around them.

The syntactic intricacy of these prefatory instructions, accomplished principally by moving *illace suouitaurilia* out of its clause (*quota ex parte . . . censeas*) to a position of prominence before the objects of the verb *lustrare*, indicates that we are already in the world of *concepta uerba*, of Roman formal solemn diction.

The landowner is then enjoined to pronounce a preliminary prayer with a libation to Janus and Jupiter[2] and to address a prayer with fixed wording to Mars. This prayer to Mars had been justly qualified by Risch 1979 as 'the oldest Latin text preserved,' 'actually older than Early Latin literature,' the monuments of authors of the third and second centuries B.C., considerably before Cato's time (ca. 234 - 149 B.C.).

1. Latin *Manius*, the equivalent of our John Doe.
2. *Ianum Iouemque uino praefamino, sic dicito.* The imperative *praefamino* is already a linguistic archaism.

The thematic and formal structure of this prayer was analyzed with characteristic lucidity by E. Benveniste, in an article of nearly a half-century ago (1945) entitled 'Social symbolism in Greco-Italic cults,' as an illustration of the principle that 'every definition of a conceptual totality tends to borrow the tripartite framework which organizes human society' among the early Indo-European-speaking peoples, that is to say, in the trifunctional schema of G. Dumézil, of which Benveniste's study provides some of the better examples.

The name of the sacrifice itself, the *suouitaurilia*, is tripartite, a three-member compound. Benveniste, following the materials amassed by Krause in the article *Hostia*, P.-W. Suppl. Bd. V, showed that this compound, a nominalization of a phrase *su oue tauro* (*facere*), combined the three animals which were typically sacrificed to Earth (pig), Jupiter (ram), and Mars (bull) respectively. The whole sacrifice is made to Mars to ward off the symbolic 'set of ills which may menace the body politic or the products of the earth' (p. 15). The threefold sacrifice recurs in Greece as the τριττύς or τρίττοια of the same three animals (in this case adult): bull, ram, and boar. It is first found in the *Odyssey*, in Tiresias' instruction to Odysseus to sacrifice to Poseidon (11.131 = 23.278),

> ἀρνειὸν ταῦρόν τε συῶν τ' ἐπιβήτορα κάπρον
>
> a ram and a bull and a boar who has been to the sows.

Poseidon receives the triple offering as the deity most appropriate, since he controls the fate of the mariner, but the sacrifice 'symbolically subsumes the whole human condition' (*ibid.*).

The scholiast to *Il.* 19.197 informs us that the same threefold sacrifice consecrated the solemn oath: πρὸς δὲ τὰ ὅρκια τρισὶν ἐχρῶντο 'Αττικοί, κάπρωι κριῶι ταύρωι 'for oaths the Athenians would use three: boar, ram, bull.' Demosthenes *Contra Aristocratem* § 68, p. 642, describes the oath-taking in a trial for murder, στὰς ἐπὶ τῶν τομίων κάπρου καὶ κριοῦ καὶ ταύρου 'standing on the cut parts (= testicles) of a boar and a ram and a bull.'

While the tripartite sacrifice here symbolically expresses a totality, we may still find in the same or similar circumstances a bipartite expression, like Paul. ex Fest. 112 L *mensa frugibusque iurato* 'he shall swear by his stores and grain', a formula which recalls the Umbrian bipartite rhyming *mefa spefa*, name of a sacrificial flatcake < **menssa spenssa* 'measured out (and) consecrated' (?). In the tradition of another Indo-European people we also find an ascending series of single, double, and triple expression in the same context of oath-taking. In the Sanskrit laws of Manu (8.113) the brāhmaṇa priest swears by his *truth* (*satyena*), the kṣatriya warrior by his *chariot* (*and*) *weapons* (*vāhanāyudhais*), and the vaiśya farmer by his *cattle*, *seed*, (*and*) *gold* (*gobījakāñcanais*), the last a three-member compound linguistically closely parallel to *suouitaurilia*.

This is not the place to debate the validity of the Dumézilian system wholly or in part. As we shall see, the triadic or tripartite organization of the Old Latin text as demonstrated first by Benveniste is a structural fact independent of any conceptual framework one might choose to superimpose upon it. Benveniste was interested above all in the structure of the *content* of Cato's prayer. Its poetic *form* did not engage his attention, and he printed the text without comment as prose, just as it was transmitted in the manuscript. This prayer, however, as I hope to show, is indeed not only the most ancient piece of Latin literature but the oldest Latin poem that we possess. As we shall see in abundant detail, its structure is far more complex than most commentators have presumed. Two characterizations of the prayer were singled out for praise by Norden. These are Leo 1913:13 'Ein Gebet, Hülfe bittend und Übel verbittend', and Wünsch 1916:176: 'Unsegen soll aufhören, Segen soll kommen; dazu sollen die Götter helfen'. Norden's book belies any 'simplicity' of the Ancient Roman priestly books, and the artistic effect both German authors strove for in their antitheses *bittend* : *verbittend*, *HÜLFE* : *ÜBEL*, *Segen* : *Unsegen* is itself an accurate rendition of the spirit of the Roman prayer.

In the following the text is printed with line division essentially as in the collective and anonymous collection *Early Roman Poetry* (Oxford 1951) 5-6,[3] but further separated into four *strophes* numbered I-IV.

1	I	Mars pater te precor quaesoque	
2		uti sies uolens propitius	
3		mihi domo familiaeque nostrae:	
4		quoius rei ergo	
5		agrum terram fundumque meum	
6		suouitaurilia circumagi iussi	
7	II	uti tu	
8		morbos uisos	inuisosque
9		uiduertatem	uastitudinemque
10		calamitates	intemperiasque
11		prohibessis defendas auerruncesque	
12	III	utique tu	
13		fruges frumenta	uineta uirgultaque
14		grandire	(du)eneque[4] euenire siris
15		pastores pecuaque	salua seruassis
16		duisque (du)onam salutem	ualetudinemque
17		mihi domo familiaeque nostrae	
18	IV	harunce rerum ergo	
19		fundi terrae agrique mei	
20		lustrandi lustrique faciendi ergo	

3. 'Edited by a subgroup of the faculty concerned.' The line division there is I believe after W. M. Lindsay.

4. In *(du)ene* here and *(du)onam* 16 I have restored the Old Latin form of later *bene, bonam*.

21 sicuti dixi
22 macte hisce suouitaurilibus lactentibus immolandis esto
23 Mars pater eiusdem rei ergo
24 macte hisce suouitaurilibus lactentibus esto

I Father Mars, I pray and beseech you
that you be favorable (and) propitious
to me, my house, and our household:
to which end
I have ordered the *suouitaurilia* to be driven around
my field, land, and farm;

II that you
forbid, ward off, and brush aside
diseases seen and unseen,
depopulation and devastation,
storms and tempests;

III and that you
let grow tall and turn out well
grains (and) corn and vineyards (and) shrubwork
and keep safe shepherds (and) cattle
and give good health and soundness
to me, my house, and our household.

IV To these ends,
to purify and perform the purification
of my farm, land, and field
so as I spoke
be magnified by these suckling *suouitaurilia* to be sacrificed;
Father Mars, to that same end,
be magnified by these suckling *suouitaurilia*.

We have here clearly a prayer within a prayer in a *nesting* arrangement:

(I (II III) IV).

Strophe I serves as the introduction and invocation, the *captatio benevolentiae*, and strophe IV as the resolution or conclusion, with the final invocation (22-24) serving as a sort of *envoi*, iterated.

I and IV formally belong together as the "wrapping" of II and III, because of their pattern of *responsions*. These verbal responsions are equivalence tokens, and they form the rings which establish I and IV as a frame. They include

Mars pater 1 : 23 Father Mars,

and the synonymous doubling figures

precor quaesoque 1	I pray and beseech
uolens propitius 2	favorable (and) propitious,
lustrandi lustrique faciendi 20	to purify and perform the purification.

For the Indo-European antiquity of the stylistic figure of the last see chap. 13.

Beside (or within) the synonymous doubling figures we have the counterpoint of synonymous or semantically similar tripling figures:

mihi domo familiaeque nostrae	3 : 17	for me, my house, and our household,

and the mirror-image repetition

agrum terram fundumque meum	5	my field, land, and farm
fundi terrae agrique mei	19	my farm, land, and field.

The last two phrases provide a link to *fundum agrum terramque meam* of the preceding prefatory instructions discussed above. In general part of the art of the whole prayer is the interplay of the bipartite with the tripartite, the doubling with the tripling figure, which creates a unique stylistic rhythm.

Further responsions between I and IV include the single postposition *ergo* in 4 and its triplication in 18, 20, 23, and the presence in I and IV of the first person singular, the persona of the worshipper as agent, in the perfects *iussi*[5] 6 and *dixi* 21.

Finally, the tripartite designation of the sacrifice itself appears only in I and IV: *su-oui-taurilia* 6 : 22, 24.

By contrast to all these links between strophes I and IV, there is only one link between them and the internal strophes II and III: *mihi domo familiaeque meae* of lines 3 and 17. The phrase in line 17 is neither thematically nor syntactically organic or necessary; its purpose is to link II-III to the farmer's personal family prayer I-IV.

Ring-composition affords a formal proof. The first word of strophe II, *morbos* 'diseases' in line 8, is answered by the last word of strophe III, *ualetudinemque* 'health' in line 16. This responsion by semantic antithesis bounds the poem proper of II-III and proves that it starts at line 8 and stops at line 16.

Strophes I and IV are stylistically careful, artfully elaborated 'ordinary' solemn religious language of 3rd-century B.C. Rome, as we can observe it for example in Plautus.[6] This sort of solemn usage was clearly traditional by that time on the evidence of its striking stylistic contrast with the colloquial speech of the same period.[7]

5. In Cato's time and before the form would surely have been *iousī*, as in the Senatus Consultum de Bacchanalibus of 186 B.C.

6. Both Plautus († ca. 184 B.C.) and Cato (234 - 149 B.C.) learned to talk in the 3rd century B.C.

7. A good example is Plautus *Trinummus* 39-42 *Larem corona nostrum decorari uolo / uxor, uenerare ut nobis haec habitatio / bona fausta felix fortunataque euenat / —teque ut quam primum possim uideam emortuam.* 'I want our Lar to be adorned with a wreath. Wife, perform your devotions that this

Yet nested within these outer layers of formal religious language, cradled and protected against the winds of change, lie the real archaisms: strophes II and III. If I and IV represent traditional language and reflect the stylistic usage of, say, a century or more before the 3rd century B.C., then strophes II-III should represent a state of the language traditional already at that time, and perhaps antedating the foundation of the Roman Republic. One must not be misled by the phonological form, which would have been continuously modernized—as was that of the Law of the XII Tables, a composition datable to 450 B.C. The central prayer to Mars, strophes II and III 'kann beliebig alt sein', 'can be as old as you want', as Rudolf Thurneysen once exclaimed over a passage in Early Irish law (fide D.A. Binchy).

For a parallel consider only that right now, toward the end of the 20th century, the basic phraseology of Christianity in the English language remains virtually unchanged from that of the Bible translation of William Tyndale in the early 16th century (New Testament 1525-6). The span is almost half a millennium. It is the text of this Latin prayer to Mars, strophes II and III—and they are indeed strophe and antistrophe—which will henceforth occupy our attention. Its composition too may well antedate by half a millennium its fixation by Cato in *De agri cultura*, ca. 160 B.C.

Benveniste's contribution was to recognize the tripartite conceptual structure of the two strophes and their homology to the hierarchy of the three functions argued for as an ideology by Dumézil. For Benveniste 'every definition of a conceptual totality tends unconsciously to borrow the tripartite framework which organizes human society' (p. 5). We may retain the key word 'unconsciously'. There may have existed an ideological tripartition into the three functions of sovereignty, force, and fecundity, though the tripartition might be simply a cognitive universal. The model might have been—as it clearly was for Benveniste—a social hierarchy, a threefold division of the classes of free males into priests, warriors, and farmers, as we can observe it in India and Iran. But that too, with all the necessary adjustments, might be a cognitive universal. It is certain in any case that the hierarchy of Roman society by the middle of the 1st millennium B.C. was based rather on birth, wealth, clientship, and the like and that the Roman 'farmer' could and did function at the same time as both 'warrior' (the Cincinnatus ideal) and 'priest' (as here in the lustration of the fields).

That said, it remains to be recognized, with Benveniste, that a tripartite hierarchy agreeing with the Dumézilian model is both present and pronounced in these two strophes of the prayer and is indeed the foundation of their grammatical and conceptual structure. The first strophe enumerates a triad of scourges the divinity is asked to avert, conceived as the totality of evils which can menace the body politic or the produce of the earth, and the second strophe (the antistrophe) enumerates a triad of benefits the divinity is asked to grant, also conceived as 'the protection and favor of the whole society'.

We may symbolize the three 'functions', giving them their reductionist Dumézilian labels, as

home turn out for us well, favorable, prosperous, and fortunate—(aside) and that I see you laid out dead as soon as possible.' The archaic subjunctive *euenat* is metrically sure.

f_1	sovereignty (including *med*icine)[8]
f_2	force
f_3	prosperity.

The strophe (II) enumerates the evils which threaten the well-being corresponding to each 'function': illness (f_1), devastation (f_2), and natural catastrophe (f_3), each associated with a particular verb of averting. As Benveniste showed, diseases visible and hidden are to be 'forbidden', cf. *Iuppiter prohibessit* Plautus *Ps.* 13f. (and *God forbid*); the devastation of war to be 'repulsed', cf. *defende hostes* Ennius *Scen.* 6 V (IE *$g^{u}hen$-); calamity to be 'swept aside', more generally 'averted', cf. *di . . . amentiam auerruncassint tuam* Pacuvius 112 R.[9] Using the symbols N for noun or noun phrase and V for verb or verb phrase, we obtain the following thematic analysis:

II strophe	8		N_1		AVERT
	9		N_2		
	10		N_3		
	11	V_1	V_2	V_3	

morbos uisos	inuisosque
uiduertatem	uastitudinemque
calamitates	intemperiasque

prohibessis defendas auerruncesque

forbid, ward off, and brush aside

diseases seen	and unseen,
depopulation	and devastation,
storms	and tempests.

The antistrophe (III) then presents, in mirror image and reverse order, the set of three benefices prayed for, again corresponding to each 'function': agricultural prosperity, safety from depredation (with *defendas . . . seruassis* . . . compare Ennius *Scen.* 6 V. *serua ciues, defende hostes* 'save the citizens, ward off the foe'), and good health:

III antistr.	13		N_3		GRANT
	14		V_3		
	15	N_2		V_2	
	16	V_1		N_1	

fruges frumenta	uineta uirgultaque
grandire	(du)eneque euenire siris
pastores pecuaque	salua seruassis
duisque (du)onam salutem	ualetudinemque

8. Compare the root **med-* of Latin *medicina*, *medērī* 'treat', and Greek μέδων, μεδέων 'ruling', μέδομαι 'provide for'.

9. The verbs are discussed also by Norden 1939:126 n. 3.

let grow tall	and turn out well
grains (and) corn	and vineyards (and) shrubwork
and keep safe	shepherds (and) cattle
and give good health	and soundness.

Benveniste's great achievement was to perceive this thematic structure as a whole for the first time. The correspondence is clear, and no other hypothesis accounts for the facts as well. Benveniste gives further a number of thematic parallels in phraseology from other Indo-European traditions; we will come to these presently.

Let us begin now to look at the poetic form of this prayer. How are the three 'functions' in fact expressed? As we stated earlier, the art of the poem is in the counterpoint of tripling and doubling, the threefold and the twofold, tripartite and bipartite. If the thematic structure as a whole is tripartite, each thematic structure point is represented by a grammatical doubling, sometimes doubled again. All of these doublings generate stylistic figures which are prototypical for the Indo-European poetic world. These categories of Indo-European bipartite noun phrase formulaic figures were discussed earlier in chap. 3. Note the following:

Argument + Negated Argument:	8 *morbos uisos inuisosque*
Argument + Synonymous Argument:	9 *uiduertatem uastitudinemque*
	10 *calamitates intemperiasque*
	16 *(du)onam salutem ualetudinemque*
Merism (copulative)	13 **fruges uinetaque*
	15 *pastores pecuaque*

The underlying bipartite 13 **fruges uinetaque* has itself undergone a further doubling (by I.2.b. Arg. + Synon. Arg.) to the alliterative (identity of phonic form) and etymological (identity of meaning) *fruges frumenta uineta uirgultaque.*[10]

Grammatical figures are a central component in the art of strophe II and antistrophe III, as is the placement of the enclitic copulative conjunction *-que* 'and'. Both strophes are penetrated by the interplay and tension double/triple and horizontal/vertical; language and the linguistic sign are not arranged only linearly. Using the + sign for 'and' (Lat. *-que*), we may observe that all doublings are A + B (A B-*que*), all triplings A B + C (A B C-*que*). Thus the three verbs of the strophe are arranged horizontally,

	V_1	V_2	+	V_3
11	prohibessis	defendas		auerruncesque.

while the three verbs of the antistrophe are deployed vertically

V_3	siris	14

10. In the latter pair the relation is one of contiguity as well as similarity, the *uirgulta* 'brushwork' grown to support the grapevines.

V_2	seruassis	15
+		
V_1	duisque	16.

Moving the last verb *duis* to the head of its clause ('fronting') is what enables it to carry the critical conjunction *-que*; all the other verbs are clause final.

The verb phrases in strophe II, diseases forbid, devastation ward off, storms brush aside, must be read "vertically":

II
morbos uisos inuisosque
uiduertam uastitudinemque
calamitates intemperiasque
prohibessis defendas auerruncesque.

The result is a structure like an upside down T:

o o
o o
o o
o o o

The same "verticality" is carried over into the first member of the triad in the antistrophe, where *fruges frumenta* 'grain' goes with *grandire* 'grow tall' (cf. *grandia farra, camille, metes* 'tall corn, boy, you'll reap' Paul. Fest. 82 L) and *uineta uirgultaque* 'vineyards' with (*du*)*eneque euenire* 'turn out well' (cf. the god *Bonus Euentus* 'Good Outcome', Varro *R.R.* 1.1.6). Thus

III	fruges frumenta	uineta uirgultaque
	grandire	dueneque euenire siris
	pastores pecuaque	salua seruassis
	duisque duonam salutem	ualetudinemque.

The underlying formula of line 13 is **fruges uinetaque*, a merism 'grain and grape' indexing the totality of the products of the earth. When each noun underwent doubling,

*fruges → fruges frumenta
*uinetaque → uineta uirgultaque

a rule moved the enclitic *-que* from *uineta* to the following *uirgulta* (which misled Benveniste to think of the whole as mere enumeration).

The greater complexity in grammatical figures of antistrophe III is apparent not only in the first member of the triad (13-14), but also in the mirror image order of the noun and verb constituents in the second and third (15, 16): Noun Noun Verb—Verb

Noun Noun. Recall finally the ring-composition which by semantic antithesis links the first word of II *morbos* 'sickness' with the last word of III, *ualetudinemque* 'health'.

We have examined the level of theme, where meaning is in play, and the level of grammar, where only grammatical meaning is relevant: the domain of the grammatical figure. We come now to the level of sound alone: the domain of the phonetic figure. Every line of II and III is marked by recurrent sound features, indeed every word is linked to another by such a figure. These equivalence tokens are remarkably varied, ranging over alliteration, homoioteleuton, internal rhyme, and phonic echo. In the following, boldface roman capitals are used for phonetic figures, and boldface italic capitals for figures that are both phonetic and grammatical. The conjunction *-que* is italicized to draw attention to its position in each strophe:

8	morbos ***VISOS***	in***VISOS****que*
9	**V**iduertatem[11]	**V**astitudinem*que*
10	c**A**l**A**mit**A**tes	intemperi**A**s*que*
11	prohibess***IS***defend***AS***	auerrunc***ES****que,*[12]
12	**FRV**ges **FRV**menta	**VI**neta **VI**rgulta*que*
13	grand**IRE**	d**VENE***que* **EVEN-IRE** s**IR*IS***
14	**P**astores **P**ecua*que*	**S**alua **S**ervass***IS***
15	**DV*IS****que* **DV**onam sal**VT**em	ualet**VD**inem*que.*[13]

My analysis of the lustral prayer has been hitherto resolutely synchronic and descriptive in character, without attention to external comparison or to diachronic, historical considerations. But the text is as rich in comparative material as it is in figures of sound and form. Let us survey these, beginning again with the thematic level and continuing through to the formulaic, and finally to the phonological level of rhythm and meter.

On the level of theme the most striking comparison in prayers across the Indo-European world is the threefold scourge which is prayed against and—less commonly—the threefold benefice which is prayed for. Benveniste[14] had already noted the Old Persian prayer of Darius at Persepolis, DPd 15-20 *imām dahạyāum auramazdā pātuv hacā haināyā hacā dušiyāra hacā drauga abiy imām dahạyāum mā ājamiyā mā hainā mā dušiyāram mā drauga* 'May Ahuramazda protect this land from enemy

11. This word is a hapax, found only here; it is properly 'widow(er)hood', 'le fait de rendre veuf' (Benveniste). It is, I suggest, formed on the surface analogy of *libertatem*: another term of civil status and, in our context, another parameter of phonic echo. Others (OLD) prefer the model to be *ubertas*, and the meaning 'dearth', from crop failure (so Norden 1939:128). But I think this is excluded by the martial verbs *defendere* and its corresponding *salua seruare*.

12. As transmitted. I think it not unlikely that the text originally had *auerruncassisque* (cf. *auerruncassint* Pacuvius 112) and *defensis* (cf. *bene sponsis* = *spoponderis* Festus 476 L). The phonetic responsions may be adjusted accordingly.

13. I have not indicated vowel quantities. Note before the iambic shortening law and with the expected elision, d**VENE**qu' **EVEN-IRE** s**IR-IS**.

14. 1945:11, reiterated 1969:1.289. Boyce 1982:2.121 (with references) terms this passage 'traditional', 'three stereotyped evils which might assail society.'

army, from bad harvest, from Deceit. Upon this land may there not come either enemy army or bad harvest or Deceit.'

Benveniste also noted a mantra from the TS 1.1.13.3 *pāhí prásityai pāhí dúriṣṭyai pāhí duradmanyaí* 'protect from bondage, protect from bad worship, protect from bad food.'[15]

Other traditions offer close parallels. In Hesiod's *Works and Days* 225-47, the good consequences of the just ruler—health, peace, and prosperity—are contrasted with the evil consequences of the unjust ruler: famine, plague, and devastation. The genre is that of wisdom literature, and as such may be in large part diffused from Mesopotamia. See the rich discussion in M. L. West's commentary.

I have further compared (Watkins 1979b:189ff.) the threefold scourge in the Hittite prayer of Mursilis II to the Sun Goddess of Arinna, which is in traditional language with an at least Middle Hittite (15th cent. B.C.) archetype (Carruba 1969:240). KUB 24.4 + Ro. 21-2:

> nu=ššan ḫinkan kūrur kaštan *ANA* KUR ^{URU}Mittanni *ANA* KUR ^{URU}Kizzuwatni *ANA* KUR ^{URU}Arzawa tarnatten
>
> Loose *plague*, *war*, *famine* on the lands of Mittanni, Kizzuwatna, Arzawa.

In that study I was concerned with parallels to the 7th-century Old Irish Mirror of Princes text *Audacht Morainn* edited by Kelly (1976), notably the phrase §12, as emended:

> Is tre fír flaithemon mortlithi
> márslóg márlóchet di doínib dingbatar
>
> It is by the ruler's Truth that *plagues*, a *great army*,
> *great lightnings* are warded off men.

As I pointed out there, the tripartite organization of the phraseology in these prayers and similar genres is a fact, whether or not one wishes to interpret them in the light of the theories of Dumézil. The most ardent Dumézilian would probably be reluctant to view as a direct Indo-European inheritance an Irish "prayer" recorded in North Mayo in the 1960's and published in 1970 by J. N. Hamilton. The speaker describes the custom of throwing away the first glass of the singlings (what first passes over in distilling), for the *daoiní maith*', the fairies, when making poteen (*poitín*, home-

---

15. The TS 'triad' is actually preceded by *pāhí mā 'dya divaḥ* 'protect me today from the sky (= lightning)' and followed by *pāhí dúścaritād* 'protect from evil deed.' Of the parallel passages in the Yajurveda VS 2.20 begins *pāhí mā didyóḥ* 'protect me from lightning', followed by the triad through 'bad food'; the older KS 1.12 has *pāhi vidyot* 'protect from lightning' with analogical ablative (Wackernagel, AiGr. 3.151) and the triad with the correct genitive-ablatives *prasityāḥ* etc. (ibid. 3.39). But since TS 1.8.14.1 has separate *mṛtyór mā pāhi didyón mā pāhi* (also ŚB 12.8.3.11) 'protect me from death, protect me from lightning', with further parallels elsewhere, the latter phrase may be an addition to the original triad, termed a *Spruch* by Wackernagel loc. cit.

distilled whiskey). 'And this is what we used to say when we were throwing out the first glass':

> Maith agus sláinte go ndéanaidh sé daoibh,
> Agus toradh agus tairbh' go gcuiridh sé 'ugainn,
> Agus go sábhálaidh sibh aig ár námhaid muid
>
> May it bring you health and goodness,
> and may it bring us good result and profit,
> and may you save us from our enemy.

Of the formulaic figures in Cato's prayer several have close verbal parallels and analogues elsewhere. The figure 'seen and unseen', Argument plus Negated Argument, is grammatically and structurally paralleled by Umbrian (*Tab. Ig.* VI b 59-60)

> nerf śihitu anśihitu
> iouie hostatu anhostatu
>
> chief citizens girt (and) ungirt
> young men under arms (and) not under arms,

a sort of "magic square" designating the totality of the four enemy armies cursed. We find the same in the great Hittite prayer of Muwatallis to the Storm God *piḫaššaššiš* (CTH 381, KUB 6.45 iii 4-8):

> [DINGIR LÚ^{MEŠ}] DINGIR SAL^{MEŠ} *ŠA* LUGAL-*RI Ù ŠA* SAL.LUGAL-*TI* kuieš daran[teš] kuieš *ŪL* daranteš kuetaš *ANA* É^{MEŠ} DINGIR^{MEŠ} LUGAL SAL.LUGAL piran EGIR-pa iyantari kuetaš=a[t] *ANA* É^{MEŠ} DINGIR^{MEŠ} *ŪL* iyantari
>
> [Male gods] and female gods of king and queen, those invo[ked] and those not invoked, those in whose temples the king and queen officiate and those in whose temples they do not officiate.

The nominal relative clauses *kueš* (*natta*) *taranteš* recall also the Archaic Latin formula *qui patres qui conscripti* designating the totality of senators, patrician and plebeian (Festus 304 L).[16]

We have even the identical semantics and root of *uisos inuisosque* in the Umbrian formula four times repeated (VIa 28, 38, 48, VIb 30) *uirseto auirseto uas* 'seen (or) unseen ritual flaw', though the morphology is different (*uīsus* < **u̯id-to-*, *uirseto* < **u̯idē-to-*), and with identical semantics but a different root, Atharvavedic *dr̥ṣṭám adŕ̥ṣṭam* (*krímim*) 'seen (and) unseen (worm)' 2.31.2, *dr̥ṣṭā́ṃś ca ghnann adŕ̥ṣṭāṃś ca* 'slaying the seen and unseen (worms)' 5.23.6, *dr̥ṣṭáś ca hanyatām krímir/ utā́dŕ̥ṣṭaś ca hanyatām* 'may the seen worm be slain, and may the unseen be slain'

16. Still valuable Benveniste 1966:208-22, esp. 220.

5.23.7. Note in these Latin, Umbrian, and Vedic formulas the three rhythmic variants of the Indo-European bipartite noun phrase: asyndeton *A B*, conjoined *A B*-$k^{u}e$, doubly conjoined *A*-$k^{u}e$ *B*-$k^{u}e$. The relevance of the Vedic to Cato's *morbos uisos inuisosque* was first seen by Durante 1958. The phrase has every right to be considered an Indo-European formula, the more so since in several traditions (Indic, Germanic) 'worm' is a metaphor for 'disease'. See in greater detail on these part VII.

We noted above on *defendas . . . seruassis* (both V_2) Ennius *Scen.* 6 V *serua ciues, defende hostes* 'save the citizens, repulse the foe'; on *fruges frumenta . . . grandire* the agricultural carmen in P. Fest. 82 L *hiberno puluere, uerno luto / grandia farra, camille, metes* 'with winter dust and spring mud, tall corn, boy, you'll reap', and on *beneque euenire* the agricultural god *Bonus Euentus* 'Good Outcome' (Varro, *R. R.* 1.1.6).

The underlying merism **fruges uinetaque* 'grain and grape' (doubled in *fruges fru. uineta ui.*) recurs over the Mediterranean world. From Homer note the flexible formula *Il.* 9.706 etc. σίτου καὶ οἴνοιο (σίτοο καὶ ϝοίνοιο) 'grain and wine' and numerous variants, as well as *Od.* 4.746 etc. σῖτον (-ος) καὶ μέθυ ἡδύ 'grain and sweet wine'. The earliest Indo-European examples are already in Old Hittite: twice in a fragment concerning Alluwamnas and Harapsilis (KUB 26.77 i 5,8) *n[u ḫ]alkieš* GEŠTIN$^{\text{ḪI.A}}$-*ešš=a ḫarki[r* 'grains and vines perished', and once in the Telepinus edict (§ 20), *n=an kiššа[(ri=šši ḫalkiuš)* DINGIR^{MEŠ}*(-iš)]* GEŠTIN$^{\text{ḪI.A}}$-*uš* GUD$^{\text{ḪI.A}}$-*uš* UDU$^{\text{ḪI.A}}$-*uš Ū[L pēter* 'and the gods did not bring (?) grains (and) vines, cattle (and) sheep into his hand'.[17] The context in both is traditional and formulaic: the consequences to the land of the wicked ruler in the *speculum principum* or Mirror of Princes.

Note that in the last passage (and also in the Telepinus myth iv 29-30) we have two inherited formulaic merisms in a row:[18] a recurrent feature of early Indo-European traditional texts, which may indicate that these formulas were learned in groups. Other instances will be noted further in this work.

'Grain (and) wine' are of course part of the common and doubtless universal formulaic verb-phrase merism 'eat (and) drink', as in *Il.* 5.341 οὐ γὰρ σῖτον ἔδουσ', οὐ πίνουσ' αἴθοπα οἶνον 'for they eat not grain nor drink flaming wine', nominalized in πόσιος καὶ ἐδητύος 'drinking and eating' (*passim*). In Old Hittite the formula 'eat (and) drink' is basically equivalent to 'live happily' Telepinus edict § 23 *pāndu=wa=z ašandu nu=wa=za* ***azzikandu akkuškandu*** *idālu=ma=šmaš=kan lē kuiški taggaši* 'Let them go (and) dwell (there); let them eat (and) drink, but let no one do harm to them.' For the condensed banishment formula cf. also KUB 26.77 i 13 (Alluwamnas fragment) *pāntu=war=i apiya aš[antu* 'Let them go (and) dwell there.' 'Eat (and) drink' figures in the Old Hittite/old script text KBo 22.1, 28′-30′, where the switch in pronominalization from 2 pl. to 2 sg. indicates the homiletic material (here enclosed in double quotes) is taken from a traditional source: . . . *ta* ^{LÚ}*ḫappinandaš īštēni parna=šša paiši ezši eukši piyanazzi=a=tta* . '. . . You (pl.) do the will of the rich man. "You (sg.) go to his house, you (sg.) eat (and) drink, and he gives you (sg.) presents."'

17. For the readings of this passage and for other examples of the phrase in Old and Middle Hittite see Watkins 1979a:283-4.

18. For 'cattle (and) sheep', Gross- und Kleinvieh, the totality of domestic animals, see the paper cited in the preceding note.

But it is the phrase *pastores pecuaque salua seruassis* which is the most astonishing in its formulaic wealth and the diachronic developments that lie behind it. These are paradigmatic for continuity and change, retention and innovation in Indo-European formulaic sequences.

The Indo-European formula is

PROTECT MEN (and) CATTLE,

which we may reconstruct lexically as

**pah₂- u̯ih̯ₓro- peḱu-*.

The history of this formula was given by me in 1979 in the article just cited, building principally on the work of Wackernagel and Benveniste. I briefly recapitulate it here.

The Indo-European folk taxonomy of wealth included inter alia the following branching semantic features:

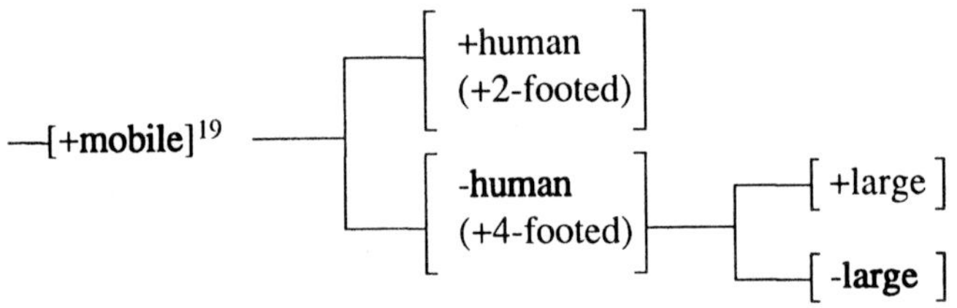

Indo-European **peḱu-* could denote any of the three in boldface, in increasing order of markedness. Compare RV 3.62.14 *dvipáde/cátuṣpade ca paśáve* '2-footed and 4-footed *paśús*', Umbrian (*Tab. Ig.* VIb 10) *dupursus peturpursus* 'for 2-footed (men) (and) 4-footed (cattle)'.

Eleven times in the Umbrian Iguvine Tables VIa-VIIa we find repeated the triadic strophe

nerf arsmo	magistrates (and) formulations,
uiro pequo	men (and) cattle,
castruo frif	heads [of grain][20] (and) crops,

followed by *pihatu* 'purify' (6x) or *salua seritu* 'keep safe' (7x). As has been known since 1910[21] *uiro pequo* is an Indo-European formulaic merism 'MEN (and) CATTLE', on the comparison of Young Avestan *pasu(.)vīra* 'id.' in the reverse order (Yt. 13.12

---

19. Compare *Od.* 2.75 κειμήλιά τε **πρόβασίν** τε 'riches which lie and riches which move'; Hittite ***iyatar*** *dametar* 'riches which go (and) riches which build' = 'plenty (and) abundance'; English *goods and* ***chattels***, Middle and Early Modern English *goodes and* ***cattel***.

20. Cf. Umbr. *pusti kastruvuf* 'per capita'. For the metaphor in 'heads of grain' compare Old Hittite *ḫalkiaš ḫaršār* ... ZÍZ$^{HI.A}$-*ašš=a ḫaršār* 'heads of grain, heads of spelt', ritual for the Royal Couple (StBoT 8) iv 19-20, cf. 32.

21. Wackernagel 1953:1.280-83, cf. Schmitt 1967.

etc.), and Gathic *pasu- vīra-* in various cases.[22] The reconstructible **u̯ihxro- peḱu-* as a merism corresponds to the middle node of the model of taxonomy of moveable wealth just given. 'Men' as a form of moveable wealth in all these traditions means 'slaves'.[23]

The Latin alliterative merism *pastores pecuaque* is the equivalent and in this formula the replacement of the same merism, as shown by Benveniste.[24] Note also *cum adhibent in pecuda pastores* 'when they bring in shepherds to the sheep' Cicero, *De rep.* 4.1. I later (1979a:275) adduced Varro, *R.R.* 2.1.12 *pecudes minores* 'small cattle' (sheep, goats, pigs), *pecus maius* 'large cattle' (cows, asses, horses)—thus the right-hand node of the model of the taxonomy [+/-large]—and continuing with *tertia pars in pecuaria . . . muli canes* ***pastores*** 'the third sort of cattle . . . mules, dogs, shepherds'. Varro's scholasticism produced this nonsense by combining and expanding two ancient and inherited paired concepts: *pecus minus, pecus maius* on the one hand, *pecus, pastores* on the other.

Benveniste in the two studies cited (1970, 1969) was also the first to recognize that the whole verb phrase of our Latin prayer had an exact cognate in the repeated Umbrian prayer:

pastores pecuaque	salua seruassis
uiro pequo . . .	salua seritu

Both go back to a Common Italic formula, and as I showed (1979a:277-80) this whole formula has correspondents in both Vedic and Avestan, a Common Indo-Iranian formula which together with that of Common Italic goes back to a Common Indo-European prototype. Both Old and Young Avestan preserve the two nouns intact, always in the order *pasu-*, *vīra-* and with the verb *ϑrā-* 'protect':

Y.50.1 kə̄ mōi pasə̄uš kə̄ mə̄nā ϑrātā vistō

Who has been found to be the protector of my cattle, who of me?

Yt.13.10 ϑrāϑrāi pasuuå vīraiiå

for the protection of cattle (and) men.

With Y.50.1 *kə̄ . . . ϑrātā* compare the strikingly similar RV 4.55.1, hymn-initial (the Avestan is line 2 of the 1st strophe):

kó vaḥ trātā́ vasavaḥ kó varutā́

22. Wackernagel analyzed the Umbrian and Young Avestan forms as dual dvandvas (acc.); the Umbrian could just be neuter plural.

23. Benveniste 1970:308 n. 3, with references to Lüders (Indic), Sittig (Italic), and Gershevitch (Iranian). Whence Greek ἀνδραπόδεσσι (Homer +) 'slaves' '2-footed chattels' beside Mycenean *qetoropopi* [kʷetropopphi] '4-footed chattels'. Note also Vergil *Georgics* 1.118 *hominumque boumque labores* 'the toil of men and oxen', as pointed out to me by Richard Thomas.

24. 1945:6,11 and more clearly in 1970:309, condensed in 1969:148-50.

who of you is the protector, o good ones, who the keeper?

Rhetorically the Vedic double agent noun parallels the Avestan double object; we may have an Indo-Iranian topos of the language of prayer.

Vedic has replaced the word for 'man' by the alliterative *púruṣa-*. In one example, 'protect' is expressed negatively, 'not harm':

AV 3.28.5,6	sā́ no mā́ hiṁsīt púruṣān paśū́ṃś ca
(refrain)	Let her not injure our men and cattle.

In another, 'protect' is the verb *trā-*, the cognate of Iranian *ϑrā-*, and the original merism has been expanded:

AV 8.7.11 trā́yantām asmín grā́me
gā́m áśvaṃ púruṣaṃ paśúm

Protect in this village
cow, horse, man, *paśu*.[25]

We may note one important fact in all the languages which attest the formula, however they may vary the order of the constituents and their morphosyntax. The reconstructible Indo-European formula PROTECT MEN (and) CATTLE, **pah$_2$- u̯ih$_x$ro- peḱu-*, is a whole verb phrase, not just the noun phrase **u̯ih$_x$ro- peḱu-*. It is furthermore as old an Indo-European formula as we can find; it is more securely based on cognates than 'imperishable fame' and syntactically more complex; and the evidence for it is not limited to the Greco-Aryan dialect area.[26] We may display the "stemma" of our formula as follows:

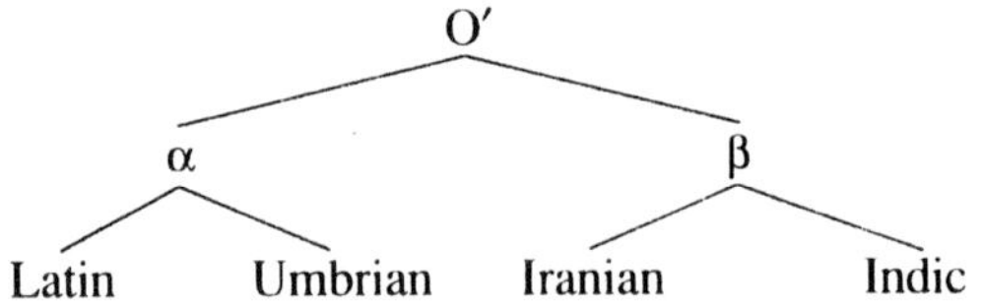

Each of the nodes α and β corresponds to an Indo-European intermediary common language (*langue commune intermédière*): Italic, Indo-Iranian. But more importantly, each is defined by a common innovation (or shared "error") in the transmission of the formula: the replacement of the verb **pah$_2$-* 'protect' in Italic by the verb phrase *salua ser*(*u*)- 'keep safe',[27] and the replacement of **pah$_2$-* in Indo-Iranian by the verb *trā-*, a root confined to this branch. Further innovations ("errors") in the transmission of

25. Here clearly the more highly marked 'small cattle', Kleinvieh, petit bétail.

26. A point also emphasized in another context in a recent work by Campanile (1987).

27. This innovation may be post-Common Italic and attributable to later diffusion in Italy (spread from one of the branches of the Italic family), as discussed in chap. 18. But the stemma is unaffected.

the formula are the Latin substitution of alliterative *pastores* for 'men' and the Indic substitution of the likewise alliterative *púruṣa-*, as well as the expansion of the original merism in

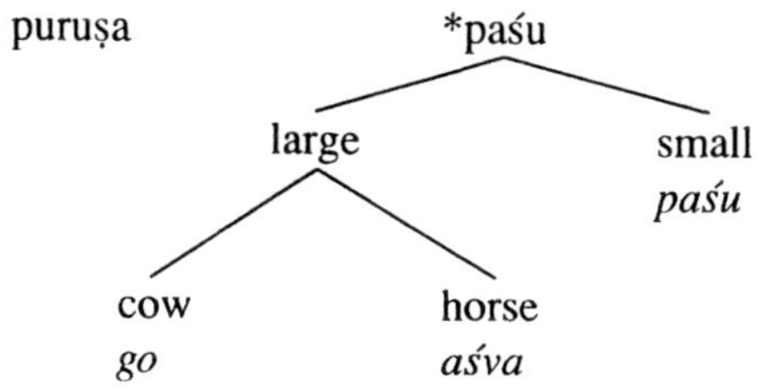

It will be observed that none of the four languages shows a direct reflex of the verb **pah$_2$-* 'protect' in the formula. Neither the Italic phrase *salua seru-* nor the Indo-Iranian *trā-* are of demonstrable Indo-European antiquity. I restore **pah$_2$-* as a likely candidate for the Indo-European lexical expression because it is used in both Indic and Iranian in the traditional trifunctional enumeration of the three scourges in the texts adduced by Benveniste.

More tricky to demonstrate but potentially of great interest are the associative semantics (contiguity relations) of the formula **pah$_2$- u̯ih$_x$ro- pek̂u-* and its various permutations. Latin *pās-tōrēs* may be a formulaic echo of **pah$_2$-*, and the Italic phrase *salua seru-*—note the echoic consonantism **s - lu̯- s - ru̯-**—which replaced **pah$_2$-* may have formulaic links with **pek̂u-* as evidenced both in Avestan *hauruua.fšu-* 'with intact livestock' (: *salua*) and Avestan (*spa-*) *pasuš.hauruua-* 'sheep-guarding (dog)' (: *seruassis*). Recall the link *defendere - seruare*, and compare Vergil *Ecl.* 7.47 *solstitium pecori defendite* 'ward off the summer heat from the flock.' To expose such formulaic links, which constitute a potentially vast network, is one of the important tasks of the future for the Indo-European comparatist-littérateur.

18

Umbria: The Tables of Iguvium

Among the most interesting texts that antiquity has left us are the seven bronze tablets discovered in 1444 in Gubbio, Latin Iguvium, a small town of Umbria, where they still remain. The Iguvine tables, by far our most extensive source of information for the Umbrian language, are no less important for the study of religion in ancient Italy, for they consist of an extremely detailed set of liturgical and cultic instructions for a college of priests, the Atiedian Brethren. As the late Arnaldo Momigliano wryly remarked (1963:115), 'Like the laws of Gortyna, the Iguvine Tables owe something of their fascination to the double fact of being preserved near the place where they originally stood, and of being very difficult to understand.'

Tablets VI and VII are written in the Latin alphabet, probably in the 1st century B.C.; their content is nearly identical to that of Tablet I, written in the native Umbrian alphabet (derived from the Etruscan) probably in the 3rd century B.C., but with the important difference that Tablets VI and VII include the full text of all the prayers and invocations only alluded to in I. They are thus invaluable for the study of the poetic form of Umbrian liturgical language as well.

I begin with the first of three virtually identical prayers accompanying the sacrifice of three oxen to Jupiter Grabovius, the first of the 'Grabovian' triad *Di*, *Marte*, *Vofione*, which strikingly recalls the old Roman triad *Iuppiter*, *Mars*, *Quirinus*.[1] Though not all scholars accept the Dumézilian account of these Roman and Umbrian deities, a more adequate hypothesis has yet to be proposed. The interpretation has in any case no consequence for the poetic analysis of the prayer itself.

In order to show the manner in which the inherited figures, many of which we saw in the preceding section, are incorporated into a liturgical whole, I present this first prayer in its entirety (VIa 22-34), dividing into line units of syntactic cohesion.[2]

teio subocau suboco	Thee I invoke an invoking,
dei graboui	Jupiter Grabovius,

1. Benveniste 1945:6-9 first provided the etymology of *Vofion-* as **leudhi̯ōno-* (**loudhi̯ōno-*) to Lat. *Līber*, German *Leute*.

2. The text is readily available in Poultney 1959. For later literature and invaluable discussion see Meiser 1986.

ocriper fisiu totaper iiouina	for the Fisian Mount, for the Iguvine State
erer nomneper erar nomneper	for the name of that, for the name of this.[3]
fos sei pacer sei	Be favorable, be propitious,
ocre fisei tote iiouine	to the Fisian Mount, to the Iguvine State
erer nomne erar nomne	to the name of that, to the name of this.
arsie tio subocau suboco	In the formulation[4] I invoke thee
	an invoking,
dei graboue	Jupiter Grabovius;
arsier frite tio subocau suboco	in trust of the formulation I invoke thee
	an invoking,
dei graboue	Jupiter Grabovius.
di grabouie	Jupiter Grabovius,
tio esu bue peracrei pihaclu	thee (I invoke) with this yearling ox as
	purificatory offering
ocreper fisiu totaper iouina	for the Fisian Mount, for the Iguvine State
irer nomneper erar nomneper	for the name of that, for the name of this.
dei grabouie	Jupiter Grabovius,
orer ose persei ocre fisie pir	in that rite if on the Fisian
orto est	Mount fire has arisen
toteme iouine arsmor dersecor	or in the Iguvine State the due
subator sent	formulations have been omitted,
pusei neip heritu	(bring it about)[5] that (it be) as not intended.
dei crabouie	Jupiter Grabovius,
persei tuer perscler uaseto est	if in your sacrifice there has been any flaw,
pesetomest peretomest	any defect, any transgression,
frosetomest daetomest	any deceit, any delinquency,
tuer perscler uirseto auirseto	(if) in your sacrifice there is
uas est	any seen or unseen ritual flaw,
di grabouie	Jupiter Grabovius,
persei mersei esu bue peracrei	if it is right with this yearling ox
pihaclu pihafei	as purificatory offering to be purified,
di grabouie	Jupiter Grabovius,
pihatu ocre fisei pihatu tota iouina	purify the Fisian Mount, purify the Iguvine State.
di grabouie	Jupiter Grabovius,
pihatu ocrer fisier totar iouinar nome	purify the name of the Fisian
	Mount, of the Iguvine State;
nerf arsmo	magistrates (and) formulations,
veiro pequo	men (and) cattle,
castruo frif	heads (of grain) and fruits
pihatu	purify.
futu fos pacer pase tua	Be favorable, propitious in thy peace,

3. Literally, 'to the name of this (masculine) [the Fisian Mount], to the name of this (feminine) [the State of Iguvium].'

4. The translation is tentative and modeled on that of Vedic *bráhman-*. Meiser 1986:194 translates *arsmor* as 'Ordnungen', *arsmo-* (and related words like *arsie(r)*) as 'Ordnung, Gesetz'. Vendryes' old etymology (1959:13) to Old Irish *ad* .i. *dliged* 'law, right' and related forms is certainly plausible, though not mentioned by Poultney or Meiser.

5. The gapped verb **fetu** is present in the parallel passage IIa 4.

ocre fisi tote iiouine	to the Fisian Mount, to the Iguvine State
erer nomne erar nomne	to the name of that, to the name of this.
di grabouie	Jupiter Grabovius,
saluo seritu ocre fisi	keep safe the Fisian Mount
salua seritu tota iiouina	keep safe the Iguvine State;
di grabouie	Jupiter Grabovius,
saluo seritu ocrer fisier totar	keep safe the name of the
iiouinar nome	Fisian Mount, of the Iguvine State;
nerf arsmo	magistrates (and) formulations,
veiro pequo	men (and) cattle,
castruo fri	heads [of grain] (and) fruits
salua seritu	keep safe.
futu fos pacer pase tua	Be favorable, propitious in thy peace
ocre fisi tote iouine	to the Fisian Mount, to the Iguvine State
erer nomne erar nomne	to the name of that, to the name of this.
di grabouie	Jupiter Grabovius, thee (I invoke)
tio esu bue peracri pihaclu	with this yearling ox as purificatory offering
ocreper fisiu totaper iouina	for the Fisian Mount, for the Iguvine State
erer nomneper erar nomneper	for the name of that, for the name of this,
di grabouie	Jupiter Grabovius,
tio subocau	thee I invoke.

The similarity in style, rhythm, and temper to Cato's *suouitaurilia* prayer has been evident to all observers over the past century and a quarter, the period of scientific study of the Umbrian language. Let us examine its devices more carefully.

The prayer is bounded by nested ring composition at a distance of more than 50 lines: 1-2 *teio subocau suboco / dei graboui* and 55-6 *di grabouie / tio subocau.*

The insistent, almost relentless doubling of grammatical parallel phrases on the "horizontal" (linear) axis—for/to the Fisian Mount, for/to the Iguvine State, lines 3, 6, 14, 37, 49, 53—is in counterpoint to the "vertical" (non-linear) reference to the following lines 4, 7, 15, 38, 50, 54, for/to the name of this (masc.), for/to the name of this (fem.):

ocriper fisiu ——— totaper iiouina
| |
erer nomneper ——— **erar** nomneper.

The remarkable play on deixis in the Umbrian passage is made possible solely by the different gender marking of the repeated pronoun: 'for the name of this (masculine)', 'for the name of this (feminine)'. The result is a sort of "magic square" which is repeated six times over 12 out of the 56 short lines.[6] See the diagrams in figure 3 below.

The perfect grammatical symmetry of these six "squares" is counterbalanced by the grammatical asymmetry of the two verb phrases which have as object first the Mount and the State and then the name of the Mount and the State: one with *pihatu* (29-

6. For a play on 'N and the name of N' in Vedic note TS 3.3.3.2 *yát te somā́dābhyaṃ nā́ma jā́gr̥vi tásmai te soma sómāya svā́hā* 'What (is) thy undeceived, watchful name, o Soma, to that of thine, o Soma, to Soma hail!'

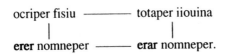

31) and the other with *saluo seritu* (40-43). These two straddle one of the squares (37-38). The symmetry is only partial; the first colon is bipartite and balanced,

29 pihatu ocre fisei pihatu tota iouina,

the second is not:

31 pihatu ocrer fisier totar iouinar nome.

The complexity is increased in 40-43 by the doubling of the sentence-initial imperative to an alliterative phrase *saluo seritu* occupying the same slot: symmetric

40-41 saluo seritu ocre fisi salua seritu tota iouina

but asymmetric

43 saluo seritu ocrer fisier totar iouinar nome.

40-3 are furthermore grammatically more complex since the adjective *saluo/a* of the phrase 'keep safe' must agree with the object of the verb. The two neuter accusatives, adjective *saluo* and noun *nome*, thus frame the whole sentence:

[**sal.** ser. [[ocr. fis. tot. iou.] **nom.**]]].

The symmetrical "squares" and asymmetrical lines occupy 17 of the 56 short lines. The name and epithet of the divinity addressed accounts for 13 more lines.

We have three instances of figura etymologica: *subocau suboco* 1, 8, 10; *pihaclu pihafei . . . pihatu* 27-29; and *pacer pase* 36, 48. In *teio subocau suboco* 1, *arsie tio subocau suboco* 8, *arsier frite tio subocau suboco* 10 we have a figure akin to the κλῖμαξ or *gradatio* of classical rhetoric. The first "square" separates the first and second of the three cola of the latter figure.

The *captatio benevolentiae* formula 'Be favorable (and) propitious' is expressed in 5 with the symmetrical clause-final 2sg. subjunctives *fos* ***sei*** *pacer* ***sei***, before the second "square", and in 36 and 49 before the fourth and fifth "square" with the clause-initial imperative and doubly alliterative but grammatically asymmetrical ***futu fos pacer pase*** *tua* "be favorable (and) propitious in thy peace." F. Leo (cited by Norden 1939:127n.) long ago compared the prayer in Plautus, *Merc.* 678-80:

Apollo, quaeso te ut des **pacem propitius**
salutem et sanitatem nostrae familiae
meoque ut parcas gnato **pace propitius**

Apollo, I beseech thee, **propitious**, that you give **peace**,
haleness, and health to our family,
and that you spare my son, **propitious in thy peace**.

The passage—'das schöne Gebet' (Norden loc. cit.)—also shows close similarities to Cato's *suouitaurilia* prayer. With the first formulation *pacer sei* 'may you be propitious' compare the closely related Marrucinian *pacrsi* 'may it be propitious, acceptable' (Vetter 218, ca. 250 B.C.)

The fourth and fifth "squares", introduced by the *futu fos* formula, are themselves framed by the third and sixth "squares", introduced by the elliptic formula *tiom esu bue peracrei pihaclu* 'thee by this yearling ox as purificatory offering (I invoke, propitiate).' The syntax of *tiom esu bue pihaclu* is identical to that of the corresponding Latin *te hoc porco piaculo* 'thee by this pig as offering (I propitiate)', Cato, *De agr.* 141.4 (and *te hisce suouitaurilibus piaculo* ibid.), down to the very ellipsis of the verb. There is no Latin verb **piaculo* 'I make atonement to', despite the Oxford Latin Dictionary s.v.,[7] as is proved by *macte* **hoc porco piaculo** *immolando esto* (ibid. 139), with the same nouns and an overt verb phrase. The elliptic expression is the rule in Umbrian, with and without *pihaklu*: VIb 28 *tiom esu sorsu persontru tefrali pihaklu* 'thee with this Tefral (divine name Tefer) pork fat as offering'; VIb 14 *tiom esa mefa spefa fisouina* 'thee with this Fisovian (divine name Fisovius) sacrificial flat cake'; VIIa 10/26 *tiom esir uesclir adrir/alfir* 'thee with these black/white vessels'. The oldest and simplest is IIa 25 in the native alphabet, **tiu puni tiu vinu** 'thee with mead, thee with wine'.

In the two phrases

tiom esu bue pihaclu	thee with this ox as offering
te hoc porco piaculo	thee with this pig as offering,

both with ellipsis (gapping of a finite verb), we have a sacrificial formula of Common Italic date, i.e., a formula which might go back to the period of community of the ancestors of Umbrian and Latin.[8]

It is in fact far more likely that this formula was *diffused* over part of the geographic area of Italy, perhaps sometime in the middle of the first millennium B.C., rather than being inherited from a period of linguistic community that might antedate the migration of its speakers into the Italian peninsula. The sacrifical formula in its particularity and cultic setting is rather more characteristic of the first millennium B.C. than an earlier period. In such cases we speak of a linguistic area (German *Sprachbund*, Russian *jazykovyj sojuz*), as in cases like the Balkans, India, or areas of Australia. The direction of the diffusion, the spread of 'areal' features is often indeterminate, particularly where the history is largely unknown. In comparative and historical poetics (and other cultural manifestations) the role of diffusion, as against either genetic transmission or occasional or systematic borrowing (for example of the

7. And Lewis and Short, Forcellini, etc.

8. Methodologically note the equation of two zero signs (the gapped verbs), plus the two accusative pronouns, the two ablative deictics and animal names, and the identical case as well as lexical form in *pihaclu/piaculo*. In both we may see partitive apposition, 'thee by the offering of this pig/ox'. Note also that to assume that *piaculo* in *hoc porco piaculo* is sometimes a 1sg. verb and sometimes an abl. sing. noun in Latin, with translators and lexicographers, is uneconomical given the unambiguous Umbrian *pihaclu*: a 1sg. verb would be **pihaclau*. The Latin ablatives in Cato's time would in any case have still ended in final *-d*, thus eliminating any possible ambiguity.

dactylic hexameter and other meters from Greek into Latin), should not be underestimated, particularly in geographically contiguous and contemporary cultures as in Ancient Italy.[9]

Lines 16-18 and 21-24 are concerned with heading off the consequences of any act which might invalidate the prayer and the ritual: a lightning fire on the mountain, incorrect formulation in the state, or omitted ritual actions: '(Bring it about) that (it be) as not intended' *pusei neip heritu.* The conjunction *pusei* recalls the use of its Latin cognate *uti* (and *utique*) in the *suouitaurilia* prayer. Lines 16-18 come the closest of any in the Umbrian prayer to unadorned prose;[10] but in the balance of *ocr. fis.* and *tot. iou.* they continue the parallelism of the "squares". In intent and function these lines are similar to Cato's instructions at the end of the *suouitaurilia* prayer (141.4): *Si minus in omnis litabit, sic uerba concipito*:

> Mars pater,
> siquid tibi in illisce suouitaurilibus lactentibus
> neque satisfactum est,
> te hisce suouitaurilibus piaculo.

Si in uno duobusque dubitabit, sic uerba concipito:

> Mars pater,
> quod tibi in illoc porco
> neque satisfactum est,
> te hoc porco piaculo.

If favorable omens are not obtained in response to all (three victims), use these words:

> Father Mars,
> if anything in the offering of those sucklings
> did not satisfy thee,
> thee by the offering of these *suouitaurilia* (I propitiate).

If there is doubt about one or two, use these words:

> Father Mars,
> what(ever) in that pig
> did not satisfy thee,
> thee by the offering of this pig (I propitiate).

---

9. For a modern example of cross-linguistic verbal diffusion compare the spread of the expression *no problem, pas de problème, kein Problem* etc. all the way to *s'ka problem* in Albania by at least 1991 (fide C. Reiss). Another typical example is the spread of jokes in contemporary folklore, down to such particulars as the characteristic phonetic distortion in the telling of "the wide-mouthed frog", which I heard exactly repeated in Paris in 1991 as "la grenouille à grande gueule".

10. It is doubtful that in *orer ose . . . ocre . . . orto* we should see intentional alliteration.

The (probably symbolic) contrast in deixis 'those (*illisce*) - these (*hisce*)', 'that (*illoc*) - this (*hoc*)' parallels Umbrian *orer* (not *erer*).

Lines 21-24 of the Umbrian prayer clearly constitute a strophe, bound together by rhythm, repetition, grammatical parallelism, and a double inherited grammatical and formulaic figure. Rhythm and morphological parallelism characterize the center two lines 22-3,

22	pesetomest peretomest	(If there has been) any defect, any trangression,
23	frosetomest daetomest,	any deceit, any delinquency,

all of four syllables (*da-etomest*), and all impersonal 3sg. perfect passives. 22a and 23a are linked by semantics (compare their Latin equivalents *peccatum - fraudatum*); 22a and b are linked by alliteration; and 22b and 23b are linked grammatically as compounds of **ei̯*- 'go', as though they were in Latin **per-itom* and **dē-itom*. We have three sides of a "magic square" again, and the linkage horizontal-sound (alliteration)/ vertical-meaning (semantics) can be exactly paralleled in another Sabellic dialect: Oscan.

The lead tablet curse Vetter 3 (ca. 100 B.C.) is a true *malum carmen*, both for its alliteration and for its semantic catagories. It contains two "magic squares", each consisting of two alliterative merisms, followed by a single merism. These five lines—2 1/2 "squares"—are flanked by the name of the intended victim and the fragmentary dative 2sg. pronoun *tíf[ei* 'to you', referring to the divinity to whom the effectuation of the curse is directed. It is interesting that there is not room in the lacuna for a verb like Latin *trado*, *mando* 'I hand over'; the verb in this utterance as well must have been gapped, understood. Strophically the lines may be presented as

aginss	urinss úlleis	his actions	utterances
fakinss	fangvam	deeds	tongue
biass	biítam	strength	life
aftiím	anamúm	ability[11]	soul
aitatum	amirikum	lifespan	livelihood.

Each horizontal line pair alliterates (boldface); the enclitic possessive *úlleis* comes after the first merism rather than the first word, by an optional poetic version of Wackernagel's rule. Each of the four vertical pairs are semantically similar, i.e. have features in common. The last merism stands alone, as a global merism designating the victim's life (Lat. *aetas*) and the means to live it (: Lat. *merx*). Observe finally that the

11. Following Pisani 1964:95. Meiser's (1986:91) 'sight' from *h_3k^w-*ti*- is semantically out of place in the above scheme, and in any case phonologically impossible.

merism *biass biítam* may be of Common Italic date; with lexical replacement of the first member ('strength') under semantic and grammatical identity (the plural number) it recurs in the alliterative Old Latin *uires uitaque* (Ennius, *Ann.* 38), as we have seen.[12]

Returning to the Umbrian prayer, we saw that lines 22-23 form a symmetrical central "square", bipartite on all sides, in the middle of the strophe. They are framed first by the repetition in 21 and 24 of the genitive *tuer perscler* 'in the sphere of your sacrifice', and then an inherited stylistic figure found in many early Indo-European traditions: the resumption or iteration of a verb form V_i by a nominal form from the same root N_i in a semantically equivalent verb phrase ($N_i + V$), including copula sentence or nominal sentence:

21	uaseto(m)[13] est	(V_i)	(If) there has been any flaw,

literally, impersonal '(if) it has been flawed', with a verb form corresponding to Latin *uacatum est*, beside

24	uas est	($N_i + V$)	If there is a flaw,

with a related abstract noun, *s*-stem **u̯ak-os*.[14] The nominalization in the last example made possible the addition of the likewise inherited merism of adjectives 'seen (and) unseen':

uirseto auirseto uas est.

The latter is the figure of Latin *uisos inuisosque*, Vedic *dr̥ṣṭā́ṁś ca adŕ̥ṣṭāṁś ca* discussed in chap. 17.

The Indo-European stylistic figure (V_i) . . . ($N_i + V$) has been discussed and illustrated in chap. 13.

Of the 56 short lines of this prayer there remain only 6 to be accounted for. These are the two three-line strophes discussed in the preceding chap. 12, the triad of asyndetic merisms

nerf arsmo	magistrates (and) formulations,
ueiro pequo	men (and) cattle,
castruo frif	heads [of grain] (and) fruits,

followed by *pihatu* (32-5) and *salua seritu* (44-7) respectively. The functional hierarchy is the same as that of the central strophes II-III of Cato's prayer, as Benveniste recognized. The structure is thus

12. For the diachronic dynamics see further in chap. 12.

13. The final *-m* is present in the second and third repetitions of the prayer.

14. Morphologically the relation of stative **u̯ak-ē-* (*uasetom*) to **u̯ak-os* (*uas*) parallels Latin *decet* : *decus* and is old.

A_1 (+) B_1
A_2 (+) B_2
A_3 (+) B_3,

and may be read both linearly (horizontally) and vertically: *nerf ueiro castruo* and *arsmo pequo frif*, as in the Oscan curse examined earlier. Note also the little phonetic ring linking the first and last words and thus delimiting the strophe. The last word provides at once a double response:

neRF ↘ FRif and neRF ↘ fRiF.

Compare the phonetic responsion of Sophocles' paean to sleep studied in chap. 55: huPN . . . PaiōN.

Of the other longer Umbrian prayers in tablets VI and VII two contain similar strophic structures. In VIb 10-11 the offering to Fisovius Sancius is accomplished by a prayer:

fisouie sanśie	Fisovius Sancius
ditu	grant
ocre fisie tote iouine	to the Fisian Mount, to the Iguvine State
ocrer fisier totar iouinar	of the Fisian Mount, of the Iguvine State
dupursus peterpursus	to the two-footed (and) the four-footed
fato fito	(success) in word (and) deed
perne postne	before (and) behind
sepse sarsite	hedged (and) whole
uouse auie esone	in vow, in augury, in sacrifice

In *dupursus peturpursus* we have another Indo-European formulaic merism, a specification (and here equivalent) of *ueiro pequo* 'men and cattle', as noted in the preceding section. In the sequence beginning *fato fito* the interpretation of some of the words is still tentative, but the structure is clear: three alliterative two-word figures followed by a three-word figure (grammatically parallel with the same locative ending, homoioteleuton). The four lines have thus the form of an inverted **T**, exactly as we noted in strophe II of Cato's prayer in Latin.

The second of the three bipartite figures belongs to I.1.b of our typology in the preceding section, argument + counter-argument, while the third is I.2.b, argument + synonymous argument. 'Before (and) behind' designates 'everywhere', whereas 'hedged (and) unbroken' is intensive, 'very protected'. The latter, if the usual connection with Latin *sarcire* 'repair, mend (as in fences)' is correct, is similar to both Latin *sane sarteque* 'safe and sound' (with the same adverbial ending as the Umbrian), and Latin *sarcta tecta* 'whole (and) roofed'. They are probably related, either by genetic filiation or by diffusion within Italy.

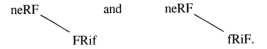

The translation of *fato fito* as 'word (and) deed' is loose, but the two must be related to Latin *fari* 'speak' and *fieri* (as passive of *facere* 'do') respectively, probably $*bhh_2\text{-}to\text{-}$ and $*bhuh_2\text{-}to\text{-}$.[15] Semantically, recall Oscan *aginss urinss* 'actions (and) utterances'.

The final strophe-like structure is found in the ritual curse pronounced on the neighboring peoples, their magistrates and armies, in VIb 58-60, repeated VIIa 47-9:

totam tarsinatem	the Tadinate State,
trifo tarsinatem	the Tadinate tribe,
tuscom naharcom iabuscom nome	the Etruscan, Narcan, Iapudic name,
totar tarsinater	of the Tadinate State,
trifor tarsinater	the Tadinate tribe,
tuscer naharcer iabuscer nomner	of the Etruscan, Narcan, Iapudic name
nerf śihitu anśihitu	the magistrates girt (and) ungirt,
iouie hostatu unhostatu	the young men under arms (and) not under arms
tursitu **t**remitu	terrify (and) make tremble,
hondu **h**oltu	destroy (and) smash (?),
ninctu **n**epitu	fall upon (and) nullify (?),
sonitu **s**auitu	overcome (and) wound (?),
preplotatu **p**reui(ś)latu	trample (and) fetter.

We saw in chap. 12 the figure of 'girt and ungirt' etc., I.1.a Argument + Negated Argument. The remaining set of five alliterative pairs are clearly all I.2.b Argument + Synonymous Argument, even if the translations of the underlined verbs are mere guesses; for the others see Meiser 1986. Both figures have exact parallels in Cato's prayer, strophes II-III. The last is finally linked both by alliteration and grammatical anaphora, the preverbs *pre- . . . pre-*. For the figure compare from the Old Latin Senatus Consultum de Bacchanalibus of 186 B.C. *neue . . . coniourase neue comuouise neue conspondise neue compromesise* 'not to swear, vow, pledge, or make promise with others', almost all hapax legomena.

The poetic units discussed through this chapter are identified and individuated by different type styles and other marks in Figure 3, beginning and ending with the ring in upper case letters.

The systematic links in poetic technique between Cato's prayer and the Umbrian prayers thus go far beyond the simple parallelism in rhythm and alliteration rightly noted long ago by F. Buecheler and E. Norden.[16] The latter could evoke with great charm 'welche Kraft und Natürlichkeit, welcher Ernst und Würde, welche sanctitas,

15. With Meiser 1986:53. Umbrian *fato* probably shows the inherited short of Latin *fat(ĕrī)* rather than the long of *fātus*.

16. 1883 and 1958 [1898[1]] respectively.

kurz welches echt italische Wesen' (p.163).[17] In the domain of poetics we may well think of Ancient Italy in the early to middle first millennium B.C. as a linguistic area. Over this territory certain poetic features, like linguistic features, could be diffused across language boundaries in an ambience of largely shared cultural institutions, both material and symbolic. The analogy with the Balkans, both in language and poetics, is illustrative. In this way we can perhaps more easily account for such "uncanny"—i.e. remarkably particular—similarities as Latin *pastores pecuaque salua seruassis* and Umbrian *ueiro pequo . . . salua seritu*, with both noun phrases occupying second place in a triadic strophic structure, or Oscan *biass biítam* and Latin *uires uitaque*, with the first member of each pair ('strength (and) life') in the plural.[18] In the first case the diffused similarities were building on a conventionally inherited material, as we saw in the preceding section; in the second case the merism may have been created on the soil of Italy. Here also doubtless belongs the shared usage with 'name' illustrated by *tuscom naharcom iabuscom nome* 'Etruscan, Narcan, Iapudic name' and *nomen Romanum* etc. (first attested in the Senatus Consultum de Bacchanalibus, *nominus Latini* 'of Latin name'). The mystical importance of the 'name' is itself probably a universal.

We have spoken frequently of strophic structures in these Italic texts, and we have posited a characteristic Italic ritual offering formula. The next sections look to other traditions to see if these very particular features of Italic verbal style have the possibility of any greater antiquity.

Figure 3

TEIO SUBOCA*U suboco*
dei graboui

ocriper fisiu	totaper iiouina
erer nomneper	erar nomneper

fos **sei** pacer **sei**

ocre fisei	tote iiouine
erer nomne	erar nomne

arsie tio *subocau suboco*
dei graboue
arsier frite tio *subocau suboco*
dei graboue

di grabouie
tio esu bue peracrei pihaclu

ocreper fisiu	totaper iouina
irer nomneper	erar nomneper

dei grabouie

17. 'What power and naturalness, what gravity and worthiness, what *sanctitas*, in short, what real Italicness.'

18. Cf. Homeric βίηφι, (ϝ)ῖφι, with the old instrumental *plural* suffix, whatever their synchronic status.

orer ose persei ocre fisie pir orto est
toteme iouine arsmor dersecor
subator sent

pusei neip heritu

dei crabouie
persei tuer perscler **uaseto(m) est**

pese*tomest* pere*tomest*
frose*tomest* dae*tomest*

tuer perscler uirseto auirseto **uas est**

di grabouie
persei mersei esu bue peracrei
pihaclu pihafei

di grabouie
pihatu ocre fisei pihatu tota iouina

di grabouie
pihatu ocrer fisier totar iouinar nome
ne**RF** arsmo
veiro pequo
castruo **fRiF**
pihatu

futu fos *pacer pase* tua
ocre fisi tote iiouine
erer nomne erar nomne

di grabouie
saluo seritu ocre fisi
salua seritu tota iiouina
di grabouie
saluo seritu
ocrer fisier totar iiouinar nome
ne**RF** arsmo
veiro pequo
castruo **FR**i
salua seritu

futu fos *pacer pase* tua
ocre fisi tote iouine
erer nomne erar nomne

di grabouie
tio esu bue peracri pihaclu
ocreper fisiu totaper iouina
erer nomneper erar nomneper
di grabouie
TIO SUBOCAU

19

Italy and India: The elliptic offering

In the preceding chapter we noted the striking parallelism of the Umbrian and Latin phrases

tiom esu bue pihaclu	thee with this ox as offering
te hoc porco piaculo	thee with this pig as offering.

Both show ellipsis (gapping) of a finite verb of the semantic type 'I propitiate' or the like. In each case the identity of the deity addressed is clearly specified by the ritual context, which involves vocatives or explicit naming in the ritual instructions. The particular similarity of the phrases with the ablative *pihaclu/piaculo* was attributed to diffusion within Italy. Other Umbrian examples were noted with and without *pihaclu*, but the oldest example, in table IIa 25 in the native alphabet, showed a "minimalist" formula simply *tiu puni tiu vinu* 'Thee with mead, thee with wine'. By the very fact of its verbal specification in the older tablets (which systematically omit the text of prayers and most other ritual utterances) this formula in its apparent simplicity may reach much further back in time than the 3rd century B.C.

The ellipsis of a verb, the pronominalization, and the same "minimalist" expression can be closely paralleled elsewhere. As S. Jamison reminds me, in ritual texts of the (Yajur-) vedic and Brāhmaṇa periods in India the almost prototypical and very widespread offering formula (*yájuṣ*) consists of just the name of the divinity in the dative and the second person singular pronoun in the accusative. The formula is thus addressed to the offering itself, whatever it may be, e.g.:

agnáye tvā	To Agni thee.	(TS)
índrāya tvā	To Indra thee.	(TS, MS, etc.)
víṣṇave tvā	To Viṣṇu thee.	(VS, TS, MS, etc.)
mr̥tyáve tvā	To Death thee.	(TS)

References may be found in M. Bloomfield, Vedic Concordance. The deity commonly may have an epithet,

agnáye tvā ā́yuṣmate	To Agni of the long life thee (MS),

or be followed by the ritual cry *svā́hā*,

agnáye tvā svā́hā	To Agni thee, hail! (TS),

or both:

agnáye tvā vásumate svā́hā	To Agni of the wealth thee, hail! (MS).

The presence of some 1sg. verb governing the pronoun 'thee' is considerably less frequent, and more particular in the semantics:

agnáye tvā juṣṭám prokṣāmi (KS, VS, ŚB)

Agreeable to Agni, I sprinkle thee,

índrāya tvā juṣṭám gṛhṇāmi (MS, VS, etc.)

Agreeable to Indra, I take thee.

The formula with just divine name and pronoun can pragmatically be very particular, as in TS 1.2.3.3:

vāyáve tvā, váruṇāya tvā, nírṛtyai tvā, rudrā́ya tvā

To Vāyu thee, to Varuṇa thee, to Nirṛti thee, to Rudra thee,

where A. B. Keith in the note to his translation ad loc. adds 'accompanying the dedication of any (cow) which may be lost or injured (to Vāyu), fallen into water or a noose (to Varuṇa); or have broken a limb or fallen into a pit (to Nirṛti); or have been attacked by a snake or a tiger (to Rudra).' It is the *deixis* (IE **deiḱ-*) implicit in the two grammatical relations, the dative argument of the god's name—the indirect object and the destination ('to Rudra')—and the accusative argument of the offering addressed ('thee')—the direct object and the governed case par excellence—which is at once pragmatically all-important and all that matters. The Brāhmaṇa to this TS passage expresses this perfectly clearly (TS 6.1.4.7):

yád evám etā́ nā́nudiśéd áyathādevataṃ dákṣiṇā
gamayed ā́ devátābhyo vṛścyeta
yád evám etā́ anudiśáti yathādevatáṃ dákṣiṇā
gamayati ná devátābhyo ā́ vṛścyate

> (He says, 'To Vāyu thee, to Varuṇa thee.') If he did not so specify them (*anu diś*, IE **deiḱ-*), he would put the offerings out of correspondence with the deities, and he would fall a victim (*ā vraśc*) to the deities. Because he thus specifies them, he puts the offerings in correspondence with the deities, and does not fall a victim to the deities.

Ritual correctness is recognized here as all-important; improper specification (IE **deiḱ-*) leads to destruction and chaos, for the verb *vraśc* 'hew' in the active is commonly used in place of SLAY (**gʷhen-*) in the basic serpent-slaying formula (on which see chap. 27.3),

HERO SLAY SERPENT (with WEAPON),

which symbolizes the destruction and elimination of chaos: RV 4.17.7 *áhiṃ vájreṇa . . . ví vṛścaḥ* 'you hewed apart the serpent with the cudgel.' Recall finally RV 3.33 examined in chap. 6, on the power of the word: the poet's narration of Indra's exploit by the basic formula using this verb first, *yád áhiṃ vivṛścát* 'when he hewed apart the serpent', then *ví . . . jaghāna* 'he smote apart', is sufficient to persuade the two torrential rivers to still their course.

The focus of the two Italic ritual formulas, Umbrian and Latin 'Thee by (this) pig/ox/wine/mead', where the deity is addressed (and specified by context), is different from the Vedic 'For god N thee', where the offering is addressed (and specified by context). But the grammatical relations of *deixis* are quite similar: accusative/instrumental argument (***tiu vinu*** 'Thee with wine') beside dative/accusative (*agnáye tvā* 'To Agni thee'). Both have a directly governed 2sg. pronoun 'thee', and both show ellipsis of any verb.

Whether there is a genetic relation between the Italic and Vedic formulas is perhaps unknowable. But more important is to recognize in these two sets of ritual formulas like grammatical responses, using cognate grammatical features, to like religious, pragmatic, and symbolic cultural features, which may themselves be cognate.

20

Strophic structures as "rhythmic prose"? Italic

Our observations of early Latin and Umbrian prayer and liturgy have led to the recognition of demarcated strophic structures which can be broken into relatively short lines which correspond to syntactic units. These lines are often ornamented by alliteration and other phonetic figures, and may and usually do exhibit characteristic rhetorical and grammatical figures (as for example those catalogued in chap. 17, merisms, Argument + Negated Argument and the like). The lines commonly involve counting entities, for example sequences of dyads followed by a triad or a monad. The entities counted are usually stressed words, accompanied or not by enclitic elements: X Y, X Y-*que*, X-*que* Y-*que* are all dyads with two stresses in Latin, but each has a different rhythmic character.

We may emphasize finally that the "lines" of these strophes are informed and penetrated by *responsions* on every level of grammar: responsions of sound and responsions of meaning, responsions of words, grammatical catagories, and syntactic structures. They are the links which articulate and index the whole. These responsions are, in short, *equivalence tokens*.

It is clear that these verbal structures in the litanies in their respective languages are very different from ordinary prose in the same languages, which shows typically longer sentences of more complex syntactic structure, absence of ornamentation, absence of systematic responsion of any sort, and in particular no attention to the quantification of rhythmic entities. Both the latter two are manifestations of Jakobson's *equivalence*.

It is equally clear in the case of Early Latin that the verbal form of these prayers is not the contemporary Saturnian verse form as we know it from third-century poets like Livius Andronicus and Naevius. Even if scholars are not agreed on just exactly how the Saturnian meter works, the interplay of rhythm, quantity, syllable count, the metrical and syntactic function of the break, and the strong sense of line-final cadence are wholly different from the style of anything in Cato's prayer. Consider such verses as Livius Andronicus 18 Buechner:

namque nullum peius | macerat homonem
quamde mare saeuom; | uires cui sunt magnae,
topper confringent | inportunae undae.[1]

For nothing torments a man worse
than the wild sea; even one of great strength
is soon brought down by the heedless waves.

Note also Naevius 5 Buechner:

| Amborum uxores
noctu Troiad exibant | capitibus opertis,
flentes ambae, abeuntes | lacrimis cum multis.

the wives of both
left Troy by night with covered heads
weeping both, departing with many tears.

The tone of these enjambed lines is "modern" and Hellenized, even if their meter were a purely native Italic one, which for the Saturnian is uncertain.

Furthermore, if we consider two good non-Latin examples of an Italic 'Segenswunsch' or blessing formula, both of which are probably metrical (whether Saturnian or not is disputed), the difference in both style and temper from either Cato's or the Umbrian prayers is marked. Compare the first line of the Faliscan inscription Vetter 241 discussed in chap. 10:

Ceres far me[la]tom | Louf[i]r ui[no]m [pa]rad

May Ceres provide ground barley, Liber wine,

with the last line of the Paelignian inscription Vetter 213:

dida uus deti | hanustu Herentas

May gracious Venus give you riches.

The initial or final position of each in its text marks the blessing formula as a self-contained, traditional poetic message. Each has a caesura and nearly the same syllable count, respectively [6 || 6] and [5 || 6]. The genre and the meter is quite possibly the same despite the half millennium which separates them: the former is from the 6th, the latter from the 1st century B.C.

For the moment let us retain only that the "strophic style" of early Latin and

---

1. Translating *Od.* 8.138-9 οὐ γὰρ ἐγώ γέ τί φημι κακώτερον ἄλλο θαλάσσης/ἄνδρα γε συγχεῦαι, εἰ καὶ μάλα καρτερὸς εἴη 'For I say there is nothing worse than the sea to confound a man, however strong he may be.'

Umbrian prayer and liturgy is neither ordinary prose nor metrical poetry in the contemporary traditions of each culture. We may leave to others to consider what to call it. The traditional label is "rhythmic prose", but that is far from being even observationally adequate, the more so since the typical responsion of equivalence tokens that "rhythmic prose" shows is precisely 'the essential characteristic of verse'.

The 'Mixed Form' of alternating prose and verse known as the *satura Menippea* (whence the word *satire*) after its alleged inventor Menippus of Gadara (first half of 3rd century B.C.) and familiar from Latin works of Varro (116-27 B.C.), Petronius († 66 A.D.), and Seneca the Younger (4-65 A.D.) is sometimes compared as a third genre, termed prosimetrum in the Middle Ages.[2] At least in its Classical Latin form this genre, with its clear alternation between ordinary prose and canonical metrical verse, is again different in kind from the rhythmic/syntactic, sentence = verse line strophic style of Cato's *suouitaurilia* prayer and the other material surveyed in chap. 17 and the following chapters.

2. See Dronke 1994.

21

Strophic structures in Iranian

We find comparable strophic structures which are generally termed "rhythmic prose" elsewhere. One such is the Old Avestan Yasna Haptaŋhāiti (YH), the 'Yasna of Seven Chapters', as recognized already by the native Iranian tradition and followed by modern editors, notably in the classic edition of Narten (1986). The text Vispered 16.4 applies to the YH the same technical terms as to the Gāthās: *hāitišca afsmanāca vacasca vacastaštīmca* 'chapters and lines and words and strophes'.[1] As Geldner points out in his edition (p. 128), the manuscript tradition marks the strophes (he terms them 'periods') by a punctuation sign. Their division into strophes or 'periods' (*vacastašti-*) is basically that adopted by Geldner and with modifications by Narten, Kellens-Pirart 1988-91, and Humbach-Skjærvø-Elfenbein 1991. Geldner however, noting that the division into verse-lines (he called them clausulae, *Sätzchen*) frequently differed in the Pahlavi and Sanskrit versions, maintained that the greater part of the YH was prose, and so printed it, within each strophe or 'period'. This practice is continued in the two most recent editions.

Narten on the other hand (p. 18ff.) had—to my mind correctly—divided the strophes into "lines" corresponding to smaller syntactic constituents. She uses the terms *cola* and *commata* from Classical metrics and rhetoric, which are the subdivisions of *strophae*; the analogy to the Avestan *hāitišca afsmanāca vacasca vacastaštīmca* is striking. She claims (p. 20) that this line division is 'arbitrary' (*willkürlich*), but the linguistic reality of the syntactic clause and constituent boundaries proves that this is not the case.

Narten does consider the YH to be prose, specifically 'liturgical recitation prose': her description is 'elevated, artfully arranged prose which is close to poetry' (p. 21). She goes on to a detailed enumeration of the stylistic figures exhibited in the YH, to which we shall return. The description is accurate enough; but the judgment of all these scholars that the YH is prose rests on the tacit assumption of a single binary opposition *prose* : *poetry*. The Gāthās are unquestionably poetry, with a variable number of strophes, each with the same number (3-5) of basically isosyllabic lines

1. Note that the Avestan technical term for 'strophe' *vacas-tašti-* as a compound 'word-fashioning' incorporates a metaphor of probably Indo-European date, discussed in chap. 2.

(occasionally ±1 syllable) with a fixed caesura or break (Kellens-Pirart 1988:89ff. with references, to which add Kellens 1991: 7-8). Thus, e.g., 3(7 ‖ 9), 5(4 ‖ 7), 4(4 ‖ 7), 3(7 ‖ 7), and the complex 2(7 ‖ 5) + 2(7 ‖ 7 ‖ 5) with a tricolon. But the fact that the lines (cola, commata) of the strophes of the YH are not syllable-counting ('metrical') does not mean that they are not verse, the more so when the native tradition speaks of them in the same terms as those of the Gāthās. Syllables are not the only equivalence tokens in which 'equivalence is promoted to the constitutive device of the sequence'. We return to the distinction below.

While the YH is clearly not Gathic verse, it is equally clearly not at all like the ordinary prose of the Younger Avesta (e.g. the Videvdat) in style. We have no other non-syllable-counting texts (i.e. non-"metrical" in the Iranian sense) from the Old Avestan period. But if the style of the Younger Avesta is projected back into the older state of the language the difference in style from that of the Yasna Haptaŋhāiti is very pronounced.

Let us then illustrate by the first five strophes of the first chapter (*hāiti*) of the YH (35.2-6):

2 humatanąm hūxtanąm huuarštanąm
    iiadacā aniiadacā
vərəziiamnanąmcā vāuuərəzananąmcā
mahī aibī.jarətārō
naē.naēstārō yaϑənā vohunąm mahī

Of good thoughts, good words, good deeds
    here and elsewhere
being done and having been done
we are welcomers;
not revilers of the good are we.

3 tat̰ at̰ vairimaidī
    ahurā mazdā
    aṣ̌ā srīrā
hiiat̰ ī mainimadicā vaocōimācā varəzimācā
yā hātąm š́iiaoϑənanąm vahištā x́iiāt̰
    ubōibiiā ahubiiā

That we have chosen
    o Wise Lord
    by the beauteous Truth
that we may think, say, and do those deeds
which are the best there are
for both existences.

4 gauuōi ad-āiš
    [tāiš š́iiaoϑənāiš yāiš vahištāiš]
    fraēšiiāmahī

rāmācā vāstrəmcā dazdiiāi
surunuuatascā asurunuuatascā
xšaiiaṇtascā axšaiiaṇtascā

To provide by them for the cow
peace and pasture
we impel
those who hear and those who do not
those who rule and those who do not.

5 huxšaϑrō.təmāi bā aṯ xšaϑrəm
ahmaṯ hiiaṯ aibī
dadəmahicā cīšmahicā huuąnmahicā
hiiaṯ mazdāi ahurāi
aṣ̌āicā vahištāi

For the one of the best rule, as far as in us lies,
the rule
we establish, we procure, we impel:
to the Wise Lord
and the Best Truth.

6 yaϑā āṯ utā nā vā nāirī vā
vaēdā haiϑīm
aϑā haṯ vohū
taṯ.ə̄ə-ād-ū vərəziiōtūcā īṯ ahmāi
fracā vātōiiōtū īṯ aēibiiō
yōi īṯ aϑā vərəziiąn
yaϑā īṯ astī

Even as either man or woman
knows the true
so (do they know) the real[2] good;
therefore let them work it for themselves
and make it known to those (others)
who will work it
as it (really) is.

The rhythmic pattern is the same as we saw in Italic: the counterpoint of triad and dyad, with the occasional monad. And the rhetorical pattern is equally plain. The figures can be described in the same terms as we saw in Italic, esp. chap. 12.1. We have Argument plus Counter Argument ('here and elsewhere'), Argument plus Negated Counter Argument ('welcomers, not revilers'), Argument plus Synonymous Argument ('peace and pasture'), and Argument plus Negated Argument ('those who hear

2. Tichy 1980:14.

and those who do not, those who rule and those who do not'). The last may be read also vertically as Argument plus Counter Argument ('those who hear and those who rule, those who do not hear and those who do not rule' = those who do or do not take orders and those who do or do not give them). It is thus a "magic square", much like Umbrian 'girt and ungirt, under arms and not under arms'.[3]

The threefold climactic anaphora of nominal *humata- hūxta- huuaršta-* is repeated by the same three verbs in the optative *mainimadicā vaocīmācā varzimācā*.[4] We have chiastic word order 'we are welcomers, not revilers are we', and the grammatical figures of present and perfect participle ('being done and having been done') and the line-framing participle and optative of 'be' *hātąm... x́iiāt* ('*are* the best there *are*').

I have cited only 5 strophes and 27 phraseological lines out of 34 strophes and some 224 lines in the YH. The remainder of the text shows the same strophic structure with the same sort of syntactic units for lines and the same stylistic figures. Compare the illustrative catalogue of the latter by Narten, pp. 21-3.

Narten in her rich commentary also calls attention to parallels with Vedic ritual language and vocabulary; these are now systematically augmented by the further collections in Kellens-Pirart at each strophe. I call attention to the strophe YH 38.2 and Narten's discussion pp. 189-210:

vaŋᵛhīm ābiš aṣ̌īm
vaŋᵛhīm īšəm
vaŋᵛhīm āzūitīm
vaŋᵛhīm frasastīm
vaŋᵛhīm parəṇdīm yazamaidē

We worship together with them[5]
good Bestowal
good Refreshment/Invigoration
good Libation
good Glory
good Plenty.

With repeated 'good' compare *(du)onam salutem* and *(du)eneque euenire* of Cato's prayer (like *Bonus Eventus*) and recall Benveniste 1945:11 on 'the notion of "wholeness" so important to every religious phenomenology, to which "good" adds its particular force.' 'Good glory' is attested elsewhere in Old Avestan, the Gāthā Y.49.7d *yə̄ vərəzə̄nāi, vaŋᵛhīm dāṯ frasastīm* 'who will give good glory to the

---

3. See on this figure Campanile 1977:97ff.

4. The same formula with nearly indentical terms in the Taittirīya Āraṇyaka 10.1.12 *manasā vācā karmaṇā vā* 'by thought, word or deed'. See Schlerath 1974. Toporov 1981:199 n. 19 terms it as an Indo-European formula. But it is natural enough to be an independent, parallel creation.

5. The divine 'women' (*gənābīš* = Ved. *gnā́-*) of the preceding strophe, personifications of feminine abstracts as daughters of Ahura Mazdā, divine blessings, like those of our strophe.

community.'[6] As Kellens-Pirart note, beside Avestan *vaŋᵛhīm parə̄ṇdīm* we can set RV 5.41.6cd *púraṃdhīr/vásvīḥ*; v. infra.

Narten (206) identifies all but the first of the personified abstracts as old ritual terms which are Common Indo-Iranian patrimony: Av. *iš-* : Ved. *iṣ-* 'strengthening, refreshment'; Av. *āzūiti-* : Ved. *ā́huti-* 'libation'; Av. *frasasti-* : Ved. *práśasti-* 'glory'; Av. *parə̄ṇdi-* : Ved. *púraṃdhi-* 'the bloom of plenty'.[7] More strikingly, from the parallels adduced by Kellens-Pirart the terms tend to occur in the same order in both Iran and India when two or more appear together. We have here a Common Indo-Iranian semantic and sequential "program" which can be poetically encoded both into the strophic style of "rhythmic prose", as in Iranian, and into the metrical strophic verse of Vedic hymnic poetry.

Compare in this respect the Old Avestan sequence *frasastīm . . . parə̄ṇdīm* beside RV 7.35.2 *śáṃ no bhágaḥ śáṃ u naḥ* ***śáṃso*** *astu śáṃ naḥ* ***púraṃdhiḥ*** 'Propitious to us be Bhaga (fortune), (Narā)śaṃsa (glory), puraṃdhi (plenty)'; RV 2.38.10 *bhágaṃ dhíyaṃ vājáyantaḥ* ***púraṃdhiṃ*** *nárā****śáṃso gnā́s****pátir no avyāḥ* 'striving for fortune, poetry, plenty—may Narāśaṃsa, master of the divine women (*gnā́-* = Av. *gənā-*), help us.' In particular Narten (207n., 210) provides many examples showing that *púraṃdhi-* almost always comes last in such enumerations in the Rigveda. The correspondence in this respect with Old Avestan would point to a common inherited ordering of shared elements of a litany. For other examples of inherited shared order of elements of a list see chap. 58 passim.

The sequence *aṣ̌īm . . . īšəm* of the first two elements recurs Y.28.7 *dāidī . . . aṣ̌īm . . . dāidī . . . īšəm* 'give bestowal . . . give invigoration'. Kellens-Pirart 3.25 cite no less than 5 examples in the Rigveda of *iṣ-* with *dā-* 'give' and 11 with *dhā-* 'place'. The epithet 'good' with *aṣ̌i-* furthermore recurs 3 times in the Gāthās (Y.43.5; 51.10, 21). The word *aṣ̌i-* 'granting, bestowal' from **árti-*[8] has no Indic equivalent.

The occurrence of *īžācā āzūitišcā* 'refreshment and libation' in the Gāthās (Y. 49.5) and in Young Avestan (V.9.53, v. infra) in that order, as well as the clearly Common Indo-Iranian formation and incorporation into shared poetical formulas of Avestan *īš-* and *īžā-*, Vedic *íṣ-*, *íḍ-*, *íḷā-*, *írā-* (50.8 *padāiš . . . īžaiiå* 'footprints of *īžā-*' = RV 3.29.4 *íḷāyās padé*, 6.1.2 etc. *iḷás padé* 'in the place of *íḷ(ā)-*') are enough to show that these are not to be separated from *īšəm . . . āzūitīm*, pace Narten 206.

Not only the individual words of this strophe, but their collocation with *vaŋᵛhī-* = *vásvī-*, their global metaphor as 'divine women' (*gənā-* = *gnā́-*), and their sequential order ending with *vaŋᵛhīm parə̄ṇdīm* = *púraṃdhīr/vásvīḥ* must reflect a ritual litany inherited 'aus urarischer Zeit' (Narten 206, of *āzūiti-* = *ā́huti-*), from Common Indo-Iranian times.

---

6. The hendecasyllable [4 ‖ 7] (*dā̃ṯ*) with syllabic cadence – ⏑ – ⏑ would scan as a perfect triṣṭubh in Vedic, n.b. See Gippert 1986 and Kellens 1991 for other views. Note also the very common figure of two-part noun phrase straddling the verb, as in 49.5c *vohū sārəštā manaŋhā* 'united with good thinking', 7d *vahištē yūjə̄n miždē* 'yoked for the best reward', 31.22c *vāzištō aŋhaitī astiš* 'will be the best fed guest' (Schwartz 1990:202), etc.

7. If IE **pl̥h_1-$h_2$andh-* with K. Hoffmann apud Narten 1986:209.

8. See Hoffmann 1992:843, who derives it from the root *ar-* 'impel' (Vedic *íyarti*, IE **$h_1$er-*). Semantically easier would be connection with Old Irish *ernaid* 'grants, bestows' if from **erh_1-*; but the latter is usually taken from **perh_3-* of πέπρωται, πόρος.

Note the same divine female metaphor and the co-occurrence of *iṣ-* in *iṣudhyú-*[9] (hapax) with *púraṃdhi-* and *vásvī-* in RV 5.41.6:

> **iṣudhyáva** ṛtasā́paḥ[10] **púraṃdhīr**
> **vā́svīr** no ā́tra **pā́tnīr** ā́ dhiyé dhuḥ
>
> May the **invigorating Bounties** caring for Truth,
> the **good wives** (of the gods) reward there our poem.

Here the alliteration ***dhiyé dhuḥ*** calls attention to and reinforces the phonetic icon linking *púraṃ**dhi**-* '(Goddess of) reward for a poem' and ***dhī́-*** '(Goddess of) hymnic poetry, poem' (Geldner ad loc., with other examples). Vedic *puraṃ**dhi**-*: ***dhī́-*** is thus an indexical figure exactly like those discussed in chap. 3: Greek νίκη : τιμή 'victory : honor (conveyed by the poet)' and Old Irish ***dúan*** : ***dúas*** 'poem' : 'recompense for a poem', or Classical Modern Irish ***clú*** : ***cnú*** 'fame (conveyed by the poet)' : 'nut, metaphor for the recompense for a poem'.

The same encoding of sequences of ritual language into metrical hymnic poetry with a personal touch is found in the exuberant first strophe of RV 8.69:

> prá-pra vas triṣṭúbham **íṣam**
> mandádvīrāya índave
> **dhiyā́** vo medhásātaye
> **púraṃdhyā́** vivāsati
>
> (Bring) forth your Triṣṭubh as **invigoration**
> to the drop which intoxicates men;
> **with Poetry**, with bounty she (? *íṣ-* fem.)
> wants to gain for you the sacrificial offering as **reward.**[11]

The poet here in the first strophe of the hymn anagrams his family name Priyamedha (Anukramaṇi):

> **prá-pra** . . . íṣam mandádvī**rāya** índave dhi**yā́** . . . **medhásā**taye.

---

9. See on these words Narten 1986:159-63 and Kellens-Pirart 1991:224. The ritual verb *išūidiia-* = Vedic *iṣudhya-* (2x, family books) is found only in the YH (3x), always in the bipartite formula *namax́iiāmahī išūidiiāmahī* 'we show reverence, we bring invigoration'.

10. The collocation *ṛtám sap-* 'care for Truth' (5.68.4 etc.) and in this compound is also a Common Indo-Iranian verb phrase: *aṣ̌əm . . . haptī* 'cares for Truth' Y.31.22. Cf. Schlerath 1968 and Kellens-Pirart 1991:76.

11. The compound *medhá-sāti-* '(having) the seeking of the sacrificial offering' (verb *san*[i]) should be compared to the Old Avestan verb phrase *mīždəm han-* (Y.44.18,19 etc.) 'win the reward', on which see Benveniste 1969:1.164. For the probable connection Ved. *médha-/miyédha-/mīḍhá-*, Av. *miiazda-/mīžda-* see Mayrhofer 1956-80 s. vv.

The name is then 'spelled out' in the last strophe of the hymn (18), as a *dānastuti* or praise of the gift, with rich alliteration:

ánu **pra**tnásya ókasaḥ
priyámedhāsa eṣām
pū́rvām ánu **prá**yatiṃ vṛktábarhiṣo
hitá**pra**yasa āśata

After their old custom the Priyamedhas, who have
twisted the sacrificial strew and set out the offering,
have regained the previous reward.

Examples such as these could be multiplied. They attest a common Indo-Iranian ritual, liturgical verbal praxis which has left its traces in Vedic hymnic poetry, and which is most clearly preserved in the strophic style of the Old Avestan YH.

A very interesting example of synchronic word and order fixation is furnished by the *āprī*-hymns in Vedic.[12] They form the litany of an ancient 'popular' family animal sacrifice, as shown by van den Bosch 1985. These hymns consist of 11 regular trimeter or dimeter strophes (plus an occasional extra), each containing a key word, and sequentially invariant:

sámiddha-	'kindled'
Nárāśáṃsa- (Tánūnápāt-)	epithets of Agni
īḷitá-	'invoked, worshipped'
bárhiṣ-	'(sacrificial) straw'
dvā́raḥ	'doors'
doṣā́- (nákta-) , úṣas-	'night and morning'
daívyā hótārā	'the two divine hotars'
Iḷā, Sárasvatī, Bhā́ratī devī́ḥ	oblation 'goddesses'
Tváṣṭṛ	Tvaṣṭar
vanaspati	'tree, sacrificial post'
svā́hā	(ritual cry, "hail!", an indexical sign like *amen* signalling the end of the ritual).

The term *āprí-* (AV +) is related to the verb *āprīṇāti* 'propitiates, pleases'. It has a cognate in Young Avestan *āfrī-* in *āfrī-uuacah-* 'having words of blessing or curse' and *āfrī-uuana-* 'blessing, curse', from *ā́* plus *prī-/frī-* 'favor/wish for (s.th. good or bad to happen to s.o.)'. The term is thus Common Indo-Iranian; though the *āprī*-hymn is purely Indic in its formal requirements, it is interesting how many of the key words have analogues in the Indo-Iranian data we have just seen. For example, the personified 'divine women' *gnā́-/gənā-* might prefigure the *devī́s* 'goddesses' of the *āprī*-hymns; *iḷā-* and *īš-/īžā-* are members of both groups.

12. RV examples are 1.13, 142, 188; 2.3; 3.4; 5.5; 7.2; 9.5; 10.70, 110. See especially Toporov 1981:251 for remarks on their synchronic poetics.

Later, Young Avestan, strophic litanies also present striking parallels with the Rigveda and other Indic texts. Schlerath 1968:10 compares Y. 4.1,

> ima humatāca hūxtāca huuarštāca,
> **imą haomąsca miiazdąsca** zaoϑrā̊sca,
> **barəsmaca** aṣ̌aiia **frastarətəm** . . .
>
> These good thoughts, good words, good deeds,
> **these haomas and solid offerings** and libations
> **and the straw spread** in accord with Truth . . .

with RV 1.177.4:

> ayáṃ yajñó devayā́ **ayáṃ miyédha**
> imā́ bráhmāṇi **ayám** indra **sómaḥ**
> **stīrṇám barhír** . . .
>
> This is the worship which goes to the gods, **this** is the **solid offering**,
> these are the formulas, **this** is the **soma**, o Indra;
> the **straw** is **spread** . . .

We saw in n. 4 above the Vedic version of the formula 'thought, word and deed'.

In Young Avestan the formula *ižāca āzūitišca* which we saw above, old ritual terms 'Labespendung und Opferguss', concretely 'milk and ghee' or 'milk and fat', is used more loosely as a symbolic representation of good things: Bartholomae's 'Glück und Fülle', much like the Hittite merism *iyata*(*r*) *dameta*(*r*) 'plenty and abundance',[13] or Greek κειμήλιά τε πρόβασίν τε and the equivalent English phrase *goods and chattels*, or outside Indo-European the biblical land flowing with milk and honey. In the Young Avestan Videvdat 9.53ff. and 13.52ff. we find the phrase incorporated in a repeated strophe describing the consequences of various impure acts: 'From this place and settlement there will depart:'

> ižāca āzūitišca
> dasuuarəca baēšazəmca
> fradaϑəmca varədaϑəmca vaxšaϑəmca
> yauuanąmca vāstranąmca uruϑəm
>
> Milk and fat,
> health and cure,
> thriving, growth and increase,
> burgeoning of grainfields and pastures.

With its rhythmic and syntactic line structure 2/2/3/2+1, an "inverted T", its concat-

13. See Watkins 1979a.

enation by *-ca*, and its morphological figure in triple *-aϑəm*, the strophe would have been immediately recognizable and familiar as a 'carmen' to a farmer of Latium or a citizen of Iguvium attentive to the verbal practice of his religious duties.

We saw in chap. 19 one critical syntactic formula, by its nature virtually confined to liturgical language, the elliptical offering, common to both Italic and Indic. The next chapter examines a syntactic figure of style which is common to the earliest Iranian and Indic.

22

'Truth of truth', 'most kavi of kavis', 'throng-lord of throngs': An Indo-Iranian stylistic figure

J. Narten, in her edition of the *Yasna Haptaŋhāiti* (1986:164), made in passing and without further explanation a remarkable equation between Indic and Iranian. She compared RV 1.113.1 (of Uṣas) in poem-initial, discourse prominent position, repeated in 10.170.3 (of Sūrya),

> idaṃ śréṣṭhaṃ jyótiṣāṃ jyótiṣ
>
> This most beautiful light of lights

with YH 36.6, in strophe initial position,

> sraēštąm aṯ tōi kəhrpə̄m kəhrpąm
>
> Thy most beautiful form of forms.

The two superlatives are of course exact cognates. While figures involving genitives (*king of kings, gentleman's gentleman, in saecula saeculorum*) and superlatives (*lowest of the low, préṣṭham u priyā́ṇām* 'dearest of the dear' (RV 8.103.10)) are fairly widespread, also outside Indo-European, the combination is much rarer and more striking.

We can be precise; the figure in Vedic has been exhaustively studied by H. Oertel (1937, cited by Narten 1986:164). He found (p. 37) a total of five examples in all of Vedic literature (counting the two instances of the same formula above as one), where 'Das regierende Nomen wird durch ein superlativisches Adjektiv qualifiziert.' All occur first in the Rigveda, and later instances are repetitions of the Rigvedic passages. That is to say that the free formation of this figure was no longer living (or in fashion) after the time of the Rigveda. If we find only five examples in the earliest Vedic, and one in the earliest Avestan, one which shares the same lexical superlative and position of discourse prominence, we are fully justified in assuming a stylistic figure proper to the ritual language of the Common Indo-Iranian period and inherited in both branches.

The other examples of this rare figure in the Rigveda are 2.23.1 *kavíṃ kavīnā́m upamáśravastamam* 'highest-famed seer of seers';[1] 10.120.6 *inátamam āptyám āptyā́nām* 'most powerful Āptya of Āptyas'; 8.40.2 *śáviṣṭhaṃ nṛṇā́ṃ náram* 'strongest man of men'; 5.74.8 *rátho ráthānām yéṣṭhaḥ* 'swiftest chariot of chariots'.

The usage in RV 2.23.1 merits special attention. It too is in poem-initial, discourse-prominent position, and the first strophe contains not just one but three similar figures:

gaṇā́nāṃ tvā gaṇápatiṃ havāmahe
kavíṃ kavīnā́m upamáśravastamam
jyeṣṭharā́jam bráhmaṇām brahmaṇas pata
ā́ naḥ śṛṇvánn ūtíbhiḥ sīda sā́danam

We invoke thee as throng-lord of throngs,
highest-famed seer of seers,
most powerful overlord of the formulas, o Brahmaṇaspati,
listening to us, sit down on your seat with your help.

Here 'throng-lord' in *a* is the equivalent of a superlative; compare *b* with RV 5.42.3 *kavítamam kavīnā́m* 'most seer (*kavi*) of the seers'. In *c* the compound of *rāj-* with superlative as the first member, followed by the divinity's name in the vocative, effects a sort of paraphrase 'most powerful Brahmaṇaspati (= lord of the formula) of the formulas'; it strains sense and syntax alike. The repetition of syntactic constituents *gaṇa- . . . gaṇa-*, *kavi- kavi-* is then followed by that of the non-constituents *brahma- brahma-*, and finally by that of the etymological figure *sīda sāda-*; the first and the last frame the whole strophe.

The genitive construction with a compound of *pati-* 'lord' as in *gaṇā́nām gáṇapati-* 'throng-lord of throngs' is by no means unique in the Rigveda, though it is clearly somewhat stereotyped and both formally and semantically restricted. It is commonest in triṣṭubh lines where it conveniently fills the seven syllables after the caesura; the construction is limited to disyllabic stems (+ disyllabic case forms of *pati-*) where the genitive plural has three syllables. Words for 'wealth' and 'riches' predominate by far: *rayipátī rayīṇā́m* 'wealth-lord of wealth' 5x (2x family books, including one vocative), *vásupatir vásūnām* 'id.' 7x (4x family books: nom. acc. voc.; one *vasupátnī* 'wealth-lady' cow). Otherwise we find one each of *dákṣāṇām dákṣapati* (1.95.6) 'strength-lord of strengths'; semantically imitated in *śácīpate śacīnām* 10.24.2a[2] 'power-lord of powers'; *índrāviṣṇū madapatī madānām* 6.69.3 'O Indra and Viṣṇu, ye two intoxicating drink-lords of intoxicating drinks.' Most interesting is 1.170.5, which shows two:

1. Beside the less rare *kavítamam kavīnā́m* 'most kavi of kavis' RV 5.42.3, 6.18.14.
2. The only example in an octosyllable; the distracted gen. pl. *-naam* is a pseudo-archaism.

tvám īśiṣe vasupate vásūnāṃ
tvám mitrā́ṇām mitrapate dhéṣṭhaḥ[3]
índra tvám marúdbhiḥ sáṃ vadasva
ádha prā́śāna ṛtuthā́ havíṁṣi

You have mastery (over wealth), o wealth-lord of wealth,
you, o alliance[4]-lord of alliances, are the most (alliance-)making;[5]
o Indra, come to an understanding with the Maruts,
and eat the offerings at their proper time.

The preceding paragraphs have presented a synchronic poetic analysis of RV 2.23.1. But there is a remarkable diachronic poetic aspect as well, which is brought out by a comparison with Iranian again. RV 2.23.1a is an invocation:

gaṇā́nāṃ tvā[6] gaṇápatiṃ havāmahe

We invoke thee as throng-lord of throngs.

Of the 17 Rigvedic examples of the construction, 10 are in the vocative or accompany a second person pronoun, and of the oldest 8 examples, in the family books, 7 are vocatives or accompany a second person pronoun. All are gods. The construction therefore clearly is originally most at home in the liturgy. Compare then 2.23.1a above, and 1.170.5b

tvám mitrā́ṇām mitrapate dhéṣṭhaḥ[7]

you, o alliance-lord of alliances, are the most (alliance-)making,

with the *single* Avestan example[8] of this construction, an invocation formula recurring five times, in Yt. 10.145, 19.35, Ny. 1.7, Y. 2.11, 1.11:[9]

miϑrəm vīspanąm daх́iiunąm
daŋ́hupaitīm yazamaide

We worship Mithra, land-lord of all lands.

3. Here the trisyllabic scansion *dhā́iṣṭhaḥ* is linguistically real. Note the same trisyllabic scansion in 1.113.1 *idaṃ śrá(y)iṣṭhaṃ jyótiṣām jyótiṣ* above.

4. In translating *mitrá* as 'alliance' (other possibilities are 'contract', 'covenant') I follow Brereton 1981.

5. As Geldner notes, the genitives are dependent both on the vocatives and the verb or verbal adjectives, and should be read with both.

6. Note that this is the only example with an enclitic intervening between the two constituents.

7. We should perhaps recognize in the superlative an asyntactic index of the previous *śrá(y)iṣṭhaṃ jyótiṣāṃ jyótiṣ, kavíṃ kavīnā́m upamáśravastamam* construction. For other asyntactic phonetic indexes of constructions and formulas see chap. 3 and chap. 5.

8. For Y. 17.11 see further below.

9. The last without *vīspanąm*.

The whole formula is metrical, occupying two octosyllables. Once again we may assume a stylistic figure proper to the ritual liturgical language of the Common Indo-Iranian period, and preserved in both branches.

The presence of the two liturgical verbs, Ved. *havāmahe* 'we invoke' and Av. *yazamaide* 'we worship', pragmatically unites two of the passages, and the presence of the Vedic word *mitrá-* 'covenant, contract, alliance', divinized as the god Mitra, and the presence of his Avestan counterpart and cognate Mithra, linguistically unites the other pair.[10]

Note that despite the verbal similarity this construction is wholly different from the purely reinforcing and redundant *nmānahe nmānō.paitiš vīsō vīspaitiš zaṇtəuš zaṇtupaitiš daŋ́hə̄uš daŋ́hupaitiš* 'house-lord of the house, village-lord of the village, clan-lord of the clan, land-lord of the land' of Yt. 10.18, 83-84 and elsewhere (Schlerath 1968:135). The latter, pluralized to *nmānanąm nmānapaitiš vīsąm vīspaitiš* etc. (Yt. 10.18) are societal designations of *men*, and have nothing to do with invocational epithets of *gods* in the liturgy. That the shared vocabulary might have led to some secondary overlap is indicated by the doubtless late[11] Y. 17.11, where in the liturgy of Fire (Ātar), son of Ahura Mazda, and of various fires by name, all in *yazamaide* 'we worship' formulas, the conclusion or summary is

> ātrəm vīspanąm nmānanąm nmānō.paitīm . . . yazamaide
>
> We worship Fire, house-lord of all the houses (Mazdā-created,
> son of A. M., Truthful, the *Ratu* of Truth).

But the phrase is probably a contamination of the Mithra epithet and the ordinary householder word *nmānahe mnanō.paiti*. Y. 6.11 has here only *ϑβąm ātrəm ahurahe mazdå puϑrəm aṣ̌auuanəm aṣ̌ahe ratūm yazamaide* 'We worship you, Fire, son of A. M., Truthful, the *Ratu* of Truth'.

What we have loosely termed stylistic features are in fact two securely reconstructible constructions which belong to the poetic grammar (O′ in our model in chap. 1) of Common Indo-Iranian. To express superlatives the ordinary common language (O) disposed of constructions like

> (*all*) $N_{gen\ pl}$ Adj_{superl}
> the most Adj of (all) N's,

or more rarely, without overt superlative marker,[12]

---

10. It is on the religious and poetic level of comparative Indo-Iranian that we should seek the meaning of this formula, and not on the level of Chorasmian (or Achaemenid or Median) political organization, with Gershevitch 1959:298-9.

11. Y. 17 is almost entirely a repetition of Y. 6., as Geldner points out in his edition ad loc. Only parts of Y. 17.11 are original: specifically the named fires.

12. And normally in languages like Hittite which lack special markers for the degrees of comparison of the adjective.

(*all*) $N_{gen\ pl}$ Adj
the [most] Adj of (all) N's,

as in Avestan *gaṇtumō yauuanąm ratufrīš* 'wheat is of (all) cereals the dear[est] to the *Ratu*'. The Common Indo-Iranian poetic language further disposed of the constructions

$N_{gen\ pl}$ N_{superl}
the most N of N's,

as in *kavítama- kavīnā́m* 'most kavi of kavi's',

$N_{gen\ pl}$ N + Adj_{superl}
the most Adj N of N's,

as in *kavím̥ kavīnā́m upamaśravastama-* 'highest-famed kavi of kavi's', and

(*all*) $N_{gen\ pl}$ N-*lord*
the N-lord of (all) N's,

as in *gaṇā́nām gaṇápati-* 'throng-lord of throngs', *vīspanąm dax́iiunąm daŋ́hupaiti-* 'the land-lord of all lands'. That both of these examples are the object of the liturgical verbs par excellence, *havāmahe* 'we invoke' and *yazamaide* 'we worship', is an index of the cultural pragmatics which explain their linguistic preservation.

There are other links of RV 2.23 to an inherited tradition reaching still further back in time. The expressive doubly-marked *upamáśravas-tama-* of *b* is superlative of *upamá-śravas-*, itself 'having the highest fame'. The latter is attested only as a personal name in the Rigveda, in 10.33.6, 7. The poet has fallen on hard times and pathetically approaches the son of his former patron:

ádhi putropamaśravo
nápān mitrātither ihi
pitúṣ ṭe asmi vanditā́

Notice (me), o son Upamaśravas,
grandson of Mitrātithi;
I am your father's praise-poet.

Upamá-śravas- is etymologically 'having the highest fame'; *Mitra-atithi-* is 'having *mitra*, the divinized "covenant", "contract", "alliance" as guest.' Such bipartite, two-member compound personal names, as is known, continue Indo-European themes, formulas, and values: they are windows into prehistory. In these two Vedic personal names we find a formulaic nexus of 'Indo-European poetic language and name giving'[13] which reaches from India to Western Europe, in some of the earliest monuments of Celtic and Germanic.

With the two names *Upama-śravas-* < **upm̥mo-k̂leu̯es-* 'having SUPREME fame' and *Mitra-atithi-* 'having M. as GUEST' compare the Lepontic Celtic personal name UVAMO-KOZIS < **upm̥mo-ghostis* 'having SUPREME GUESTS'; the Runic Germanic personal name (Gallehus horn) *hlewa-gastiR* < **k̂leuo-ghostis* 'having famous guests'; and the Venetic personal name *ho.s.tihauo.s.* < **ghosti-ghou̯ó-* 'who honors guests'.[14] The nexus linking 'fame', 'lofty', and 'guest' (Indo-European **ghos-ti-*, with the same suffix Indo-Iranian **atH-ti-* in Ved. *átithi-* = Av. *asti-* (Schwartz 1990:200-7)) is precisely a 'contract' or 'covenant': that of *hospitality* between patron and poet.[15]

The purpose of this excursus has been to point up the close linkage of the verbal practice of the author of RV 2.23 (which we also examined in chap. 8) with a poetic tradition reaching back to the proto-language and manifesting itself in a number of traditions outside India. To those we have surveyed comes another, which incorporates the rare grammatical figures of RV 2.23 and the same wording, in a specifically liturgical context, in the strophic style with largely non-metrical mantras in "rhythmic prose", in a Vedic Indian ritual which is widely regarded as reflecting Common Indo-European religious practice: the Horse-Sacrifice or *Aśvamedha*.[16] Before examining in detail the poetics of the *Aśvamedha* litany (chap. 25) we must consider the non-metrical strophic style of "rhythmic prose" in three other Indo-European traditions: Celtic, Armenian, and Anatolian. To these the next chapters are devoted.

---

13. The phrase is drawn from Schmitt 1973, who himself consciously evoked Schramm 1957. For a provocative and challenging presentation of the same phenomenon ("nexus") in Slavic onomastics see the two works of Ivanov and Toporov 1965 and 1974.

14. Lejeune 1974:47, 169, no. 137 (Este III, 5th cent. B.C.). I prefer to see in the second member the cognate of Latin *fauēre*, OCS *gověti* 'revere, show reverence', Vedic *gho-rá-* 'fearsome' (Caland-system), Pokorny 453 *ghou-*, rather than Pokorny 513 *ghau-* 'invoke, call', with Lejeune ('qui interpelle l'étranger').

15. The prominence of the theme of *commensality* in the hospitality relation (Pindar's ξενία . . . τράπεζα 'hospitable table') inclines one to see in European **ghos-(ti-)* (Lat. *hostis, red-hostire*, Sikel *gosti-*, Goth. *gasts*, Slavic *gos-podь, gostь*), zero grade **ghs-* in Greek ξένϝος, the cognate of Vedic *ghas-* 'eat'. Compare the suffixed **ghos-ti-* 'guest' with the zero-grade **sm̥-ghs-ti-* in Vedic *ságdhi-* 'eating together, communal meal' (TS 4.7.4 and parallels, mantra; AVP 19.22.6).

16. Compare Toporov 1981:231f: "The Aśvamedha . . . permits the uncovering of a layer which connects it to ritual texts in other Indo-European languages. It may be suggested that the rituals of animal sacrifice (*aprī*-hymns) and some soma-worship are likewise connected with corresponding liturgical texts which go back to Indo-European times." For a comparison of the soma ritual with certain Greek ritual practices in the early texts, and with features of the Eleusinian Mysteries, cf. Watkins 1978b.

23

More strophic structures

1. Anatolian Hittite and Palaic

It has long been recognized that Hittite texts which appear to be regarded as poetry by their own culture, for example those referred to by the Sumerogram SÌR 'song' or the common verb form SÌR^{RU} (Akkadian *izammaru* 'they sing'), Hittite stem *išḫamāi-* noun and verb, do not show any recurrent syllabic count or stress-timed rhythmic pattern. Rather they exhibit precisely what we have seen in the many traditions surveyed: a strophic/stichic style of rhythmic/syntactic units, with a principled equivalence verse-line = clause or sentence.[1] In the Hittite clay tablets themselves the verse lines are written continuously, as in Early Greek epigraphic practice and that of the Semitic-speaking scribes of Ugarit, whereas in Sumerian and Akkadian poetry each verse is written on a separate line. The Hittite clay tablets regularly divide texts into 'paragraphs' by a horizontal line across the column, and the practice is found in these poetic texts as well, which led Güterbock to recognize them as 'stanzas', in other words a strophic style. The last (and only legible) line of the first paragraph/strophe of the Song of Ullikummi (i 3-4) is

dapiyaš šiunaš addan Kumarbin išḫamiḫḫi

I sing of Kumarbi, father of all the gods.

The Song (SÌR) of Ullikummi is translated from Hurrian, and it is always possible that the translation imitates the poetic form of the source language. Other texts of Hurrian provenience, like the tale of the hunter Keššе, are labeled 'Song' (SÌR)[2] and show similar prosodic and stylistic features, like the Song of Silver,[3] whose second paragraph begins

---

1. Fundamental is Güterbock 1952, esp. 7-11. See also Güterbock 1964, on the Sun Hymns adapted from Akkadian.

2. Cf. E. Neu 1988:248.

3. Edited by H. A. Hoffner, Jr. 1988a.

išḫamiḫḫiy=an KÙ.BABBAR-an šanizzi[

I sing of him, Silver the unique (?).

Whether there is a connection between these Hittite 1sg. forms and the Homeric epic and hymnic practice of ἀείδω 'I sing' / ἄρχομ' ἀείδειν 'I begin to sing' is not known, but it is not impossible.

We now have the recently published text (KUB 32.10-104) of the lengthy Hurrian-Middle Hittite bilingual SÌR *parā tarnumaš* 'Song of emancipation', which shows in fact a number of poetic features in the Hurrian original such as strophic cola with lines of smaller syntactic units, verb phrases, repeated in successive lines with the verb fronted (E. Neu, loc. cit.). The Hittite translator in these cases appears to have altered, misinterpreted, or ignored the Hurrian stylistic figure, as Neu shows.

We need not, however, rely on translation literature for glimpses of Hittite or other Anatolian poetry, stichic/syllabic or strophic/rhythmic-syntactic.

A clear example of the former is the oft-treated soldiers' dirge KBo 3.40 = BoTU 14α 13′-15′ (duplicate KBo 13.78 Vo. 12′-14′), CTH 16b.[4] It is preceded by *nu=zza išḫamaīzzi* 'he sings' (duplicate *išḫamiškanzi* 'they sing'):

Nešaš wašpeš Nešaš wašpeš
tiya=mmu tiya
nu=mu annaš=maš katta arnut
tiya=mmu tiya
nu=mu uwaš=maš katta arnut
tiya=mmu tiya

Shrouds of Nesas, shrouds of Nesas,
bind me, bind.
Bring me down for burial with my mother,
bind me, bind.
Bring me down for burial with my *forefather*,
bind me, bind.

While the translation is in part controversial and the syllable count partly indeterminate, the poetic form is self-evident with its 8/9 syllable lines [4 || 4]/[5 || 4], grammatically parallel, alternating with an invariant refrain of 3 or 5 syllables. Nesas is the old city of Kaneš, modern Kültepe, the cradle of the Hittites. With line three of these still moving verses compare the expression (written in Sumerograms) UD AMA-*KA* 'day of your mother' = 'your death day, dying day.'

From another ancient Anatolian language we may cite what I have referred to

4. See most recently Soysal 1987 (with partly differing interpretation) as well as Gamkrelidze-Ivanov 1984:839-840 and (partly superseded) Watkins 1969b.

as a Palaic *carmen*:[5] two almost identical prayers accompanying the sacrifice of first a ram and then a bull to the Palaic god Zaparwa. The text is contemporary with Old Hittite. The evident organizational principle is grammatical parallelism and the equivalence verse-line = sentence or clause. We may therefore regard the texts as rhythmic/syntactic strophes of six lines:

> nū Zaparwa šameriš šameriš
> (*variant* nū Zaparwa tiunaš tiunaš)
> ḫalāiš=ta nī
> purtaḫḫiš=ta nī
> wašḫullatiyaš nī waḫarianza/i
> ḫāpnaš=ta nī tekanza
> ḫašīram=pi nī padāmman.

I forbear to offer a connected translation as too conjectural. What we do know is that *nī* appearing in five of the six lines is the negation; *ḫāpnaš* must be 'river' and *ḫašīram* 'dagger' because they alternate in the texts with the familiar Sumerograms ÍD and GÍR;[6] *=ta* and *=pi* are enclitic particles.

The last two particles must cliticize to the first word in their clause or sentence. This fixes the clause and therefore verse-line boundaries as I have given them; no other arrangement is possible. The negations in *ḫalāiš=ta nī*, *purtaḫḫiš=ta nī* must therefore be emphatically extraposed to the right, a syntactic option shared with Hittite.[7]

The grammatical parallelism is given by the two noun forms *ḫalāiš*, *purtaḫḫiš* on the one hand, forming a dyad 'let there be (or there is) no *ḫ.*/*p.*', and the three nouns *wašḫullatiyaš*, *ḫāpnaš*, *ḫašīram*, each with an agreeing participle: *waḫariy-anza*, *tek-anza* (passive), and the middle *pad-āmman*. The result is a triad: 'let the *w.*/*ḫ.*/*ḫ.* not be (or the *w.*/*ḫ.*/*ḫ.* is not, has not been) *w.*-ed/*t.*-ed/*p.*-ed.' Whatever the lexical meaning, we have the same contrapuntal articulation of two- and three-member cola that we saw in Italic and Iranian prayer and liturgy.

The extensive Hittite-Luvian Kizzuwatnean ritual texts grouped under CTH 760 contain a number of litany-like spells and incantations spoken by the 'Old Woman' (^{SAL}ŠU.GI).[8] Some are enumerations of body parts which are 'fitted' (*ḫandant-*) to those of a "scapegoat" sheep, §§1-3 of Tablet Two. It begins 'head is fitted to head, throat is fitted to throat' and continues through the canonical '12 body parts'—17 are in fact mentioned—ending with

---

5. Watkins 1978d. Much of the interpretation offered there is obsolete. See Melchert, forthcoming.

6. Both are inherited Indo-European lexemes, **$h_2$ab(h)-no-* : Welsh *afon* (*Avon*), Latin *amnis* 'river', and **h_2n̥si-ro-* : Vedic *así-*, Latin *ēnsis* 'sword'.

7. Compare from the instructions for Bēl Madgalti officials (v. Schuler 1957:48) iii 27-8, where the extraposition of *lē* emphasizes the figure of antithesis: *DINAM šarazzi katteraḫḫi lē* , *kattera<n> šaraz<zi>ya<ḫ>ḫi lē* 'Let him not bring low a good (lit. high) case, let him not hold up a bad (lit. low) case'. The image is clearly drawn from scales; cf. *Il.* 22.209ff. The metaphor of the scales of justice is confirmed in the next line of the text, *kuit ḫandan apāt īšša* 'What is right (lit. fitting), do that'.

8. A number of these are edited by Hutter 1988 and Beckman 1990. I take my examples from the latter.

ḫaštai=kan ḫaštai ḫandan
UZUSA=kan *ANA* UZUSA ḫandan
ēšḫar=kan ēšḫani ḫandan

bone to bone is fitted
sinew to sinew is fitted
blood to blood is fitted.

The enumerations are identical to those in the Germanic, Indic, and Irish healing charms to be discussed below (chapters 56 and 57).[9] The body parts of the ram will call out (*wewakkanzi* §4) the sickness of the body part of the mortal: 'head will lift sickness of head' etc.

Subsequent sections (§24ff.) of this and related rituals involve the (somewhat inept) image of the pig that roots (*mūtaizzi*) meadow and mountain and gets plants and water, so it should root out illness of body parts, wrath of gods (DINGIR^{MEŠ}-*aš karpin*), and slander (literally 'tongue', EME = *lala-*) of people and palace, priests and priestesses, troops, army camp and palace guard. It then continues (§§28-29) in merism style:

aggantaš ḫuišwantaš lalan mūdaiddu[10]
ŠA ÌR GEME lalan mūdaiddu
adandaš akuwandaš lalan mūdaiddu
tangarandaš lalan mūdaiddu

Let it root out the slander of the dead, of the living
let it root out the slander of male slave, of female slave,
let it root out the slander of the one who has eaten, who has drunk,
let it root out the slander of the one who has gone hungry.

The function of the merisms is as usual to indicate a totality: all persons living or dead, all unfree male or female, all persons satisfied or hungry. 'Satisfied' is split into 'eaten and drunk', in accord with Common Anatolian formulaic practice. Once again we find rhythmic/grammatical counterpoint of dyad and triad. These merismatic lines in an otherwise enumerative litany are directly comparable to similar structures in the Aśvamedha liturgy; see chap. 25.

An obscure conjuration in Tablet Five of the same text, col iv 8ff., reads 'Afterwards she takes a rope and waves it over him. She conjures (*ḫukkiškizzi*) as follows:'

9. Since the external series runs from 'head' (SAG.DU-*aš*) to 'sole (of the foot)' (*ḫarganau*), just before the internal triad cited, the latter may well be *genetically* related to the Old High German second Merseburg spell and other passages discussed in section VII below.

10. The tablet has Sumerograms TI-*andaš*, EME-*an*, and for some of the verbs the graphic convention KI.MIN 'ditto'. KUB 9.4 iv 11 splits the first line into 'let it root out the slander of the dead, let it root out the slander of the living'.

arunaš āḫriyatta
aruni=ma=kan anda šumanzan daškupāit
arunaz=kan šumanza ḫuittiyami

The sea was unclean(?).[11]
But in the sea the rope cried out.
From the sea I draw the rope.

The anaphora and polyptoton of fronted sentence initial *arunaš—aruni—arunaz* is surely an intentional figure; but the meaning of the whole spell is completely opaque to me, and I cannot say whether the spell is poetry or prose.[12]

A full study of the poetics and stylistics—as well as the syntax—of the enormous number of spells, litanies, and other utterances in our vast corpus of Hittite rituals would require a monograph, but the rewards would be great. Compare the very valuable collection of Hittite similes by A. Ünal in Mikasa 1988:52-85. Note only in closing the example in our same ritual, Tablet Five iv 1ff., of Behaghel's law of increasing members, with the epithet confined to the last: 'If he has seen something with his eyes (IGI.ḪI.A-*it*), or taken something with his hand (ŠU-*it*), or trodden something with his powerful foot (*innarawantet* GÌR-*it*).'

For Luvian poetry see chap. 11.2.

2. Armenian

The Armenian historian Moses of Chorene (Movsēs Xorenacʿi) writing probably in the early ninth century A.D. is one of the few Classical Armenian authors to preserve actual fragments of pre- (or para-)Christian Armenian epic poetry, historical 'songs' (*erg, ergel* : Vedic *ṛc-* of *ṛg-veda-*) and 'fables' (*aṙaspelkʿ*). Some of these recount events and figures of the early second century B.C., notably the king Artašēs (Greek Artaxias I), a younger contemporary and friend of Hannibal the Carthaginian.

These texts are clearly poetry within their own tradition, though they are neither isosyllabic, nor syllabotonic, nor for example rhyming. In these as for that matter much late (Medieval and Early Modern) Armenian poetry I may quote the eminent specialist J. R. Russell: 'It is more fruitful to look at word-plays and sound patterns within the poem . . . and to draw the connections between ecclesiastical *taɫ*s and gnomic

11. I take this verb to be a denominative to the first member of the magical rhyme-word pair *aḫran waḫran*, etwa "Unreinheit (und) Unheil" to be spat out in many Hittite and Luvian rituals. See Hutter 1988:81 for other examples, like *ain wain*. A Luvian substantivized participle of the same verb is found in KUB 9.34 i 22 *tarnaššan āḫraman* (parallel to SAG.DU-*aš ḫultaramman*) 'the "unclean-sickness" of the throat', Hutter 27.

12. J.R. Russell (p.c.) ingeniously compares the old Armenian proverb quoted by Movsēs Xorenacʿi (I.13) *ulunkʿ Šamiramay i cov* 'the beads of Semiramis into the sea', adding '—beads on a *string* of course'.

songs . . . or . . . string poems . . .'[13] The same pre-Christian thematic and formulaic tradition continued intact down to modern times, for the great Armenian folk epic David of Sassun (Sasunc῾i Davit῾), or The Crazy Ones of Sasun (Sasna cṙer), collected in the 19th and early 20th centuries, shows the same prosodic form. Compare the description of its French translator F. Feydit: 'L'épopée se présente sous la forme d'un récit rhythmé,—dont le rhythme est obtenu par l'équilibre entre les diverses périodes de la phrase,—et coupé de passages chantés, assez rarement rimés.'[14]

Movsēs quotes the epic description of the abduction by King Artašēs of the Alan princess Sat῾inik (II 50):[15]

hecaw ari ark῾ayn Artašēs
i seawn gełec῾ik
ew haneal zoskeawł šikap῾ok parann
ew anc῾eal orpēs zarcui srat῾ew ənd getn
ew zgeal zoskeawł šikap῾ok parann
ənkēc῾ i mēǰk῾ awriordin Alanac῾
ew šat c῾awec῾oyc῾ zmēǰk῾ p῾ap῾uk awriordin
arag hasuc῾anelov i banakn iwr.

The brave King Artašēs
rode on a black handsome horse,
and he drew the gold-ringed red leather lasso,
and he crossed the river like the sharp-winged eagle,
and he threw the gold-ringed red leather lasso.
He threw it around the waist of the maiden of the Alans,
and much he made the waist of the tender maiden suffer
by carrying her swiftly back to his camp.

Note the discourse initial finite verb *hecaw* 'rode' (IE **sed-i̯e/o-* 'sit'), the grammatical parallelism *haneal . . . anc῾eal . . . zgeal*, and the many word and phrase repetitions.

Movsēs continues with what 'they sing' (*ergen*) in the fables:

teł oski tełayr
    i p῾esayut῾eann Artašisi
tełayr margarit
    i harsnut῾ean Sat῾inkann.

A rain of gold it rained
    when Artašēs became a groom;

13. Letter of 5 February 1992. I have seen his Carmina Vahagni (*Acta Antiqua*, Budapest) only in manuscript.

14. David de Sassoun (1964). Text: Sasunc῾i Davit῾. Hayakan Žołovrdakan Epos. Erevan: Haypethrat 1961. The most informative study of this work is the still unpublished Paris thesis of Ch. de Lamberterie, Mythe et langue en Armenie. La geste de Vahagn. 1981.

15. For the critical edition see chap. 13 n. 2. Other fragments of this epic are discussed in Russell 1986-7 and Dowsett 1986.

it rained pearls
        when Saťinik became a bride.

Note the etymological figure, the shift in position of the repeated verb *tełayr*, the grammatical parallelism of the two nominal expressions (lit. 'at the groom-ness of A.', 'at the bride-ness of S.') syntactically skewed by the different positioning of the two demonstrative suffixes *-n*.

Otherwise in these verse lines there is no trace of syllable or stress counting, or other discernible "metrical" structure. The metric line is commanded by the syntactic boundaries, as in the other traditions we have examined, and larger "strophic" unities such as these examples selected for quotation by Movsēs were demarcated by grammatical signals like the discourse-initial verb. This was to be the form of Armenian epic poetry for millennia.

To conclude we may cite the full text of the Birth of Vahagn quoted by Movsēs (I 31), the beginning of which we saw in chap. 13. It too begins with a discourse-initial, "cataphoric" verb. The continuation shows other figures, notably phrasal and verbal anaphora:

erknēr erkin erknēr erkir
erknēr ew covn cirani
erkn i covun unēr[16]
zkarmrikn ełegnik.

ənd ełegan ṗoł cux elanēr,
ənd ełegan ṗoł boc' elanēr,
ew i boc'oyn vazēr
xarteaš patanekik.

na hur her unēr,
boc' unēr mawrus,
ew ac'kunk'n ēin aregakunk'.

Heaven was in labor, earth was in labor,
the purple sea too was in labor.
Labor pangs in the sea seized
the little crimson reed.

Along the reed stalk smoke ascended,
along the reed stalk flame ascended,
and from the flames there leapt
a golden-haired little youth.

16. Russell (p.c.) calls attention in Heaven and Earth to the 1/2 + 1/2 = 2 motiv; the Sea as the third element is indexed by the alliterative *c- c-*. See also chap. 13 n. 2.

He had fire for hair,
flame he had for beard,
and his little eyes were suns.

Note the (quasi-universal) stylistic device of diminutivization in *ełegnik*, *patanekik* (double, *patani* + *ak* + *ik*), and *ačkunk'*.[17]

This Armenian hymn from the Zoroastrian tradition is directly comparable to the hymning of *apā́m nápāt*, Descendent or Grandson[18] of the Waters, the kenning for Fire (Agni), doubtless of Indo-European date (Old Norse *sævar niðr* 'descendent of the sea'). Compare J. R. Russell (loc. cit.): 'the concepts of physics implied in the song of the birth of Vahagn are archaic and find a parallel in the Vedas, where plants, born of water, become sticks, which rubbed together give birth to fire.'[19] The parallelism to RV 2.35, to Apām Napāt as deity and as the sacrificial fire, is even more striking: he is nurtured as a youth (*yúvānam* 4) and is of overwhelming golden aspect (*híraṇyarūpa*, *híraṇyasaṃdṛk*, *híraṇyavarṇa* 10).

17. For the effect compare Latin *animula uagula blandula*, the emperor Hadrian's poetic farewell to his soul (*Poetae Lat. Min.*, 3.1).

18. The gender-marked kinship term *nápāt* reflects the masculine *Agni*, a grammatical icon beloved of poets in the languages with gender down to modern times. Note that Indo-European had two words for fire (and water, mutatis mutandis) one masculine or animate **ognis* (> Lat. *ignis*) and one neuter or inanimate **peh₂ur* (> Umbr. *pir*).

19. He refers to Boyce 1975:1.45, who refers to Oldenberg 1917:101, 117.

24

Early Irish *rosc*

Liam Breatnach observed in an important article (Breatnach 1984, with references) that 'Old Irish texts appear in three forms: prose, rhyming syllabic verse, and *rosc*. The simplest definition of *rosc* is that it is neither of the other two.' There were several stylistic varieties of prose in Early Irish, associated with such genres as law texts, saints' lives, and sagas. There was a large number of syllable-counting meters with varying patterns of rhyme (end-rhyme, *aicill*-rhyme of line-final with line-internal), lines of different syllable length (most commonly seven), always organized in strophes (most commonly quatrains).[1]

Breatnach goes on to point out that in the case of *rosc* (or *roscad*, plural *roscada*)[2] 'we can distinguish three main types: the first consists of syllabically regular lines with fixed cadence and alliteration, but without rhyme; the second of lines with regular number of stressed words per line and alliteration; while the third type shows no apparent regular syllabic or stress pattern, but is heavily alliterative. Furthermore, *rosc* is characterized by various linguistic features, usually referred to as 'Archaic Irish', which are not found in prose but are found in Old Irish rhyming syllabic verse.' I would add that *roscada* may be then stichic (line-by-line) or strophic in arrangement; unlike the quatrains of rhymed syllabic verse, strophes if present are irregular and of variable length, sometimes demarcated by reduction in cadence and syllable count.

The first of these three types of *rosc* or *roscad*[3] is the 'heptasyllabic' [4 || 3] verse (variants [5 || 2], [6 || 1], [4 || 1], etc.) with fixed caesura or word boundary, which

---

1. An early example of rhymed syllabic verse is studied in chap. 9. For a detailed discussion of rhymed syllabic verse see the indispensable work of Murphy 1961.

2. Cf. Binchy 1972.

3. From Proto-Celtic (and Indo-European) **pro-sk*^{u}*o-m*, cf *árosc* 'maxim' < **ad-ro-sk*^{u}*o-*, Middle Welsh *dihaereb* 'proverb' < **dē-ad-ro-sk*^{u}*o-*. Old Irish *rosc* also means 'eye, sight'. The basic meaning of the root **sek*^{u}- must refer to perception: 'see' (as in Germanic, Gothic *saiƕan*, Old English *sēon*, and probably Anatolian, Hittite *šākuwa* 'eyes' if from **sok*^{u}-). The retention (cf. *be**hold***) and transmission of cognition resulted semantically in 'cause to see, show; tell' (as in Greek [*Od.* 1.1] ἄνδρα μοι ἔννεπε, Μοῦσα 'Tell me, o Muse, of the man . . .'). We can observe the same semantic development with other verbs of perception and cognition which are part of the vocabulary of Indo-European poetics, like **men-*, **u̯et-*, on which see chap. 9.

The composition with preverb as in **pro-sk*^{u}*o-* (Irish *rosc*), **en-s(e)k*^{u}- (Greek ἔννεπε, Latin *inquit*,

generates the fixed cadences 'x x x, 'x x ('x), etc. by the Irish word stress on the initial syllable. For the psychological reality of the word boundary at least in the seventh century see chap. 9. I surveyed these mostly heptasyllabic, fixed cadence verse lines in Watkins 1963b. It is perfectly clear that these were regarded as poetry in Irish from the first attestations through the Middle and Modern periods; they were simply non-rhyming, stichic or in irregular strophes but not quatrains, with rhythmically fixed cadence but freer initial, and considerable use of alliteration—line-internal, concatenating, or serial. An example of the last, from the end of the Old Irish period, can be taken from Breatnach's edition of the *Amra Senáin* (n. 7 below), verses 1-3, with his translation:

Senán soer sídathair	'x x 'x	'x x x
síلem soáilche,	'x x	'x x x
sainemail suíb srethamra	'x x x 'x	'x x x
curson cadb, calb cletharda	'x x 'x x	'x x x
cuipe co fín.	'x x x	'x
fó lúin lainderda,	'x 'x	'x x x
loo laissem luamna	'x 'x x	'x x x
asa laís lúan	x x 'x	'x
lán fuach fírinde	'x 'x x	'x x x
for-osna iltúatha	x 'x x	'x x x
Érenn úas maig	'x x x	'x

Senán, noble father of peace, a sower of virtues,
unique, beautiful, marvellously arranged, a fine sage,
a sheltering head, a goblet with wine.

Good is the radiant moon, in the daytime a blazing light,
whose praise is radiance.

Full of words of rightousness, he illuminates many
kingdoms above the plain of Ireland.

---

insece) is characteristic. Note the common Hittite *anda memai-* 'say into' of a spell or utterance in a ritual. For an inherited compound with **pro* compare J. Narten's equation (1960) of Vedic *pra math* 'rob, carry away, steal away with' and Greek Προ-μηθ-εύς (Doric Προ-μαθ-εύς). Her establishment of the necessary separation of *math* 'rob' from *manth* 'twirl', together with the many textual collocations of the name of Mātariśvan who brought fire to man and *math* 'rob' demonstrates, as she shows, that the Mātariśvan-Prometheus myth, long assumed to be cognate and inherited in Greek and Indic (Kuhn, Charpentier), agreed also in the motifeme of the **theft** of fire. S. Insler (IVth East Coast Indo-European Conference, Cornell, June 1985) has argued convincingly that the name *mātaríśvan-* was built on Indo-Iranian **ātar-* 'fire'; the initial *m-* of *math-*, Indo-European **math*$_2$- may well have played a role in its deformation.

The effect may be described in Pokorny's translation of *rosc* as 'dithyrambic'.[4] Beside the syllabotonic features of regular cadence and free initial, and the lengthy alliterative strings, note the 'poetic' linguistic features such as recherché vocabulary (*curson cadb*, *calb*, identified by the native glossatorial tradition as *Bérla na Filed* 'Language of the Poets' [chap. 16]), and the word order perturbation (preposed genitive) in the last line, *Érenn uas maig*.

Over more than a decade Breatnach has produced an impressive set of text editions of *roscada* material from the 'poetico-legal' traditions of the learned and ecclesiastical classes with full discussions of their poetic form.[5] Several are relatively lengthy compositions showing a variety of poetic forms, both *rosc* and rhymed syllabic meter, as well as both straightforward prose and "rhythmic alliterative" prose. The 'Caldron of Poesy' and *Bretha Nemed Toísech* are compositions of the eighth century, *Amra Senáin* of the end of the ninth, and *Cáin Fhuithirbe* of the latter seventh century, ca. 680. All are products of what D. A. Binchy termed a 'poetico-legal' school (Binchy 1955), with heavy ecclesiastical influence. As Breatnach showed, some of the *Bretha Nemed* texts were compiled in Munster between 721 and 742 by three kinsmen: Forannán, a bishop; Máel Tuile, a poet; and Báethgalach hua Búirecháin, a judge. The *Nemed* texts are in part translations of the Latin of the Collectio Canonum Hibernensis, and show for the eighth century an artificially archaizing style incorporating many linguistic features (listed in Breatnach 1984:453) associated with what is frequently termed Archaic Irish. As an example with variable (serial, concatenating, or internal) alliteration and stress count we may cite the 'Caldron of Poesy' §§1-2, after Breatnach:

1. Moí **c**oire **c**oir **g**oiriath
gor rond-n-ír **D**ía **d**am a **d**úile **nd**emrib
dliucht **s**óer **s**óeras **br**oinn
bélrae **mb**il **br**úchtas **ú**ad.
Os mé Amar**g**en **gl**úngel **g**arrglas **gr**élíath, . . .

2. Ara-**c**aun **c**oire **s**ofis
sernar **d**liged cach **d**áno
dia **m**oiget **m**óin
móras **c**ach **c**eird **c**oitchunn
con-utaing[6] **d**uine **d**án.

Mine is the proper cauldron of *goiriath*;
warmly God has given it to me out of the mysteries of the elements;
a noble privilege which ennobles the breast
is the fine speech which flows forth from it.
I being white-kneed, blue-shanked, grey-bearded Amairgen . . .

4. Or in the irrepressible verbal icon of *dithyrambic* in New Orleans Dixieland jazz, *Didn't he ramble*.

5. Breatnach 1981, 1984, 1986, 1989a, 1989b, 1991.

6. Note the stressed-unstressed concatenating alliteration ***dáno*** : ***dia***, ***coitchunn*** : ***con-***. The stressed syllable ['ud] of *con-utaing* is linked by inversion to the following ['du] of *duine*.

I acclaim[7] the cauldron of knowledge
where the law of every art is set out,
as a result of which prosperity increases,
which magnifies every artist in general,
which exalts a person by means of an art.

The next 10 'strophes' or paragraphs are in prose, followed by a strophe (§13) of more than 30 short lines of two stresses each (the first and last lines of three stresses) and concatenating or internal alliteration:

Ar-**c**aun **c**oire **n-é**rmai
intlechtaib **r**aith
rethaib **s**oḟis
srethaib **i**mbais
indber **n-é**cnai . . .

I acclaim the cauldron of *érmae*
with understandings of grace,
with accumulations of knowledge,
with strewings of *imbas*,
the estuary of wisdom . . .

§15 is built on the grammatical figure of parallelism, which continues for 10 lines:

Coire **é**rmai
ernid **e**rnair
mrogaith **m**rogthair
bíathaid **b**íadtair . . .

The cauldron of *érmae*,
it grants, it is granted,
it extends, it is extended,
it nourishes, it is nourished . . .

The final §16 closes the composition with two quatrains in syllabic verse $5^2 5^2 5^2 5^2$ with rhyme between *b* and *d*, *rinnard bec* or *anamain* (Murphy 1961:57, cited by Breatnach):

Fó **t**opar **t**omseo
fó **a**trab n-***i**nsce*
fó **c**omar **c**oimseo
con-utaing *firse*.

7. *Ara-caun* literally 'I sing'; the cognate of Latin *canō* is the usual verb of the 'poetico-legal' tradition.

Is mó cach ferunn
is ferr cach *orbu*
berid co hecnae
echtraid fri *borbu.*

Good is the source of measuring
good is the acquisition of speech
good is the confluence of power
which builds up strength.

It is greater than any domain
it is better than any patrimony
it brings one to wisdom
it separates one from fools.

Alliteration is present throughout, either line-internal or line-linking. In *orbu* : *berid* we have the freer *fidrad freccomail* type of the latter.[8]

Another form of *rosc* in which the principal device is grammatical parallelism is the series of brief complex sentences of identical structure, noun with gapped copula plus relative verb with 3 sg. feminine pronominal object, in a legal text (Kelly 1986). The editor, Fergus Kelly, has taken them as a sequence of riddles, the answer being the feminine gender noun *breth* 'judgement':

ántengthaid ar-da-feith[9]
airecht no-dan-aig
brithem no-da-mbeir

It is a clear spokesman who tends it,
it is a court which impels it,
it is a judge who delivers it.

Use of the pronominal object as a grammatical figure recurs outside the riddle genre in the mantic style of *Baile Chuind* (Murphy 1952), with repeated *íbthus* 'will drink it', i.e. the sovereignty of Ireland (*flaith*, feminine).

The same rhetorical strophic style is found in compositions of a couple of generations earlier, in the seventh century, in the fragments of *Cáin Fhuithirbe* (ca. 680, as Breatnach has shown), and more significantly in the 'Mirror of Princes' (*Speculum Principum*) text of advice to a king, *Audacht Morainn* 'The Testament of Morann'.[10] The text is extensive, consisting of 164 lines in three strophes or prose sections. Kelly dates its compilation to ca. 700, with 'much of Recension B composed a good deal earlier' (p. xxxiii), on linguistic grounds. It belongs to the same 'poetico-

8. Cf. Carney 1981.

9. Note the strong verb, an exact cognate of Vedic *ápi vatati*, Avestan *aipi vataiti* 'perceive, be aware of'. See the discussion in chap. 9.

10. Edited from the older recension B by Kelly (1976).

legal' tradition as the *Bretha Nemed* collection and shows the same obscure rhetorical style characterized by alliteration, grammatical parallelism, and older syntactic constructions employed as grammatical figures.

From *Cáin Fhuithirbe* we may note the following example, with relative clauses and word order perturbation (Breatnach 1986:39). The lines have two or three stresses, and are linked by alliteration:

> Indles cach n-indred
> íar cumalaib slóig segar.
> Díles cach forloscud
> fedar i fithisib ríg
> ro n-íacht élud . . .
>
> Every spoiling by a host which is pursued after *cumals* (have been given up) is liable. Every burning which is carried out in the circuits of a king when he has bewailed evasion is immune.

Prose order would be . . . *indred slóig segar íar cumalaib.*

From *Audacht Morainn* note first the same active-passive grammatical figure we observed in the 'Caldron of Poesy' above:

> (§62) to-slaid to-sladar
> ar-clich ar-clechar
> con-claid con-cladar
> ad-reith ad-rethar
> to-seinn to-sennar
>
> He strikes, is struck,
> wards off, is warded off,
> roots out, is rooted out,
> attacks, is attacked,
> pursues, is pursued.

The same reciprocal figure is the grammatical basis, variously realized, for a formulaic figure of pan-Indo-European distribution discussed in chap. 31, as in Old Irish *gonas géntar* 'he who slays will be slain', or Greek κτανέοντα κατέκτα 'he slays him who would slay', or Vedic *yó no . . . jighā́ṁsati/ . . . hantanā tám* 'he who would slay us . . . slay him!'

A grammatical variant of the reciprocal figure is §§6ff.,

> comath fírinni, cotn-ofathar
> turcbath fírinni, tan-uircéba . . .
> coicleth a thúatha, cot-céillfetar . . .
>
> Let him preserve justice, it will preserve him.

Let him raise justice, it will raise him . . .
Let him care for his tribes, they will care for him . . .,

with three parallel verbs with 'justice' and three with 'tribes'.

The central formula of *Audacht Morainn*, which introduces each alliterative sentence of §§12-21, Kelly's section three which according to him forms with section five the oldest stratum of the text, is

Is tre f̊ír flathemon

It is through the ruler's truth . . .

This formula introduces each alliterative sentence of §§12-21. I have treated elsewhere (Watkins 1979b) the close verbal fit of this formula with that of the Hindu act of truth

(téna) r̥téna / satyéna

By (this) truth . . .

discussed in chap. 5. Together with Avestan *aṣ̌a* and Greek δίκηι in cleft sentences like the Old Irish *is tre f̊ír* (*flathemon*) we have 'not only a cultural institution common to Indo-Iranian, Greek and Celtic, the mystical power of the ruler's truth, but a Common Indo-European syntactic construction which continues the linguistic expression of this cultural institution in each tradition' (p. 189). Runs of alliterative strophes like

§12 Is tre f̊ír flathemon mortlithi márṡlóg márlóchet
  di doínib dingbatar.
§14 Is tre f̊ír flathemon fo- síd sámi sube soäd
  sádili -slána.
§20 Is tre f̊ír flathemon to- aidbli éisc
  i sruthaib -snáthar

It is through the ruler's truth that plagues, a great host,
  and great lightnings are warded off from people.
It is through the ruler's truth that he secures peace,
  tranquillity, joy, ease, comfort.
It is through the ruler's truth that abundance of fish
  swim in streams,

are directly comparable to runs of triṣṭubh strophes in Vedic like RV 4.3.9a, 10a, 11a, 12a, all beginning with *r̥téna*.

In these seventh-century texts the sheer variety of strophic structures observable in a single composition like *Audacht Morainn* is striking. Each section has its own style, its own metrics and alliteration, its own rhetoric. To the examples given we may add the two invocations to *aí* 'poetic art' in *Ériu* 13.38f. and 39f. (CIH 1128.20ff. and 1129.11ff.) printed and discussed in Breatnach 1981:58-9 and Watkins 1963b:239-40:

> fo chen aí
> ilchrothach ilgnúisech ilbrechtach
> bé sóer sonaisc
>
> ar dligid tuarastal
> ar ní tualaing as-rinde cen tuarastal
> ar dligid cach aisndis a tuarastal
> . . .
> fo-glinn fo-glennar
> do-eim do emar
> for-reith for-rethar
> for cúartaib cloth
>
> Welcome, poetic art,
> of many forms, many faces, many spells,
> noble, well-linked lady.
>
> For she is entitled to reward,
> for she does not tolerate telling without reward,
> for every telling is entitled to its reward.
> . . .
> She studies, she is studied,
> she protects, she is protected,
> she proceeds, she is proceeded to
> on circuits of fame.
>
> Fo chen aí
> ingen soïs
> sïur chéile
> ingen menman
> míadach mórdae . . .
>
> Welcome, poetic art,
> daughter of learning,
> sister of reason,
> daughter of mind,
> noble, exalted . . .

The first is stress-counting, each strophe totaling eight or ten according to Breatnach, while the second is syllable-counting, with 12 lines of four syllables each after the first line of three. Both clearly belong to the same 'Creed' of poetry (*crédha na filidheachta ann so*, CIH 1128.14). The personification as woman in each is an icon of the feminine gender of the word *aí*.

We have examined instances of the strophic style in Early Irish, with lines of rhythmic-syntactic units sometimes stress-timed, sometimes syllable-timed. The lines are usually heavily alliterative, long, short or alternating, and exhibit characteristic figures of grammar, perturbations of word order, and straining of syntax or sense. They coexist, sometimes in the same document, with both normal prose and 'normal' early rhymed syllabic verse, of which we have some very fine examples from the first half of the seventh century like *Tiughraind Bhécáin* and *Fo réir Choluimb* (chap. 16), both about St. Columb Cille (St. Columba).[11] Compare from the former (§5):

> Cechaing tonnaig tresaig magain mongaig rónaig
> roluind mbedcaig mbruichrich mbarrḟind faílid mbrónaig
>
> He traversed the wavey, tumultuous place, foaming, full of seals,
> very rough, leaping, turbulent, white-topped, joyful, sorrowful.

The same 'poetico-legal' cum ecclesiastical tradition which we have noted above, following Binchy and Breatnach, in the production of important but obscure rhetorical *roscada* through the seventh and eighth centuries, is probably responsible for the late sixth-century *Amra Choluimb Chille* 'Wonders of St. Columba' as well, composed shortly after the saint's death in 597. In Kelly's words (1975:74-5), 'It is written in a complex and obscure style with many learned references and unusual Latin loanwords (see RC 20.33). The lines are generally unrimed, irregular in length, and are not always connected by alliteration.'[12] We find also the same variations of word order ('Bergin's law', tmesis, preposed genitive) as we have observed earlier, and many examples, with elaborate variations, of Breatnach's first type of *rosc*, syllabically regular lines with fixed cadence and alliteration. I have cited a number of these in 1963b:228, 237, 243-4. They make extensive use of grammatical parallelism. The most noteworthy are the runs of three or four parallel tricolic long lines, like §12:

> ar di-n condiath || con-roeter | bïu -bath
>
> For the leader (?) who protected the living has died on us.

Stylistically compare the antithesis in the last colon *bïu -bath* 'living died' with that of the last colon of the verse of *Tiughraind Bhécáin* just cited: *fáilid mbrónaig* 'joyful, sorrowful'. Metrically the line is directly comparable to the Vedic tricolic triṣṭubh/jagatī, and mutatis mutandis the Greek iambic trimeter catalectic/iambic trimeter and other meters, and doubtless the Old Avestan [4 || 7] line. The Old Irish lines like those of Vedic and Old Avestan are grouped into strophes.

11. Both edited by Kelly (1973) and (1975), and both attributed by him to Bécán mac Luigdech, surely correctly.

12. Kelly goes on to show that the difference in temper and style between the *Amra* and *Tiughraind Bhécáin* is such that their attribution to the same author is less than credible; *Tuighráind Bhécáin* and *Fo réir Choluimb* on the other hand are probably by the same poet, Bécán mac Luigdech. Both poems of the latter do show clear verbal influence of the *Amra*, for all that they are aesthetically more pleasing to us.

In the two lengthy compositions in *rosc* we have looked at, *Audacht Morainn* and *Amra Choluimb Chille* we find clear instances of Indo-European tradition both in cultural institutions and their linguistic and poetic expression. The genre of each, wisdom literature/mirror of princes and eulogy/lament, are ancient and widespread, at once universal and particular in their traditions.

To the degree that the strophic style of rhythmic/syntactic phrases as verse lines, grouped together as variegated units, exhibits particular similarities in each of the related traditions where we observe it and is not simply one of a set of independent but parallel creations based on universal characteristics of human speech and discourse, to that degree we may speak of Indo-European inheritance in so-called "rhythmic prose".

It is clear that Irish compositions in *rosc* of the late ninth century are direct continuations of a very specific poetic tradition which we can observe fully developed in Ireland in the late sixth century. While the stamp and flavor of Christian learning on this tradition is obvious and recognized, especially and most understandably in the *Amra(e)* 'Wonders' of St. Columba, the similarities in strophic style to Latin and Umbrian prayer, Avestan liturgy, Hittite and Anatolian ritual utterance and, as we shall see, Old Indic ritual litany are too strong to allow an explanation of the poetic style of *Audacht Morainn* or *Amra Choluimb Chille* from Christianity, the Bible, or the Liturgy alone. The native component of *rosc* is real.

The similarity of certain Medieval Latin texts in the Menippean tradition to the *rosc*(*ad*) style of Early Irish, rightly noted by P. Dronke (1994), is probably to be attributed to Irish influence on Hiberno-Latin, diffused to the continent. Dronke, like W. M. Lindsay, suggests that 'Aethicus Ister', the 8th-century author of the *Cosmographia* (ed. M. d'Avezac, 1852) was in fact an Irishman. On the Irish influence on Hiberno-Latin meters see also now the recent work of Herren (1991), which would support the same conclusion which I suggested in 1963b:247-8.

25

The *Aśvamedha* or Horse Sacrifice: An Indo-European liturgical form

At the Journées de synthèse historique of 1938 E. Benveniste presented a communication on 'The Indo-Europeans and the populating of Europe'.[1] He listed in the resumé as one of 'the distinctive features of [the Indo-Europeans'] first community,' along with 'patriarchal structure of the extended family, ancestor cult, agriculture and pastoralism, the aristocratic style of a society of priests, warriors and farmers,'

> worship of "natural forces" and royal sacrifices (of which the most important is that of the horse, the Vedic *aśvamedha*).

We may legitimately look upon the Aśvamedha as the principal Indo-European kingship ritual.

The traditional comparanda are three: the richly documented Indian *aśvamedha*, the Roman *October Equus*, and the Irish kingship inauguration rite known as *feis* (e.g. *Temro*) 'Feast (of Tara)',[2] known principally from the (doubtless biased) description of the 12th-century Welshman Giraldus Cambrensis. Three involve the sacrifice of a horse; the Indic and Irish versions show in addition symbolic or real copulation with the horse, on the part of the queen with a dead stallion in India, of the king with a live mare in Ireland. To these three comparanda a fourth may now be added: see below.

Giraldus de Barri, called Cambrensis 'of Wales', was born in the castle of Manorbier, in Pembrokeshire around 1146, to a Norman father and a Welsh mother. He visited Ireland in 1183 and again in 1185; his family the fitzGeralds were important principals in the Norman conquest of Ireland in that century. The first recension of his *History* or *Topography of Ireland* was composed between 1185 and 1188. The Latin text was edited by O'Meara 1949, and a newly revised translation is found in O'Meara 1982. I quote the relevant passage from the latter (p. 109-110):

---

1. Quoted at length at the end of chap. 4.

2. Literally 'sleeping with', verbal noun of *foaid* 'spends the night, sleeps (with)'. *Feiss Temhra la Diarmaid* (Annals of Ulster 559) should thus be understood as 'Sleeping with (the sovereignty of) Tara by Diarmaid.' Cf. Schröder 1927, Carney 1955, J.F. Nagy 1985, McCone 1990.

> There are some things which, if the exigencies of my account did not demand it, shame would discountenance their being described. But the austere discipline of history spares neither truth nor modesty.
>
> There is in the northern and farther part of Ulster, namely in Kenelcunill, a certain people which is accustomed to appoint its king with a rite altogether outlandish and abominable. When the whole people of that land has been gathered together in one place, a white mare is brought forward into the middle of the assembly. He who is to be inaugurated, not as chief, but as a beast, not as a king, but as an outlaw, has bestial intercourse with her before all, professing himself to be a beast also. The mare is then killed immediately, cut up in pieces, and boiled in water. A bath is prepared for the man afterwards in the same water. He sits in the bath surrounded by all his people, and all, he and they, eat of the meat of the mare which is brought to them. He quaffs and drinks of the broth in which he is bathed, not in any cup, or using his hand, but just dipping his mouth into it about him. When this unrighteous rite has been carried out, his kingship and dominion has been conferred.

The slaughter of the mare with a blow of the axe, a boiling cauldron, and the naked king in a large wooden barrel surrounded by an entourage, all gnawing on pieces of flesh, is depicted in an illustration in ms. Nat. Libr. Irel. 700, from ca. 1200, reproduced in O'Meara, loc. cit.

For the other rituals themselves, their description, and their comparative study we may refer to the work of J. Puhvel.[3] He presents an analysis of the *October Equus* (known principally from Festus 190 L), which was sacrificed to Mars and then dismembered. Its tail was brought on the run from the Campus Martius to the Regia to sprinkle its fire altar with blood.

Puhvel's description of the Indian Aśvamedha is as follows:

> The main ritual took three days. On the principal, second day of the sacrifice the king drove in a war chariot drawn by the stallion and three other horses. The victim was anointed by the king's three foremost wives, and its mane and tail were adorned with pearls. The sacrifice took place at twenty-one stakes . . . The stallion was smothered to death, whereupon the principal queen symbolically cohabited with it under covers, while the entourage engaged in obscene banter. Then followed the cutting up of the victim, disposal of the parts, further blood sacrifices, ablutions, and disbursement of priestly honoraria.

Puhvel (p. 276) goes on rightly to note the articles in the Hittite Law Code (§§199-200a) which prescribe capital punishment for bestiality with pig, dog, or cattle, but states that for a man with horse or mule it is not an offense, but 'he cannot become a priest'. This may be a relic of a similar practice.

More interestingly, it is now known from the scenes depicted on the recently published large relief vase from İnandık (Özgüç 1988, with rich illustrations) that in a ritual in Old Hittite times a couple, probably the king and queen, apparently engaged in a public, ritual copulation, even if our texts are silent on the practice.

3. Puhvel 1987. On the Aśvamedha see also O'Flaherty 1980, and especially Jamison (to appear), Part III.D, Sexuality and Fertility. The *Aśvamedha*.

The vase, of considerable interest for the art historian, presents the sequential *narration* of the ritual by four friezes of appliqué relief figures and images, beginning with the preparation of foodstuffs by cooks, and continuing with processions of musicians with various instruments and other ritual personae familiar from our texts, leading up to the sacrifice of a bull before a bull-statue. The third frieze, again "reading" from bottom up and left to right depicts a procession of musicians moving to a temple with a veiled woman and two musicians on the roof, followed and concluded by a sort of zoom-focus to two figures on an elaborate bed: a male figure preserved only below the waist, reaching out to remove the veil from the head of the female figure. With Özgüç I believe the female figure on the roof and the one in the bed are the same person, but I believe she is the queen and that the male and the female are not god and goddess, with Özgüç , but the royal couple. The scene is rendered with characteristic Hittite delicacy and restraint, but the fourth and final frieze with its "small goddess Inanna lyre" (GIŠ ^{D}INANNA.TUR) player, cymbalists, other musicians, and tumbling acrobats clearly establishes the theme. The last cymbalist in the procession has her back turned to the final relief; a standing man grasps from behind a standing woman bent double, with her skirt raised and falling to the ground, and they copulate *more ferarum*, in the manner of beasts. The symbolism is clear.

Our concern in the present chapter is only the liturgical aspect of the Indian Aśvamedha, the litany of mantras or *yajūṁṣi* 'spells' recited at each sequential ritual act in the Vedic Aśvamedha, which are given with greater or lesser variation in the various saṁhitās of the White (Vājasaneyī-Saṁhitā) and Black (Kāṭhaka-, Maitrāyaṇī-, Taittirīya-Saṁhitā) Yajurvedas, and in part their respective Brāhmaṇas and Sūtras, notably the Śatapatha Brāhmaṇa to the Vājasaneyī-Saṁhitā and the Āpastamba and Baudhāyana Śrauta Sūtras to the Taittirīya-Saṁhitā.

What for our purposes is most noteworthy is that the litany of mantras in the Horse Sacrifice are not all in regular isosyllabic verse, as is found most frequently in these Yajurvedic texts. Rather, in the Aśvamedha we find regular verses interspersed with metrically irregular strophes held together more by grammatical parallelism than by meter, as well as long litanies of repetitive devotions.

I take as reference point the text as given in the TS and ĀŚS, since they are both more extensive than the other three Yajurvedas and accessible to readers in translation.[4] The ordering of the liturgy is better preserved in the other three, however, especially MS, and we will treat some of the four sections in TS books 4 and 5 after the litany proper, which begins at TS 7.1.11 = MS 3.12.1 = KAśv 1.2 = VS 22.1.

4. Text: Indische Studien 11-12, ed. A. Weber, Leipzig: Brockhaus 1871-2. Translation: A. B. Keith, The Veda of the Black Yajus School entitled Taittiriya Saṁhita, Harvard Or. Ser. 18-19 [1914], reprinted Delhi: Motilal 1967. For the Āpastamba Śrauta Sūtra the text edition is by R. Garbe, (1882-1902) repr. New Delhi 1983, and the very valuable translation by W. Caland (1928) repr. Wiesbaden 1969; for the Baudhāyana Śrauta Sūtra the text edition is by W. Caland (1904-13), repr. New Delhi 1982. For the MS and KS (KAśv = vol. 3, p. 151 ff.) the editions are those of L. von Schroeder, 1881-6 and 1900-10, both reprinted Wiesbaden: Steiner 1972; for the VS A. Weber 1852, repr. Varanasi: Chowkhamba 1972. For the Śatapatha Brāhmaṇa the text is A. Weber (1855) repr. 1964, and the translation J. Eggeling (1880-1900), Sacred Books of the East, repr. Delhi 1978.

The *aśvamedhamantrāḥ* begin with a formulaic non-metrical strophe, spoken by the *adhvaryu*-priest as he takes up the rope to put on the horse as a halter, TS 7.1.11-20:

devásya tvā savitúḥ prasavé	On the impulse of the god Savitar thee
aśvínor bāhúbhyām	I take with the arms of the Aśvins,
puṣṇó hástābhyām ā́ dade	with the hands of Pūṣan,

This strophe recurs with variants literally hundreds of times in Yajurvedic, Brāhmaṇa, and Sūtra texts (Bloomfield, Vedic Concordance). The same god Savitar is addressed in the final mantra of the Aśvamedha ritual in the TS, 7.5.24:

> yé te pánthānaḥ savitaḥ purvyā́so
>
> Your ancient paths, o Savitar,

taken from RV 1.35.11 with some variation. The name of the god Savitar thus makes a ring. In the KAśv on the other hand the latter mantra comes at the very beginning, KAśv 1.1. The symbolism is appropriate for both: RV 1.35 celebrates Savitar as both morning and evening god. There follows a metrical strophe, then a litany to the halter (TS 7.1.11c),

> abhidhā́ asi bhúvanam asi yantā́ 'si dhartā́ 'si . . .
>
> Thou art the surrounder, thou art the world, thou art the restrainer,
> thou art the holder . . .,

picked up and echoed by the grammatical figure

> . . . yantā́ 'si yámano dhartā́ 'si dharuṇaḥ
>
> Thou art the restrainer who restrains, thou art the holder who holds.

Then the horse is apostrophized in the elliptic figure discussed in chap. 19 (TS 7.1.11e):

> kṛṣyaí tvā kṣémāya tvā
> rayyaí tvā póṣāya tvā
> pṛthivyaí tvā 'ntárikṣāya tvā divé tvā
> saté tvā́ 'sate tvā . . .
>
> For ploughing thee, for dwelling thee,
> for riches thee, for increase thee,
> for earth thee, for atmosphere thee, for sky thee,
> for being thee, for non-being thee . . .

The following passage 7.1.12, the *aśvanāmāni* or horse-names, is a liturgical synonomy, an invocation by all the names of the horse:

> áśvo 'si háyo 'si . . . árvā 'si . . . vājy àsi . . .
>
> Thou art horse, thou art steed, . . . thou art courser, . . . thou art racer . . .

This invocation prefigures the penultimate sentence of the TS, the brahman following the final mantras of the Aśvamedha (7.5.16-24), which is TS 7.5.25.2:

> háyo devā́n avahad
> árvā́ 'surān
> vājī́ gandharvā́n
> áśvo manuṣyā̀n
>
> As steed it carried the gods,
> as courser the Asuras,
> as racer the Gandharvas,
> as horse men.

The whole of TS 7.5.25 is repeated with minor variations in ŚBr 10.6.4.1, from which this passage was first quoted by H. Güntert over 70 years ago (Güntert 1921) as an example of the Indo-European metaphor of 'language of gods and language of men', and further examined in subsequent studies by myself (Watkins 1970a) and Toporov (1981:204-5). See chap. 3. The opposition between the ordinary and poetic-language denominations of the horse is found already in the Rigveda hymns to the sacrificial horse 1.162 and 163, which contain some of these very names.

TS 7.1.11 through 17 continue with lengthy litanies of ultra-short mantras, linked by loose parallelism: *ā́yanāya svā́hā, prā́yanāya svā́hā* . . . 'to the going, hail! to the advancing, hail!' . . . *agnáye svā́hā* . . . *pṛthivyaí svā́hā* 'to Agni, hail! . . . to earth, hail! . . .' In 18 we get the seasonal consecrations (*ṛtudīkṣā́ḥ*), with the strophe

> vásubhir devébhir devátayā
> gāyatréṇa tvā chándasā yunajmi
> vasanténa tvartúnā havíṣā dīkṣayāmi
>
> With the Good Gods as deity,
> with the gāyatrī as meter I yoke thee,
> with the spring season as oblation I consecrate thee,

repeated verbatim with four other groups of gods, four more meters and four more seasons (summer, rainy, autumn, winter). Verse 19 brings a series of over 80 invocations to the horse, his movements and actions past, present, and future, including such grammatical figures as 'To him about to scratch, hail! To him scratching, hail! To him having scratched, hail!'[5]

Verse 20 closes this section with further offerings and the very emblematic example of the stylistic and grammatical figure 'Truth's Truth' which H. Oertel took as the title of his work cited in chap. 22:

> ṛtám asy ṛtásyartám asi
> satyám asi satyásya satyám asi
>
> Thou art Truth; thou art the Truth of Truth;
> thou art Verity; thou art the Verity of Verity.

The next section, TS 7.2.11-20, gives mantras for offerings to the numbers (To one, hail! . . .); then 7.3.11-20 intersperses some irregular verse triadic sets with the refrain *váśaṭ svā́hā námaḥ*, 'dithyrambic' sequences, and finishes with a litany (with *svā́hā* 'hail!') to the parts of the horse. Noteworthy in the metrically and otherwise irregular 11b is the sentiment (common in Vedic) we saw expressed in the Umbrian prayer in chap. 18: (*yajñaśamalám*) . . . *tásmin hīyatām̥ yó 'smā́n dvéṣṭi* . . . *yajñaśamalám . . . tásmint sīdatu yó 'smā́n dvéṣṭi* 'Let (the fault in the worship) settle on him who hates us, let the fault in the worship rest with him who hates us.'

The last major section in the TS, 7.4.12-22, culminates dramatically with the symbolic copulation scene in 19. (TS and the other two Black Yajurveda Saṁhitās MS and KAśv omit the actual killing of the horse altogether; for the mantras to that we have VS (and ŚB), as well as the detailed description of the ritual in ĀŚS, which we will see presently.)

TS 7.4.13-18 leads up to the killing (itself omitted) with a series of *svā́hā* 'hail!' and *námaḥ* 'reverence' formulas and interspersed verses, including one which is found in MS 3.12.1 at the beginning of the Aśvamedha:

> yó árvantaṃ jíghāṁsati, tám abhy àmīti váruṇaḥ
> paró mártaḥ paró śvā́
>
> He who would slay the courser, him Varuṇa punishes;
> away the man, away the dog!

It ends with a series of riddles (*brahmodya*) and answers in verse, some built on RV 1.164.34-5, the riddle hymn which follows the two horse-sacrifice hymns RV 1.162-3. The riddle style is surely common Indo-Iranian, and probably Indo-European. Compare e.g. TS 7.4.18e:

---

5. *kaṇḍūyiṣyaté/kaṇḍūyámānāya/kaṇḍūyitā́ya*. The humor—which I think we should recognize as such—recalls the mock-heroic in genre, as do such continuations as *yán méhati* (VS 22.8 *yán mū́traṃ karóti*) *tásmai svā́hā, yác chákṛt karóti tásmai svā́hā* 'To what he stales, hail! To the dung he makes, hail!' Both MS and VS omit these participles of 'scratch' and other verbs of ordinary equine activities, as well as the dung. As we shall see, many of the texts omit the cruder part of the symbolic copulation liturgy as well.

pr̥cchā́mi tvā (RV yátra) bhúvanasya nā́bhim
pr̥cchāmi tvā vŕ̥ṣṇo áśvasya rétaḥ[6]

I ask thee about the navel of the earth
I ask thee about the seed of the stallion,

like Old Avestan Y. 44.1 etc. (even to the position of the caesura)

taṯ ϑβā pərəsā, ərəš mōi vaocā ahurā

This I ask thee, tell me truly, Lord,

and save for the absence of a reflex of IE **pr̥(k̂)-sk̂oh$_2$* 'I ask', Old Norse *Alvíssmál* 9.1 etc.:

Segðu mér þat, Alvíss

Tell me that, All-knower.

For the actual sacrificial act of killing we may turn to the Āpastamba Śrauta Sūtra 20.17.1 ff. It begins with the recitation by the adhvaryu priest of a non-metrical strophic mantra, given in full in TS 7.5.19.1-2, consisting of four triplets of the type

ā́ 'krān vājī́ pr̥thivīm
agním̐ yújam akr̥ta vājī́ árvā

The racer has come to the earth;
the swift courser has made Agni his yoke-mate,

repeated with atmosphere and Vāyu, sky and Sūrya:

cákṣur asi cákṣur mayi dhehi

Thou art the eye; place the eye in me,

repeated with 'ear' and 'life'. This is followed by a verse with *kram* 'stride' and *vājī́*, then another parallel mantra strophe ('Thy back is the sky . . . Thine eye the sun . . .'),

---

6. The answers are respectively the worship (*yajñā́ḥ*) and the soma. For the metaphor of 'where (RV *yátra* < IE **i̯o-tro*) is the navel of the earth' compare *Od.* 1.50, of Calypso's sea-girt island ὅϑι (IE **i̯o-dhi*) τ' ὀμφαλός ἐστι ϑαλάσσης 'where the navel of the sea is,' as well as (of the stone in the religious center of Delphi) Bacchylides 4.4 παρ' [ὀμφα]λὸν ὑψιδείρου χϑονός 'by the navel of the high-cliffed land', Pind. *Py.* 4.74 πὰρ μέσον ὀμφαλὸν εὐδένδροιο ῥηϑὲν ματέρος '(the oracle) spoken by the middle navel of well-treed mother earth', and Aeschylus *Eumen.* 166 πάρεστι γᾶς τ' ὀμφαλὸν προσδρακεῖν 'one can see the very navel of the earth,' with a deft phonetic figure in the strophic responsion, 160 **πάρεστι μαστί**κτορος ~ 167 **πάρεστι γᾶς τ'**.

both given in full in TS 5.7.24-25, then a passage of stylistically Brāhmaṇa-like prose, TS 5.7.26, repeated exactly for the three deities Agni, Vāyu, Āditya:

> agníḥ paśúr āsīt, ténāyajanta, sá etáṃ lokám ajayad
> yásminn agníḥ, sá te lokás, táṃ jeṣyasy, áthā́va jighra vāyúḥ . . .
>
> Agni was an animal, they sacrificed him; it won this world,
> where Agni is; this is thy world, thou wilt win it, and so sniff![7]
> Vāyu . . .

ĀŚS at this point prescribes the *āprī*-hymn to the sacrificial horse found in TS 5.1.11 and in the three other Saṁhitās. It is a well-formed metrical hymn of eleven verses, correctly fulfilling the requirements of the genre: see chap. 21 with n. 16.

VS 23.13-17 present further non-metrical strophic mantras, ending with the prose part just cited. Strophe 16 is a verse the first half of which is RV 1.162.21ab:

> ná vā́ u etán mriyase ná riṣyasi
> devā́n íd eṣi pathíbhiḥ sugébhiḥ
>
> You do not die of this, indeed, you come to no harm;
> You go to the gods on easy paths.

The moment of reassurance is the moment of putting to death, in the ageless, universal rite. The horse is suffocated by a woolen or linen cloth (*śyāmūlena kṣemena vā* ĀŚS 17.9); no blood is shed.

The king's chief wife is then led by a priest to lie down beside the dead stallion for a symbolic act to assure fertility. Both are covered by a cloth (*tārpya*). She says in singsong verse,[8]

> ámbe ámbike ámbālike
> ná mā nayati káś caná
> sásasty aśvakáḥ
>
> Mother, dear mother, little mother!
> No one takes me to wife,
> the bad little horse is sleeping.

She or the other wives of the king as they go around the horse (both in ĀŚS) then utter(s) a strophe taken precisely from RV 2.23.1, the Brahmaṇaspati/Bṛhaspati hymn

7. The ĀŚS says the formula is to make the horse drink, and the parallel VS 23.17 has in place of the last imperative *píbetā́ apáḥ* 'drink these waters.' On sniffing of animals and the 'sniff-kiss' in Vedic ritual and mythology see Jamison 1991:115-20.

8. From here on I give a composite text, based on TS 7.4.19, VS 23.18-32, MS 3.12.20, KAśv 5.4.8 (both considerably abridged), and ĀŚS 20.17.12-18.7. I do not discuss the variants, except as explicitly noted.

studied in chap. 22 with the Common Indo-Iranian stylistic figure:

gaṇānāṃ tvā gaṇapatiṁ havāmahe
vaso mama
priyāṇāṃ tvā priyapatiṁ havāmahe
vaso mama
nidhīnāṃ tvā nidhipatiṁ havāmahe
vaso mama

Throng-lord of throngs we invoke thee,
o my good one;
precious-lord of the precious we invoke thee,
o my good one;
treasure-lord of treasures we invoke thee,
o my good one.

The adhvaryu says (TS):

suvargé loké sám prórṇvāthām

In the heavenly world be you two completely covered.

The queen says:

ā́ 'hám ajāni garbhadhám ā́ tvám ajāsi garbadhám
táu sahá catúraḥ padáḥ sám prá sārayāvahai.[9]

I will urge on the impregnator, you will urge on the impregnator;
let the two of us together stretch out our four legs.

The adhvaryu says:

vṛ́ṣā vājī́[10] retodhā́ réto dadhātu

Let the stallion, semen-producer, produce semen,

and continues with 7 octosyllabic pādas (the last four only in TS and ĀŚS):

---

9. ĀŚS 20.18.1 gives as well the variant, apparently from another śākhā or Vedic school (Caland):

ahaṃ syām tvaṃ syāḥ surādhāḥ kulajaḥ syāt
imāś caturaḥ pado vyatiṣajya śayāvahai

I'd like to be, you'd like to be, let there be a wealthy, well-born (sən)
let us two lie down, entwining our four legs

10. Reading *vājī́* with VS (MS *vām aśvó*, TS *vām̐*), cf. *vṛ́ṣṇo aśvásya rétaḥ* TS 7.4.18e. Note the total phonetic figure, *vṛ- v- r-t-dh r-t d-dh-t*.

út sakthyò̀r gr̥dám dhehi
añjím údañjim ánv aja
yá strīṇā́ṃ jīvabhójano
yá āsām biladhā́vanaḥ
priyá strīṇā́m apīcyàḥ
yá āsām kr̥ṣṇé lákṣmaṇi
sárdigr̥dim parā́vadhīt.[11]

Bring the penis into the two thighs,
drive along the erect and unctuous one
which is women's living enjoyment,
which is their hole-runner,
women's dear secret (pleasure)
which has hit the sardigr̥di (clitoris?)
in their black(haired) mark.

The queen then repeats her litany, scolding the horse (or its member) with a cruder variant:

ámbe ámbike ámbālike
ná me yabhati káś caná
sásasty aśvakáḥ

Mother, dear mother, little mother,
no one is fucking me;[12]
the bad little horse is asleep.

She repeats this three more times, each of the four followed by a bantering erotic verse spoken by one of the other wives of the king while slapping her thighs:

ūrdhvā́m enām úc chrayatād, veṇubhārám girā́v iva
áthāsyā mádhyam edhatām̐, śīté vā́te punánn iva

Raise her on high, like a load of bamboo on a mountain,
and let her middle prosper, like someone winnowing in a cool wind.

Mother, dear mother, little mother,
no one . . .

11. For *gr̥dá-* (m.) and the echoic expressive form *sárdigr̥di-* (f.), which make ring-composition, see Mayrhofer, EWA s.v. *gr̥dá-* with references to Hoffmann (1975:570 n. et al.). In these and *gudá-* 'gut, arse' and °*gadá-* 'sickness, delirium' the non-canonical sequence *gVd-* has the same expressive value as noted for the root *GAD* by Thieme 1972: 80: 'symbolic imitation of abnormal speech'. See Mayrhofer EWA s.v. *GAD*. One may be permitted to think of English *god*. An expressive figure here also in *añj- -añj- an(v) aj-*.

12. The verb is as vulgar in Sanskrit as its English translation or Russian cognate and translation: IE **i̯ebh-*.

yád dhariṇī́ yávam atti, ná puṣṭám paśú manyate
śūdrā́ yád áryajārā, ná póṣāya dhanāyati

When the (wild) doe is eating grain, she doesn't think the
(domestic) animal is fatted;
when the śūdra-woman has an Ārya as lover, she doesn't
seek wealth (= has no need) for fattening.

Mother, dear mother, little mother,
no one . . .

iyáṃ yakā́ śakuntikā́ 'hálam íti sarpati
ā́hataṃ gabhé páso ní jalgulīti dhā́ṇikā

This little bird which creeps around saying 'ā́halam'[13]
knocks the penis into the slit; the vulva devours it.

Mother, dear mother, little mother,
no one . . .

mātā́ ca te pitā́ ca te (á)gram vṛkṣásya rohataḥ
prá tilāmī́ti[14] te pitā́ gabhé muṣṭím ataṁsayat

Your mother and your father are climbing to the top of the tree;
'I'm passing over' says your father (as) he moved his fist (= caput
penis Caland and commentators, but perhaps to be taken literally)
to and fro in the slit.

The sexual litany is turned off as suddenly as it was begun: the next mantra, spoken by all the wives, hymns the mythical stallion Dadhikrāvan of the Rigveda:

dadhikrā́vṇo akāriṣam, jiṣṇór áśvasya vājínaḥ
surabhí no múkhā karat, prá ṇa āyūṁṣi tāriṣat

I have glorified Dadhikrāvan, the victorious race horse;
may he make our mouths fragrant, may he lengthen our days.

With three mantras to the healing waters they wash themselves, then proceed to marking out with needles the lines of eventual dismemberment of the horse. A litany of *svā́hā*-formulas to the horse follows, some of the familiar Argument plus Negated Argument form:

13. There is probably a play on *ā́halam* (VS, MS *āhalak*) and *ā́hatam* 'knocked' (VS *ā́hanti*).

14. Perhaps with popular *l* for *prá tirāmi*. Meaning 'I'm coming' in the sexual sense? TS *prá sulāmi* '?' (comm. *praveśayāmi* 'I (make) enter').

sitā́ya svā́hā ásitāya svā́hā
abhíhitāya sv. ánabhihitāya sv.
yuktā́ya sv. áyuktāya sv. . . .

To the bound, hail! to the unbound, hail!
to the fastened, hail! to the unfastened, hail!
to the yoked, hail! to the unyoked, hail! . . .

The whole Aśvamedha ritual must have been quite a show.

This ritual has the longest litany and the most extensive in non-metrical, strophic mantras and spells (*yajūṁṣi*) alternating with metrical verses in Vedic. The ritual itself has long been held to be an Indo-European inheritance; to the Irish and Roman comparanda we were able to add the veiled but evocative representation of a ritual public copulation of the royal couple in Old Hittite times on the recently published great İnandık vase.

We must add that the verbal elaboration of the liturgy, the stylistic alternation between metrical and non-metrical strophic runs, points also and independently to the inheritance of the Aśvamedha as a ritual. In short the Aśvamedha with its preponderance of strophic "rhythmic prose" litanies is also the most Indo-European of Indic rituals. When we compare the Vedic non-metrical strophic mantras in the liturgy of the Horse Sacrifice with the strophes (*vacastašti*) of the Zoroastrian liturgy of the Yasna Haptaŋhāiti, with the strophes of the ancient Roman lustration of the fields, the Umbrian purification of Iguvium, the Old Irish invocation to the Caldron of Poesy and the eulogy of Saint Columba, the Old Hittite funeral verses, and the Palaic sacrificial carmen addressed to the victim, we are forced to one conclusion. The strophic and stichic structures are all the same, with short lines commanded by phraseology, parallelism, and syntactic constituency; the stylistic figures are the same, down to such particular features as the elliptic offering; and the pragmatics are the same, ranging beyond general and quasi-universal characteristics of religious and liturgical language—compare the Book of Common Prayer—to features particular to only these traditions in this context.

I submit that these are cognate poetic forms in the several Indo-European traditions, including the most ancient. These strophic and stichic forms, these *vacastašti*'s 'word-craftings' of Indo-Iranian, Anatolian, Armenian, Italic, and Celtic are cognate just as surely as the Greek 11-syllable Sapphic/Alcaic line and the Vedic 11/12 syllable triṣṭubh/jagatī, or the 8-syllable dimeter verse lines of Greek and Vedic.

Both the metrical and the non-metrical mantra and strophic style are of comparable age at the beginnings of each of these traditions. As parallel inheritances from Indo-European poetic language the two styles of liturgy, metrical hymnic and non-metrical rhythmic/syntactic, are of equal antiquity. The latter, improperly termed "rhythmic prose", thus differs entirely from narrative prose as a consciously elaborated art form, which is a younger development in each of the traditions.[15]

15. That is not, of course, to say that the Indo-Europeans did not tell stories, fables, and tales in "prose", which they surely did and continue to do. Our earliest representative examples are in Old Hittite, like the Palace Chronicle and the Zalpa tale.

26

Orphic gold leaves and the great way of the soul: Strophic style, funerary ritual formula, and eschatology

We have no examples of early liturgical texts in Greek, and no principled way of knowing whether or not they involved the sort of non-metrical rhythmic/syntactic style which we have observed elsewhere. But we might suggest that in the syntactic and lexical *responsions* of the non-syllable-counting strophic style in the traditions examined, we may find the background of the metrical, syllabic, and phonetic-echoic *responsions* which are the primary poetic feature of the fully developed strophe, antistrophe, and epode of Greek choral lyric.[1]

The single genre of Classical Greek texts which affords us a glimpse of the inherited strophic style, including both hexameter verse and what has—to my knowledge uniquely for Greece—been termed 'rhythmical prose',[2] are the famous 'Orphic gold leaves'. These are inscribed *lamellae*, rectangular gold leaf sheets sometimes even in the shape of ivy leaves, found with burials from the 5th and mostly the 4th century B.C., in sites from Southern Italy, Thessaly, Crete, and Lesbos (unpublished). They give instructions to the dead about the way to be followed in the other world and have sometimes, rather unfairly, been styled 'passports of the dead'.

Scholars are agreed now that these texts reflect contemporary currents of Dionysiac-Orphic (or Orphic-Dionysiac) views of the afterlife, to a considerable extent overlapping with views associated with Pythagoras and the Pythagoreans.[3] Zuntz's earlier view that the texts were wholly Pythagorean has had to be modified, but his appreciation for the tone of the texts still stands: 'I can imagine that they contain

1. See Schürch 1971.

2. Zuntz 1971:341, the classic study before the new finds of the 70's and 80's.

3. Cf. Burkert 1985:293ff., 1987:21f., 33f., and for useful discussion and references Segal 1990:411-19. All the texts except Pelinna and a small fragment in the Getty Museum may be found, with Italian translation, in Colli 1977:1.172ff. Fundamental on Pindar and these texts is Lloyd-Jones 1985. The best and most up-to-date discussion, with composite texts (established by West, Janko, and himself) and fresh translations of the whole corpus, is Obbink 1992.

main items—verses and ritual prose—of a Pythagorean *Missa pro defunctis* celebrated at the burial of those who took the tablets with them to the other world' (1971:343). Discounting the specifically Pythagorean this view is wholly comparable with Segal's (1990:413), that 'the repetitive, rhythmic, and formulaic qualities of the new texts, as of many of the previously discovered texts, would make them highly suitable for oral . . . funerary performance . . . Identical texts of the two [Pelinna] inscriptions . . . suggest that both are copies of a preexisting ritual formula, rather than an *ad hoc* creation for this burial'.

The most recently discovered of these texts are two ivy-shaped gold leaves found in Pelinna, Thessaly, and first published in 1987.[4] The two are identical save that the shorter omits lines 4 and 7 of the longer. The latter reads:

> νῦν ἔθανες καὶ νῦν ἐγένου, τρισόλβιε, ἄματι τῶιδε.
> εἰπεῖν Φερσεφόνᾱι σ' ὅτι Βάκχιος αὐτὸς ἔλυσε.
> ταῦρος εἰς γάλα ἔθορες
> αἶψα εἰς γάλα ἔθορες.
> κριὸς εἰς γάλα ἔπεσες.
> οἶνον ἔχεις εὐδαίμονα τιμ<ά>ν
> κἀπιμένει σ' ὑπὸ γῆν τέλεα ἅσσαπερ ὄλβιοι ἄλλοι
>
> Now you died and now you were born (a god),
> o thrice-happy one, on that day.
> Tell Persephone that Bakkhios himself set you free.
> A bull, you rushed into the milk.
> Suddenly you rushed into the milk.
> A ram, you fell into the milk.
> You have the fortunate wine as your honor
> (or, you have wine as your fortunate honor)
> And there await you beneath the earth rewards even such as the other blessed ones (have). (tr. after Segal)

The parallelism of the gold leaf text from Thurii 4 θεὸς ἐγένου ἐξ ἀνθρώπου· ἔριφος ἐς γάλα ἔπετες 'From a man you were born a god; a kid, you fell into the milk', suggests that we understand θεός with ἐγένου in line 1. The phrase ἐγένου τρισόλβιε, recalls also Thurii 1 ὄλβιε καὶ μακαριστέ, θεὸς δ' ἔσηι ἀντὶ βροτοῖο 'Happy and most blessed one, you shall be a god instead of a mortal'. It is not excluded that some archetype could have read (or said) ἐγένου θεός, ὄλβιε, for the later unmetrical ἐγένου, τρισόλβιε, though this is only a tentative solution. The curious "animal falling in the milk" phrases are evidently metaphorical '*symbola*' or "passwords", tokens of identity of the addressee or speaker as an initiate, one 'set free'.

Lines 1-2 and 7 are long lines, dactylic hexameters, even if the first is irregular in the (iconic or expressive?) lengthening τρισ(σ)όλβιε. Lines 3-5 are non-metrical short lines, but isosyllabic[5] and clearly governed by grammatical parallelism, syntac-

4. Tsantsanoglou and Parássoglou 1987. Cf. also Luppe 1989 and Merkelbach 1989.

5. The exact syllable count depends on whether all possible elisions are observed, as in 7 to be read τελε' ἅσσαπερ.

tic, semantic, and phonetic. Line 6 shows the first two and last two feet of a dactylic hexameter; it is thus a truncated long line and functions as such in the closure of the shorter version. (Burkert apud Obbink suggests that something has dropped out between its two constituents). The strophic alternation of metrical long lines and non-metrical short lines closely recalls the liturgical pattern of the Vedic Aśvamedha.

Attention to phonetic figures is also a feature of this and other gold leaf texts. In particular note the anaphora-like beginning sequences of lines 3-7:

ταῦρος **εἰς** . . .
αἶψα **εἰς** . . .
κριὸς **εἰς** . . .
οἶνον ἔχ**εις** . . .
κάπιμεν**ει σ**' . . .

Grammatical "otherness" is clearly sought after in these five phonetic "samenesses", the identical strings of preposition εἰς, 2sg. pres. -εις, and 3sg. pres. -ει plus elided 2sg. pronoun σ'.[6] The technique is thus identical with that of RV 8.103.11a ***úditā*** *yó **níditā** **véditā** vásu* 'who at sunrise (*úd-itā*) produces (*védi-tā*) the tethered (*ní-ditā*) wealth', discussed in chap. 16, which likewise opposes phonetic "sameness" and grammatical "otherness". The invariant unstressed *eis*, preceded by two then three syllables, is in the Pelinna gold leaf the link between the short and the long lines and concludes the strophe. We are thus justified in seeing with Segal a ring between 1 τρισόλβιε and 7 ὄλβιοι.

R. Merkelbach discussed the Pelinna text in 1989 and specifically suggested that Bacchios' act of releasing was a freeing of the defunct initiate from the 'ancient grief' of mankind as sprung from the ashes of the Titans 'thunderbolted' by Zeus for tearing to pieces and devouring Dionysus/Zagreus, the son of Persephone. The 'ancient grief' is from a fragment of a threnos of Pindar (fr. 133 Snell-Maehler), which Merkelbach printed in a strophic form recalling that of the Pelinna leaf in its opposition of long and short lines:

οἷσι δὲ **Φ**ερσε**φ**όνα **π**οινὰν **π**αλαιοῦ **π**ένθεος
δέξεται, ἐς τὸν **ὕ**περθεν **ἅ**λιον κείνων **ἐ**νάτωι **ἔ**τεϊ
ἀνδιδοῖ **ψ**υχὰς **π**άλιν,
ἐκ τᾶν βασιλῆες ἀγαυοί
καὶ **σ**θένει κραιπνοὶ **σ**οφίᾱι τε μέγιστοι
ἄνδρες **αὔ**ξοντ'· ἐς δὲ τὸν λοιπὸν χρόνον **ἥ**ροες **ἁ**–
γνοὶ πρὸς ἀνθρώπων καλέονται

For those from whom Persephone exacts the penalty of
the ancient grief, in the ninth year she restores
their souls again to the sun above; from these
come august kings, and men who are swift in strength

6. Segal 1990, followed by Obbink, notes just the first four as 'particularly striking'.

and great in wisdom; for the rest of time by men
they are called saintly heroes.

The lines, of dactylo-epitrite rhythm, are arranged differently by different editors. The sheer amount of alliteration (noted in boldface) is striking; attention to such poetic embellishment appears to be a characteristic of these Orphic-Dionysiac cum Pythagorean texts.

According to Walter Burkert (1985:293) 'most impressive is the oldest text' setting forth these eschatological doctrines of metempsychosis: Pindar's second *Olympian* Ode written in 476 for Theron of Akragas. We have already seen in chap. 18 Pindar's Saussurian hypograms of the patron's name (THĒRŌN) in line 2 of this ode (*tina* THE*eon*, *tin'* *h*ĒRŌ*a tin'* *a*N*dra*), and of his city (AKRAGANT-) in line 87 (AKRANTA GA*rueton*). Burkert (ibid. 299) paraphrases the fourth choral triad of strophe, matching antistrophe, and epode (56-80): 'Whoever has led a pious and just life finds a festive existence in the underworld, free from all cares in a place where the sun is shining at night; but evildoers suffer terrible things. The soul thereafter returns to the upper world where its fate is determined by its previous deeds; whoever stands the test three times enters the Island of the Blessed forever.' The strophe is shot through with responsions, figures, and parallelisms:

61 ἴσαις δὲ νύκτεσσιν αἰεί,
ἴσαις δ' ἁμέραις ἅλιον ἔχοντες, ἀπονέστερον
ἐσλοὶ δέκονται βίοτον, . . .
66 . . . οἵτινες ἔχαιρον εὐορκίαις ἄδακρυν νέμονται
αἰῶνα, τοὶ δ' ἀποσόρατον ὀκχέοντι πόνον

Having the sun forever for equal nights and equal days,
the good receive a life free from toil . . .
but those who rejoiced in fidelity to oaths spend a life
without tears; while the others endure toil that cannot
be looked upon.

Between the iconic pair ἴσαις . . ἴσαις 'equal . . . equal' the word αἰεί at line end links with its line initial cognate αἰῶνα, and strophe-final πόνον etymologically echoes line-final ἀπονέστερον. The syntactic core is formed by three verb phrases of the familiar Indo-European poetic type with distracted noun phrase (Adj + N) straddling the verb. All the adjectives are privative (the boldface **ἀ**-), and the syntactic parallelism is intersected by and in counterpoint to the verse-line boundaries until resolved in the last:

ἀπονέστερον | . . . δέκονται βίοτον, . . .
ἄδακρυν νέμονται | αἰῶνα, . . .
ἀποσόρατον ὀκχέοντι πόνον |

receive a life free from toil, . . .
spend a life without tears, . . .
endure toil that cannot be looked upon.

Note finally the iconic lengthening of the consonant in ὀ(κ)χέοντι 'endure', iterative of ἔχω 'have, hold' (cf. πόνον ἔχειν Soph. *OC* 232, πόνους ἔχω Aristoph. *Eccl.* 972). Other examples of the lengthening deformation process are given in chap. 3. Compare the spelling BAXXOI (= βάκχοι 'bacchants') in the Hipponion text.

The antistrophe (68) beginning ὅσοι δ' ἐτόλμασαν ἐστρίς 'whosoever had the courage three times. . .' by contrast, matching syllable for syllable, is almost entirely lacking in phonetic or grammatical figures. The crucial exception, however, is the key word. In the third line of the strophe (63) ἐσλοὶ δέκονται βίοτον, οὐ and antistrophe (70) ψυχάν, ἔτειλαν Διὸς ὁδόν (both – – ᴗ – – ᴗ ᴗ ᴗ –) the vowel sequence of the three shorts in **βίοτον** is exactly echoed by that of **Διὸς ὁδόν**, the 'road of Zeus', the 'sacred way' traveled by the soul (ψυχά) to the Island of the Blessed.

We find this expression 'Sacred Way' in the oldest of the Orphic gold leaves, that from Hipponion - Vibo Valentia in Calabria, dated around 400. It contains 16 hexameter lines, probably drawn from an old oral tradition of hexameter recitation. Compare the hemistich ἐν<ὶ> φρασὶ πευκαλίμαισι (8) 'in their keen mind' beside the Homeric phrase (4x) (ἐνὶ) φρεσὶ πευκαλίμῃσι(ν); the Hipponion leaf preserves the old zero-grade dative plural φρασί beside the φρεσί ubiquitous in our text of Homer, just like the sixth century Attic grave elegiac IG I^2 971 (Hansen CEG 28) : φρασιν : αλα μενοίνōν : beside the Homeric *h.Merc.* 62 φρεσὶν ἄλλα μενοίνα 'set his mind on other things'.[7]

The last line finishes στειχōσι κλεινοι, which to scan must be restored as στείχουσι κλεεινοί 'they tread in glory'. Attic κλεινός shows contraction.[8] The uncontracted form κλεεινός < *κλεϝεσνός (cf. Aeolic κλεεννός) is otherwise unattested; the word is not found in our corpus of Homeric and Hesiodic poetry.

The forms φρασί and κλεεινοί must come from somewhere; they are perhaps the best evidence for the correctness of Obbink's thesis that the compositors of these texts are not 'producing at best a derivative hodge-podge of formulae pirated from the language of earlier, canonized poems', but rather that 'the texts of the gold leaves are poetry, but they are neither arbitrarily, nor affectedly, nor derivatively so.' 'In all three texts some type of ritual (probably funerary or initiation) is closely connected with the performance and ritual context of poetry'—in a word, liturgy. Compare the rich anthropological literature cited by Obbink on the stylistics of ritual language.[9]

7. Janko 1984:98, followed by Obbink, puts the Homeric form φρεσί back into the composite text but wisely cautions against so doing in a note.

8. Since the text spells the spurious diphthong E (as in εμι 'I am') and reserves EI for a real diphthong (στειχōσι, εξερεεις, μελλεισι, ελθεις) or a disyllabic vowel sequence (βασελεϊ) we should perhaps see in ΚΛΕΙΝΟΙ a spelling of trisyllabic κλεενοι. I do not understand the hiatus or the diphthong in line 8 [h]οι δε σε ειρεσονται 'they will ask you'.

9. To which one may add Michael Silverstein, "Parallelism in ritual speech", Chicago Ling. Soc. Parasession 1979.

The Hipponion text shows a fine (false)[10] etymological figure in **ψυχ**αὶ νεκύο̄ν **ψύχ**ονται 'the souls of the dead cool themselves' ("chill themselves out", perhaps) in the baneful spring of oblivion on the right by the ghostly cypress tree, which the initiate is warned against. In the context of Orphic eschatology a "folk"-etymology of the word for 'soul' is to be taken seriously; it is phonetically linked as well with the true 'chill water flowing from the pool of Memory' **ψυχ**ρὸν ὕδωρ προρέον τε̄ς Μνεμοσύνε̄ς ἀπὸ λίμνε̄ς, which the instructed soul will ask for and be given, the water of Memory which confers immortality and divinity.

The final lines 13-16 of Hipponion show the same sort of linking phonetic echo which we saw in Pelinna:

> **καὶ** δε **τοι** . . .
> καὐτοί **σοι**[11] . . .
> **καὶ** δε **καὶ** . . .
> μύσται **καὶ** . . .

The link connects us with the last lines of Hipponion and the 'Holy Way' of the soul:

> καὶ δε καὶ σὺ πιο̄ν[12] | **hoδὸν** ἔρχεαι, hάν τε καὶ **ἄλλοι**
> μύσται καὶ βάχχοι | **hιερὰν** στείχο̄σι **κλ<ε>εινοί**.
>
> Then you too, having drunk, walk the **holy way**
> which **other** initiates and bacchants tread **in glory**.

The two constituents of the noun phrase, hoδὸν . . . hιερὰν, distracted to a full line's distance, are placed in the identical position of metrical prominence, following the penthemimeral caesura of these enjambed lines. Note the similarly distracted appositional ἄλλοι . . . κλεεινοί, both line-final. The last constituents of each pair straddle the verb στείχο̄σι in a variation on the familiar and inherited pattern of poetic syntax.

In several of the gold leaf texts the strophic style is evident from a contrast in meters, as ably discussed by Obbink. Thus in texts 2 and 3 from Thurii six lines of hexameter are followed by a final pentameter. Such use of catalectic or shorter lines commonly has a demarcative function in the strophic style, transforming a stichic series into a bounded set (Watkins 1963b passim). Text 1 from Thurii has a different final short line, the prose *symbolon* or *synthema* "password" ἔριφος ἐς γάλ' ἔπετον 'A kid, I fell into the milk', and lacks the pentameter altogether. I am therefore somewhat sceptical of Obbink's composite text of Thurii including both the pentameter and the *symbolon*. It is a characteristic of the originally oral style to have available such different but functionally equivalent 'closures'.

Zuntz eloquently discussed the force of the "rhythmic prose" *symbola* in Thurii

---

10. Cf. Chantraine, DELG s.v., citing Benveniste; ψύχω 'breathe' / ψυχή 'soul' is a different family from ψύχω 'chill' / ψυχρός 'cool'.

11. Restored by Janko from the Petelia gold leaf; Hipponion has dittographic καὶ δή τοι.

12. Janko, for previously read συχνο̄ν.

1 and 4, noting that 'the transition from verse to prose is a uniquely effective means of conveying the significance of an important statement.' His view is confirmed by the prosodic, strophic structure of the Pelinna text subsequently unearthed (cited above), as Obbink notes. The short version in Thurii 4 follows three hexameters with

> ϑεὸς ἐγένου ἐξ ἀνϑρώπου·
> ἔριφος ἐς γάλα ἔπετες
> χαῖρ<ε>, χαῖρε· δεξιὰν ὁδοιπόρ<ει>
>
> From a man you were born a god;
> a kid, you fell into the milk.
> Rejoice, rejoice; travel the road to the right.

There follows a single hexameter. The two *symbola* in rhythmic prose of nine and eight syllables (with elision), respectively with three stresses in each, are followed by a catalectic series of trochees. The first *symbolon* is paraphrased as a normal hexameter in the utterance of Persephone at the closure of Thurii 1, the second *symbolon* is spoken by the initiate:

> "ὄλβιε καὶ μακαριστέ, ϑεὸς δ' ἔσηι ἀντὶ βροτοῖο."
> "ἔριφος ἐς γάλ' ἔπετον."
>
> "Happy and blessed one, you shall be a god instead of a mortal."
> "A kid, I fell into the milk."

The difference in person in the various gold leaf texts might well reflect a real ritual scene in which the *symbolon* is uttered first by a mistress of ceremonies (or the like) in the second person and then repeated by the initiand in the first person.

If we simply enumerate the key words and phrases of this Dionysiac-Orphic, in part Pythagorean eschatology as we observe them in the gold leaf texts, together with passages of Pindar and references in Plato, that is to say in the fifth and fourth centuries, we obtain a picture something like the following (compare the discussion in Burkert 1985:289ff.):

The souls of the dead, initiate and uninitiate, good and evil, journey to the underworld, where two springs or pools or rivers are portrayed topographically. The first is that of Oblivion (Lethe), to drink from which entails forgetting past life, Plato's myth (*Resp*. 621a) of the plain of Lethe and the river of Ameles, Indifference, which souls drink from for the forgetfulness of death before reincarnation; the souls of evildoers undergo suffering not to be looked upon, lying in the mire. The second, to which the initiate is directed, is that of Memory, remembrance of past lives, which confers, through rebirth and Persephone's grace, external bliss and apotheosis: to die and be reborn a god, to travel the way of Zeus, the way which is holy, to the Isle of the Blessed and the company of heroes. The verbal *symbolon* of that blessed state is the utterance 'I/you as domestic animal fell into the milk'.

These are manifestations, in the fifth and fourth centuries, of metempsychosis, which Burkert termed 'a speculative doctrine more characteristic of India, which remained a kind of foreign body in the framework of Greek religion' (p. 298). Whether the gold leaf texts presuppose it is not clear, but not excluded. In India it is known as *saṁsāra* 'transmigration' and *punarmṛtyú* 'dying again', a term recalling Greek παλιγγενεσία 'being born again'. Similar doctrines are ascribed to the druidical teachings of the Celts, and have left traces in Irish myths like the Dagdae's cauldron of rebirth. Let us look at what an adjacent and linguistically related culture had to offer: an extraordinary Old Hittite text composed some 1200 years before these Greek documents.

The main text has been available hitherto only in cuneiform autograph, and that only since 1972: KUB 43.60. A join of two further fragments, KBo 22.178 (+) KUB 48.109, was presented by Harry Hoffner to the American Oriental Society in 1987 and published in 1988.[13] In 1990 Hoffner published a translation of the whole text,[14] drawing (of course with acknowledgement) for KUB 43.60 also on an unpublished transcription and translation I had made available to him in 1978.

Hoffner entitles the text 'The Voyage of the Immortal Human Soul', but in fact the soul is in the text never called 'immortal', for which there is no ready Hittite equivalent. The Hittite word for 'soul' is *ištanza* (stem *ištanzan-*), in this text written Sumerographically as ZI-*anza*. Its regular accompanying word or epithet is *dandukiš* 'human, mortal' (lines 4, 27 [*-ieš* gen. sg.?]) abstract *dandukišnaš* (gen. sg.) in line 32, taken by Hoffner and myself as elliptic for *dandukišnaš* DUMU-*aš* 'son of mortality' = 'mortal'. The word *dandukiš* 'human being' is opposed to DINGIR 'god', e.g. KBo 3.60 ii 14-16. On the other hand the soul clearly survives the death of the body, and the dead person (*akkant-*) has a soul (ZI).[15] In that sense we may perhaps understand 'immortal'.

The Hittite text is a late copy, but the language of the archetype is clearly Old Hittite, and evidently caused difficulty for the later scribe. The ritual dialogue style of 26ff. is very reminiscent of that in KBo 21.22 and other texts quoted in chap. 11.1. I give here my own text and translation of KUB 43.60, which differs in several places from Hoffner's version; that of the joining fragments is his. The difficult text is fragmentary and often barely comprehensible; my version is tentative and meant to be an incitement to others to work on this rewarding challenge. KUB 43.60 (Bo 2533):

Ro. i

[-a]z GUD-uš šuppatta UDU-uš
2 [šuppa]tta nepiš šupp[at]att[a
[KI šuppa]tta ullāpa kadanki
4 [ ]dandukiš ZI-anza

13. Hoffner 1988b. He includes the very fragmentary and unenlightening columns ii and iii of KUB 43.60.

14. Hoffner 1990. My edition has benefitted from comments and suggestions made by Erich Neu and Craig Melchert in 1978 and 1980 as well as from Hoffner's translation. I have not been able to follow them in all their suggestions—nor doubtless they me in mine.

15. Cf. Kammenhuber 1964-1965.

[kuwapi]t=še=pa uitta ḪUR.SAG-i=kuw=at=šan
[NI]M.LÀL=at udau š=an pēdi=šši dāu
[takš]anni=ku!w=<at=>ša<n> NIM.LÀL=at <udau> (tab. dāu)
[n=]at pēdi=šši dāu kuit=a
[ter]ippiaz=ma n=at NIM.LÀL^{MEŠ} udandu
[n=]at pedi=šši tiandu NIM.LÀL teriyaš UD-aš
[m]īuwa<š> UD-aš KASKAL-an pāndu n=apa iyatar=mit
udandu takku arunaz=ma n=at laḫanza
udau n=at=šan pēdi=šši dāu
takku ÍD-az=ma n=at ḫuwalaš udau
n=at=šan pēdi=šši dāu

---

kuit=a nepišaz=ma n=at tapakaliya<š?>
ḫaraš^{MUŠEN} kad!dut udau ilalianza kaddu=šmit
walḫanza ēšdu MAŠ.GAL-š=an šappuit
walaḫdu UDU-ušš=an SI$^{\text{ḪI.A}}$-andu walaḫdu
annaš=an UDU-uš titittet walaḫdu
annaš DINGIR^{LIM}-aš išḫaḫruanza n=aš išḫaḫruit
walḫanza nu=šši=ššan kue āššū
9!-andaš ḫappešnaš šer ḫāššan n=e
walḫanza ēšdu ZI-anza=ma iyatniyanza
[ḫapp]ešnianza nu=šši=kan lē areškatta

[Z]I-anza=wa=kan uriš! ZI-anza=wa=kan uriš
kuel=wa=kan ZI-anza uriš tandukieš=wa=kan
ZI-anza uriš nu kuin KASKAL-an ḫarzi
uran KASKAL-an ḫarzi marnuwalan KASKAL-an ḫarzi
š=an=z=apa KASKAL-ši LÚ.KASKAL-laš ḫandāit
šu!ppi ^{D}UTU-aš ZI-anza DINGIR-nan (annan?) ZI-anza
dandukišnaš kuwat arušan paimi
dāšanatan paimi ÍD-p[a m]ūḫḫi luli[ya
muḫḫi tenawa=šan paim[i l]ē pai[mi lē
tēnawaš idāluš KASKAL?-š[a?
uellawa l[ē
šiuniya[ḫ-

[. . .] The ox is sleeping. The sheep
[is sleep]ing. Heaven is sleeping.
[Earth is sleep]ing . . .
[ ] the human (or mortal) soul.
[Wher]e did it come for it? If it is on the mountain,
let the bee bring it and put it in its place.
And if it is on the plain, let the bee bring it
and put it up in its place. But whatever is
from the ploughed field, let the bees bring it

and put it in its place. Let the bees go a journey of three days,
of four days, and let them bring my 'plenty'.
If it is from the sea, let the *laḫanza*-duck
bring it and put it in its place.
But if it is from the river, let the *ḫuwalaš*-bird (owl?)[16] bring it
and put it in its place.

But whatever is from the sky, let the . . .
eagle bring it in his defenses (= talons). Let the desired one be
struck with their defenses. Let the goat strike her
with his *šappu*-horns. Let the ram strike her with his horns.
Let the mother sheep strike her with her nose.
The Mother Goddess (?) is tearful. She is struck
with tears. Whatever good things are born (? opened?)
over the nine body parts, let her be struck
(with regard to) them. The soul is thriving,
with (all) its parts (?). Let there be no . . . for it.

"The soul is great. The soul is great."
"Whose soul is great?" "The mortal('s ?)
soul is great." What road does it have?
It has the great road. It has the road that makes things disappear.
The Traveler (? man of the road) has fitted it out for the road.
A holy thing of the Sun Goddess (of the Earth) is the soul. To the
gods (Mothers?)
belongs the soul. Why should I, (a) mortal, go . . .
(or, ...belongs the soul of mortality/ a mortal. Why should I go . . .)
I will go . . . I will fall into the river. I will fall
into the pool. Let me not go to the *tenawaš*, let me [not go.(?)]
The *tenawaš* is evil [
Let [me] not [go?] to the meadow [
[Let me not be] struck down by a god (?) [

KBo 22.178 (+) KUB 48.109 Ro. ii

		n=an ḪU]L-lu[š/n?	
tēnau[waš/n?	. . .	*Ū*]*L* kanē[šzi	
araš ar[an	*ŪL*	kanē]š	-zi
annanekē[š	*ŪL*	kanē]ššan	-zi
pappa(-) ŠE[Š^{MEŠ}	*ŪL*	kan]ēššan	-zi
annaš=za DUMU-a[n=šan	*ŪL*	k]anēš	-zi
[DUMU-aš=za A]MA-a[n=šan	*ŪL*	k]anēš	-zi

---

16. The equation of Hittite *ḫuwalaš* with Old High German *ūwila*, German *Eule*, English *owl*, was made by Ben Fortson.

] x [*ŪL* ka]nēš -zi
] LÚ? [*ŪL*] kanēš -zi

Vo. iii

[šaniz]ziya[z=ka]n ^{GIŠ}BANŠUR-az
2 [*Ū*]*L* adanzi [šan]izziyaz=kan ḫapš[al!iaz]
[*Ū*]*L* adanzi [šan]izziyaz=kan GAL-az
4 *ŪL* akuwanzi [āšš]u adatar *ŪL* adanz[i
āššu akuwatar=mi[t *Ū*]*L* akuwanzi
6 šaluinuš az[zikan] -zi
mirmirruš [akkuška]n -zi
8 uētriš[(-)
šer=šamaš [
10 nu add[aš
ḫa[z-

Vo. IV
3′ w]ā!tar eku
lē

Ro. II
2′ the evil
tēnauwaš . . . . . . does not recognize.
4′ One doesn't recognize the other.
Sisters by the same mother [do not re]cognize each other.
Brothers by the same father [do not re]cognize each other.
A mother does [not] recognize [her] own child.
[A child] does [not] recognize [its own] mother.
. . . does [not] recognize . . .
. . . does [not] recognize . . .

Vo. III
From a [fi]ne table
2 they do [no]t eat. From a [fi]ne stool
they do [n]ot eat. From a [fi]ne cup
4 they do not drink. They do not eat
[goo]d food. They do not drink my good drink.
6 They eat bits of mud.
They drink muddy waters.
8 emaciation
over them
10 and the fath[er
dri[ed

Vo. IV
3′]drink water!
do not [

Thematically the text begins apparently by setting the scene for an epiphany or birth of the human soul.[17] There follows a characteristically Anatolian section about the mission of the bee or bees (compare the several versions of the Vanishing God myth). They are to bring back from mountain, plain, or ploughed field 'my plenty', where the curious possessive appears to refer to the soul's plenty or nourishment. Three birds are envisioned if the 'plenty' is from sea or river or sky: duck, owl, and eagle. Note that *lahanza*-ducks, both images and live (when in season, as the text specifies), figure in the rituals for the dead king or queen.[18]

The text moves then to the mysterious 'desired one', who is successively struck by three domestic animals, all Kleinvieh, 'small cattle'. The function of the striking is apparently maieutic. The Mother (Goddess?) cries, and is struck by her very tears, but seems then (line 22) to have given birth; Hittite birth rituals speak of 'the good things (*āššū*) of a boy', 'the good things of a girl'.[19] It is evidently the soul itself which has been born as a result; the text says the soul is thriving, healthy, and whole. The last sentence of the paragraph is uncertain, but *areškatta* may mean 'let no oracle be taken for it (the soul)'—since it not necessary—, as suggested by Melchert (letter of 12/18/78), similarly Puhvel 1984:137 'Let no oracle be taken for her'.[20]

The new paragraph begins with a veritable choral celebration of the soul. The particle -*wa*(-) in each of the sentences in 26-7 marks them formally as direct, quoted speech, and the question and answer as dialogue. The dialogue stichomythic—or perhaps catechetical—style probably continues at least through line 29; the particle -*wa*(-) is not obligatory.

The 'great way' *uran* KASKAL-*an* which the soul has cannot but recall the Orphic 'holy way' of the gold leaves, or 'Zeus's way' in Pindar. Its epithet is *marnuwalan*, apparently a derivative of the verb *marnu-/mernu-* 'cause to disappear' (see CHD s.v.). The same expression also cannot but recall the Hieroglyphic Luvian inscription on the inside of the tomb destined for Suppiluliumas II, (DEUS) STONE + EARTH + ROAD, Hittite ^{D}KASKAL.KUR 'divine land way', indicating an entrance to the underworld (David Hawkins). See the references in chapters 40 and 46.

17. Cf. Alcman 89P. εὕδουσι 'sleep' . . . εὕδουσι 'sleep' . . . and Pfeiffer 1959.

18. Otten 1958, a systematic edition of the Hittite ritual texts of the *šalliš waštaiš*, the 'Great Wrong' which is the death of the king or queen. The standard expression for the royal 'dying' is 'become a god'; the apotheosis is viewed as real, as Otten notes (12, 106) since the dead king is addressed 'o god'. But apotheosis is apparently confined to the royal family. The first tablet begins (p. 18): 'When in Ḫattusas the Great Wrong occurs, either the king or the queen becomes a god (DINGIR^{LIM}-*iš kišari*), everyone great (and) small take their straws (?) and begin to lament. On which day he/she becomes a god, on that day (cf. Pelinna 1 νῦν ἔθανες . . . ἄματι τῶιδε 'now you have died . . . on that day') they do as follows: they sacrifice a plough ox of 'raising' (?) to his/her soul. They slaughter it at his/her head and speak as follows: "As you have become, lo, let him become likewise. Let down your soul to this ox.'

19. KBo 17.62 + 63 iv 14, 17; cf. Beckman 1983:32ff.

20. I do not understand Hoffner's 'Let nothing be impossible for it'.

The continuation is obscure; then we find an abrupt shift to the first person. Who is speaking? The narrative structure with ZI-*anza* 'soul' twice in 3rd person nominal sentences in line 31 argues that it must be the soul who is speaking, of its fearful journey (*paimi* 'I (shall) go'). 'I (shall) fall into the river, I (shall) fall into the pool' sounds strangely like the Dionysiac-Orphic *symbolon* 'a ram/kid, I fell into the milk'. They contrast with the following negative, 'Let me not go to the *tēnawaš*, the *tēnawaš* is evil . . .' The 'meadow' of l. 36 is probably another topographical feature of the underworld. From Hoffner's addition we are afforded a fearful and cruel picture of the oblivion caused by the evil *tēnawaš*: The souls do not recognize their dearest relatives in their former life. Hoffner glosses *tēnawaš* (p. 85) as 'An evil force, sometimes portrayed topographically, which seizes souls in the afterlife, causing forgetfulness. It may be compared to Lethe . . .' The word is found only in these two tablets.

A key is the unexpected 1sg. pronominalization in *aššu akuwatar=mit ŪL akuwanzi* 'they do not drink *my* good drink'. Hoffner correctly saw that this parallels the equally surprising line 11 of KUB 43.60: *pāndu n=apa iyatar=mit údandu* 'Let (the bees) go and bring *my* plenty'. Together with the phrase 'evil *tēnawaš*' it is the strongest verbal proof that both tablets are part of a single composition. And in both cases we must conclude that the 1sg. possessive, like the 1sg. verb forms, refer to the soul: 'my plenty', 'my good drink'. Specifically it is the nourishment of the fortunate, perhaps instructed or "initiated" soul, not that of the souls who went to the evil *tēnawaš* of oblivion and who eat only clay and drink muddy water.

The cheerless diet of the dead is a Mesopotamian topos, as Hoffner notes in his original edition (note 13 above, p. 193): the dead eat clay (Akkadian *ṭiddu*) and drink muddy water (*mē dalḫūti*). Compare Biggs 1993 and Malul 1993, references I owe to Gary Beckman. But a curious and arresting verbal similarity exists between this Hittite text and alphabetic Greek a millennium later. The Hittite word for the filthy muddy water that the damned must drink is *mirmirr-uš* (accusative plural), a noun with expressive reduplication apparently built on the root of Hittite *mer*(*r*), *mir*(*r*)- 'disappear, vanish, cease to exist', the cognate of the verb 'to die' in other Indo-European languages.[21] While this could be only a folk etymology, the sinister, dismal drink of the dead contains two repeated syllables beginning with a labial and ending with an *r*. The same sequence is found in the Greek word for 'liquid mire, muddy liquid, filth' βόρβορ-ος, likewise with expressive reduplication. In Aeschylus, *Eumenides* 694 βόρβορος makes clean water undrinkable:

> κακαῖς ἐπιρροαῖσι βορβόρωι ϑ' ὕδωρ
> λαμπρὸν μιαίνων οὔποϑ' εὑρήσεις ποτόν

> Polluting[22] clean water with filthy effluents of mire
> you will never find a drink.

21. Hittite would seem to attest the variant forms **mer*- (*merzi*, *mirzi*), **mr̥*- (*martari*) and **merh*$_x$-*o*- (*merrăntaru*).

22. The vowel sequence of **μιαίνων** 'polluting' repeats that of μὴ **'πικαινούντων** νόμους 2 lines above and spreads the semantic overtones of the former onto the latter, as translators have seen: 'do not pollute the laws with innovation'.

More than a generation earlier Heraclitus of Ephesus (in Asia Minor!) (Diels-Kranz 22 B 13, cf. 37) noted that pigs preferred βόρβορος to clean water (καθαρῶι ὕδατι). The earliest attestation of the word in Greek is the 7th or 6th century poet Asius, in a mock-heroic elegiac description of the parasite (IEG 2.46):

> ἤρως εἰστήκει βορβόρου ἐξαναδύς
>
> The hero stood, rising up out of the mire.

Asius came from the island of Samos off the coast of Asia Minor, and his name is of certain Asianic origin (*Aswios*, cf. Hitt. *Aššuwa*) even if at home in Greece since Mycenean times (Myc. *Asiwijo*).

The Asianic connections of the earliest attested users of the word βόρβορος in Greek may be just coincidental, and the phonetic similarity of Hittite *mirmirr-* and Greek βορβορ- may be only an illusion. We have no explicitly "Orphic" uses of the Greek word. But it remains the case that the semantic overtones of both the Greek and the Hittite are those of something very unpleasant to drink. The possibility of an areal semantic feature and term diffused from Anatolian-speaking Asia Minor to Greek-speaking Asia Minor and thence to Greece cannot be rejected out of hand.

We began our consideration of the Dionysiac-Orphic gold tablets as an example, rare in Ancient Greek, of the inherited Indo-European strophic style of ritual, liturgical language. From these texts and the speculative notions of the soul and the afterlife which are their *raison d'être* we were led to comparison of the content and form of an Old Hittite text (17th or 16th century B.C.) preserved in 13th-century Neo-Hittite copies. The Hittite composition likewise involves speculations on the human soul and the afterlife, presented in dramatic narrative form involving direct speech, with lyrical and dithyrambic interludes.

I do not want to insist on a thematic connection between the two sets of texts in the two languages. The similarities—even those which are most striking, like the "singular detail" of the Greek and Hittite word for muddy water—may belong to the plane of imaginative universals of eschatology. But I do wish to emphasize that speculations very similar to those of the Dionysiac-Orphic and Pythagorean "mysteries", both in content and in the form of artistic verbal presentation, were being made and written down in a geographically adjacent and genetically related language some 1200 years earlier and continued to be copied until some 800 years earlier. If we are to believe in an Indo-European eschatology,[23] a common core of inherited beliefs about final things and a common core of style of verbal expression in the (inherently conservative) service of the dead, then it is to such comparisons that we should look.

For a single final example compare the high degree of alliteration in Pindar's fragmentary funeral dirge (*thrēnos*, fr. 133) quoted above early in this chapter with the

---

23. Note chap. 12 and especially chapters 34 and 35. It is curious that the activity of the Pythagoreans was centered in Southern Italy and especially Tarentum (Greek Ταραντ-), whose name looks like another derivative of the Indo-European eschatological verb root *$terh_2$- par excellence.

striking instantiation of the same figure (boldface) in the address to the dead in the Rigvedic hymn to Yama 10.14.7ab:

préhi **p**réhi **p**athíbhiḥ **pū**rvyébhir
yátrā naḥ **pū́**rve **p**itáraḥ **p**areyúḥ

Go forth, go forth, on the prior paths
where our first fathers fared.

HOW TO KILL A DRAGON IN INDO-EUROPEAN

A CONTRIBUTION TO THE THEORY OF THE FORMULA

IV

The basic formula and its variants in the narration of the myth

27

Preliminaries

1. The myth

One or more myths about a god or hero killing a dragon or other reptilian adversary, usually just called 'snake, serpent', is found in a vast number of cultures around the world; it may be a quasi-universal. We cannot speak of an exclusively Indo-European dragon; our task rather is to sort out the Indo-European modalities of the myth as a verbal message and to underline the peculiarities which characterize the Indo-European version and which allow us to assert that it existed. We are looking, in short, for "the Indo-European touch", and it is in the *formula* that we will find it.

A vast amount of evidence of dragon-myths from Classical, Near Eastern, Indian, Germanic, and other sources has been assembled by Fontenrose 1959 (repr. 1980), with rich documentation and bibliography.[1] The dragon-slaying myth has been studied in several places over the past two decades by the two Russian linguists V. V. Ivanov and V. N. Toporov.[2] Following in part their predecessors, but in greater part on the basis of their own collections, Ivanov and Toporov have analyzed a considerable amount of data from Indic, Iranian, and Hittite, a vast amount from Baltic and Slavic—the great originality of their work—and some from Germanic and still other Indo-European traditions. Greek occupies a relatively small place in their system, though, as will appear, its evidence for the formulas is both extensive and critical.

The two authors are primarily concerned with the structural and semiotic analysis of the whole myth itself and of the mythological protagonist, the Storm God, his attributes and exploits, and connected themes. While formulas engage their attention and are the subject of frequent probing observations, they are fundamentally a means to an end. I will not here go into all the *themes* reflected in these various traditions. I prefer only to keep to their linguistic form, as inherited *formulas*.

1. Older studies such as Siecke 1907 contain useful materials but are basically flawed by their antiquated naturistic approach, e.g. explaining the myth by the phases of the moon. On the other hand there is much material, ancient and modern, Eastern and Western, with an informed discussion in Evans 1987:27-58; I owe the reference to J. Ziolkowski. Note also Athanassakes 1988:41-63.

2. Most extensively in Ivanov and Toporov 1974. In a Western language note also their contribution in Mélanges C. Lévi-Strauss 1970.

We owe to Emile Benveniste and Louis Renou (1934) a profoundly innovative study of what we may loosely (and inaccurately) term the Indic and Iranian dragon-slaying myth. Their attention was again primarily focused on the myth itself and the protagonists: in Benveniste's words (177): 'Dans l'Iran, on s'est préoccupé de restaurer l'exacte signification du terme fondamental de vr̥ϑra-, et de définir . . . la nature . . . du dieu Vr̥ϑraγna. Du côté védique, l'étude a été centrée sur le démon Vr̥tra et a montré comment le foisonnement de traits secondaires et la tendance à une figuration toujours plus concrète ont enrichi et diversifié un simple schème formulaire.' The role of formulaics has been thus in a sense trivialized.

For Benveniste (182 ff.) there are in Vedic three separate themes: (1) a religious motif, the exploits of a victorious god; (2) an epic motif, the struggle of the hero with a usually reptilian monster; (3) a mythical motif, the freeing of the waters. For him (1) is an Indo-Iranian warrior god, with the epithet **u̯r̥tra-ǰhan-* 'smashing resistance', who embodies the potential of victorious offensive, irresistible force; (2) on the other hand is a sort of universal, both within and outside the Indo-European world, a theme worked and reworked on a traditional canvas, with varying protagonists but the same frame: Indra and Vr̥tra, Trita and Viśvarūpa, Thraētaona and Aži Dahāka, Kr̥sāspa and Sruuara, Zeus and Typhon, Herakles and Geryon, Apollo and Python, Herakles and the Hydra, Perseus and the Gorgon, Thor and the Serpent, etc. The only inheritance is the Indo-Iranian designation **aǰhi-* 'serpent'; (3), the releasing of the pent-up waters, is a properly Indo-Iranian myth and hardly represented elsewhere, linked with the importance and scarcity of water in Aryan lands. Its origin for him may lie in the chthonic springs and waters so frequently inhabited or guarded by dragons and other creatures like the Hydra, "Water-beastie".

We can surely retain their thesis that the Vedic "dragon" Vr̥tra owes his personalized existence to an Indo-Iranian divine epithet **u̯r̥tra-ǰhan-* 'smashing resistance'. There was at the outset no dragon named Vr̥tra: he was just the Serpent, *ahi*, and Indo-Iranian **u̯r̥-tra-* was a neuter noun of instrument (*-*tro*-) from the root *vr̥*- 'block, obstruct, close, cover'.

But the rigorous separation of themes asserted by Benveniste is in fact illusory. The Indo-Iranian warrior god of (1) is simply the incarnation of the compound epithet **u̯r̥tra-ǰhan-*, whose second member is the verb of the basic dragon slaying formula of (2), the 'hero slew the serpent'. The root *vr̥*- of *vr̥tra*- in (1) is the verb of (3), the 'blockage' of the waters, and the same verb furnishes the name *Vala*[3] of the cave where the (rain-)cows are pent up and of the demon who holds them prisoner. Otherwise the chthonic water-element of (3) is just a general attribute of the dragon of (2). Benveniste himself (p. 195) notes the significance of the linkage, both syntagmatic and paradigmatic, of the warrior god of (1) with the mortal hero of (2) both in India and in Iran (discussed in chapters 28 and 29). And the opposition Benveniste would see between god in (1) and human hero in (2) is not valid; the subject of (2), the dragon-slayer, is indifferently god (Zeus, Apollo, Thor, Indra) or man (Perseus, Kadmos, Herakles, Trita).

In concentrating on the protagonists, the hero/subject and monster/object, Benveniste to a certain extent—less so Renou (chap. 28)—failed to recognize the posi-

3. With 'popular' *l* for *r*.

tive aspect of the formulas themselves as the actual vehicle for the long term preservation of tradition. In particular the verb phrases, where the hero/subject is not even mentioned, turn out to be extremely conservative; these verb phrases are precisely that aspect of the formulas which least claimed the attention of the two great French scholars.

Benveniste described his and Renou's task in their monograph (p. 3) as 'a question of discovering, beneath the developments which a supple phraseology had extended and infinitely varied, the fundamental data of the myth: the scheme which generates the amplification (*le schème générateur de l'amplification*).' In good ring-composition fashion Benveniste used the same phrase in the concluding paragraph of the book: 'Every study of a mythological fact must strive to reconstitute its formation within the framework of the Veda, to discover *le schème générateur* as well as the process of development'. My own study is primarily the formulas themselves as linguistic and poetic entities. I hope first to define more precisely the set of formulas and their properties, to show just how exiguous a base is that "schème générateur". And secondly I intend to show by wider-ranging comparison in the Indo-European world, with attention to time as well as space, just how enduring and pervasive was this "schème générateur" and what a powerful device it is for the reconstruction of linguistic, cultural, and literary history.

2. The function of the myth

To all the works cited in the preceding section, notably Fontenrose, Benveniste and Renou, Ivanov and Toporov, we may make global reference for the various dragon-slaying myths. They are all ultimately variations and elaborations of a single theme: 'hero slays serpent'. Compare Renou 1934:108: 'Le mythe de Vṛtra se résume pour l'essential en la formule "Indra tua Vṛtra": le fait brutal est cent fois répété avec des variations diverses qui la plupart du temps n'apportent aucune précision supplémentaire. Mais un trait domine d'abord, à savoir que cet acte est considéré comme important . . .'[4]

We must ask the question, Why does the hero slay the serpent? What is the function of this widespread if not universal myth, or put another way, what is its meaning? The question has been discussed fully by Fontenrose, Ivanov, and Toporov, building on classical anthropological work. The dragon symbolizes Chaos, in the largest sense, and killing the dragon represents the ultimate victory of Cosmic Truth and Order over Chaos. As a part of the Frazerian 'dying god' myth, it is a symbolic victory of growth over stagnation or dormancy in the cycle of the year, and ultimately a victory of rebirth over death.[5]

4. 'The myth of Vṛtra can be subsumed essentially in the formula "Indra slew Vṛtra": the brute fact is repeated a hundred times with different variations which most of the time bring no additional information. But one feature predominates, namely that this act is considered important . . .'

5. Compare Beckman 1982, with references.

Indeed for Fontenrose the ultimate adversary with whom the hero must do battle is Death. While I cannot follow him in seeing the two antagonists, hero and serpent, as "Eros" and "Thanatos"—a view which rings too closely to Woody Allen's film *Love and Death*—the theme of Death as an adversary of the hero is certainly real, as with the prototypical hero Herakles and the tale of Alkestis. This theme is examined in chap. 40.

This myth must be regularly and cyclically retold—and the attendant rituals re-performed—in order to perpetuate its effectiveness. It is in several traditions associated with the turning of the year: compare chapters 46 and 47. In the winter of the old year the forces of Chaos are in the ascendancy: stagnation, dormancy, and death. With the new year the slow ascendancy of Order, rebirth, and growth begins; but the myth must be re-narrated and the ritual re-enacted to assure the triumph of the Power of Active Truth (M. Witzel), Vedic *ṛta*, Avestan *aṣ̌a*, over Chaos.

The Chaos which the dragon symbolizes may take many manifestations in the different traditions. In Indo-Iranian it is the theme of the pent-up waters, the "resistance" (**u̯ṛ-tram*) which is the blockage of life-giving forces, which are released by the victorious act of the hero. As Benveniste saw (188), the development of this theme and its verbal expression, culminating in India in the personalized dragon *Vṛtra* (and the demon *Vala*), is a function of the particular importance of water in the arid Aryan lands (*Īrān* < *aryānām*), before the easternmost *āryas* reached the fringe of the Indian subcontinent. On the other hand Benveniste was basically not correct (ibid.) in dissociating this theme from that of the Zoroastrian Evil Spirit *Aŋra Mainiiu* keeping the newly-created waters from flowing and the plants from growing in Yt. 13.78 (cited and discussed in chap. 35). Both are manifestations of the prevalence of Chaos, and the formulaic patterns and lexicon selected in the narrative of Yt. 13.78 demonstrate its identity with the dragon-slaying theme.

In Ireland and Anatolia, as examined in chap. 45, and in Ancient Greece as well (chap. 41),[6] one manifestation of Chaos is societal in character: the figuration of all that is "anti-social". This includes all that disrupts the established hierarchy of gods and men, free and unfree, noble and common, patron and client, rich and poor. It particularly includes all that violates hospitality: the institutionalized gift-exchange relation termed **ghos-*, which lies at the very center of interpersonal, interfamilial, and intertribal relations in the Indo-European world. In the Germanic world we find yet another modality of symbolic Chaos. It is the dragon's "job", as Professor William Alfred has put it, to guard treasure. That is, the dragon keeps wealth from circulating: the ultimate evil in society in which gift-exchange and the lavish bestowal of riches institutionalized precisely that circulation.[7]

The dragon symbolizes finally everywhere the chaos of destruction, the threat to life and property, the ravager of man and beast, which we find formulaically expressed, and will examine in detail, in a variety of traditions throughout the Indo-European world.

---

6. Compare also Vermeule 1979, in connection with G. Beckman, note 5 above.

7. On gift-exchange and reciprocity in Indo-European language and society see Benveniste 1969 and, more generally, the classic work of Mauss 1924.

3. The basic formula, its nature and function

Most students of mythology, from Apollodorus to Lévi-Strauss, tend to throw language—diction—out the window as somehow irrelevant to the establishment of plot or semiotic structures of particular myths. But in cases where we can know, as in that of the dragon-slaying myth here considered, we can observe that language or diction, the precise verbal form of the narration of myth, is almost incredibly persistent.[8]

We saw in the preceding section the statement of Renou that 'the myth of Vṛtra can be subsumed essentially in the formula "Indra slew Vṛtra".' He continues (110), 'The basic formula (*la formule de base*) designating the slaying of Vṛtra is (*índro*) *vṛtrám* (or *áhim*) *jaghāna* or *ahan*' ((Indra) slew (perfect or imperfect) Vṛtra (or the serpent)).

To demonstrate the specificity of this very formula and this verbal tradition not only in Indic but across most of the related older Indo-European languages over several thousand years in the narration of a specific theme, the central act of the serpent or dragon-slaying myth, is the principal contribution of the present work. That is to say that we can extend to the whole early Indo-European world, on the comparative, diachronic plane, what Renou recognized for Vedic on the descriptive, synchronic plane.

To anticipate the results detailed below, we may postulate a common Indo-European verbal formula expressing the central act of the inherited serpent-slaying myth. The *theme* or semantic structure, following the conventions explained in chap. 3, may be presented as

HERO SLAY SERPENT.

It is a single sentence, which following Renou I will term the *basic formula*. The verb phrase involves a single verb, in the original or underlying formula, a form of the Indo-European root **g^uhen-* 'to smite, slay'.[9] The basic formula may optionally include the presence of a marginal element (in the instrumental case or its equivalent), the specification of either a weapon or a companion (normally not both). The formula

8. For the principle compare the work of Stephanie Jamison quoted in chap. 46, with note 12.

9. Note for the present the quasi-equations ('slew', 'slay') Vedic (*a*)*han*(*n*) = Avestan *jan*(*aṯ*) = Hittite *kuenta* = Old Irish *gono* = Greek (ἔ)πεφνε(ν); ('slain') Greek -φατος = Vedic *hatas* = Pahlavi *-zad*; ('slaying', 'slayer') Greek φόνος = Vedic *ghanás* = Germanic *bana*, English *bane*.

More formally, we may state that the comparative facts allow us to posit for this verb in Indo-European an ablauting athematic present/preterite in Vedic *hánti*/*ghnánti*, Avestan *jaiṇti*/(-*γn*-), Hittite *kuenzi*/*kunanzi*, the generalized zero-grade thematized in Celtic **g^uane-* of Old Irish *gonid*, Welsh *gwanu* 'stab', and Balto-Slavic **gine-* 'pursue'; imperative Vedic *jahí*, Avestan *jaiδi*; participle Vedic *ghnánt-*, Greek (aorist) θενών; subjunctive Vedic *hanat*, secondarily thematized in Avestan *janāṯ* and Greek (aorist) μὴ θένηις (Ps.-Eur. *Rh.* 687); reduplicated thematic intensive present/preterite form (Hoffmann 1975:562-69 and Thieme 1929:34) Avestan *-jaγnaṯ*, mediopass. *-jaγnəṇte*, Greek (aorist) ἔπεφνεν; reduplicated athematic intensive Vedic *jaṅghán-ti* and the base of Hittite NA4*kunkun-uzzi-* 'basalt'; reduplicated perfect Vedic *jaghāna*, Avestan (pple.) *jaγnuuå*, Old Irish *geguin*, Greek πέφαται; reduplicated desiderative Vedic *jighāṁsati*, Old Irish (future) *génaid*; and the *-tó-* verbal adjective forms just cited, plus Lithuanian *giñtas* 'pursued', and Old Irish *do-gét* 'was violated'.

sentence frequently exhibits marked word order (Verb-Object), and typically lacks an overt hero subject. With the optional marginal weapon or companion and lexical specification of the verb, we have the boxed

HERO	SLAY (*g^{u}*hen-*) SERPENT (with WEAPON) (with COMPANION).

Compare Vedic *áhann áhim* (RV 1.32.1, etc.) 'he slew the serpent', *vádhīd vṛtrám vájrena* (4.17.3) 'he slew Vṛtra with his cudgel', or Greek ἔπεφνεν τε Γοργόνα (Pindar *Pyth.* 10.46) 'he slew the Gorgon', κτεῖνε . . . ὄφιν (Pindar *Pythian* 4.249) 'he killed the serpent', or Avestan *yō janat̰ ažīm dahākəm* (Y. 9.8) 'who slew Aži Dahāka', all with Verb-Object order. With unmarked Object-Verb order, note Vedic . . . *vájram . . . yád áhiṃ hán* (5.29.2) '. . . cudgel . . . when he slew the serpent', or Avestan **vaδəm . . . yat̰ ažiš dahākō jaini* (Yt. 19.92) 'weapon . . . when Aži Dahāka was slain', or Hittite ^{MUŠ}*illuyankan kuenta* (KUB 17.5 i 17) 'he slew the serpent', or Greek ἔνθα δράκαιναν / κτεῖνεν ἄναξ, Διὸς υἱός, ἀπὸ κρατεροῖο βιοῖο (*h.Ap.* 300f.) 'there the lord, son of Zeus, slew the she-dragon with his strong bow'.

The semantic constituents of the basic theme may undergo paradigmatic (commutational) variants: for the HERO's name there may appear an epithet (e.g., slayer); for SLAY we may find KILL, SMITE, OVERCOME, BEAT, etc.; for the SERPENT (ADVERSARY) we may find MONSTER, BEAST, but also HERO$_2$ or ANTI-HERO. The constituents may undergo syntagmatic variants: the Verb Phrase may be passivized as in Greek πέφαται . . . Πάτροκλος (*Il.* 17.689f.) 'slain is Patroklos', Vedic *ható rā́jā kṛ́mīnām* (AV 2.32.4) 'slain is the king of the worms', Pahlavi *-zad* of *ōzad* = Vedic *ávahata-* in Kārnāmag 9.1 *ān kirm ōzad būd* 'had slain that dragon/worm',[10] historically 'anguis occisus'. HERO and ADVERSARY may switch grammatical roles, as in Greek τὸν . . . πέφνε . . . δράκων (Bacchylides 9.12f.) 'whom the dragon slew', or Hittite ^{MUŠ}*illuyankaš* ^{D}IM-*an tarḫta* (KBo 3.7 i 11) 'the serpent overcame the Storm God'. The WEAPON may be promoted to direct object and the ADVERSARY assigned a marginal role in the utterance as in Vedic *jahí vádhar* (4.22.9), etc), Avestan *vadarə jaiδi* (Y. 9.30), both 'strike the weapon'. The WEAPON may also be promoted to grammatical subject of the verb SLAY or equivalent, as in Vedic *só asya vájro hárito yá āyasáḥ . . . tudád áhiṃ hárisipro yá āyasáḥ* (10.96.3-4) 'This is his golden yellow weapon, the brazen; the golden yellow (weapon), the brazen, smote the serpent'.

The Indo-European expressions for these semantic constituents can be reconstructed without difficulty. Basic to the theme is the Verb Phrase, the boxed formula above; basic to the Verb Phrase is the Verb, typically *g^{u}*hen-*. But we find also by lexical substitution **u̯edh-*, **terh$_2$-*, **u̯aĝ-*, in Greek **dk̑en-* (κτεν-) and others. It is characteristic that the same root may appear in different semantic slots, with the appropriate derivational and inflexional morphology, as subject, verb, object, instrument: thus Vedic *vṛtra-hā́, áhan . . . vadhéna* (1.32.5), but also *vádhīt . . . ghanéna* (1.33.4), both 'SLEW with the WEAPON'.

10. The Kârnâmê î Artakhshîr î Pâpakân, ed. D. P. Sanjana, Bombay, 1896. I am grateful to P.O. Skjærvø for the reference and discussion.

The 'purpose' of the central theme and its expression in the basic formula is predication: it is a definition of the HERO. Compare the series of relative clauses and main clause refrain in RV 2.12, e.g. 3ad, where the basic formula is only one of many definitions:

> yó hatvā́him . . .
> . . . sá janāsa índraḥ
>
> He who slew the serpent (and) . . .
> . . . He, o people, is Indra.

At the same time the function of the basic formula is indexical and memorative. It makes reference to the myth and calls it to the mind of the listener and at the same time makes reference to and reminds the listener of all other instances of the basic formula. As such it serves to locate the hero and the narrated event in a cosmology and ideology perceived as permanent and everlasting.

The thematic pattern we term the basic formula will turn out to be an integral part, indeed the principal constituent of the associative semantics—the connotations, the overtones—of the derivatives of the root *g^{u}hen-* 'smite, slay' in their mythographic, heroic, and literary deployment in most of the earlier branches of the Indo-European family.

These various phrases may legitimately, indeed must be looked upon as formulas in the sense of contemporary theory of oral or traditional literature. The variations rung on them constitute a virtually limitless repository of literary expression in archaic Indo-European societies, and their careful study can cast light in unexpected places and bring together under a single explanation a variety of seemingly unrelated, unconnected text passages.

The formula is a precious tool for genetic as well as typological investigation in the study of literature. The fact is well known to Indo-Europeanists, but less so to philologists, historians of literature, and literary critics.

It is the claim of the present work that the "intertextuality" of these versions of the basic formula we have established, varying in time, place, and language but taken collectively, constitute a background without which one cannot fully apprehend, understand, and appreciate the traditional elements in a given ancient Indo-European literature. In this sense we may speak of a genetic Indo-European comparative literature. The claim will doubtless seem to some exaggerated, even to the point of fancy. But it follows from a rigorous application of the comparative method as we know it. If it is once admitted that an Indo-European verb *g^{u}hen-* is the common ancestor of Greek πεφν-, φον-, Vedic *han-*, Avestan *jan-*, Hittite *kuen-*, and Germanic *ban-*, then the burden of proof is on the skeptic who would deny that the semantics of that verb, and its formulaic deployment in traditional literature, cannot be likewise inherited.

28

The root *$g^{u}hen$-: Vedic *han-*

I begin with Indic. In India the hero par excellence is the god Indra, the prototypical gargantuan, gourmandizing, soma-swilling warrior-hero. His primary exploit is the slaying of the serpent-monster Vṛtra, which releases the pent-up waters. As Renou and Benveniste showed, the name Vṛtra is a personification—confined to India—of an Indo-Iranian abstract noun **u̯ṛtrám* meaning 'resistance'; the channel is the divine epithet *vṛtra-han-* (Iranian *vṛϑra-jan-*), originally 'smashing resistance'. The original and inherited designation of the Indo-Iranian dragon adversary is just 'serpent, snake': Sanskrit *áhi-*, Avestan *aži-*.

The well-known Rig-Vedic hymn to Indra 1.32 presents the myth *in nuce* in its first strophe:

> índrasya nú vīryā̀ṇi prá vocaṃ
> yā́ni cakā́ra prathamā́ni vajrī́
> **ā́hann ā́him** ánv apás tatarda
> prá vakṣáṇā abhinat párvatānām
>
> I tell now the manly deeds of Indra,
> the foremost which he did armed with the cudgel.
> He **slew the serpent**, drilled through to the waters,
> he split the belly of the mountains.

The key phrase is *áhann áhim* 'he slew the serpent'; RV 1.32 continues with the same phrase, in a figure of anaphora in each of the two succeeding verses (2a):

> **ā́hann ā́him** párvate śiśriyāṇám
>
> He **slew the serpent** who had encamped in the mountain,

the last expanded to (3d)

> **ā́hann** enam prathamajā́m **ā́hīnām**

He **slew** him, firstborn **of serpents**.

The same verbal linkage as between 1 and 2 (*áhann áhim* bis, *párvatānām ~ párvate*) is the complete phrasal repetition in the second person in the immediately following verse (4ab),

yád indr**ā́han** prathamajā́m **áhīnām**
ā́n māyínām áminā̄ḥ próta māyā̄ḥ

When, o Indra, **you slew** the firstborn **of serpents**,
then did you outtrick the tricks of the tricksters,

with a threefold etymological figure. Only then do we find the personalized Vṛtra in the basic formula, expanded by appositions, another play on words, and a kenning (5ab):

áhan vṛtrám vṛtratáraṃ vyàṁsam
índro vájreṇa mahatā́ vadhéna

He slew Vṛtra, the *vṛtrá-* ['obstruction'] par excellence,
the cobra (Schmidt 1964),
he Indra with the cudgel, the great smiter.

Note the alliterations in *v-*, which run through the whole hymn (Renou 1934:104).

The crucial phrase *áhann áhim*, the figure of this hymn and many others, has a clearly formulaic character, long ago recognized by Sanskritists. Its affect is underscored by the phonetic figure *áh- áh-*, and by the marked word order V(erb) O(bject), with the verb sentence-initial.

The whole phrase is inherited lexical material: the Vedic root *han-* is from IE **g^{u}hen-* 'smite, slay', and Vedic *áhi-* from IE **og^{u}his* 'serpent, snake'. Both contain the voiced aspirate labio-velar *$g^{u}h$*, which together with *b* is the rarest of Indo-European obstruent consonants, and thereby inherently most expressive.[1]

The formulaic phrase *áhann áhim* occurs 11 times in the Rigveda, with half of these in the older family books (2-7).[2] The formula is always sentence-initial and verse-initial. The subject is always Indra, who however is only once overt as grammatical subject, otherwise only as vocative and the verb in the 2sg. In the single exception with Indra as apparent overt subject, 5.29.3., we have in fact overlapping of two formulas and themes:

utá brahmāṇo maruto me asya
índraḥ sómasya súṣutasya peyāḥ

---

1. For the inverse correlation of frequency and affectiveness or expressivity in phonology compare the high proportion of French slang words in /gV-/ (*g* before *e, i, a* has no Latin source), or the nature of Irish words in /p-/ (IE **p* > Ø), or of Japanese words in /p-/ (Old Jap. *p-* > *h-*), etc.

2. 3sg. 1.32.1,2; 1.103.2; 4.28.1; 5.29.3; 10.67.12; 2sg. 2.11.5; 3.32.11; 4.19.2; 6.30.4; 10.133.2.

tád dhí havyám mánuṣe gā́ ávindad
ā́hann ā́him papivā́m̐ índro asya

And, o formulator Maruts,
may Indra drink of it, my well-pressed soma;
for this oblation found the cows for Manu.
He **slew the serpent**, Indra, having drunk of it.

Here the focus is on the soma offering and drinking, and the whole myth is, as it were, hung on it; the formula *áhann áhim* is intercalated between *índraḥ . . . peyāḥ* and *papivā́m̐ índraḥ*, with the result an (awkward) apposition. The first line is curious in showing only one accented syllable; atonic *asya* at the end of 3a echoes in *sóm**asya** súṣut**asya*** and is repeated at the end of 3d. In each case its position is a syntactic anomaly.

The phrase *áhann áhim* is moreover a flexible formula (cf. Hainsworth 1968), allowing syntactic and morphological variants: thus in the injunctive 5.29.2 *ā́datta vájram abhí yád áhiṃ hán* 'He took the cudgel when he slew the serpent', and the other examples, e.g. 2.15.1 perfect *áhim índro jaghāna*, relativized 2.12.11 *yó áhiṃ jaghā́na* 'who slew the serpent', subordinate 5.29.8 *yád áhiṃ jaghā́na*, with variant word order and enjambment 6.17.9cd *áhiṃ yád índro* . . . | . . . *jaghā́na* ||. The phrase occurs with the verb nominalized, with participles of present, perfect, and desiderative: 5.13.7 *áhiṃ yád ghnán*, 5.32.3 *áhiṃ . . . jaghanvā́n*, 1.80.13 *áhiṃ . . . jíghāṁsatas*. This verb phrase expressing the myth is finally encapsulated in the compound *ahihán-* 'serpent-slaying', epithet of Indra, and the abstracts *ahihátya-* and *áhighna-*. Note that all but one of these variant formulas come from the family books.

The full phrase *áhann áhim* in a repeated formulaic whole line (RV 4.28.1 = 10.67.12 and recurring AV 20.91.12, MS 4.11.2, KS 9.19),

ā́hann ā́him áriṇāt saptá síndhūn

He **slew the serpent**, let flow the seven streams,

is transformed to a gerund phrase, likewise repeated, in RV 2.12.3 and AV 20.34.3, MS 4.14.5:

yó hatvā́him áriṇāt saptá síndhūn

He **who slew the serpent** and let flow the seven streams.

As with all cases of the gerunds *hatvā́*, *hatvī́* there is no overt subject. The infinitive phrase *áhaye hántavā u* 'to slay the serpent' 5.31.4, 8.96.5 likewise shows no subject.

For the basic formula and others involving nominal forms of the root *$g^{u}hen$- in both Indic and Iranian and either accusative rection or objective genitive (e.g. *hántā vṛtrám* 'slayer of V.'), see chap. 41 n. 7.

In only two of the preceding flexible formulaic variants, 2.15.1 and 6.17.9, is

Indra an overt grammatical subject, and both are special cases. 2.15.1ab begins with an anaphoric reference to Indra (unstressed *asya* 'his'), as yet unnamed, and a chiastic grammatical figure, gen. sg. (of Indra) - neut. pl. (of the deeds) - neut. pl. (of the deeds) - gen. sg. (of Indra):

prá ghā nv àsya maható mahā́ni
satyā́ satyásya káraṇāni vocam

Now I will tell his, the great one's great (deeds),
the true one's true deeds.

The myth is then narrated in the imperfect without overt subject Indra, which is deferred to the last sentence of the verse and with a verb in the perfect: 1cd

tríkadrukeṣu apibat sutásya
asyá máde **áhim** índro **jaghāna**

In the Trikadrukas he drank of the pressed (soma);
in its exhilaration Indra **slew** the **serpent**.

The narration continues but with a repeated refrain at line d of each of the following eight verses:

sómasya tā́ máda índraś cakāra

These things Indra did in the exhilaration of soma. (tr. Jamison)

Line 1d thus forms a bridge between the narrative and the refrain, and it is only in these lines, 1d and the refrain, and in the vocative of the final line 9b that Indra is overtly mentioned at all.

In 6.17.9cd we have both shift of subject from 2sg. to 3sg. (ab 'Even heaven retreated from your weapon, and doubly in fear of your wrath'), as also in verses 7 and 11, and a long separation of object and subject from the verb:

áhiṃ yád índro abhy óhasānaṃ
ní cid viśvā́yuḥ śayáthe **jaghā́na**

when Indra the lowering **serpent**
in his lair for all time **slew**.

The normal state of affairs for the Vedic formula is clearly the absence of overt subject, both with the marked (VO) and unmarked (OV) order: *áhann áhim, yád áhiṃ hán/jaghā́na*.

While the Verb-Object formula is characteristic, the full structure with overt Subject is, not surprisingly, possible, with various permutations of word order, as we have seen. Indeed the fullest expression of the mythological *theme* includes the specification of the Weapon, typically a cudgel; this type will be considered separately later. With overt subject, yet still distanced from the verb phrase, compare 5.29.4:

> jígartim índro apajárgurāṇaḥ
> práti śvasántam áva dānaváṃ **han**
>
> Calling out the swallower (= Vṛtra), Indra **hit** back
> the snorting demon.

Note the the final phonetic echo (*áva dānavam han* [2 sg.] also found in 5.32.1):

> **apa-** – ∪ – ∪
> **ava** dāna**va**ṃ,

as well as the complex phonetic and grammatical figure

> jigar-ACC -jargur-NOM,

which is iconic to the verb with double preverb *práti . . . áva . . . han* 'hit back, smote in return'.

The present tense of *han-* is never used with object *áhim*, only *vṛtrám*/ *vṛtrā́(ṇi)* etc., where we find both root athematic *hánti* and the reduplicated thematic middle *jíghnate*. Renou (1934:110-111) noted a clear tendency for the former to take singular object, the latter plural. Compare the equally timeless and permanent senses in the following two passages, both describing Indra (contrasted with Varuṇa):

6.68.3 vájreṇānyaḥ . . . hanti vṛtrám

> The one smites obstruction (Vṛtra) with his cudgel. . .

7.83.9 vṛtrā́ṇy anyáh . . . jighnate

> The one smashes obstructions. . .

Just so the intensive usually takes the plural, 4.24.10 *yadá vṛtrā́ṇi jáṅghanat* 'if he smashes obstructions'. The lone exception is serially plural: 3.53.11 *rājā́ vṛtrám jaṅghanat prā́g ápāg údag* 'may the king smash obstruction in the East, in the West, in the North'.[3] For Renou (ibid.) these are just formulaic expansions into a verb phrase—'la simple mise en syntaxe'—of the ancient compound *vṛtrahán-* = Av. *vərəϑrajan-* 'smashing resistance'. But the aspectual contrast adds more semantic information than the nominal compound shows. The infrequent compound *ahihán-* simply nominalizes the ancient verbal syntagmas like *áhann áhim*.

3. For the morpho-syntax of these verbs with singular and plural objects compare that of Hittite simple verbs versus *-šk-* iteratives: see Dressler 1968.

Other verbs than *han-* are occasionally found, by lexical substitution and variation, like *vi vraśc-* 'split apart, split open' (for *vadh-* and *tar-* see chapters 32 and 34). Thus 3.33.7b *índrasya kárma yád áhiṃ vivṛścát* 'Indra's deed, when he split open the serpent'. These often co-occur with phrases with *han-*, as here 3.33.7c *ví vájreṇa pariṣádo jaghāna* 'He smote apart the surroundings'. The effect is to "spread" the semantic overtones of *han-* onto the other verb (note the common preverb *ví*). We will have occasion to observe the same phenomenon in Greek, where a form of φόνος 'murder' (IE **g^u^hen-*) may spread its root semantics to a verb κτείνω and raise it to full basic formulaic status of the verb πεφνέμεν (IE **g^u^hen-*). Compare also 4.17.7d *áhiṃ vájreṇa . . . ví vṛścaḥ* 'you split apart the serpent with the cudgel' ~ 8c *hántā yó vṛtrám* '(Indra) who is the slayer of Vṛtra', or with overt subject 2.19.2 *áhim índro . . . ví vṛścat* 'Indra split apart the serpent' ~ 3 *ahihā́* 'the serpent-slayer'. In 1.61.10 *ví vṛś cad vájreṇa vṛtrám índraḥ* the alliteration is clearly sought after; note also the fronting of both preverb and verb. The verb *vraśc-* is of uncertain etymology, with no clear cognates. Its employment in the basic formula would seem to be an Indic innovation.

It is unnecessary to multiply examples further; a vast number may be found in Renou's contribution to Vṛtra et Vṛϑragna, with attention to their development and proliferation. Nor have we cited examples from the Atharvaveda, which presents essentially the same picture. Given the subject matter of the latter text, white and black magic, appropriate examples will be reserved for discussion in part VII on the language of charms.

It is a characteristic of the HERO in general, and of Indra in particular, that his exploits or deeds (*cyautnā́ni, ápas, kárma, kárana*) involve victorious combats with many other adversaries, some monstrous, some anthropomorphic. It is further characteristic of Indic, Iranian, and Greek formulaic narrative of these exploits that they are syntactically conveyed by one or more relative clauses, with the name of the adversary and a form of the basic verb root **g^u^hen-* (occasionally another verb by lexical substitution). We have a (Late) Indo-European, at least Greco-Aryan inherited stylistic figure. This figure is one of the syntactic and stylistic variations of the Indo-European basic formula, and it functions as an index and a definition of the Indo-European HERO.

Compare RV 1.101.1ab, 2:

prá mandíne pitumád arcatā váco
yáḥ kṛṣṇágarbhā **nirā́hann** ṛjíśvanā
. . .
yó vyàṃsaṃ jāhṛṣāṇéna manyúnā
yáḥ śámbaraṃ **yó ā́han** pípruṃ avratám
índro yáḥ śúṣṇam aśúṣaṃ ny ā́vṛṇaṅ
marútvantaṃ sakhyā́ya havāmahe

Sing a hymn full of drink for him who loves intoxication,
who smote (*han-*) **down** (i.e. caused to abort, metaphorically) those

(citadels) pregnant (metaphorically) with black ones, accompanied
by Ṛjiśvan[4]

. . .

who (slew) Vyaṁsa, in aroused rage,
who (slew) Śambara, **who slew** (*han-*) Pipru[5] with whom
there is no covenant, Indra, who hurled down
Śuṣṇa the greedy (?)[6]—We call (Indra) together with
the Maruts to friendship.

We have already (chap. 27.3) seen RV 2.12, with its relative clauses defining the god hymned, who is then named in the refrain 'He, o people, is Indra'. Some of the definitions are the generalized basic formula, like (10) *yó dásyor hantā́* 'he who(se function) is *dasyu*-slayer', (11) *yó áhiṃ jaghā́na dā́nuṃ śáyānam* 'who slew the serpent, the *dānu* as he lay there'.[7] But in the stylistically and rhetorically closely parallel adjacent hymn 2.14, also of the Gṛtsāmada family, we find the defining relative formula *yó* NN *jaghā́na*, followed by epexegetic variants of 'Give this Indra the soma', in verses 2 (Vṛtra), 3 (Dṛbhīka), 4 (Urana), and in 5 the whole list:

ádhvaryavo **yáḥ** sv áśnam **jaghā́na**
yáḥ śúṣṇam aśúṣaṃ yó vyàṃsam
yáḥ píprum námuciṃ yo rudhikrā́m

Adhvaryu's! **Who slew** well Aśna,
who Śuṣṇa aśuṣa, who Vyaṁsa,
who Pipru, Namuci, who Rudhikrā.[8]

For Avestan and Greek we may anticipate a couple each of the examples to come in chapters 29 and 36. From the Avestas note Yt.19.40-43, of the hero Kərəsāspa:

(40) yō janat̰ ažīm sruuarəm . . .
(41) yō janat̰ gaṇdarəβəm . . .
yō janat̰ hunauuō yat̰ paϑanaiia nauua . . .
yō janat̰ . . . hitāspəm . . .
(42) yō janat̰ arəzō.šamanəm . . .
(43) yō janat̰ snauuiδkəm . . .

4. King Ṛjiśvan is thus the COMPANION in the basic formula. His name, 'having swift dogs', is itself an Indo-European formula, cf. from the same roots Homeric Greek κύνες ἀργοί 'swift dogs' and the Caland composition form ἀργι- (IE *h_2ṛǵ-ró-, *h_2ṛǵ-i-). The episode of Odysseus' dog Argos is also a topos built out of the same formula, as is shown by the careful ring-composition which introduces him in *Od.* 17.291-2, discussed in chap. 3.

5. It is the citadels of Pipru which Indra smashed, with and for King Ṛjiśvan, in RV 1.53.8, 6.20.7, 10.138.3. Here verses 1b and 2b have seemingly split a single legend.

6. Here and elsewhere *aśuṣa*, of uncertain meaning (: *aś* 'eat'??) makes a play on the name of *śuṣṇa*, as though they were a merismatic pair '*śuṣ-*' / 'un-*śuṣ-*'. Cf. ᾽Ιρος ἄϊρος *Od.* 18.73.

7. I take *áhi* and *dā́nu* here to refer to Śambara (11a *yáḥ śámbaram anvávindat* 'who found Śambara'), as against Geldner, ad loc.

8. Possibly rather an epithet (RV 1x).

Who slew the horned serpent . . .
who slew Gaṇdarəβa . . .
who slew the nine sons of the Pathana clan . . .
who slew Hitāspa . . .
who slew Arəzō.šamana . . .
who slew Snauuiδka . . .

For Greek we may note first Pindar's rhetorical question at *Isth*. 5.39-41 (478 B.C.?):

λέγε, τίνες Κύκνον, τίνες Ἕκτορα **πέφνον**,
καὶ στράταρχον Αἰθιόπων ἄφοβον
Μέμνονα χαλκοάραν;

Say, who **killed** Kuknos, who Hektor, and the
fearless leader of the Ethiopians,
Memnon of the bronze arms?

The traditional answer preexisted; in *Ol*. 2.81-3 Pindar speaks of the just heroes in the Isles of the Blessed, Peleus and Kadmos and Achilles:

ὃς Ἕκτορα σφᾶλε, Τροίας
ἄμαχον ἀστραβῆ κίονα, Κύκνον τε θανάτωι πόρεν,
Ἀοῦς τε παῖδ' Αἰθίοπα

Who felled Hector, the irresistible, unswerving
pillar of Troy, and gave to death Kuknos,
and the Ethiopian son of Dawn.

In the preceding century a different answer for a different Kuknos had been given in the *Shield of Heracles* (57), attributed to Hesiod, namely Herakles:

ὃς καὶ Κύκνον ἔπεφνε

Who slew Kuknos as well.

The relative clauses underline the thematic and formulaic link, and σφᾶλε is one of the many lexical substitutes for the basic verb πέφνε.

In RV 1.32.11 the personalized 'dragon' Vṛtra is referred to both as *áhi-* 'serpent' and as *dāsá-*: *dāsápatnīr áhigopāḥ . . . níruddhā ápaḥ* 'the pent-up waters with the *dāsá* as husband, the Serpent as guardian'. Geldner regularly leaves the word untranslated; the meaning is 'hostile demon', 'enemy', but also on the human plane, by opposition to *ā́rya*, 'non-āryan, barbarian', and finally 'slave'. Similarly in 2.11.2 Indra released the waters *páriṣṭhitā áhinā* 'surrounded by the Serpent', and struck down the *dāsá* who thought himself immortal, *ámartyaṃ cid dāsám mányamānam ávābhinad.* In verse 5 the basic formula recurs, *áhann áhiṃ śūra vīryèṇa* 'you slew the serpent, Hero, with your manly strength'. The monster is called *vṛtra* at verses 9 and 18, as well as *dā́nu-*, another designation for hostile demons: *yéna vṛtrám avā́bhinat dā́num* 'by which he struck down Vṛtra, the *dānu*'. In the same verse the demon is called *dásyu-* 'enemy (demon), stranger': *ní savyatáḥ sādi dásyuḥ* 'the *dásyu-* has sat down on the left', while in the next, 19, the same word is applied on the human level to the hostile non-āryan strangers: *yé . . . táranto víśvā spṛ́dha ā́ryeṇa dásyūn* '(we) who are overcoming all adversaries, *dasyu*'s by the *Ārya.*' Note that in both the latter the verb precedes the object (or subject of passive), just as in *áhann áhim.*

The other adversaries of Indra have the same system of sobriquets: Pipru is *áhimāya-* 'having the magic power of an *ahi*' (6.20.7), Śambara is an *áhi*, a *dā́nu* (2.12.11), a *dā́sa-* (6.26.5), a *dásyu-* (6.31.4), Śuṣṇa a *dā́sa-* (7.19.2), a *dásyu-* (8.6.14), Namuci a *dāsá-* (6.20.6).

The terms *dāsá-*, *dā́sa-*, and *dásyu-*, with *dása-* (6.21.11, legendary ancestor of the *dāsá*'s) and other forms, are doubtless related, as Indo-Iranian **dāsá-*, **dásiu-* 'enemy, stranger', **dasiú-* 'land (orig. of the enemy)', Av. *daxiiu-/daŋhu-*. A likely cognate outside Indo-Iranian is Greek δοῦλος 'slave' Myc. *doero* [do(h)-elo-]. See Mayrhofer EWA s.vv. The nomenclature of Indo-Iranian demonology would thus be drawn from the terms for the hostile, non-āryan peoples with whom they came in contact (and whom on occasion they enslaved). We may pose a link which joins the serpent and the sobriquet in Indo-Iranian

*aǰhi- dāsa-,

whence both Vedic *áhi- . . . dāsá-* and the Iranian name of the dragon par excellence, *Aži Dahāka*[9] slain by Thraētaona, on which see the following chapter.

9. With trisyllabic shortening from **dāhāka-* (P.O. Skjærvø, p.c.)

29

The root *g^{u}hen-: Avestan *jan-*

In RV 2.11.19 Indra is hymned by recalling his previous aid:

asmā́bhyaṃ tát tvāṣṭrā́ṃ viśvárūpam
árandhayaḥ . . . tritā́ya

To us then you delivered the son of Tvaṣṭṛ,
Viśvarūpa, to Trita.

Trita is the legendary Trita Āptya, slayer of the three-headed, six-eyed dragon Viśvarūpa, with the aid of Indra. Benveniste (1934:195) pointed out the all-important structural similarity between this Indic dragon-slaying episode and the Iranian legend of the (mortal) hero Thraētaona, who slew the three-headed, six-eyed dragon Aži Dahāka, with the aid of Vərəϑraγna (Yt. 14.38,40):

aməmca vərəϑraγnəmca
. . .
yim ϑraētaonō taxmō barat̰
yō janat̰ ažīm dahākəm
ϑrizafanəm ϑrikamərəδəm
xšuuaš.ašīm hazaŋrā.yaoxštīm . . .

The power and offensive force[1]
. . .
which brave Thraētaona bore
who slew the dragon Aži Dahāka,
the three-jawed, three-headed,
six-eyed one of a thousand skills . . .

1. Vərəϑraγna's aid to Thraētaona can be compared to his aid to Zarathustra earlier in the same hymn (Yt. 14.29), giving him, in an arresting metaphor, *ərəzōiš xå* (*bāzuuå aojō*, . . .) 'the wellspring of the scrotum, (the strength of the two arms . . .)'

As we noted in the previous chapter, using Jakobson's terms, the similarity is both syntagmatic and paradigmatic: syntagmatic in the sequential linkage of the two stories themselves, the aid brought by Vərəϑraγna to Thraētaona to enable him to slay Aži Dahāka, and the aid brought by Indra to Trita to enable him to slay Viśvarūpa (contiguity relations); paradigmatic in the near-identities of the names (*Thraēt-* ~ *Trit-*) of the hero and attributes (3-headed, 6-eyed) of the dragon, the protagonists of the two myths (similarity relations).

The basic formula in Old Iranian *yō janaṯ ažīm* is an exact cognate of Vedic *áhann áhim*, in both words; the phrase is relativized, but the marked word-order Verb-Object is preserved.[2] The relative verb phrase *yō janaṯ ažīm* is always sentence- or clause-initial in Avestan (further examples below). The word order is precisely that of the Vedic relative verb phrase *yó áhan píprum* 'who slew Pipru' in 1.101.2b cited above.

These names and phrases in both traditions recount traditional mythology which must be common Indo-Iranian patrimony, as has been recognized for over a century.[3] I note here only the linguistic equations. In Iran, as recounted in Yasna 9, the Hōm Yasht, *Vivaŋ^vhant* (= Vedic *Vivasvant*) was the first man to press *haoma* (= Vedic *soma*), and his reward was to beget *Yima* (=Vedic *Yama*), the first ruler, who presided over the golden age. The second man to press haoma was *Āϑβiia* (~ Vedic *Āptya*), whose reward was to beget *Thraētaona* (~ Vedic *Traitana*, on whom see further below), who slew *Aži Dahāka*. The third man to press haoma was *Thrita* (= Vedic *Trita*, both "third"), whose reward was to beget *Uruuāxšaiia*, a lawgiver, and *Kərəsāspa*, the warrior hero who slew *Aži Sruuara*, the horned serpent.

Avestan *Thrita* and *Thraētaona* seem to be ablaut variants of the same name and identical with Vedic *Trita Āptya*, who is also associated with *soma*. *Āptya* itself is in origin identical with Avestan *Āϑβiia* < **ātpi̯a* (or *ātu̯i̯a* ?), remade with metathesis by association with *āp-* 'water'.[4]

Compare then, beside RV 2.11.19 cited above, the specifications in book 10 of the Rigveda about the legend of Trita Āptya and Viśvarūpa, 10.8.8:

> sá pítryāṇy ā́yudhāni vidvā́n
> índreṣita **āptyó** abhy àyudhat
> triśīrṣā́ṇaṃ saptáraśmiṃ[5] **jaghanvā́n**
> tvāṣṭrásya cin níḥ sasṛje **tritó** gā́ḥ
>
> This one, **Āptya**, knowing his paternal weapons,
> set on by Indra, went forth to battle;

2. For the thematization of the Avestan 3sg. imperfect *janaṯ* beside Vedic (*á*)*han* = Old Persian *aja*, cf. Hoffmann 1975:73.

3. Cf. Reichelt 1968:95-7, and in greater detail Boyce 1975-82:I.85-108, esp. 97-104. Boyce is doubtless right (pp. 99-100) in assuming that Trita Āptya - Thrita Thraētaona, son of Āϑβiia, were originally in Indo-Iranian times regarded as mortal rather than divine (as in India), though whether we should think of them as euhemerized "real" *Ātpi̯as living sometime before 2000 B.C. is open to question.

4. Gershevitch 1969:188-9, making more precise the identification long assumed. Cf. also Mayrhofer EWA s.v. *āptyá-*.

5. Cf. 1.146.1a of Agni *trimūrdhā́nam saptáraśmim* 'three-headed, seven-bridled', and see below.

having slain the three-headed, seven-bridled (Viśvarūpa),
Trita let out even the son of Tvaṣṭṛ's (Viśvarūpa's) cows.

Or 10.48.2 (Indra's self-praise):

tritā́ya gā́ ajanayam **áher** ádhi

For Trita I brought forth the cows from the **serpent**
(i.e. which the serpent Viśvarūpa had swallowed).

Note the association of the two names with the perfect participle of *han-* (**gʷhen-*) and the word *áhi-* (**ogʷhi-*). For the same association in Avestan cf. Y. 9.7:

āϑβiiō mąm bitiiō maṣ̌iiō
. . . hunūta . . .
tat̰ ahmāi jasat̰ āiiaptəm
yat̰ hē puϑrō us.zaiiata
vīsō suraiiā̊ **ϑraētaonō**

Āϑβya was the second mortal to press me (Haoma)
. . .
That fortune came to him,
that a son was born to him,
Thraētaona, of heroic family.

This is followed immediately by strophe 8:

yō **janat̰ až̌īm** dahākəm
ϑrizafanəm etc. (Yt. 14.40 supra)

Who **slew Aži** Dahāka
the three-jawed, etc.

For the epithets compare RV 10.99.6:

sá íd **dā́saṃ** tuvīrávam pátir **dán**
ṣaḷakṣáṃ triśīrṣā́ṇaṃ damanyat
asyá tritó nv ójasā **vṛdhānó**
vipā́ varāhám áyoagrayā **han**[6]

This lord in the house (Indra) overpowered
the loud-roaring, **six-eyed, three-headed dāsa**;

---

6. Note the triple alliterations **d**, **d**, **d**; **v**, **v**, **v**, the end-rhyme *dán* : *han*, and the two injunctives. The verb *damanya-* is a hapax in the Rigveda.

strengthened by his (Indra's) power, Trita **slew**
the boar with his iron-tipped arrow.

The MONSTER is here assimilated to a 'boar', *varāhá*; see below for the Iranian HERO Vərəϑraγna in his furious onslaught also assimilated to a 'boar', the exact cognate *varāza-*. Further connections of this ancient Indo-Iranian word, borrowed into Finno-Ugric (see Mayrhofer, KEWA s.v.), are unknown. But the Indo-Iranian word is not only a shared lexical item; it is also a shared cultural and mythological icon.

With the similar description of the monster we have again Y. 9.8, of the hero Thraētaona:

yō janat̰ ažīm dahākəm
ϑrizafanəm **ϑrikamərəδəm**
xšuuaš.ašīm hazaŋrā.yaoxštīm
aš.aojaŋhəm daēuuīm drujim . . .[7]

Who slew Aži Dahāka
the three-mouthed, **three-headed**,
six-eyed one of a thousand tricks,
the very powerful Demoness, the Druj . . .

Note that Vedic *ṣaḷakṣa-* (*ṣaḍ-akṣ-a-*) 'six-eyed' and Avestan *xšuuaš.aš-i-* are exact cognates up to the suffixes. Note also that Avestan *ϑrikamərəδəm* (*ϑri-ka+ mərəδa-*) is almost identical to Vedic *trimūrdhā́nam* (*tri-mūrdhan-*) 'three-headed', epithet of Agni (note 5 above).

Before continuing with Yasna 9.10 and the third presser of *haoma* we must examine another Indo-Iranian link. Mary Boyce in discussing the Iranian and Indic traditions around Avestan Thrita and Thraētaona son of Āϑβya, and Vedic Trita Āptya, notes that the Vedas mention once (RV 1.158.5) a Traitana, 'who appears obscurely, in a context which does not suggest any connection with the Avestan Thraētaona' (p. 99).

Now the names are similar enough to arouse an interest (*trit-/ϑrit-*, *ϑraēt-/trait-*; for the suffix cf. Greek κέρ-αυνος, Slavic *Per-unъ*, Hittite [D]IM-*unnaš* [*Tarḫunnaš*] beside Vedic *Parj-an-ya*), and when they are syntagmatically associated with other key lexical expressions of the myth, I would suggest the connection becomes perfectly real and self-evident.

The name is found in the Saga of the ṛṣi Dīrghatamas 'Of the long darkness', the

7. The Avestan lexicon includes synonyms opposed dualistically as applying to "good" and "evil" beings, Ahuric and Daēvic. These body parts are those of Daēvic creatures: *zafar/n-* 'mouth, jaws, set of teeth' (Vedic *jámbha-*, IE **ĝm̥bh-* ~ **ĝm̥ph-* as in Germ. *Kiefer*), *kamərəd-* 'head' (literally 'what a head' *ka-mərəd-*, Ved. *mūrdh-an-*), *aš-* 'eye' (Ved. *ákṣi*, *an-akṣ-*), opposed to those of Ahuric creatures, resp. *āh-* 'mouth', *vaγδana-* 'head', *dōiϑra-*, *casman-* 'eye' (the cognate of Ved. *śíras*, *sarah-* 'head' is neutral). This part of the Iranian lexicon is of great theoretical and metalinguistic interest. It has received a fair amount of attention; the classic study is Güntert 1914, and the best recent studies (both with the intervening literature) are by Gercenberg 1972:17-40, and Toporov 1981:205-14. As Toporov notes in this seminal work, the question is complex, and still not settled.

blind poet, son of Ucathya and Mamatā.[8] It is one of the many examples of the Power of the Word in ancient India. The legend is told in Bṛhad-Devatā 4.21-24, and recalls that in MBh 1.104.23ff. As an old man Dīrghatamas' slaves bound him and threw him into a river. But his prayer saved him: one of the slaves, Traitana, tried to behead him with a sword, but instead cut off his own head, shoulder, and breast (Bṛh. Dev. 4.21, cited by Geldner). The waters carried Dīrghatamas safely to shore. RV 1.158.4-5 gives the words of his prayer: 'May the song of praise (*úpastuti*) save the son of Ucathya . . .'

(5) ná mā garan nadyò mātṛ́tamā
dāsā́ yád īṃ súsamubdham avā́dhuḥ
śíro yád asya **traitanó** vitákṣat
svayáṃ **dāsá** úro áṃsāv ápi gdha.

The most mothering rivers will not swallow me.
When the **Dāsas** put him in, well bound,
when **Traitana** tries to hew off his **head**,
the **Dāsa** eats up his own breast and two shoulders.[9]

Traitana is a *dāsa* in the sense of 'slave', but he is at the same time a *dāsa* 'demon': the HERO has become the MONSTER. The power of Truth, of the spoken word, drives his WEAPON back on himself, and instead of Dīrghatamas' head (*śíras*) he cuts off his own 'breast and two shoulders' (1 + 2 = 3) in the Rigveda, or 'head and shoulders and breast' (1 + 1 + 1 = 3) in the Bṛhad-Devatā. The tone is grimly mock-heroic: Traitana has become precisely the three-headed serpent which Thraētaona slew, and the three-headed *dāsa* which Trita Āptya slew. Cf. RV 10.99.6 (quoted in full above) for the identical key words,

dāsám . . . **triśīrṣāṇam** . . . **tritó** . . . **han**,

or the same elements in Avestan (Y. 9.7-8) with a different order:

ϑraētaonō . . . **janaṯ** . . . **ϑrikamərəδəm** . . . **dahākəm**.

There should be no doubt that this legend is only another version of the same common Indo-Iranian myth, with its same formulaic diction.[10]

Yasna 9.10, with which we began, continues exactly parallel to strophe 7 quoted above, with Thrita, the third man to press haoma, whose fortune was

8. Cf. RV 1.32.11 etc.

9. The present tense of the English translation of cd attempts to capture the Vedic injunctives. 'Put' of b is preterite, corresponding to the Vedic aorist.

10. Just *why* in India the original hero Traitana has become both monstrous and servile, an inept buffoon and the complete inversion of his heroic self, I cannot say. The mock-heroic is perhaps universally not far removed from the heroic, and perhaps coeval with it. Compare the beggar and anti-hero (W)Iros in *Odyssey* 18 (Ved. *vīrás* 'man, hero'), and Bader 1976.

yat̰ hē puϑra us.zaiiōiϑe
uruuāxšaiiō kərəsāspasca
t̰kaēšō **aniiō** dātō.rāzō
āat̰ **aniiō** uparō.kairiiō
yauua gaēsuš gaδauuarō

That to him two sons were born,
Urvāxšaya and Kərəsāspa:
the one a judge, a lawgiver,
and the other one of superior deeds,
a young (hero), curly-haired, bearing the cudgel.

For the compound *gaδauuarō* in the last line note also Yt. 10.101, of Mithra, with a compound of *gan-* (**g^u̯hen-*) and the weapon itself as object:

hō paoiriiō gaδąm **nijaiṇti**
aspaēca paiti vīraēca

He first **strikes** his cudgel
at horse and man.

As an illustration of a Common Indo-Iranian topos we may compare the figure of the two Iranians Urvāxšaya and Kərəsāspa, *aniiō* . . . *aniiō* . . . 'the one . . . the other . . .', with RV 7.83.9ab, to the gods Indra and Varuṇa:

vr̥trā́ṇy **anyáḥ** samithéṣu **jíghnate**
vratā́ny **anyó** abhí rakṣate sádā

The one smashes the hostile defenses in battles,
the other protects alliances always.

Even the second position of *aniiō/anyá-* is common to both.[11] Note in the Vedic the poetic antithesis under partial phonetic identity in the identically fronted ***vr̥trā́ṇi*** : ***vratā́ni***. The figure is exactly that of ***last but not least***.

Kərəsāspa is with Mary Boyce 'the other great Avestan hero', and 'many more stories are told of him than of Thraētaona' (op. cit. 100). Yasna 9.11 continues immediately:

yō janat̰ ažīm sruuarəm
yim aspō.garəm nərə.garəm
yim vīšauuaṇtəm zairitəm

11. Cf. also the similar 6.68.3. S. Jamison has shown that Vedic *anyá-* (. . . *anyá* . . .) in second position is definite, 'the one (. . . the other . . .)', while in first position it is indefinite, 'someone'. These examples would indicate the syntactic feature is Common Indo-Iranian.

Who slew the horned Aži,
the horse-swallowing, man-swallowing,
venomous, yellow-green . . .

With *aspō.gar- nərə.gar-* compare *aspaēca paiti vīraēca* 'against horse and man' of Yt. 10.101, together with the compound (ibid.) *aspa.vīraja* 'smiting (*gan-*) horse (and) man', also of Mithra.

We have already seen in the preceding section the enumeration of the other men or monsters slain by Kərəsāspa in Yt. 19.40-43, all in the identical formula *yō janat̰* NN. Again the subject Kərəsāspa is not overt in the sentences.

The verb phrase is nominalized to agent noun plus genitive in V. 1.17 *ϑraētaonō* ***jaṇta ažōiš*** *dahākāi* 'Thraetaona slayer of Aži Dahāka'.[12] For this and other Iranian nominal forms of *gan-* in the basic formula see chap. 51.

The final Old Iranian example is furnished by three verses in Yt. 19.92 (cf. 93):

*vaδəm vaējō yim vārəϑraγnəm
yim barat̰ taxmō ϑraētaonō
yat̰ **ažiš** dahākō **jaini**

Swinging the weapon which smashes resistance
which brave Tharaetaona carried,
when **Aži** Dahākā **was slain**.

Similarly in the continuation of the passage (describing the future coming of the Savior Astuuat̰.ərətō), 93 (*yim barat̰ . . .*) *yat̰ druuå zainigāuš jaini . . . yat̰ tuurō jaini fraŋrase . . .* '(which NN bore) when evil Zainigu was slain . . . when the Turanian Fraŋrasyan was slain . . .' Note the variation in word order of the last, with the familiar distraction of noun (name) and adjective by intervening verb.[13]

The reading *vaδəm* for *vaēδəm* (anticipation of the following *vaējō*) is due to J. Schindler (p.c.). Avestan *vaδa-* equals Vedic *vadhá-* 'weapon, Totschläger', specifically Indra's cudgel in RV 1.32.6 et alibi.

We may juxtapose the Avestan sentence of Yt. 19.92 with the Vedic of RV 5.29.2 (cited in full above) to illustrate the close similarity of expression in the two languages:

vaδəm . . . yat̰ ažiš . . . jaini
vájram . . . yád áhiṃ hán.

All five collocations of *jan-* and *aži-* in Avestan are metrical; they are all

12. For the agent noun with accusative construction cf. Yt. 17.12 *vītārəm paskāt̰ hamərəϑəm / jaṇtārəm parō dušmainiiūm* '(who is) the pursuer of the adversary from behind, the slayer of the enemy from in front' see chap. 50 n. 3. *hamərəϑa-* and *dušmainiiu* are a figure of hendiadys.

13. The passage concludes with 'which Kavi Vīštāspa bore,' *aṣ̌ahe haēnaiiå caēšəmnō* 'going to avenge Aša on the enemy army'. (Read *aṣ̌əm*; the error was induced by the line-initial *aṣ̌ahe* two lines later.) Here the participle of *kay-* 'avenge', IE *$k^{u}ei$-, occupies a position parallel to *jaini* 'was slain', IE *$g^{u}hen$-. For other examples from Avestan and especially Greek see chap. 49.

octosyllabic verse lines.[14] There can be no doubt that these cognate verb phrases continue an ancient poetic tradition, a verbal flexible formula which is at least common Indo-Iranian in date.

We may illustrate the various forms of the root *gan-* in Avestan with a passage from Yt. 10.71, the hymn to Mithra, describing the onslaught of *vərəϑraγnō ahuraδātō* 'Ahura-created Vərəϑraγna' in the shape of a wild boar: a common and frequent image of the heroic deity,[15] which emphasizes his fearsome monstrous qualities. The verb *nijaiṇti* is in a relative clause, the syntactic definition of the hero, in accord with the pattern described at the end of the preceding section:

> yō fra̧štacō hamərəϑāδa
> . . .
> stija **nijaiṇti** hamərəϑə̄
> naēδa maniiete **jaγnuuå**
> naēδa cim **γəna̧** sadaiieiti
> yauuata aēm **nijaiṇti**
> mərəzuca stūnō gaiiehe
> mərəzuca xå uštānahe
>
> Who, running before the adversary, . . .
> **smashes** the adversaries in battle;[16]
> he does not think that he **has struck**
> nor has he the impression he **is striking** anyone,
> until he **smashes**
> even the vertebras, the pillars of life,
> even the vertebras, the wellspring of vitality.

The echoic *stija nija(iṇti), naēδa . . . naēδa, mərəzuca . . . mərəzuca* form a counterpoint to the different forms of basic verb *gan-*: general present *nijaiṇti*, perfect participle *jagnuuå*, present participle *γəna̧*, repeated *nijaiṇti*. The metaphors with *stūna* 'pillar' are widespread[17] and those with *xå* 'wellspring' common in Indic as well: *rāyás khā́m* 'wellspring of riches' RV 6.36.4, and the Common Indo-Iranian *khā́m ṛtásya* 'wellspring of Truth' RV 2.28.5, *aṣ̌ahe xå* 'id.' Y. 10.4. Cf. note 1 above. Finally the parallel *gaiia-* 'life' and *uštāna-* 'vitality' recall the Italic merism in Latin *uires uitaque*, Oscan *biass biítam*, discussed in chap. 18.

14. For a recent discussion of YAv. metrics see Lazard 1984.

15. Cf. Benveniste and Renou 1934:34-5, 69, 73, and Gershevitch 1959:219.

16. The interpretation of *stija* is controversial. For discussion see Kellens 1974:84.

17. Cf. Watkins 1990:52-5, and Hektor Τροίας . . . κίονα 'pillar of Troy' in the preceding chapter.

30

The root *$g^{u}hen$-: Hittite *kuen*- and the Indo-European theme and formula

That the Common Indo-Iranian verbal formula *áhann áhim*, *janaṯ ažīm* is even older, and of Common Indo-European date, is proved by the presence of the same syntagma in Old Hittite. We find it as the dénouement of the Hittite myth entitled by Laroche (CTH 321) Combat contre le Dragon ou "Illuyanka".[1] KUB 17.5 i 17 §12:

> ^{D}IM-aš uit nu=kan ^{MUŠ}**illuy**[(**ankan**)]
> **kuenta** DINGIR^{MEŠ}-š=a katti=šši ešer
>
> Tarḫunnas came and he **killed the serpent**;
> and the gods were with him.

The Hittite verb *kuenta* 'killed' makes an exact equation with Vedic *áhan*(*n*), *hán*, and Avestan *jan*(*aṯ*), reflecting Indo-European *$g^{u}hen$-*t*.[2]

It is most important to note that the Hittite sentence, like the Vedic and Avestan, focusses on the object; the subject is known from the preceding clause, but not overt in its own clause, regardless of the order of Verb and Object. As in normal unmarked word order in Hittite narrative prose, the sentence begins with a particle sequence and concludes with the verb:

(marked word order)	(unmarked word order)
áhann áhim	yád áhiṃ hán
yō janaṯ ažīm	yaṯ ažiš jaini
	nu=kan illuyankan kuenta.

From these sentences we may extract an Indo-European mythological *theme* with partial lexical expression:

1. The myth is edited and translated by Gary Beckman (1982), who doubtless correctly takes *illuyanka*- as the Hittite common noun for 'snake' or 'serpent.'

2. For the thematization of the Avestan form cf. K. Hoffmann 1975:73.

HERO SLAY (*$g^{w}hen$-) SERPENT.

The verbal *formula* which is the vehicle for this theme—asymmetrically—is boxed:

HERO | SLAY (*$g^{w}hen$-) SERPENT. |

This asymmetry in the correspondence of formula to theme is precisely the "Indo-European touch" that we were looking for. G. Nagy calls my attention to M. L. West's observation (ad Hesiod, *Th.* 112) on the widespread omission of an overt subject in Hesiod, 'where it is the thing dominant in Hesiod's mind'. The boxed verb phrase 'slay the serpent' constitutes, as we have seen, the predicate which *defines* the Indo-European hero. Thus in RV 2.12, following a series of relative clauses like *yó áhiṃ jaghā́na* 'who slew the serpent' which describe the exploits of the god without mentioning his name, the Vedic poet proclaims at the end of each strophe *sá janāsa índrah̩* 'He, o people, is Indra'.

Unexpected confirmation of the stylistic significance of the 'asymmetrical' verb phrase formula without overt subject comes from Middle Iranian; I am indebted to S. Jamison for calling it to my attention. The Pahlavi version of the legend of the hero Kərəsāspa, the richest and most detailed Iranian tradition, is found in the Rivāyāt; it represents the Pahlavi redaction of a chapter of the lost Sassanian Avesta.[3] The passage in question reads as follows (the soul of Kiršāsp is pleading with Ohrmazd that he should forgive him for killing the fire, Ohrmazd's son, and grant him paradise in view of his major feats) PR p. 66:[4]

> . . . u-m Garōdmān bē dah až ī srūwar bē ōzad ī asp-ōbār ī mard-ōbār
>
> . . . and give me Paradise: the horned dragon was killed, the horse-devouring and man-devouring one.

The lack of an overt subject here is quite noteworthy, as the parallel passages describing his other feats are expressed in normal Pahlavi prose, PR p. 67:

> ān-im . . . Garōdmān dah čē-m Gandarw bē ōzad
>
> Therefore give me Paradise, because I killed the Gandarβa,

and PR p. 69:

> Garōdmān bē dah čē-m rāhdār ōzad hēnd (for mss. hēm)
>
> Give me Paradise, because I killed the highwaymen.

3. See Nyberg 1964-1974 and 1933.

4. The Pahlavi Rivâyat accompanying the Dâdistân-î Dînîk, ed. B.N. Dhabhar, Bombay, 1913. I thank P.O. Skjærvø for clarifying my presentation here.

In contrast to the last two feats, which are introduced with the expected causal conjunction *čē* and contain an overt subject, the first feat, which is also his greatest, is introduced by nothing and lacks an overt subject, and we can safely assume that it is taken directly from the Pahlavi version of an Avestan text, cf. Y. 9.11 (above IV.29) *yō janat̰ ažīm sruuarəm yim aspō.garəm nərə.garəm* with its Pahlavi translation *kē-š zad až ī srūwar ī asp.ōbār ī mard-ōbār* as well as Yt. 19.92 *yat̰ ažiš dahākō jaini* (ibid.).

Pahlavi *ō-zan-*, *(ō-)zad* continues Iranian **aua jan-*, **(aua) jata-*, Indo-European **g^{u}hen-*, **g^{u}hn̥to-*. We shall see in the discussion to come how the Greek evidence completely confirms that the formula for killing the serpent could typically lack an overt subject.

My concern in this chapter is simply the Indo-European basic formula and the Hittite evidence for it. Further modalities of the formula in the Hittite *illuyankas* myth are explored in chap. 35. The whole myth is analyzed from a comparative standpoint in chap. 45, and its diffusion studied in chap. 46.

31

The slayer slain: A reciprocal formula

In the model of the mythological theme presented heretofore the narrative action proceeds from left to right: it is the hero who kills the serpent. But there is always the real or potential danger that the serpent will slay the hero, or someone else. AV 6.56.1:

> mā́ no devā áhir **vadhīt**
>
> O gods, let not the serpent **slay** us.

In both versions of the Hittite myth of the *illuyankas* (§§3,21):

> nu=za ^{MUŠ}illuyankaš ^{D}IM-an **taraḫta**
>
> The serpent **overcame** the Storm God.

In Bacchylides 5.115-16 the hero Meleager's duty is

> ϑάπτομεν οὓς **κατέπεφνεν**
> σῦς
>
> to bury those whom the boar
> **had slain**.

The subject of the relative clause is the Calydonian boar. A similar relative clause, also dependent on an infinitive, is found in *Beowulf* 1054-5, where the hero ordered

> golde forgyldan þone þe Grendel ǽr
> máne **ácwealde**

> compensation to be paid for the one whom Grendel
> wickedly **killed**.

Beowulf himself will die of the Worm's venom after slaying it, and Odin and the Miðgarð Serpent will meet the identical fate.

Hence we have the possibility that the action can go in either direction: the HERO may be the subject and the SERPENT the object, or the SERPENT may be the subject and the HERO the object. Rather than duplicating the basic formula I prefer to capture this reciprocal, reversible, or bidirectional thematic relation by the notation

$$\underleftarrow{\overrightarrow{\text{HERO}\qquad\text{SLAY } (^{*}g^{w}hen\text{-})\quad\text{SERPENT.}}}$$

These relations are particularly evident in the case of a non-monstrous, heroic adversary, to be treated in detail in part VI. The typical basic theme is here

$$\text{HERO}_1\qquad\text{SLAY } (^{*}g^{w}hen\text{-})\quad\text{HERO}_2.$$

HERO_1 and HERO_2 are "shifters"; like certain linguistic categories (e.g. *I* : *you*, *this* : *that*, present tense : past tense) they cannot be defined without reference to, and their meaning is dependent on, the particular context (e.g. the speech situation, for these linguistic categories) in which they occur. Thematically compare in the *Iliad* Hektor and Patroklos on the one hand, Achilles and Hector on the other.

The interplay of bidirectionality and the linguistic and literary notion of *focus* is well-illustrated when the ADVERSARY is a monstrous boar. The action moves from right to left when the boar is the subject,

$$\overleftarrow{\text{(HERO)}\qquad\text{SLAY } (^{*}g^{w}hen\text{-})\quad\text{BOAR}}$$

as in Bacchylides (cited above)

> **κατέπεφνεν** σῦς,

but from left to right when the boar is the object,

$$\text{HERO}\qquad\text{SLAY } (^{*}g^{w}hen\text{-})\quad\text{BOAR,}$$

as in RV 10.99.6

> tritó . . . varāhám . . . **han**.

But the hero may be assimilated to a boar, as Vərəϑraγna in Yt. 10.71 (cf. 24.3 above), in which case the focus becomes rather

$$\text{HERO-BOAR}\qquad\text{SLAY } (^{*}g^{w}hen\text{-})\quad\text{(ADVERSARY),}$$

as in

varāzō . . . **nijaiṇti**,

with the exact cognate of the Vedic boar-word *varāhá-*, discussed in chap. 29: a Common Indo-Iranian theme or topos thus differently realized in focus.

The reciprocal theme

$$\overrightarrow{\overleftarrow{\text{HERO}_1 \quad \text{SLAY } (^*g^{\mu}hen\text{-}) \quad \text{HERO}_2}}$$

gives rise to an endless series of iconic grammatical figures in the various traditions.[1] Compare Old Irish (ZCP 11.86 §40)

gonas géntar

He who kills will be killed,

from *gonid* 'kills, slays' (**gʷhen-*, Celtic **gʷaneti*), or Early Welsh (*Llawsgrif Henregadredd* 60a4, an example I owe to John Koch)

ef wanei wanwyd

He who would slay was slain,

from the same root and preform.

Homeric Greek, with lexical replacement, offers an example which is clearly proverbial, with gnomic τε (*Il.* 18.309):

ξυνὸς Ἐνυάλιος, καί τε κτανέοντα κατέκτα

Alike to all is the War God, and him who would kill he kills.

On the antiquity of the ancient god Enualios and his epithet see chap. 39. Line-final (κατ)έκτα may recover an old athematic *(κατ)έκτεν from **ekten-t* like *áhan* from **egʷhen-t.* This Iliadic line could go back to the Bronze Age.

Nominal forms may participate. Euripides is fond of the figure, as in

φόνον δικάζων φόνος (*El.* 1094)

murder judging murder,

ὡς φόνωι σβέσηι φόνον (*Herc.* 40)

as if to extinguish murder with murder.

1. I discussed some of these from the standpoint of comparative-historical Indo-European syntax in Watkins 1976c. Here as elsewhere a syntactic equation rests on an inherited poetic formula.

Simple variations alter the focus; so beside Old Irish *gonas géntar* 'he who kills will be killed' above we find in *Togail Bruidne Dá Derga* both

> **génait** ⁊ ní génaiter (783)
>
> **They will kill** and not be killed,

and

> sech ní génaiter ní génat nech (1335)
>
> Not only will they not be killed, they will not kill anyone.

Basically just a figure of antithesis, the "slayer slain" may be either the sole feature, as in the examples we have seen so far, or it may be woven into more complex sentences and thematic structures. The figure is simply doubled in Euripides, *Suppl.* 614:

> δίκα δίκαν ἐκάλεσε καὶ φόνος φόνον
>
> Justice has called for justice and blood for blood.

The semantic contrast of the "slayer slain" is preserved, but the verbs are divergent in the famous simile of Achilles before the combat with Aeneas (*Il.* 20.172-3), 'like a lion . . .':

> ἤν τινα **πέφνῃ**
> ἀνδρῶν, ἢ αὐτὸς φθίεται
>
> . . . whether he **slay**
> some man, or perish himself.

'Perish' here clearly stands for 'be slain'—as the passage is frequently translated; the reciprocal passive is not formed from the verb πεφνέμεν in this tense and aspect in Greek, so the etymological figure was blocked.

In RV 7.59.8 the formulaic structure incorporates other themes as well as an additional etymological figure:

> yó no maruto abhí durhṛṇāyús
> tirā́ś cittā́ni vasavo **jíghāṁsati**
> druháḥ pā́śān práti sá mucīṣṭa
> tápiṣṭhena **hánmanā hantanā** tám.
>
> Whoever, o Maruts, seeks in his envy,
> unperceived, o good ones, to **slay** us.

let him himself be caught in the snares of Deceit;
slay him with your hottest "**slayer**".

Note that the desiderative *jíghāṁsati* is an exact cognate of the Old Irish future *génaid* (examples supra). The rhyming jingle *hánmanā hantanā* is an etymological figure in deadly earnest.

'Deceit' itself is the object of the desiderative of *han* in 4.23.7a *drúhaṃ jíghāṁsan* 'seeking to smite Falsehood', which continues with its antithesis (.8b) *ṛtásya dhītír vṛjinā́ni hanti* 'devotion to Truth smites the wicked'. Geldner ad loc. notes that Vedic *druh-* and *ṛta-*, 'Falsehood' and 'Truth', are here opposed exactly like their dualistic cognates in Iranian Zoroastrianism, *Druj* and *Aṣ̌a*: a Common Indo-Iranian theme.

Another variant, expanded with other material, is found in RV 8.84.9, significantly the last verse of a three-triplet (*tṛcas*) hymn:

kṣéti kṣémebhiḥ sādhúbhir
nákir yáṃ **ghnánti hánti** yáḥ
ágne suvī́ra edhate

He dwells in right safe dwellings,
whom none **slay**, who **slays**;
o Agni, he thrives rich in sons.

The sacrificer is referred to. Like the Old Irish variant above, this is the "slayer not slain", but with the focus on the positive and active '*he* slays'. This verse should be compared to 2.27.13, which shares the same themes and vocabulary, but with only the "not slain" motif and no verbal antithesis:

śúcir apáḥ suyávasā ádabdha
úpa kṣeti vṛddhávayāḥ suvī́raḥ
nákiṣ ṭáṃ **ghnanty** ántito ná dūrā́d
yá ādityā́nām bhávati práṇītau.

The pure one dwells undeceived by waters of good pasture,
he of ripened age, rich in sons;
none **slay** him from near nor far
who is under the leadership of the Ādityas.

Here the antithesis is only in *ná . . . ántito ná dūrā́d* 'not from near nor from far', a universal figure.

With the same verbal antithesis as in 8.84.9, the same focus on the positive and active but a different verb, compare RV 10.108.4a, in the dialogue between the divine bitch Saramā and the Paṇis. Saramā defines Indra in response to the Paṇi's question 'what is Indra like?' (*kīdṛ́ṅṅ índraḥ*) and his deceitful offering of friendship:

nā́hám̩ tám̩ veda **dā́bhyam̩ dā́bhat** sá

I do not know him as one to **be deceived**; *he* **deceives**.

Such antithetical figures, building on an underlying or overt passive : active focus on the subject, HERO or otherwise, rest ultimately on the bidirectional, reversible character of any hostile action between adversaries. Negation of right-to-left action and affirmation of left-to-right in a generalized structure,

$$\overrightarrow{\underleftarrow{\text{HERO}\quad\text{VERB}\quad\text{ADVERSARY}}},$$

is yet another way to praise the hero. It is also only another, syntactic, verbal, and linear manifestation of the same inherited stylistic figure we have studied earlier (chap. 3) in bipartite noun phrases,

Argument + Negated Counter-Argument

and its many variants.

Stylistically these doubtless go back to Proto-Indo-European. But at the same time they are universal, transcendent, and enduring. There is in the last analysis little difference except pronominalization between the Vedic poet's *ná . . . dábhyam̩ dábhat sá* and Berthold Brecht's

Wie man sich bettet, so liegt man.
Es deckt einen da keiner zu.
Und wenn einer tritt, dann bin ich es.
Und wird einer getreten, dann bist's du.

As you make your bed, so you lie in it,
nobody tucks you in;
and if someone steps, then it's me,
and if someone gets stepped on, then it's you.

32

First variant: The root *u̯edh-

In Vedic, *vadh-* forms the suppletive aorist to *han-*, which (like Iranian *gan-*) forms only a present and perfect system. With *vadh-* in Vedic we find the same gamut of associated themes as with *han-* (Benveniste and Renou 1934:107). Renou recognized that in 1.51.4 *vr̥trám yád indra śávasā́**vadhīr áhim***, in appearance 'When, o Indra, you slew Vr̥tra the serpent with your strength', we have actually a fixed verse-initial formula *vr̥trám yád* (Bloomfield, Vedic Concordance, s.v.) to which *ávadhīr áhim* has been added: schematically the familiar

HERO *u̯edh- SERPENT,

with the subject grammatically 'outside' the sentence, in the vocative. For the attendant *śávasā* cf. RV 4.17.1 *vr̥trám śávasā jaghanvā́n* 'having slain (*han-*) Vr̥tra with your strength'.

The beginning strophes of the latter hymn with its series of 'memorative' injunctive verb forms recalling the scene of Indra's birth and deeds are effectively analyzed in Hoffmann 1967:178-80. The remarkable grammatical figure of ten, perhaps originally twelve, successive injunctives in strophes 1-4 is forcefully underlined by the word order: all but the last of the twelve verbs are phrase-initial.

manyata dyáuḥ	'heaven acknowledged'
sr̥jáḥ síndhūm̐r	'you released the rivers'
rejata dyáu	'heaven trembled'
(r)éjad bhū́mir	'earth shivered'
r̥ghāyánta . . . párvatāsaḥ	'the mountains shook'
ā́rdan dhánvāni, saráyanta ā́paḥ	'the plains sank, the waters flowed'
bhinád girím	'he split the mountain'
vádhīd vr̥trám	'he smote Vr̥tra'
sárann ā́po	'the waters flowed'
manyata dyáur	'heaven was acknowledged'
índrasya kartā́ svápastamo bhūt	'the maker of Indra is the supreme craftsman'

Here 1b *ánu . . . manyata dyáuḥ* and 4a *manyata dyaur* make a ring-composition framing the series of injunctives, and the abrupt shift of 'resultativ konstatierende' *bhūt* (Hoffmann) to line final position in the cadence transforms the series of injunctives to a closed set. Verse 3c like the others lacks an overt subject but shows the weapon in the instrumental and an alliterative string:

> **vádhīd vṛtrám̐ vájreṇa** mandasānáḥ
>
> He **slew Vṛtra** with his **weapon** in his intoxication.

In one hymn, telling an obscure myth where the adversaries are *dasyu* demons, the verb is **u̯edh-* and the weapon itself a derivative of the root **gʷhen-*, *ghaná-*, 1.33.4:

> **vádhīr** hí dásyum̐ dhanínam̐ **ghanéna**
>
> For you **slew** the rich dasyu with your "**slayer**".

Compare chap. 28 for the Indo-Iranian linkage of **dā̆sa-* and **aǰhi-* 'serpent'.

The basic general grammatical meaning of the instrumental case in an Indo-European case system is to signal that the entity occupies a marginal or peripheral position in the message, as Jakobson showed for Russian in 1936 (reprinted in 1971:23ff., esp. 45ff., and cf. 154ff.). This marginal role may be filled by an abstract (here *śávas-* 'strength'), as in *śávasā́vadhīr áhim, vṛtrám śávasā jaghanvā́n* cited above, which we may symbolize as follows (the parentheses indicate the marginal entity):

> HERO SLAY SERPENT (by MEANS).

But more frequently the marginal role may be filled by a concrete noun, the WEAPON, as in ***vádhīd*** *vṛtrám* ***vájreṇa***, or with another designation of the weapon, as in 1.32.5 ***áhan*** *vṛtrám . . .* ***vadhéna***. We obtain a fuller structure

> HERO SLAY SERPENT (with WEAPON),

where it is to be noted that the marginal role of the WEAPON may be expressed by the very roots **u̯edh-* (*vadhá-*) and **gʷhen-* (*ghaná-*) themselves. In 1.33.4 *vádhīt . . . ghanéna* is a sort of formulaic mirror image of 1.32.5 *áhan . . . vadhéna*; their proximity in the collection is not accidental. Allowing for the difference of tense-aspect and mood (aorist injunctive - imperfect indicative) the parts of speech and the focus (central vs. marginal) are exactly reversed, but the semantics are unchanged. Put in terms of the lexical expression of the basic formula we have thus:

HERO	SLAY	SERPENT	(with WEAPON)
	*gʷhen-		*u̯edh-
	*u̯edh-		*gʷhen-.

Other roots are of course possible in any of the slots: Indra's cudgel is usually termed *vájra-*, like Mithra's *vazra-*, from the root **u̯aĝ-* of Greek (ϝ)ἄγνυμι. Other aspects of the WEAPON, whose linguistic expression is likewise inherited, will be taken up in subsequent chapters.

Iranian shows an exact cognate of the noun *vadhá-* as WEAPON in *vaδa-*, which we saw in chap. 29 (Yt. 19.32):

> **vaδəm** vaējō yim vārəϑraγnəm
> yim baraṯ taxmō ϑraētaonō
> yaṯ ažiš dahākō jaini
>
> Swinging the **weapon** which smashes resistance
> which brave Thraētaona carried,
> when Aži Dahāka was slain.

Another comparison may be suggested. RV 1.33.4-7 narrates an obscure Indra myth where his adversaries are *dasyu*'s. The passage is described by Geldner as 'dunkel'. It begins with the line we have already cited:

> **vádhīr** hí dásyuṃ dhanínaṃ **ghanéna**
>
> For you **slew** the rich *dasyu* with your "**slayer**"

The *dasyu*'s are further called *áyajvānaḥ sanakā́ḥ* 'impious old men' who have no worship (*yaj-*), with whom there is no covenant (*avratá-*):[1]

> **áyajvāno yájvabhiḥ** spárdhamānaḥ
>
> the **impious** contending with the **pious**.

By burning down the *dasyu*'s from heaven,

> prá **sunvatáḥ stuvatáḥ** śáṃsam āvaḥ
>
> (Indra) favored the hymn of the **soma-presser** (and) the **praiser**.

Note the phonetic figure indexing and calling attention to the latter pair: *sunv-* and *stuv-* differ by a single feature (*n* : *t*) and a single inversion (*un* : *tu*) alone.

Comparison with Iranian sheds light on this myth. There is just one locus in Avestan where the same themes come together, the same conflict of the true versus the false religion and culture, expressed by the same cognate lexical items. It is the beginning of Fargard 19 of the Videvdat, known as the "Temptation of Zarathustra". The Prince of Evil Aŋra Mainiiu says to Zarathustra (5),

1. Cf. Schmidt 1958.

apa.**stauuaŋᵛha** daēnąm mazdaii**asn**īm

Renounce the Mazdayasnian religion,

in order to obtain the boon,

yaϑa viṇdaṯ **vaδaγanō daŋ́hu**.paitiš

as **Vadagana** lord of the **land** obtained (it).

Zarathustra refuses, and invokes as his weapons the words of the Wise Lord,[2] as well as (9)

hāuuanaca taštaca **haomaca**

the **presser**, the vessels, and **haoma**,

and the demons are confuted.

The name of Vadagana would appear to prolong a tradition of Common Indo-Iranian date. The correspondences with RV 1.33.4-7 are striking, beginning with

vádhīr hí **dásyum** . . . **ghanéna**
vaδa-γanō daŋ́hu.paitiš (*dahyu-pati-*).[3]

The conflict is religious, the Mazdayasna (Avestan *yaz-*) and the *yájvan*'s with the *áyajvan*'s (Vedic *yaj-*). The Avestan compound verb *apa.stauua-* 'renounce' is the antithesis of the Vedic participle *stuvat-* 'praising, proclaiming', the action of the pious worshiper (both from IE **steu̯-*). The other action of the pious worshiper, the Vedic participle *sunvat-* 'pressing', finds its counterpart in the weapons of the victorious Zarathustra, *hāuuana* 'the pressing' and *haoma* = Vedic *soma* (all from IE **seu-*). Compare the Common Indo-Iranian formula preserved in Avestan *haomō hutō* 'pressed *haoma*' and Vedic *sómaḥ sutáḥ* 'pressed *soma*'. I leave it to historians of religion and students of mythology to sort out and interpret the modalities of this myth and the light it may shed on the Indic and Iranian past, as well as their common material and symbolic culture.

This lengthy excursus into the historical implications of the associative chains evoked by formulas with Indo-Iranian *vadh-* may serve as an argument for the 'practical' utility of such speculations.

To conclude the survey of Vedic passages with *vadh-* we may consider three

2. Martin Schwartz on a number of occasions has called attention to the anagrammatic correspondence of the Prince of Evil **Aŋ**ra **Mai**niiu and the Wise Lord **A**hura **Ma**z**da**. See his 1986 study.

3. On the relation of Iranian *dahyu* and Indic *dasyu* see Benveniste 1969:1.318-19; for the form see Hoffmann apud Mayrhofer, EWA s.v. *dásyu-*. For *daŋ́hu.paiti-* in a liturgical figure of Common Indo-Iranian date see chap. 22.

whose poetics are entirely synchronic. The first is RV 4.41.4ab:

> índrā yuvám̥ varuṇā didyúm asminn
> ójiṣṭham ugrā ní vadhiṣṭam̥ vájram
>
> Indra and Varuna, strike down your missile on him,
> the most powerful weapon, o powerful ones.

Here the weapon is the direct object of the verb, as in the Common Indo-Iranian formula of the imperative *jáhi vádhar* = *vadarə jaiδi* 'strike the weapon' (chap. 44); the eventual victim is indicated by a cataphoric locative. Line 4b is framed by the distracted adjective-noun phrase *ójiṣṭham . . . vájram* 'most powerful weapon' and contains no less than four separate linkages: the figura etymologica ***ójiṣṭham ugra***, the alliteration ***vadhiṣṭam vájram***, and the phonetic figures *ój**iṣṭham*** . . . *vadh**iṣṭam*** and ***ugrā*** . . . *vá**jram***.

In the second passage (RV 8.101.15) the Cow is speaking to those who understand (*cikitúṣe jánāya*), and uses a deft phonetic figure:

> **mā́ gā́m ánāgām** áditim̥ vadhiṣṭa
>
> Do not kill the innocent cow, the Aditi.

The third is a version of the basic formula with marginal instrumental. RV 1.187.6:

> távā́him ávasāvadhīt
>
> With your help he slew the serpent.

The octosyllable begins and ends with the same sound (*t-* . . . *-t*), and six of its eight syllables are the balanced sequence

> avā . . . ava . āva . . .,

a phonetic icon echoing 'help . . . help . . . help . . .' These figures, like the threefold alliteration ***vádhīd vr̥trám vájreṇa*** of 4.17.3c above, function as powerful indexes, forcing the listener's attention to the message, to the deployment of the mythographic formulas themselves.

33

'Like a reed': The Indo-European background of a Luvian ritual

Among the more or less fragmentarily preserved but extensive Luvian rituals (SISKUR) is one entitled *dupaduparša* or *dupiduparša*.[1] The lengthy ritual against evil-doing and for purification took up at least nine tablets, following the colophon of KUB 35.40 + KBo 29.8 iv 6-8: DUB IX KAM *ŠA* SISKUR *dupidupar*[*ša AWAT* / ^{f}*Šillaluḫi* ^{SAL}ŠU.GI / *U* ^{f}*Kuwattalla* ^{SAL}SUḪUR.LAL 'Ninth tablet of the *dupiduparša* ritual: the words of ^{f}Sillaluhis the "Old Woman" and ^{f}Kuwattalas the "Hierodule".' The texts and the textual tradition are fully described and presented by Starke 1985:79ff. and 104ff. Starke notes that this ritual must go back to the 15th century B.C., as its composer ^{f}Kuwattalla the hierodule received a landgrant (KBo 5.7) from the Middle Kingdom royal couple Arnuwanda and Asmunikal, and another ritual by the same woman is found in tablets paleographically datable to the 15th century. As a traditional composition of hieratic and strictly formulaic context the wording of this ritual certainly goes back to an even earlier period.

The title SISKUR *dupaduparša* / *dupiduparša* must mean 'Ritual of the Beating', with 'case' in *-ša* (not, I think, with Starke 104 nominative plural neuter) to an abstract in *-(w)ar* from an intensive reduplication of *dup-* 'beat'. The action and the verb form a sort of leitmotiv of the ritual; Starke 104 n. 2 notes the 'beaten hand' *dūpaimin iššarin* and 'beaten tongue' *dūpaimin* EME-*in* in one fragment, and 'they beat' *dupainti* in broken context in another. Another verb of similar semantics is *puwa-* 'pound' (cf. Güterbock 1956:123), occurring in broken context after the phrase *kuiš-tar malḫaššaššan* EN-*ya ādduwāl ānnīti, a=du=tta* . . . 'whosoever does evil to the celebrant, to him . . . ' We shall see the same phrase and the same theme in the passage to be studied below; it is one of those which Starke (p. 106 and foldout) rightly focuses on as recurrent 'characteristische Begriffe und Wendungen' of the 18 fragmentary tablets which are the basis of our text of the Ritual of the Beating.

1. A version of this chapter first appeared in Die Sprache 32, 1986 [1988], 324-333, dedicated to Manfred Mayrhofer.

Like most Luvian and Anatolian rituals the basic principle is sympathetic or homeopathic magic. We see the action unfold, and the action is *explained* in the bilingual ritual by the 'Old Woman', the ^{SAL}ŠU.GI, through the interaction of *word* (in Luvian) and *deed* (described in Hittite).

Let us look at a single "episode" in tablet three of this lengthy and rambling SISKUR *dupaduparša*. I give the text as in Starke 1985:115, but in broad transcription. The first, second, and fourth paragraph are Hittite; the third is Luvian. KUB 9.6 + [his I.2] iii 19″ ff.:

ŠA GI=ma II ^{GIŠ}PISAN$^{\text{ḪI.A}}$ *ANA* EN S[ISKUR par]ā ēpzi

nu II ^{GIŠ}PISAN$^{\text{ḪI.A}}$ *ŠA* GI appizz[iya]z
^{SAL}ŠU.GI ḫarzi EN SISKUR=ma=ššiy=aš mena[ḫḫ]anda
IŠTU QATI-ŠU ēpzi n=uš anda
uešuriyanzi n=uš arḫa duwarnanzi
^{SAL}ŠU.GI=ma kiššan memai

kuiš=tar malḫaššaššanzan EN-ya
āдduwala ānniti a=an DINGIR^{MEŠ}-inzi
āḫḫa nātatta tatarḫandu
uitpanim=pa=an uidāindu
a=duw=an annān pātanza dūwandu

nu ^{SAL}ŠU.GI GI$^{\text{ḪI.A}}$ *ANA* EN SISKUR
ŠAPAL GÌR^{MEŠ}-*ŠU* dāi . . .

[The Old Woman] proffers two reed baskets from the back; opposite her the celebrant takes them in his hands, and they crush them by twisting (*anda uešuriyanzi*), and they break them apart (*arḫa duwarnanzi*). The Old Woman speaks as follows:

"whosoever does evil to the celebrant, may the gods crush him (*tatarḫandu*) like reeds, and may they smash him (*widaindu*) a *witpani*-?, and may they put him under his feet."
The Old Woman places the reeds under the celebrant's feet . . .[2]

The Hittite and Luvian passages and their interpretation have been discussed by Melchert (1984a:157-8). As the latter rightly notes, Luvian *tatarḫ*- is a reduplicated form of the root seen in Hittite *tarḫ*- 'overcome, overpower, compel', and in Luvian the name of the Storm God Tarḫunzas, IE **terh*$_2$-.[3] But the Luvian verb need not be

2. The Hittite passage was translated by Carruba (1966:50), whom I basically follow.

3. The reduplication of Luvian *tatarḫ* - is comparable in function to that of the Greek aorist πεφνέμεν. It shows intensive character, like Vedic *apaptat* 'has flown', *avocat* = Greek εἶπε, ἔειπε, *anesán* = GAV. *nąsaṯ*, *anąsaṯ*, 'perished', *atatanat* 'thundered'. See Thieme 1929:34, Hoffmann 1975:569.

exactly equated semantically with Hittite *anda wešuriya-*; the latter may mean 'press, oppress', but also carries the notion 'choke, strangle, throttle' (= Akkadian *ḫanāku* KBo 1.42 ii 40), which is I believe the image of the two participants' action: the natural way for two people to break reed baskets is by twisting them in opposite directions. The Hittite descriptions are precise and particular: the two baskets having been twisted, 'throttled in' (*anda wešuriya-*), are then 'broken apart' (*arḫa duwarna-*). But the Luvian curse is much more general: the evil-doer is to be crushed like reeds (not 'like baskets'), and we do not expect a specific verb (and preverb) like 'break apart' (*arḫa duwarna-*). Melchert loc. cit. for etymological reasons (Sanskrit *vi-dhā-* lit. 'put apart') would assign to the Luvian verb *widai-* a meaning 'divide'. But such is surely rather flat for a ritual imprecation with the gods as subject. Since the reed baskets in the ritual and the reeds of the Luvian simile are not 'divided' but utterly destroyed and trampled underfoot, we expect a more violent verb like 'smash'. I find it etymologically more reasonable to see in Luvian *widāi-* the same Indo-European root **u̯edh-* which Melchert himself identified in Hittite *uizzai* and Glossenkeil ⸗*wi-ú-i-da-i*, *wi-ú-i-ta-i* 'strikes, urges' (1979:265ff., cf. 1984:151). The lengthened grade **ē* appearing in Luvian *widāi-* and *wiwidai* recalls in formation the Gathic Avestan verb in Y. 29.2 *yə̄ drəguuō.dəbiš aēšəməm vādāiiōit̰* 'who would destroy the fury caused by the deceitful'.[4] Luvian *witpani-* in our passage is obscure in form and meaning, but Melchert is perhaps right in taking it as making a real or imagined etymological figure with *widāi-*: 'smash him with a smashing' or the like, cf. RV 5.54.15 *yásya tárema tarasā́* 'by whose crossing power may we cross' from the root **terh₂-* of Luvian *tatarḫ-*.[5]

In this brief episode of the Ritual of the Beating the symbolism is plain enough, as is the interaction of word and deed. The ritual proceeds from the particular to the general and analogizes from specific ritual acts, described in Hittite, to the generalized homeopathic ritual imprecation in Luvian.

Ritual utterances are by their nature traditional, frozen, and enduring. Ritual and myth are furthermore inextricably linked, in ancient Anatolia as elsewhere, where the narration of a myth is itself usually a ritual act, a single action as a part of a larger whole. The pattern is familiar to us from other traditions within and outside the Indo-European world. But where we can observe a set of verbal similarities with other Indo-European traditions in the domain of ritual and myth, then we may legitimately inquire whether we have to deal with manifestations of inherited common cultural tradition.

The basic formula which we have seen in the preceding chapters, as in Vedic *vádhīd vr̥trám̐ vájreṇa* 'he smote Vr̥tra with his cudgel' RV 4.17.3, transposes into the realm of myth the effective overcoming of adversaries and obstacles which is precisely the business of the "real" world of ritual.

Recall now the key words and themes of our Luvian ritual. The actions are performed as it were in pantomime; it is in the symbolic transfer to the words of the

4. See Kellens 1984:15, 134 for alternative views.

5. For another suggestion see Garrett and Kurke 1994. Note that in *tárema tarasā́* we have a figura etymologica at two structure points of a variant of the basic formula: the verb and the marginal noun of means in the instrumental. Compare AV 10.4.9 *ghanéna hanmi* 'I smite with the "smiter"', the object being a real snake. For other examples of the last see chapters 56 and 59.

spell that we find the true meaning of the acts, and it is the words we look for. The gods are adjured—in the 3rd person—to crush (*tatarḫ-*) the evil-doer like reeds (*aḫḫa natatta*), to smash (*widāi-*) him, and to lay (*duwa-*) him beneath their feet (*pad-*). Etymologically these Luvian lexemes are clear, and all inherited. To express their Indo-European exponents: the gods (HEROES) are to CRUSH (*$*terh_2$-*) the evil-doing ADVERSARY, with the simile like REEDS (**nedo-*), to SMASH (**u̯edh-*) him, and to lay (*$*dheh_2$-*) him under their feet (**ped-*).

As a semantic structure in its verbal expression, the Luvian imprecation is only an elaborated imperative variant of the *basic formula*.

At this point a specific comparison is in order. The first five verses of RV 1.32 successively repeat, then elaborate the basic formula, then add a simile and a static image of the vanquished adversary:

1c **áhann** áhim

he slew the serpent

2a **áhann** áhim

he slew the serpent

3d **áhann** enam prathamajā́m áhīnām

he slew him, the firstborn of serpents

4a yád . . . **áhan** prathamajā́m áhīnām

when you slew the firstborn of serpents

5a **áhan** vṛtrám . . . vájreṇa . . . **vadh**éna

he slew Vṛtra with his cudgel, the weapon

cd skándhāṃsīva kúliśenā vívṛknā / áhiḥ **śay**ate

like branches lopped by an axe the serpent lies.

The roots of the forms in boldface are successively *$*g^{u}hen$-* 1-5, **u̯edh-* 5a, **k̂ei̯-* 5d. The stage is set.

The Luvian spell has *aḫḫa* ***nat**atta* *ta**tarḫ**andu* 'crush him like reeds' . . . ***wid**aindu* 'smash him': 'like **nedo-* *$terh_2$-* . . . *u̯edh-*'. Compare then the next three verses of RV 1.32, of the beaten *ahi* Vṛtra:

6c nắ**tārī**d asya sámṛtiṃ **vadhắ**nām

he did not withstand the onslaught of his weapons.

We have the same sequence of roots *$terh_2$- and *u̯edh-, which continues with a verbal echo of the latter in

7cd . . . **vádh**riḥ . . . / . . . vṛtró a**śay**at . . .

. . . the eunuch . . . / . . . Vṛtra lay . . .

The similarity of *vadh*ⁱ and *vádhri-* —whether a real (**u̯edh-*) or a folk-etymology (cf. Mayrhofer, KEWA III 135-8) is immaterial—would hardly be lost on the Indian poetic mind. The root **k̂ei̯-* 'lie' recurs twice more, again of the dead *ahi-* in another simile, this time exactly corresponding to the Luvian *aḫḫa natatta* 'like **nedo-*':

8a **nadá**m ná **bhin**nám amuyắ **śáy**ānam

lying that way like a broken reed

with the simile 'like **nedo- bheid-* . . . *k̂ei̯-*'. The Luvian continues *a=duw=an annān* ***pāt**anza **duwa**ndu* 'may they put him under their feet', **ped-* . . . *$dheh_1$-*. The Vedic strophe continues:

8d tắsām áhiḥ **pat**sutaḥ**śī́r** babhūva

at the feet (of the waters) lay the serpent,

with the roots **ped-* and **k̂ei̯*, which functions as the passive of **$dheh_1$-*. The phrase *annān pātanza duwa-* 'place under the feet' is traditional in Luvian and clearly attested in the 1st-millennium B.C. Hieroglyphic Luvian royal inscriptions of local kings.[6]

The lexical expression of the thematic structures in the two languages may be juxtaposed, together with their respective reconstruction:

aḫḫa natatta	tatarḫ-	nắtārīd . . . vadhá-
	widāi-	vádhri-
		nadáṃ ná bhinnám . . . śáy-
pata- . . .	duwa-	patsutaḥśi-
like *nedo-	$terh_2$-	*$terh_2$- . . . u̯edh-
	*u̯edh-	*u̯edh- (?)
		like *nedo- bheid- . . . k̂ei̯-
*ped- . . .	$dheh_1$-	*ped- k̂ei̯-

6. Like KARATEPE, SULTANHAN, cf. Morpurgo Davies 1987.

Lying or being placed at or under the feet of the victor is of course a universal image of the vanquished. But the collocation of the remaining roots is in no way universal.[7] Anatolian ritual and Indic myth, separated in time, space and genre, here preserve two enduring semantic and thematic structures which are ultimately the same.

The Anatolian text is a hortatory magical ritual, while the Rigvedic hymn is a paean of mythological victory, whose use in the ritual we are largely ignorant of. But the Atharvaveda with its more homely world of black and white magic presents contexts which are much more similar in genre to the Anatolian ritual. And here we find thematic, semantic, and lexical contexts which are directly comparable to the structures of our Anatolian ritual and Vedic mythical "episodes". The key theme is the simile of the *reed*, of which we have three examples in the Atharvaveda. AV(Ś) 4.19 = AV(P) 5.25 apostrophizes a plant (*oṣadhi*) used for counter-magic against enemies and sorcerers. I am grateful to Michael Witzel for making available to me the Orissa mss. variants of the unpublished Paippalāda text. Compare the following:

1cd utó kr̥tyākŕ̥taḥ prajā́m **naḍám ivā́ cchindhi** vā́rṣikam

and **cut off** the offspring of the witchcraft-maker **like a reed** of the rainy season

3cd utá **trātā́si** pā́kasyā́tho (Ppp. pākasya trātāsy uta) **hantā́si** rakṣásaḥ

you are **protector** of the simple, likewise you are **slayer** of the demonic

5 **vibhindatī́** śatáśākhā **vibhindán** nā́ma te pitā́
pratyág **ví bhindhi** tvám̐ tám̐ yó asmā́m̐ abhidā́sati

splitting apart, hundred-branched-"**Splitting-Apart**" by name is thy father; in return do thou **split apart** him who assails us.

The word order *taṃ tvaṃ* of 5c in the Orissa text (Ś reverses the two, K has *vibhitaṃ tvaṃ*) confirms Whitney's note ad loc. Verse 1d *naḍám ivā́ cchindhi vā́rṣikam* is one syllable too long, and Whitney notes that 'The Anukr. seems to sanction abbreviation to *'va*.' In view of RV 1.32.8a *nadáṃ ná bhinnám* it is tempting to assume an early error, common to all our mss., for *nadáṃ nā́* (*ná ā́*) *cchindhi*. In any case the thematic and verbal similarity of the AV and RV is clear, and the rhyming *chindhi* and *bhindhi* of the AV passage (1 and 5) together with the participles *vibhindatī́*, *vibhindán* explicate the root **bheid-* in the RV *nadáṃ ná* ***bhin****nám*. Finally the Vedic coordinated imperative and relative clause 'split apart him who assails us' exactly parallels the Luvian 'whosoever does evil to the celebrant, may the gods crush him . . .' The rhyme *chindhi* : *bhindhi* is an index of semantic equivalence, and we may regard as underlying 'transformational' syntactic equivalents the imperative *split/crush* (*him*) *like a reed* of

7. On the dialectology of **nedo-* (first securely reconstructed by Bailey 1952:61-2) and its history in India see most succinctly Mayrhofer 1956-80:2.127-9, 3.742-3.

the Luvian and Atharvavedic passages and the participial-adjectival *like a split reed* of the Rigvedic passage.

That the collocation of **nedo-* 'reed' and **bheid-* 'split' is a real cultural semantic nexus, where 'split' is just a variant of the verb of the *basic formula* (prototypically **g^whe n-*) is shown by another passage in the Atharvaveda. AV(Ś) 6.138 is an incantation to make a certain man impotent and a eunuch. The concluding verses 4 and 5 are closely linked by phonetic figures (*yé te nāḍyàu/yáthā́ naḍám*, repeated ***amúṣ****yās* . . . ***muṣ****káyoḥ*) and the phonetic and grammatical figures of the basic formula itself (*bhinadmi* ***śám****yayā/bhindánty* ***áśm****anā*) and like positioning of the same or similar words. The translation is Whitney's; that of pada d in both is very uncertain, and the text is unsound.

4 yé te **nāḍyàu** devákṛte yáyos tíṣṭhati vŕ̥ṣṇyam
té te **bhinadmi śámyayā** (a)múṣyā ádhi muṣkáyoḥ

The two god-made **tubes** that are thine, in which stands thy virility,
those **I split** for thee with a **wedge**, on yon woman's loins,

5 yáthā **naḍáṃ** kaśípune stríyo **bhindánty áśmanā**
evā́ **bhinadmi** te śépo (Paipp. muṣkau) (a)múṣyā ádhi muṣkáyoḥ

As women **split reeds** with a **stone** for a cushion, so do **I split**
thy member (Paipp. testicles), on yon woman's loins.

Verses 4 and 5 are respectively AVP 1.68.5 and 1, with variants 1d *amuṣyādhi muṣk°* 'on yon man's testicles', 5d *tasmai tvām avase huve* (= AVŚ 5.25.2d) 'for that I call thee for aid', which need not concern us here further.

Beyond the vivid and arresting images of the Atharvan black magic we may discern clearly the same semantic and thematic structures which we found in the episodes of the Luvian ritual and Rigvedic myth, the *basic formula.* The central simile of each is that of the beaten ADVERSARY likened to a broken *reed* (**nedo-*): the verb of violent action BEAT, BREAK, SPLIT is variously a reflex of **terh₂-*, **u̯edh-*, **bheid-*, ultimately equivalents of **g^whe n-*. In AV(Ś) 6.138.4-5 the object of the verb of the basic formula is by synecdoche the ADVERSARY's body-part, and the optional instrumental WEAPON or tool is present. Schematically, the two verses may be reduced to a 'syllogism' of sorts:

	SPLIT (*bheid-)	*nedo-BODY-PART	(with WEDGE)
as	SPLIT (*bheid-)	*nedo-	(with STONE)
	SPLIT (*bheid-)	BODY-PART	

Both the WEDGE and the STONE are entirely appropriate to the instrumental WEAPON slot in the basic formula in Indo-Iranian. Indra's *vájra* is also called *áśman-* 'stone' (RV 4.22.1, cf. Hoffmann 1975:395), and we have the basic formula in a charm against poisonous insects in RV 1.191.15 *takám bhinadmy áśmanā* 'I squash the little one with a stone'. In Avestan Skjærvø (p.c.) notes inter alia the stones (*asānō*) given by Ahura Mazdā to Zarathustra with which to smite (*janāni*) the evil one in V. 19.4-5, the "Temptation of Zarathustra". For the *śámyā* 'wedge' we have even a collocation with the root **g^{u}hen-* in a passage in the Śatapatha-Brāhmaṇa: 1.2.1.17 *tásmāc chámyayā samā́hanti* 'That is why he beats (the millstones) with a wedge'.

34

Second variant: The root *$terh_2$-

It remains to examine another alternative verbal lexical expression of our mythological theme which is likewise inherited. It involves the root *$terh_2$-, with derivatives meaning 'to cross over, pass through, overcome, vanquish'; the English cognate is *through*.

The Hittite dragon-slayer is the Storm God ᴰU/ᴰIM in Sumerographic writing; the Hittite reading of the name is **Tarḫunnaš* or **Tarḫuntaš* the "Conqueror", derived from the verb *tarḫ-* 'to overcome, vanquish'.[1] Compare then the first episode in the narration of the Illuyankas myth KBo. 3.7 i 11:

nu=za ᴹᵁŠilluyankaš **ᴰIM-an tarḫta**

The serpent **defeated the Storm God**.

Note the iconic etymological figure in the Hittite, phonetically *Tarḫunnan tarḫta* or *Tarḫuntan tarḫta*.

We have in fact a whole nexus of inherited themes in the Hittite narration of the myth, for the verb *tarḫta* 'vanquished' makes a nearly exact equation with Vedic *atārīt* 'withstood, overcame', a "sigmatized" root aorist (cf. *átārima* RV 8.13.21).[2]

---

1. As usually inferred from the phonetic writing ᴰIM-*unnaš* in our oldest Hittite source, the Anittas text (ed. Neu 1974) for the first, ᴰU-*taš* for the second, together with the well-attested phonetic spelling of the Cuneiform and Hieroglyphic Luvian equivalent, ᴰ*Tarḫunzaš*. The formal etymology of his name is discussed by Eichner (1973:28).

Mark Hale pointed out to me a number of years ago the suspicious similarity of the name of the Hittite Storm God **Tarḫunnaš* to that of his closest equivalent in the Germanic pantheon, Old Norse *Þórr*. For the former we may reconstruct *$t\text{r̥}h_2Vno$-, for the latter *$t\text{n̥}h_2Vro$-, and the two look like metathesis variants of each other. Both ostensible roots *$terh_2$- 'overcome' and *$tenh_2$- 'thunder', are firmly established in the proto-language. But on the other hand folk etymology or tabu deformation by metathesis are well-documented precisely in divine names; we can observe the process from **per*[*k*]-*aunos* (Slavic god *Perunъ*) and **ker*[*p*]-*aunos* (Greek κέραυνος 'thunderbolt') to English *doggone* and *goddam*. The result is an etymological quandary: is the similarity just accident, or is one divine name metathesized from the other by folk etymology or other deformation—and if so, which?

2. IE *(*e*)$terh_2$-*t*, with analogical lengthening of the root vowel in Vedic. On the regular laryngeal reflex *ī* in closed final syllables see Jamison 1988.

The nominal composition forms in Vedic *-tur-* and Greek -ταρ reflect a zero-grade **-tr̥h₂-*. The verb is amply attested in the older Indo-European dialects. We have root athematic Hittite *tarḫ-*, *taraḫzi-* 'overcomes; is able' beside thematic *tarratta* 'is able' < **terh₂-o(r)*. Cuneiform Luvian shows reduplicated *tatarḫandu*. Note also Indo-Iranian reduplicated *títar-* 'cross, overcome' in Rigvedic *títrat-* 'crossing', Avestan *titarat̰*. Other formations of possible Indo-Iranian date are Rigvedic *tū́rvasi* and Gathic Avestan **tauruuāmā* (Y. 28.6 for mss. *tauruuaiiāma*, for metrical reasons), as well as Rigvedic *turáyati* 'rushes' and Old Persian *vi-taraya-* 'cross'. We have **tr̥h₂-i̯o-* in the imperative in RV 8.99.5 *viśvatū́r asi / tvám̐ tūrya taruṣyatáḥ* 'you are all-overcoming; do you overcome those who would overcome (you)!' Hittite *tariya-* 'tire' might belong here as well. Vedic shows further *tárati* (active frequent but rare in the middle) and, with preverb, *-tiráti*. The *u̯* of Vedic *tū́rva-* and Gathic Avestan *tauruua-* recurs in Rigvedic *tarute*, *taruṣa-*, and further in Hittite *taruḫzi* and the nominal forms *tarḫu-ili-*, and the divine names cited below.

Thematized participial forms recur in the Vedic personal name *Váidadaśvis Tarantáḥ*, and especially in the Anatolian name of the Storm God, Hittite ᴰU-*taš* (**tarḫuntaš*) and Cuneiform and Hieroglyphic Luvian ᴰ*Tarḫunzas* (= Rigvedic present participle *tū́rvant-*, Eichner 1973:28).[3] Compare also Atharvavedic *jīvantá-* 'living'. The thematic formation is reminiscent of Vedic *vā́ta-*, *váata-*, Lat. *uentus* 'wind'.

The Vedic form *atārīt* and the root *tarⁱ* in general figure prominently in the Indic narration of the myth. Compare from the hymn first cited, RV 1.32.6,

> **nā́tārīd** asya sámr̥tim **vadhā́nām**
>
> He (Vr̥tra) **did not withstand** the onslaught of his (Indra's) **weapons**.

Note also the epithet (perfect participle) of Indra *titirvas-* 'overcoming' in 6.41.4, or the morphologically parallel epithets of Indra *vr̥trahán-* and *vr̥tratúr-*, cf. 4.42.7c *vr̥trā́ṇi . . . jaghanvā́n . . . indra* 'Vr̥tra slayer', 8d *índraṃ na vr̥tratúram* 'overcoming Vr̥tra'. In Maitrāyaṇi Saṁhitā 4.14.13 (mantra) we have the full Vedic verb phrase in an etymological figure:

> índro vr̥trám **atarad** vr̥tra**tū́rye**
>
> Indra **overcame** Vr̥tra at the Vr̥tra-**overcoming**.

It is likely that the verb phrase here has been generated from the nominal compound *vr̥tratū́rye*, which is attested earlier in the Rigveda and is formulaic there in verse-final position.[4] But that a verb phrase with *tarⁱ* is inherited is shown by other Vedic evidence, combined with that of Hittite and Iranian. In three verses of a single hymn (RV 8.99) we get no less than six occurrences of the root:

---

3. The Etruscan royal name *Tarquinius* is probably a theophoric from the same Anatolian stock. Cf. Oettinger 1979:220-222.

4. In the family books it is more frequently 5 syllables than the contracted 4 as here.

5 tvám indra **prátūrtiṣv**
abhí víśvā asi spŕ̥dhaḥ
aśastihā́ janitā́ **viśvatū́r** asi
tvā́ṃ **tūrya taruṣyatáḥ**
6ad ánu te śúṣmaṃ **turáyantam**
. . .
vr̥trā́ṃ yád indra **tū́rvasi**
. . .
7d **átūrtaṃ** tugryāvŕ̥dham

At the lists, o Indra, you are superior to all contestants;
overcoming all, you smash the un-song (for the loser) and engender (it for the winner).
Overcome those who would overcome!
Your **rushing** power . . .
when you **overcome** Vr̥tra, o Indra
. . . the **insurpassable** fosterer of the son of Tugra;

RV 7.48.2:
índreṇa yujā́ **taruṣema** vr̥trám

with Indra as comrade **may we overcome** resistance;

KBo. 3.7 iii 24-5:
n=an=za namma ^{MUŠ}illuyanka[n] **taraḫḫūwan** dāiš

[the Storm God] began **to overcome** him (the serpent);

Yt. 13.38:
tauruuaiiata vərəϑrəm dānunąm tūranąm

you overcame the resistance of the Turanian Dānu's.

Note also the Avestan nominal compound *vərəϑra.tauruuan-* 'overcoming resistance', of Haoma.

All these examples permit us to reconstruct an additional mythological theme with its verbal lexical expression in the formula

HERO **terh$_2$-* ADVERSARY.

Like the basic formula with **g^{u}hen-* that with **terh$_2$-* is bidirectional: the HERO may be object and the ADVERSARY may be the subject, as in the first Hittite example, with which we began, or the HERO may be the subject and the ADVERSARY the object, as in the second Hittite example we have just seen. Both subjects may be overt, but we find here as the characteristic asymmetry in the formula noted earlier,

HERO	*$terh_2$-* ADVERSARY.

A striking semantic feature of the verbal root **terh*$_2$- is precisely to mark a conditional, transitory, or non-permanent victory of one adversary over the other. It is just this pathetic or ominous semantic overtone which we hear in a widely attested Indo-European tradition in which the ultimate adversary is death. Synoptically the formula may be noted

HERO	OVERCOME (**terh*$_2$-) DEATH.

While reserving the detail for the succeeding chapters 35 and 40 we may note only the Greek compound νέκταρ from **neḱ-tr̥h*$_2$- to the root of Latin *nex*: the nectar which "overcomes death" and gives immortality.

35

Latin *tarentum*, the *ludi Saeculares*, and Indo-European eschatology

Varro, *L.L.* 6.23-4, preserves for Latinity the precious phrase *tarentum Accas Larentinas*; it was rescued for us by Emil Vetter (1958:274-276), resuming earlier publications.[1] The meaning of *tarentum* is 'grave, tomb'. Acca Larentina (with the archaic genitive in *-as*), also called Acca Larentia, was a former prostitute and benefactress of the Roman state in the time of the king Ancus Marcius by one account, the nurse and foster-mother of Romulus and Remus by another. The passage is given in the Teubner edition of Varro by Goetz and Schoell (1910) as follows:

> Larentinae . . . ab Acca Larentia . . . †qui atra dicitur diem tarentum accas tarentinas. (24) hoc sacrificium fit in Velabro . . . ut aiunt quidam ad sepulcrum Accae. . .

Various attempts have been made to heal this 'locus corruptissimus' (Scaliger). Mommsen, followed by R.G. Kent in his Loeb edition, emended *tarentum* out of existence, and read

> qui *ab ea* dicitur die*s P*arent<ali>um Accas *L*arentinas.

It remained for Vetter to propose a viable solution to the crux, and in doing so to rescue the word *tarentum*. His restoration of the passage reads as follows, together with his translation in Vetter 1957:80:

> Larentinae . . . ab Acca Larentia . . . qui atra dicitur die<s ad locum dictu>m **tarentum Accas** Larentinas. (24) Hoc sacrificium fit in Velabro . . . ut aiunt quidam ad **sepulcrum Accae** . . .

1. This chapter summarizes the conclusions of a paper of the same title in Lehmann and Jakusz Hewitt 1991. For the philological details of the argumentation, see that study.

> Die (*feriae*) *Larentinae* sind nach *Acca Larentia* benannt—der Tag heisst *dies atra*—<an einem Platze, der als> '*tarentum Accas Larentinas*' <bezeichnet wird>. Dies Opfer wird auf dem *Velabrum* dargebracht . . . am Grabe der *Acca*, wie manche sagen . . .

Vetter was eminently justified in referring to *tarentum* as das kostbare alte Wort, 'the precious old word', even if no one seems to have taken note of the form since, not even to register its existence. From the context the meaning is clearly 'tomb.' It is 'ein altes Appellativ für "Grab",' more specifically 'eine unterirdische Kultstätte für das Totenopfer am Grabe,' and finally 'mit dem Namen der Stadt Tarentum nur zufällig zusammengefallen.'

Though not mentioned by Vetter—perhaps because it seemed evident to him—the meaning follows directly from the text, for Varro glosses the form *tarentum Accas* in the very next paragraph by *sepulcrum Accae*, modernizing both the lexical form and the old genitive singular feminine.

Better known in Latin, as Vetter notes, is *Tarentum*, name of a spot in the Campus Martius where the secular games, the *ludi Saeculares*, were performed once a century. It is still the only *tarentum* to be recognized by the Oxford Latin Dictionary (the relevant fascicle appeared in 1982). Compare the following citations from Festus:

478 L <**Terentum**>
in campo Martio loc[
dicendum fuisse, quod te[<*ludos*>
Secularis Ditis patris [

479 L (Paul.) **Terentum** locus in campo Martio dictus, quod eo loco
ara Ditis patris terra occultaretur

440 L <***Saeculares ludi***>
Tarquini Superbi regis i[
Marti consecrauit [
cos., quod populus Romanus in l[
aram quoque Diti ac <*Proserpinae in*>
extremo Mart<io campo *quod* ***Tarentum*** ap->
pellatur ho->
stis furuis est[<*tribus diebus totidem*->
que noctibus, ac de[<cen->
tum post annos u[<sae->
culares appella[
saeculi habetur.

Though the two *tarentum*'s in Rome were in different locations (that of Acca in the Velabrum), there can be no doubt that the lexical items in each are identical.

Some uncertainty persists in the shape of the name of the place in the Campus Martius. The variation *Tarentum / Terentum* was phonetically real by 204 A.D., since both are now attested in the inscription of the *ludi Saeculares* of Septimius Severus (CIL VI 32328, 15), Pighi 1965:149:

> Pompei]us Ru[so]nian[us] magister **Tarentum** / lustravit s[
> lus]trandi piandique saecularis sacri / ludorumque causa

Ibid. 162:

> cum pr.pr. et ceteris XVuir. praetextati coronatique de Pa[latio
> in T]**erentum** uenerunt.

But the preponderance of *Tarentum*, the invariant *tarentum* (*Accas*) of Varro, and the same author's *ludi Tarentini* (= *ludi Saeculares*), together with the tradition of homophony with the city of South Italy *Tarentum* / Tarant-, show that the variant *tarentum* is the older. See Latte 1960:246 n. 6.

In a passage cited by Censorinus, Varro *gram.* 70 (Funaioli), too, lets us know that the *ludi Saeculares* were also called *ludi Tarentini*:

> et ideo libros Sibyllinos XV uiri adissent, renuntiarunt uti Diti patri et Proserpinae **ludi Tarentini** in campo martio fierent tribus noctibus, et hostiae furuae immolarentur utique ludi centesimo quoque anno fierent.

The close verbal similarity, indeed identity, between his description of the Tarentine games and that in Festus (440 L) of the secular games leaves no room for doubt.

A Roman etiological tale on the origin of the *ludi Saeculares* is given by Valerius Maximus (*De institutis antiquis* 2.4.5 [1st century A.D.]) and Zosimus (2.1-3 [5th century A.D.]). The children of a certain Valesius—note the pre-rhotacism form—a rich farmer (*uir locuples rusticae uitae*) lie mortally sick; a voice tells the father to take them down the Tiber to *Tarentum* and there warm water on the altar of the gods of the underworld and give it to the children. Though disturbed by the prospect of a long and dangerous sea voyage (to Tarentum in South Italy) he nonetheless sets sail down the Tiber, only to disembark by night at a mysterious spot in the Campus Maximus which exhaled smoke and was called *Tarentum.* Needless to say he performs the required rites there, on an altar conveniently labelled 'to Dis and Proserpina', the children are restored to health, and the ritual duly instituted.

It has often been suggested that the *ludi Saeculares* are a cultural import from Magna Graecia, specifically Tarentum, at the time of the secular games of 239 B.C. This rests entirely on the Greek origin of the cult of the underworld divinities Dis (Πλούτων) and Prōserpina. But while Dis translates Πλούτων, the latter is an earlier borrowing via Etruscan: Περσεφόνα > *Φersipnai*, *-nei* > Etr.-Lat. *Proserpina*, attested on a mirror from Cosa (de Simone in Campanile 1988:37). Despite the widely shared view of historians of Roman religion,[2] there is nothing whatever to link the South Italian city to a toponym in Rome associated with a much older cult. *Tarentum Accas Larentinas* is associated with the mythologico-historical traditions surrounding the very beginnings of the city itself.

What then of the *ludi Saeculares* = *ludi Tarentini*, the 'secular rite' (*saeculare*

---

2. Nilsson, P.W. RE s.v. Saeculares ludi: Wissowa 1971:309; Weinstock, RE s.v. Tarentum²; Latte 1960:246-248; Dumézil 1966:431-2.

sacrum) of Septimius Severus? These were in the historical period 'games and sacrifices performed by the Roman state to commemorate the end of one *saeculum* and the beginning of a new one.'[3] But they are celebrated precisely at the *Tarentum*, the place of the cult-offering for the dead. As Merkelbach puts it (1961:90), 'Wer das Opfer am Tarentum darbrachte, zelebrierte eine Katabasis. Ein solcher Altar heisst *mundus*, und auch das Tarentum ist als solcher anzusehen; . . ."eine für gewöhnlich geschlossene und nur am Tag des Festes geöffnete Grube, wie sie nach römischer Vorstellung eine geeignete Opferstätte für die di inferi abgab [Wissowa]".' The liminal nature of the *Tarentum* of legend is equally clear: an underground spot, marked by exhalations of smoke and accessed by crossing water.

The secular games were associated in origin with the gens Valeria, as L. R. Taylor (1970) notes (Valerius Maximus cited above, and independently also Festus 440 L), and she sees Valerius Corvus' consulship of 349 B.C. as a possible date for their first celebration. But we should recall that the societal prominence of the gens Valeria is now epigraphically attested by the lapis Satricanus as already well established in 500 B.C. (·]*ei steterai popliosio ualesiosio suodales mamartei*). Festus 440 L furthermore links the secular games with the Etruscan king Tarquin and the cult of Mars (<*saeculares ludi*> *Tarquini superbi regis i*[ ] *Marti consecrauit* [ ); compare Satricum *mamartei* = *Marti*. Public games (*ludi*) in Rome were themselves recognized to be of Etruscan mediation already in antiquity.[4] Again all the indications favor a much more ancient origin than third century Magna Graecia for the cult at the Tarentum, the secular rite, and the games.

'Die Säkularspiele sollen Segen and Glück für die Zukunft bringen' (Merkelbach 1961:90). Following in part J. Gagé and L. R. Taylor we may see in the secular rite an old gentilicial cult associated with the Valerii, perhaps already in the 6th century, a ritual 'commemorating the end of one *saeculum* and the beginning of a new one,' a periodic reaffirmation and renewal of life by the cult of the dead. The rite is associated with the beginnings of Rome (*tarentum Accas*), and was conceivably taken over by the state as early as the time of the Etruscan kings. The cult of the dead would have involved ancient and inherited underworld deities (*di inferi* = Gaulish *anderon* = English *under* etc., IE **n̥dhero-*) long predating the introduction of Dis and Proserpina.

'The *saeculum*, defined as the longest span of human life, was fixed in the Republic as an era of a hundred years' (Taylor 1970). Compare the definition of *saeculum* in Censorinus 17.2,

> spatium uitae humanae longissimum partu et morte definitum,

and in Varro *L.L.* 6.11:

> s<a>eclum spatium annorum centum uocarunt, dictum a sene, quod longissimum spatium senescendorum hominum id putarunt.

---

3. Taylor 1970, based on the sensible discussion in Taylor 1934. Other useful recent discussions include Gagé 1932 and Merkelbach 1956. Wagenvoort 1956 is linguistically unsound ('Sabine' *Terentum* from a **tēr̥u̯entum* 'earthy, terrosum', 'a striking definition of an underground altar'!), and Brind'Amour 1978 simply fantastic (Egyptian origin!).

4. Livy 1.35.8; Bloch 1981:136; Thuillier 1985; de Simone in Campanile 1988:37-8.

This ideal human lifespan of 100 years is certainly older than the Roman Republic. We find it commonly in Vedic as in RV 3.36.10, *asmé śatáṃ śarádo jīváse dhāḥ* 'grant us to live 100 autumns', RV 2.27.10 *śatáṃ no rāsva śarádo vicákṣe* 'grant us to see 100 autumns', etc. Like another multiple of 10, the gestation period of Vergil's *decem menses* (*Ecl.* 4.61), Hittite ITU 10 KAM (KUB 33.119+ iv 15,16), and Vedic *dáśa mā́sān* (RV 5.78.9), all 'ten months', it is Indo-European patrimony.

Etymologically, *saeculum* agrees exactly with Welsh *hoedl* 'lifespan', and that may be taken as the meaning of their common IE ancestor **sah₂i-tlo-m* (< **seh₂i-tlo-m*). Though this **-tlo-* derivative is confined to Italic and Celtic, the complete absence of the verbal root in either proves the formation must be considerably older. The root is the verb 'to bind', Hittite *išḫai, išḫiḫḫi, išḫiyanzi* and its derivative *išḫiul* 'contract'. Compare the Indo-Iranian perfect Vedic *siṣāya* = Gathic Avestan *hišāiiā,* and the figura etymologica in RV 8.67.8 *mā́ naḥ sétuḥ siṣed ayám* 'may this fetter not bind us'. Vedic *sétuḥ* is also the word for 'bridge'. In the ancient metaphor which underlies IE **sah₂i-tlo-m* (**-tlo-* nomen instrumenti) the 'lifespans', the generations are 'links' in the chain of human life.[5]

We have seen the Indo-European ideological background of Lat. *saeculum* and the *ludi Saeculares*. Let us return to the term with which we began. Varro glosses *tarentum Accas* with a modernized *sepulcrum Accae. Sepulcrum* has a perfectly good Indo-European etymology: **sepel(i)-tlo-* to Latin *sepeliō* 'bury; lay out', Vedic *saparyati* 'honor, worship', both from 'handle carefully, reverently', and Greek (ἀμφι)έπω in the service of the dead (*Il.* 24.804, the final line of the epic). For the semantics of IE **sep-* and its other reflexes, notably in Anatolian, see now Vine 1988. We should therefore expect the older *tarentum* likewise to have an Indo-European etymology. And so it does. Purely formally, by regular Latin phonological rules (cf. *parens*), *tarentum* continues IE **tr̥h₂-ent-o-*, an individualizing thematic vowel derivative of the regular participle **tr̥h₂-ént-* of the athematic present **terh₂-* 'pass over, cross, overcome'.

The *Tarentum* is thus originally the "crossing place". In formation and literal meaning *tarentum* < **tr̥h₂-(e)nt-ó-* closely parallels Vedic *tīrthám* 'crossing place, ford; watering place', Wackernagel-Debrunner AiGr II 2.718. But what does the grave as crossing place mean? To answer we must look to what is the associative semantics of the root **terh₂-* in Indo-European. The verb involves a notion of overcoming adversity, hostilities, the enemy, conceived of as a difficult passage to be gotten through. One may compare the remarkably similar semantics of Vedic *pánthāḥ* and its Indo-European forebear as described by Benveniste 1966:297-8: 'il implique peine, incertitude et danger . . . C'est bien plutôt un "franchissement" tenté à travers une région inconnue et souvent hostile . . . un moyen de parcourir une étendue perilleuse ou accidentée.' We have common Indo-Iranian figures in Ved. *tarád-dveṣas-* = Av. *tarō.ṯbaēšah-* 'overcoming hostility'; RV 3.27.3 *áti dvéṣāṁsi tarema,* Y. 28.6 *duuaēšå tauruuāmā* 'overcome hostilities'; RV 6.2.4. *dviṣó áṁho ná tarati* 'he goes through the enemy as through straits'. In both Neo- and Old Hittite note LÚKÚR

5. For other metaphors in this semantic realm, cf. Old Irish *glún* 'knee; knee-joint, generation', or Vedic *párus* 'joint; generation' (Hoffmann 1975:327). Yet another appears in *Il.* 6.146 οἵη περ φύλλων γενεή, τοίη δὲ καὶ ἀνδρῶν.

*IŠTU*NI.TE-*YA tarḫḫun* (*Ḫatt*. ii 39) 'I overcame the enemy on my own', $^{\text{LÚ.MEŠ}}$KÚR-*uš=muš* [*tarḫḫu*]*n* 'I overcame my enemies' (HAB ii 28).

Noteworthy are examples where what is crossed, passed over, is water: RV 9.107.15 *tárat samudrám* 'he crossed the ocean', with marked verb initial position like *áhann áhim*; Old Persian DB I 88 *vašnā Auramazdāha Tigrām viyatarayāmā* 'by the will of Ahuramazda we crossed the Tigris'; and Old Hittite KUB 31.4 Ro. 19 *arunan=a tarḫuen* 'but we overcame, crossed over (the way to) the sea'.[6] In the latter two examples the sentence marks a dramatic turning point in the narrative sequence. The associations of Sanskrit *tīrtha* in later Hinduism are likewise with water: 'stairs for descent into a river, place of pilgrimage on the banks of sacred streams' (Monier-Williams).

But it is one very specific Indo-European formula with **terh₂-* which explains the semantics of Latin *tarentum*. What is the ritual of the secular games for? The answer is furnished by Indo-European eschatology, the Indo-European doctrine of final things: what is crossed over, overcome, is death. The formula was given above, with the example of Greek νέκταρ:

HERO OVERCOME (**terh₂-*) DEATH.

Further illustrations are given in chap. 40.

Significantly in Vedic what is crossed over is more frequently 'life, lifespan'. The formula is *prá tar^{i}* + *ā́yus-* 'lifespan' (**h₂ói̯u-*): the lifespan is 'gotten across', whence 'lengthened, prolonged'. This variant is well discussed by Geib 1975, who notes the etymological figure in RV 8.79.6:

prém ā́yus tārīd átīrṇam

May (soma) bring him across the uncrossed lifespan.

More recently, following Geib, Lazzeroni 1988 puts it 'nominando, anzichè la morte, la vita', possibly by 'una motivazione tabuistica', the formula may be glossed 'portare la vita al di là degli ostacoli', 'fare attraversare la morte alla vita', whence 'prolungare la vita'. Cf. RV 8.18.22:

yé cid dhí **mṛtyubándhava**
ā́dityā mánavaḥ smási
prá sū́ na **ā́yur jīváse tiretana**

Though we men are **companions of death**,
o Adityas, **you should prolong our lifespan for living**.

6. Otherwise Otten 1963:161 'Und das Meer haben wir bezwungen', followed by Soysal 1987:180 'So haben wir das Meer bezwungen', and in part Bernabé 1988:8 'hemos dominado [. . .] y el mar' (but *arunan=a* without gemination!)

Cf. also RV 8.44.30, 1.44.6, 1.89.2, the latter two also with *jīváse* and the first with ***vaso*** in the same slot, which may be a play on words.

Vedic *ā́yus* 'lifespan' is a virtual synonym of Latin *saeculum* and Welsh *hoedl*; we may pose an Indo-European equivalence *$*h_2$óiu* = *$*sah_2$itlom*.

The final and most striking Vedic passage to cite is RV 5.54.15 cd, from one of the family books. The lines are hymn-final; on the significance of this locus in Vedic and Indo-European poetics see Toporov 1981:239. Recall that for the Roman and the Indian the ideal human lifespan was a century:

idáṃ sú me maruto haryatā váco
yásya **tárema tárasā śatáṃ** hímāḥ

Accept well this hymn, o Maruts,
by whose **"crossing-power" may we cross 100** winters

For the *s*-stem noun *táras-* 'force permettant de traverser' (Renou, EVP ad loc.) compare the frozen zero-grade adverb Ved. *tirás*, Avestan *tarō* 'across', Old Irish *tar h-* 'over'.

The Roman ritual for the dead at the *Tarentum*, the 'crossing place', is at the same time a ritual to assure the long life and orderly succession of the generations; it is a reaffirmation of the crossing of the *saecula* of a hundred years. The rite and its associated vocabulary faithfully continue different facets of a single, unitary Indo-European formulaic spectrum:

$*terh_2$-	$*terh_2$-	$*terh_2$-	$*terh_2$-	$*terh_2$-
|	|	|	|	|
$*sah_2$itlom	$*h_2$ói̯u	*dk̑m̥tóm	*mr̥ti-	*nek̑-

These formulas are the vehicles for the verbal transmission of a coherent eschatological doctrine which goes back to the remotest reconstructible Indo-European times.

This doctrine is wholly consistent with the greater formulaic context whereby certain important features of Indo-European culture find their expression. The mythological basic formula

HERO SLAY (*$*g^when$-*) ADVERSARY

of *áhann áhim*, ἔπεφνέν τε Γοργόνα, MUŠ*illuyankam kuenta*, *orms einbani*, is reciprocal and reversible. We find as well

ADVERSARY SLAY (*$*g^when$-*) HERO,

as in the death of Beowulf.

The basic formula which we have seen,

HERO OVERCOME (*$*terh_2$-*) DEATH,

as in Greek νέκταρ and the preceeding formulaic spectrum, is again only a variant of

HERO OVERCOME (*$terh_2$-) ADVERSARY

and its reciprocal,

ADVERSARY OVERCOME (*$terh_2$-) HERO.

Both roots, *$g^u hen$- and *$terh_2$-, as well as the formula and its reciprocal, with subject and object 'waters' as noted above, are in play in Maitrāyaṇi-Saṁhitā 4.3.4:

ā́po vaí rakṣoghnī́r
apó rákṣāṃsi ná taranti
rákṣasām ápahatyai

The waters are really Rakṣas-smashing (*$g^u hen$-).
The Rakṣases do not cross over/surpass waters (*$terh_2$-).
(This is) for the smashing away of Rakṣases (*$g^u hen$-).

The ambiguity of the root *$g^u hen$-, both 'slay, kill' and 'smite, strike', renders the verb apt for expressing the hero's sequential defeat by and then victory over his adversary. In RV 4.18.7c-9d we have no fewer than six phrases of self-justification spoken by Indra's mother to Indra, each beginning with the 1sg. pronoun form *máma*(*t*). The first (7cd) sets the stage by the familiar formula with *$g^u hen$-:

mámaitā́n putró ṃahatā́ **vadhéna**
vṛtráṃ jaghanvā́ṁ asṛjad ví síndhūn

My son, **having slain/smitten Vṛtra** with the great **weapon**,
released those rivers.

The last (9a-d) recounts both the defeat and the victory in turn, in verbally parallel fashion, beginning with *$g^u hen$- 'strike' and then with an equivalent substitution 'smash' (*peḭs-):

mámac caná te maghavan vyàṁso
nivividhvā́ṁ ápa hánū **jaghā́na**
ádhā nívíddha úttaro babhūvā́ñ
chíro dāsásya **sám piṇak vadhéna**

Not on my account, o generous one, did Vyaṁsa **smite** off your
two jaws, having wounded you; then, though wounded, you
smashed in the head of the Dāsa with your **weapon**.

The unity of the passage is marked by the verse-final instrumental *vadhéna* 'with the weapon' at beginning (7c) and end (9d), a good example of ring-composition framing.

A striking semantic feature of the verb **terh₂-* as we have noted is precisely temporariness, transitoriness, non-permanence, which made it pathetically apt in the context of the object DEATH. To illustrate we may take two mythological passages, from Avestan (the paean of victory in the Fravardin Yasht), and from Hittite (the Illuyanka myth).

13.77 yaṯ **titaraṯ** aŋrō mainiiuš
dāhīm ašahē vaŋhāuš
aṇtarə pairi.auuāitəm
vohuca manō ātaršca

When the Evil Spirit **was about to overwhelm** the creation of
the good truth, both Good Thinking and Fire intervened.
(tr. Insler 1967)

78 tå hē **tauruuaiiatəm** ṯbaēšå
aŋrahe mainiiāuš druuatō
yaṯ nōiṯ āpō takāiš staiiaṯ
nōiṯ uruuarå uruϑmabiiō

They two **overcame** the hostilities of the deceitful Evil
Spirit, so that he could not hold up the waters in their
flowing, nor the plants in their growing.

In Avestan the temporary ('prospective') victory is expressed modally by a subjunctive, contrasting with the indicative of the final victory in the following verse. Both verbs are forms of *tar-*, **terh₂-*.[7]

In the Hittite each of the two successive narrations of the Illuyanka myth in the course of the New Year's ritual (for the text see Beckman 1982) involves the opposition of the roots *tarḫ-*, (**terh₂-*) and *kuen-* (**gʷhen-*). In the first,

§3 nu=za ᴹᵁŠilluyankaš ᴰIM-an **taraḫta**,

The serpent **overcame** the Storm God

§12 nu=kan ᴹᵁŠilluyankan **kuenta**

The Storm God) **killed** the serpent.

The second begins alike,

7. Insler's interpretation and translation of *titaraṯ* is controversial, see Kellens 1984:193. Even if the form is indicative (injunctive), not subjunctive, the imperfect of an iterative (with reduplication) is equally apt here: 'was overwhelming'.

§21 [=za (^{MUŠ}il)luyankaš ^{D}IM-an] **taraḫta**

The serpent **overcame** the Storm God,

and continues with a periphrastic 'prospective' of the same verb,

§25 n=an=za namma ^{MUŠ}illuyanka[n] **taraḫḫūwan dāiš**

and (the Storm God) **was about to overcome** the serpent,

to conclude with the final victory:

§26 nu=kan ^{D}IM-aš ^{MUŠ}illiyankan *Ù* DUMU-*ŠU* **kuenta**

The Storm God **killed** the serpent and his (own) son.

As I have said elsewhere of other passages, from the vantage point of Indo-European oral literature we are looking at two performances of the same text. Like RV 4.18.7-9 above (with verbal root **g*^{w}*hen-*), the two are narratologically identical in their responsion: a sequence of conditional or temporary victory of the one adversary and the final victory of the other. The structure of the narrative in the Hittite and the Avestan is the same and its lexical expression identical, whether in Hittite myth or the hagiography of the archangels of Zoroastrianism. Both victories, provisional and final, are doomed to be repeated with every retelling of the myth and every re-performance of the ritual, whether the cycle is a year or a century.

36

The myth in Greece: Variations on the formula and theme

How does one kill a dragon in Greek? What is the lexicon and syntax, the verbal means? The verb 'to kill' in Greek is ordinarily (κατα)κτείνω, yet precisely not here.

In the *Iliad*—a text which describes a lot of killings—there is only a single instance of a mythological narration of a hero killing a dragon. But it is very instructive. In book 6 the Trojan warrior Glaukos sets forth his genealogy to the Greek warrior Diomedes. The two will end up by recognizing they are linked by the relation of hospitality, ξενία, and they will not fight each other. Glaukos begins his narrative exactly like a folktale (152-5):[1]

> ἔστι πόλις ᾽Εφύρη μυχῷι Ἄργεος ἱπποβότοιο
> ἔνθα δὲ Σίσυφος ἔσκεν, ὃ κέρδιστος γένετ᾽ ἀνδρῶν
> Σίσυφος Αἰολίδης ὁ δ᾽ ἄρα Γλαῦκον τέκεθ᾽ υἱόν,
> αὐτὰρ Γλαῦκος τίκτεν ἀμύμονα Βελλεροφόντην
>
> There is a city, Ephyre, in the corner of horse-pasturing
> Argos; there lived Sisyphus, that sharpest of all men
> Sisyphus, Aiolos' son, and he had a son named Glaukos,
> and Glaukos in turn sired Bellerophontes the blameless.

Stylistically we have left epic narrative behind, and we are in the domain of storytelling. From that point the genealogy is interrupted until l. 191 by the tale of the trials of Glaukos' ancestor Bellerophontes (Bellerophon).

Whatever the first member of the compound may be, the name of the hero

---

1. Compare Hesiod *fr.* 240.1 M.-W. ἐστί τις ῾Ελλοπίη πολυλήιος ἠδ᾽ εὐλείμων 'there is a place Hellopie, with many grain fields and fair meadows,' of the land of Dodone sacred to Zeus. The tradition is old; note that for the old name of Corinth we must restore πόλις Ϝεφύρη (which invalidates Puhvel's etymology of the name, HED s. v. *epurai-*).

Βελλεροφόντης identified him to the Greek consciousness as a "slayer": the second member *-phontēs* is, or was perceived as, an agent noun from the root of Greek φόνος 'slaying, murder', the same IE root **g*ʷ*hen-* as Vedic *han-*, Avestan *jan-*, Hittite *kuen-*, and Old English *bona* 'killer, *bane*'. Compare the Avestan agent noun *jaṇta* 'slayer'. Mycenean names like *da-i-qo-ta* Daikʷhontas (Δηιφόντης), *ra-wo-qo-ta* Lawokʷhontas, *po-ru-qo-ta* Polukʷontas (Πολυφόντης) indicate the genuineness and antiquity of the onomastic stock.[2]

As the result of a false accusation by his king's wife, Bellerophon is banished and sent to Lycia in Asia Minor, where he must execute a series of perilous tasks by order of the king (*Il.* 6.179-86):

πρῶτον μέν ῥα Χίμαιραν ἀμαιμακέτην ἐκέλευσε
πεφνέμεν. ἡ δ' ἄρ' ἔην θεῖον γένος, οὐδ' ἀνθρώπων,
πρόσθε λέων, ὄπιθεν δὲ δράκων, μέσση δὲ χίμαιρα,
δεινὸν ἀποπνείουσα πυρὸς μένος αἰθομένοιο.
καὶ τὴν μὲν **κατέπεφνε** θεῶν τεράεσσι πιθήσας
δεύτερον αὖ Σολύμοισι μαχέσσατο κυδαλίμοισι
καρτίστην δὴ τήν γε μάχην φάτο δύμεναι ἀνδρῶν.
τὸ τρίτον αὖ **κατέπεφνεν** Ἀμαζόνας ἀντιανείρας.

First he sent him away with orders **to slay** the Chimaira
none might approach; a thing of immortal make, not human,
lion-fronted and snake behind, a goat in the middle,
and snorting out the breath of the terrible flame of bright fire.
He **slew** Chimaira, obeying the portents of the immortals.
Next after this he fought against the glorious Solymoi,
and this he thought was the strongest battle with men that he entered;
but third he **slew** the Amazons, who fight men in battle.[3]

The verb 'to kill' in boldface has the stem πεφνε-, reduplicated thematic aorist of the root **g*ʷ*hen-*, again the same root as Greek φόνος, -φόντης, Ved. *han-*, Av. *jan-*, Hitt. *kuen-*, and Germanic *ban-*. The repetition ensures the importance of the choice of this verb, and not (κατα)κτείνω.

The burden of this and the chapters following will be a systematic examination of most of the attestations of the verb (κατα)πεφνέμεν[4] and their associative semantics in Ancient Greek through the fifth century B.C. This verb is confined to poetry, and does not occur in prose authors; it is furthermore bookish from the fourth century on, and its relatively infrequent appearance in Hellenistic poetry is a matter of reminiscence of epic diction. But as will become clear the verb πεφνέμεν, particularly in

2. For recent discussions see Moreschini 1985 and Ruijgh 1985:158ff.

3. Unless otherwise noted the translations are those of R. Lattimore.

4. The verb lacks a present, since historical θείνω was at least semantically differentiated to 'strike'. I will cite the verb πεφνέμεν in its Homeric aorist infinitive, since the expected Attic πεφνεῖν, to judge by the Thesaurus Linguae Graecae computer files, is never actually found. We will examine below evidence to show that the lexically differentiated θείνω still functions as a constituent of the basic formula with **g*ʷ*hen-*.

traditional early Greek poetry, is the "dragon-slaying" verb par excellence, the verb to describe in poetic language the "terrifying exploit of the hero".[5] In its poetic function just as in its linguistic form the Greek verb πεφνέμεν, like the Indo-Iranian, Anatolian, Germanic, and Celtic avatars of the root *$g^{w}hen$-, is an inheritance from Indo-European itself.

The same mythological episode as in *Iliad* 6, the trials of Bellerophon, is evoked in the same words by Pindar in *Ol.* 13.87-90:

σὺν δὲ κείνωι καί ποτ' Ἀμαζονίδων
αἰθέρος ψυχρῶν ἀπὸ κόλπων ἐρήμου
τοξόταν βάλλων γυναικεῖον στρατόν
καὶ Χίμαιραν πῦρ πνέοισαν καὶ Σολύμους **ἔπεφνεν**

So mounted, out of the cold gulfs
of the high air forlorn, he smote
the archered host of women, the Amazons;
and the Chimaira, breathing flame; and the Solymoi, and **slew** them.

Compare ἀποπνείουσα πυρὸς μένος αἰθομένοιο 'breathing the holy force of burning fire' in *Il.* 6.182 just cited. While πῦρ πνέοισαν might be only a Homeric reminiscence (adjusted for dialect), the fact that Pindar uses the verb πεφνέμεν of the Amazons, the Chimaira, and of the Solymians (the second of Bellerophon's three tasks in Homer)—note the three καί's—indicates that he is independently drawing on traditional verbal material, in which all three tasks are expressed by the verb πεφνέμεν. Note also the absence of an overt subject in Pindar's phrase: we have only verb and object, in the unmarked OV order.

In line 88 Schroeder's correction from ψυχρᾶς is surely right, and adopted by Snell and Bowra. The concentric nesting around the preposition of the two noun phrases, both in the relational case and each of equal syllabic weight, is a remarkable grammatical and metrical figure. It may be diagrammed as follows; word boundaries are marked, and subscripts identify agreement:

– ⏑ –	– –	⏑ ⏑	– –	⏑ – –
N_i	A_j	P	N_j	A_i
αἰθέρος	ψυχρῶν	ἀπὸ	κόλπων	ἐρήμου
		out		
	of cold		gulfs	
of high air				forlorn.

Pindar proceeds to follow these feats of poetics and formulaics with a metalinguistic boast (*Ol.* 13.93-5):

5. See especially Chantraine 1949, Visser 1988, and for Homer Bechert 1964. While I cannot follow the latter in every detail, I can only applaud his statement that 'der besondere Klang von (κατα)πεφνέμεν ist nicht zu überhören.'

ἐμὲ δ' εὐθὺν ἀκόντων
ἱέντα ῥόμβον παρὰ σκοπὸν οὐ χρή
τὰ πολλὰ βέλεα καρτύνειν χεροῖν

It becomes me not, spinning
the shaft's straight cast beside the mark, to speed
too many bolts from my hand's strength.

We will see other such boasts; like a Vedic *kavi* Pindar is highly conscious of his art.

The same phraseology probably recurs, though it is mostly by Wilamowitz' conjecture, in a fragment of Hesiod (43a.87 M.-W.), which tells the myth of Bellerophon and Pegasus:

σὺν τῶι πῦρ [πνείουσαν ⏑ – κατέπεφνε Χίμαιραν][6]

With whom he slew the fire-breathing Chimaira.

With Hesiod's σὺν τῶι 'with whom' compare Pindar's σὺν δὲ κείνωι 'with that one' above, also of Pegasus. We have here an optional further extension of the basic formula to specify the companion, expressed originally by an instrumental case of accompaniment, with or without preposition:

HERO	SLAY (*g^{w}*hen*-) SERPENT (with COMPANION)

With other adversaries Pindar uses the same phrase of the hero Herakles and his companion Telamon in *Isth.* 6.31-2:

εἷλε δὲ Περγαμίαν, **πέφνεν** δὲ **σὺν κείνωι** Μερόπων
ἔθνεα . . .

He took the city of Pergamon, and in the same hero's company
(lit. **with that one**) **slew** the hosts of the Meropes . . .

Note the coordinated unaugmented verb forms in clause-initial position. The passage will be treated at greater length in chap. 38:

From Vedic among many examples note RV 6.20.2:

áhim yád vr̥trán . . . **hánn** . . . **víṣṇunā** sacānáḥ

When you **slew** . . . the **serpent** Vr̥tra . . . accompanied **by Viṣṇu.**

On the verse see also chap. 42.

6. West's ἀπηλοίησε is cleverer than it is plausible, in view of the massive evidence here and below that one kills a Greek dragon with πεφνέμεν.

Recall the dénouement of the Hittite myth cited earlier,

> nu=kan ^{MUŠ}illuyankan **kuenta**
> DINGIR^{MEŠ}-š=a **katti=šši ešer**
>
> he **slew** the serpent, and the gods **were with him,**

where the notion of accompaniment has been expanded to a clause.

This extended version of the basic formula should be compared with that including the weapon above (chap. 27.3):

HERO | SLAY (*$g^{u}hen$-) SERPENT (with WEAPON) |

In each the marginal component of the semantics of the instrumental case is reflected both in the optionality of the specification and in its frequent syntactic extra-position. More importantly, it appears that the two optional specifications of the formula are in complementary distribution; if one is present the other is almost obligatorily absent:

$$\text{HERO} \quad \text{SLAY } (*g^{u}hen\text{-}) \quad \text{SERPENT} \begin{Bmatrix} \text{(with WEAPON)} \\ \text{(with COMPANION)} \end{Bmatrix}$$

A single formulaic instance (for example, a sentence) will not normally contain both. We have a sort of formulaic/thematic redundancy rule. If both notions, weapon and companion, are present on the level of *theme*, as for example in the final dragon-combat of Beowulf, they must be independently motivated. Significantly they are sequential in time: Beowulf's sword *Nægling* breaks before the entry of his companion *Wiglaf.* We may call attention to the phonetic index **-gl-** which both Old English names share: an icon of identity.

Further modalities of these relations are discussed below in chap. 42, on the name of Meleager.

Nominal derivatives of the root *$g^{u}hen$- in Greek, just as in Indic, Iranian, and especially Germanic, can also alone carry the full weight of the inherited formula. Aeschylus likens the Persian monarch to a murderous dragon: nominal φόνιος δράκων is the "transformational" equivalent of πέφνε δράκων 'the dragon slew' (*Pers.* 81-2):

> κυάνεον δ' ὄμμασι λεύσσων
> **φονίου** δέργμα **δράκοντος**
>
> In his eyes lazuli flashing
> like a **snake's murderous** glances.

S. Bernadete's translation perfectly renders the Greek meter.

As will be discussed and illustrated more fully in chap. 53, Euripides shows only a single, and uncertain, instance of the verbal reflex of the root *$g^{u}hen$- in the meaning of SLAY, πεφνέμεν (*πεφνεῖν).[7] Yet he is well aware of, and makes full use of, the basic formula as the vehicle for themes which are common in his dramatic oeuvre, whence the title of chap. 52, 'The formula without the word'. Euripides' technique is lexical substitution (κτείνω, ὄλλυμι SLAY) and semantic spreading typically from a nominal form of **g^w^hen-* like φόνος or φόνιος. But his deployment can be subtle indeed. A passage in the *Phoenissae* (657-65) manages to narrate the central formula of the myth twice:

> ἔνθα **φόνιος** ἦν **δράκων**
> . . .
> ὃν. . .
> Κάδμος **ὄλεσε μαρμάρωι·**
> κρᾶτα **φόνιον ὀλεσίθηρος**
> ὠλένας δικὼν **βολαῖς**
>
> There was the **murderous dragon** . . . which . . . Kadmos **slew** with a **stone**, hurling the **casts** of his **beast-slaying** arm at the **murderous** head.

The presence of the epithet φόνιος with its root **g^w^hen-* associated with the SERPENT permits the deployment of a lexical substitute for 'kill' (ὄλλυμι). With this displacement the formula remains the same, the familiar

HERO SLAY [**g^w^hen-* + SERPENT] with WEAPON.

It occurs first (undoing the relative clause) in

Κάδμος ὄλεσε [φόνιος + δράκων] μαρμάρωι,

and is then immediately repeated, without overt subject and with remarkable syntactic and semantic variation, in

ὀλεσί- [φόνιον -θηρ] βολαῖς.

Here the compound ὀλεσίθηρ 'beast-slaying' (compare *Od.* 11.572-5 of Orion, θῆρας . . . τοὺς . . . κατέ**πεφνεν**, 'beasts . . . which . . . he slew') is actually an epithet of the HERO (in fact, his arm), φόνιον with the root **g^w^hen-* is an epithet of the SERPENT (in fact, his head), and the verb of the clause is a semantic doubling of the WEAPON: δικὼν βολαῖς 'hurling with casts'. Yet through these artful transformations the fundamental ancient underlying formula can still clearly be perceived.

In Euripides' *Bacchae* the dragon lineage of the doomed Pentheus runs through as a leitmotif, accompanied by a derivative of φον-. Like his name which points to calamity, ἐνδυστυχῆσαι 'be luckless' in the words of Dionysus, Pentheus

7. *Andr.* 655 Πάρις γάρ, ὃς σὸν παῖδ' ἔπεφν' Ἀχιλλέα, a passage suspected of interpolation, cf. Stevens 1971 ad loc.

(πένθος 'grief') bears an ominous aura of the basic formula SLAY SERPENT:

538-44   χθόνιον
           γένος ἐκφύς τε **δράκοντός**
           ποτε Πενθεύς· ὃν **Ἐχίων**
           ἐφύτευσε χθόνιος,
           ... **φόνιον** δ' ὥσ-
           τε γίγαντ' ...

           Earth-born race
           and offspring of the **dragon**,
           Pentheus whom earth-born **Ekhion**
           sired ... like a **murderous**
           giant ...

The name Ἐχίων contains ἔχις 'serpent', another inherited designation (*eĝhi-, Armenian *iž* 'serpent'); his epithet χθόνιος 'from the earth, chthonic' rhymes with φόνιος.[8]

991-6   ἴτω δίκα ...
           φονεύουσα λαιμῶν διαμπὰξ
           τὸν ἄθεον ἄνομον ἄδικον **Ἐχίονος**
           γόνον γηγενῆ

           Go, Justice ...
           smiting through the throat
           of the godless, lawless, unrighteous son
           of **Ekhion**, born of earth.

1154-5   ἀναβοάσωμεν ξυμφορὰν
           τὰν τοῦ **δράκοντος** Πενθέος ἐκγενέτα

           Let us raise a song and shout over the fall
           of Pentheus, offspring of the **dragon**.

1178   **καταφόνευσέ** νιν

           ... **slaughtered** him.

Euripides uses the infrequent compound verb καταφονεύω only twice. Further examples of his practice of the basic formula with Herakles are found in chap. 38, and with other heroes in chap. 52.

---

8. Compare the play in the names of Kreousa's father Ἐρεχθεύς king of Athens and his ancestor Ἐριχθόνιος together with the massive serpent imagery permeating Euripides' *Ion*.

Other passages complete in striking fashion the Homeric and Pindaric mythopoeic deployments of the basic formula with the inherited finite verb 'slay' just presented. The Chimaira is not the only "dragon"; the Gorgon is another monster who can be assimilated to a dragon or serpent. In the same legend of Bellerophon we have in Pindar (*Ol.* 13.63-4):

> ὃς τᾶς **ὀφιήδεος** υἱόν ποτε **Γοργόνος** ἦ πόλλ' ἀμφὶ κρουνοῖς
> Πάγασον ζεῦξαι ποθέων ἔπαθεν
>
> who beside the Springs, striving to break the **serpent Gorgon's**
> child, Pegasos, endured much hardship.

Note the phonetic figure **POTHEōN ePATHEN** 'struggling suffered', which calls attention to, indexes the narration of the theme. Pegasus is the offspring of the Gorgon, whose epithet is ὀφιήδης, serpent-like. Recall that ὄφις 'snake' is the cognate of Vedic *áhi-* and Avestan *aži-*.

The killing of the Gorgon by Perseus is given by Pindar in *Pyth.* 10.46-8:

> ἐς ἀνδρῶν μακάρων ὅμιλον· **ἔπεφνέν** τε **Γοργόνα**
> καὶ ποικίλον κάρα
> δρακόντων φόβαισιν ἤλυθε νασιώταις
> λίθινον θάνατον φέρων
>
> . . . to that throng of blessed men. He **slew** the **Gorgon**,
> came bearing the head, intricate with snake hair,
> the stony death to the islanders.

Pythian 10 is Pindar's earliest attested ode, composed in 498 B.C., and the story of Perseus slaying the Gorgon is the first myth we have that he narrated. And there in Greek is precisely our Vedic *áhann áhim*, down to the very word order. Combining the syntagms ὀφιώδεος . . . Γοργόνος and ἔπεφνεν Γοργόνα we can restore the real mythographic formula, just below the surface:

> *ἔπεφνεν ὄφιν
>
> he slew the serpent.

Note again, just as in the case of Vedic *áhann áhim*, the absence of an overt subject and the presence of a phonetic figure (**phn** . . . **ph.n**). For the formulaic adversary, just ὄφις 'snake', recall also the name of the "philosophical dragon" ***Ophi**oneus* (or ***Ophi**on*), the earth-born snake-god challenger to the cosmic order of Chronos, Zas, and Chthonie in the cosmogony of the 6th-century thinker Pherecydes of Syros (Schibli 1990), whose father Βάβυς bore an Anatolian name.[9]

9. I owe the indication of this "dragon" and the reference to Hayden Pelliccia.

That is not all. Pindar lets us see the same formula elsewhere, and in a wholly conscious fashion. Toward the end of *Pythian* 4 (463 B.C.) Pindar claims to be in a hurry and wants to abridge his narrative. He says, 'I know a shortcut' and then, 'I am a leader in the lore of song', i.e., 'a master of poetic tradition'. The next line proves his assertion, for the shortcut is the traditional basic formula itself.[10] Lines 247-50:

> μακρά μοι νεῖσθαι κατ᾽ ἀμαξιτόν· ὥρα γὰρ συνάπτει· καί τινα
> **οἶμον** ἴσαμι **βραχύν**· πολλοῖσι δ᾽ **ἅγημαι σοφίας** ἑτέροις.
> **κτεῖνε** μὲν γλαυκῶπα τέχναις ποικιλόνωτον **ὄφιν**,
> ὦ ᾽Αρκεσίλα, κλέψεν τε Μήδειαν σὺν αὐτᾶι, τὰν Πελίαο(-)**φονόν**
>
> The high road is long for me to travel, and time closes. I know
> a **short path**, I that **guide** many another in the **craft of singers**.
> By guile he **slew** the green-eyed **serpent** of the burnished scales,
> o Arkesilas, and stole away Medeia, with her good will,
> she that was **bane** to Pelias.

It is a remarkable bit of pragmatics, of poet-performer/audience interaction, an indexical reference to the poetic message within the message itself. Encapsulating the myth of Jason and the Golden Fleece—without overt subject—, Pindar begins the sentence and the verse line with the verb κτεῖνε 'slew', ends the verse-line with the object ὄφιν 'serpent', and ends the sentence and the next verse-line with a form of the root **g^{w}hen-*, φονός 'murderess'. Braswell 1980 argues for keeping a compound Πελιαοφόνον, with an analogical composition vowel *-o-*, noting Λαμνιᾶν . . . ἀνδροφόνων 'the Lemnian women who murdered their husbands' only two lines later (252). Snell's text reads Πελίαο φονόν, with a feminine agent noun φονός 'murderess' (conjectured by Wackernagel 1953:1199-200) which would be found only here in all of Greek literature. But speaking for it, *pace* Braswell, would be precisely the feminine compound ἀνδροφόνος 'who murdered their husbands' two lines later in the same verse-final focus position.

It is interesting that Lattimore chose to translate the latter by its cognate, *bane*. The effect is the same with either reading; the form (-)φονος reintroduces the marked root for 'kill' **g^{w}hen-*, vis-à-vis the common, unmarked κτείνω. By a process of semantic spreading it has given to κτεῖνε (in emphatic line-initial position) the semantics of πέφνε; with the object ὄφιν (distracted to line-final focus position) the effect is to restore the Indo-European basic formula:

(HERO) | SLAY (**g^{w}hen-*) SERPENT (**$og^{w}hi$-*) |

κτεῖνε . . . ὄφιν
(πέφνε)

Beside Πελιαοφόνος (?) and ἀνδροφόνος, Pindar's remaining compound of the nominal form of the root **g^{w}hen-* is ταυροφόνωι τριετηρίδι 'at the bull sacrifices at the

10. The stylistic figure is well described by Bundy 1962:13 n. 10.

triennial festival', which occurs in *Nem.* 6.40, in a context rich in allusions to the sophistication of poetic art. Compare the immediately following responsion figure, **τίμασε** . . . /**νικάσαντ'** . . . (41-3) 'brought honor . . . to the victor . . .' with the iconic phonetic figure discussed in chapters 3 and 12.

Pindar makes another conscious reference in *Nemean* 6 (465? B.C.) to the basic formula, while at the same time using it. Achilles' killing of Memnon is here preceded by line 45:

> **π**λατεῖαι **π**άντοθεν λογίοισιν ἐντὶ **π**ρόσοδοι
>
> Wide are the ways from all sides, for the tellers of tales.

where we may note the triple alliteration. The brief tale is then told (52-4) precisely in the heroic version of the basic formula (chap. 49):

> HERO_1 SLAY HERO_2 (with WEAPON)
>
> φαεννᾶς υἱὸν εὖτ' **ἐνάριξεν** 'Αόος ἀκμᾶι
> ἔγχεος ζακότοιο. καὶ ταῦτα μὲν παλαιότεροι
> ὁδὸν ἀμαξιτὸν εὗρον· ἕπομαι δὲ καὶ αὐτὸς ἔχων μελέταν
>
> (Achilles) when he **slew** the son of shining Dawn with
> the point of his angry spear. Such is the passable way that
> men before me discovered long ago; but I follow it also, carefully.

Lines 47 and 53-4 are another explicit reference to the basic formula with the same language; (πρόσ)οδος, ἀμαξιτός, like the 'shortcut' (οἶμος βραχύς) of *Pyth.* 4.247-50.[11] The HERO_1 Achilles, named only in the preceding clause, SLEW (ἐνάριξεν) HERO_2 (Memnon) with a WEAPON (ἀκμᾶι ἔγχεος). That Pindar uses the verb ἐνάριξεν here as a variant of πέφνεν is indicated by the use of the latter in the reference to the same myth in the earlier ode *Isth.* 5.39-41 (478? B.C.):

> λέγε, τίνες Κύκνον, τίνες Ἕκτορα **πέφνον**,
> καὶ στράταρχον Αἰθιόπων ἄφοβον
> Μέμνονα χαλκοάραν;
>
> Say, who **slew** Kuknos, who Hektor,
> and the fearless marshal of the Aithiopians,
> Memnon armored in bronze?

Yet even more striking is Pindar's motivation for this substitution of ἐνάριξεν—his only attested use of this verb—for πέφνεν. In *Nem.* 6.52 (465? B.C.) Pindar uses **ἐνάριξεν** 'slew' in a version of the basic formula with a periphrasis of Memnon: 'the son of shining Dawn'. A dozen or so years before in *Isth.* 5.39ff. (478? B.C.) he had

11. Compare Odysseus' hurried summation to his father in *Od.* 24.324-26. See chap. 49.

given the killing in a rhetorical question, but with the verb πέφνον and a straightforward naming and identification of the victim:

πέφνον – στράταρχον Αἰθιόπων – ∪ ∪ Μέμνονα

slew . . . the marshal of the Aithiopians . . . Memnon.

The latter too had a formulaic precursor a dozen years before, in 490 B.C. In *Pyth.* 6.31-2 Pindar referred to Memnon in the context of his killing of Nestor's son Antilokhos, with the same straightforward name and identification, but with another epithet clearly of his own creation:

ἐναρίμβροτον . . . στράταρχον Αἰθιόπων Μέμνονα

the **man-slaying** marshal of the Aithiopians, Memnon.

It is the inexorable logic of the basic formula that Memnon once identified as 'man-**slaying**' (**ἐναρι-**) for the killing of Antilokhos must then be **slain** with the same root (**ἐνάριξεν**) in the formulaic reciprocal, the "slayer slain" (chap. 31).

The death of Memnon at the hands of Achilles, avenging the death of Antilokhos, was narrated in the Epic Cycle, in the *Aithiopis* of Arktinos. The summary of Proklos (p. 106.4-6 Allen) laconically gives the heroic basic formula: 'Antilokhos is killed by Memnon in an encounter, and then Achilles kills Memnon.' These Pindaric passages and the figure of Memnon are discussed in the context of Pindar's relation to Homer and the Epic Cycle by Nagy 1990a:212ff. and especially 415ff., with reference to earlier commentators. While the story of Memnon that 'haunted Pindar's imagination' (Farnell, cited by Nagy) may well be drawn from the Cycle (the *communis opinio*), or from a 'continuum of epic tradition' (Nagy), the wording of Pindar's narration of it appears to go back straight to Homer, as does indirectly the very epithet ἐναρίμβροτος which Pindar coined.

We can observe the channel for its formation in the other Pindaric use of the word, in *Isth.* 8.48-55 (478 B.C.), again linked with Achilles and the killing of Memnon. The passage is introduced by the familiar inherited stylistic figure of the relative clause defining the Indo-European hero (chap. 28):

'Αχιλέος·
ὃ καὶ Μύσιον ἀμπελόεν
αἵμαξε Τηλέφου μέλα-
νι ῥαίνων **φόνωι** πεδίον
γεφύρωσέ τ' 'Ατρεΐδαι-
σι νόστον,'Ελέναν τ' ἐλύσατο, Τροΐας
ἶνας ἐκταμὼν δορί, ταί νιν ῥύοντό ποτε
μάχας **ἐναριμβρότου**
ἔργον ἐν πεδίωι κορύσ-
σοντα, Μέμνονός τε βίαν

ὑπέρθυμον Ἕκτορά τ' ἄλ-
λους τ' ἀριστέας

. . . Achilles; who made bloody the vine clad plain of Mysia,
sprinkling it with the black **blood** of Telephos,
and bridged the way for the Atreidai to return home,
and released Helen, cutting out with his spear
the sinews of Troy, who once had hindered him
from marshalling on the plain the work of **man-slaying** war:
Memnon of overweening power, and Hector, and the other heroes.

Homeric formulaic reminiscences—down to the order of the elements—include γεφύρωσε . . . νόστον (*Il.* 15.357 γεφύρωσεν δὲ κέλευθον 'bridged a way'), ἶνας ἐκταμὼν (*Il.* 17.522 ἶνα τάμηι διά 'cut through the sinew'), μάχας . . . ἔργον κορύσσοντα (*Il.* 2.273 πόλεμόν τε κορύσσων 'marshalling war'). The immediate model for (μάχας) ἐναρίμβροτου, as noted already by Frisk (GEW s.v. ἔναρα), is *Il.* 13.339 μάχη φθεισίμβροτος 'man-destroying war', following ἐναιρέμεν ὀξέϊ χαλκῶι at the end of the immediately preceding line 338 (and cf. *Od.* 22.297, of Athena's aegis). The word φθεισίμβροτος occurs only once in the *Iliad*, but we have four examples there of the semantically nearly identical πόλεμον φθεισήνορα 'man-destroying war'.

Returning to *Pyth.* 6 and the death of Antilokhos at the hands of Memnon, we find the compound Homeric formulaic epithet of war φθεισίμβροτος transformed and transferred to each of the two heroes in one of its two constituents each. The root φθι- of φθεισίμβροτος is first extracted, and then the compound is semantically copied as ἐναρί-μβροτος. Lines 30-32 of *Pyth.* 6 introduce the subject by the familiar device of the relative:

Ἀντίλοχος . . .
ὃς ὑπερ**έφθιτο** πατρός, **ἐναρίμβροτον**
ἀναμείναις στράταρχον Αἰθιόπων
Μέμνονα

Antilokhos . . ., who **died for** his father, standing up to the
man-slaying marshal of the Aithiopians, Memnon.

Pindar in his reworking of the formula has taken the Homeric epithet and deftly created out of it the setting for a "slayer slain" theme. Both the compound verb ὑπερέφθιτο 'perished for, died for' and the epithet ἐναρίμβροτος 'man-slaying, man-killing' are as far as we can tell creations of Pindar himself, and they stretch the limits of syntax and morphology alike. But their effect is to recreate the ancient theme and formula far older than Pindar:

$$\overrightarrow{\underleftarrow{\text{HERO}_1 \quad \text{SLAY} \quad \text{HERO}_2}}.$$

And again it is the inexorable logic of the bidirectional, reciprocal basic formula, asymmetrically loaded with active epithet for Memnon 'man-**killing**' (**ἐναρι-**), but passive-equivalent verb **'died** = was killed' (**-ἔφθιτο**) for Antilokhos, which requires the expression of the killing of Memnon at the hands of Achilles by the same active verb ἐνάριξεν.

That 25 years of Pindar's active creative life would elapse between his *Pythian* 6 (490 B.C.) and *Nemean* 5 (465 B.C.) is an interesting fact, but not necessarily a surprising one. The phrasing of the latter has in a sense a potential synchronic existence from the time of the creation of that of the former, and can be realized at any point. Just so the creation of ἐναρίμβροτος in 490 on the model of μάχη φθεισίμβροτος presupposed the intermediate formula μάχα ἐναρίμβροτος, even though the latter surfaces only in 478 (*Isthmian* 8). It is in this sense that I would interpret Nagy's notion of the 'continuum of epic tradition' which Pindar was dependent on—and contributed to.

Pindar was a highly self-conscious verbal artist, as we noted, just as were the Vedic kavis, and in the passages cited earlier from *Nemean* 6 (465 B.C.) and *Pythian* 4 (463 B.C.) he makes explicit reference to the basic formula, the basic formulaic system which is far older than he. In the passable way (ὅδον ἁμαξιτόν) discovered of yore (παλαίτεροι ... εὗρον), the shortcut which Pindar knows (οἶμον ἴσαμι βραχύν) and follows (ἕπομαι δὲ καὶ αὐτός) to be a leader in poetic art (ἄγημαι σοφίας), we have the answer to Helmut Rix's question,[12] 'How did Pindar learn Indo-European poetics?' Pindar learned the formulas that vehicled in unbroken fashion the Indo-European poetic tradition just as he learned the language that continued unbroken the Indo-European linguistic tradition.[13]

---

12. In a review of an earlier version of this essay (1990).

13. Recall Meillet's famous dictum (1937:35): 'We will call *Indo-European language* every language which at any time whatever, in any place whatever, and however altered, is a form taken by this ancestor language, and which thus continues by an uninterrupted tradition the usage of Indo-European.'

Snorri Sturluson (1179-1241), Icelandic author of the handbook for poets which is the *Prose Edda*, learned Old Norse, Germanic, and Indo-European poetics in the same way, be it noted.

37

Expansion of the formula: A recursive formulaic figure

We saw in the preceding chapter Pindar's *Pyth.* 4.249-50 with its tripartite formula,

> **κτεῖνε** μὲν γλαυκῶπα τέχναις ποικιλόνωτον **ὄφιν**,
> ὦ 'Αρκεσίλα, κλέψεν τε Μήδειαν σὺν αὐτᾷ, τὰν Πελίαο(-)**φονόν**
>
> By guile he **slew** the green-eyed **serpent** of the burnished scales,
> O Arkesilas, and stole away Medeia, with her good will,
> she that was **bane** to Pelias.

with each member at both verse- and clause- or sentence-boundary focus position. The use of the nominal form of *$g^{u}hen$- φονός/-φόνος here has an etymological consequence, for it is an etymological figure. According to the principle of ring-composition it re-establishes the underlying form of the initial verb κτεῖνε: the repetition repeats not the surface form but the underlying, "deep" form of the ancient formula. Beneath

> κτεῖνε . . . ὄφιν . . . φονός,

with preposed verb and object, we can read

> *πέφνε . . . ὄφιν . . . φονόν,

with etymological and phonetic figure (πέ**φν**ε . . . ὄ**φι**ν . . . **φ**ονόν) superimposable on Vedic

> áhann áhim.

Both reflect an Indo-European prototype

> *(é)g^{u}hent óg^{u}him.

It is rare for an Indo-European poetic formula to be so surely identifiable. The Indo-European formula has two members, but this version of the formula in Greek has three.

Let there be no doubt about the etymological figure κτεῖνε . . . ὄφιν . . . φονός from underlying *πέφνε . . . ὄφιν . . . φονός. Pindar says of Orestes in *Pyth.* 11. 36-7:

> ἀλλὰ χρονίωι σὺν Ἄρει
> **πέφνεν** τε **ματέρα** θῆκέ τ' Αἴγισθον ἐν **φοναῖς**
>
> and with late-visited Ares
> **slew** his **mother**, and laid Aigisthos low in his **blood**

Here again we have an etymological figure πέφνεν . . . ματέρα . . . ἐν φοναῖς, with the keywords at verse boundary, functioning as a phonetic ring-composition; we have again no overt subject in the sentence; and we have again the word order Verb - Object for the narration of the killing of the monster, who is this time the hero's mother.

Hayden Pelliccia (p.c.) points out that Clutaimestra is thus formulaically identified as a snake, just as she is called ἔχιδνα at Aeschylus *Ch.* 249 and 994, a μύραινα at 994, one of two δράκοντε at 1047, and an ἀμφίσβαινα ἢ Σκύλλα τις at *Ag.* 1233, there following θῆλυς ἄρσενος φονεύς 1231.[1]

Yet another example of the basic formula with the same tripartite etymological figure in ring-composition recurs in Bacchylides, with the inverse or reciprocal version of the formula which we saw in Vedic and other languages in chap. 31. Beside the accusative of the serpent as object in the cases we have seen, all of the underlying pattern

> πέφνε . . . ὄφιν . . . φόνο-,

Bacchylides furnishes the inverse, with the nominative of the serpent as subject (*Ode* 9.12-14):

> ἄθλησαν ἐπ' Ἀρχεμόρωι, τὸν ξανθοδερκής
> **πέφν'** ἀωτεύοντα **δράκων** ὑπέροπλος
> σᾶμα μέλλοντος **φόνου**
>
> contested over Arkhemoros, whom the enormous
> tawny-eyed **dragon slew** in his sleep,
> a sign of the **slaughter** to come.

1. There are older precedents. The dying king Hattusilis I disinherits his son for heeding not his word but that 'of his mother, the snake', *annaš-šaš* MUŠ[*-aš*] HAB ii 10 (Akkadian AMA-*ŠU ŠA* MUŠ), repeating ten lines later 'his mother is a snake!' *annaš-šiš* MUŠ*-aš* ii 20. As noted by Sommer in his and Falkenstein's classic edition (1938), the old king held to the metaphor: KBo 3.27 = BoTU 10β 25-27 (Edict, CTH 5) 'When you don't fan the fire on the hearth, then the snake will come and wrap the city of Hattusas in its coils,' *m*[*ān*]*-šan haššī p*[*aḫ*]*ḫur natta paraišteni ta uizzi* ^{UR}[^{U}*Ha*]*tt*[*ušan*] MUŠ*-aš ḫulāliazzi*. For other Greek and Hittite thematic coincidences see chap. 46, as well as Puhvel 1991.

Again we find the key words of the ring-composition etymological figure in verse-initial and verse-final focus position. Underlyingly the pattern is the same, save that the case marking has been switched:

πέφνε . . . ὄφις . . . φόνο-

Bacchylides furnishes another good example of the use of πεφνέμεν in the basic formula when a dragon or other fabulous beast kills a man. In *Ode* 5.115-16 the subject is the Calydonian boar:

θάπτομεν οὓς **κατέπεφνεν**
σῦς ἐριβρύχας ἐπαίσσων βίᾳ

To bury those whom the bellowing
boar had **slain** in his charge.

The Calydonian boar is also in *Il.* 9.540 the subject of the rare participle ἔθων from the basic formula variant root **u̯edh-* discussed in chapters 32 and 42.[2] For formulaic inversion in Indo-Iranian and Hittite see chap. 31.

Note finally that in both Bacchylides passages πέφνε precedes its object, dragon or other beast, just as the verb preceded its object the Gorgon in Greek and the serpent in Vedic and Avestan. The formula is once again asymmetric, but this time the focus is on the subject:

SERPENT (MONSTER) SLAY (**gʷhen-*) (ADVERSARY).

The final proof of the reality of the ring-composition etymological figure in the basic formula comes from a text older than Pindar, the Pythian sequence of the Homeric *Hymn to Apollo*, which must date from the beginning of the sixth century. The place of the foundation of the temple is that of the god's heroic exploit (300-4):

ἀγχοῦ δὲ κρήνη καλλίρροος, ἔνθα **δράκαιναν**
κτεῖνεν ἄναξ Διὸς υἱὸς ἀπὸ κρατεροῖο βιοῖο,
ζατρεφέα, μεγάλην, τέρας ἄγριον, ἣ κακὰ πολλὰ
ἀνθρώπους ἔρδεσκεν ἐπὶ χθονί, πολλὰ μὲν αὐτούς,
πολλὰ δὲ μῆλα ταναύποδ', ἐπεὶ πέλε πῆμα **δαφοινόν**.

But near by was a sweet flowing spring, and there with his strong bow the lord, the son of Zeus, **killed** the bloated, great **she-dragon**, a fierce monster wont to do great mischief to men upon earth, to men themselves and to their thin-shanked sheep; for she was a very **bloody** plague. [tr. Evelyn-White]

---

2. Meleager's killing of the Calydonian boar is assimilated to Apollo's killing of the dragon Python in the Sikyonian version of the myth, according to Fontenrose 1980:38 n. 4.

The enjambment of lines 300/301 δράκαιναν / κτεῖνεν . . . is the equivalent of the phrase κτεῖνε . . . ὄφιν of *Pyth*. 4.249; in both cases the verb is line-initial. And by a folk etymology which was manifest throughout antiquity, φοινός and δαφοινός 'blood-red, bloody' (the latter first attested here) were related to φόνος 'murder' and 'blood'. This relation between δαφοινόν, which closes the narration of the killing, and the semantically marked root φον- for 'kill', re-establishes an underlying formula δράκαιναν / *πέφνεν. The choice of the final adjective δαφοινός assures us that the sentiment for the inherited formula was still living and structured the narration.

The perceived relation (folk-etymology) of φόνος and (δα)φοινός is shown to be real by *Il*. 16.159 αἵματι φοινόν '(cheeks) red with blood' and *Il*. 16.162 φόνον αἵματος '(belching) blood and gore', in the same simile.[3] One should finally compare *Il*. 12.202 (= 220) φοινήεντα δράκοντα 'a blood-red serpent', where the epithet and noun, phonetically coordinated (φοινήεις is a Homeric hapax), echo the basic formula itself. D. Fehling's monumental work (1969) takes no notice of any of these figures, but their reality is certain.

Smitten by Apollo's arrow (the WEAPON), the she-dragon gives up the ghost in 361-2:

λεῖπε δὲ θυμὸν
φοινὸν ἀποπνείουσ', ὁ δ' ἐπηύξατο Φοῖβος 'Απόλλων

She left her life-spirit,
breathing out **gore**. And Phoibos Apollo boasted over her.

Here φοινόν closes the narrative begun with 300-4 δράκαιναν / κτεῖνεν . . . δαφοινόν above.

The participle ἀποπνείουσα describes other dragons as 'fire-breathing'. We saw above *Il*. 6.181-2:

χίμαιρα,
δεινὸν ἀποπνείουσα πυρὸς μένος αἰθομένοιο

The chimaira, breathing out the terrible power of burning fire.

The poet of the *Hymn to Apollo* lets the dragon give up the ghost with the echoing φοινὸν ἀποπνείουσα 'breathing out gore', which makes, as we have seen, a remarkable Saussurian anagram or hypogram of the name of the dragon-slayer, Phoibos Apollo, to complete the frame (362):

ΦΟΙνὸν **ΑΠΟ**πνείουσ', ὁ δ' ἐπηύξατο **ΦΟΙ**βος **ΑΠΟ**λλων.

. . . breathing out gore. And Phoibos Apollo boasted over her.

3. As pointed out by Bechert 1964, following Leaf[2] ad loc. and Chantraine 1949:146.

38

Herakles, the formulaic hero

The prototypical Greek hero is Herakles, and it is not surprising that we find the verb πεφνέμεν of his exploits and his labors, especially those involving giant- or monster-killing. In this respect he is like the Germanic god Thor and the Vedic god Indra. See in general the discussion and commentary in Bond 1981.

There is no overt subject in Hesiod *fr*. 43a 65 M.-W. (of Herakles):

ἐν Φλέγρηι δ]ὲ Γίγαντας ὑπερφιάλους **κατεπέφ[νε**

[In Phlegra] he **slew** the overweening Giants.

In Pindar *fr*. 171 the subject is probably Herakles (so Snell), but he is again not overt. The verb is in tmesis:

κατὰ μὲν φίλα τέκν' **ἔπεφνεν** θάλλοντας ἥβαι δώδεκ'

He **massacred** twelve dear children in the bloom of youth.

One should note the sentence-initial verbs and the deferred object and even further deferred subject in Pindar, *Isth*. 6.31-5:

εἷλε δὲ Περγαμίαν, **πέφνεν** δὲ σὺν κείνωι Μερόπων
ἔθνεα καὶ τὸν βουβόταν οὔρεϊ ἴσον
Φλέγραισιν εὑρὼν **Ἀλκυονῆ**, σφετέρας δ' οὐ φείσατο
χερσὶν βαρυφθόγγοιο νευρᾶς
Ἡρακλέης.

He **took** the city of Pergamon, and in the same hero's company **slew**
the hosts of the Meropes and the oxherd mountain-high,
Alkyoneus, encountered in the Phlegraian Fields. The hand
of **Herakles** spared not his deep-voiced bowstring.

We examined the first lines of the passage in chap. 36 for σὺν κείνωι 'with that one', the COMPANION in the basic formula.

Isthmian 6 just cited continues with a prayer of Herakles in whch he evokes his lion skin (48),

> ϑηρός, ὃν **πάμπρωτον** ἀέϑλων **κτεῖνά** ποτ' ἐν Νεμέαι
>
> of the beast that, **first** of all my labors, I **slew** long ago in Nemea.

The theme recalls the deeds of Indra *yā́ni cakā́ra prā́thamāni* 'which first he did' in RV 1.32.1.[1] In the Greek the verb is the unmarked κτείνω, and the word order is likewise unmarked. But in the context we may view that verb here as a resumption of the marked lexeme πέφνεν in marked clause-initial position earlier in line 31: the phenomenon of semantic spreading of the features of the first verb (πέφνεν) to the second (κτεῖνα). Note that both are unaugmented. That πεφνέμεν was long traditional in narrating the slaying of the Nemean lion may be gathered from *Anthol. graec.* 16.92.1 **πρῶτα** μὲν ἐν Νεμέῃ βριαρὸν **κατέπεφνε** λέοντα 'First he slew the mighty lion in Nemea.'

Such echoes with lexical substitution may extend even further, as we might expect with flexible formulas. Indeed, lexical substitution under semantic identity is one of the principal ways in which formulas undergo diachronic change. Hesiod, *fr.* 43a65 and Pindar, *Isth.* 6.31-3 above clearly point to πεφνέμεν as the traditional verb of narration of Herakles' exploits in the battle of the Gods and Giants on the plain of Phlegra. The phrases of *Isthmian* 6, composed in 480, are echoed by those of *Nemean* 1, composed in 476, in which Tiresias prophesies the future deeds of the infant Herakles, 62-3 and 67-8:

> ὅσσους μὲν ἐν χέρσωι **κτανών**
> ὅσσους δὲ πόντωι ϑῆρας ἀϊδροδίκας
> . . .
> καὶ γὰρ ὅταν ϑεοὶ ἐν
> πεδίωι Φλέγρας Γιγάντεσσιν μάχαν
> ἀντιάζωσιν
>
> all the beasts he must **slay** by land,
> all the beasts of the sea, brutes without right or wrong;
> . . .
> and how, when the gods in the plain of Phlegra meet the
> Giants in battle.

The mention of the beast adversaries and the Giants at Phlegra in *Nem.* 1.62 and 67

---

1. The theme is an enduring one. Compare from the Middle Irish (free) version of Statius' *Achilleid*, (ed. D. Ó hAodha), §6 *is é-seo dano cetgnim Aichil iarna geinemuin* 'This is moreover the first manly deed of Achilles after his birth.' Both the prose text (c 1150-1250) and the verse text (c. 1150) develop the inherited theme, dear to the Irish, of the "boyhood deeds" (*macgnima*) of Achilles. See chap. 54.

echoes that of *Isth.* 6.33 and 48 and enables us to invest κτανών in *Nem.* 1.62 with all the semantic overtones of a πεφνών.

Synchronically the text is a good example of a chiastic figure of ellipsis (gapping):

> ὅσσους μὲν ἐν χέρσωι [θῆρας] κτανών
> ὅσσους δὲ πόντωι θῆρας ἀϊδροδίκας [κτανών].

In view of the parallel, the gapped verb of *Nem.*1.63 could as well be [πεφνών].

Note also that there is another echo of *Isth.* 6.48 in *Nem.* 1.43:

> πειρᾶτο δὲ **πρῶτον** μάχας
>
> (the infant Herakles) made his **first** try of battle,
>
> θηρός, ὃν **πάμπρωτον** ἀέθλων κτεῖνά ποτ' ἐν Νεμέαι
>
> of the beast that, **first** of all my labors, I slew long ago in Nemea.

We find the same echo or resumption of marked πεφνέμεν by unmarked κτείνω in a heroic context in Bacchylides, *Dith.* 18.18-25, narrating the early heroic deeds of Theseus:

> ἄφατα δ' ἔργα λέγει κραταιοῦ
> φωτός· τὸν ὑπέρβιόν τ' **ἔπεφνεν**
> Σίνιν, ὃς ἰσχύι φέρτατος
> θνατῶν ἦν, Κρονίδα Λυταίου
> σεισίχθονος τέκος·
> σῦν τ' **ἀνδροκτόνον** ἐν νάπαις
> Κρεμμυῶνος ἀτάσθαλόν τε
> Σκίρωνα **κατέκτανεν**·
>
> Telling of deeds incredible done by
> a strong man. He **killed** overpowering
> Sinis, once the greatest in strength
> of men, being son to Kronid Lytaios
> (earthshaker, that is, Poseidon)
> killed, too, the **manslaughtering** wild boar
> in the valley of Kremmyon, and **killed**
> wicked and cruel Skiron.
> (tr. Lattimore)

Here ἔπεφνε (Σίνιν, VO) is gapped in the second exploit (σῦν) and resumed in the third by unmarked (Σκίρωνα) κατέκτανεν, in unmarked OV word order. Note that in the second exploit the epithet ἀνδροκτόνον 'man-slaying' of the boar furnishes an overt inverse of the basic formula, again with semantic spreading from the first ἔπεφνε to the unmarked -κτόνον. Theseus is not mentioned by name; at this point in the narrative the hero's identity is not yet known, and he is simply defined by his exploit. Like Kərəsāspa's in Iran, the Greek hero's monstrous adversaries can be robbers and highwaymen like Sinis and Skiron—outlaws who are as ἀϊδροδίκας 'lawless' as the θῆρας 'beasts' of *Nem.* 1.62. Compare Indra's adversaries who are *anyavratá-* 'who follow another commandment' (chap. 8), and Achilles to Hector at *Il.* 22.262-4.

Bacchylides' ἔπεφνε / Σίνιν is itself artfully echoed in Callimachus' only attested use of the verb (*Hymns* 2.91-2):

ἧχι λέοντα
Ὑψηῒς **κατέπεφνε** βοῶν **σίνιν** Εὐρυπύλοιο

where the daughter of Hypseus
slew the lion, **plunderer** of the cattle of Eurypylos.

In Sophocles *Trachiniae* we have an instance of lexical, indeed phrasal substitution. Herakles in his agony recounts six of his labors, addressing his hands, shoulders, breast and arms. Recall Achilles' 'man-**slaying** hands' (χεῖρας . . . ἀνδρο**φόνους**), thrice in the *Iliad* (18.317, 23.18, 24.478-9). *Trach.* 1089-1100:

ὦ χέρες χέρες,
ὦ νῶτα καὶ στέρν', ὦ φίλοι βραχίονες,
ὑμεῖς ἐκεῖνοι δὴ καθέσταθ' οἵ ποτε
Νεμέας . . .
λέοντ' . . .
βίᾳ κατειργάσασθε, Λερναίαν θ' ὕδραν,
διφυᾶ τ' . . ., στρατὸν
θηρῶν, . . .
Ἐρυμάνθιόν τε θῆρα . . .
. . .
. . . τόν τε . . .
δράκοντα μήλων φύλακ' ἐπ' ἐσχάτοις τόποις

O hands, hands, o shoulders and breast, o dear arms,
you it was who were there, when you subdued by force
the Nemean lion, . . . and the Hydra of Lerna,
and the two-natured host of beasts . . . and the
Erymanthian boar . . . and the dragon that
guarded the apples of the Hesperides.

With the phrase βίᾳ κατεργάζομαι 'overcome, subdue by force, finish off, kill' (cf. Herodotus 1.24.4) with the many monsters as object we are still in the world of the basic formula.

A series of good examples of semantic spread from nominal forms of the root

*g^{w}*hen-* are found in the great lament celebrating in narration the labors of Herakles in Euripides' play of that name (*Herc.* 348-450, esp. 359-435), where we find the following collocations, associating φον- with a constituent of the basic formula (e.g. the WEAPON) or other element:

364-7 τάν . . . Κενταύρων . . . γένναν
ἔστρωσεν τόξοις **φονίοις**
ἐναίρων πτανοῖς βέλεσιν

He laid low the race of Centaurs with **deadly** shafts,
slaying them with winged missiles,

375-9 τάν τε . . . δόρκα . . . συλήτειραν . . .
κτείνας, θηρο**φόνον** θεὰν
Οἰνωᾶτιν ἀγάλλει

And he **slew** the ravaging hind, and adorned the shrine
of Oinoë for Artemis **slayer** of beasts,

381-2 καὶ ψαλίοις **ἐδάμασσε** πώλους
Διομήδεος, αἳ **φονίαισι** φάτναις . . .

And with bridle he **mastered** the foals of Diomedes,
who in **gory** stables . . .

The next two exploits are told with the usual verbs of killing and no associated φον-:

391-2 Κύκνον ξεινο**δαΐκταν**[2]
τόξοις **ὤλεσεν**

He **slew** Kuknos **slayer** of strangers with his shafts,

compare τόξοις **φονίοις** in 366 above, and of the guardian of the apples of the Hesperides, simply

397-9 δράκοντα . . . **κτανών**

killing the dragon.

The last labors involving killing reintroduce φον-, reconfirming the investiture of its

2. The epithet may be imitated from Pindar *fr.* 140a.56 ξενοδα[ΐ]κτα βασιλῆος (King Laomedon of Troy), as suggested by Rutherford 1994. For other parallels see Bond 1981 ad loc. Euripides uses ξενοδαΐκτα of Kuknos at *Herc.* 391; also ξενοδαίτας 'devouring strangers' of the Kuklops (another opponent of Herakles) at *Cyc.* 658.

associative semantics into the unmarked κτείνω and transforming the latter into the dragon-killing, giant-killing verb par excellence:

419-24 τάν τε μυριόκρανον
πολύ**φονον** κύνα Λέρνας
ὕδραν ἐξεπύρωσεν,
βέλεσι τ' ἀμφέβαλ' ἰόν,
τὸν τρισώματον οἶσιν **ἔ-**
κτα βοτῆρ' Ἐρυθείας

And he burned out the thousand-headed Hydra, the **murderous** hound of Lerna, and spread her venom on the shafts with which he **slew** three-bodied Geryon the herdsman of Erytheia.[3]

From the first to the last of these exploits the themes are variations rung on the single formula

HERO | SLAY MONSTER (with WEAPON).

In the 102 lines of the choral passage the name of Herakles appears only in the final epode (442-50), which is no longer part of the narration of the labors nor of the lament proper. It is dramatically only a transition to the dialogue which follows. Once again the asymmetry of the basic formula is constant.

In the *Herakles* φόνος appears repeatedly (1016, 1021, 1034, 1052) in the lines following the herald's announcement of the hero's awful deed, the murder of his children and his wife.[4] The nouns invest Amphitruon's words to the chorus in 1061-3 with the full power of the basic mythographic formula:

Χο. εὕδει; Ἀμ. ναί, εὕδει γ' ὕπνον ἄυπνον ὀλόμε-
νον, ὃς **ἔκανεν** ἄλοχον, **ἔκανε** δὲ ψαλμῶι
τέκεα τοξήρει

Chorus: Does he sleep?
Amphitruon: Yes, he sleeps, but sleeps the un-sleep of the dead, for he **slew** his wife and **slew** his children with the twanging bow.

The pathos of the lines is heightened by the dochmiac meter, whose 'tone is always urgent or emotional', serving to express 'strong feeling, grief, fear, despair, horror

3. There must be a relation, conscious or otherwise, between this passage and (Ps.-)Euripides, *Rh.* 61-2, πρὶν ναῦς **πυρῶσαι** καὶ διὰ σκηνῶν μολεῖν / **κτείνων** Ἀχαιοὺς τῇδε **πολυφόνωι** χερί 'before burning the ships and going through the tents, slaying Achaeans with this murderous hand.' I leave to others the question of its relevance to the date and authorship of the *Rhesus*.

4. See chap. 41, on the saga of Iphitos and the hero as monster.

. . .', here against a background of verbal tradition (West 1982:108; Dale 1968:110). The sequence of two maximally resolved dochmiac metra, each metron-end coinciding with word-end, yields an extraordinary run of 16 short syllables, through the SLEEP, the KILLING, and the VICTIM; it is followed in Diggle's text by the two repeated metra ⏑ ⏑ ⏑ – – –, where the shorts carry more KILLING and VICTIMS, and the longs carry the WEAPON.

– – – – – | ⏑ ⏑ ⏑ ⏑ ⏑ ⏑ ⏑ ⏑
⏑ ⏑ ⏑ ⏑ ⏑ ⏑ ⏑ ⏑ | ⏑ ⏑ ⏑ – – –
⏑ ⏑ ⏑ – – – |

It is a remarkable interplay of synchronic metrics and diachronic verbal and thematic tradition. In the identical last two metra note that *ékane* and *tékea* in the three shorts are near-perfect anagrams of each other; *n* and *t* differ by only a single feature. See further on this passage and the theme of SLEEP chap. 56.

Some hundred lines further we find a recurrence of the link of κτείνω, καίνω with φόνος, φόνιος, and in the same dochmiac cola. Theseus asks Amphitruon over their corpses, 'Who are these children?' He answers (*Herc.* 1182-3):

ἔτεκε μέν νιν οὑμὸς ἶνις τάλας
τεκόμενος δ' **ἔκανε**, **φόνιον** αἷμα τλάς

My poor son begot them, and having
begotten them **slew** them; he bears the guilt of their **blood**.

The juxtaposition of the two is indexed by a double phonetic figure of repetition which serves as a frame: **ete**ke . . . **tek**omenos **d' ek**ane, **talas** . . . **tlas**. Both are at the same time etymological figures (with the phonetic echo of the first), and the first also involves the grammatical figure of the opposition of voice, active ἔτεκε and middle τεκόμενος.

Theseus then asks, 'Who is that among the corpses?' and Amphitruon answers (1190-3):

ἐμὸς ἐμὸς ὅδε γόνος ὁ πολύ**πονος**, ὃς ἐπὶ
δόρυ γιγαντο**φόνον** ἦλθεν σὺν θεοῖ-
σι Φλεγραῖον ἐς πεδίον ἀσπιστάς

This is my son, my son of the many **labors**, who
came with giant-**slaying** spear to the Phlegraian plain,
a fellow-warrior with the gods.

Note that *polúponos* 'of many labors' here differs from *polúp*^{h}*onos* 'of many slaughters' (line 420) by only a single feature, and is probably meant to suggest it. Theseus' final question is 'Why does he hide his head with his robes?', to which Amphitruon replies (1199-1201):

αἰδόμενος τὸ σὸν ὄμμα
καὶ φιλίαν ὁμόφυλον
αἷμά τε παιδο**φόνον**

Shame to meet your eye,
shame for the love of kinsmen, shame for the
blood of his **murdered** sons.

The tricolon of hemiepe with catalexis of the last (Dale 1968:175) is indexed by remarkable phonetic figures: the anaphoric initial rhymes αἰ- . . ., καὶ . . ., αἷ- . . ., παι- . . ., the internal φιλ- . . . -φυλ-, and the closing παιδοφόνον which echoes the opening αἰδόμενος.

In Amphitruon's last utterance in this whole lyric stichomythic dialogue with Theseus (1177-1213) he implores his son to uncover his face, and restrain his monstrous wild lion spirit, which impels him

δρόμον ἐπὶ **φόνιον** ἀνόσιον

to **murderous** unholy rage.

The horror of the slaying, as told by Amphitruon to Theseus, is eloquently foregrounded by the deployment of these four nominal forms in φον-: φόνιον αἷμα, δόρυ γιγαντοφόνον, παιδοφόνον and δρόμον . . . φόνιον.

In this moment of extraordinary dramatic tension the hooded Herakles himself is uncovered by Theseus and begins speaking. The verbal echoes of φόνος and φόνιος still lurk in the background, and emerge as he catalogues his labors:

1275 ὕδραν **φονεύσας** . . .

Slaying the Hydra . . .

followed by a clear indexical similarity, in verse-final position:

1279-80 τὸν λοίσθιον . . . **πόνον**,
παιδο**κτονήσας**

The last labor, . . .
slaying my children . . .

Compare Herakles' descent into Hades as πόνων τελευτάν 'the end of labors' (429) in the choral passage cited earlier. The mounting effect, sustained over 90 lines, of πολύπονος . . . γιγαντοφόνος (1192-3), παιδοφόνον (1201), φόνιον ἀνόσιον (1212), serves to spread over the newly minted verb παιδοκτονέω (first found in Euripides) the monstrousness of every unjust slaying in Greek literature heretofore. The HERO Herakles' realization that he has himself become a MONSTER is grist for Euripides' particular tragic mill; but it is only another parameter of the basic formula.

Herakles finally is dissuaded from suicide and resolves to keep his bow, the WEAPON that has been his companion through all his labors and trials, including the last, the slaying of his family. He imagines the bow saying to him, in the language that warriors speak (1380-1):

> ἡμῖν τεκν' **εἷλες** καὶ δάμαρθ'· ἡμᾶς ἔχεις
> παιδο**κτόνους** σούς.
>
> With us you **took** out children and wife; you bear us
> as your children's **slayers**.

In ἡμῖν 'with us' in the first clause the WEAPON occupies focus position, and is in the marginal instrumental dative case; for the verb SLAY is substituted the colloquial εἷλες 'took out'. In the second clause by the appositional παιδοκτόνους the WEAPON has been promoted to underlying grammatical subject of the verb SLAY in the second element of the compound παιδοκτόνους, with the same pregnant semantics as the participle παιδοκτονήσας in the same verse-initial position 100 lines before. When the hero's weapons talk to him, they use the basic formula.

39

Hermes, Enualios, and Lukoworgos: The Serpent-slayer and the Man-slayer

The anonymous tragic fragment Tr G F 2, Adesp. 199,

> ἀργῆν ἔπεφνεν
>
> slew the serpent,

gives the bare basic formula, with an obscure word for a kind of snake, also found as ἀργᾶς, and probably a derivative of ἀργός 'white, brilliant; swift' (Chantraine, DELG s.v. ἀργός).[1] The meaning is clear, cf. Hippocrates, *Epid.* 5.86 ἀργῆς ὄφις, and the citation in Hesychius (α 7040 L.) from which the fragment comes: ὄφιν· ἔστι δὲ ἐπίθετον δράκοντος. Cf. also Sud. ἀργόλαι· εἶδος ὄφεων.

Hayden Pelliccia pointed out to me years ago that the formulaic fragment ἀργῆν ἔπεφνεν must provide the explanation of the compound divine epithet or epiclesis 'Αργεϊφόντης, notably of Hermes (as always in Homer) and, rarely, of Apollo (Sophocles, *fr*. 1024).

This explanation 'serpent-slayer' was clearly current already in antiquity; compare the references in LSJ s.v., especially Eustathius p. 183.12 ἐν τῷ Παυσανίου λεξικῷ φέρεται ἀργεϊφόντης· ὁ ὀφιόκτονος. ἄργην γάρ, φησιν, ἔνιοι τὸν ὄφιν καλοῦσιν 'In Pausanias' lexicon ἀργεϊφόντης is glossed "serpent-slayer". For some, he says, call the snake ἄργης'.

That the epithet meant 'slayer of Argos' is morphologically and phonologically very unlikely, *pace* Chantraine, Frisk, and the Lex. frühgriech. Ep. Compare the discussion of 'Αργεϊφόντης in M.L. West's commentary on Hesiod, *Works and Days* 368-9, though his adoption of the suggestion 'dog-slayer' is no better; there is no

1. Semantically compare the formulaic Old Norse phrase *enn fráne ormr* 'the speckled worm', of the dragon Fáfnir (*Skírnismál* 27.4, *Fáfnismál* 19, 26, and nearly a half-dozen other passages).

reasonable explanation for the replacement of a perfectly well-attested Caland form ἀργι- by an opaque ἀργεϊ-. Nor is F. Bader's 'qui maîtrise la brilliance/vision' at all convincing, either semantically or thematically (1984:102-8; 1985:107; 1986:132-5; 1989:27). The suffix of ἀργῆς/ᾶς 'serpent', whatever its preform may be—the handbooks are of no help—must be a component of the pseudo-Caland form Ἀργεϊφόντης, from an **arge*X-*i*-.[2]

The compound ἀργεϊ-φόντης with its peculiar suffix form in the first member is clearly the source of the Homeric ἀνδρεϊφόντης 'man-slaying' epithet of the ancient war god Enualios, of Mycenean age.[3] As has been long known, this epithet must be scanned ⏑ ⏑ – ⏓ in *Il.* 2.651 etc. (hexameter final)

Ἐνυαλίωι ἀνδρεϊφόντηι,

and must therefore be restored with first member *anr̥*- (West 1982:13; Watkins 1986: 286ff.):

Ἐνυαλιωι ἀνr̥φόντηι (Com. Gk. -*tāi*).
⏑ – ⏑ ⏑ – ⏑ ⏑ – ⏓ #

The form *anr̥phóntās* thus arrived at can be equated exactly with the Mycenean Greek name *a-no-qo-ta* /anorq^{w}hontās/ (Lejeune 1972:203). The form in the *Iliad*, with its syllabic *r̥* still intact and counting metrically as a short vowel, preserves a shape linguistically older than the Mycenean name with the change *r̥* > *or* already accomplished; the Mycenean form would scan ⏑ – – ⏓, not ⏑ ⏑ – ⏓. Homeric Ἐνυαλίωι ἀνδρεϊφόντηι thus continues a poetic formula in epic meter which belongs linguistically to the Bronze Age, to the mid-second millennium B.C. The divinity himself is attested precisely in that period, Mycenean *e-nu-wa-ri-jo* (KN V 52).

The second compound member -φόντης (-ᾱς), Myc. /-q^{w}hontās/ thus belongs to the Bronze Age as well, and the compound Ἀργεϊφόντης, whose Homeric scansion is always the line-final adonic – ⏑ ⏑ – ⏓, can certainly claim the same antiquity. The formulaic phrase ἀργῆν ἔπεφνεν provides the syntactic link to its interpretation.

Pelliccia himself in a personal communication very aptly adduced to ἀργῆν ἔπεφνεν Aeschylus, *Eum.* 181-4 (Apollo threatening the Furies and driving them out of Delphi):

μὴ καὶ λαβοῦσα πτηνὸν **ἀργηστὴν ὄφιν**
χρυσηλάτου θώμιγγος ἐξορμώμενον
ἀνῇς ὑπ' ἄλγους μέλαν' ἀπ' ἀνθρώπων ἀφρόν,
ἐμοῦσα θρόμβους οὓς ἀφείλκυσας **φόνου**

Lest you receive a **glistening** winged **snake**
sped from my gold-wrought bowstring,

2. Like ἐγχεσ-ί-μωρος (Celtic -*māros* in compounds), with analogically restored -σ-.
3. West ibid., citing Debrunner 1917:17.

and heave up in torment the black froth of men,
vomiting the clots which you have drained from **slaughter**.

We can observe in this magnificent inversion of the basic formula the same lexical elements in collocation, reinforced by the framing verse-final focus position (and the intervening homoeoteleuton **-ον** . . . **-ον** preparing φόν**ον**). The two tragic passages are sufficient to anchor Ἀργεϊφόντης as encapsulating a variant of the basic formula of Indo-European poetic tradition—whatever underlies its application to Hermes[4] — just like *vərəϑrayan-* and *ahihan-* or *nərə.gar-*, *nr̥han-*, *jə̄nnar-*, *vīrənjan-*, and *a-no-qo-ta* /anorqʷhontās/, or later Greek Γιγαντοφόνος, Γοργοφόνος (Euripides), Κενταυροφόνος (Theocritus), and, replacing /anorqʷhontās/, ἀνδροφόνος (already Homer).

The last compound, ἀνδροφόνος 'man-slayer', is found eleven times in the *Iliad* as an epithet of Hector, three times of Achilles' hands and once of the hero Lukoworgos (*Il.* 6.134). The "new" epithet ἀνδρο**φόνος** seems to have sinister or at least ambiguous overtones; Hector of course will be slain by Achilles, and Lukoworgos, whose saga is briefly told by Diomedes in *Il.* 6.130ff., comes to a bad end, blinded by Dionysus the son of Zeus for his hybris (*Il.* 6.139).[5]

Another Lukoworgos figures also in old Nestor's harangue of the battles of his youth in *Iliad* 7. The two are unrelated, but thematically and formulaically they pattern alike in the text. The god Ares had given a suit of armor to the club-wielding (n.b.) hero Areïthoos. In an unheroic, 'ANTI-HERO' version of the basic formula (7.142-3),

τὸν Λυκόοργος **ἔπεφνε** δόλωι, οὔ τι κρατεΐ[6] γε,
στεινωπῶι ἐν ὁδῶι

Him Lukoworgos **slew** by guile, not by strength at all,
in a narrow road,

---

4. We can only speculate that the myth of the slaying of *Argos* represents in its particulars a reworking of an older myth in which the god Hermes' adversary was a SERPENT, styled ἀργῆς or an ancestor thereof. That the name Ἀργεϊφόντης was still applied to another known dragon-slayer like Apollo is significant, as is the morphological parallelism of the even more opaque name Βελλεροφόντης. Bader's invocation of the root *$g^{w}el$- 'throw; die; cause to die' (Luvian, Germanic) is in view of the opaque morphology a mere guess devoid of substance. Kirk in his commentary notes that 'Zenodotus' preference for ***Ellerophontes*** (so Eustathius p. 289.39 etc.) remains obscure.' Should we think of Hittite ***Illuyankaš***, variant ***Elliyankuš***?

5. Recall that Pindar uses ἀνδροφόνων (*Pyth.* 4.252) only of the Lemnian women, 'who murdered their husbands'. The sense of the Pindaric compound is different from that of the Homeric one in that the former is an "event agent noun", which presupposes that the event has occurred—the Lemnian women *had* slain their husbands—whereas the latter is a "non-event agent noun", which does not presuppose that the event has taken place: it is irrelevant to the epithet in 'man-slaying Lykourgos' whether he has slain anyone yet or not. He has the potential, or the function. Both values are found in English: a *coffee-grinder* may never have been used, but a *cradle-robber* is usually so styled only after the fact. I follow M. Hale, 'The syntax of agent nouns in Sanskrit' (forthcoming) in interpreting Vedic *-tŕ̥* (and Greek -τήρ) as "non-event agent noun" and *-́tr̥* (and Greek -τωρ) as "event agent noun". He follows Levin and Rappaport 1988:1067-83 on the similar values of English *-er*, as well as Benveniste 1948.

6. Perhaps a reference to the epithet 'strong', κρατερὸς Λυκόοργος at *Il.* 6.130.

where his club was of no avail. Lukoworgos stripped him of his armor (ἐξενάριξε, which metonymically has come to be a synonym of πεφνέμεν itself), and when he was old (ἐγήρα 7.148) gave it to Ereuthalion. He in turn was killed by Nestor, who boasts in the basic formula (7.155),

> τὸν δὴ μήκιστον καὶ κάρτιστον **κτάνον ἄνδρα**
>
> Him I **slew**, tallest and strongest of **men**.

For the stylistic force of the superlatives see chap. 50. Here unmarked κτάνον is a substitute and alternative for marked πεφνέμεν used 13 lines before.

The object ἄνδρα 'man' in line-final focus position is significant; the verb phrase is a syntactic realization of the compound ἀνδροφόνος. As such it effects an assimilation of Nestor—'I slew a man' (κτάνον ἄνδρα) in youth and have now grown old—to 'man-slaying' Lukoworgos (ἀνδροφόνοιο *Il.* 6.134), who killed a man in youth and then grew old (ἐγήρα *Il.* 7.148). We could as well translate ἄνδρα and ἀνδρο- in these phrases and compounds as 'hero'; and growing old is not the hero's end. The 'sinister or at least ambiguous overtones' of the epithet ἀνδροφόνος in epic context find their ready explanation in the heroic version of the basic formula, in which the adversary is not a monster but another hero:

> HERO_1 SLAY (*g^{u}*hen-*) HERO_2

Given the reciprocal, ambidirectional character of the action either Hero is potentially the slayer, and either is potentially the slain. The heroic versions of the basic formula and theme will be taken up in detail in part VI.

Let us return to the passages in *Iliad* 6 with which the discussion of the basic formula in Greece began: the meeting and verbal exchange on the battlefield between the Trojan Glaukos and the Greek Diomedes. As well as myths and legends it contains many cultural themes of great antiquity.

One such is the brief tale of Axulos, slain by Diomedes in 6.12 (Ἄξυλον δ' ἄρ' **ἔπεφνε** βοὴν ἀγαθὸς Διομήδης), who was rich and generous and lived by a high road whence he could dispense hospitality (14-15):

> **ἀφνειὸς** βιότοιο, **φίλος** δ' ἦν **ἀνθρώποισι**·
> πάντας γὰρ φιλέεσκεν **ὁδῷ ἔπι** οἰκία ναίων
>
> A **wealthy** man, and one **dear** to all **men**,
> for he dwelt in a home **by** the high **road**, and used to give
> entertainment to all.

He is a "brewy", in the Hiberno-English tradition, the reflex of Old Irish *briugu* 'hospitaler', the rich person whose societal *obligation* is to dispense hospitality to all wayfarers.[7] F. Motta astutely recognized a Celtic ancestor of the Irish *briugu* in the tradition of the (Celtic) Galatians in Asia Minor in Phylarchus, as quoted in Athenaeus, *Deipnosophistae* 4.150d-f (Motta 1985). The figure of Axulos and the etymology of *briugu* show that the tradition is far older than Irish or Celtic; his is an Indo-European societal function: the oldest philanthropist.

Another is the final ritual exchange of armor by Glaukos and Diomedes as pledge-tokens of mutual fidelity (πιστώσαντο, IE **bhidh-to-*), 6.233-6. Homer comments on the delusion of the senses which induced Glaukos to exchange gold armour for bronze—the Early Irish *diupert* 'unequal bargain'—but the anthropologist knows that in a potlatch the more flamboyantly and destructively generous one 'wins' (cf. Benveniste 1969:76). We should therefore pay close attention to the verbal expression of these traditional themes.

Diomedes begins the verbal exchange by asking the identity of his adversary (Glaukos), and in particular whether he is a man or god, for he would not wish to fight with immortal gods. He then tells the tale of Lukoworgos precisely as an exemplum of the latter folly, framing it with another 'I wouldn't like to fight with the blessed gods' (140), and an abrupt warrior's challenge, if he is mortal, to 'come closer, to get quicker to the ends of death' (143):

ἇσσον ἴθ', ὥς κεν **θᾶσσον** ὀλέθρου πείραθ' ἵκηαι.

The grammatical figure ('the closer, the quicker') is heightened by the phonetic figure, a perfect rhyme. Both words adjoin a metrical boundary, verse initial and caesura.

The nucleus of Diomedes' speech is the sacrilege of Lukoworgos, his frightening away the young god and attacking the nurses of Dionysos, making them drop their holy ritual objects (θύσθλα), (*Il.* 6.134-5):

ὑπ' ἀνδρο**φό**νοιο Λυκούργου
θεινόμεναι βουπλῆγι

Being **beaten with a cattle whip** by man-**slaying** Lukourgos.

The verb θείνω 'strike, beat' is the old present of the root **g^u^hen-* 'smite, slay'. It was semantically differentiated in Greek from the aorist and perfect system of the verb and the nominal derivatives, (ἐ)πεφν-, πεφα-, φατός, φόνος, by the phonological change of the labiovelar **g^u^h*, Mycenean Greek q^wh, to *th* before *e*, *i*, but to *ph* before *a*, *o* or consonant. Since the labiovelar is still intact in Mycenean Greek, the sound changes must have taken place at some point or points during the half millennium between Mycenean Greek and Homer, roughly the same distance as between Tyndale and today. It is thus not surprising that the verb θείνω, as in this example, has retained its special position in the basic formula, qua root **g^u^hen-*, despite its synchronic semantic differentiation.

7. For the social institution see D.A. Binchy, *Críth Gablach* s.v. Old Irish *briugu* is etymologically IE **bhr̥ĝh-u̯ōs* 'lofty, great', an epithet of 'wealth' in Vedic (*br̥hántaṃ ráyim* RV 9x, *br̥ható rāyáḥ* 2x etc., *br̥hádrayi-*).

Another example of ϑείνω (*g^{u}*hen-i̯o-*) retaining its linkage to the basic formula is furnished by Pindar, *Ol.* 7.27-30. The subject is Herakles' son Tlepolemos:

> καὶ γὰρ 'Αλκμήνας κασίγνητον νόϑον
> **σκάπτωι ϑενών**
> σκληρᾶς ἐλαίας **ἔκτανεν** Τίρυνϑι Λικύμνιον
> ἐλϑόντ' ἐκ ϑαλάμων Μιδέας
> τᾶσδέ ποτε χϑονὸς οἰκιστὴρ χολωϑείς
>
> For the destined founder of this land once in a rage
> **slew** in Tiryns the bastard brother of Alkmene,
> Likumnios, as he came from Midea's chamber,
> **smiting** him with a **stick** of hard olive.

Here the archaism ϑενών, originally the participle of the old athematic present of *g^{u}*hen-* (Ved. *hánti*) but revalued as aorist in Greek, spreads to the aorist ἔκτανεν from unmarked κτείνω the semantics of marked ἔπεφνεν. The formula is reinforced:

HERO	SLAY	ADVERSARY	with WEAPON
	(ἔκτανεν ϑενών)		(σκάπτωι ἐλαίας).

Note that it is heavily indexed by the extraordinary cluster of phonetic figures of partial similarity: *kasig***nēton** ***not**^{h}**on***, ***skap****tōi* . . . ***sklē****ras*, ***t**^{h}**enōn*** . . . *ek**tanen***, ***Tirunt**^{h}**i Likumn**ion*, ***Mideas tasde***, ***k**^{h}**t**^{h}**on**os* . . . ***k**^{h}**olōt**^{h}**eis***. The sentence is a thematic, formulaic, and artistic tour de force.

In *Il.* 6.134-5 we have a passive variant of the basic formula; but instead of a focus on the underlying object, the SERPENT, as in *ažīš . . . jaini* 'the serpent was slain', *ható vr̥tráḥ* 'slain is Vr̥tra', we find the focus on the underlying subject, the HERO as the overt agent of the passive verb: a relatively rare early Indo-European syntactic type and a correspondingly infrequent formulaic pattern. Syntactically,

by HERO are BEATEN (*g^{u}*hen-*) with WEAPON (ADVERSARIES).

The effect of this manipulation of the formula is to promote the underlying objects, the ADVERSARIES, to innocent victims, and to transform the underlying subject HERO into a monster. The root *g^{u}*hen-* in an epithet of the HERO (ἀνδρο**φόν**οιο) in this example enhances that effect.

It is notable that in 4 of the 5 Homeric occurrences of the name Λυκοόργος (*Lukoorgos*) the name resists contraction of the two identical short vowels, which elsewhere is the synchronic norm in Homer.[8] These include κρατερὸς Λυκόοργος in this very passage (*Il.* 6.130) and the three mentions of Λυκόοργος in Nestor's speech, *Il.* 7.142, 144, 148. The contraction of the name in this example in *Il.* 6.134, in an artistically manipulated and archaic occurrence in the basic formula is surprising, the

8. The name originally had a digamma, with retracted accent from a *luko-worgós* 'shutting out the wolf', to (ἐ)έργω (Frisk, Chantraine)

more so since the passage as a whole, Diomedes' homiletic address, is a unified whole, demarcated by a near-repetition at beginning and end.

The metrical form of the name in *Il.* 6.134 in fact presents two anomalies: the contraction of Λυκοοργ- to Λυκουργ-, and the verse-final genitive in -ου,

ὑπ' ἀνδροφόνοιο Λυκούργου
⏑ | – ⏑ ⏑ | – ⏑ ⏑ | – ⏑̄ #,

unresolvable into any of the older monosyllabic variant forms of the thematic genitive singular like -οι', -ο'.[9]

Now the passive participle θεινόμεναι in our example has an agent, as above: syntactically the 'classical' Greek ὑπὸ + genitive. But historically in Greek and all the other Indo-European languages attested in the second millennium B.C., the agent of the passive is expressed by the instrumental case.[10]

The consensus of scholars is that Mycenean Greek has an instrumental case. The instrumental plural case marker *-pi/-phi* was clearly recognized at the very outset of Mycenean studies, and since no language has more cases in the plural than in the singular, it follows a priori that there must have been an instrumental singular. As indeed most Mycenologists assume, the form of this case in the Mycenean Greek thematic *o*-stems was doubtless *-ō*, in the syllabary <-o>, thus falling together graphically with the nominative and other cases as well. The ending is cognate with the Indic and Iranian instrumental in *-ā* and the Lithuanian instrumental in *-u* from **-uo*.

Both metrical anomalies in *Il.* 6.134 disappear if for the agent of the passive verbal participle θείνομεναι, the epithet and name

ὑπ' ἀνδροφόνοιο Λυκούργου,

we restore the instrumental case forms which the syntax and morphology of the Greek language a few centuries before Homer would have required:

*[hup'] andraphónō Lukowórgō
*[ὑπ'] ἀνδραφόνω Λυκοϝόργω.
[⏑] – ⏑ ⏑ – ⏑ ⏑ – ⏑̄ #

The instrumental would have been originally used without preposition, as in cognate languages in the second millennium B.C. The thematic instrumental in **-ō* probably first merged with the thematic ablative in **-ōt* (**-ōd*), obligatorily by the time of the loss of final stops in pre-Greek. The new instrumental-ablative case in **-ō* might have been used with the preposition *hupo* to express the agent of a passive, and our reconstructed half-line could equally well reflect that stage.[11]

9. Cf. for the classic discussion of the issues Chantraine 1973:166, 194.

10. See Jamison 1979a and 1979b, and Melchert 1977.

11. See now in detail Hajnal 1994:§27. Subsequently the ablative-instrumental merged functionally with the genitive in the thematic declension in Greek (in athematics the genitive functioned also as ablative since Proto-Indo-European); whence alphabetic Greek ὑπὸ + gen., ἀπὸ + gen. etc.

If it is objected that the earlier composition form of 'man' would have been **anr̥-* (whence Mycenean *anor-* but *andr-* before vowel, and also Old Attic *andra-* < *anra-* < *anr̥* in ἀνδραφόνος itself [on which see chap. 52]), we may as easily assume a metrical lengthening:

ānr̥phonō
– ᴗ ᴗ –

just as in ἀνέρε(ς), ἀνέρα, – ᴗ ᴗ in Homer in the same metrical slot, and doubtless the instrumental and locative plurals **ānr̥phi, *ānr̥si.*

In either case *Il.* 6.134 has every likelihood of containing a striking linguistic archaism. It is scarcely accidental both that such archaisms often tend to occur at thematically archaic junctures like the basic formula, and that their elimination in the text produces a cluster of characteristically 'late' features such as contracted Λυκούργου and verse-final genitive in -ου.

40

Nektar and the adversary Death

At the conclusion of chap. 34, as well as several times in chap. 35, we noted the formulaic manifestation of an Indo-European eschatology, a doctrine of final things: what is crossed over and thus overcome is death. The formula is:

HERO | OVERCOME (*$terh_2$-) DEATH. |

The presence of a HERO is unnecessary, and reflects a personalization of the verbal action viewed as agonistic: only the predicate, the boxed formula, is essential.

This formula is most familiar in the etymological analysis of the Greek compound νέκταρ proposed first by Jakob Grimm and vigorously championed by Paul Thieme (1952). Nectar and ambrosia are the nourishment of the blessed gods, and magically protect the corpse of a mortal from corruption (*Il.* 19.38f.):

Πατρόκλωι δ' αὖτ' ἀμβροσίην καὶ νέκταρ ἐρυθρὸν
στάξε κατὰ ῥινῶν, ἵνα οἱ χρὼς ἔμπεδος εἴη

On Patroklos she shed ambrosia and red nectar
through his nostrils, so that his flesh might be lasting.

Greek νέκταρ reflects *neḱ-tr̥h_2-* to the root of Latin *nex*: 'das über die (Todes-) Vernichtung hinwegrettende', the nectar which 'overcomes death'. It remained for Thieme's student Rüdiger Schmitt (1961) to show the same formula analytically deployed in Vedic, in a repeated verse of the Atharvaveda, again, like nectar, of a comestible (4.35.1, 6 and 2):

ténaudanénā́ti **tarāṇi mr̥tyúm**

by that rice-mess let me **overpass** death,

yénā́**taran** bhūtakr̥tó 'ti **mr̥tyúm**

by which the being-makers **overcame death**.

Thieme 1965 adduced Iśopaniṣad (= VS 40) 14:

vināśéna **mṛtyúm tīrtvā́** sámbhūtyāmṛ́tam aśnute

after having **crossed death** by destruction, he reaches immortality by becoming.

It is striking that in this passage the three inherited lexical items

vi**nāśé**na . . . **tīr**tvā́ . . . **amṛ́t**am . . .

recapitulate in the same order the Homeric Greek (*Il*. 19.347) noun phrase

νέκ-ταρ τὲ καὶ **ἀμβροσί**ην

nectar and ambrosia.

The two nouns in early Greek may appear in either order, cf. the Homeric passage cited above. Together they are the formulaic expression of an Indo-European eschatological doctrine. Schematically, in root form:

*neḱ- terh$_2$- n̥-mṛto-.

The adjective **n̥-mṛto-* 'undying, immortal' sets off the gods from human beings and defines them in the Indo-European world. Like Greek ἀμβροσία, Vedic *amṛ́tam* is also the food or drink of immortality. To reach *amṛ́tam*, **n̥-mṛto-*, is to reach the gods.[1] Just this doctrine recurs in the Hittite rituals for the dead: having passed over death the defunct is with the gods beyond. Compare the following (Otten 1958:96):

akkanza kuiš n=an=kan *ŠUM-ŠU* ḫalziššai n=aš=kan DINGIR^{MEŠ}-aš kuedaš anda, nu apuš DINGIR^{MEŠ} kattan šarā memiškanzi *INA* ^{É}šinapši=war=aš pait

He calls the dead man by name, and the gods with whom he is say up: "He has gone to the Cedar-House".

Compare also the Hieroglyphic Luvian inscription on the tomb destined for the last Hittite king Suppiluliumas II, discovered in 1988, as read by David Hawkins: "this is actually the building inscription . . . the structure is described as a (DEUS) *202 . . ., a ligature of STONE + EARTH + ROAD . . ., the hier. equivalent of cun.

1. Cf. Grassmann s.v. *amṛ́tam*: 'das Unsterbliche als Gesamtheit der Götter; das Unsterbliche als Götterwelt; der Unsterblichkeitstrank, ἀμβροσία'.

DKASKAL.KUR. The term should indicate an entrance to the Underworld . . ."[2] The "divine stone earth road" is precisely a *tarentum*, a *tīrthám*, a 'crossing place', overcoming death into the great beyond.

Overcoming death is only a special variant of the basic formula,

(HERO) OVERCOME (*$*terh_2$-*) ADVERSARY.

This formula is as we have seen reciprocal and reversible; we find also

ADVERSARY OVERCOME (*$*terh_2$-*) HERO,

as in the Hittite and Avestan texts in chap. 35. Here OVERCOME (*$*terh_2$-*) is itself only a special lexical variant of the basic formula with SLAY / SMITE (*$*g^{u}hen$-*, **u̯edh-*); as in

HERO SLAY (**u̯edh-*) ADVERSARY,

with its reciprocal

ADVERSARY SLAY (**u̯edh-*) HERO.

With the ultimate adversary Death we find precisely the last formula in a healing spell in the Atharvaveda (8.2.5):

áyaṃ jīvatu mā́ mr̥ta
imā́ṃ sám īrayāmasi
kr̥ṇómi asmai bheṣajám
mŕ̥tyo mā́ púruṣaṃ vadhīḥ

Let this man live; let him not die;
him we send together;
I make a remedy for him;
Death, do not slay the man.

In a three-verse strophe (*tr̥cas*) in RV 1.38.4-6, the poet asks the Maruts for immortality; he expresses himself obliquely, and his tone suggests he knows he will be disappointed. 'If I were in your place,' he implies,

stotā́ vo amŕ̥taḥ syāt

Your singer would be immortal.

2. Letter of 8 May 1989 to Heinrich Otten, as cited in Neve and Otten 1989. On the Hittite term and the geographical feature in Turkey see Gordon 1967.

. . .
mā́ vo . . . jaritā́ . . .
pathā́ yamásya gād úpa

Let not your singer
wander over the paths of Yama (god of the dead).

mó ṣú naḥ párāparā
nírr̥tir durhā́ṇā vadhīt
padīṣṭá tŕ̥ṣṇayā sahá

Let not baneful Nirr̥ti slay
us well, sooner or later;
let her perish together with drought.

The subject of SLAY (*u̯edh-) is not Death but the closely linked Indic notion of nírr̥ti 'dissolution, destruction, chaos, goddess of death (devī́ RV 7.37.7)'.

We noted in the earlier chapters the theme of overcoming death with the root *terh₂- marking the conditional or temporary victory. The arch-hero Herakles is involved in two separate episodes where the adversary whom he bests is Death.

One is the Alkestis myth, in which he wrestles with Death (Θάνατος) and succeeds in winning back Alkestis—temporarily, we understand—for her husband Admetos. The Admetos-Alkestis myth with its combat of Herakles and Thanatos is first narrated in full by Euripides in his play *Alcestis*; it was told earlier by Phrynichus, whose play survives only in a few fragments. But the scholiast to Euripides, *Alc.* 1 notes that the story was 'orally transmitted and popular': ἡ διὰ στόματος καὶ δημώδης ἱστορία (see Alexiou 1978). The theme probably belongs to the plane of universals—in the Thompson Motif-Index of Folk-Literature it is no. R.185, Mortal fights with "Death". Within Indo-European traditions we find an equivalent again in Norse mythology, as one of the feats of the visiting Æsir, visiting Jǫtunheim, the land of the giants: Thor's wrestling the old crone Elli, who turns out to be Old Age and who forces him to one knee (Snorri Sturluson, *Gylfaginning*).[3]

One should note as well the line of Herakles in Euripides, *Herc.* 1351 (with the manuscripts):

ἐγκαρτερήσω θάνατον

I shall endure against death.

Diggle and Murray prefer Wecklein's conjecture βίοτον 'life'. But the heroic motif in its Indo-European context favors the manuscript reading. The verb ἐγκαρτερέω as well recalls its other compound ἀποκαρτερέω 'starve oneself to death, go on a hunger

---

3. Thompson classifies this as motif no. H1149.3, under miscellaneous superhuman tasks. But the two tales are very similar.

strike against someone', which is an institution known also to Euripides (*I.T.* 973-4). This legal institution—the last recourse of the weak against the strong—is itself of Indo-European provenience and, as well as in Greece, is attested in India from the Dharmasūtras to Mahātma Gandhi and in Ireland from the Senchas Mār to Bobbie Sands (see Gernet 1982b:80).

As noted in chap. 27.2, J. Fontenrose in Python *passim* (and others before him) would identify many of Herakles' adversaries like Geryon, Cacus, and Antaeus as symbols of Death. I think rather that when the hero's monstrous adversary is Death he is called just that. Death is only one of the many manifestations of Chaos; he is just one of many monsters.

The other combat of Herakles and the adversary Death is narrated in *Il.* 5.395-404, where Herakles fights with Hades ('Αΐδης) at Pylos, wounds him with an arrow (the WEAPON), and drives him from the fray. Hades in this passage is described as a πελώριον 'monster'. Here again the Hero can overcome Death in a temporary victory. But Death cannot die or be killed, *Il.* 5.402:

οὐ μὲν γάρ τι καταθνητός γε τέτυκτο

For (Hades) was not made to be mortal.

Death is never the object of the verb *g^{u}hen-*.

Yet a number of indications point to the existence of an underlying "ideal" theme

HERO SLAY (g^{u}hen-*) DEATH,

that never surfaces in overt formula.[4] One may note first that this potential formula is in a sense the definition of the divine, of the gods as im-mortal (securely reconstructed as **n̥-mr̥to-*). The Hero may transcend his own mortality—'slay Death'—and attain immortality, as the arch-hero Herakles did in one Greek tradition. For India compare the Iśopaniṣad passage cited above.

The root **g^{u}hen-* does in fact occur in the narrative of the combat of Herakles and Hades. Herakles wounded Hades with the arrow and

ὀδύνῃσιν ἔδωκεν

gave him to pain.

The phrase recalls the solemn proclamation, *funeris indictio*, at the Archaic Roman burial ritual:[5]

ollus quiris leto datus

4. For another example of an underlying formula, vehicle of a theme that never surfaces overtly, see Watkins 1977.

5. Festus 304. 2 L. See Norden 1939:61ff. Cf. also the Law of Numa (Leg. Reg. Num. 12 Bruns) *si quis hominem liberum morti duit* 'If anyone gives to death (kills) a free man'.

This citizen is given to death.

In *Il.* 5.401, immediately preceding the line just cited, the physician of the gods had to heal Hades of Herakles' wound:

τῶι δ' ἐπὶ Παιήων ὀδυνή**φατα** **φάρμακα** **πάσσων**

Paieon rubbed pain-killing drugs on him.

The root **gʷhen-* of -**φατα** (**gʷhn̥-to-*) is indexed by an insistent phonetic figure: *pa- pʰa- pʰa- pa-*.

But most telling of all is that the reality of the unattested, "ideal" formula,

*HERO SLAY (**gʷhen-*) DEATH,

is proved by the existence of its inverse, the reciprocal formula

DEATH SLAY (**gʷhen-*) HERO.

Tiresias foretells to Odysseus his death in *Od.* 11.134-6 (= 23.281-3):

θάνατος δέ τοι ἐξ ἁλὸς αὐτῶι
ἀβληχρὸς μάλα τοῖος ἐλεύσεται, ὅς κέ **σε πέφνηι**
γήραι ὕπο λιπαρῶι ἀρημένον

Death will come to you from the sea, in
some altogether unwarlike way, and it **will slay you**
in the ebbing time of a sleek old age.

In a bold figure it is Death himself 'who will slay you', as the text says literally. Compare the remarks at the end of chap. 28 on the inherited figure of the relative clause in the basic formula with **gʷhen-* as an index of the Indo-European hero. By their manipulation of the formula these gentle lines effectively elevate and transform Death from a monstrous adversary to another HERO.

The same inverted formula is used by Euripides in the *Alcestis* with an entirely different tone. The coldness, impersonalness, and inflexibility of Death come through vividly in the abrupt shift in pronominalization from the first person singular (before and after) to first person plural in his dialogue with Apollo, line 49 (Death speaking):

κτείνειν γ' ὃν ἂν χρῆι; τοῦτο γὰρ τετάγμεθα

To slay whom we must? Those are our orders.

As we will see in detail in a subsequent chapter, Euripides no longer uses the verbal derivatives of the root **gʷhen-*, but uses κτείνειν for both ordinary, unmarked 'kill', and for semantically charged 'slay' as a substitute for earlier πεφνέμεν. The emphatic initial position here, together with the formulaic character of the figure, suggests the latter interpretation.

41

The saga of Iphitos and the hero as monster

We must consider a particular aspect, and a particular thematic variant, of the dragon-killing myth and its expression. There is a negative aspect of the hero; he can be a sort of monster. In the figure of Herakles, the Greek hero par excellence, just as in such characters as Indra, Thor, or Bhīma in the Mahābhārata, unpredictable violence is always latent. The theme is an inherited one. Compare Indra's *kílbiṣāni* 'misdeeds', on which see Jamison 1991:64-7, citing Oertel 1898, and for a full and able discussion of the theme in Greek, Detienne 1986.

The term *kílbiṣam* makes its first appearance in the Rigveda, occurring once already in a family book (5.34.4). It is doubtless a loanword, by its phonological shape (cf. Mayrhofer, KEWA and EWA s.v.); the source is uncertain. In this Indra hymn (and 5.33, by the same author) the opposition between Ārya and Dāsa is in the foreground (5.34.6):

índro . . .
yathāvaśám̐ nayati dā́sam ā́ryaḥ

Indra . . . the Ārya leads the Dāsa where he will.

It is therefore not unreasonable to see in *kílbiṣām* a "Dāsic" borrowing, a word borrowed from hostiles relating to hostile behavior or actions, somewhat like English borrowings from the language of erstwhile enemies like *blitzkrieg*, *U-boat* (calqued), *panzer*, *jiujitsu*, *kamikaze*, *bushido*, and the like.

RV 5.34.4 furnishes illustrations of the *kílbiṣam*:

yásy**ā́vadhīt** pitáraṃ yásya mātáraṃ
yásya śakró bhrā́taraṃ nā́ta īṣate
vétī́d v asya práyatā yataṃkaró
ná **kílbiṣā́d** īṣate vásva ākaráḥ

The mighty one does not shy away from him
whose father, whose mother, whose brother **he has slain**;
he even demands presents from him, the present-giver,
he does not shy away from any ***kilbiṣam***, the giver of good things.

Indra as praised in this hymn behaves thus differently from the Indra of 1.32.14:

áher yātā́ram kám apaśya indra
hṛdí yát te **jaghnúṣo** bhī́r ágacchat
náva ca yán navatím ca srávantīḥ
śyenó ná bhītó átaro rájāṁsi

What avenger of the serpent did you see, o Indra,
that fear came into your heart, you **the slayer**,
when you crossed the ninety-nine streams,
crossed the spaces like the frightened eagle?

Like Apollo after slaying Python, Orestes pursued by the Furies after slaying Klutaimestra, Indra after slaying the serpent Vṛtra must run away.[1]

The HERO and the MONSTER are in fact frequently ambiguous and ambivalent. Pausanias (6.6.7-11) records a tale about a monster who in the usual fashion had to be appeased by annual sacrifice of a maiden and who when finally defeated 'sank into the sea'. This monster was called simply ὁ Ἥρως 'the Hero'; Pausanias also saw a picture dealing with the same subject, a copy of an ancient picture, in which the black-skinned monster wore a wolf's pelt and was apparently labeled Λυκας 'Wolf'.[2]

The focus of "sympathy" may be on the MONSTER adversary rather than on the HERO, as in Stesichorus' portrayal of Geryon, slain by Herakles; see chap. 48. One of the few thematically "original" uses of πεφνέμεν in Greek poetry of the Hellenistic or Imperial periods is found in the Orphic *Argonautica* 415-6, the Centaur Kheiron singing of the Centaurs whom the Lapiths had slain:

ὃς δ' ἄρ' ἄειδε μάχην Κενταύρων ὀμβριμοθύμων
οὓς Λαπίθαι **κατέπεφνον** ἀτασθαλίης ἕνεκα σφῶν

Who sang of the fight of the Centaurs of violent spirit
whom the Lapiths **slew** in their recklessness.

Here again the focus of "sympathy" is on the slain monsters, half-horse, half-man, rather than on their civilized slayers. The use of a form of *g^{w}hen-* in the narration of the conflict between Centaurs and Lapiths, an old and enduringly popular motif in

1. Geldner ad loc. gives references to the myth in the Brāhmaṇas. For Apollo see Detienne 1986.
2. MS acc. λυβαν; β and κ are frequently confused. Fontenrose's Αλυβαν (1980:19-20) is unnecessary.

visual art as well—the friezes of the Parthenon—, is likely to be traditional and ancient.

Typically of great size, the hero approaches in this respect his giant adversaries. Orion is such a figure; a giant, ultimately slain by a goddess, he is nonetheless the "hero", and subject of the formula in *Od.* 11.572-5:

τὸν δὲ μετ' Ὠρίωνα πελώριον εἰσενόησα
θῆρας ὁμοῦ εἰλεῦντα κατ' ἀσφοδελὸν λειμῶνα,
τοὺς αὐτὸς **κατέπεφνεν** ἐν οἰοπόλοισιν ὄρεσσι
χερσὶν ἔχων ῥόπαλον παγχάλκεον, αἰὲν ἀαγές

After him I was aware of gigantic Orion
in the meadow of asphodel, rounding up and driving together
wild animals he himself **had killed** in the lonely mountains,
holding in his hands a brazen club, forever unbroken.

Note that he too, like Vedic Indra, Iranian Mithra or Thraetaona, Greek Herakles, Germanic Thor and the Irish Dagdae, wields a cudgel. See further on this feature in chapters 42 and 44.

Monstrosity is not a matter of size alone. At the end of Sophocles' *Oedipus Rex*, in the last speech of the hero (1496-9):

τί γὰρ κακῶν ἄπεστι; τὸν πατέρα πατὴρ
ὑμῶν **ἔπεφνε**· τὴν τεκοῦσαν ἤροσεν,
ὅθεν περ αὐτὸς ἐσπάρη, κἀκ τῶν ἴσων
ἐκτήσαθ' ὑμᾶς ὧνπερ αὐτὸς ἐξέφυ

What curse is not there? Your father **killed** his father;
he ploughed his mother
from whence he himself was sown,
and begot you from the same source whence he sprang.

Patricide comes first in a series of acts which provoke horror; the hero, stained by his crime, becomes himself a monster.[3]

In the *Seven against Thebes* Aeschylus builds a crescendo of horror as the Chorus recounts the curse of Oedipus and his house: Laios begot his own doom, πατρο**κτόνον** Οἰδιπόδαν 'father-killing Oedipus', who (*Sept.* 783) with

πατρο**φόνωι** χερὶ

father-**slaying** hand,

3. This is one of only three examples of (κατ)ἔπεφνε in all of Sophocles. For the others see chapters 44 and 53.

reft himself of the eyes that were dearer to him than his children. The phrase is then echoed by (788-9),

> σιδαρονόμωι διὰ χερὶ
>
> with iron-giving hand,

of the antistrophe, Oedipus' curse proper, which sets forth the manner—by fighting—in which his sons will divide their inheritance.

Just such an act of unpredictable violence, an awesome, unjustified, and unethical act, is Herakles' killing of Iphitos, a guest in his own house. The story is narrated in *Od.* 21.11-38 and merits close attention.

Penelope goes to get the great bow which Iphitos had given Odysseus when they met in Lakedaimon and exchanged weapons as tokens of guest-friendship (*Od.* 21.11-14):

> ἔνθα δὲ τόξον κεῖτο . . .
> δῶρα τά οἱ ξεῖνος Λακεδαίμονι δῶκε τυχήσας
> Ἴφιτος Εὐρυτίδης, ἐπιείκελος ἀθανάτοισι
>
> There lay the bow . . .
> gifts that a guest-friend gave him,
> Iphitos son of Eurutos, like to the immortal gods.

Both came on lawful, legal business: Odysseus to collect a debt incurred by the Messenians, carrying off 300 sheep and their shepherds from Ithaca, and Iphitos to recover 12 mares, each with a mule colt, which had been rustled from him. Odysseus' mission was successful, but the mares would be Iphitos' doom, when he met Herakles (27-9),

> ὅς μιν ξεῖνον ἐόντα **κατέκτανεν** ᾧι ἐνὶ οἴκωι
> σχέτλιος, οὐδὲ θεῶν ὄπιν αἰδέσατ' οὐδὲ τράπεζαν,
> τὴν ἥν οἱ παρέθηκεν
>
> who **killed** him though he was a guest in his own house,
> merciless man, without regard for the watchfulness of the gods
> or the rights of the table, the one he had set for him.

The first clause narrates the legal facts and circumstances, and uses the unmarked verb κατακτείνω. But the immediately following continuation, which resumes it, uses the marked πέφνε, VO word order, and a more emotional conclusion (29):

> ἔπειτα δὲ **πέφνε** καὶ αὐτόν
>
> and he **slew** him afterwards . . .

and kept the mares for himself. And in a recapitulation Iphitos gave Odysseus the bow (31 δῶκε δὲ τόξον) as a token of guest-friendship to come, but they never knew each other's hospitality (36-8):

> πρὶν γὰρ Διὸς υἱὸς **ἔπεφνεν**
> Ἴφιτον Εὐρυτίδην, ἐπιείκελον ἀθανάτοισιν,
> ὅς οἱ τόξον ἔδωκε
>
> Before that, the son of Zeus **slew**
> Iphitos, son of Eurutos, one like the immortal gods,
> who gave Odysseus the bow.

The conclusion makes a perfect Irish *dúnad* or ring composition with the beginning of the episode,

> ἔνθα δὲ τόξον . . .
> δῶρα τά . . . δῶκε
> Ἴφιτος Εὐρυτίδης, ἐπιείκελος ἀθανάτοισι
>
> There was the bow . . .
> The gift was given by . . .
> Iphitos son of Eurutos, like to the immortal gods,

as well as echoing the key verb πέφνε of 29.

What function is served by the carefully wrought demarcation of the Iphitos tale, its indexing by ring composition? The purpose is to highlight the episode of Iphitos as a thematic foil, a formulaic photographic negative of the narrative to come. To balance the wrong of Herakles slaying Iphitos, a guest (ξεῖνος) in his own house, will come a dramatic right: Odysseus as guest-stranger (ξεῖνος) who will slay the suitors, non-guests and anti-heroes, in his own house. The correspondence is rigorous, mathematical:

	(Herakles)			
wrong:	HERO	SLAY	HERO_2	(in OWN HOUSE)
			guest	
	(Odysseus)			
right:	HERO	SLAY	SUITORS	(in OWN HOUSE)
	guest		non-guests	

The monstrous behavior of the hero Herakles abases him to the level of a monster, and in terms of formulaic echoes, to one in particular: the Kuklops. The utter wantonness and lawlessness of the Kuklops lies not in his cannibalism, but in his eating guests. The importance of the guest-relationship in the episode is made plain and underscored in Odysseus' first speech to the Kuklops Poluphemos, which uses a derivative of ξεῖνος 'guest' five times in as many lines (*Od.* 9.267-71):

εἴ τι πόροις **ξεινήϊον** ἠὲ καὶ ἄλλως
δοίης δωτίνην, ἥ τε **ξείνων** θέμις ἐστίν.
ἀλλ' **αἰδεῖο**, φέριστε, θεούς· ἱκέται δέ τοί εἰμεν.
Ζεὺς δ' ἐπιτιμήτωρ ἱκετάων τε **ξείνων** τε,
ξείνιος, ὅς **ξείνοισιν** ἅμ' αἰδοίοισιν ὀπηδεῖ.

if you might give us a **guest present** or otherwise
some gift of grace, for such is the right of **strangers**. Therefore
respect the gods, o best of men. We are your suppliants,
and Zeus the **guest** god, who stands behind all **strangers** with honors
due them, avenges any wrong toward **strangers** and suppliants.

Here αἰδεῖο θεούς 'respect the gods' will be echoed in the description of Herakles οὐδὲ θεῶν ὄπιν αἰδέσατ' 'he did not respect the watchfulness of the gods' of *Od.* 21.27-9 cited above, just as the same latter passage's ξεῖνον ἐόντα κατέκτανεν ᾧι ἐνὶ οἴκωι / σχέτλιος echoes Odysseus' final speech to Poluphemos, with its grim enjambment (9.478-9):

σχέτλι' ἐπεὶ ξείνους οὐκ ἅζεο σῶι ἐνὶ οἴκωι
ἐσθέμεναι

merciless man, since you fear not **to eat** guests
in your own house.

The foil to this formulation of evil is Odysseus' final triumph over the suitors. Slaying the non-guests who abuse hospitality is an act of vengeance, Greek τίσις, τίνω, ποινή (IE **k^uei-*), and the formula is expressed by Odysseus' old nurse Eurukleia to Penelope as (23.57):

μνηστῆρες, τοὺς πάντας **ἐτείσατο** ᾧι ἐνὶ οἴκωι

he has **taken revenge** on all the suitors in his own house.

Odysseus can summarize the whole denouement in a single line when he is pressed for time; compare Pindar's "shortcut", the οἶμος βραχύς which is the formula itself. Odysseus reveals himself to his father (24.324-6):

ἐκ γάρ τοι ἐρέω μάλα δὲ χρὴ σπευδέμεν ἔμπης·
μνηστῆρας κατέπεφνον ἐν **ἡμετέροισι δόμοισι,**
λώβην **τινύμενος** θυμαλγέα καὶ κακὰ ἔργα

For I tell you this straight out; the need for haste is upon us.
I have killed the suitors who were **in our palace, avenging**
all their heart-hurting outrage and their evil devisings.

In chap. 49 we will see further examples of the root **k*^{u}*ei-* as a corollary or reciprocal, depending on voice, of **g*^{u}*hen-*.

We may postpone a fuller exploration of the formulaic vehicles of the all-important nexus in archaic Greek and Indo-European society which is guest-friendship. Suffice it here to state that the array of formulas we have examined may be reduced to two reciprocal counterparts:

ANTI-HERO	SLAY	GUEST	(in OWN HOUSE)
HERO	SLAY	ANTI-GUEST	(in OWN HOUSE).

We noted above that Odysseus is also frequently called ξεῖνος GUEST-'stranger' in his own house, and in the cave of the Kuklops. Greek ξεῖνος (Indo-European **ghs-*) at the same time means 'host', the dispenser of hospitality, exactly like Indo-European **ghos-*(*ti*)-, English *guest*, Slavic *gostь*, Latin *hostis*. Herakles as anti-hero who abuses his hospitality is thus an anti-guest (using English *guest* now as a portmanteau for the Indo-European semantics), and the two formulas may be rewritten respectively as:

ANTI-GUEST	SLAY	GUEST	(in OWN HOUSE)
GUEST	SLAY	ANTI-GUEST	(in OWN HOUSE).

These are evidently only a special case of the fundamental bidirectional basic formula and theme: respectively, as we have represented it,

$$\xrightarrow{\hspace{6cm}}$$

HERO	SLAY	SERPENT
HERO	SLAY	SERPENT.

$$\xleftarrow{\hspace{6cm}}$$

It should be noted that the (in OWN HOUSE) element, an accessory, attendant circumstance, grammatically signalled by a local, peripheral case (here locative), is indifferently the house of the GUEST/HERO (Odysseus slaying the suitors) or of the ANTI-GUEST/SERPENT (Herakles slaying Iphitos [subject], Odysseus blinding Poluphemos [object]).[4] In chap. 44 we will see the same indifferent assignment of the attendant WEAPON to either of the two adversaries.

Two final comparative details may be adduced, which I believe demonstrate both the well-foundedness of our identification HERO = GUEST, SERPENT = ANTI-GUEST, and its inheritance, that is, its legitimate status as an Indo-European theme. The first is the fact that the Hittite *illuyanka*-serpent is an invited guest at a feast, where he is made drunk and thereby overpowered: the same stratagem employed by

4. In the case of formulas with OWN this value is conditioned by Indo-European syntax; **su̯o-* 'own' normally refers to the subject of the clause, but refers to the Topic of the sentence if that differs from the grammatical subject. Compare *Od.* 9.369 Οὖτιν ἐγὼ πύματον ἔδομαι μετὰ οἷς ἑτάροισιν 'Noman I will eat last, after his companions'.

Odysseus against Poluphemos, and by other heroes from Iranian Kiršāsp to Macbeth. Compare KUB 17.5 i 4-16 (§9-11):[5]

DInarašš=az
unuttat n=ašta MUŠilluyank[an]
ḫantešnaz šarā kallišta
kāša=wa EZEN-an iyami
nu=wa adanna akuwanna eḫu

---

n=ašta MUŠilluyankaš *QADU* [DUMUMEŠ-*ŠU*]
šarā uēr nu=za eter ekuir
n=ašta DUGpalḫan ḫumandan ek[uir]
n=e=za nininkēr

---

n=e namma ḫattešnaz kattanda
nūmān pānzi mḪūpašiyašš=a uit
nu MUŠilluyankan išḫimanta
kalēliet

Inaras dressed herself up
and invited the serpent up from his hole (saying):
"I'm preparing a feast—come eat and drink!"
Then the serpent came up together with [his
children], and they ate and drank—they drank of all
the vessels and were sated.
They were no longer able to go back
down into their hole, and Hupasiyas came
and tied up the serpent with a cord.

In Greek, compare ϑεοὶ ϑάνατόνδε κάλεσσαν, two 'invitations to death' ... given by the gods to Patroklos (*Il.* 16.693) and Hektor (*Il.* 22.297) . . . like an invitation to a banquet (Vermeule 1979:105). Greek κάλεσσαν is of course cognate with Hittite *kallišta*. The verb recurs in the sinister invitation to the feast of Tantalos in Pindar (*Ol.* 1.37-8):

ὁπότ᾽ ἐκάλεσε πατὴρ τὸν εὐνομώτατον
ἐς ἔρανον

when your father invited the gods to that most
honorable feast.

The second is a "singular detail" (cf. chap. 27.3) in a dragon-slaying episode of the Old Norse *Grettissaga*. When Grettir came to the young wife Steinvǫr's house,

---

5. Text and translation (slightly modified) from Beckman 1982.

with the purpose of ridding it of the unknown monster who has carried off her husband, 'he concealed his identity and called himself *Gestr/Guest*' (§64) *Hann dulðisk ok nefndisk Gestr*. It is under the assumed name of *Gestr* that he meets and fights and finally overcomes the monster, a great troll-woman who comes into the house-hall with a trough in one hand and a cleaver in the other, the better to eat her intended human prey; she is the ultimate anti-guest. We are back in the cave of Poluphemos: just as the stranger Odysseus assumes the name of Noman (Οὖτις), so must the outlaw (*útlagi*) Grettir, legally a non-person, assume the name of Guest. The semantic identity of ξεῖνος and *gestr*, as well as their common etymological origin, Indo-European **gh(o)s-*, points to two manifestations of an inherited Indo-European theme:

ξεῖνος (Οὖτις)
GUEST SLAY ANTI-GUEST.
Gestr (útlagi)

The same version of the basic formula applies to one of the labors of *Herakles* himself, in a passage from Euripides (*Herc*. 391-2):

Κύκνον ξεινοδαΐκταν
τόξοις **ὤλεσεν**

He **slew** Kuknos slayer of strangers with his shafts.

Two formulaic features of the Iphitos episode remain to be examined. The first is a comparative syntactic remark. We saw above that the verb form ἔπεφνεν was the main verb of the conclusion (lines 35-8) of the episode, which formed a ring-composition with the beginning (lines 11-14). The verb ἔπεφνεν has no counterpart in 11-14, but it does in the noun φόνος 'murder, death, bane' in 24. Iphitos came to recover his mares, but

αἳ δή οἱ καὶ ἔπειτα **φόνος** καὶ μοῖρα **γένοντο**

but thereafter these **became** his **death** and doom.

In φόνος γένοντο (+ dative) we can see the origin of the Germanic construction of Old English *to bonan weorðan* 'to become the bane'. See chap. 43.1 for a full discussion of the Germanic forms and chap. 51 for more on the figure.

The last formulaic feature of the Iphitos episode to claim our attention is the phrase ϑεῶν ὄπις, the 'watchfulness of the gods' which Herakles had no regard for. Chantraine DELG translates it well—pace Considine 1966—as 'la vigilance vengeresse des dieux pour toute faute commise.' The phrase is found only once in each of the Homeric poems (here and *Il*. 16.388) but enters into a complex network which I have examined in detail elsewhere (1977:209). In particular I postulated a virtual semantic identity ϑεῶν ὄπις = ϑεῶν μῆνις,[6] a reciprocal relation in the attitude of gods toward men and vice-versa:

GODS (θεῶν) ὄπις = (θεῶν) μῆνις
|
MEN (θεῶν) μῆνιν ὀπίζεσθαι

The latter formula is applied to Zeus Xeinios, the protector of the rights of hospitality, in *Od.* 14.283-4 Διὸς δ' ὠπίζετο μῆνιν / ξεινίου 'he was mindful of the (potential) wrath of Zeus Xeinios', cf. *Il.* 13.624-5 Ζηνὸς . . . ἐδείσατε μῆνιν / ξεινίου 'you feared the (potential) wrath of Zeus Xeinios'. And it is Zeus Xeinios whom Odysseus evokes in his first speech to the Kuklops (cited above), formulaically in the same metrical slot. These successive formulas, part of the repertoire of the poet-performer and shared by his audience, evoke an associative chain that links the watchfulness of the gods to the vengefulness of Zeus the protector of guests. The effect is stark and awesome contrast in the final formula of the brief saga of Iphitos: it is the very son of Zeus who slays his guest (*Od.* 21.36-7):

Διὸς υἱὸς **ἔπεφνεν** / Ἴφιτον

ANTI-GUEST SLAY GUEST (with WEAPON).

It is this unholy guest-murder which sacrificially *consecrates* the bow (Burkert 1983 passim), a holy guest-gift; with this bow Odysseus will slay the suitors, and right will triumph:

GUEST SLAY ANTI-GUEST (with WEAPON).

6. This equation ὄπις = μῆνις and the etymology of μῆνις (Doric μᾶνις) there proposed, a deformation of *μνᾱ-νις, are mutually supported by the discovery that the root *mnā-* (**mnah₂-*) in Luvian means 'to see', just like the root ὀπ- of ὄπις. See Starke 1980.

42

The name of Meleager

In Bacchylides' fifth victory ode Herakles in Hades meets the shade of Meleager (68-70):

> ταῖσιν δὲ μετέπρεπεν εἴδω-
> λον θρασυμέμνονος ἐγ-
> χεσπάλου Πορθανίδα
>
> Clear showed among them the shade of the
> brave spirited wielder of spears, (Meleager),
> descendant of Porthaon.

Meleager is here the formulaically prototypical HERO, who μεταπρέπει by the spear like Hektor (*Il*. 16.834-5), is θρασυμέμνων like Herakles (*Il*. 5.639, *Od*. 11.267), and ἐγχέσπαλος like Ares (*Il*. 15.605), Polydamos (*Il*. 14.449), and the nameless Trojan allies (*Il*. 2.131). On seeing and being addressed by Meleager, Herakles' reply is the recognition of a hero (86-9):

> τίς ἀθανάτων
> ἢ βροτῶν τοιοῦτον ἔρνος
> θρέψεν ἐν ποίαι χθονί;
> τίς δ' ἔκτανεν;
>
> What god or man reared such a scion
> as this, and where? Who slew him?

He knows: marvelous birth, semi-divine lineage, and extraordinary death, a *Heldentod*. τίς δ' ἔκτανεν is a formulaic topos: cf. (*Od*. 3.248) πῶς ἔθαν' Ἀτρείδης; 'how was Agamemnon slain?', (Pindar, *Isth*. 5.39) τίνες Κύκνον, τίνες Ἕκτορα πέφνον; 'who killed Kuknos, who Hector?'

In the narration of Meleager's greatest exploit, killing the Calydonian boar, he and the other Aitolians are called by Bacchylides Ἑλλάνων ἄριστοι 'best of the Hellenes' (111), a characteristic formulaic index of the HERO.[1] The formula is indexed by phonetic figures and homoioteleuton in the immediately following στασάμεϑ' **ἐνδυκέως** / ἓξ ἅματα **συν(ν)εχέως** 'we stood steadfast for six days continually'; note the iconic length of **ν** in the last. The monster boar is itself subject of the verb SLAY in Bacchylides 5.115-6 οὓς κατέπεφνεν/σῦς 'whom the boar slew', with the reciprocal of the basic formula, as discussed above (chap. 31).

We find another formulaic Homeric reminiscence in a metrical feature of this ode of Bacchylides: the placement of the name of Meleager in verse-final position at the close of a dactylic unit, with muta cum liquida making position, in all three of its occurrences: 5.77 ψυχὰ προφάνη Μελεάγρου, 93 τὸν δὲ προσέφα Μελέαγρος, 171 ψυχὰ προσέφα Μελεάγρου.

While postverbal position of the subject is what we expect in such formulas introducing quoted speech, Bacchylides' placement of the name echoes that of line-final *Il.* 2.642, ϑάνε δὲ ξανϑὸς Μελέαγρος, 9.543 τὸν . . . ἀπέκτεινεν Μελέαγρος, or Hes. *fr.* 25.10 [. . . κρατερ]ὸν Μελέαγρον. It is probably significant that once the line-final name is preceded by a verse with line-final verb μέλει 'has as a care' (92-4):

> "τὰ δέ που
> Παλλάδι ξανϑᾶι **μέλει**."
> τὸν δὲ προσέφα **Μελέ**αγρος
>
> "But that, somehow, is the **concern**
> of blonde Pallas Athena."
> **Mele**ager answered him . . .

We would have an etymological figure, as well as an echoic link of ξανϑᾶι μέλει to Homer's ϑάνε δὲ ξανϑὸς Μελέαγρος.

Note finally that in the same victory ode the final exploit of 'spear-wielding' ἐγχέσπαλος Meleager, the slaying of his mother's brothers, also involves weapons thrown like spears: τυφλὰ δ' ἐκ χειρῶν βέλη (132) 'bolts thrown blind from our hands'.

The tale of Meleager is told by Phoinix to Achilles in the mission in *Iliad* 9, as an exemplum. Here as in Bacchylides we find the reciprocal of the basic formula, this time with the Calydonian boar as subject of the exceedingly rare Greek reflex of **u̯edh-*, the participle ἔϑων 'smiting, wasting'.[2] *Iliad* 9.539f. σῦν **ἄγρ**ιον **ἀργ**ιοδόντα . . . (note the phonetic figure indexing the name Μελέ**αγρ**ος) / ὅς κακὰ πολλ' ἔρδεσκεν ἔϑων Οἰνῆος ἀλωήν 'a wild boar white of tusk . . . / that wrought much ill, wasting the garden land of Oineus'. *Iliad* 9.543 continues τὸν ἀπέκτεινεν Μελέαγρος 'him . . . Meleager killed', thus re-establishing the usual grammatical role of the constituents

1. On the notion see Nagy 1979; it is taken up in an Indo-European context in chap. 50. This chapter first appeared in the Festschrift for Ernst Risch.

2. This analysis of the word is rightly upheld by Leumann 1950:212-3, with literature, and followed by Chantraine and Frisk. Note also Melchert 1979 on *uizzai*, *wiwidāi*, and chap. 33.

of the basic formula, but with the name of the HERO in line-final position and no mention of a WEAPON.

The other Homeric occurrence of the ancient participle (ϝ)έθων is in a simile in *Il.* 16.259ff., where the Myrmidons pouring forth into battle with Patroklos are likened to a swarm of wasps that boys in their foolishness (**παῖδες . . . νηπίαχοι**) smite and goad into fury (ἐριδμαίνωσιν **ἔθοντες**). Here too we have a variant of the basic formula: the foolish boys are ANTI-HEROES who SMITE (**u̯edh-*) the 'HERO'-WASPS to whom the Myrmidons are compared.

Now we find just such a theme and variant of the basic formula in another and instructive Iliadic simile in 11.558 ff. The Greek hero Ajax slowly giving ground before the Trojan onslaught is likened to 'a donkey, stubborn and hard to move, who goes into a cornfield in despite of boys (**παῖδες**), and many sticks have been broken upon him (ᾧι δὴ πολλὰ περὶ **ῥόπαλ'** ἀμφὶς **ἐάγηι** line-final) but he gets in and goes on eating the deep grain, and the children beat him with sticks (οἱ δέ τε **παῖδες / τύπτουσιν ῥοπάλοισι**) but their strength is infantile (βίη δέ τε **νηπίη** αὐτῶν) . . .'. The weak boys are again ANTI-HEROES, who BEAT the 'HERO'-ASS (≅ Ajax) with WEAPONS (ῥοπάλοισι); we have the full version of the basic formula. And in ᾧι . . . ῥόπαλ' . . . ἐάγηι 'upon him . . . sticks . . . have been broken' we have the variant with WEAPON promoted to grammatical subject of the intransitive verb ἐάγηι, IE **u̯aĝ-*. Compare RV 4.41.4 (*asmin*) *ní vadhiṣṭaṃ vájram* 'strike down the weapon on him', with the WEAPON (*vájra*, IE **u̯aĝ-*) promoted to grammatical object of the transitive verb *vadhiṣṭaṃ*, IE **u̯edh-*.

The word ῥόπαλον occurs only here in the *Iliad*; as in the Aesop tales, it is just a stick to beat with, but it occurs in a definable locus of a formulaic nexus. In the *Odyssey* the word has more legendary associations, and in the same formulaic nexus: the WEAPON. In *Od.* 17.195 it is the staff requested by Odysseus from Eumaios, which in 236 is potentially a deadly weapon. In *Od.* 9.319-20 it is the great club of the MONSTER Poluphemos, which Odysseus will use to blind him: μέγα . . . ῥόπαλον . . . χλωρὸν ἐλαίνεον 'of yellow-green olive wood'. Elsewhere it is the club of the HERO Herakles: Soph. *Trach.* 512 (lyr.), Aristoph. *Ran.* 47, 495, and Pindar *fr.* 111, with the epithet τραχύ 'rough, jagged'.

But the most interesting is the final attestation of ῥόπαλον in the *Odyssey*, in book eleven, the Nekuia (11.572-5 cited in chap. 41). 'After him I was aware of gigantic Orion/in the meadow of asphodel, rounding up and driving together/wild animals (**θῆρας**) whom he himself had killed (κατέ**πεφνε**) in the lonely mountains/holding in his hands a brazen club, forever unbroken'; χερσὶν ἔχων **ῥόπαλον**, παγχάλκεον, αἰὲν **ἀαγές** (tr. Lattimore).

We observe here not only another instance of the basic formula

HERO SLAY BEAST (with WEAPON),

but another collocation of the WEAPON and the root **u̯aĝ-* as well, this time as an epithet ἀαγής, hapax in Homer.

Orion's cudgel here is the most fully described in early Greek literature. There can be no doubt that this is an ancient and inherited thematic nexus, for the same features recur in the description of Indra's cudgel in Vedic and Mithra's mace in Avestan. And the word for the WEAPON in both languages is a derivative of the root **u̯aĝ-* (Mayrhofer, KEWA s. v. with references, also Nachträge): Ved. *vájraḥ* = Av. *vazrō*, IE **u̯aĝros*.

With χερσὶν ἔχων ῥόπαλον . . . ἀᾱγές 'holding in his hands the club . . . unbroken' compare Vedic *vájrahasta-* 'having the bolt in his hand', 17x of Indra; for Avestan, Yt. 10.96 *vazrəm zastaiia dražəmnō* 'holding his mace in his hand'. With παγχάλκεον 'all brazen' compare RV 1.80.12 *vájra āyasáḥ* 'cudgel of bronze', as well as 10.96.3-4 cited above, and Yt. 10.96 *zarōiš aiiaŋhō frahixtəm* 'cast in yellow bronze'. With the χλωρόν 'yellow' cudgel of Poluphemos note RV 3.44.4 *hárim . . . vájram* 'the yellow cudgel', as well as 10.96.3-4 and the Avestan epithet just cited. For the τραχύ 'rough' cudgel of Herakles, the studded club familiar in Greek iconography, cf. Ved. *sahásrabhr̥ṣṭiḥ* 'with 1000 studs' (1.80.12 above), or Av. *sata.fštanəm* 'with 100 bosses'. Such was the Indo-European **u̯aĝros*; see chap. 44.

It is well-known that both the verb form ἐᾱ́γῃ and the adjective ἀᾱγές in the above passages show 'metrical lengthening', and that the other Homeric instances of ἐάγη (3x *Il.*, 1x *Od.* repeated) do not. The participle (ϝ)αγνυμενάων occurring (at verse-end) once in each epic (*Il.* 16.769, *Od.* 10.123) points to a digamma and a short vowel.[3] How is this metrical lengthening generated? ἐᾱ́γῃ and ἀᾱγές have the same metrical position (verse-final) as Μελέαγρος in *Il.* 2.642 and 9.543; Hesiod's ἔᾱγε the same position (before feminine caesura) as Μελέαγρος in *Il.* 9. 550, 553, 590. The long syllable in (⏑) ⏑ – ⏒ # and (⏑) ⏑ – ⏑ || is primary in (Μελέ)αγρος, secondary in ἐᾱ́γῃ, ἀᾱγές, ἔᾱγε. I suggest the latter three are based on the former.

The hiatus in Μελέαγρος is most easily explained by a lost ϝ. If a line or hemistich-final *(Μελε-)ϝαγρος (⏑ ⏑) – ⏒ # is responsible for the lengthening in *ἐϝάγη, *ἔϝαγε, *ἀϝαγές ⏑ – ⏒ # then the link must be semantic, and therefore *(-)ϝαγρος must have been perceived as containing ϝαγ- 'break'. If so, then either *(-)ϝαγρος forms an equation with Vedic *vájraḥ*/ Avestan *vazrō* 'WEAPON' or is wholly independent. In view of the clear association of the Greek root ϝαγ- with the WEAPON in these contexts, variants of the basic formula (ῥόπαλ'. . . ἐᾱ́γῃ, ῥόπαλον . . . ἀᾱγές), and in view of the formal identity of Greek *(-)ϝαγρος and Indo-Iranian **u̯ájras* 'WEAPON', we are led to conclude—as the simplest hypothesis to account for the facts—that Greek *(-)ϝαγρος meant 'WEAPON', and made a word equation with the Indic and Iranian forms.

The metrical evidence indicates that the original locus of the root ϝαγ- in the Greek version of the basic formula was verse-final (⏑)(⏑) -- ⏒ # or hemistich-final (⏑)(⏑) – ⏑ ||, and that the only form apt to fit that slot was *ϝαγρο-, the nominal derivative 'WEAPON'. A tendency to verse- and clause-final position is also characteristic for the position of the instrumental WEAPON in the (boxed) basic formula in Vedic,

HERO	SLAY	MONSTER	(with WEAPON),

3. Hiersche 1966 has suggested that the perfect in Hesiod *Op.* 534 ἐπὶ νῶτα ἔᾱγε and Sappho 31.9 (2.9 D2) γλῶσσα ἔᾱγε reflects an Aeolic poetic tradition outside Homer with lengthening (and digamma), whence Ionic ἔηγε. The two traditions with lengthening are I think one and the same.

notably when the verb is clause-initial.

If the original locus of *ϝαγ-ρο- in the Greek formula was the WEAPON, the other cases show transference of the root to other semantic constituents. Given in our myth

HERO	SLAY	MONSTER	(with WEAPON),
1	2	3	4

the (VERB$_{intr}$ ἐάγη) shows 4 → 2, while (ADJECTIVE ἀαγές + WEAPON) shows 4 → $_{NP}$[x + 4]. At a certain time in the hexameter tradition (or its ancestor) these constituents underwent semantic 'movement' in the underlying structure, but remained metrically static; their position in the metrical line remained unchanged. The necessary consequence was the deformation we know as 'metrical lengthening'.

The final semantic 'movement' was simply 4 → 1: the WEAPON became the name of the HERO, or a constituent of it. This transference could be the more favored by the existence of the thematic and formulaic variant

WEAPON KILL MONSTER,

with the WEAPON promoted to grammatical subject, as discussed and illustrated above. The Maruts' bolt is a *gohā́* (IE **gʷou̯-gʷhen-*) *nṛhā́ vadháḥ* 'cattle-slaying, man-slaying weapon' in RV 7.56.17, just as Mithra's weapon is *aspa.vīraja* 'horse- and man-slaying' in Yt. 10.101. That such a semantic structure was profoundly rooted in early Greek culture is proved by a curious feature of the ancient Athenian ritual of the Bouphonia (IE **gʷou- gʷhon-*), the sacrifice of an ox to Zeus of the city: the sacrificial axe is ritually tried for murder.[4]

The creation of the compound name Μελέ-ϝαγρος 'having the care of *ϝαγρος', 'he who cares for the *ϝαγρος' could have been at the outset a nonce-formation; names in Μελε- (var. Μελι-) are infrequent but do occur. See Bechtel 1917 who notes that the type was first analyzed already by August Friedrich Pott.[5]

That the HERO of such a mythological episode in the basic formula may owe his name to a (synchronically no longer perceived) transference of the WEAPON can be exactly paralleled in Vedic. For as Stanley Insler will show in a future study,[6] the Hindu God *Viṣṇu* himself was originally only the name of Indra's cudgel, his *vájra*. Compare the clear basic formula in RV 6.20.2:

áhiṃ yád vṛtrám . . . **hánn** . . . **víṣṇunā** sacānáḥ

When you **slew** . . . the **serpent** Vṛtra . . . together with **Viṣṇu.**

4. See the penetrating analysis of Burkert 1983:136ff. It is curious that an apparent cognate of Βουφονία recurs in a Middle Irish place-name *Benn Bóguine*, with its dindšenchus (Metr. Dinds. 4.70), a tale of cattle-slaying. See Thurneysen 1921:320. If the compound were genuinely old, we should expect syncope; but since it was etymologically transparent it could have been re-formed.

5. 1857:129: 'Er [Μελέαγρος] bedeutet cui curae cordique est (μέλει) venatio (ἄγρα).' But the second member (so etymologized already by Euripides, v. infra) will not account for the hiatus.

6. Referred to by permission, for which I am grateful.

Etymologically the WEAPON *(-)ϝαγρος was the 'breaker' in Greek (ϝάγνυμι).[7] The root **u̯aĝ-*—otherwise not found in Indo-Iranian—recurs in Tocharian AB *wāk-* 'split, open (intr.)', pres. B *wokotär* < **u̯aĝ-o-*,[8] and in the Hittite ḫi-verb *wāki* 'bites'. The weapon might have been originally the 'biter'; for the semantics compare IE **bheid-* in Germanic (*bite, beissen*) and its association with the WEAPON in Germanic legend. Beowulf's sword Hrunting was useless against Grendel's mother: ***bitan** nolde* (1523) 'would not bite'; from Old Norse (*Helgakviða Hundingsbana* II.33) *bítia þér þat sverð* 'that sword will not bite for you'. The weapon with which Beowulf finishes off the Worm in the final, fatal conflict is ***biter** and beaduscearp* (2704) 'biting ("bitter") and battle-sharp': **bhid-ro-* is formed just like **u̯aĝ-ro-*.[9]

Formally **u̯aĝ-ro-* suggests a Caland adjective in *-ró-*, with substantivation and accent shift to *vájra-*. The stative **u̯aĝ-ē-* in Greek ἐάγη is likewise at home in a Caland-system, as is the *s*-stem **u̯aĝ-es-* of the Hesychean gloss ἄγος· κλάσμα, θραῦμα 'fragment', and its internal derivative ἀαγής 'unbroken'.

Hidden in the name of Meleager, but recoverable by the techniques of formulaic analysis, we have a Greek word *ϝαγρος which makes an exact word equation, both linguistically and in its poetic deployment, with Vedic *vájraḥ* and Avestan *vazrō*. That word and its associative poetic semantics and formulaics must go back directly to the period of community of Greek and Indo-Iranian, to the period of both linguistic and poetic community. The explanation of the name of Meleager is only a by-product of the understanding of the nature and extent of that Indo-European poetic tradition.

Jochem Schindler points out that this analysis of the name of Meleager is not new, but was published over a century ago.[10] He referred me to Hermann Osthoff (1878:140), who wrote of Μελέαγρος, 'besser ist aus lautlichen Gründen diejenige Etymologie, auf deren Urheber wir uns aber leider nicht besinnen, nach welcher in dem etymologisch zu deutenden Namen das Schlussglied Skr. *vájra-* m. n. 'Donnerkeil', Abaktr. *vazra-* m. 'Keule' enthalten sein soll.' The etymology in fact was made by none other than Berthold Delbrück, at the age of 23.[11] He quite correctly saw the figure of Meleager in the framework of what I term the basic formula. Nihil novi sub sole. But Delbrück's etymology, based explicitly on a long-antiquated view of mythology as a reflection of phenomena of nature, failed to convince the few Hellenists who knew of it. I believe it is the formulaic analysis alone which can demonstrate the correctness of the equation and explain the genesis of the name.

---

7. Burrow 1973:26, Thieme 1984:765, Mayrhofer, KEWA 126 and 790. I leave to others to consider whether the Germanic name of history and legend *Odoacer*, *Odovacar*, OEng. *Éadwacer*, Gmc. **Auða-wak-raz* might still contain our WEAPON (**u̯aĝros*) rather than the apparent *u̯oĝros* of ON *uakr*, OE *wacor*, German *wacker*. See Schönfeld 1911:174.

8. Jasanoff 1978:41, 120.

9. The following line *forwrat Wedra helm wyrm on middan* (2705) '(B.) cut open the belly of the Worm' also recalls RV 1.32.1d *prá vakṣáṇā* ***abhinat*** *párvatānām* '(Indra) split the belly of the mountains', or 4.17.3 ***bhinád*** *girím* 'he split the mountain'.

10. Schindler also notes Euripides' etymology in *Meleager* fr. 517 Nauck: Μελέαγρε, μελέαν γάρ ποτ' ἀγρεύεις ἄγραν with a double figura etymologica (ἄγραν ἠγρευκότες recurs at *Bacchae* 434). As Nauck notes, the paronomasia was castigated already in antiquity: ἵνα μὴ τὸν Μελέαγρον ὥσπερ Εὐριπίδης κακῶς ἐτυμολογήσῃ . . .

11. Delbrück 1865:282-3, as can be learned from van der Kolf, Pauly-Wissowa RE 29 (1931), col. 446 (who however remained unconvinced).

43

The Germanic world

1. Myth and Hero

The earliest Germanic literature, Old English, Old High German, Old Saxon, and Old Norse, knows a great many combats between heroes and dragons or heroic adversaries, epical conflicts which have continued to seize popular imagination from the Dark Ages right down to the 19th and 20th centuries, in the response to the operas of Richard Wagner, the still unabated vogue of the literary creations of the distinguished philologist J. R. R. Tolkien, and the immense success of the game Dungeons and Dragons. The themes of all these epic poems and tales have been repeatedly studied, catalogued, and analyzed by philologist and folklorist alike, and their similarity to the themes of Greek, Indic, and other legendary material has been noted since the 19th century.[1] The thematic similarities may be presumed as given; our concern here is language.

A number of verbal parallels among the various Germanic dragon-slaying legends have been adduced,[2] which prove, by the tenets of the comparative method, that they are genetically related and common inheritance. Such is the remarkable and methodologically indispensable agreement in what Meillet (1925:3) would term the critical 'détail singulier', the *hepti-sax* 'hilted knife', WEAPON of Giant adversary in the *Grettissaga* (§66) and a hapax in Old Norse, and the *hæft-méce* 'hilted sword' Hrunting which Unferth loaned to Beowulf (1457) and which was useless against Grendel's mother (1523 *bitan nolde* 'would not bite'). The equation of the compounds is notable for two reasons. The first is that both contexts refer to the antiquity of the weapon: *Beowulf* 1458 *án foran ealdgestréona* 'foremost of the ancient treasures'; *Grettissaga* §66 metalinguistically as *þat kolluðu menn þá heptisax* 'such men called

1. Compare the bibliography in Klaeber 1950. Perhaps the finest appreciation is still Tolkien 1938. For extra-Germanic comparisons cf. recently, and in some detail, Fontenrose 1980:Appendix 5.

2. Cf. Klaeber 1950:xv-xviii and note to line 1457. That the Germanic names of the dragon-slaying hero in their first element (cf. Gothic *sigis* 'victory') have the same root **seĝh-* 'overcome, conquer' as the Greek name Ἕκτωρ (Hektor) is perhaps accidental, but still worth pointing out. The semantics of the formation of the name Ἕκτωρ are older than those of the synchronic verb ἔχω in Homeric Greek. Cf. Ved. *sáhate* 'conquers, overpowers, wins over'.

then heptisax'. The second is that *Beowulf* and Grettissaga come respectively at the beginning and the end of the attested Old Germanic heroic literary tradition. The two are separated by nearly 600 years (8th to 14th century), yet they are very close to each other, perhaps identical, in theme and message, i.e. in "meaning". It is a remarkable testimony to the tenacity of the Germanic tradition.

Perhaps the clearest evidence for a common Germanic (at any rate West and North Germanic) dragon-slaying myth are the respective genealogies of the heroes Sigemund in *Beowulf* and Sigmundr-Sigurðr ("Siegfried") in Old Norse:

Wæls			Vǫlsungr		
*Sister	(*=)	Sigemund (the Wælsing)	Signý	(=)	Sigmundr = o
Fitela (*nefa* of Sig.)			Sin-fjǫtli [cf. OHG PN (Sintar-)Fizzilo]		Sigurðr [MHG Sigfrit]

The identity of the names and their relations, the mythopoeic incest motif (probably reconstructible for Old English as well), all point unequivocally to a common Germanic mythographic background, whether the dragon-slayer is Sigemund as in *Beowulf*, or his son Sigurðr/Sigfrit as elsewhere. It is with this myth that we may begin.

Sigemund's exploit is narrated as part of the victory song composed to celebrate Beowulf's victory over Grendel (867ff.). In this victory song we have a treasure house of the metalanguage of Old Germanic poetry. 'Mindful of lays' (*gidda gemyndig*) the poet 'found another poem, truly bound [i.e. rightly alliterative]' (*word óðer fand / sóðe gebunden*). (With the neuter plural *word* compare Greek ἔπεα.) He began to 'vary words' (*wordum wrixlan*), as Klaeber puts it (ad 874) 'in the customary manner of Germanic poetry', and told of the deeds of Sigemund:

884-7 Sigemunde gesprong
æfter déaðdæge **dóm unlýtel,**
syþðan wíges heard **wyrm ácwealde,**
hordes hyrde.

To Sigemund came, after his death-day, **no little fame**,
since the handy battler **killed a serpent**,
the guardian of a treasure.

'Great fame' is expressed in the ancient figure of litotes, literally '*un*little fame' (*dóm unlýtel*), like Greek κλέος ἄφθιτον and Vedic *ákṣiti śrávaḥ* '*im*perishable fame'; compare also with the same semantics, Greek μέγα κλέος and Vedic *máhi śrávas* 'great fame'.[3] And embedded in the phonetic figure ***heard . . . hordes hyrde*** we find one of the traditional Old English dragon slaying formulas: *wyrm ácwealde* 'killed the worm'.

3. See on these Schmitt 1967:79ff.

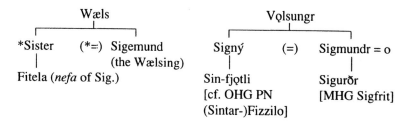

Germanic has no cognate of *áhi-*, *aži-*, ὄφις; the word for 'worm, serpent, dragon' is Old English *wyrm*, Old Norse *ormr*, Old Saxon and Old High German *wurm*, Gothic *waurms*: Germanic **wurmiz*, exactly cognate with Latin *uermis*, and presupposing Indo-European **u̯r̥mis*. The word is a rhyme formation in Indo-European to **k^ur̥mis*, probably for reasons of tabu; **k^ur̥mis* is found in Celtic, Balto-Slavic, Albanian, and Indo-Iranian. The usual meaning of **k^ur̥mis* is just 'worm' in most traditions, but in Middle Iranian it is also the word for 'dragon'; compare the Pahlavi version of the familiar Indo-European formula: *kirm ōzad būd* 'had slain the dragon' (chap. 29). There can be no doubt that in **u̯r̥mis/k^ur̥mis* we have two variants of the same alternative designation of the Indo-European mythological serpent-adversary.[4]

Old English here uses *cwellan* as the unmarked verb for 'kill', the causative of *cwelan* 'die': Indo-European **$g^uel(h_1)$-*, Cuneiform and Hieroglyphic Luvian *wal-* 'die', Old Irish *at-baill* 'dies', Greek βάλλω 'throw'. The causative formation **kwaljan*, anachronistically **$g^uol(h_1)$-éi̯e-*, appears to be confined to Germanic, and its use in the dragon-slaying formula is apparently an innovation confined to Old English.[5] *Beowulf* furnishes two further instances, both precisely in that formula:

1053-5 ond þone ǽnne heht
golde **forgyldan** þone þe Grendel ǽr
máne **ácwealde**

and he ordered the compensation **to be paid**[6]
for the one whom Grendel wickedly **killed**,

1334 þé þú gystran niht Grendel **cwealdest**

(the fight) in which **you killed** Grendel last night.

The two well illustrate the inherited bidirectionality of the formula

→
KILL SERPENT,
←

even where the lexical expression of KILL has been renewed, from IE **$g^{uh}en$-* to Germanic **kwaljan*, Old English *cwellan*.

Other verbs as well are associated with the narration of dragon combat in both

4. See further below (chap. 56) on the Charm.

5. Likewise proper to Old English is the use of the verb *overcome* with the dragon as object. It is used twice of Grendel: *Beowulf* 845 *niða ofercumen* 'overcome by the fight', 1273 *þy he þone feond ofercwom* 'then he (Beowulf) overcame the adversary'. Since Grendel is only the first of Beowulf's monstrous adversaries we could see in *ofercuman* here the continuator of IE **terh₂-*, expressing the preliminary victory of one of the protagonists. IE **seĝh-* shows a similar meaning; compare n. 2 above, and recall only that Hektor too won a preliminary victory.

6. Compare the Greek τίνω, ποινή below in the same context.

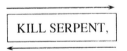

West and North Germanic. The Old Norse verb *vega* 'fight' pret. *vá* < IE **u̯oik-* (**u̯eik-*) is attested in the fragments of the *Vǫlsungasaga* (3. Brunnhildr to Gunnarr): *sigurðr* ***vá*** *at Fáfni / ormi* 'Sigurd fought with Fáfni / the serpent'. In the *Vǫluspá* (53), the Sybil's prophecy, Odin will fare forth

við úlf **vega**

to fight the Wolf,

and perish in the attempt. But he will be avenged: as the next stanza relates, the 'mighty son of Sigfadir' *mikli mǫgr Sigfǫður* ("Victory-Father", epithet of Odin) will come

vega at valdyre

to fight with the corpse-monster (the wolf Fenrir),

and spear him through the heart. Formulaically note the same collocation of the verb and the epithet in *Lokasenna* 58: Loki taunts Thor that he will not dare fight with the wolf (*við úlfinn* ***vega***) and the latter will swallow Odin (***Sigfǫður***). The verb is found only once in *Beowulf* (2400), but in the identical context and again a prophecy of doom: 'So he survived (*genesan*) every battle

oð ðone ánne dæg
þé hé wið þám **wyrme** **gewegan** sceolde

till that one day
when he had to **fight** against that **serpent**.

The verb is IE **u̯eik-*, with an old athematic ablauting paradigm with shifting accent **u̯éik-ti* / **u̯ik-énti* which accounts for the Germanic hesitation in root final consonant, Gothic *weihan*, but Old English, Old Norse (-)*wegan*. Among cognates note Old Irish *fichid* 'fights', Old High German *ubarwehan* 'conquers', with nasal infix Latin *uincō* 'conquers', perfect *uīcī* < **u̯oik-* = Old Norse *vá*, and Homeric Greek οὐκ ἐπίεικτον 'unconquerable, insuperable', which if correctly transmitted in vocalism looks like the obscure Old Irish form *fíacht* (Thurneysen 1946:422).

Old Norse provides us with a precious piece of evidence for the channel for the renewal and replacement of IE **g$^{u̯}$hen-* by other verbs like Germanic **kwaljan* or **wigan* (**weihan*), which we can only present now; the explanation will come in the pages immediately following. In the *Vǫlundarkviða* 33, one of the oldest of the Eddic poems, the smith Vǫlundr makes the King Niðuðr swear an oath, 'by ship's sides, shield's rim, horse's withers and sword's edge', *at skips bordi ok at skialdar rǫnd / at mars bógi ok at mækis egg*, clearly traditional language. Ship and horse, shield and sword are together the warrior's transport and arms; compare the instruction in the Sanskrit laws of Manu (8.113) that the man of the warrior caste (*kṣatriya*) must swear by his 'chariot and weapons' (*vahanāyudhais*), and with the arms alone, the Old Irish oath *tar mo scíath ⁊ tar mo c*[*h*]*loidim* 'over my shield and over my sword' (*Fled Bricrenn* §99). Vǫlundr makes the Norse king swear

> at þú **kveliat** kván Vǫlundar
> né brúði minni **at bana verðir**
>
> that you will not **kill** Vǫlundr's wife,
> nor **become the bane** (= killer) of my bride.

Here *kvelja* and the periphrasis *at bana verða* (on which see below) are semantically identical; the choice of each is governed by the alliteration.

The Old English noun *bona* (*bana*), Old Norse *bani* 'slayer, killer', is frequent in poetic texts in both languages. In *Beowulf* it is applied both to heroes and to monsters; the dragon is the subject. Cf. Grendel in 1743 *bona swíðe néah* 'a killer is very near', 2082 *bona blodigtóð* 'the bloody-toothed killer', and of the Worm who killed Beowulf and was killed by him, 2824 *bona swylce læg* '(his) killer also lay dead'. In Old Norse the dragon is the object. It is used twice with the dragon Fáfnir as object, once of the WEAPON and once of the HERO.[7] *Grípisspá* 15:

> þú munt hǫggva hvǫsso sverði
> brynio rísta með **bana Fáfnis**
>
> You will hew with sharp sword,
> cut her byrnie with **Fáfnir's bane** (the sword Gram),

Oddrúnargrátr 17:

> iǫrð dúsaði ok upphiminn
> þá er **bani Fáfnis** borg um þátti
>
> Earth and Up-heaven shook
> when **Fáfnir's bane** (Sigurðr)
> looked at (Brynhildr's) fortress.[8]

---

7. *inn fráni ormr* 'the speckled snake' *Fáfnismál* 19, 26; for the perseverance of this frequent Eddic formula cf. Faroese *frænorormur*, New Norw. dial. *franarormen* 'the snake with yellow spots'. Cf. Greek ἀργῆν ἔπεφνεν and chap. 39.

8. 'Earth and Up-heaven' is itself an old formula in the Old Norse tradition, indeed probably of Indo-European age. The connection is natural enough, to be sure, but compare in Hittite such collocations, all from mythological or ritual texts, as *Ù* DUMU ^{D}IM ^{MUŠ}*illuyankaš katta nu* ***šarā nepiši*** *attišši ḫalzāiš* 'But the Storm God's son was with the Serpent; and he called up in heaven to his father . . .' (Illuyankas §25); ***šarā nepiši*** *kuwat šakueškizzi* 'Why does it keep looking up to heaven?' (KUB 7.41 Ro. 10-11). Both probably originally would have showed the directive case *nepiša*; for the locative cf. *šēr=a=ššan nepiši šiunaleš ueškanta* 'up in heaven the divine ones are shrieking' (KBo 10.24 iii 13-14). The topos of the stormy agitation of Earth and Heaven is widespread in early Indo-European literatures.

We find finally the collocation with the generic word for serpent in a kenning for the god Thor. *Hymiskviða* 22:

orms einbani uxa hǫfði

The serpent's single bane (used as bait) the head of an ox.

Here the compound *ein-* is there only to alliterate with *orms* and *uxa*; the underlying phrase is *orms bani*, which nominalizes the familiar formulaic verb phrase

KILL SERPENT.

The noun phrase 'serpent's killer' is itself here a definition of the Germanic divine HERO par excellence, the warrior god Thor himself, Nordic counterpart of Indra.

There is in fact no primary, non-derived verb in Germanic which is related to the noun of Old English *bona* etc.[9] To express such a notion verbally by this root all the early North and West Germanic languages have recourse to a periphrasis meaning literally 'become slayer to', which semantically means just 'slay': Old English *tó bonan weorðan* (+ dat.), Old Norse *at bana verða* (+ dat.), Old High German *ti banin werdan* (+ dat.), Old Saxon *te banon uuerðan* (+ dat.). This periphrastic verb phrase is regularly used of more than ordinary killings: it is semantically marked. It is found characteristically in narration of killing of or by a dragon or other monster (bidirectionality), of fratricide or other kin-slaying, of awesome exploits of the hero, or of awesome victims. The context is not indifferent. The examples from *Beowulf* are the following:

1330-1 **Wearð** him on Heorote **tó handbanan**
wælgǽst wǽfre

A wandering murderous sprite (Grendel's mother)
slew him in Heorot.

Note the sentence-initial verb and the postposed, indefinite subject, who is not identified by name.

2078-9 him Grendel **wearð**
mǽrum maguþegne **tó múðbonan**

him, the famous young retainer, Grendel **slew by mouth**.

The first compound members *hand-* and *múð-* are for alliteration. Beowulf taunts Unferth:

9. Old Norse does show the denominative weak verb *bana* (+ dat.), already once in the *Poetic Edda* (*HHv* 26). It is comparable to the Greek creation φονεύω, which as we have seen increases dramatically in frequency in the course of the fifth century B.C.

587 þéah ðú þínum bróðrum **tó banan wurde**

though you **killed** your brothers,

and the same verb describes the primeval fratricide in

1261-2 siþðan Cáin **wearð**
tó ecgbanan ángan bréþer

since Cain **killed** his only brother by the sword,

and the death of Hygelac's son in

2202-3 ond Heardréde hildeméceas
under bordhréoðan **tó bonan wurdon**

and battle-swords **killed** Heardrede under shield-covering.

After Heardrede's death Beowulf legitimately succeeded to the kingship of the Geats:

460 **wearð** hé Heaþoláfe **tó handbonan**

He (Beowulf's father) **slew** Heatholaf,

2501-2 syððan ic for dugeðum Dæghrefne **wearð**
to handbonan Húga cempan

since I (Beowulf) in the presence of the hosts
slew Dæghrefne, champion of the Franks.

From the Old Norse *Poetic Edda* we may cite the following. Of dragons (*Grípisspá* 11):

þú munt báðom **at bana verða**
Regin ok Fáfni

You will **slay** both, Reginn and Fáfnir.

Of brothers (*Reginsmál* 5):

brœðrum tveim **at bana verða**

to **slay** the two brothers,

Helgakviða Hundingsbana I.36 (a taunt, as in *Beowulf* 587 above):

(þú hefir . . .) brœðr þínom **at bana orðit**

you have **slain** your brother.

And finally Odin's question and the witch's answer in *Baldrs Draumar* 8-9:

hverr man Baldri **at bana verða**?
hann man Baldri etc.

Who will **slay** Baldr?
He (Baldr's blind brother Hoðr) will etc.

In Old High German note only the single but telling example of the periphrasis, of tragic adversaries doomed to an ineluctable conflict. Hildebrand says of his son Hadubrand, who does not recognize his father (*Hildebrandslied* 54):

eddo ih imo **ti banin werdan**

or I (shall) **kill** him.

The construction is finally found in Old Saxon Christian poetry as well; for examples, see the work of Rosemarie Lühr cited below.

Old Norse knows another periphrasis with the same word *bani* in the same meaning 'slay': *ban(a)orð bera af* (+ dative), literally 'bring the killer('s) word from', the 'death message'. The expression is explained by Gering s.v. as derived from the legal obligation of a murderer to acknowledge himself as such.[10]

Compare *Fáfnismál* 39 *at Reginn skuli / mitt* ***banorð bera*** 'that Reginn should slay me'; *Landnámabók* iv. 17 (the forge-song of the smith Vǫlundr):[11]

Ek **bar** einn af ellifu
banaorð. Blástu meirr!

I **killed** eleven alone. Blow harder!

10. One might also however imagine a directly created metaphor, the act of killing itself being the word, the message. In RV 8.101.3 the missile of Mitra and Varuṇa is called their 'swift messenger' *ajiró dūtás*. The 'swift messenger' is formulaic in Vedic, *dūtó ajirás* RV 10.98.2, *āśúṃ dūtám ajirám* 3.9.8. It is also in Greek ταχὺς ἄγγελος *Od.* 15.526 and especially Sappho 44.3L-P, where it is line final in the same metrical slot as that occupied by κλέος ἄφθιτον in the next line. See on the latter Nagy 1974:117. Greek ἄγγελος 'messenger' lacks an etymology; should we equate it with Vedic *ajirás* 'swift', via the transferred epithet? A mechanical preform **h₂n̥ĝh₁lo-* will account for both. For examples of the transferred epithet in etymology see chap. 12.

11. Cited from Gordon 1949:134. For the meter see ibid. 294. Note also the enjambment which permits a "vertical" as well as "horizontal" alliterative linkage in *b-*, and the "Irish" rhyme (by consonant-class) *einn* : *meirr*.

Atlakviða 43:

> hon hefir þriggia þiódkonunga / **banorð borit**
>
> She **killed** three kings.

In the *Prose Edda* of Snorri Sturluson the description of Ragnarök, the Twilight of the Gods, presents the whole gamut of Old Norse phrases with *bani* in the space of a few lines: the hound Garmr will fight Tyr, *ok* ***verðr*** *hvárr ǫðrum* ***at bana*** 'and each will kill the other', *Þórr* ***berr banaorð*** *af Miðgarðsormi* 'Thor will slay the Miðgarð serpent', *Ulfrinn gleypir Óðin;* ***verðr*** *þat hans* ***bani*** 'the wolf will swallow Odin; that will be his death'. Note once again the role of Thor as formulaic dragon-slayer: *berr banaorð af ormi* is equally

KILL SERPENT

like *orms einbani* above.

The construction 'became the bane' in Old English *to bonan weordan*, Old High German *ti banin werdan* etc. is discussed by Rosemarie Lühr 1982: 2.652-4, in her exhaustive study with rich comparative material and secondary literature. She shows that it is common West and North Germanic. Lühr rightly explains the meaning 'death, destruction, *bane*' found in all the medieval Germanic languages as a development of this construction, where the subject is not a person but a thing. (Compare the rich proliferation of Medieval and Early Modern English plant names like *henbane, wolfbane, cowbane, dogbane, fleabane*.)

On the other hand, Lühr's identification of this construction with certain others in Germanic misses the point. Old English and Old High German constructions like Laws *Grið* 21.2 *þræl wearð to ðegene* 'slave became noble', *Tat.* 15,2 *steina zi brote uuerden* 'stones to become bread' are not equivalent to a finite verb, and *Otfr*. III 19,25 *uns zi frúmu wurti* '(that) it become of use to us' is just the equivalent of a Latin (etc.) "double dative" (*nobis auxilio*) construction. OHG *ti banin werdan*, OSax. *te banon uuerðan*, OEng. *to bonan weorðan*, ON *at bana verða* are not 'fientive'; they are periphrases which mean 'to slay'. As such they are the exact semantic equivalent of the primary finite verb from the root which produced the Germanic **banan-* 'slayer, bane': a primary verb which does not exist in Germanic.

We have seen the contexts where we find the phrases *to bonan weorðan* and cognates (for convenience I will use the Old English formula as a portmanteau form) or Old Norse *bera ban(a)orð*: slaying of or by a "dragon" (bidirectionality!); killings of heroic dimension; fratricide. These are precisely the context for the appearance of the Indo-European formula

HERO SLAY (**g*^{w}*hen-*) SERPENT/HERO$_2$,

and we pose as equivalent Germanic

to bonan weorðan

HERO SERPENT/HERO$_2$.

bera ban(a)orð

In Germanic as well the subject HERO is frequently not overt, the more readily since he is the *bona*.

The equivalence *$g^{u}hen$-: *tó bonan weorðan* and *bera ban*(*a*)*orð af* must finally be recognized as not merely a typological semantic parallel, but a genetic equation. For E. Seebold and others have made a convincing case for *b* as the typical reflex of Indo-European *g^{u}h*,[12] citing the family of Old English *bona* as part of the evidence; we may equate *bona* exactly[13] with Greek φόνος and Vedic *ghaná*-: Indo-European **g^{u}hon-o-*, *o*-grade of the root **g^{u}hen-*. Indeed, it should be emphasized that the *poetic* equation **g^{u}hen-* : *tó bonan weorðan* is additional and independent evidence for the correctness of Seebold's *phonological* equation and of the sound law. It is yet another argument for the proposition that linguistics needs poetics.

Skeptics of the equation like Meid 1984:104, who prefer to regard the equation as reflecting a borrowing into Germanic from a related "Northwest block" Indo-European dialect would have to assume that the traditional phrasing of the dragon-slaying mythology of the Germanic peoples was also borrowed at the same time from this mysterious source. I doubt they would find that a congenial hypothesis.

Note finally that in the expression φόνος γενέσθαι (+ dative) of *Od*. 21.24

αἳ δή **οἱ** καὶ ἔπειτα **φόνος** καὶ μοῖρα **γένοντο**

but thereafter these **became** his **death** and doom,

we can see in Greek the precise syntactic conditions for the development of the Germanic periphrastic construction 'become the bane' of Old English *tó bonan weorðan* (+ dative). A similar phrase is found in *Od*. 11, when the shade of Agamemnon says (444),

ἀλλ' οὐ **σοί** γ', Ὀδυσεῦ, **φόνος ἔσσεται** ἔκ γε γυναικός

and yet **you**, Odysseus, will never **be murdered** by your wife.

Lattimore's translation clearly captures the verbal force of the periphrasis. Compare also the legal formula in a fifth-century Arcadian inscription, Schwyzer 661.25-6 (Buck 16):

---

12. Seebold 1967, 1980. Note also Cowgill 1980:53, 65, citing with approval Martinet 1972: 89-93.

13. Gmc. **bana-* + *n*-, cf. Lühr 1982:651. Strictly the equation is with the oxytone agent noun *ghaná-* rather than the barytone action noun φόνος. But Indo-European and Germanic could well have had both, as was conjectured by Wackernagel for Greek (ἡ φονός, chap. 36).

ει Иις ιν το(ι) ιεροι τον τοτ[ε απυθανοντον]/ **φονες εστι**

If anyone (present) in the temple is a murderer of those
who were killed at that time.

We may add Germanic to those branches of the Indo-European family which continue the ancient mythological and heroic formulas

HERO	SLAY (**g*^{w}*hen-*)	SERPENT

and

$HERO_1$	SLAY (**g*^{w}*hen-*)	$HERO_2$

The Germanic innovations are only to lose the verbal root **g*^{w}*hen-* and to develop, using inherited morphological, syntactic, and poetic means, a periphrasis with the agent noun derivative **g*^{w}*honó-*, and to utilize the inherited **u̯r̥mi-*, rhyme-form to **k*^{w}*r̥mi-*, for the serpent. The Indo-European asymmetry of the formula is well attested in Germanic, and the bidirectionality is perhaps more prominent in this family than any other due to the pessimistic Germanic view of "final things": Beowulf slays the Worm and is slain by him; at Ragnarök Thor will slay the Miðgarð Worm and die of its poison.

2. Applied myth as charm

We may examine here briefly, as a sort of appendix in anticipation of part VII below (From myth to charm), an Old English dragon-slaying narrative that is incorporated into a longer metrical piece known as the Nine Herbs Charm. It is edited by Dobbie 1942: 119-21, 210, from the unique manuscript Harl. 585, dated by Ker to the 10th/11th century.[14] The relevant episode in the edited text begins with an introduction (27-30):

Þis is seo wyrt   ðe wergulu hatte;
ðas onsænde seolh   ofer sæs hrycg
ondan attres   oþres to bote.
Ðas viiii magon   wið nygon attrum

This is the plant that is called *wergulu* (crabapple);[15]

---

14. I am indebted to Daniel Donoghue for this and many of the references cited below, and am particularly indebted to Joseph Harris for corrections and suggestions, not all of which—at my peril—I followed.

15. So Cockayne 1961:3.34, and the lexica, most recently Bierbaumer 1976:127-8. The word is found only here. Cockayne's justification for the meaning 'crabapple' is presented at 3.348.

16. The reference to the seal is obscure. With the metaphor in *ofer sæs hrycg* 'over the sea's ridge,

a seal sent it over the sea's ridge[16]
to compensate for the malice of other venom.
Those nine are efficacious against nine venoms.

The narrative of the dragon myth proper (31-35) begins a new folio page (161b) and is demarcated by a cross before the first word of l. 31 and another cross at the beginning of line 36.[17] The text then runs:

Wyrm com snican, toslat he man;
ða genam Woden viiii wuldortanas,
sloh ða þa næddran, þæt heo on viiii tofleah.
Þær geændade æppel and attor,
þæt heo næfre ne wolde on hus bugan

A worm came sneaking, it bit someone;
then Woden took nine glory-twigs,
he smote then the adder, so that it flew in nine (pieces).
There the apple ended (it) and (its) venom,
so that it never should go into house.

I translate thus in the light of common sense (the 'apple' as direct object is much more difficult) and the cross-linguistic commonplace of a third person object unexpressed or expressed by a zero sign. Joseph Harris (p.c.) very tentatively suggests as an Old English parallel *Andreas* 1221-2 *bæron ut hræðe / ond þam halgan þær handa gebundon* 'they quickly carried (him) out and bound the saint's hands'. The alliteration requirement (*halgan* : *handa*) may have entailed a movement from the more expected '. . . carried the saint out and bound his hands', leaving the pronoun as a trace. For a similar zero subject with a conjoined noun phrase compare Old Irish *téit ⁊ a máthair* '(he) goes and his mother' = 'he and his mother go'.

The text has given rise to considerable discussion and some controversy. The medical historian Charles Singer (1920: 15) recognized the notion that diseases arose from the nine fragments into which Woden smote the reptile. The healing virtues of the nine herbs mentioned in the text before and after our passage are then to be understood as directed each against a particular 'venom' (*áttor*). The arithmetic of the nine herbs is itself unclear, as noted by H. Meroney,[18] who points out that even for an Old English botanist the (crab)apple is hardly an 'herb'.

In my view (partly building on Meroney) at least two originally distinct metrical charms have been combined by the compilator of ms. Harl. 585 or its source: an 'apple charm' with the dragon-slaying narrative of Woden and a 'nine herbs charm'. The link

back' compare the Old Irish phrase *fairrge al druim* 'over the sea's ridge, back' from the 7th-century poem on St. Columba discussed in chap. 9. We may have diffusion here. The same Archaic Irish poem attests the kenning *nemeth mbled* 'whales' sanctuary' for 'ocean', like Old English (*Beowulf* et passim) *hronrád, hranrád* 'whale-road'.

17. As can be learned from Cockayne's original edition.

18. Meroney 1944. I cannot follow him in his eventual equation of *wergulu* with *lombescyrse* 'lamb's cress'.

is either just the magic number nine or the apple pulp (*þæs æpples gor*), which along with 'old soap' (*ealde sapan*) provides in the prose 'recipe' the base into which the ground herbs are mixed. The 'nine herbs charm' will no longer concern us here; we are interested in the other, whose text has been given.

The name of the pagan god Woden is very rare in Old English literature; aside from genealogies Bosworth-Toller cite only this passage and one other from the Exeter Book (Krapp and Dobbie 1936:161, Maxims 1, line 132):

> Woden worhte weos,   wuldor alwalda,
> rume roderas
>
> Woden wrought idols, the Almighty (wrought) glory,
> the heavens far and wide.

That both this passage and the 'apple charm' should show the collocation *Woden . . . wuldor* 'Woden . . . glory, fame' is probably more than coincidence, the more so since the Old Norse cognate of the latter, *Ullr*, is a divine name or epithet, 'eine Form des alten idg. Hochgottes' (de Vries, s.v.). Like Woden (IE **u̯et-* 'see, be cognizant of', Latin *uātēs* and Old Irish *fáith*), *wuldor* and *Ullr*, Goth. *wulþus* 'δόξα, splendor' are derivatives of a root meaning 'see', IE **u̯el-*, with close links to poetry and mantic prophetic wisdom as well, Old Irish *fili* 'learned poet'. See on these the discussion in chap. 9.

The narrative itself is 'classical' basic formula, with lexical renewal of the basic verb of violent action. First comes the preliminary victory of the serpent,

> SERPENT (*wyrm*) *toslítan* 'lacerate by biting' MAN,

then the reciprocal, the hero's smiting of the beast with a weapon:

> HERO (*Woden*) SMITE (*sléan*) SERPENT (*næddre*) with WEAPON (*tān*).

The verb is precisely Modern English *slay*; the Old English *sléan* is also used reciprocally with the snake as subject, *gif næddre sléa man* 'If a serpent bites a man' (Cockayne 1961:2.110.14).

The weapon is a magical twig (*tán*). The Old Norse cognate *teinn* appears notably in the compound *mistil**teinn***, English *mistleTOE*, the sinister twig which is the WEAPON with which blind Hǫðr will kill—become the bane of, *at bana verða*—Odin's son Baldr (*Vǫluspá* 31, *Baldrs Draumar* 9). The word is also used for a twig cast as a lot, and we know from Tacitus, *Germania* 10.1, that these were cut from fruit trees (*virgam frugiferae arbori decisam in surculos amputant*)—and *agrestia poma* 'wild fruit' along with fresh game and curds were alleged to be the principal diet of the ancient Germans (ibid. 23.1).[19] Such are the overtones of Woden's weapon against the serpent in this ancient Germanic myth narrated as part of the charm.

The brief and formulaic myth is framed, both preceded and followed, by the

19. Cf. the edition and commentary of Anderson 1938, and Much 1959.

reference to the apple: first under the name of *wergulu*, mediated by the mysterious seal over the sea's ridge to remedy venom, then as the *æppel* which finished off the serpent and his venom. What is the connection, or more simply, what is the apple doing in this charm?

The apple is an Indo-European fruit; see the discussion of Gamkrelidze and Ivanov 1984: 2.637-43, with attention to language, botany, ethnography, and mythology. The apple is prominent in several myths among various Indo-European peoples, such as the apple of discord, or the golden apples of the Hesperides (guarded by a dragon), or the golden apples conferring eternal youth and immortality which belong to Idunn, wife of Bragi, the Norse god of poetry (: Vedic *bráhmaṇ-* 'formulation', perhaps Iranian *brazman-*). For Slavic and Baltic compare the references cited by the Georgian and Russian scholars in their work.

I suggest, however, that a much simpler and humbler homeopathic image underlies the function of the apple in this Old English charm against venom (*áttor*). Venom is conveyed by the serpent's tooth; elementary observation teaches that it is the bite of the serpent which is toxic.

Consider then a formulaic curse in Hittite, attested from Old Hittite times down into texts of the New Kingdom and recently discussed by Soysal 1989. KBo 3.46+ Ro. 12′-13′:

> ^{GIŠ}]šamluwanza gakuš=(š)muš [dāu
>
> May the apple take your (or their) teeth!

The reference is clearly to the danger of eating an unpeeled apple for one with poor teeth or ailing gums: one may leave one's teeth in the apple.[20]

As such the apple is a natural homeopathic symbol of defense against the serpent's tooth and its venom. The worms and their venom (Old English *áttor*) are at the same time a metaphor for diseases in Germanic (and Atharvavedic) thought (chap. 56). Add that diseases in the Germanic Middle Ages were themselves metaphorically known as wolf's tooth; compare from Middle High German, Wolfram von Eschenbach, *Parzifal* 7591 *ir truogt den eiterwolves zan* 'you bear the toothmark of the pus-wolf', with *eiter* the German cognate of Old English *āttor*.[21]

The logic of the whole charm then becomes perfectly clear and perfectly natural. It begins with an 'external' narrative:

> The apple is sent against venom.

Then the 'internal' narrative, the myth proper:

> The Serpent bites Man;
> Woden smashes the Serpent into nine pieces with magic twigs.

20. Rather than Soysal's view that it is the sourness of the wild apple which is envisaged. Apples and corn on the cob are routinely proscribed to those with dentures.

21. Cited in Gerstein 1974.

The pieces are venoms, diseases; the venoms are (wolf's)tooth; the apple takes the tooth. Therefore, returning to the 'external' narrative,

> The apple ends (the Serpent) and the venom.

The terms *apple*, *serpent* (both *adder* and *worm*), and *Woden* are all Common Indo-European as well as Common Germanic, and *venom* (*áttor*) and magic *twigs* (*tánas*), and the 'external' verbs *send* and *end* (rhyming!) and the 'internal' verbs *bite* (*slítan*) and *smash* (*sléan*) are all Common Germanic. The Old English charm as we have it lexically may thus be legitimately projected back into, that is, reconstructed for, Proto-Germanic. We are that much closer to the goal expressed by Gamkrelidze and Ivanov 1984:2.643, that the commonality of motifs about the apple in the various traditions may point to a 'reflexion of Common Indo-European ritual and mythological concepts'.

44

Thor's hammer and the mace of Contract

In the preceding chapters we have studied the formulaic aspects of the narration of the dragon-slaying myth in a variety of early Indo-European languages. It was noted that the fullest expression of the mythological theme involved the specification of the WEAPON, typically identified as a mace, cudgel, or war club, often a metaphor for the thunderbolt.

Compare Thor's hammer, named *Mjǫllnir* in Old Norse (*minn þrúðhamarr, Mjǫllnir* 'my power-hammer, M.', *Lokasenna* passim). The Germanic word *hammer* itself belongs together with cognates of variable shape meaning 'stone' (Vedic *áśman-*, Lithuanian *akmuõ*, Old Church Slavonic *kamy*, *kamene*), 'anvil' (Greek ἄκμων), and doubtless the Germanic family of *heaven*, German *Himmel*, Gothic *himins*, and Old Norse *himinn*. It is conceivable that an original meaning like 'meteorite stone' lies at the back of these forms, but it seems not to have been taken up for pre-Germanic poetic or mythographic purposes, and Thor's hammer is just that, a massive smith's tool functioning as a weapon.

The name *Mjǫllnir* (Germanic **melð[u]nijaz*) on the other hand is clearly a Northern European mythographic term, since it can be directly compared with Latvian *milna* (Baltic **mildnā*), the name of the chief pagan god Perkun's hammer. The two together can then be related to the Balto-Slavic and Welsh words for 'lightning', 'thunderbolt': Old Prussian *mealde*, Byelorussian *maladńa*, Church Slavonic *mlъnьji*, Russian *molnija*, and apparently, despite its isolation in Insular Celtic, Welsh *mellt* 'lightning', singulative *mellten* 'bolt of lightning' ('with secondary *t*', according to Pokorny).

Pokorny (IEW s.v.) sets up a root **meldh-* for these Northern European forms, with zero-grade **m̥ldh-*; the form is not demonstrably Common Indo-European, and it is probably best to speak only of a Northern European **m(e)ld-*. The semantics however are much older, for they agree with Greek and Indo-Iranian in designating the metaphorical weapon of a warrior god or sky god, hero or giant. Northern European Germanic Thor the thunder god or Baltic Perkūnas (Slavic Perunъ) with their hammers are in this respect directly comparable to Indra with his *vájra* or his *vadhá*,

Mithra with his *vazra* or his *gaδa*, Astuuaṭ.ərəta or Thraētaona with their *vaδa*, and Herakles or Orion or Poluphemos with their *ropalon*, or maceman Areithoos with his *korunē*.

The Anatolian Storm God ᴰIM-*unnaš*, *Tarḫunt-*, Luvian ᴰ*Tarḫunzaš* in representations carries in his left fist a three-pronged lightning bolt as his symbol and ideogram (Laroche 196), as in the procession in the sanctuary of Yazılıkaya (41 ᴰTONITRUS). A cursive variant of the same hieroglyphic sign (Laroche 199) is that conventionally and iconically transcribed (ᴰ)W, ideogram of the Storm God (Cuneiform ᴰU or ᴰIM), well-attested in the 2nd millennium. In his right fist the Storm God already in the 2nd-millennium iconography (seals, etc.) holds a *vajra*-like scepter similar to the hieroglyphic sign MALLEUS (Laroche 280); in later representations the weapon in his right hand is a battle axe, like the sign ASCIA (Laroche 281). The associated verb in Anatolia is a form of the root *zaḫ(ḫ)*- 'strike', of uncertain origin: Hittite *zaḫḫiškizzi* (Telipinus myth §16), Hieroglyphic Luvian *za-ha-nu-wa-ta* (KARKEMISH A 1 a 6).

In Indic and Iranian there are three common designations of the weapon, from two roots: Vedic *vájraḥ* = Avestan *vazrō*; Vedic *vadháḥ* = Avestan *vaδō*; Vedic *vádhar* = Avestan *vadarə*. The first, as noted in chap. 42, is from the root **u̯aĝ-* of Greek ϝάγνυμι 'break';[1] the other two are both from the root **u̯edh-* (**u̯edhhₓ-*) discussed in chap. 32. The first is another verb of violent action, and the second is in Indic suppletive to the very root **gʷhen-* of the basic formula. Recall from chap. 27.3 the quasi-etymological figures *áhan . . . vadhéna* (RV 1.32.5) and *vadhīt . . . ghanéna* (RV 1.33.4), both 'SLEW with the WEAPON', and note also AV 8.8.3,4, with a derivative of *vadh-* also as subject: *hántv enān vádhako vadháiḥ* 'Let the slayer (*vádhaka-*) slay (*han-*) them with his slayers (*vadhá-* = weapons)'. Compare the etymological figure in RV 5.32.4 *vájreṇa vajrī́ ní jaghāna śúṣṇam* 'The cudgel-bearer struck down Śuṣṇa with the cudgel'.

All three are formulaic and occur in collocations that are of Common Indo-Iranian date; see Mayrhofer, KEWA s. vv. Examples of both *vájra* and *vadhá* have already been given in chap. 28.

For Vedic formula and both weapon words compare RV 1.32.5:

áhan vṛtráṃ vṛtratáraṃ vyàṁsam
índro vájreṇa mahatā́ vadhéna

He slew Vṛtra, the worst obstacle, with shoulders apart (= the cobra),
he Indra, with his mace, his great weapon.

The enjambment of the subject heightens the distancing; each noun has an alliterative noun phrase in apposition to it, and the subject *índra* is in apposition to the immanent subject of the 3 sg. verb. Schematically the formula is double: the familiar verb phrase

1. The Tocharian cognate AB *wāk-* 'split' also points to IE *a*-vocalism. If the isolated Homeric noun ἰωγή 'shelter, windbreak' is from ϝιϝωγ- and related, the ablaut is peculiar.

áhan vṛtrám plus enjambed appositional material and then another formula, this time the instrumental noun phrase *mahatā́ vadhéna*:

*g^{u}*hen*- SERPENT	+	with great WEAPON

The same formula appears in the curse of Vasiṣṭha (RV 7.104.16 a-c):

yó mā́yātuṃ yā́tudhānéty ā́ha
yó vā rakṣā́ḥ śúcir asmī́ty ā́ha
índras táṃ **hantu** mahatā́ **vadhéna**

Whoever says to me, no sorcerer, "Sorcerer!",
or whatever demon says "I am innocent!"
let Indra **smite** that one with his great **weapon**.

We have in 16c the maximal and unified structure

HERO	*g^{u}*hen*-	ADVERSARY	with WEAPON.

Curses of this sort have every likelihood of reflecting ancient—and enduring—verbal habits.

The weapon is not always in the 'marginal' instrumental case. It may instead, for example, be either subject or object of the verb *g^{u}*hen*-, and thus a noun in the nominative or accusative case, as a substitute for either the HERO or the SERPENT.

As object of Vedic *han-* (*g^{u}*hen-*) we find the neuter *vádhar-* (**u̯edh-r̥*) in 2.34.9 *áva . . .* ***hantanā vádhaḥ*** 'beat off the weapon!' The same syntagma underlies the Iranian daēvic personal name *Vaδaγan-*, literally 'weapon-striking', (***vaδa-*** + ***-γan-***). The verb phrase is Common Indo-Iranian.[2]

The structure of the last formula, at least of Common Indo-Iranian age, is

HERO	*g^{u}*hen*-	WEAPON.

For an even fuller structure we must consider the repeated Vedic line (RV 4.22.9 = 7.25.3):

jahí vádhar vanúṣo mártyasya

strike the weapon of the jealous mortal!

The last is of particular interest, for as Bartholomae first noticed, the verb phrase is identical with that of the final litany of the Avestan Hōm Yašt (Y. 9.30-32) *vadarə jaiδi*

2. The Lithuanian word *vedegà* 'axe, pick, esp. for maintaining an ice-hole' is conceivably a remade distant reflex of just such a formation, but this is speculative. Cf. Leskien 1891 on the Lithuanian suffixes *-egas, -ega, -agas, -aga*, and especially Jakobson 1985:25ff. on the pagan Slavic divine names *Svarogъ, Rarogъ, Tvarogъ*.

'strike the weapon!', repeated six times. The first strophe (30) refers precisely to the dragon-slaying myth:

> paiti ažōiš zairitahe
> sīmahe vīšō.vaēpahe
> kəhrpəm nāṣ̌əmnāi aṣ̌aone
> haoma zāire **vadarə jaiδi**
>
> Yellow Haoma, **strike the weapon** against
> the body of the yellow serpent, dirty, poison-spewing,
> for the pious one who is about to perish.

The litany continues in parallel fashion with the invocation to strike the weapon against the 'robber', the 'deceitful mortal' (*maṣ̌iiahe druuatō*, cf. *vanúṣo mártyasya* 'jealous mortal' of the Vedic parallel just cited), the 'heterodox teacher', and the 'bewitching whore'. The *-d-* of *vadarə* (rather than *-δ-*) could show that the word in the formula belongs to the oldest, Gathic Avestan dialect. The phrases in the two languages are a syntactic mirror image, Vedic *jahí vádhar* in sentence- and verse-initial, Avestan *vadarə jaiδi* in sentence- and verse-final position. There can be no doubt that we have a Common Indo-Iranian poetic formula.

The first may be schematized as

HERO | $*g^{w}hen$- WEAPON SERPENT, |

again boxing the verbal formula which is the vehicle of the theme; the second where the adversary is the hostile, deceitful mortal, Indo-Iranian **martii̯a-*, is

HERO | $*g^{w}hen$- WEAPON MORTAL. |

It is significant that the WEAPON in question is indifferently that of the hero, or that of the adversary; using the linguistic convention of the subscript i to mark this linkage, we obtain

HERO$_i$ | $*g^{w}hen$- WEAPON$_i$ SERPENT, |

on the one hand, and

HERO | $*g^{w}hen$- WEAPON$_i$ MORTAL$_i$ |

on the other. In Indo-Iranian phonetic shape,

HERO$_i$ **ǰhan-* *u̯adhar*$_i$- *aǰhi-*
HERO **ǰhan-* *u̯adhar*$_i$- *martii̯a-*$_i$

The weapon is the serpent's in RV 5.32.2-3:

áhim . . .
jaghanvā́n . . .
tyásya cin maható nír mr̥gásya
vádhar jaghāna táviṣībhir índraḥ

Having slain . . . **the serpent** . . .
Indra with all his strength **struck aside the weapon**
of that great monster.

We find the same indifferent attribution of the weapon either to the hero or to his monstrous adversary in Germanic, precisely in the "singular detail" (discussed in chap. 43) of the shared compound element Old Norse *hepti-* and Old English *hæft-* in the formulaically and thematically inherited weapon word. The ***heptisax*** is the weapon of the monstrous adversary in the Old Norse *Grettissaga*, while the Old English cognate ***hæftmece*** is the weapon of the hero Beowulf.

The Iranian god Mithra, whose name means Contract, is armed with a mace (*vazra-*, the cognate of Vedic *vájra-*), carefully and formulaically described in Yašt 10, the Avestan hymn to Mithra edited by Gershevitch. Compare the verses of 10.96:

vazrəm zastaiia dražəmnō
satafštānəm satō.dārəm
frauuaēγəm vīrō.niiā̊ṇcim
zarōiš aiiaŋhō frahixtəm
amauuatō zaraniiehe
amauuastəməm zaiianąm
vərəϑrauuastəməm zaiianąm[3]

Holding the mace in his hand
with a hundred bosses, a hundred blades,
felling men as it swings forward,
cast in yellow bronze,
strong, gilded,
strongest of weapons,
most irresistible of weapons.

Strophe 101 furnishes the construction with the weapon as direct object of the verb *jan-* (IE *$*g^{\mu}hen$-*) with the victims in the locative, then repeats the basic formula with the victims as underlying direct objects in a compound with the same root:

hō paoiriiō **gaδąm nijaiṇti**
aspaēca paiti vīraēca,
haϑra.taršta ϑrā̊ŋhaiiete
uuaiia aspa.vī**raja.**

3. For the pair *amauuastəməm*, *vərəϑrauuastəməm* compare the formulaic *aməmca vərəϑraγnəmca* Yt. 14.38.

It is he who first **strikes** his **club**
at horse and man;
he frightens both with sudden fright
smiting horse and man.

Further on, all of Mithra's weapons on his chariot are catalogued and described, a thousand each of bowstrings, arrows, spears, hatchets, knives, hurling clubs (*gaδā-*), and a single mace, described with an expansion of 96 cited above (132):

hištaite aom vāṣ̌ahe
miϑrahe vouru.gaoiiaoitiš
vazrəm srīrəm huniuuixtəm
satafštānəm. . .
vərəϑrauuastəməm zaiianąm
mainiiauuaså vazəṇti
mainiiauuaså patəṇti
kamərəδe paiti daēuuanąm

There stands on the chariot
of Mithra of the wide pastures
the beautiful mace, easily brandished,
with a hundred bosses . . .
most irresistible of weapons.
through the spirit-place they fly,
through the spirit-place they fall
on the heads of the daēvas.

Yašt 6.5 in a strophe to Miϑra gives the variant:

yazāi vazrəm huniuuixtəm
kamərəδe paiti daēuuanąm

I will worship the mace, easily brandished
on the heads of the daēvas.

The Indic cognate and counterpart of Avestan Mithra is the god Mitra 'Contract, Ally'; attested already in Mittanni and Middle Hittite documents of the middle of the second millennium B.C., Mitra the god Contract is clearly a Common Indo-Iranian divinity.[4] The concept itself and its societal valuation are much more ancient, going back to the community of Indo-European itself, including Anatolian. The earliest attested word of any Indo-European language is the word for contract, borrowed from Hittite *išḫiul* into the Old Assyrian of the Cappadocian merchant colonies (*kārum Kaneš*, *kārum Ḫattuš*) in the 19th century B.C.[5]

4. The fundamental study is Thieme 1975:21-39.
5. In Hittite the word continued down to the end of the empire over six centuries later as the unique

If the notion of the sacredness of Contract is Common Indo-European and the divinity of Contract *Mitrá/Miϑra* Common Indo-Iranian, it remains a fact that the Mace of Contract is only an Iranian topos. Mitra in Vedic India (and earlier in Anatolian Mittanni) had no weapon. We must seek some explanation for the Iranian development of this theme.

We already saw in chap. 42 that the formulaic deployment of Mithra's *vazra* in Iran can be thematically and verbally exactly paralleled in India in the descriptions of Indra's *vájra*, and in Greece as well in the descriptions of the club or mace (ῥόπαλον) of many heroes and giants like Herakles, Poluphemos, or Orion. The epithet ἀ(ϝ)αγές 'unbroken' of ῥόπαλον (*Od.* 11.575) contains the same root as *vazra/vájra*, and the name of the hero Μελέ-(ϝ)αγρος is identical to the Indo-Iranian weapon name down to the very suffix: we have a Common late Indo-European **u̯aĝros.*

Not only this but the other weapon words *vádhar/vadarə* and *vadhá/vada* are common to Indic and Iranian, with Greek showing the verbal cognate in the isolated participle (ϝ)έϑων 'striking'. The epithet of the *vazra* in Avestan *(fra-)hixta* 'cast', belongs to the technical vocabulary of metalworking. It recurs in Vedic of the *vájra* and *vadhá*, collocated with the cognate *sic-* in the meaning 'cast', as well as with *han-* 'slay, smite'. AV 11.10.(12,)13:

vájraṃ yám **ásiñcata**
asurakṣáyaṇaṃ **vadháṃ**
ténāhám amū́ṃ sénāṃ
ní limpāmi bṛhaspate
amítrān **hanmy** ójasā

The **vajra** which (Bṛhaspati) **cast**,
the asura-destroying **weapon**,
with that I blot out yonder army, o Bṛhaspati;
I slay the enemies with force.

From another myth, Indra's fear after slaying Tvaṣṭṛ's son Viśvarūpa, note TS 2.5.2.2 (cf. 2.4.12.2) *tásmai* ***vájraṁ siktvā́*** *prā́yacchad eténa* ***jahī́ti*** 'having cast the *vájra* he gave it to him, saying, "slay with it!".'

Combining these passages with those cited in chap. 42, we may display in three columns the verbal equations of form or meaning collocated in these three traditions describing the hero's great weapon:

	Iranian	Indic	Greek
'weapon'	vazra	vájra(-)	-(ϝ)αγρος, ἀ(ϝ)αγές
'hand'	zasta	-hasta	χερσίν
'100(0)-bossed'	satafštāna	sahasrabhṛṣṭi	(τραχύ)
'yellow'	zairi	hári	χλωρός

designation for the binding (Hittite *išhiya* 'bind, tie') contract or alliance of the Hittite king, ranging from treaties on the international level to 'contracts' and 'instructions' on the interpersonal level. Cf. Laroche 1971:35.

'golden'	zaraniia	híraṇya	
'bronze'	aiiaŋhō	āyasá	παγχάλκεον
'weapon'	vaδa	vadhá	((ϝ)έϑων)
'cast'	frahixta	siktvā́	
'slay'	nijaiṇti, -ja	jahi, hanmi	(κατέπεφνεν)
'beast'	aspaēca	gohā́	(βουφονία)
	aspa.vīraja		
'man'	vīraēca	nṛhā́	(Myc. Anorphontās)

The massive coincidences of these three languages must surely reflect a common and inherited traditional topos of the description of the WEAPON. In each of the three the words describe the weapon of different divinities (Mithra, Indra, the Maruts), heroes or anti-heroes (Orion, Herakles, Poluphemos), but who all belong to the warrior class of gods or heroes. The equation of Thor's hammer *Mjǫllnir* and Perkun's hammer *Milna* points to the same thematic context in the respective pantheons, but on a younger and dialectally more restricted layer: the geographically contiguous Germanic and Baltic.

It is finally in this formulaic set that we must find the explanation for the particular Iranian creation and development of the "Mace of Contract", *vazrəm miϑrahe*, the weapon of the divinity personified already in Indo-Iranian times (Thieme 1975). For Iranian alone preserves clearly the expression *miϑrəm jan-* 'break [literally 'smite, slay'] a contract'; Hymn to Mithra (Yt. 10) 2:

miϑrəm mā janiiā̊ spitama

Never break a contract, o Spitama (Zarathustra).

Avestan *miϑra-* is both the abstract and the divinity. The "logic" of the basic formula presupposes that beside the evil action 'smite contract' *miϑrəm jan-* (*miϑrəm* accusative), there exists the reciprocal good action 'Contract smites' *miϑrō jan-* (*miϑrō* nominative). From there the way stands open to *gadąm nijaiṇti*,

Mithra STRIKE (*jan-*) WEAPON,

at horse and man. The whole formulaic development we have seen in the passages from Yašt 10 could then be transferred from an Indo-Iranian Indra-divinity to the new, aggressive Iranian Mithra who partly took the latter's place, his function, and his epithet system.

Thieme 1975:26 did point out the existence in epic of *Mitraghna*, name of a Rākṣasa (Rāmāyaṇa), and *mitrahan-* (Mahābhārata). But the meaning 'Kontraktbrecher' (so also Mayrhofer, KEWA 3.778) is only reconstructed; synchronically they must mean 'friend-slaying'.

Much older, however, and more relevant as well, is the verb phrase we have seen in the Atharvavedic passage cited earlier, AV 11.10.13 *amítrān han-* 'slay the enemies', which is clearly formulaic in Vedic. Compare RV 4.12.2 *ghnánn* ('slaying') *amítrān* of the pious worshipper (as in AV 11.10.13), 6.44.17 *jahí* ('slay!') ... *amítrān* of Indra, 7.85.2 *amítrān hatám* ('ye two slay!') of Indra and Varuṇa, as well as the compound *amitrahán-* 'enemy-slaying', of Indra and other divinities. Vedic *a-mítra-* is a negative bahuvrīhi compound formed directly from *mitrá-* 'contract, alliance': our 'enemies' are those with whom we have no alliance or covenant. As such Vedic *amítrān han-* qua 'slay/smite those with whom we have no contract' is directly comparable to Avestan *miϑrəm mā janiiā̊* 'do not break/smite contract', and on a much older level than the purely Indic semantic development of *mitrá* to 'friend'. Schematically,

NEG (*a-)mitra- *ǰhan-

and

*mitra- NEG (mā) *ǰhan-

are syntactic variants of the same Common Indo-Iranian poetic formula. The reciprocal of the same formula in Iran, with *miϑra* as subject, entailed as formulaic consequence the poetic creation of the Mace of Contract.

To the chart of interlingual formulaic collocations given above we can certainly add

	Iranian	Indic
'contract'	miϑra	(a-)mítra,

both with *jan-/han-*. These have been compared, speculatively, with Homeric Greek μίτρη, a piece of armor girded around one, ἀμιτρο-χίτωνες, epithet of Lydian warriors, and ἄμιτρος 'ungirdled' (i.e. not of marriageable age) in Callimachus. Formally the equations are perfect; but they seem to suppose a basic root meaning of 'bind, tie' and a lengthy semantic history, both of which elude demonstration.[6]

On the chart Vedic *gohā́* (*g^{u}ou-g^{u}hen-*) epithet of the Maruts' weapon, was compared to the Greek *Bouphonia* (*g^{u}ou-g^{u}hon-*) discussed in chap. 42, the ritual ox-sacrifice in Athens after which the sacrificial axe is tried for murder. I conclude with some purely synchronic remarks on a passage from Sophocles' *Electra*, where another axe, a famous murder weapon, is animatized, endowed with memory, metonymically just called 'cheek' (γένυς, of feminine gender), and made the subject of the verb κατέπεφνεν 'slew' in one of the three attestations of the verb *g^{u}hen-* in Sophocles. *Electra* 482-91, a choral passage:

οὐ γάρ **ποτ' ἀμναστεῖ** γ' ὁ φύ-
σας σ' Ἑλλάνων ἄναξ,
οὐδ' ἁ παλαιὰ χαλκόπλη-

6. Cf. Chantraine, DELG, s.v.; Mayrhofer KEWA s.v. *mitrá-*; and for the μίτρη in Homer, Kirk 1985 ad 4.137, 187, and 5.707.

κτος ἀμφάκης **γένυς**,
ἅ νιν **κατέπεφνεν** αἰσχίσταις ἐν αἰκείαις.
ἥξει καὶ πολύπους καὶ πολύχειρ **ἁ**
δεινοῖς κρυπτομένα λόχοις
χαλκόπους **'Ερινύς**.

For he who begot you, king of the Greeks,
has **never forgotten**,
nor the ancient **cheek** of the axe
double-bladed, smiting with brazen edge,
which slew him in most shameful outrage.
There will come with many feet and many hands,
hiding in terrible ambush,
the brazen-footed **Fury**.

The strong figure of litotes in **οὐ** γάρ **ποτ' ἀμναστεῖ** 'is never unmindful, has never forgotten', the negation of negation which affirms the positive, cannot but recall the last phrase of Kalkhas' prophecy reported by the chorus at the beginning of Aeschylus' *Ag.* 155: **μνάμων** Μῆνις τεκνόποινος 'unforgetting, child-avenging Wrath' (Denniston and Page ad. loc.).

The iconicity of the feminine gender of ἁ . . γένυς, ἅ . . κατέπεφνεν 'the cheek which slew' is a powerful indictment of the real murderess Klutaimestra, and the identical gender of the like-ending γέ**νυς** and 'Ερι**νύς**, both line-final and clause- or sentence-final, indexes the inexorable logic of the link **χαλκ**όπληκτος . . πολύ**πους** . . **χαλκόπους** 'brazen-edged . . many-footed . . brazen-footed'. The murder weapon has become the agent of its vengeance.

V

Some Indo-European dragons and dragon-slayers

45

Fergus mac Léti and the *muirdris*

The 'Saga of Fergus mac Léti' was edited by D. A. Binchy (1952), from the originally Old Irish text of the 16th-century legal ms. H 3.18 (CIH 882.4ff.); a somewhat later version in Harl. 432 (CIH 354.27ff.), Binchy's L, is also reprinted and translated in Anc. Laws of Ireland 1.64ff. The first text of the *Senchas Már*, the collection of legal texts known as the 'Great Tradition', is the lengthy treatise on distraint, *Cetharslicht Athgabála*, from Harl. 432 (CIH 352.25ff.) and H 3.17 (CIH 1897.16ff.). It begins in both with a paragraph of archaic prose (Binchy, p. 48), starting *teora ferba fīra* 'three milk cows', which sets forth what was intended as a 'leading case' of distraint. This is followed by an archaic poem in heptasyllabic meter giving a condensed version of the legal aspects of the saga of Fergus mac Léti, with its reference to the forfeiture and eventual restoration of land. It is edited by Binchy, ibid. 45-7.

Binchy recognized that these two leading cases were drawn from native mythology and pressed into service by the jurists; that the two were 'traditionally associated from a very early period' is perhaps due in part to the name *Asal* (*mac Cuinn Chétchathaig*) occurring in both.

The myth of the first of the two leading cases, *teora ferba fíra* 'three milk cows', contains both themes and key vocabulary going back to the Indo-European times: in a lecture in Dublin I styled it 'The Milk of the Dawn Cows'. For this reason alone the second myth, the events culminating in Fergus' vanquishing the monster in an underwater combat, also deserves our close attention. As we shall see, the resultant set of themes and vocabulary of Indo-European antiquity amply repay that attention.

The archaic poem itself clearly belongs to the legal tradition by its style and subject matter. Its focus is land (*tír*), as demarcated by ring composition, here the word for 'land', as a frame. I give Binchy's text save for two controversial 3 sg. relative preterite forms:

> **tīr** ba[ä] Chuind chētchoraig
> asa-ngabtha ilbenna
> bertai Fergus ferglethech
> i ndīgail a thromgreise
> di **guin** Echach bēlbuidi.

Brethae Dorn i n-ansoīri,
do-cer inna **fīrinni**
s(e)iche i ngnūis Fergusa.
Ferais Fergus ferḟechtas
finech i lloch Rudraige
dia-**marbad** i mārchinta.
Taisic a **tīr** immurgu
fo selba Cuind comorbae.[1]

Land which belonged to Conn of the hundred treaties, out of which many horned beasts were taken, Fergus the manly warrior took it as atonement for the grievous outrage done to him by the **slaying** of Eochu of the yellow lips. Dorn was sentenced to captivity; she perished in atonement for her **truth** which she uttered in Fergus's face. Fergus of the kindreds made a manly incursion in Loch Rudraige, on account of which he **was killed** for his grave wrongdoings. The **land**, however, reverted to the estates of Conn's heirs.

As Binchy saw, the poem is a condensed version of the saga itself, to the point of being largely unintelligible without knowledge of the latter. The central dragon-slaying is barely alluded to; the jurists were concerned with law and not myth. Hence the framing by 'land' (*tír*) and the generalized balance of slaying (*guin*, IE **gʷhen-*) requited by killing (*-marbad*, IE **mr̥-u̯o-*). At the very center of this thematically nested poem is *fírinne* 'truth'.

I give in the following a brief synopsis of the prose saga, with attention to selected themes and their verbal expression:

Conn and Eochu were in rivalry over the kingship of the Fēini.

Eochu went in exile to Fergus, king of Ulster.

While under the latter's protection, Eochu was killed (*marbs-i*, IE **mr̥-u̯o-*) by 6 men: Asal son of Conn, the four sons of Buide, and the son whom Dorn ('hand'), daughter of Buide, had borne to an 'outlander' (*deorad*, one without legal status). Note that these are an alliance both of kinsmen by blood and kinsmen by marriage.

1. Disyllabic *baä* (mss. *ba*) for Binchy's conjecture *boíe* was suggested by David Greene 1977:31. We expect also a relative form 'which she uttered' (mss. *sich*, *seiche*); with some misgivings I follow Carney's suggestion *sīche*. The verb must have been originally strong; we might have expected **sāche*, but cf. Umbrian *prusikurent*. For *Fergus . . . finech* I follow a suggestion of John Carey's (1988). The importance of the epithet will emerge below.

This chapter was first presented in 1993 as a Michael Devlin lecture at St. Patrick's College, Maynooth.

> Fergus's protection was violated (*do-gét*, IE **gʷhn̥-to-*),[2] and he sought vengeance for the violation (*siacht a díguin*, IE **sag-* [**sh₂g-*] . . . **gʷhen-*).[3]
>
> Fergus was given land (*tír*) from Conn, and received Dorn in servitude for life.[4]
>
> Fergus got from a dwarf/sprite[5] he had captured the magic power to travel under any body of water save Loch Rudraige (which was forbidden to him).
>
> Fergus did go under Loch Rudraige, where he saw a *muirdris*, a fearful water monster. At the sight of it (*la diuterc do foire*, lit. 'by his gazing at it') he came out on land with his face permanently disfigured by terror.
>
> Kept from seeing his reflection for seven years and thus unaware of the blemish,[6] he once ordered his bondswoman Dorn to wash his face. When she was slow to respond he struck her with a whip. Resentment overcame her and she taunted him with the blemish; and he killed her.
>
> Then he went under Loch Rudraige and fought the *muirdris* for a day and a night. He emerged from the bloody lake with the monster's head saying, 'I am the survivor' (*messe is tiugbae*), and fell dead (*marb*, IE **mr̥-u̯o-*).

We have intertwined in the dragon-killing tale proper a remarkable set of themes and "motifemes": those of (1) abnormal or inverse social and sexual relations (Dorn's son by an 'outlander' without legal status); (2) the abuse or violation of hospitality (the killing of Eochu in violation of Fergus's protection, *díguin*); (3) the abnormal servitude of Dorn; (4) the injunction (against going into Loch Rudraige) and (5) the violation of the injunction; (6) the temporary victory of the *muirdris* over the hero; as a result (7) the hero's disfigurement or mutilation, itself causing real or potential loss of status or power; (8) the abuse or violation of the responsibility of "hospitality"to an inferior in

2. This is one of the very few examples in Early Irish of the etymologically regular preterite passive *-gét* < **gʷhn̥-to-* (= Ved. *hatá-*, Av. *-zata-*, Gk. -φατος) of *gonid -guin* and its compounds. So *Buile Suibhne* 1077 (: *éc*), as John Carey notes. Otherwise we find the obscure reformed *-goít*.

3. Compare the legal expression for 'seek vengeance for murder' in Hittite *ešḫar šanḫ-* , Albanian *gjak kërkoj*, both literally 'seek blood'.

4. Binchy suggests that originally Dorn went into servitude volutarily to save her son and perhaps brothers from noxal surrender and death. The very obscure *rosc* in §2 seems to indicate that her kin-group (that of Buide, her and her brothers' father) refused to pay compensation; in any case it is important for focusing on her central role on the narrative.

5. Called both *abacc* 'dwarf' and *lúchorpán* 'little-bodied', which occurs here for the first time: later deformed to *luchrapán*, *luprachán*, (Hiberno-English *leprechaun*), *lúrapóg*, etc. A striking feature of this episode is the practice of fealty by nipple-sucking, the pagan Irish custom called by St. Patrick *sugere mamillas*.

6. Which would have put him out of the kingship, according to the ancient Irish and Indic institution.

Fergus's treatment of Dorn; (9) the underwater locale of the combat; and (10) the final paean, in direct speech of the victory which reestablishes order over chaos, followed by the death of the hero.

At the heart of the narrative linguistically is the root **gʷhen-* in the ancient compound with **dē-*: verbal noun *díguin*, pret. pass. *do-gét*, act. 3pl. *di-tn-gegnatar*, compare Latin *dē-fen(-dō)*. Other lexical reminiscences of inherited themes have been noted above; add to these the name of the hero *Fergus* < **u̯iro-ĝustu-* 'having the strength of men' (echoed in the archaic legal poem by *ferglethech* 'manly warrior' and *ferḟechtas* 'manly incursion'), which recalls Indra's first *vīryám* 'manly deed' of slaying the serpent. For the word *muirdris* see further below.

While the narrative of the tale of Fergus mac Léti and the slaying of the *muirdris* is markedly 'saga-like' and Irish in temper and style, an extraordinary number of the associated themes and 'motifemes' we have noted recur in the central Hittite myth of the Storm God and the slaying of the *illuyankaš*, the serpent. These turn out to be so numerous and so precise, I suggest, that we must assume a common prototype: the Indo-European dragon-slaying myth par excellence.

Again I give a synopsis of the text of the myth,[7] identifying these themes and their verbal expression where relevant. As commonly in Hittite, the narration of the myth is an integral part of a ritual, that of the new year:[8] 'In order that the land grow and prosper, they perform the *purulli* festival:'

> When the Storm God and the serpent did battle, the serpent overcame the Storm God. [temporary defeat of the hero]
>
> The goddess Inaras made a feast and invited all the gods. She met the mortal Hupasiyas and said, 'I am going to do such-and-such. Come join up with me too (*ziqq=a ḫarapḫut*[9]).' [abnormal and inverse social relations, goddess to mortal]
>
> Hupasiyas replied, 'I'd like to sleep with you; then I will come and do your heart's desire.' And[10] he slept with her (*n*[*u* (*katt*)]*i=ši šešta*). [abnormal and inverse sexual relations, mortal to goddess]
>
> She hid him, bedecked herself, and invited the serpent and his children. They drank, became drunk, and could not get back into their hole. Hupasiyas tied up the serpent. [violation of hospitality]

---

7. Following the edition and analysis of the text (CTH 321) by Beckman 1982. The serpent ᴹᵁˢ̌*il*[*luyanka-*] is plausibly restored by Otten and Rüster in the newly published fragment KBo 34.23 Ro. 16′, which seems to be from a different text than CTH 321. Cf. KUB 36.97?

8. MU.KAM-*aš* SAG.DU 'head of the year', KUB 36.97 iii 3′.

9. The Hittite verb *ḫarp* - IE **h₃orbh-*, means to transfer oneself or be transferred from one sphere of physical or social appurtenance or allegiance into another. It is used concretely of divorce, and of cattle getting out of a pen and into someone else's property (Laws §§ 31,66), or more abstractly, as here. In other Indo-European languages the root gives rise to such divergent notions as 'bereft' (Lat. *orbus*), 'orphan' (Gk. ὀρφανός), 'inheritance' (Irish *orbbe*, Goth. *arbi-*), and 'slave' (OCS *rabъ*, doubtless originally 'enslaved free man').

10. Read *n*]*u* with B i 2 rather than Beckman's restoration [*na-aš*].

> The Storm God killed the serpent (*kuenta*, IE *g^{w}*hen*-), and the gods were with him.
>
> Inaras installed Hupasiyas in a house, saying, 'When I go out, don't look out the window, you will see your wife and children.' [the injunction]
>
> After twenty days he looked out and saw them. [violation of the injunction] He began to weep, and implored Inaras to let him go home.
>
> [At this point the text becomes too fragmentary; probably Hupasiyas is killed. But we clearly have the themes of abnormal and inverse social and sexual relations, violation of hospitality, and abuse of the responsibility to an inferior.]

The second version of the myth, on the same tablet, is also narrated in the same ritual, as shown by Beckman (cf. chap. 46). It begins:

> The serpent overcame (*tarḫta*, IE **terh*$_2$-) the Storm God [temporary victory of the monster] and took his heart and eyes. [mutilation of the hero, leading to diminution of his status]
>
> The Storm God married the daughter of a poor man and begot a son. [abnormal and inverse social and sexual relations, god to poor mortal]
>
> The Storm God's son grew up and married the serpent's daughter, and went to live in his bride's house. [again abnormal and inverse socioeconomic[11] and sexual relations]
>
> The Storm God instructed his son when he went to his wife's house to ask for his heart and eyes. The son did so, and brought them back to his father. [betrayal or violation of his father-in-law's hospitality]
>
> Restored to his former status by the recovery of his heart and eyes the Storm God went into the sea to fight the serpent. [underwater locale of the combat]
>
> When the Storm God was about to overcome (*taraḫḫuwan daiš*, IE **terh*$_2$-) the serpent, the Storm God's son was with his father-in-law. He shouted up to heaven to his father: 'Include me in! Do not show me mercy!' [a paean of reaffirmation, in direct speech, of the son's morally

11. Hittite society was normally patrilocal. When as here a poor man took a rich man's daughter as bride and went to live in her father's house, the groom was called LÚ *antiyant-* 'in-going man', 'eingeheirateter Schwiegersohn', Turkish *içgüvey* (*iç-* 'in-'). The same custom and the same label persisted in 20th-century rural Latvia, where the *iegātnis*, literally 'in-gone one', used to suffer a good deal of abuse from his in-laws (fide Joseph Lelis). The specific parallel to Dorn's son is striking, even if their roles are different.

correct but tragic new allegiance,[12] which by his death will reestablish order over chaos]

Then the Storm God killed the serpent and his own son. [*kuenta*, IE *$*g^{w}hen$-*]

The dragon-killing myth represents a symbolic victory of order over the forces of chaos, as we have seen; of growth over stagnation in the cycle of the year, of rebirth over death, which must be perpetually and cyclically retold to maintain its effectiveness.[13] The comparison of the tales of Fergus and the *muirdris* and the Storm God and the *illuyankaš*, at opposite ends of the Indo-European world, shows that the chaos symbolized by the Indo-European dragon was fundamentally social in character. An Irish storyteller would say immediately, as one once did say to the folklorist and collector Seamus Delargy (*fide* Edgar Slotkin): "This is about *cleamhnas* and *gaol*," (Old Irish *cleamnas*, *gáel*) 'kinship by marriage' and 'kinship by blood'.

A Hittite chronicler with the same image could speak of the conditions under the just ruler, as in the preamble to the Proclamation of King Telepinus of the early dynasts Labarnas, Hattusilis, and Mursilis (§§ 1,5,8):

DUMU^{MEŠ}-*ŠU* ŠEŠ^{MEŠ}-*ŠU* $^{\text{LÚ.MEŠ}}$gaenaš=šešš=a
LÚ^{MEŠ} ḫaššannaš=šaš *Ù* ERÍN^{MEŠ}-*ŠU* taruppanteš ešer

His sons, his brothers, and his relatives by marriage,
the members of his kindred and his soldiers were united.

The formula is expressed twice, with ever widening circles of social appurtenance: the ruler's close relatives by blood and close relatives by marriage, then his partisans by kin-fealty and his partisans by allegiance.

Soldiers of the Hittite army (ERÍN^{MEŠ}) took an oath of personal allegiance to the King; the texts are edited by N. Oettinger 1976. Old Irish *cliamain* (genitive *clemna*) 'relative by marriage, alliance' probably contains the same **k̂li-* 'lean' as Latin *cliens* 'client', with another modality of allegiance (to the *patronus* 'patron').

That is to say, the evil or chaos that must be overcome by the narration of the myth, the telling of the story, is all that is 'anti-social', anti-traditional, anti-hierarchical, and that is in violation of the fundamental institutionalized gift-exchange relations and consecrated customs which are alliance and blood kinship, symbolized by hospitality. These are characteristic notions for a society where the highest ethical ideal is that Cosmic Truth which is 'fitted, ordered', and therefore 'right, true': Hittite *ḫandant-* and its abstract *ḫandantatar*, Vedic *r̥ta*, Avestan *aša*, which corresponds in Ireland to the *fírinne* 'truth' at the very center of the legal poem with which we began, and to the ancient Irish ethical notion of the Ruler's Truth, *fír flathemon*.

12. Compare note 10, on the meaning of Hittite *ḫarp-* and IE **h₃orbh-*.
13. Compare Beckman's discussion and the extensive literature there cited.

Appendix: *muirdris*

This word for the dragon or 'sea-monster' (*peist uiscide*) is apparently confined to this text alone.[14] The first element is evidently *muir* 'sea'; the element *dris* may therefore convey the notion 'monster', 'dragon', or the like. That it is the same as *dris* 'bramble, briar' seems unlikely; the creature is not a sea urchin. It is doubtful whether *dris* is identical with the first element of the name of a (low) poetic grade (a *doerbard* of the third degree) *drisiuc*, gen. *driscon*, a compound of *cú*, *con* 'dog' with hypocoristic gemination (**drissiccū*).

Now it was the sight of the creature which terrorized Fergus into disfigurement: the archaic word is *diuderc* 'gazing' from *dī-uss-derc-*, with the cognate of Greek δέρκομαι 'look, see', perfect δέδορκα = Vedic *dadárśa* = Old Irish (*ad-con*)-*darc*. This dangerous or lethal property is shared with some dragons in Greece, notably the Gorgon, the sight of whom turned the beholder to stone. Compare Pindar, *Pyth.* 10.46-8 (cited in chap. 36):

> **ἔπεφνεν** τε **Γοργόνα**
> καὶ ποικίλον κάρα
> **δρακόντων** φόβαισιν ἤλυθε νασιώταις
> λίθινον **θάνατον φέρων**

> And he **killed** the **Gorgon**,
> came **bearing** the head, intricate with **snake** hair,
> the stone **death** to the islanders.

As we noted, the story of Perseus slaying the Gorgon is the first myth we have that Pindar narrated; composed in 498 B.C., *Pythian* 10 is his earliest attested work. In this single sentence we find not one but two formulas of Indo-European date: the basic ἔπεφνεν . . . Γοργόνα, and θάνατον φέρων, the equivalent of φόνον . . . φέροντες, φόνον φέρει (*Il.* 2.352, 17.757) discussed in chap. 51. And nestled between these two formulas we find the snakes' hair, **δρακόντων** φόβαισιν, with the Greek word δράκων 'dragon, serpent', the source of our own word *dragon*. The connection of δράκων with the verb δέρκομαι, aorist ἔδρακον, was in antiquity psychologically real enough, whether a 'true' or a folk etymology; cf. the dictionaries of Chantraine and Frisk.

I suggest that in the second element of the Old Irish compound *muir-dris*, 'sea-*dris*' we see a cognate of the Greek word δράκων 'dragon, serpent'. The zero-grade of the root is common to both, **dr̥k̂-* > Greek *drak-*, Celtic *drik-*. A suffixed form **dr̥k̂-si-* (or feminine **dr̥k̂-sih*$_2$) would yield precisely Primitive Irish **drissi-*, Irish *dris*.

Both branches then, Greek and Celtic, would attest both the verbal root **derk̂-* 'see' and a word for 'dragon, serpent' **dr̥k̂-*. If the latter two should turn out not to be cognate—which I doubt—the folk etymology itself could be of Indo-European date, since the danger of the sight of the dragon is found in both traditions, Greek and Irish.

---

14. The monster in Loch Lurgan called *sm(e)irdris* (*Acall. na Sen.*) is a late variant of the same name (M.A. O'Brien apud Binchy 1952).

46

Typhoeus and the Illuyankas

It is now generally assumed, by 'inspection', that the myth of Typhoeus or Typhon (Τυφωεύς, Τυφάων, Τυφώς, Τυφῶν), the monster who threatened the sovereignty of Zeus, whom Zeus overcame and cast into Tartarus, was diffused into Greece from Anatolian Hittite, where it is attested as the myth of *Illuyankas*, the serpent-adversary slain by the Storm God. Though the time and the manner of this diffusion may be uncertain or unknown—but see further below—'the basic similarity of the Hittite and the Greek version has struck scholars ever since the Hittite text became known,' as Walter Burkert (1979:8) states in an influential work. Compare also especially M.L. West's important discussion and bibliography in his edition of the *Theogony*. The systematic comparison was first made overs 60 years ago and the similarities noted and discussed in detail by Walter Porzig (1930), and many scholars between him and West have taken up the issue.[1]

Subsequent to West, Marcel Detienne and Jean-Pierre Vernant (1978:115-125) give a lengthy and insightful examination of the earlier and later versions (v. infra) of the myth in Greek in the context of the union with *mētis* and the conquest of power. They focus on the motif of trickery in the defeat of Typhon in the later versions, notably those of Apollodorus and Oppian, somewhat paradoxically maintaining at once their indebtedness to Anatolian myths and at the same time their quintessential hellenism (p. 120).

In a more recent work, W. Burkert states simply,[2] 'There are detailed Hittite parallels; hence these myths must be regarded as borrowings from Asia Minor.' While recognizing the value of the oriental analogues to Hesiod, Gregory Nagy (1990b:81) on the other hand cautions against the danger of mere typological similarity: the standard dilemma of the comparative method. We shall see how the study of the detail of verbal expression—the mythographic equivalent of Meillet's 'détail singulier'—can obviate this danger, and vindicate the Anatolian origin of the myth in Greece. More specifically, we shall see how the linguistic evidence points unequivocally to the

1. Note Lesky 1950 and 1963 passim; Heubeck 1955; Fontenrose 1980; Vian 1960; Walcot 1966, the year of publication of West's *Theogony*; Bernabé 1986 and 1988.

2. 1985:123 with n. 31, cf. 127 with n. 21.

Bronze-Age second millennium as the time of the transmittal of the tale from Anatolia to Hellas. The manner of the transmittal must be assumed a priori to be a classic language contact phenomenon, and the place the Western coast of Anatolia where Mycenean settlements as well as artifacts attest just such contact. Emily Vermeule points out to me 'the importance of places like 14th-century Panaztepe, Ephesus, Miletos, Müskebi/Episkopi, for Mycenean fathers with Anatolian wives and bilingual children.'

The *illuyankaš* myth in Hittite is now available in the edition of Beckman 1982, which supersedes all others. In particular Beckman shows that MUŠ*illuyankaš*[3] is not a name, but simply the Hittite for 'snake, serpent', like *áhi* in India and *aži* in Iran. Beckman also lays to rest the notion (going back to Goetze, *ANET*) that the two versions of the myth narrated during the New Year's *purulli*-ritual are respectively 'old' and 'new', a view which has misled several Classical scholars, notably Walter Burkert (1979:7-10) in his excellent work.

The Greek sources on the Typhoeus myth fall naturally into three groups: epic, 5th-century, and Hellenistic. Here the first two will be referred to as 'earlier', and the last as 'later'. The epic passages include *Il.* 2.781-83, Hesiod, *Th.* 304-307, 820-68, and the Homeric *Hymn to (Pythian) Apollo* 300-340, with which we may associate Stesichorus 239 PMGF and the mid-6th-century Chalcidian hydria (Fontenrose 1980:71 (fig. 13)). The fifth-century version is found in closely similar passages in Pindar, *Pyth.* 1.20-28, *Ol.* 4.6-7, *frags.* 92-93, and Aeschylus *P.V.* 353-74, *Sept.* 493, 511. The Hellenistic group includes Apollodorus 1.6.3-6, Oppian *Hal.* 3.15-25, and Nonnus *Dion.*, books 1, 2. In epic the monster is called *Typhōeus* and *Typhaōn* , and for simplicity I will use *Typhoeus*; in Pindar and Aeschylus *Typhōs* (stem usually *Typhōn-*), and later *Typhōn*. For the latter two I will again for simplicity use Typhon, though perhaps with some overlap all around.

The version of the myth in Apollodorus, with its temporary victory of the monster over Zeus, most strikingly recalls the second narration of the *illuyankaš* myth: "the serpent overcame the Storm God". This was shown already by Porzig 1930, discussed most fully (supra, n. 1) by Vian and independently Fontenrose, summarized in West ad *Th.* 820-80, and systematically juxtaposed in Burkert 1979. West follows Vian in thinking the diffusion of this particular Anatolian version of the myth to Greece is a phenomenon of Hellenistic times or slightly earlier. Though we may wonder how the diffusion is to have taken place, perhaps this is so. It is clear from reading Strabo—himself an Anatolian Greek—that local legend in Southern Anatolia and Cilicia would have been far more accessible to Apollodorus or his possible sources in Hellenistic times than before. If this chronology is correct, then of course the source language was no longer Hittite, and the language of the Hittite *illuyankaš* myth is only indirect testimony. In any case the Hellenistic and later versions and their Hittite parallels have already received a great deal of careful attention over the past half-century, and I will not discuss them further. It is the earlier sources which will engage our attention.

Francis Vian, followed by Scott Littleton 1982:179, cf. also Puhvel 1987:29-31, raised the question of grafting or fusion in Greece of inherited Indo-European motifs,

3. MUŠ is the Sumerogram determiner for 'serpent'.

a fight between a Dumézilian second-function figure and a three-headed monster, and a non-Indo-European dragon-slaying account also diffused to the Hittites; Littleton himself envisaged a similar fusion among the Hittites a millennium before that among the Greeks. Rather than speculate about such hypothetical constructs, let us be guided by the language and diction of the texts, and hug the formulaic ground closely. For, as we have seen throughout this book, formula is the essence of myth and ritual.

If the kingship-in-heaven story and the song of Ullikummi are of Hurrian provenience in Hittite, the dragon-slaying *illuyankaš* myth itself is native 'Anatolian'. As we saw in chap. 30, on the basis of the particular formula with the root *$g^{w}hen$- 'slay', it is a direct Indo-European inheritance in Hittite. The dénouement of both the first and the second narration of the myth is ^{MUŠ}*illuyankan kuenta* 'he slew the serpent' resp. ^{MUŠ}*illuyankan Ù* DUMU-*ŠU kuenta* 'he slew the serpent and his own son'. Compare our now familiar *áhann áhim*, ἔπεφνε τε Γοργόνα, *orms einbani*, etc.

The temporary victory of the serpent over the Storm God in the second narration of the myth is itself likewise a motif inherited from Indo-European, as is proved by the recurrent verbal formulas with the root *$terh_1$- 'overcome' (cf. chapters 34-35): ^{MUŠ}*illuyankaš* ^{D}IM-*an taraḫta* 'the serpent overcame the Storm God' ... ^{MUŠ}*illuyankan taraḫḫuwan dāiš* '(the Storm God) was about to overcome the serpent'.[4] Compare from the Avestan Fravardin Yasht 13.77 *yat̰* ***titarat̰*** *aŋrō mainiiuš dāhīm aṣ̌ahe vaŋhāuš* 'When the Evil Spirit was about to overwhelm the creation of the good truth', Yt.13.78 *tå hē* ***tauruuaiiatəm*** *t̰baēšå aŋrahe mainiiāuš druuatō* 'These two overcame the hostilities of the deceitful Evil Spirit'.

We must ask ourselves what the nature of the evidence is for any presumptive earlier diffusion of this myth from Anatolia to Greece. It is in the first place clear from the internal evidence of geographical names that Typhoeus/Typhon is associated with Southern Asia Minor, 'at least as early as Pindar'; as West states, (*loc. cit.*), e. g. the Cilician cave. He continues, 'and perhaps in the pre-Homeric tradition that located him εἰν 'Αρίμοις, see on 304.' In the latter discussion West states, 'We can safely say that εἰν 'Αρίμοις was a phrase known only in connexion with Typhon, and this was probably true even in Hesiod's and Homer's time.'

Antiquity was unanimous in locating the Arimoi in Southern Anatolia (West or East). Though the segmentation is admittedly arbitrary, I would suggest that we may see the name in either or both the 2nd-millennium southern Anatolian cities *Arimm-atta* or *Att-arimma*.

^{URU}Attarimma in the Lukka-lands (classical Lycia) is familiar from the Tawagalawa-letter; from it is derived (by regular apheresis) the self-designation of the Lycians Trm̃mili- in classical times.[5]

^{URU}Arimmatta in the newly-found Bronze Treaty Tablet[6] was a boundary of Kuruntas' kingdom of Tarḫuntassa. It was known for its underground water-course or *katabothron*, Turkish *düden*, Hittite ^{D}KASKAL.KUR, equated by David Hawkins

4. As noted before, there is a play on the verb form *taraḫta* (*tarḫ-ta*) and the name of the Storm God *Tarḫunnan* or *Tarḫuntan* (acc.), from the same root.

5. Carruba 1964/65, and independently Eichner 1983. Contra, Bryce 1988, but the two viewpoints may still be reconciled.

6. Edited by Otten 1988:i 24, 26, cf. the similar KBo 4.10 Ro. 19.

with Hieroglyphic Luvian (DEUS) STONE + EARTH + ROAD[7] (Laroche no. 202) 'The term [Hier. Luv. (DEUS) STONE + EARTH + ROAD] should indicate an entrance to the underworld,' as Hawkins writes; as such, a prominent example like *Arimm-atta* might well commend itself to the Greek imagination as a locale for Typhoeus. It is worth noting that Nonnus speaks of going εἰς 'Αρίμων φόνιον σπέος 'to the bloodstained cave of the Arimoi', *Dion*. 1.140. Nonnus had some acquaintance with Anatolian lore two thousand years older than he: *Dion*. 1.408-9 κερόεντι πανείκελος ἔσσυτο ταύρῳ / ἔνθεν ὄρος πέλε Ταῦρος ἐπώνυμον '(Zeus) went in the shape of the horned bull, from which the Taurus mountain takes its name,' as A. Bernabé has shown (note 3 above), reflects the Hittite text (CTH 16) I have called 'The cow with the crumpled horn', Otten 1963 'An aetiological tale of the crossing of the Taurus,' and Soysal 1987 'Puhanu's tale'. Early tradition then puts the locale of the mythical actants in Anatolia. With this in mind let us now turn to the earliest Greek texts themselves, to see if they offer any clues.

The principal methodological lesson in an important new work by Stephanie Jamison (1991) is extremely simple, and remarkably rare in structural studies of myth and mythologies. It is to pay attention to the precise verbal form of the narration of myth. As she states (p. 39),

> I assume that the language in which a myth is told is an integral part of the telling, not a gauzy verbal garment that can be removed without damage to the real meaning of the myth. The clues to contemporary understanding of myth often lie in its vocabulary and phraseology, which have complex and suggestive relationships with similar vocabulary and phraseology elsewhere. Examining other instances of the same words and phrases will often allow us to see these associations.
>
> I think this is probably true of all mythology: that the verbal expression is of major importance and that abstracting themes or archetypes or patterns from their verbal expression does violence to the 'meaning' of the myth.

This principle will be our guide.

Typhoeus is mentioned in the Homeric epics only once. *Il*. 2.780-5 wraps up the Catalogue of Ships, forming both the continuation and the closure of the series of similes at 2.455-83, describing the marshaled host of the Argives marching on Troy, with which the Catalogue began. Line 455 begins ἠΰτε πῦρ, echoed in 780 ὡς εἴ τε πυρί, thus forming a frame around the whole Greek Catalogue. The Typhoeus simile is itself nested in the very middle of a smaller ring or *omlijsting*, as van Otterlo noted in his classic discussion of ring-composition (1948:10 et passim):

> οἱ δ' ἄρ' **ἴσαν** ὡς εἴ τε πυρὶ χθὼν πᾶσα νέμοιτο·
> **γαῖα δ' ὑπεστενάχιζε** Διὶ ὣς τερπικεραύνωι
> χωομένωι, ὅτε τ' ἀμφὶ Τυφωέι γαῖαν ἱμάσσηι
> εἰν 'Αρίμοις, ὅθι φασὶ Τυφωέος ἔμμεναι εὐνάς·

7. Letter of 8 May 1989 to H. Otten on the inscription of the newly discovered tomb for Suppiluliumas II; reference in chap. 40 n. 5.

ὣς ἄρα τῶν ὑπὸ ποσσὶ μέγα **στεναχίζετο γαῖα**
ἐρχομένων

So they **went**, as if all the earth were swept with fire; and
Earth moaned beneath them as beneath Zeus of the thunderbolt
in his rage, when he lashes the ground about Typhoeus
among the Arimoi, where they say is the couch of Typhoeus. Even so
Earth moaned greatly beneath their feet as they **came**, and swiftly
they sped across the plain.

The striking mirror-image ring γαῖα δ' ὑπεστενάχιζε . . . στεναχίζετο γαῖα serves to demarcate and index these lines as the conclusion to the Catalogue and at the same time reintegrates the Catalogue into the narrative. This Homeric passage with its unique Typhoeus reference is also valuable precisely for being a simile, in that as such it presupposes known familiar information. On φασί 'they say' as 'traditional in speaking of Typhon' see West at *Th.* 306.

In the *Theogony* of Hesiod lines 820 ff. narrate the combat of Zeus and Typhoeus; the monster is described, and the fight and its outcome: 853-855 Ζεὺς . . . πλῆξεν 'Zeus . . . smote' with the thunderbolt. The text continues (857-8):

αὐτὰρ ἐπεὶ δή μιν δάμασε πληγῇσιν ἱμάσσας,
ἤριπε γυιωθείς, στονάχιζε δὲ γαῖα πελώρη

But when Zeus had conquered him and lashed him with strokes,
Typhoeus fell down, lamed, and the monstrous earth moaned.

Here at 858 γαῖα πελώρη 'monstrous earth' closes the episode, making a ring-composition with 821 ὁπλότατον τέκε παῖδα Τυφωέα Γαῖα πελώρη 'monstrous Earth bore her youngest child Typhoeus'.

The monster is mentioned once elsewhere at *Th.* 304-8, in the form Τυφάων, whom 'they say' (φασί, again traditionally) lay with the dragoness Echidna and sired Orthus, Cerberus, Hydra, and Chimaira. In ἔχιδνα, ἔχις we have a good Indo-European word for 'snake', as well as in the 'hedgehog' ἐχῖνος as 'snake-eater', both with cognates in Germanic (German *Igel*), Balto-Slavic, and Armenian.

We come finally to the Homeric Hymn to Pythian Apollo, which syntagmatically links the dragon Typhaon to the dragoness Pytho, who served as Typhon's foster mother.[8] The latter is introduced with a recapitulation of the myth (300-304), narrated with a particular stylistic variant of the basic dragon-slaying formula as we have seen in chap. 37:

ἀγχοῦ δὲ κρήνη καλλίρροος, ἔνθα **δράκαιναν**
κτεῖνεν ἄναξ, . . .
. . . ἐπεὶ πέλε πῆμα **δαφοινόν**

8. See the following chapter for the paradigmatic linkage Τυφ- ~ Πυθ- (*Tuph-* ~ *Puth-*) and the Indo-European doublets *dhubh- ~ *bhudh-.

Nearby was a sweet flowing spring, and there the lord
killed the she-dragon . . .
. . . for she was a **very bloody** plague.

The narration is classical Greek and Indo-European drakontomakhia.

The passage then continues (305-309):

καί ποτε δεξαμένη χρυσοθρόνου ἔτρεφεν Ἥρης
δεινόν τ' ἀργαλέον τε Τυφάονα πῆμα βροτοῖσιν
ὅν ποτ' ἄρ' Ἥρη ἔτικτε χολωσαμένη Διὶ πατρὶ

She it was who once received from gold-throned Hera
and brought up full, cruel Typhaon, a plague to men.
Once Hera bore him because she was angry with father Zeus,
when he bore glorious Athena in his head.

Hera in her anger harangues all the gods with her stratagem; then she prays (333), striking the ground flatwise with her hand:

χειρὶ καταπρηνεῖ δ' **ἔλασε χθόνα** καὶ φάτο μῦθον.

The prayer itself follows, and at its conclusion, thus functioning with 333 as a frame, we have 340:

ὣς ἄρα φωνήσασ' **ἵμασε χθόνα** χειρὶ παχείῃ

speaking thus she lashed the earth with her stout hand.

In the fulfillment of her prayer she bears Typhon and gives him to the she-dragon Pytho, κακῶι κακόν 'evil to evil' (354), to foster. The same genealogy (Typhon born of Hera) is reported in Stesichorus (PMGF 239) by the *Etymologicum Genuinum* and *Etymologicum Magnum*.

The whole passage was examined by van Otterlo 1948:72-73 as a good example of a multi-member ring (*meerledige ringsysteem*). Lines 300-309 narrate in reverse chronological order the themes of (III) the slaying of the she-dragon, (II) Typhaon's fosterage, (I) Typhaon's birth, which are then recapitulated with close verbal parallels in lines 349-74 in the order (I) birth of T., (II) fosterage of T., (III) slaying of the she-dragon, and etymology of the name. It is worth pointing out that line 340 just cited is nested almost in the exact middle of these three concentric rings.

These are the earliest Typhoeus narratives in Greek. As we have seen, each is heavily indexed by ring composition in its own narrative. What have they in common verbally? Consider the following:

Homer:	Zeus	ἱμασσ-	earth around Typhoeus, earth moans;
Hesiod:	Zeus	ἱμασσ-	Typhoeus with thunderbolts (πληγ-), earth moans;
h.Ap.:	Hera	ἱμασ-	earth with hand, praying for Typhoeus.

Martin West on *Th.* 857-8 rightly sees that ἱμασσ- 'is especially used with reference to Typhoeus,' comparing the *Iliad* passage. But then he goes on to say that 'the lashing of Typhoeus was apparently a mythical explanation of earthquakes.' For him also at 820 on the *Iliad* passage the lashing of Typhoeus is 'evidently a mythical interpretation of some natural phenomenon, probably the earthquake.'

Now there has been no talk of earthquakes at all in either passage, and the "explanation of natural phenomena" is not any longer regarded as a likely rationale for myth. Moreover this account will not do for the *Hymn to Apollo* passage, where the link ἱμασ-—Τυφ. is arbitrary; it cannot refer to a 'lashing of Typhoeus', who is yet unborn. It is the arbitrary link ἱμασσ-—Τυφ. in all three versions (for it is explainable in two of them only by a gratuitous and discredited assumption) which must serve as our point of departure.

Greek ἱμάσσω 'lash' is a denominative verb, formed from ἱμάς 'thong', stem ἱμαντ-. The latter is a derivative of an Indo-European verb root **seh₂i-*/**sh₂i-* 'to bind, tie', Hittite *išḫai-*, *išḫiya-*, Skt. *syáti*. In Greek, binding was normally with thongs, and we find such typical verb phrases with the verb 'to bind' (δέω, δίδημι) and instrumental datives as *Il.* 21.30 δῆσε δ' ὀπίσσω χεῖρας ἐυτμήτοισιν ἱμᾶσι, 10.567 κατέδησαν ἐυτμήτοισιν ἱμᾶσι, 10.475 ἱμᾶσι δέδεντο, 8.544 δῆσαν δ' ἱμάντεσσι, whence Pindar, *Nem.* 6.35 χεῖρας ἱμάντι δεθείς 'with hands bound with the thong', i.e., wearing the cestus. These will figure in the discussion below.

As stated above, it is generally assumed that the Typhoeus myth was diffused to the Greeks from Anatolia, in a way that is not clear. Now it is a basic tenet of sociolinguistics that "diffusion" implies language contact and bilingualism; in our case it implies specifically a narrative act *n* from a speaker of a language L_1 to a speaker of a language L_2. At least one of these is bilingual in L_1 and L_2. We may model this as

$$L_1 \xrightarrow{n} L_2$$

More strictly, we can state that a narrated event E^n in L_1 becomes by this bilingual narrative act a narrated event in L_2:

$$E^nL_1 \longrightarrow E^nL_2$$

What I propose is to explain an apparently arbitrary linguistic feature of the narrated event in L_2 as a reflex of the narrated event in the source language L_1.

The arbitrary feature of the narrated event in Greek (L_2), the myth of the vanquishing of Typhoeus, is the associative presence of the verb 'lash', a derivative of ἱμαντ- 'thong'. I suggest its presence is a cross-linguistic verbal echo. It is the echo of a non-arbitrary "motifeme" of the narrated event in the Hittite (L_1) myth of the vanquishing of the serpent, which is itself absent from these Greek versions: the **binding** of the serpent **with a cord**, Hittite instrumental *išḫimanta*.

In the dénouement of the first version of the Hittite myth §11-12, with the paragraphing of manuscript tablet H,

^{m}Ḫūpašiyašš=a uit
nu ^{MUŠ}illuyankan **išḫimanta**
kaleliet ^{D}IM-aš uit nu=kan ^{MUŠ}illuya<n>gan
kuenta DINGIR^{MEŠ}-š=a katti=šši ešer

And Hupasiyas came and
bound the serpent **with a cord**. The Storm God
came and killed the serpent, and the gods
were with him.

Hittite *išḫimāš*, *išḫimān-* 'rope, cord' and Greek ἱμάς, ἱμάντ- 'thong' are in fact cognates, but more importantly they are sufficiently similar in sound and meaning to be compared by speakers in a language-contact situation. In this way we can account naturally for the seemingly surprising transfer of the narrative assocative form of *išḫimāš* to the narrative associative semantics of ἱμάσσω. It is a phonetic echo, and the link is the formally similar and semantically identical pair *išḫimanta* / ἱμάντι.

The foregoing would perhaps seem altogether too circumstantial and too fanciful a scenario to be believed, were it not for the evidence of our middle group of fifth-century Typhon texts, in Pindar and Aeschylus, to which I now turn.

In these two authors, principally in *Pythian* 1 and *Prometheus Bound*, Typhon is felled by the thunderbolt and then cast down under Mt. Aetna; the 'Sicilian connection' is marked, perhaps for sound reasons of patronage. The versions in the two authors share so many verbal similarities that they must be connected; whether this is due to influence of one on the other or to both drawing on an earlier common source (Sicilian? Stesichorean?) I leave to others to ponder.[9] But the two may be juxtaposed, taking Pindar (without prejudice) as the point of departure:

	Pindar, *Pyth.* 1		Aeschylus, *P.V.*
15	ὅς . . . κεῖται 'who lies'	364	κεῖται
16	Τυφὼς ἑκατοντακάρανος 'hundred-headed T.'	353-4	ἑκατογκάρανον . . .Τυφῶνα
17	Κιλίκιον . . . ἄντρον 'Cilician cave'	351-2	Κιλίκιων . . . ἄντρων
	νῦν γε 'but now'	363	καὶ νῦν
19	Σικελία . . . πιέζει 'Sicily presses tight'	369	Σικελίας

9. Cf. Fontenrose 1980:73 n. 7, citing von Mess 1901 and Solmsen 1949:131. Note also P. Mazon, ed., *Eschyle* 1.iv, and A. Puech, ed., *Pindare* 2.22. n. 2.

20	κίων . . . συνέχει . . . Αἴτνα 'the column, Aetna, holds (him)'	cf. 365 infra	
21-22	ἐρεύγονται . . . ἀπλάτου πυρὸς / παγαί 'springs belching unapproachable fire'	370-71	Τυφὼς ἐξαναζέσει / ἀπλάτου . . . πυρπνόου ζάλης 'T. will boil up with an unapproachable rain of fire'
(*fr.* 93	ἄπλατον Τυφῶνα) 'unapproachable T.'	(*Sept.* 493,511	Τυφῶνα . . . πυρπνόον) 'fire-breathing T.'
25-26	κεῖνο . . . Ἁφαίστοιο κρουνοὺς ἑρπετόν / ἀναπέμπει 'that serpent sends up fountains of fire'	367 cf. 370	Ἥφαιστος ἐξαναζέσει
26	τέρας 'prodigy'	352	τέρας
27	Αἴτνας ἐν . . . δέδεται κορυφαῖς 'is bound in the heights of A.'	366	κορυφαῖς
(*fr.* 92	Αἴτνα δεσμός . . . ἀμφίκειται 'A., the bond, lies about (him)'		
(*Ol.*4.6-7	Αἴτναν . . . ἶπον . . . Τυφῶνος 'A., the weight that presses on T.'	365	ἰπούμενος ῥίζαισιν Αἰτναίαις ὕπο 'pressed down beneath the roots of A.'

Vernant and Detienne 1978:90 have the merit to call attention to the **binding** (δέδεται) of Typhon in *Pyth.* 1.27, whom Sicily presses tight (πιέζει 19). For the precise force of the latter verb they note *Od.* 8.336, where Apollo asks Hermes if he too wouldn't mind lying with Aphrodite even though pressed tight by strong **bonds**,

ἐν **δεσμοῖς** . . . κρατεροῖσι **πιεσθείς**,

and *Od.* 12.164, when Odysseus to resist the Sirens asks his men to press him tight with yet more **bonds**,

δεσμοῖσι πιέζειν.

I add only that it is clear formulaically that here πιέζω equals δέω, δίδημι 'bind', because of the preceding *Od.* 12.54,

δεσμοῖσι διδέντων,

with the etymological figure of *Il.* 5.386 δῆσαν κρατερῷι ἐνὶ δεσμῶι, and similarly Hesiod *Th.* 618.

In Pindar, Sicily and Aetna are the binding force (δεσμός *fr.* 92, δέδεται *Pyth.* 1.27), just as in Aeschylus Typhon is pressed down (ἰπούμενος *P.V.* 364) beneath the roots of Aetna, and in Pindar Aetna is the weight (ἶπος *Ol.* 4.7) that presses down on

Typhos.[10] We retain that in the fifth century versions of the myth the **binding** of the thunderbolted Typhon is a clear "motifeme".

Where does it come from? Given that the binding of the serpent is a distinct motif in the Anatolian source myth, it is difficult to avoid the assumption that its presence in Greek myth is due to the original transmittal. Let us return to the model of our scenario of the bilingual narrative act, by which the narrated event E^n in L_1 becomes a narrated event in L_2. Simply put in concrete terms, this means only one thing: the translation of a Hittite verb phrase into a Greek verb phrase. Anachronistically in the language of Homer,

E^nL_1	$\longrightarrow$	E^nL_2
išḫimanta kaleliet		δῆσεν ἱμάντι/ἱμᾶσι

The Hittite instrumental is indifferent to number, hence the option of singular or plural in the Greek version.

The anachronism of Homeric Greek beside 2nd-millennium Hittite is only superficial. The verb δέω, reduplicated δίδημι, perf. mid. δέδεται is attested in 2nd-millennium Mycenean Greek in the perfect participles *de-de-me-no*, *de-de-me-na* in both Pylos and Knossos, as is the related noun in *de-so-mo* (KN) and *o-pi-de-so-mo* (PY). The verb δέω and its family is, like ἱμάς, an Indo-European inheritance.

We have noted Hittite *išḫimāš*, *išḫimān-* and Gk. ἱμάς, ἱμάντ-; together with Vedic *sīmán-* 'part (in the hair)' and Old English *sīma*, Old Norse *sími* 'rope, cord' they point to an Indo-European word **sh₂i-món-* securely reconstructible down to the accent on the suffix.[11] Greek ἱμάς therefore may also be projected back to the second millennium, whatever the precise form of the suffix,[12] particularly in the instrumental singular or plural which the Greek syntax would probably require at this point.[13]

Once transmitted by translation from Anatolian to Greek, I would suggest the tradition of this phrase as a "motifeme" at some time before our documentation underwent a split. In one tradition, reflected in Homer, Hesiod, and the *Hymn to Apollo*, we have perseverance of FORM of the noun ἱμάς in the new denominative ἱμασσ-, but loss of the semantics of binding: the new motif of lashing. In the other, reflected most clearly in Pindar, we find perseverance of MEANING of the verb δέω in the motif of binding, with the semantics of the old noun ἱμάς transferred to the noun δεσμός (Pindar *fr.* 92) related to δέω (Pindar *Pyth.* 1.27).

The last fact makes it possible to suggest an even more precise channel for the split. The etymological figure of verb and noun is attested in *Od.* 12.54 ἐν δεσμοῖσι διδέντων. Such a widespread and natural figure could have been created at any time; etymological figures are found outside Indo-European as well, for example in Semitic.

---

10. One wonders whether this noun and its derived verb might have had some precise technical meaning in "correctional" vocabulary. Cf. πλίνθους ἐπιτιθείς Aristophanes *Ran.* 621.

11. For the Hittite, cf. Oettinger 1982:165-68; for the Greek, the dictionaries of Frisk and Chantraine s.v.; and for the Germanic family, Lehmann 1986 s.v. *in-sailjan*. Note also in extenso Bader 1990b.

12. Frisk and Chantraine suggest a ἱμων (sic).

13. See Morpurgo Davies 1988b:98-100.

I suggest that the split of the formulaic tradition involved the creation of not one but two etymological figures:

(išḫimanta kaleliet ⟶) δῆσεν ἱμάντι/ἱμᾶσι

↙ ↘

δῆσεν δεσμῶι/δεσμοῖσι 'bound with bonds' | ἱμάσσεν ἱμάντι/ἱμᾶσι '*corded with cords'

The second of these involves the formation of a new denominative verb ἱμάσσω from ἱμάς 'thong, cord' and therefore meaning '*to cord, *to tie'. Indirect support for this meaning for the verb comes from the only attestation of its derivative ἱμάσκω, in an Elean inscription (Schwyzer 409, Buck 61) dated 475-450 by Jeffery 1990:218-20 and Pl. 43, 215: αι ζε τις τον αιτιαθεντα ζικαιον ιμασκοι . . . αι ϝειζος ιμασκοι 'If someone maltreats someone accused in a matter of fines . . . if he does so wittingly.' Buck's meaning 'maltreat', adopted by Jeffery, is readily derivable from 'oppress' from 'bind'; the meaning 'fetter' suggested by Schwyzer and Chantraine would prove the same meaning for ἱμάσσω. Even clearer semantically is the recent suggestion 'spellbind' for ἱμάσκω by Weiss 1994.

A figura etymologica in a verb phrase is a sort of doubling or iteration of semantic features in verb and noun, and is readily reduced; 'bind with bonds', 'cord with cords', are merely emphases of 'binding', 'cording', and may be reduced to the verb or noun alone. Both are found in the Pindaric tradition about Typhon:

δῆσεν δεσμῶι

↓

Αἴτνας ἐν . . . **δέδεται** κορυφαῖς
Αἴτνα **δεσμός** . . . ἀμφικεῖται

In the Homeric, Hesiodic, and Hymnic tradition the same reduction took place:

ἱμάσσεν ἱμάντι

↓

ἱμάσσεν

but with a semantic specialization: the denominative verb is restricted to continuing only the special sense 'lash' of its base noun.[14] With the development of a special sense of the base noun, the derivative verb must follow suit; the original '*corded with a cord', '*"thonged" with a thong', becomes 'lashed with a lash'. Reduction of the etymological figure to the verb alone yielded ἱμάσσεν 'lashed'. This new primary meaning then served as base for a new derivative noun: ἱμάσθλη 'lash, whip'. In this way we can account naturally for the loss of the motifeme of **binding** in the epic tradition and its replacement by the motifeme of **lashing**, henceforth arbitrarily linked to the Typhoeus myth.

14. Similarly in my dialect of American English, in the absence of any other context the denominative verb 'to rope' means only 'to lasso'.

To recapitulate the development here envisaged,

išḫimanta kaleliet ⟶ δῆσεν ἱμάντι/ἱμᾶσι

↙ ↘

δῆσεν δεσμῶι/δεσμοῖσι ἱμάσσεν ἱμάντι/ἱμᾶσι

↓ ↓

Pindar δέδεται/δεσμός Homer ἱμάσσηι/ἱμάσθλη

In Pindar we find the perseverance of MEANING of the Anatolian motifeme of binding the serpent; in epic we find the perseverance of FORM: the verb ἱμάσσω from ἱμάντι (or the like) translating *išḫimanta*. The new meaning of ἱμάσσω, the new motifeme of lashing, is dependent on that of ἱμάντ-; the original meaning 'bind' survives in Elean ιμασκοι 'maltreats, fetters', or 'spellbinds'.[15]

The essential correctness of this scenario is finally suggested by the distribution of ἱμάσσω in Greek, which forms no compounds. For the word is basically confined to epic. It is wholly absent from lyric, drama, and prose throughout the classical period.

Of the nine Homeric examples (6 *Il.*, 2 *Od.*, 1 *Hy.*), four (3 *Il.*, 1 *Od.*) show the same formula ἵμασεν καλλίτριχας ἵππους 'lashed the fair-maned horses'. Of the remainder three are precisely the Typhoeus passages; this is to say that nearly half the few attestations of ἱμάσσω in Classical Greek are narratives of the Typhoeus myth.

Thereafter, to judge from the TLG corpus, we find only scattered and rare attestations, with the bizarre exception of no less than 72 examples in Nonnus. The verb is particularly frequent in books 1 and 2 of the *Dionysiaca*, which tell precisely of Zeus' combat with and defeat of Typhoeus, as Ian Rutherford points out to me.

Attention to the language and the formulas of the Typhoeus myth in Greek permits us to be that much more precise about its Hittite and Anatolian origin, and the time and manner of its transmission: language contact in the mid-second millennium. It is yet another testimony to the cultural contacts between Mycenean Greece and Hittite Anatolia. And for ἱμάς and ἱμάσσω it is a chapter in that French ideal in etymology: 'l'histoire des mots'.

15. At the risk of triviality it is of course possible to postulate an Indo-European verb phrase *BIND / BOUND + WITH A CORD (**sh*$_2$*imón-*), on the comparison of *išḫimanta kaleliet*, δῆσαν τ' ἱμάντεσσι/ἱμάντι δεθείς with Old English (*Genesis* 764-65) *læg / sīmon gesæled* '(Satan) lay bound with cords', and Old Icelandic *sím-bundinn*. Various roots may supply the verb, like **deh*$_1$*-* (δέω, Vedic *dyáti*, Hittite *tiya-mmu tiya* 'bind me, bind', *tiyamar* 'rope'), **bhendh-*, etc. We find a diachronic etymological figure in the Old English example above, a synchronic one in RV 7.84.2 *yáu setŕ̥bhir arajjúbhiḥ sinītháḥ* 'you two who bind with cordless binders', both from our root IE **sh*$_2$*i-* (with laryngeal metathesis **sih*$_2$*-*).

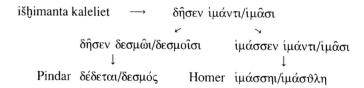

47

Python and Ahi Budhnya, the Serpent of the Deep

The Rigvedic pantheon includes a hazily defined elemental and primordial Serpent of the Deep, *Ahi Budhnyà*.[1] Vedic *áhi-* is the familiar word for 'serpent, snake', Greek ὄφις, IE **og^whis*. *Budhnyà-* is an adjectival derivative of *budhnás* 'bottom, base', Greek πυθμήν, Latin *fundus*, and the Germanic family of Old High German *bodam*, German *Boden*, Old English *botm*. Ahi Budhnya's origin and abode is the dark bottom of the waters, but he is not a mythological actant; he is mentioned only in stereotypical contexts, and as Oldenberg notes, he no longer has the ability to appear independently and seems to be preserved only as a relic, an 'Überlebsel'.

Of the dozen or so Rigvedic attestations[2] perhaps the fullest is 7.34.16-17:

> abjā́m ukthā́ir áhiṃ gṛṇīṣe
> budhné nadī́nāṃ rájassu ṣī́dan
> mā́ no áhir budhnyò riṣé dhān
> mā́ yajñó asya sridhad ṛtāyóḥ

> With songs I praise the water-born serpent
> sitting in darkness in the depths of the rivers.
> May the Serpent of the Deep not bring us to harm;
> may the worship of this (singer) who seeks truth not go wrong.

The comparison of Ahi Budhnya, the primordial serpent of the depths, with the Old Norse serpent *Níðhǫggr* at the bottom (in the roots) of the world tree *Yggdrasil*, was made by Dumézil 1959a and further explored by Ström 1967. The comparison permitted the reconstruction of a plausibly Indo-European theme or motifeme. RV *budhnás* is used of the root (in heaven) of the cosmological *Nyagrodha*-tree at 1.24.7. It remained for V. V. Ivanov and V. N. Toporov (1974:37-8) and more extensively

1. Cf. Oldenberg 1917:70, and Hillebrandt 1929:2.305-6.
2. 1.186.5; 4.55.6; 6.49.14; 50.14; 7.34.16-17; 35.13; 38.5; 10.64.4; 66.11; 92.12; 93.5.

Toporov 1976[3] to extend the comparison by first one then a second equation corroborating it in the linguistic plane.

The first was to equate the base of the epithet of (*Ahi*) *Budhnya-* with Serbo-Croatian *bȁdnjāk* (Slav. **bъdьnj-*), the word for '"Yule" log, oak log lit on Christmas Eve'. The associated ritual of felling the *badnjak*, bringing it in after sundown on Christmas Eve, and the personification of *Stari Badnjak* ('old B.') and his son *Mladi Bog/Božić* ('young god'), make it clear, as Toporov elegantly shows, that we have to deal with equivalents respectively of the mythological dragon and its adversary.[4] *Old Badnjak* is a symbol of the last day of the Old Year—when the forces of Chaos are in the ascendancy—and his divine young son symbolizes the first day of the New Year—when Cosmic Order begins to be victorious.

The narration of the *illuyankaš* myth as part of the New Year's ritual comes immediately to mind, as do aspects of our own contemporary New Year's Eve rituals and symbols, like the outgoing year as an old decrepit man (a euphemism for dying) and the incoming year as a baby.

The second linguistic equation (Toporov 1974) was of the root of the second element of (*Ahi*) *Budhnya*—the *-ya-* is suffixal—with the Greek dragon *Python* (Πύθων), slain by Apollo with his arrows.[5] The phonology is perfectly regular: IE **bhudh-* > Vedic *budh-* and Greek **phuth-* > *puth-* by the (independent) action of Grassmann's aspiration dissimilation law in each. The long *ū* in Πῦθων, not mentioned by Toporov, is doubtless due to expressive lengthening, like the *ū* of Greek κλῦθι 'hear!' (Ved. *śrudhi*), West Germanic **hlūd* 'loud' (Greek κλυτός).[6] The name of the dragon *Python* thus shows the inherited designation of a serpent creature of the watery depths. Compare the underground spring where the dragoness dwelt (ἀγχοῦ δὲ κρήνη . . . *h.Ap.* 300). In the Homeric Hymn the dragoness is not named; later tradition called her Delphunē. The water nymph Telphousa in the *Hymn to Apollo* (the name is attested elsewhere in Greece as a hydronym) is also a dragoness figure and adversary of Apollo,[7] who buried her spring under a shower of stones. Her name may also be Indo-European and cognate with English *delve* (**dhelbh-* > *θελφ- > τελφ-, Neumann 1979); it is attested in numerous Germanic and Slavic water spring and river names (*Delft*).

Toporov 1974:5 with notes 12-14 recognized the importance of the already Indo-European doublets **bhudh-n-* and **dhubh-n-* under semantic similarity or identity: both refer to bottom, foundation, depths, and related notions which recur both

3. Cf also now Gamkrelidze and Ivanov 1984:528.

4. Toporov notes the simile in RV 1.32.5 where the slain serpent lies 'like branches lopped by an axe', *skándhāṁsīva kúliśenā vívṛkṇā*. One can add RV 2.14.2 *yó . . . vṛtráṃ jaghánāśányeva vṛkṣám* 'who struck Vṛtra like a tree by lightning', and others; see Renou in Benveniste and Renou 1934:132. West (1988:154) states that the simile of the adversary felled by the hero like a tree struck by lightning or chopped down by a woodcutter is common Greco-Aryan patrimony: he cites RV 2.14.2, 6.8.5, 1.130.4, and *Il.* 14.414, 4.482-7, 13.178-80, 389-91, after Durante 1976:121. Durante and West cite a number of such shared features, topoi or themes.

5. Homer *h.Ap.* 300 ff.; cf. Simonides 511.1(a) 6-7; Euripides *I.T.* 1239-53 (the last cited in chap. 52). See in detail the vast treatment of Fontenrose 1980.

6. The expressive *ū* may have favored the connection with πύθω 'rot' (*h.Ap.* 363ff.), but the latter clearly remains a folk etymology.

7. Discussed extensively by Fontenrose 1980:366ff.

as lexical exponents and as motifemes in the mythology. We have seen **bhudh-n-o-* in Vedic *budhná-*; **dhubh-n-o-* recurs in Slavic *dъno*, Russian *dno* 'bottom'. The specific mythographic associations of Ahi **Budh**nya, 'water-born, sitting in the depths of the rivers' (supra) are mirrored both in Celtic ***dub**no-* 'deep' and ***dub**ro-* 'water'.

Now beside *Pythōn* from **phuth-* from **bhudh-* Greek mythological tradition knows another dragon figure, adversary of Zeus: *Typhōn*, or in earlier variant forms *Typhāōn, Typhōeus, Typhōs*. We saw in the preceding chapter that significant features or motifemes of this myth were borrowed into Greece from Hittite Anatolia. But the names of the actants are pure Greek out of Indo-European: *Zeus* from **di̯eu̯-s* and *Typh-* from **thuph-* from **dhubh-*. The quantity of the *u* varies: the etymological short in *Typhaōn, Typhōeus*, the expressively lengthened *ū* in *Typhōn, Typhōs*.

Fontenrose showed at considerable length, without comparing the two names linguistically, that the Python and Typhon myths largely coincide, and must be at the outset developments of a single 'earlier form of the Greek dragon myth in which Typhon and Python were not distinguished' (1980:193).

The syntagmatic link between the dragon Typhon (Τυφάων) and the dragoness Pytho (Πυθώ) is furnished by the Homeric *Hymn to Apollo*, in which Pytho served Typhon as a foster mother. The paradigmatic link is precisely the fact that *Tuph-* and *Puth-* are poetic linguistic doublets as inversions, underlying **thuph-* and **phuth-*, and have been since Indo-European times (**dhubh-* ~ **bhudh-*).

We have finally a syntagmatic comparandum in Greek to the two constituents of the Vedic name *Ahi Budhnya*. Callimachus, *Hymn* 2.100-101 reads:

> **Πυθώ** τοι κατιόντι συνήντετο δαιμόνιος θήρ,
> αἰνὸς **ὄφις**
>
> Going down to **Pytho** you were met by a marvelous beast,
> the terrible **serpent**.

Vedic *áhir budhnyàḥ* is Indo-European **og^u̯hi- bhudh-*. Greek Πυθώ and ὄφις syntactically occupying sentence-initial and sentence-final position, respectively, and metrically forming an enjambed unit from verse initial of 100 to the trithemimeral caesura of 101, continue Indo-European **bhudh- . . . *og^u̯hi-* in the reverse sequence.

This sentence in the Callimachean hymn is then followed immediately by a narration of the Pythoctony in the basic formula, 101-102:

> τὸν μὲν σὺ κατήναρες ἄλλον ἐπ' ἄλλωι
> βάλλων ὠκὺν ὀιστόν
>
> You slew him, shooting one swift
> arrow after another.

Both subject and object are pronominalized, the latter anaphoric to the immediately preceding ὄφις:

(HERO) SLAY (SERPENT) with WEAPON.

For the second person note that Vedic *áhann áhim* is frequently second person addressing Indra. The Callimachean passage continues with the aetiology of the paean cry;[8] for the basic formula as victory paean see chap. 55.

8. Discussed by Rutherford 1991.

48

Aži Dahāka, Viśvarūpa, and Geryon

From the evidence surveyed in chap. 29 it is clear that a Common Indo-Iranian myth underlies the slaying of the dragon Aži Dahāka by Thraētaona and the slaying of Tvaṣṭṛ's son, the monster Viśvarūpa, by Trita Āptya. Thraētaona was a mortal hero, while Trita appears to have been a god. Both are enabled to perform their valorous deed by a god: Thraētaona by Vərəϑraγna and Trita by the (higher) god Indra, whose epithet is *vṛtrahán-*. Both monsters, the Iranian and the Indic, share the same physical attributes: they have three heads (*ϑrikamərəδa-*, *triśīrṣán- / trimūrdhán-*) and six eyes (*xšuuaš.aši-*, *ṣaḷákṣa-*). The Indic monster kept cows, which Indra (or Trita? cf. Geldner ad loc.) carried off in RV 10.8.9:

> tvāṣṭrásya cid viśvárūpasya gónām
> ācakrāṇás trī́ṇi śīrṣā́ párā vark
>
> Having driven off for himself some of the cows of Viśvarūpa son of Tvaṣṭṛ
> he twisted off the three heads.

While Iranian Aži Dahāka had no cows, the hero Thraētaona requested of the goddess Arəduuī Sūra Anāhitā in Yt. 5.34 (and of the goddess Aši Vaŋᵛhī in Yt. 17.34), and was granted, the boon 'that I may become the winner over Aži Dahāka, the three-jawed, three-headed, six-eyed...' (quoted in chap. 51), moreover:

> uta he vaṇta azāni
> saŋhauuāci arənauuāci
>
> And that I may carry off his (Aži Dahāka's) two beloved wives
> Saŋhavac and Arənavac . . .[1]

1. Reichelt, Av. Reader 103 and 96 (1911), where the comparison with Viśvarūpa's cows (and those of Geryon) is explicitly made. His explanation, on the other hand, that Thraētaona delivered wives

On the passage see Hoffmann 1975:374-7. The two women were sisters of Yima and had been carried off earlier by Aži Dahāka. The verb *az-* 'drive', cognate with Vedic *aj-*, Greek ἄγειν, and Old Irish *agid*, is like them used with both cattle and women as object, in the sense of 'carry off as booty'.[2] As we saw in the preceding note, this Common Indo-Iranian myth has been compared, for almost a century at least, with the Greek legend of the tenth labor of Herakles, the stealing of the cattle of Geryon (Gēryoneus, Gēryonēs, Gāryonās). For references in classical sources see Page 1973 and Fontenrose 1980:334ff. with n. 31. The myth is first alluded to in Hesiod's *Th.* 287-94. Poseidon lay with Medusa, and when Perseus cut off her head Chrysaor and the horse Pegasus sprang forth:

> Χρυσάωρ δ' ἔτεκεν τρικέφαλον Γηρυονῆα
> μιχθεὶς Καλλιρόηι κούρηι κλυτοῦ Ὠκεανοῖο.
> τὸν μὲν ἄρ' ἐξενάριξε βίη Ἡρακληείη
> βουσὶ παρ' εἰλιπόδεσσι περιρρύτωι εἰν Ἐρυθείηι
> ἤματι τῶι, ὅτε περ βοῦς ἤλασεν εὐρυμετώπους
> Τίρυνθ' εἰς ἱερήν, διαβὰς πόρον Ὠκεανοῖο.
> Ὄρθον τε κτείνας καὶ βουκόλον Εὐρυτίωνα
> σταθμῶι ἐν ἠερόεντι πέρην κλυτοῦ Ὠκεανοῖο
>
> Chrysaor begot three-headed Geryoneus
> joining in love with Kallirhoe, daughter of glorious Ocean;
> him in might Herakles slew
> beside his shambling cows in sea-girt Erytheia,
> on that day when he drove the wide-browed cows
> to holy Tiryns, having crossed the ford of Ocean
> and killed (the monstrous dog) Orthos and the herdsman Eurytion
> in the airy stead out beyond glorious Ocean.[3]

Hesiod repeats the story in condensed form in 981-3: 'Kallirhoe bore a son, strongest of all men,'

> Γηρυονέα, τὸν κτεῖνε βίη Ἡρακληείη
> βοῶν ἕνεκ' εἰλιπόδων ἀμφιρρύτωι Ἐρυθείηι

---

instead of cows because Aṣ̌i Vaŋᵛhī (Yt. 17) was 'the protectress of matrimony', seems farfetched. Heracles' taking of Geryon's cows was already compared with Indra's freeing the cows held by Vṛtra, or in the cave of Vala, by M. Bréal in 1863 (*Hercule et Cacus*) and later by L. von Schroeder in 1914 (*Herakles und Indra*).

2. Thraētaona's *vaṇta azāni* (1sg. subj.) 'that I may carry off his two beloved wives' is identical to Agamemnon's ἐγὼ δέ κ' ἄγω Βρισηΐδα 'I will take Briseis' *Il.* 1.184.

3. The ring κλυτοῦ Ὠκεανοῖο in 288 and 294, first the god and then the place, indexes the remoteness of the island Erytheia; West points out wryly that the difficulty of capturing Geryon's cattle 'consisted in the remoteness of the ranch.' The name Ἐρυθείη is probably a derivative of 'red' or so understood, like *Loch Rudraige* in Ireland, scene of another drakontomakhia (chap. 45). Such associations are fairly frequent, cf. the Vedic demon *Rudhikrā*, and the Avestan 'red serpent' *aži raoδita*, and probably not very significant. Cf. also chapters 56 and 57, for A. Kuhn, the Vedic worms, and the Germanic *red* : *dead* rhymes.

Geryoneus, whom mighty Herakles killed
in sea-girt Erytheia for the sake of his shambling cows.

The lines have two irregularities, Γηρυονέα and βοῶν, on which see West ad loc. The verb ἐξενάριξε of the first, longer version is a common lexical substitute for πέφνε, as we have seen; κτεῖνε in the second is neutral, and in the first version used for the ancillary killing of Geryon's dog and herdsmen. We may retain as central the epithet 'three-headed' (for the metrical lengthening τρικέφᾱλος see West ad loc.), and the formula βοῦς[4] ἤλασεν (εὐρυμετώπους) 'drove off the cows', which recurs in the *h.Merc.* 102 of Hermes rustling the cattle of Apollo, and *Il.* 1.154.

Pindar shows the same words of the formula distracted in *fr.* 169a6-8: ἐπεὶ Γηρυόνα[5] βόας . . . ἀπριάτας ἔλασεν 'when he (sc. Herakles) drove off the unbought cows of Geryon.'

The poet Stesichorus, active from the latter seventh to the mid-sixth century, composed a mini-epic of over 1500 lines on this legend, the *Geryoneis*. The work is preserved only in a handful of fragments, fortunately augmented by extensive papyrus finds.[6] The sympathetic portrayal of Geryon is the most striking feature of the new text: his tragic sense of inescapable conflict and impending death, the colloquy with his mother and her passionate concern, and finally the infinite tenderness of the portrayal of the dying Geryon stricken by the poisoned arrow (SLG 15 ii 14-17):

ἀπέκλινε δ' ἄρ' αὐχένα Γαρ[υόνας
    ἐπικάρσιον, ὡς ὅκα μ[ά]κω[ν
ἅτε καταισχύνοισ' ἁπαλὸν [δέμας
    αἶψ' ἀπὸ φύλλα βαλοῖσα ν[

And Geryon bent his neck over to one side,
like a poppy that spoils its delicate shape,
shedding its petals all at once . . . (tr. Page).

Page notes (1973:152) that the model of the poppy is *Il.* 8.306ff. (well imitated by Vergil, *Aen.* 9.435ff.), but as he emphasized, 'the development of the drooping poppy is unique to Stesichorus'. We are a long way from a monster, and a long way from the topos of the adversary felled by the hero like a great tree (chap. 47 n. 4). Though Geryon had three heads (Hesiod) and 'the body of three men joined at the waist, which became threeform at the flanks and thighs' (Apollodorus, *Bibl.* 2.5.10, probably taken from Stesichorus' poem [Page 1973:144-5]), it is curious that in the attested fragments the words for 'head', 'helmet', and 'shield' are only singular: SLG 15 ii 3 κεφαλά, i 16 τρυφάλει', i 12 ἀσπίδα, ii 10-11 ἐπ' ἀκροτάταν κορυφάν. Contrast the black-

4. The monosyllabic acc. pl. is probably an archaism, equatable with Vedic *gā́s*.

5. For the non-appearance of the Doric form Γαρυόνας, cf. Forssman 1966. He rightly notes the form Γαρυϝονες on a sixth-century (Ionic) Chalcidian vase, Schwyzer 797.2 (Kretschmer, Vaseninschr. §40,2).

6. See the editions of Davies 1991, Page 1962 and 1972, as well as his 1973 study. Cf. also Lerza 1982, with bibliography.

figured amphora, illustrated in Fontenrose 1980:335 (fig. 26), Br. Mus. B155, cat. II fig. 26, where Geryones (so labeled) has clearly three heads, three helmets, and three shields, as well as two wings and two feet.

We should note in the same representation that Athena (Αϑεναιε) stands directly behind Herakles and obviously brings him divine aid, as she does in Stesichorus *frg.* 3. Athena thus has the same functional role toward Herakles in the myth as Vərəϑraγna toward Thraētaona and Indra toward Trita.

Despite the singular 'head' in these fragments a three-form Geryon can be inferred for Stesichorus both because of Apollodorus' description above, and because a scholiast to Hesiod *Th.* 287 tells us that Stesichorus in an innovation presented Geryon winged and with six hands and feet: cf. PMG 186 ἓξ χεῖρας ἔχειν φησὶ καὶ ἓξ πόδας. The wings are attested on the Chalcydian vase painting illustrated in Fontenrose 1980:335, but Geryon there has two feet. According to Page 1973 this representation is clearly inspired by Stesichorus. Note that this vase has the expected Ionic spelling Γερυονες (it is Kretschmer, Vaseninschr. §40,9) whereas in the same scene illustrated in Kretschmer §40,2 (Schw. 797.2 and note 5 above), the spelling Γαρυϝονες would seem to be directly due to the influence of Stesichorus. Other forms on both vases are perfectly good Chalcidian Ionic. Combining the traditional epithet τρικέφαλος in Hesiod, the description in Apollodorus, the Chalcidian vase paintings, and the scholiast's statement we are justified in making the linguistic inference that Stesichorus in the Geryoneis described the adversary of Herakles as THREE-HEADED and SIX-somethinged. It may be that those somethings were 'feet', by an innovation of the poet; but I suggest that what they replaced was an earlier epithet 'six-eyed' identical in meaning to the Indic and Iranian epithets:

THREE-HEADED and SIX-EYED.

We may regard this as a poetic and mythographic formula common to Indo-Iranian and Greek, and resting on the semantic equations

tri-śīrṣán- tri-mūrdhán-	ṣaḷ-ákṣa-
ϑri-kamərəδa-	xšuuaš-aši-
τρι-κεφαλο-	ἑξ(α)-.

Such a formula is of course trivially easy to imagine on the plane of universals. To anchor it more firmly on the diachronic plane we can point to the association of the monster with wealth in cows, which are driven off by the hero as part of his exploit. Here the Vedic accusative plural *gā́s* (RV 10.8.8, 48.2) can be even morphologically equated, mutatis mutandis, with the Homeric and Hesiodic accusative plural βοῦς (*Th.* 291). We saw the forms in Pindar; and Stesichorus SLG 11.27-9 (PMGF S11, p. 156) adds the tantalizing fragment in broken context περὶ βουσὶν ἐμαῖς

. . .

]κλέος[

. . . about my cows

. . .

]fame[.

We may then, however tentatively, suggest a specific late Indo-European (Greco-Indo-Iranian) myth whose semantic structure and signature formulas deploy the lexical items or names HERO (variable), SLAY (*$g^{w}hen$-*, replaced in Hesiod by ἐξενάριξε), a MONSTER (*$og^{w}hi$-*, not in Greek) who is THREE (*tri-*)-HEADED (variable) and SIX (*su̯eḱs-*)-EYED (*$h_3ok^{w}p$-*, not in Greek), with the aid of a GOD (variable). As a result HERO DRIVE OFF (*$h_2a\hat{g}$-*, replaced in Greek by ἤλασε) MONSTER's COWS (*$g^{w}\bar{o}s$*, replaced in Avestan by WOMEN). A simple story perhaps, but one with enough arbitrary linkage (contiguity relations) for us to be unsatisfied with the explanation of mere fortuitous resemblance.[7]

The *names* of the actants in the three traditions are, as usual, variable and of little use, whether they are descriptive like Aži Dahāka 'the Serpent-D.', transparent like Viśvarūpa 'having many forms', or simply obscure, like Geryon. The name looks like the noun γᾶρυς 'voice, cry' as noted by Forssman, loc. cit., but the name 'Shouter' is without semantic relevance for the myth.

7. We may also be unsatisfied with Fontenrose's conclusion, that Geryon is 'the king of the dead, a form of Thanatos of Hades' (1980:335). The new Stesichorus fragments (published after the appearance of the book) weaken the claim seriously for Greek, and the Indo-Iranian facts never fit it at all. Cf. chap. 40. Ours is only a variant of the same myth.

VI

From myth to epic

49

From god to hero: The formulaic network in Greek

The verb πεφνέμεν in Greek, which we discussed at length in chap. 36 and following, is of course not confined to the dragon-slaying formula and its transformations. The serpent adversary of myth can easily become the human adversary of epic "reality".

We find here two possible themes, expressed again in variations rung on the basic formula:

$$\overleftrightarrow{\text{HERO}_1 \quad \text{SLAY } (^*g^{\mu}hen\text{-}) \quad \text{HERO}_2}$$

and

$$\overleftrightarrow{\text{HERO} \quad \text{SLAY } (^*g^{\mu}hen\text{-}) \quad \text{ANTI-HERO.}}$$

The first is an equipollent opposition of noble adversaries, like Hector and Patroklos, Achilles and Hector; an example of the second, where the anti-hero is assimilated to a monster, would be Odysseus and the suitors, or Orestes and Klutaimestra. In both the action is bidirectional, potentially reciprocal; either member may be the subject of the verb.

We find πεφνέμεν frequently here in Greek, as well as the common κτείνειν and others. But πεφνέμεν is always the semanticaly *marked* verb for the notion of 'killing', much like English marked *to slay* versus unmarked *to kill*. It is the verb, as we noted earlier, which Greek poetic language utilizes to describe the "terrifying exploit of the hero". In the majority of occurrences of πεφνέμεν the context is not indifferent. They regularly present killings of fable, or crimes beyond the norm. If it is a question of the killing of one human being by another, the seriousness of the action is a function of the relations among the protagonists. We saw πεφνέμεν in Pindar, *Pyth.* 11.36-7 above (chap. 37) in the case of Orestes killing Klutaimestra and Aigisthos; in the *Odyssey* the verb is used four times of the murder of Agamemnon.

The contexts of the legend of the return of Agamemnon are instructive and well illustrate the interplay of the verbs πεφνέμεν, κτείνειν, and others, as well as the echoes from one part of the text to another.

In book four of the *Odyssey* Menelaos, summing up the story to Telemakhos, says (4.91-92):

τῆός μοι ἀδελφεὸν ἄλλος **ἔπεφνε** . . . δόλωι οὐλομένης ἀλόχοιο

Meanwhile another **slew** my brother . . . by his wife's treachery.

As Menelaos recounts, the Old Man of the Sea first told him, again using πεφνέμεν, and emphasizing the violation of hospitality (4.534-5):

τόν δ' οὐ εἰδότ' ὄλεθρον ἀνήγαγε, καὶ **κατέπεφνε**
δειπνίσσας, ὥς τίς τε κατέκτανε βοῦν ἐπὶ φάτνηι

Led him in all unsuspicious of death, and feasted him
and **killed** him **feasting**, as one strikes down an ox at his manger.

Both sets of formulas are repeated by the ghost of Agamemnon to Odysseus in book eleven, but with a late and unhistoric form of unmarked κτείνειν (11.409-11):

Αἴγισθος . . .
ἔκτα σὺν οὐλομένηι ἀλόχωι, οἶκόνδε καλέσσας,
δειπνίσσας, ὥς τίς τε κατέκτανε βοῦν ἐπὶ φάτνηι

Aigisthos . . . **killed** me with the help of my cursed wife,
inviting me and **feasting** me, as one strikes down an ox in its manger.

Note that the younger and analogical form ἔκτα (for *ἔκτεν) could have replaced πέφνε here.[1] Agamemnon's bitter and circumstantial narrative continues for some 40 lines; in summation he says curtly (11.453),

πάρος δέ με **πέφνε** καὶ αὐτόν

Before that she **slew** me myself.

In epic as in myth, part of the function of the root *g^{w}*hen*- in Greek is 'memorative':[2] a form of πεφνέμεν functions as a summation, recalling to the mind

1. 3 sg. ἔκτα and other forms of the singular have been analogically spread from forms like ἔκτατο < ἐ-κτη̥-το, κτάμενος < κτη̥-μενος, ἔκταμεν < ἐ-κτη̥-μεν, regular athematic root aorists: Chantraine 1973:381. The form (κατ)έκτα occurs 9 times in the *Iliad* and twice (one repeated four times) in the *Odyssey*. Of these only one in each epic (as here) is not line final. Line-final *ἔκτεν could continue an athematic aorist to **dḱen*- (**kþen*-), a rhyme-form to *g^{w}*hen*-. For the root of κτείνω and Vedic *kṣan*- 'wound' cf. perhaps **deḱ*- in Gothic *tahjan* 'tear'.

2. To borrow Karl Hoffmann's term for his view of the function of the Indo-European injunctive (1967:passim). There is to my mind no direct link between the memorative function of this (and other!) formulas, and the unaugmented form πέφνε. The formula is equally memorative with augmented verb form

of the epic audience what it knows already. This feature is, as we have already suggested, the Homeric equivalent of the Pindaric 'shortcut', the οἶμος βραχύς. The *Odyssey* furnishes no less than six or seven separate instances of this function of πεφνέμεν: it must be recognized as a component of the semantics of the root *g^{w}hen-*.[3]

This whole formula of *Od.* 11.453 recurs in book 21, in the Iphitos saga discussed above (chap. 41), *Od.* 21.29:

> ἔπειτα δὲ πέφνε καὶ αὐτόν
>
> But slew him afterwards.

The first person object is not organic, and in the formula in both cases the unexpressed agent has by his or her action become a monster.

Book three of the *Odyssey* contains a recapitulation of the Agamemnon *nostos* or Return. Athena in the guise of Mentor reminds Telemakhos of the death of Agamemnon, *Od.* 3.232-8:

> βουλοίμην δ' ἂν ἐγώ γε καὶ ἄλγεα πολλὰ μογήσας
> οἴκαδε τ' ἐλθέμεναι καὶ νόστιμον ἦμαρ ἰδέσθαι,
> ἢ ἐλθὼν **ἀπολέσθαι** ἐφέστιος, ὡς 'Αγαμέμνων
> **ὤλεθ'** ὑπ' Αἰγίσθοιο δόλωι καὶ ἧς ἀλόχοιο
> ἀλλ' ἤ τοι θάνατον μὲν ὁμοίιον οὐδὲ θεοί περ
> καὶ φίλωι ἀνδρὶ δύνανται ἀλαλκέμεν, ὁππότε κεν δὴ
> Μοῖρ' **ὀλοὴ** καθέλῃσι τανηλεγέος θανάτοιο.[4]
>
> I myself would rather first have gone through many hardships
> and then come home, and look upon my day of returning,
> than come home and be **killed** at my own hearth, as Agamemnon
> was **killed**, by the treacherous plot of his wife, and by Aigisthos.
> But death is a thing that comes to all alike. Not even
> the gods can fend it away from a man they love, when once
> the **destructive** doom of leveling death has fastened upon him.

Athena as a goddess, of course, knows; but Telemakhos asks Nestor the full story (3.248):

(*Od.* 21.36), and unaugmented πέφνε need not be memorative (*Il.* 13.363). See, however, Pelliccia to appear (1985).

3. Compare the immediacy of Odysseus' first narration of the killing of the cattle of the Sun, *Od.* 12.375 ὅ οἱ βόας **ἔκταμεν** ἡμεῖς 'that we had killed his cattle', with his brief recapitulation of the story to Penelope, *Od.* 23.329 ἠδ' ὡς 'Ηελίοιο βόας **κατέπεφνον** ἑταῖροι 'how his comrades had slain the cattle of the Sun' Others are *Od.* 3.252, 11.453, 516-18, 23.84, and especially 24.325 (infra).

4. Note the ring-composition with the forms of the root ὀλ- and the phonetic echoes 232 βουλ- [o:l], πολλ- [oll], 234 ἀπολ- [ol], 235 ὠλ- [ǫ:l], ἀλοχ- [lo], 237 φίλωι [lǫ:], 238 ὀλο- [olo].

πῶς **ἔθαν**' 'Ατρείδης

How did Atreus' son **die**?

i. e., 'how was he killed?', for in Greek 'die' is the passive of 'kill'. Telemakhos continues, echoing first Athena's verb (and Nestor's formula of 3.194 ἐμήσατο λυγρὸν ὄλεθρον), then using a neutral one (3.249-50):

τίνα . . . μήσατ' ὄλεθρον
Αἴγισθος . . . ἐπεὶ **κτάνε** πόλλον ἀρείω;

What scheme of death did Aigisthos have,
to **kill** one far better than he was?

He concludes his question with the final summary verb which establishes the monstrousness of the action (3.252):

ὁ δὲ θαρσήσας **κατέπεφνε**;

And the latter took courage and **slew** (him)?

Telemakhos' question is equally bounded by ring-composition: πῶς **ἔθαν**' 'Ατρείδης is the passive of (κατε)**πέφνε**, and the ring explains the absence of an object of the latter.

Nestor narrates the tale of Agamemnon's death in the following words (3. 193-8):

'Ατρείδην δὲ καὶ αὐτοὶ ἀκούετε[5] νόσφιν ἐόντες
ὥς τ' ἦλθ' ὥς τ' Αἴγισθος ἐμήσατο λυγρὸν ὄλεθρον.
ἀλλ' ἤ τοι κεῖνος μὲν ἐπισμυγερῶς **ἀπέτεισεν**,
ὡς ἀγαθὸν καὶ παῖδα καταφθιμένοιο λιπέσθαι
ἀνδρός, ἐπεὶ καὶ κεῖνος **ἐτείσατο** πατρο**φον**ῆα,
Αἴγισθον δολόμητιν, ὅ οἱ πατέρα κλυτὸν ἔκτα.

You yourselves, though you live apart, have heard of Atreides,
how he came home, and how Aigisthos devised his wretched
death; but Aigisthos too paid for it, in a dismal fashion;
so it is good, when a man **has perished**, to have a son left
after him, since this one took **vengeance** on his father's **killer**,
the treacherous Aigisthos, who cut down his glorious father.

The reciprocity of the basic formula when it involves two adversaries, whether hero or anti-hero, has a very precise foundation in the culture: among men the taking of life requires vengeance, requital, atonement. The simplest expression of this in

5. Note the stylistic device of a form of the verb 'hear' to introduce a poem or episode.

Homer is just a postpositional phrase, as in *Il.*13.447 τρεῖς ἑνὸς ἀντὶ πεφάσθαι 'three to be slain in exchange for one', cf. also 14.471, 24.254.[6] But more frequently we find a reflex of the Indo-European verbal root for the notions of vengeance and requital, **kʷei-* in Gk. τίνω, τίνυμαι 'atone, pay the price for', middle 'take vengeance on, have a price paid one', τίσις 'vengeance', ποινή 'blood-money, penalty'. There is an implicational relation between the two roots. **gʷhen-* requires **kʷei-*, which finds its expression in their frequent juxtaposition in epic, as in *Il.* 15.116 **τείσασθαι φόν**ον υἷος 'to avenge the slaying of my son', *Od.* 24.470 **τείσεσθαι** παιδὸς **φόν**ον 'id.', *Il.* 17.34-5 **τείσεις** γνωτὸν ἐμόν, τὸν **ἔπεφνες** 'you will pay the price for my brother whom you slew.'

In the Odyssey passage just given above the focus is on Orestes the avenger of his father, as an intended model for Telemakhos son of Odysseus. The focal verb is the bidirectional active and middle voice **τεισ-** (**kʷei-*). Aigisthos plotted Agamemnon's death (ὄλεθρον) for which he paid (active ἀπέτεισεν): the son Orestes avenged himself (middle ἐτείσατο) on his father's slayer (πατροφονῆα). It is the second member of the nominal compound -φον- which points to and identifies the real verbal and nominal forms (as bracketed) of the obligatory sequence:

> Aigisthos **ἐμήσατο ὄλεθρον** = [**πέφνε**] Agamemnon
> Aigisthos **ἀπέτεισεν** [φόνον]
> Orestes **ἐτείσατο** πατρο-**φον**ῆα.

The final line Αἴγισθον . . . ὅ οἱ πατέρα ἔκτα is simply epexegetic to, explains πατροφονῆα, and makes ring composition with line 194. For line-final ἔκτα see note 1 above.

That this sequence is lexically, formulaically and culturally predetermined is proved by its overt expression in the *Iliad*, 21.133-5:

> ἀλλὰ καὶ ὧς **ὀλέεσθε** κακὸν μόρον, εἰς ὅ κε πάντες
> **τείσετε** Πατρόκλοιο **φόνον** καὶ λοιγὸν 'Αχαιῶν
> οὓς ἐπὶ νηυσὶ θοῇσιν **ἐπέφνετε** νόσφιν ἐμεῖο
>
> And yet even so, die all an evil death, till all of you
> **pay** for the **death** of Patroklos and the slaughter of the Achaeans
> whom you **killed** beside the running ships, when I was not with them.

Here the root **gʷhen-* is not underlying, but overt. Schematically,

ANTI-HERO	**gʷhen-*	HERO_1
ANTI-HERO	**kʷei-*$_{\text{act.}}$	HERO_1 **gʷhon-o-*

6. The associative presence of a form of ἄξιος 'worthy, worth, of equal weight' in the first two of these, with its implied image of balanced scales, is noteworthy. Compare ἀτάλαντος 'of equal weight on the scales' and Watkins 1987b.

HERO$_2$ $\left\{ \begin{matrix} *g^{u}hen- \\ *k^{u}ei-_{\text{mid.}} \end{matrix} \right\}$ ANTI-HERO

We discussed earlier the memorative function of the root *$g^{u}hen$-, as a summation, the epic equivalent of Pindar's 'shortcut', the οἶμος βραχύς which is the formula itself. We can observe the same with the co-occurrence of the root *$k^{u}ei$-. In the last book of the *Odyssey* Odysseus has just revealed himself to his father. He is in a hurry, like Pindar, but is speaking concisely to an older generation (24.324-6):

ἐκ γάρ τοι ἐρέω· μάλα δὲ χρὴ σπευδέμεν ἔμπης·
μνηστῆρας **κατέπεφνον** ἐν ἡμετέροισι δόμοισι
λώβην **τινύμενος** θυμαλγέα καὶ κακὰ ἔργα

For I tell you this straight out; the need for haste is upon us.
I have killed the suitors in our own house
avenging their heart-hurting outrage and their evil devisings.

Formulaically and culturally no further justification is needed, and none is asked for or given.

These passages illustrate the importance of the derivatives of the root *$k^{u}ei$- and the theme of their cooccurrence with derivatives of *$g^{u}hen$- in Greek epic on the level of the hero, the warrior. It should be noted that the same theme holds true on the level of myth, of the conflict of the hero with the monster adversary.

In chap. 41 we noted the figure of the Kuklops Poluphemos as monster or pre-civilized anti-hero for his violation of hospitality. As just noted, the verb in the formula may be replaced by the middle of *$k^{u}ei$- 'PUNISH, take vengeance on'. The Kuklops' crime is eating guests: ξείνους . . . ἐσθέμεναι (*Od.* 9.478-9). The last line, concluding Odysseus' address to the Kuklops after escaping him, continues:

τῶι σε Ζεὺς **τείσατο** καὶ θεοὶ ἄλλοι

For that Zeus **punished** you, he and the other gods.

Formulaically,

HERO (*$di̯eu$-) | PUNISH (*$k^{u}ei$-$_{\text{mid.}}$) ANTI-HERO (with COMPANIONS).

The HERO is Zeus (*$di̯eu$-), the Indo-European word for 'god', and the COMPANIONS are the other gods.

The similarity of the Poluphemos episode to other dragon-slaying myths is evident; in particular the blinding of the drunken Kuklops reminds us of the trussing up and slaying of the drunken Illuyankas. We can observe another formal—i.e., verbal formulaic—link with the dénouement of the Illuyankas myth: the phrase *nu=kan* ^{MUŠ}*illuyankan kuenta* DINGIR^{MEŠ}-*š=a katti=šši ešir* 'he killed the serpent; and the gods were with him'. In this Hittite version of the basic formula,

HERO	SLAY (*$g^{u}hen$-) SERPENT (with COMPANIONS),

the HERO is the Storm God, head of the pantheon, and the COMPANIONS are the other gods, as in the *Odyssey* passage. In the latter the HERO is Zeus (IE **di̯eu-s*); in the Hittite myth, where behind the Sumerogram DINGIR^{MEŠ} 'gods' lies the Hittite word *šiuneš*, we find a suffixed form of Indo-European **di̯eu-* as well.

Crime and punishment is a natural collocation, and it is not surprising to find it in other traditions. In some the very roots are the same, as in Iranian. From Avestan compare Yt. 15.28 *yaṯ* ***kaēna*** *nijasāni azəm brāϑrō uruuāxšaiia yaṯ* ***janāni*** *hitaspəm raiϑe paitivazaiδiiāi* '(grant me this boon,) that I may come down as avenger of my brother Urvāxšaya, that I may slay Hitāspa and drag him behind my chariot' (Bartholomae s.v. *vazaiδiiāi* already compared *Il.* 22.395ff.). From Middle Iranian compare from the Pahlavi Dēnkard VII (4521 ff.) *mā mān abar* ***zanē*** . . . ***kēn*** *tōzēd* . . . *Zarduxšt* 'Do not kill me . . .' (Mid. Pers. *zan-* < Old Iran. *jan-* 'slay' < IE *$g^{u}hen$-), 'He will take revenge, Zarathustra . . .' (Mid. Pers. *kēn* < Old Iran. *kaēnā-* 'punishment' < IE *$k^{u}oin\bar{a}$-, Greek ποινή). In other traditions one or both roots have undergone lexical replacement: *Beowulf* 1576-7 *hé hraþe wolde / Grendle* ***forgyldan gúð****ræsa fela* 'he intended to pay back (IE **gheldh-* or **ghelt-*) Grendel quickly for the many raids (IE *$g^{u}hen$-)'; 1053-5 *ond þone ǽnne heht / golde* ***forgyldan*** *þone þe Grendel ǽr / máne* ***ácwealde*** 'and he ordered compensation in gold to be paid (**gheldh-*) for the man whom Grendel had wickedly killed (IE *$g^{u}el$-) earlier'. The formulaic system is an index to Indo-European customary law.

These patterns which we have examined hitherto mostly in the *Odyssey* are equally characteristic of the deployment of πεφνέμεν in the *Iliad.* We have the straightforwardly "heroic" exploit involving a major figure, as in 4.397: Agamemnon chides Diomedes by recalling—the memorative function—the exploits of his father Tydeus, who killed 49 of the 50 sent to ambush him, but left one to return home: πάντας **ἔπεφν'**, ἕνα δ' οἶον ἵει οἶκόνδε νέεσθαι. Nestor in 7.142 recalls the background of his own exploits, of Areïthoos the mace-wielder (κορυνήτης, compare chap. 44) 'whom Lykoorgos slew by guile, and in no way by strength': τὸν Λυκόοργος **ἔπεφνε** δόλωι, οὔ τι κράτεΐ γε. He uses κτάνον for his own deed (155).

Iliad 15.638ff. tell of Hector's rout of the Achaeans:

ὁ δ' οἶον **ἔπεφνε** Μυκηναῖον Περιφήτην
Κοπρῆος φίλον υἱόν . . .
τοῦ γένετ' ἐκ πατρὸς πολὺ χείρονος υἱὸς ἀμείνων

But he **slew** only the Mycenean Periphetes
son of Kopreus ["Dungman"] . . .
From him was born, from a father baser by far, a noble son.

The mock-heroic, barnyard bow to upward mobility may have its roots in the second millennium, for the name of the Mycenean Kopreus seems to be found in Mycenean Greek, twice each in Pylos (nom. *ko-pe-re-u*, gen. *ko-pe-re-wo*) and Knossos (*ko-pe-re-u*, dat. *ko-pe-re-we*).[7] If for the unresolvable τοῦ at verse initial of 15.641 we read a Mycenean genitive or genitive-ablative *tō < *tōd,[8] the whole line will still scan perfectly transposed into Mycenean Greek.

In *Il.* 10.476ff., when Odysseus and Diomedes are rustling the horses of Rhesos, Odysseus says 'Here is the man and here are the horses told of to us two (νῶϊν) by Dolon, whom we slew (Δόλων ὅν ἐπέφνομεν ἡμεῖς). You take the men and I'll get the horses.' Athene breathes power into Diomedes:

κτεῖνε δ᾽ ἐπιστροφάδην· . . . στόνος ὄρνυτο . . . ἄορι θεινομένων

He was killing right and left; the groaning arose of those **being struck** by the sword.

So Diomedes went like a lion among a flock, ὄφρα δυώδεκ᾽ ἔπεφνεν 'until he had killed twelve'. The king as the thirteenth he robbed of honey-sweet life (μελιηδέα θυμὸν ἀπηύρα, for which see further below), a bad dream (κακὸν ὄναρ) standing over his head by the ruse (μῆτις) of Athene. The whole is presented as a thoroughly satisfying caper, in the language of warriors' slang with its mixture of archaic and colloquial, which characterizes much of *Iliad* 10.[9]

The verb may be epexegetic to minor exploits, as in *Il.* 15.338-39, the beginning of a catalogue of ἀνὴρ ἕλεν ἄνδρα 'man took out man' as the Trojans storm the wall: Ἕκτωρ μὲν Στιχίον τε καὶ Ἀρκεσίλαον ἔπεφνεν 'Hector slew S. and A.' Cf. also *Il.* 16.547, 17.539. This usage is easily amenable to mock-heroic parody, as 6 times in the Battle of Frogs and Mice.

In *Il.* 3.281-4 Agamemnon's prayer and oath before the single combat is both a grammatical and a pragmatic antithesis, heavily indexed by phonetic figures:

εἰ **μέν** κεν **Με**νέλαον Ἀλέξανδρος καταπέφνηι
. . .
εἰ **δέ** κ᾽ Ἀλέξανδρον κτείνηι **ξαν**θὸς Μενέλαος
. . .

If Alexandros slay Menelaos . . .
But if fair-haired Menelaos slay Alexandros . . .

That we have to do with the basic formula is shown by the focus on the object of the

---

7. For the attestations and on the phonological problems and possible solutions see Chadwick and Baumbach 1963:211 and Baumbach 1979:171, respectively.

8. For which see Morpurgo Davies 1988b:100, as well as Hajnal 1994.

9. Expanding θυμόν by the adjective 'honey-sweet', ironic in the context of the verb phrase 'rob of life', the equivalent of the basic formula with *gʷhen-, recurs in Euphorbos' warrior-taunt to Menelaos, *Il.* 17.17. The effect is that of saying "you bet your sweet life . . ." in a comparable pre-fight exchange. Cf. also *Od.* 11.203, also in dialogue, Odysseus' dead mother's reproach.

verb rather than the subject, as shown by their respective order, the object preceding the subject.[10] As elsewhere, the semantic mark of καταπέφνηι carries over to unmarked κτείνηι, much as that of a compound verb (P + V_i) carries over to a subsequent and resumptive simple (V_i); both processes may be at work in καταπέφνηι . . . [κατα]κτείνηι = [κατα]πέφνηι.

Andromache in her meeting with Hector in *Iliad* 6 knows and says that she will soon be a widow, for the Achaeans will soon kill him: 408-9 ἦ τάχα χήρη/σεῦ ἔσομαι· τάχα γάρ σε **κατακτανέουσιν** 'Αχαιοί. She has neither father nor mother; she says simply (414-16),

> ἤτοι γὰρ πατέρ' ἁμὸν **ἀπέκτανε** δῖος 'Αχιλλεύς
> . . .
> . . . κατὰ δ' **ἔκτανεν** 'Ηετίωνα
>
> For godly Achilles **killed** my father as you know
> . . .
> . . . He **killed** Eetion,

using the unmarked verb, but continues (421-23):

> ἑπτὰ κασίγνητοι
> . . .
> πάντας γὰρ **κατέπεφνε** ποδάρκης δῖος 'Αχιλλεύς
>
> Seven brothers . . .
> . . .
> swift-footed godly Achilles **slew** them all.

The reversion to the marked verb after the litany of the three unmarked ones has a summational, but also a climactic value.[11] The function of ἔπεφνε is clearly memorative in the nearly identical *Il.* 23.828: Achilles sets as a game the mass of iron which Eetion used to throw, ἀλλ' ἤτοι τὸν **πέφνε** 'but Achilles slew him, as you know', and carried it off as booty.

The death of Patroklos echoes and reverberates in verbal formulas over many thousands of lines. Menelaos says at 17.564 Πατρόκλωι· μάλα γάρ με θανὼν **ἐσεμάσσατο θυμόν** '. . . Patroklos; for his death has touched me to the heart'. The verb ἐσεμάσσατο applies indifferently to the victim and his killer: Achilles on seeing Hector in the fray says to himself at 20.425-6,

> ἐγγὺς ἀνὴρ ὃς ἐμόν γε μάλιστ' **ἐσεμάσσατο θυμόν**
> ὅς μοι ἑταῖρον **ἔπεφνε** τετιμένον

10. On the inherited legal theme of this episode see Jamison 1994.

11. The inherent pathos of Andromache's situation would have a legal foundation as well, in Indo-European tradition. Compare Thurneysen 1936 and the texts cited there.

Near is the man who above all **grieved** me **to the heart**,
who **slew** my honored comrade.

The verb is confined in Homer to these two instances. The formula ὅς μοι ἑταῖρον ἔπεφνε will be used—as though he had heard it—by Priam's son Lycaon begging Achilles for his life (21.95-6):

μή με κτεῖν', ἐπεὶ οὐχ ὁμογάστριος Ἕκτορός εἰμι,
ὅς τοι ἑταῖρον **ἔπεφνεν** . . .

Don't kill me, for I am not of the same womb
as Hector, who **slew** your comrade . . .

These formulas are poetic discourse 'shifters', applying indifferently to the *I* or the *You.*

Homer had said of Patroklos, just before his fortunes changed (16.784ff.), 'Thrice he rushed in with a terrible cry,'

. . . τρὶς δ' ἐννέα φῶτας ἔπε**φν**εν
ἀλλ' ὅτε δή τὸ τέταρτον . . .
ἔνθ' ἄρα τοι, Πάτροκλε, **φ**ά**ν**η βιότοιο τελευτή

. . . thrice he slew nine men,
but when for the fourth time . . .
then for you, Patroklos, did the end of life appear.

The dramatic address is indexed by a phonetic figure linking *epePHNē* and *PHaNē*. That this link between the two verbs is real is indicated by the gnomic neologism at 15.140,

ἢ πέφατ', ἢ καὶ ἔπειτα **πεφήσεται** . . .

either **has been slain**, or will be later,

where the epic future has been cloned from that of φαίνω, which is regular and expected, and which appears in the same metrical slot in 17.155:

Τροίῃ δὲ **πεφήσεται** αἰπὺς ὄλεθρος

For Troy **will appear** sheer destruction.

For the real suppletive future of πεφνέμεν see chap. 51.

Patroklos' death is formulaically and thematically prefigured by that of Sarpedon, felled like a great tree (16.487-9):

ἠΰτε ταῦρον **ἔπεφνε λέων** . . .

. . .

ὤλετό τε στενάχων ὑπὸ γαμφηλῆισι **λέοντος**

As a **lion slays** a bull . . .

. . .

and with a groan he **perishes** beneath the jaws of the lion.

At the death of Patroklos, run through by Hector's spear, the verb stands outside the simile:

16.823 ὡς δ' ὅτε σῦν ἀκάμαντα **λέων ἐβιήσατο**

. . .

826 . . . **λέων ἐδάμασσε βίηφιν**

827 ὣς πολέας **πεφνόντα** Μενοιτίου . . . υἱὸν

828 Ἕκτωρ . . . ἔγχεϊ **θυμὸν ἀπηύρα**

As when a **lion overpowers** an untiring boar

. . . **the lion overcomes him by his power**.

So did Hector by spear **rob of life** of the son of Menoitios

. . . who had **slain** many.

In lines 823-26 we find not merely ring-composition, but also another characteristic stylistic figure of Indo-European date discussed earlier: the resumption or iteration of a finite verb form by a semantically equivalent nominal form from the same root in a Verb Phrase: . . . ἐβιήσατο 'over**powers**' . . . ἐδάμασσε βίηφιν 'overcomes by **power**'. Compare the examples in Greek and elsewhere of this Indo-European stylistic figure given in chap. 13.

Positioning both Verb and related Noun adjacent to the verse boundary points up and indexes the parallelism. Within this four-line simile the ring involves both a lexical responsion **λέων ἐβιήσατο** : **λέων** . . . **βίηφιν** and a grammatical responsion **ἐβιήσατο** (V_i) : **ἐδάμασσε βίηφιν** ($V + N_i$). In the grammatical responsion V_i and ($V + N_i$) are semantically equivalent.

The aorist in the verb phrase θυμὸν ἀπηύρᾱ of 828 'took away, robbed of life', participle ἀπούρας (i.e. ἀπ-ή-ϝρα, ἀπό-ϝρᾱς) in both vocalism and accent is regarded as an Aeolism (Chantraine 1973:191), whether in the traditional sense or that of the 'Peloponnesian Aeolic' linguistic and poetic tradition of the Ἀχαιοί argued for recently by Peters 1986 and 1989. The verb is clearly old, though it has no certain cognates outside Greek. Within Homer the verb phrase is clearly an equivalent of πεφνέμεν in the basic formula. We saw above *Il.* 10.488-95: ὄφρα δυώδεκ' ἔπεφνεν . . . τὸν τρισκαιδέκατον μελιηδέα θυμὸν ἀπηύρα 'until he had slain twelve . . . the thirteenth he robbed of honey-sweet life . . .' The function of the verb phrase is demarcative, like that of the ordinal. It closes the set: 12 ἔπεφνεν (V) . . . the 13th θυμὸν ἀπηύρα (V + N).

In chap. 53 we will examine in detail the inherited theme that links **gʷhen-* in the basic formula with **k̂ei-* 'lie'. In the death of Asteropaios at the hands of Achilles we see the same link between θυμὸν ἀπηύρα and κεῖμαι; the verb πεφνέμεν is not present in the passage at all, because θυμὸν ἀπηύρα is its substitute and equivalent. The whole verb phrase is another form of the basic formula. Achilles robs Asteropaios of life with his sword (the WEAPON), 179 ἄορι θυμὸν ἀπηύρα. He taunts him in death, saying (184) κεῖσ' οὕτως 'lie as you are . . .' After speaking he leaves him, 'when he had robbed him of life, lying in the sands', 201-2 ἐπεὶ φίλον ἦτορ ἀπηύρα/κείμενον ἐν ψαμάθοισι.

In chap. 31 we discussed the inherited figure of the reciprocal formula "the slayer slain", a variant of the basic formula, with such phrases as 'he who slays will be slain'. One of the verbs may be nominalized, as in the future participle (*Il.* 18.309) τὸν κτανέοντα κατέκτα 'he kills him who would kill'. It is just such a topos that we have here in *Il.* 16.827-28: Hector slew Patroklos who had slain. The figure begins with the verb SLAY of the basic formula nominalized: the aorist participle πεφνόντα. The accusative marks the object of the underlying reciprocal verb SLAY of the formula, transformed into the Verb Phrase θυμὸν ἀπηύρα, and including the WEAPON ἔγχεϊ. Schematically, the reciprocal figure of "the slayer slain", with two forms of the same verb V_i : V_i has been renewed by replacement of the second verb by a semantically equivalent Verb Phrase, V_i : $(V + N)_i$.

At this point we can understand what is going on in *Il.* 16.823-28. The inherited stylistic figure in the simile (823-26) of verb (V_i) repeated by verb plus semantically equivalent noun ($V + N_i$), which is at the same time a ring composition demarcating the simile, is echoed by grammatical parallelism. The next two lines present yet another inherited stylistic figure, the reciprocal basic formula of "the slayer slain". The first verb is the participle πεφνόντα (V_i), and its reciprocal counterpart is the semantically equivalent verb phrase θυμὸν ἀπηύρα $(V + N)_i$. The correspondence is complete:

ἐβιήσατο	V_i	πεφνόντ'	V_i
ἐδάμασσε βίηφιν	$(V + N_i)$	θῦμον ἀπηύρα	$(V + N)_i$

Such is the first token of the verbal art inherited from Indo-European which marks the death of Patroklos in Homer's *Iliad*.

50

The best of the Achaeans

We can observe the transition from mythical combat to the reality of war in the account of the trials of Bellerophontes in *Iliad* 6 with which we began chap. 36. The passage concludes with the slaying of the warriors sent against Bellerophontes by the king of Lycia after his victory over the Chimaira, the Solymians, and the Amazons, *Il.* 6. 188-90:

> κρίνας ἐκ Λυκίης εὐρείης φῶτας **ἀρίστους**
> εἷσε λόχον· τοὶ δ' οὔ τι πάλιν οἶκόνδε νέοντο·
> πάντας γὰρ **κατέπεφνεν** ἀμύμων Βελλεροφόντης
>
> He chose out of wide Lycia the **best men**
> and set an ambush; but these did not return home in any way,
> for peerless Bellerophon **slew** them one and all.

The choice of verb remains the same, but note that the hero's adversaries have the epithet ἀρίστους: they are the best and the bravest.

The equipollent opposition of two heroes in the epic context is reflected in their system of epithets: each of the two can be qualified as ἄριστος 'best'. The notion has been studied in depth by Nagy 1979, in an influential book. Achilles and Patroklos are both 'best of the Achaeans' (ἄριστος 'Αχαιῶν); bestriding Patroklos' corpse Menelaos killed Euphorbos, *Il.* 17.80:

> Τρώων τὸν **ἄριστον ἔπεφνε**
>
> He **slew the best** of the Trojans.

Reciprocity finds its grammatical expression in Achilles' cry to Zeus when hard-pressed by the River Skamandros, *Il.* 21.279-80:

> ὥς μ' ὄφελ' Ἕκτωρ **κτεῖναι**, ὃς ἐνθάδε γ' ἔτραφ' **ἄριστος**
> τῶ κ' **ἀγαθὸς** μὲν **ἔπεφν'**, **ἀγαθὸν** δέ κεν **ἐξενάριξε**

Would that Hector **had slain** me, **the best** of the men
bred here; then **a brave man** would have been the **slayer**,
and he would have **slain a brave man**.[1]

And the Trojan ally Glaukos says of Patroklos and Achilles (17.164),

τοίου γὰρ θεράπων **πέφατ**᾽ ἀνέρος, ὃς μεγ᾽ **ἄριστος**
᾽Αργείων

Such a man is he whose squire has been **slain**, **the best**
of the Argives.

The Odyssean passage linking SLAY and BEST is also put in the mouth of Achilles, speaking to Odysseus in the underworld: 11.499-500 'I am not such as I was, when in broad Troy I slew the best of the host', **πέφνον** λαὸν **ἄριστον**. It is a part of the formulaic definition of the HERO that he is BEST, or vanquishes the BEST.

This Greek usage has parallels in other Indo-European traditions. Indra is addressed as *vasiṣṭha* 'best' in RV 2.36.1, and Agni at 7.1.8 (with a play on the poet's family name, which is the same). The hero-king Purūravas calls in vain after his former lover, the vanishing apsaras Urvaśī, at RV 10.95.17 *úpa śikṣāmy urváśīṃ vásiṣṭhaḥ* 'I the best (lover) long for Urvaśī' (where there may be a play *ur*VAŚ*iṃ* VAS*iṣṭhaḥ* and an unspoken VAŚ*mi* 'I want').[2] These three are the only beings in the Rigveda to receive the epithet, which is otherwise only a name.

As in Greek the positive 'good' is common as well as a divine epithet. In the Rigveda the positive *vásu* is also very common as a divine epithet, and frequent as an absolute in the vocative, particularly of Indra and Agni. Examples from religious language could be multiplied indefinitely, from multiple traditions, from Latin *bona dea* and Old Irish *in Dagdae* to *Le Bon Dieu*. We are here in the realm of universals.

In the Rigveda we find superlatives in *-iṣṭha-* as epithets clustered around the mythologeme, the basic formula of the hero Indra and his adversary. In 6.37.5

índro **vṛtrám hániṣṭho** astu sátvā

Let Indra be **the best** warrior to **have slain Vṛtra**,

we have the unique occurrence of the superlative of the root *han-*, an inherited formation (compare Greek φέριστος, Avestan *bairišta-*), which functions in Indo-Iranian as suppletive to the agent noun, with verbal rection.[3] Much more frequent is

1. ἀγαθός is the positive of the superlative ἄριστος.

2. The word is not found in the prose version of the tale, ŚB 11.5.1., which quotes only RV 10.95. 1-15.

3. Compare stylistically and grammatically RV 6.44.15 *pā́tā sutám índro astu sómaṃ/* ***hántā vṛtrám*** *vájreṇa mandasānáḥ* 'let Indra be the one who has drunk the pressed soma, who has slain Vṛtra with his cudgel in exhilaration.' The agent noun with root accent assigns case like a verb. For the verbal rection of the adjectives note also RV 9.61.20 *jághnir vṛtrám* 'slaying Vṛtra' and Avestan (*ni*)*jaγništa* (*tāyūm* Y. 12.7,8) 'best smiting the thief'. Positive and superlative behave alike. See also chaps. 29 n.12 and 39 n. 5.

the compound adjectival superlative *vṛtrahántama-* (RV 23x) 'most smashing resistance, most smiting the foe'.

The same hymn furnishes another superlative in the preceding verse, 6.37.4:

> **váriṣṭho** asya dákṣinām iyarti
>
> (Indra) **the broadest** sets in motion his reward (to the poet).

Geldner ad loc. terms the superlative hypallage (interchange in syntactic relationship between two terms), since it should properly go with the reward (to consist of the broadest herd of cattle). We can say that by a rule or license of poetic grammar Indra the subject HERO has attracted the superlative.

In RV 1.32.5 we find a comparative in *-tara-* made to the adversary which is scarcely translatable:

> áhan vṛtráṃ vṛtratáraṃ vyàṁsam
>
> He slew Vṛtra, the Vṛtra among all the *vṛtrá* with shoulders apart.

The formation is again unique. The translation 'Vṛtra entre tous les *vṛtrá*' is Renou's (1952:170); the interpretation of v*yàṁsam*, as a kenning for 'cobra', is due to H. P. Schmidt (1964).

A primary comparative from the root *han-* is attested in a repeated mantra in the Yajurvedas: *námo hantré ca hánīyase ca* 'reverence to the slayer and the better slayer' (TS 4.5.8.1, MS 2.9.7, Kāṭh. 17.15, Kap. 37.5, VS 16.40).

In the Gathas the Wise Lord Ahura Mazdā is addressed as *vahištā* 'Best One' in Y. 28.8 and 33.7 (the latter pluralized in an inclusive syntagma, see S. Insler 1975 ad loc.).[4]

Exactly comparable usages of 'best' are found in the language of Germanic epic. Beowulf is addressed by Hrothgar as *secg betsta* 'O best of men' at 947 (after the fight with Grendel and Hrothgar's homily on Heremod the bad king) and 1759 (after the fight with Grendel's mother, and Hrothgar's second homily on Heremod). At 1405-6 Grendel's mother

> magoþegna bær
> þone sélestan sáwolleasne
>
> bore the lifeless body
> of the best of young thanes,

Æschere, whom she had slain in vengeance for the death of Grendel. Unferth lent

4. The stylistic figure of the triad of superlatives *mazišta-ca vahišta-ca sraēšta-ca* 'greatest and best and most beautiful', both of gods and men (Y. 1.1, V. 2.27, etc.), is related, and clearly cognate with the Roman cult title *Iuppiter Optimus Maximus* and Homeric Ζεῦ πάτερ . . . κύδιστε μέγιστε. See Watkins 1975a.

Beowulf his sword Hrunting *sélran sweordfrecan* 'to the better swordsman' at 1468.

The hero's arms and armor are similarly described; Beowulf refers to his corselet, the work of the smith Wēland, as *beaduscrúda betst* (453) 'best of battle-garments' and *hrægla sélest* (454) 'best of corselets'. On the promotion of the WEAPON to the status of subject/HERO see chap. 27. The marvelous sword with which Beowulf can kill Grendel's mother is described in the half-line formula *þæt* [*wæs*] *wæpna cyst* 'that was the best of weapons' at 1559, with a noun (Gmc. **kustiz* < IE **ĝus-ti-*) which in form and meaning iconically recalls a superlative.

Just as we have seen the positive ἀγαθός in Achilles' formulation cited above (*Il.* 21.280), so we should see the familiar and striking half-line formula (*Beowulf* 11 et passim)

> þæt wæs **gód** cyning
>
> That was a **good** king,

in the same light as these superlatives.

The usage recurs in North Germanic as well. In the *Poetic Edda*, in the first *Lay of Helgi Hunding's Bane* 2 the Norns or Fates prophesy at Helgi's birth that he will be called *buðlunga betstan* 'the best of rulers'. The phrase reflects the same ideology as the Old English *þæt wæs gód cyning.*

I suggest that in this 'heroic' use of the superlative 'best' in Greek ἄριστος, Vedic *vasiṣṭha-*, Avestan *vahišta-*, Old English *betst*, *sélest*, and Old Norse *betstr* (*beztr*), as well as of the pregnant positives ἀγαθός, *vásu*, *bonus*, and *gód*, we have an inherited, Indo-European theme and stylistic figure. To the Best of the Achaeans (ἄριστος 'Αχαιῶν), the Best of the Hellenes ('Ελλάνων ἄριστοι, Bacchylides 5.111), the Best of the Trojans (Τρώων . . . ἄριστος) we can add *Beowulf* 1684-6:

> woroldcyninga
> þǽm sélestan be sǽm twéonum
> þára þe on Scedenigge sceattas dǽlde
>
> to the Best of World-kings between the seas
> of those who have distributed treasures in Scandinavia.

External comparison enables us to move from the domain of synchrony to that of diachrony. The variations rung on these superlatives and their lexical expression may be a function of the individual branches or languages and their histories; but the underlying system which formulaically conveys the definition of HERO is a linguistic and socio-cultural inheritance from common Indo-European times.

We may conclude with a recollection of the formulation of the closing lines of *Beowulf*, with their implicit definition of the ideal king-hero (3180-2): 'They said that of world kings he was

> manna mildust ond monðwǽrust
> léodum liðost ond lofgeornost

gentlest of men and most gracious
kindest to his people and most desirous of renown.

One cannot fail to be moved by the solemnity and nobility of these metrically identical, isosyllabic, grammatically parallel "spondaic" lines.

A far more sophisticated man writing at an earlier time but in a more sophisticated cultural environment had recourse to the same grammatical figure in recounting the death of his own intellectual hero: 'Such was the end, Ekhekrates, of our friend, of a man, as we may say, of all those of that time whom we have known,

ἀρίστου καὶ φρονιμωτάτου καὶ δικαιοτάτου

The best and the wisest and the most just.
(Plato, *Phaedo* 118).[5]

5. I print the text with Schanz' bracketing of ἄλλως '(and) besides' before φρονιμωτάτου. Those who would retain it (like LSJ) could point to the contrast in suffixal morphology as well as meaning between the first and the next two superlatives.

51

To be the death of: Transformation of the formula

Some instances of the basic formula in Greek show a more complex grammatical responsion. Two sets involve minor players in the *Iliad*. We may think of them as little sagas, like that of Iphitos (chap. 41). The first is the saga of Tlepolemos of Rhodes, the son of Herakles and grandson of Zeus. In the Catalogue of Ships we learn that he killed his own father's maternal uncle: *Il*. 2.662 πατρὸς ἑοῖο φίλον μήτρωα **κατέκτα**.[1] For this kin-slaying (Old Irish *fingal*) he fled to Rhodes, to escape the revenge of his father's kin-group, sons and grandsons. And in book 5 he will indeed be killed by Sarpedon, son of Zeus. Before the fateful combat they taunt each other, 5.633ff., 648ff. Sarpedon promises him (5.652-3):

> **σοὶ** δ' ἐγὼ ἐνθάδε φημὶ **φόνον** καὶ κῆρα μέλαιναν
> ἐξ ἐμέθεν **τεύξεσθαι** . . .
>
> I say that **death** and black fate
> will be **wrought** here from me for **you**.

Here the verb of slaying has been replaced by a verb phrase whose object is a noun (**g^{w}hon-o-*) from the same root. But the effect is the same.[2]

The same figure is found in *Iliad* 11 in the little saga of Sokos ('Strong'), whose brother Odysseus kills. Sokos joins the fight, taunting Odysseus (430 ff.): 'Today you will either boast of having slain two such men (dual, τοιώδ' ἄνδρε **κατακτείνας**), or you will perish (ὀλέσσῃς) by my spear.' Odysseus replies (443-4), with a repeat of 5.652:

1. On archaic (κατ)έκτα in line-final position see chap. 49 n. 1. Line-finally we find complementary distribution according to the final of the preceding word: - V̆ κατέκτα / -V̆C ἔπεφνεν /. The former is more frequent with the preverb, the latter without it.

2. With the same verb compare *Od*. 4.771 οὐδέ τι οἶδεν ὅ οἱ **φόνος** υἷι **τέτυκται** 'she does not know that murder has been made ready for her son.' But here the clearly prospective sense of φόνος τέτυκται is not in any way equivalent to πέφαται.

> **σοὶ** δ' ἐγὼ ἐνθάδε φημὶ **φόνον** καὶ κῆρα μέλαιναν
> ἤματι τῷιδ' **ἔσσεσθαι** . . .
>
> I say that here on this day **death** and black fate
> **will be** upon you. . .

The same verb is found in *Od.* 11.444, when the shade of Agamemnon says,

> ἀλλ' οὐ σοί γ', 'Οδυσεῦ, **φόνος ἔσσεται** ἔκ γε γυναικός
>
> And yet you, Odysseus, will never **be murdered** by your wife.

(Lattimore's translation clearly captures the verbal force of the periphrasis.) Similarly *Od.* 21.24 αἵ δή οἱ καὶ ἔπειτα **φόνος** καὶ μοῖρα **γένοντο** 'but thereafter these became his death and doom'. An example in the present tense is *Il.* 16.144 = 19.391, Achilles' spear given to his father by Chiron **φόνον ἔμμεναι** ἡρώεσσιν 'to be the death of heroes'. Compare also the legal formula in a fifth-century Arcadian inscription, Schwyzer 661.25-6, Buck 16 ('a little later than 460', Jeffery 1990:214):

> ει Иις ιν το(ι) ιεροι τον τοτ[ε απυθανοντον]/**φονες εστι**
>
> If anyone present in temple **is a murderer** of those who
> were killed at that time . . .

Here the noun is a derived agent noun.

The use of the periphrastic 'be death (φον-) for someone, be a murderer (φον-) of someone, prepare death (φον-) for someone' has a clear advantage over the use of finite forms of πεφνέμεν: they can be used in tenses and aspects which are missing or barely developed in the latter, like present and future, and it is no accident that the Homeric examples are mostly confined to these tenses.

Three examples remain in the *Iliad*, all presents, with the alliterating verb φέρειν 'bear': 2.352/3.6 **φόν**ον καὶ κῆρα **φέρ**οντες / **φέρ**ουσαι 'bearing death and fate (to Trojans/Pygmies)'; 17.757 σμικρῆισι **φόν**ον **φέρ**ει ὀρνίθεσσιν '(the hawk) brings death to small birds'.

All these cases of Verb + φον- are semantically and affectively equivalent to a finite form of πεφν-, but one which happens not to be found in this "defective" verb. The periphrastic verb phrase made possible the expression of the basic formula in Greek in these tenses; the process was suppletion.

We saw in the preceding section an instance of the inherited stylistic figure of Verb_i iterated by synonymous Verb + Noun_i where Verb_i and Noun_i are from the same root: βιήσατο . . . / ἐδάμασσε βίηφιν, like ἐρᾶι . . . / ἔρως . . . λαμβάνει. The function of the figure may be conclusory, summational, or climactic; but it is older than Greek. That is to say that the stylistic option of iterating or resuming a finite form of the Verb **gʷhen-* by a Verb Phrase consisting of Verb + **gʷhon-o-* existed since Indo-European times. Two examples of such Indo-European Verb Phrases, reconstructible on the basis of the Homeric examples cited, are

**h₁es- g^whon-o-*	'be the death (of)'
**bher- g^whon-o-*	'bring death (to)'.[3]

There is thus both grammatical and stylistic motivation for Greek φόνος ἔσσεται 'will be the death' (*Od.* 11.444).

This periphrasis is not confined to Greek. Column IV of Darius' great inscription at Bisutun, the conclusion of his account of his first regnal year, contains two warnings in traditional formulaic language, on the person who conceals and does not tell the people of this record, and on the person who destroys and does not protect this inscription. The topos is a familiar one in the Ancient Near East in the second and first millennia in a variety of languages. But the blessing and curse formula itself is strictly Indo-European Iranian: if you do not conceal etc., and do not destroy etc. (DB 4.55-6, 74-5),

auramazdā ϑuvām **dauštā** biyā

May Ahura Mazdā **love** you (lit. *te amator sit*);

but if you do conceal etc. and do destroy etc. (DB 4.58-9, 78-9),

auramazdā=taiy **jatā** biyā

May Ahura Mazdā be a **slayer** to you (= may he slay you).[4]

As Benveniste saw (1948:20-1) the two must be functionally parallel agent nouns *dauštar-* 'amātor', *ja(n̥)tar-* 'slayer', as the author of an act, despite the different constructions of the two pronouns. Originally we should expect accusative rection of this agent type, as in RV 4.17.8 (6x) *hántā yó vr̥trám* '(Indra) who (is) slayer of Vr̥tra = who slew Vr̥tra'[5] RV 2.12.10 *yó dásyor hantā́ sá janāsa indraḥ* 'he who is slayer of (= whose function is to slay) the *dasyu*—he, o people, is Indra.' With Y. 57.15 *jaṇta . . . drujō* of n. 5 compare RV 2.23.17 *druhó hantā́* 'destroyer of falsehood (Brahmaṇaspati)' (Schlerath 1968:160).

As we saw in the preceding chapter, in Indo-Iranian verbal roots could be suffixed for degrees of comparison, and the forms were taken by the Indian grammatical tradition as suppletive to these agent nouns.[6] They carry accusative rection. We

3. Such Verb Phrases enter into well-attested and open-ended syntactic categories in Indo-European which persist in the historical languages sometimes down to the present day. See Watkins 1975b.

4. Cf. Bartholomae, Air. Wb. 929f., Reichelt 1967:§625, 671.

5. In Young Avestan (Videvdat 1.17) *ϑraētaonō jaṇta ažōiš dahākāi* 'Thraētaona the slayer of (= who slew) Aži Dahāka', the genitive is probably a later construction. The genitive is appropriate, on the other hand, in Y. 57.15 *sraošəm . . . yō jaṇta daēuuaiiā̊ drujō* 'Sraoša the slayer of (= whose function is to slay) the daēvic Druj', Benveniste 1948:20, 26.

6. Debrunner, AiGr. II 2.443ff., citing Pāṇini 5.3.59 and 6.4.154. This is unlikely to be original, in the light of the unique equation with Greek φέριστος 'best' : Avestan *bairišta-* 'best helping, caring for',

have precisely the 'be the death of' predication in RV 6.37.5:

> índro vr̥tráṃ **háni̦ṣṭho** astu sátvā
>
> Let Indra be **the best slayer** (most slaying warrior) of Vr̥tra.

Avestan shows the superlative of the reduplicated root, Yt. 11.3:

> sraošō . . . yō vərəϑraja drujəm **jaɣništō**
>
> Sraoša . . . (is) the victorious, **best smiter** (most smiting) of the Druj,

like RV 9.61.20 *jághnir vr̥trám amitríyam* (*asi*) 'You are smiting Vr̥tra, with whom there is no alliance.'

The comparative *hánīyaṁs-* is not found in the Rigveda, but occurs in a later Vedic mantra in the liturgy to the god Rudra (MS 2.9.7, TS 4.5.8.1, VS 16.40 etc.):

> námo **hantré** ca **hánīyase** ca
>
> Homage to the **slayer**, and to **the better slayer**.

While Avestan has no corresponding form (**janiiå̊*) from the root *jan-*, it shows a rhyming form *aiβi.vaniiå̊* 'winner, conqueror' (+ accusative) in a very common formula first used in the words of the hero Thraētaona in Yt. 5.34: 'Give me that fortune',

> yat̰ bauuāni **aiβi.vaniiå̊**
> ažīm dahākəm
> ϑrizafanəm ϑrikamərəδəm . . .
>
> That I become the **winner**
> over Aži Dahāka,
> the three-mouthed, three-headed . . .

Yt. 5 continues with the same formula spoken by Kərəsāspa about the adversary Gaṇdarβa, and five further heroes and their respective opponents. It clearly belongs to the narration of the myth in Iran by the basic formula with a lexical variant.

So in the combat between the star *Tištriia* (Sirius) and the Demon of Drought *Apaoša*, according to a familiar pattern (chapters 35 and 46) the evil one defeats the hero, and then is finally defeated by him. The formulation is identical in the two verse narratives; only the case marking switches (Yt. 8.22 and 28):

---

and the semantic distance from the Avestan agent nouns *bāṣ̌ar-* 'bridle, halter' from Ir. **bártar-* (Hoffmann 1992:163-83) or *bərətar-* (Ir. **bŗtár-*) in V. 2.3.4 *mərətō bərətaca daēnaiiāi* 'remembrancer and propagator for the religion' (Benveniste 1948:23), or from the Umbrian *ařfertur* priest. There is no Greek *φέρτωρ and was no IE **bhér-tor-*. Compare the syntactic discussion at chap. 39 n. 7.

ā dim bauuaiti aiβi.aojō
ā dim bauuaiti **aiβi.vaniiå**
daēuuo yō apaošo tištrīm
raēuuaṇtəm x͏ᵛarənaŋᵛhuaṇtəm

He becomes the overpowerer of him,
he becomes the **winner** over him,
the daeva Apaoša (over) Tištrya
the splendid, glorious.

ā dim bauuaiti aiβi.aojō
ā dim bauuaiti **aiβi.vaniiå**
tištriiō raēuuå x͏ᵛarənaŋᵛhå
daēūm yim apaošəm

He becomes the overpowerer of him,
he becomes the **winner** over him,
Tištrya the splendid, glorious,
(over) the daeva Apaoša.

The root *van-* (IE **u̯en-*) like *tar-* (IE **terh₂-*) had the advantage over *jan-* (IE **gʷhen-*) that it was not irreversible, and could be applied to an only temporary victory. But these Iranian and Indic forms are all variants of 'be the death of', 'become the death of', and stylistic variants of a verbal sentence with a finite form of **gʷhen-*.

One other branch of the Indo-European family attests reflexes of these very Verb Phrases in Indo-European. We have already seen the evidence in chap. 43: Germanic. For the Indo-European formula

HERO (**gʷhen-*) SERPENT/HERO$_2$.

we posed as equivalent Germanic (represented by Old Norse)

at bana verða
HERO$_1$ SERPENT/HERO$_2$.
ban(a)orð bera

The first, 'become the bane', is common to all of North and West Germanic in the early period; the second, literally 'bring the killer-word, the death-word', is confined to Old Norse. The 'word' is a North Germanic innovation, but *bani* is for **gʷhon-o-* and *bera* is **bher-*; North and West Germanic 'become' is semantically a (slight) innovation, from IE **u̯ert-* 'turn' (cf. φόνος καὶ μοῖρα γένοντο). The finite verb **gʷhen-* has disappeared in Germanic, just as it was on the way out by the end of the fifth century B. C. in Greek. The periphrastic Verb Phrases assured the verbal continuity of this root in the basic formula for over two more millennia in Germanic, and their Indo-European origin could not be clearer.

52

The formula without the word: A note on Euripides and Lysias

As we saw in detail in chapters 38 and 40, in the context of mythical dragon-slaying, Euripides no longer uses the verb πεφνέμεν. The verb to SLAY for him is typically κτείνω; but it can continue the semantics of πεφνέμεν, assured by the presence of a nominal derivative of *g^{u}*hen-* in φον- as an auxiliary epithet of the MONSTER (πολύφονον κύνα), the WEAPON (τόξοις φόνιοις), or some other element in the message (θηροφόνον θεάν, φονίαισι φάτναις). We observe exactly the same in Euripides' handling of the basic formulas of heroic, "epic" killing. It is possible to see in this pattern a development of the earlier

> *πέφνε . . . ὄφιν . . . (-)φόνον
> πέφνε . . . δράκων . . . φόνου (Bacchylides)
> κτεῖνε . . . ὄφιν . . . -φόνον (Pindar),

discussed above (chap. 37). A transitional variant of the Pindaric formulation can perhaps be seen in [Ps.-]Euripides, *Rh.* 61-2, with -φονος in penultimate, not final position:

> πρὶν ναῦς **πυρῶσαι** καὶ διὰ σκηνῶν μολεῖν
> **κτείνων** Ἀχαιοὺς τῆιδε πολυ**φόνωι** χερί

> Before **burning** the ships and going through the tents,
> **slaying** Achaeans with this **murderous** hand.[1]

Here πολυ**φόνωι** χερὶ may also recall the adjective ἀνδρο**φόνος** 'man-slaying', which in the *Iliad* is basically an epithet of Hector (11x), but by an awesome synecdoche is three times an epithet of the hands of Achilles.

---

1. For the wording cf. Euripides *Herc.* 420ff. πολύφονον . . . ἐξεπύρωσεν . . . ἔκτα, whatever its relevance to the date and authorship of the *Rhesus*.

The figures of Agamemnon, Klutaimestra and Orestes cry out for the basic formula. Typical is Euripides *El.* 1086-95 (the heroine is speaking to her mother):

> σὴν θυγατέρ' **ἔκτεινεν** πατήρ
> ...
> ... πόσιν **κτείνασα**
> ...
> ... ἐμὲ **κτείνας** ... εἰ δ' ἀμείψεται
> **φόνον** δικάζων **φόνος**, **ἀποκτενῶ** σ' ἐγὼ
> καὶ παῖς 'Ορέστης πατρὶ **τιμωρούμενοι**.
>
> If our father **killed** your daughter
> ...
> ... having **killed** your husband
> ...
> ... having **killed** me ...
> If **murder** judges and calls for **murder**,
> I will **kill** you and your son Orestes will, to **avenge** our father.

In the context of patricide—the ring πατήρ ... πατρί—the reciprocal figure φόνον ... φόνος, "the slayer slain",[2] informs the four climactic verbs with the full force of *$*g^{u}hen$-* SLAY, and the new verb in τιμωρούμενοι continues the semantic role of *$*k^{u}ei$-* AVENGE (τίνυσθαι).[3] The basic formula has undergone almost total lexical renewal, but its structure shines through intact.

As well as κτείνω Euripides makes frequent use in the basic formula of the denominative verb φονεύω, originally 'be a φονεύς, murderer', transitively 'murder, slay'. This prose verb (Herodotus, passim) increases markedly in frequency in poetry in the course of the fifth century. Both Pindar and Aeschylus show only a single instance each; Sophocles has 6, but Euripides 37 (including two of καταφονεύω). Dividing the latter figure by three to give a commensurable corpus we still have for the three tragedians an ascending ratio of 1 : 6 : 12.

Two passages from Euripides' *Iphigenia in Aulis* show the basic formula with φονεύω and an interesting phonetic figure. The old man announces to Klutaimestra at 873-5:

> παῖδα σὴν **πατὴρ** ὁ φύσας αὐτόχειρ μέλλει **κτενεῖν**
> ...
> **φασγ**άνωι λευκὴν **φον**εύων τῆς ταλαιπώρου δέρην.
>
> Her father who sired her is about to kill your child with his own hand
> ...
> slaying the poor girl with a sword to her white throat.

2. Cf. Euripides *Suppl.* 614 δίκα δίκαν ἐκάλεσε καὶ φόνος φόνον 'justice called for justice and murder for murder'. See chap. 31.

3. Cf. Euripides *Phoen.* 935 δράκοντι τιμωρεῖ φόνον 'avenges the slaying of the dragon'.

And Iphigenia herself says with echoing words at 1317-18:

> **φον**εύομαι, δι**όλλ**υμαι
> **σφαγ**αῖσιν ἀνοσίοισιν ἀνοσίου **πατρός**
>
> I am murdered, I am killed
> by the unholy sacrificial strokes of my unholy father.

SLAY (φον-) in both is reinforced by a near-synonym (κτεν-, ὀλ-), and both share the monstrous father as agent. But the WEAPON of the first (φασγάνωι), with its sound sequence **p^{h}asg**-, has resurfaced in the second in the sequence **sp^{h}ag**-, a nominal form of the verb σφάζω 'slaughter' which is an equivalent of **g^{u}hen*- SLAY. Both **p^{h}asg**- (**φασγ**άνωι) and **sp^{h}ag**- (**σφαγ**αῖσιν) are in the "marginal" dative case, without preposition, and each is verse-line initial.[4]

The linking of both words to the verb φονεύω can be paralleled elsewhere in Euripides. Note *Herc.* 319-20

> πάρεστιν ἥδε **φασγ**άνωι δέρη
> κεντεῖν **φον**εύειν
>
> This throat is ready for the sword,
> to stab, to slay,

beside *Andr.* 412

> **σφάζ**ειν **φον**εύειν δεῖν ἀπαρτῆσαι δέρην
>
> (Here I am) to slaughter, slay, bind, strangle,

and *Hel.* 1594

> **σφάζ**ειν **φον**εύειν βαρβάρους
>
> to slaughter and slay the enemy.

The effect of the nominal form φόνος, typically placed by Euripides in the prominent verse-final position, can extend over a number of lines, as a sort of overtone. Compare from *Iphigenia in Tauris*, Orestes speaking:

> 72 καὶ βωμός, Ἕλλην οὗ καταστάζει **φόνος;**
>
> And the altar, where Greek blood drips?

---

4. Skeptics of the reality of the phonetic transposition should note the perennial frequency of ***pasgh**etti* for ***spagh**etti* in American child language. But more to the point, the same figure is found with the same collocations in Sophocles, *Aj.* 898ff. See chap. 53.

78 πατρὸς αἷμ᾽ **ἐτεισάμην**
μητέρα **κατάκτας**

I avenged my father's blood and **slew** my mother.

In the same play we have three striking repetitions of 'embracing arms', linked with φόνος and the dragon context. Orestes imagines the dragon-like Furies:

286 Ἅιδου δράκαιναν . . .
δειναῖς ἐχίδναις . . .
288 ἡ 'κ γειτόνων δὲ πῦρ πνέουσα καὶ **φόνον**
πτέροις ἐρέσσει, **μητέρ᾽ ἀγκάλαις ἐμὴν**
ἔχουσα, πέτρινον ἄχθος, ὡς ἐπεμβάληι

A dragoness from hell . . .
with fearful snakes . . .
Another of her fellows breathing fire and **gore**,
rowing with her wings, **holding my mother** in
her arms, a stony burden to throw on me.

Iphigenia recalls Orestes:

834 . . . ἔτι βρέφος
ἔλιπον **ἀγκάλαισι** νεαρὸν τροφοῦ

. . . whom I left still a new born
babe **in the arms** of his nurse.

Finally Iphigenia, with a reference to the figure of 'the slayer slain', reinforced by a ring, introduces the Chorus' hymning of Apollo's slaying Python as a 'boyhood deed', which links it to 834:

1223 ὡς **φόνωι φόνον**
μυσαρὸν ἐκνίψω . . .
1230 ἣν νίψω **φόνον**

To wash out foul **blood**
with **blood** . . .
If I can wash out the **blood** . . .

1250 (δράκων) ἔτι νιν ἔτι βρέφος, ἔτι φίλας
ἐπὶ **ματέρος ἀγκάλαισι** θρῴσκων
ἔκανες

(A dragon) . . . You leapt up and

> **slew** it when still a new born
> babe, still in your **mother's arms**.

We have a visual representation of the same scene on an early fifth-century black figured lekythos (thus prior to Euripides), with 'the infant Apollo shooting his arrows from Leto's arms at a snake of many coils, who appears among rocks in a hollow.'[5]

The contexts of these three interlinked occurrences of ἀγκάλαισ(ι) suggest the complete antithesis of the nurturing arms of a mother; most appropriately, where the hero is a matricide.

Examples such as these show that in the world of heroic internecine conflict just as in the world of dragon-slaying the basic formula is still very real to Euripides. Even if the simple verb πεφνέμεν is no longer part of his active usage, he can develop and extend the basic formula with extraordinary suppleness and art.

A final token is the threefold multiplication of synonyms of 'kill', with φονεύω (*$g^{\prime h}$en-) in first place, in Electra's frenzied cry directed against Helen in the *Orestes* 1302-3:

> φονεύετε καίνετε ὄλλυτε
>
> Slay, kill, slaughter!

We will discuss in chap. 56.1 its Old Irish pendant, also with *gono* (*$g^{\prime h}$en-) in first place,

> gono mīl orgo mīl marbu mīl
>
> I slay the beast, I slaughter the beast, I kill the beast.

The beginning paragraphs of Lysias 10, *Against Theomnestus* 1, provide graphic testimony for the changing vocabulary of killing inside a functioning legal system.[6] Lysias' dates are ca. 458-380 B.C.; the delivery of the speech in question can be dated on internal grounds to 384/3 B.C. It is a private action against Theomnestos for slander, for having accused the speaker of 'having killed [his] own father': τὸν πατέρα μ' ἔφασκεν **ἀπεκτονέναι** τὸν ἐμαυτοῦ (1). Theomnestos then 'had the audacity to say before the arbitrator that it was not using a forbidden word to say that someone had killed his father; for the law does not forbid that, but does not allow calling someone a "murderer" ["man-slayer"]': ἐτόλμα λέγειν καὶ πρὸς τὸν διαιτητήν, ὡς οὐκ ἔστι τῶν ἀπορρήτων, ἐάν τις εἴπῃ τὸν πατέρα ἀπεκτονέναι· τὸν γὰρ νόμον οὐ ταῦτ' ἀπαγορεύειν, ἀλλ' **ἀνδροφόνον** οὐκ ἐᾶν λέγειν (6). The speaker goes on to aver to the judges that they are well aware 'that those who have killed someone are "murderers", and those who are "murderers" have killed someone': ὅτι ὅσοι

5. Fontenrose 1980:16, where it appears as figure (1), and on the front cover of this paperback edition.

6. I am grateful to Hayden Pelliccia for calling my attention to the passage.

<**ἀπεκτόνασί** τινας, καὶ **ἀνδροφόνοι** εἰσί, καὶ ὅσοι> **ἀνδροφόνοι** εἰσί, καὶ **ἀπεκτόνασί** τινας (7). After pointedly noting some synonymy that has no legal effect—ῥῖψαι versus ἀποβεβληκέναι τὴν ἀσπίδα (9) 'fling' versus 'throw away your shield', an accusation previously leveled at Theomnestos—he says that when they try 'cases of "murder"' (τὰς τοῦ **φόνου** δίκας), 'they do not use this term in making the sworn statements, but the one which was used for slandering me: the prosecutor swears that the other party has "killed", the defendant that he has "not killed"': οὐ διὰ τούτου τοῦ ὀνόματος τὰς διωμοσίας ποιοῦνται, ἀλλὰ δι' οὗπερ ἐγὼ κακῶς ἀκήκοα· ὁ μὲν γὰρ διώκων ὡς **ἔκτεινε** διόμνυται, ὁ δὲ φεύγων ὡς **οὐκ ἔκτεινεν** (11). One would scarcely acquit someone who had said he was a "murderer" (ἀνδροφόνον) on the grounds that the prosecutor deposed on oath that he had "killed" (ὡς ἔκτεινε). The law is read; and then the speaker requests for the edification of the defendant that some other laws be read, 'those ancient laws of Solon' (τούτους τοὺς νόμους τοὺς Σόλωνος τοὺς παλαιούς [15]), to show 'that things are the same now as they were long ago, but we don't use some of the same words now as before': ὅτι τὰ μὲν πράγματα ταὐτά ἐστι νῦν τε καὶ πάλαι, τῶν δὲ ὀνομάτων ἐνίοις οὐ τοῖς αὐτοῖς χρώμεθα νῦν τε καὶ πρότερον (20).

The argument of the case has a strikingly modern ring to it, and a direct appeal.[7] But it establishes on the one hand that the verb corresponding to the noun ἀνδροφόνος[8] was κτείνω and vice-versa; on the other hand that the noun ἀνδροφόνος carried enough special semantic mark vis-à-vis the verb κτείνω, of venerability or whatever, to induce a native speaker to attempt the claim that only the use of the former, not the latter, was actionable as slander. Such was the power of the root **g^{w}hen-* even when it no longer was synchronically a verbal root.

A further point might be considered. Our manuscripts of Lysias show only the usual form ἀνδροφόνος, and the text of the relevant law of slander cited in this passage is not given, nor is it stated to be a law of Solon.[9] But it is interesting that the ninth-century Byzantine lexicographer Photius, in a manuscript which came to light and was published only early in the present century (p.126 Reitzenstein) gives the lemma Ἀνδραφόνων· οὕτως Σόλων ἐν τοῖς Ἄξοσιν <ἀντὶ> τῶν ἀνδροφόνων ἀεί φησιν 'Solon always used the form ἀνδ**ρα**φόνοι instead of ἀνδ**ρο**φόνοι in the Axones (wooden tablets of the laws, publicly displayed)'. This form was immediately recognized as a real archaism, being the normal Attic-Ionic phonological reflex of IE **h$_2$nr̥-g^{w}hon-(o-)*, via **anr̥-* > **anra-* > *andra-*, as in Vedic *nr̥-hán-*, Avestan *nərə-gar-* 'man-devouring', and Greek **anr̥-k^{w}hon-tā-* in Homeric Ἐνυαλίωι ἀνr̥φόντηι (Lejeune 1972:§202), on which see chap. 39.

It is not excluded that Theomnestos' defence might have been a reaction to the opaque Solonian form ἀνδρα-φόνος (rather than expected ἀνδρ-ο-φόνος), whether it once appeared in the list of ἀπόρρητα in the law of slander, or merely in the law of homicide. But this is simple speculation.

---

7. I have personally had to testify as an 'expert witness' (as have many other linguists) about comparable, seemingly silly verbal quibbles with legal consequences.

8. And φόνος.

9. It is 'probably' a later law, according to MacDowell 1978:127.

53

The basic formula and the announcement of death

The *Iliad* is the epic of two deaths: much of the dramatic structure rests on the death of Patroklos (alter ego, θεράπων of $HERO_1$) by the hand of Hector ($HERO_2$), which is counterbalanced by the death of Hector at the hand of Achilles ($HERO_1$). The two deaths are in fact equivalent and interchangeable. They are presented in identical verses of evident antiquity, 16.856-7 (death of Patroklos) = 22.362-3 (death of Hector):

> ψυχὴ δ' ἐκ ῥεθέων πταμένη Ἄϊδόσδε βεβήκει
> ὃν πότμον γοόωσα, λιποῦσ' ἀνδροτῆτα καὶ ἥβην
>
> his soul flying from his limbs was gone to Hades,
> bemoaning her fate, leaving manhood and youth.

It has been recognized for some time[1] that this description of the soul leaving the body is linguistically very old; ἀνδροτῆτα must be scanned ⏑ ⏑ – ⏑, with a syllabic liquid unchanged; i. e. **anr̥tāta*, like the epithet ἀνδρειφόντης scanned ⏑ ⏑ – – (*Il.* 2.651), i. e. **anr̥kʷhontās* as just noted in chap. 52. Since we know that the change *r̥* > *or*/*ro* (other dialects *ar*/*ra*) had taken place in Greek by the time of the Linear B tablets in Greek (*topeza* [torpeza], *qetoropopi* [kʷetropopphi], *anoqota* [Anorkʷhontās]),[2] the lines with **anr̥tāta* could not have been composed any later than 1400 B.C. or so. They furnish us thus with a terminus ante quem for the fixation of the formulaic vehicle of a key feature of the thematic structure of the *Iliad*: these two deaths in equipoise.[3]

---

1. Wackernagel 1953:1116 n. 1, cf. 1170 n. 1 originally published 1909; Leumann 1950:221 n. 16; West 1982:15.

2. See C. J. Ruijgh 1967:69, Wathelet 1970:171f., Watkins 1987b, and West 1988a:156-7 with references.

3. The similarity of ψυχὴ δ' ἐκ ῥεθέων πταμένη Ἄϊδόσδε βεβήκει, ὃν πότμον γοόωσα, λιποῦσ' ἀνδροτῆτα καὶ ἥβην with Beowulf's departing soul at 2819-20 *him of hræðre gewát / sáwol sécean sóðfæstra dóm* 'from his bosom went his soul to seek the glory of the true' has surely been noted long before.

The two deaths are formally announced by the basic formula in the interior of the text. Again we find the asymmetry of focus, as in the boxed

HERO$_1$ | SLAY (**g^{u}hen-*) HERO$_2$. |

The first announcement uses a syntactic variant: the passive. Menelaos announces the death of Patroklos to Antilokhos, who is to run and bear the news to Achilles, *Il.* 17.689-90:

νίκη δὲ Τρώων· **πέφαται** δ' ὥριστος Ἀχαιῶν,
Πάτροκλος

Victory belongs to the Trojans; **slain** is the best of the Achaeans, **Patroklos**.

Here the formula is given with enjambment; it begins with the clause-initial verb following the caesura, and ends with the hero's name at the beginning of the next line. This is the underlying formula for the pitiless words spoken by Achilles to Lykaon whom he will not spare, *Il.* 21.107:

κάτθανε καὶ **Πάτροκλος**, ὅ περ σέο πολλὸν ἀμείνων

Patroklos also **died**, who was far better than you.

Again, 'die' is the passive of 'kill' in Greek, and for this death Lykaon must pay with his life.

The words of Antilokhos' announcement of the news to Achilles likewise hark back to an ancient mythographic formula. In chap. 28 we examined the co-occurrences of various elements in the narration of the dragon-slaying myth in Rigveda 1.32. One of these was the insistent presence of the root *śi* 'to lie', IE **k̂ei-*:[4]

5cd skándhāṁsīva kúliśénā vívr̥knā / áhiḥ **śayate**

like branches lopped by an axe the serpent **lies**,

It would indicate that the Old English passage was not unequivocally the expression of Christian salvation, as has been argued. Meaning, "location", and etymology of *of hræðre* (Gothic *hairþra* 'σπλάγχνα') are uncertain, as are the same of ἐκ ῥεθέων (schol. 'σπλάγχνων'); connection of the two is of course just 'die Sirene des Gleichklangs'. Germanic 'soul' (Gothic *saiwalo*) has no etymology; it is clearly a pre-Christian term.

4. As Geldner notes ad RV 2.12.11, this use of 'lie' in 1.32 in the context of the dragon-slaying myth is different from that of the same verb in similar contexts where it must mean 'lying inattentively (and liable to be taken by surprise)', as also 3.32.6 and 5.32.2 (explicitly *práyutaṃ śáyānam*). Likewise different is *áhann áhim pariśáyānam árṇaḥ* 'you slew the serpent who lay encircling the flood' 3.32.11, 4.19.2, 6.30.4. But we will see other Vedic examples of the sense in 1.32 presently.

7d vr̥tró **aśayad** vyàstaḥ

Vr̥tra **lay** torn apart,

8a nadám̐ ná bhinnám amuyā́ **śáyānam**

lying that way like a broken reed,

8d tā́sām áhiḥ patsutaḥ**śī́r** babhūva

at their feet **lay** the serpent,

9d dā́nuḥ **śaye** sahávatsā ná dhenúḥ

The she-demon (Vr̥tra's mother) **lies** like a cow with her calf,

10d dīrghám̐ táma **ā́śayad** índraśatruḥ

He whose rival is Indra **lay** down for a long darkness.

Similarly in RV 2.12, which hymns Indra's exploits with a sequence of relative clauses without overt subject, followed by the same triumphal refrain, verse 11cd reads

ojāyámānam̐ yó áhim̐ **jaghā́na**
dā́num̐ **śáyānam̐** sá janāsa índraḥ

He who **slew** the swelling serpent,
the demon **lying** there—he, o people, is Indra.

The Rigvedic hymn is a paean of mythological victory, while the slaying of a hero is an occasion of grief and lamentation for the losing side.[5] But the formulaic language of hymnic paean in India and epic narrative in Greece is the same. Menelaos says to Antilokhos, *Il.* 16.689-90:

πέφαται . . . Πάτροκλος

Slain is Patroklos,

like *áhann áhim* 'he slew the serpent', and Antilokhos goes and says to Achilles, *Il.* 18.20:

κεῖται Πάτροκλος

5. Compare Nagy's valuable discussion of πένθος ἄλαστον 'unforgettable suffering' as antithesis of κλέος ἄφθιτον 'undying fame' (1979 passim).

> Patroklos **lies**,

like *áhiḥ śayate* 'the serpent lies'.

The one other place in the *Iliad* to show this verb line-initial followed by a personal name is at 16.541, where Glaukos announces to Hector:

> **κεῖται** Σαρπηδών
>
> Sarpedon **lies**,

the king of Lycia slain by the hand of Patroklos. The very enjambment of Menelaos' announcement of Patroklos' death at 16.689-90 is prefigured in Patroklos' announcement to Ajax and his brother, *Il.* 16.558-9:

> **κεῖται** ἀνὴρ ὃς πρῶτος ἐσήλατο τεῖχος 'Αχαιῶν
> Σαρπηδών
>
> There **lies** the man who was first to leap the wall of the Achaeans,
> Sarpedon.

The marked line-initial verb in **πέφαται** . . . Πάτροκλος, **κεῖται** Πάτροκλος, **κεῖται** Σαρπηδών, and **κάτθανε** καὶ Πάτροκλος (*Il.* 21.107 above)[6] is cut from the same formulaic stuff as that of **ἔπεφνεν** τε Γοργόνα, **κτεῖνε** . . . ὄφιν . . . φόνον, ***áhann*** *áhim*, ***vádhīd*** *vṛtrám*, ***ható*** *rā́jā krimīṇām* (see below).

We find the same link in a passage in Sophocles' *Ajax*, with one of the three instances of (κατ)έπεφνε in the tragedian's work (898-902):

Tekmessa	Αἴας ὅδ' ἡμῖν ἀρτίως νεο**σφαγ**ὴς **κεῖται**, κρυφαίωι **φασγ**άνωι περιπτυχής.
Chorus	ὤμοι ἐμῶν νόστων· ὤμοι, **κατέπεφνες**, ἄναξ, τὸνδε συνναύταν, τάλας.
Tekmessa	Here before me **lies** Ajax, just newly slain his fallen body enfolds and hides the sword.
Chorus	O woe for my return; O woe, my lord, my wretched lord, you have **slain** your shipmate.

The phonetic figure in -**σφαγ**- . . . **φασγ**- (-***sphag***- . . . ***phasg***-) indexes the semantic

6. Worth exploring is potentially the "Luvo-Lycian connection" linking these two deaths, both indexed by the basic formula: that of Sarpedon king of Lycia and that of Priam's son Lukāōn, whose name must mean 'from the Lukka-lands', the KUR.KUR$^{MEŠ\ URU}$*Luqqā* of Hittite texts, with the Luvian suffix of ethnic names -*wann*(*i*)-.

identification with κατέπεφνες from **g^when-*. We have seen the same figure exploited by Euripides in the preceding chapter.

The inherited formulaic link of **g^when-* and **k̑ei-* casts light also on a form in Hekabe's *goos*, lament or keening—the formal antithesis of the victory paean—for her son Hector in *Il.* 24.757-8:

> νῦν δέ μοι ἑρσήεις καὶ **πρόσφατος** ἐν μεγάροισι
> **κεῖσαι**, τῷ ἴκελος ὅν τ' ἀργυρότοξος Ἀπόλλων
> οἷς ἀγανοῖσι βέλεσσιν ἐποιχόμενος κατέ**πεφνεν**
>
> Now you **lie** in my halls dewy-fresh and as newly **slain**
> like to one whom Apollo of the silver bow
> approaches with his gentle shafts and **slays**.

For a pendant of this Greek passage in all three of morphology, lexicon, and pronominalization compare Hekabe's

> **πρόσφατος** ἐν μεγάροισι **κεῖσαι**
>
> Newly **slain** you **lie** in my halls,

with RV 10.108.4d, spoken by Saramā the divine bitch:

> **hatā́** índreṇa paṇayaḥ **śayadhve**
>
> **Slain** by Indra, o Paṇis, may you **lie** there.

An Atharvan curse (AV 6.134.2) gives

> ádharo 'dhara úttarebhyo gūḍháḥ pṛthivyā́ mót sṛpat
> vájreṇā́va**hataḥ śayām**
>
> Under, under those above, hidden, may he not crawl out of the earth;
> let him **lie slain** by the cudgel.

Add finally from the Avesta (Yt.10.80), with the archaic 3 pl. mid. ending of the verb 'to lie' **k̑ei-ro(i)*, and perhaps archaizing diphthong *ōi* instead of *aē* (Skjærvø and Fortson, p.c.),

> yahmi **sōire** miϑrō.drujō
> aipi vīϑiši **jata**
> pauruua mašiiākåŋhō
>
> At whose divinatory trial men false to contract
> **lie** in masses, **slain**.

These collocations support the derivation of πρόσφατος from **gʷhn̥-to-*, whatever the precise force of προσ-.[7] Greek -φατος from **gʷhn̥-tó-*, as in Hom. μυλήφατος 'crushed by the mill', Ἀρείφατος 'slain by Ares', is one of the most securely reconstructible lexemes in the language: cf. Ved. *hatás* and *ádri-saṁhatas* 'squeezed by the pressing stones', Avestan and Old Persian *jata-* and *avajata-*, Lith *giñtas* 'driven (of cattle)', Old Irish *do-gét* 'was violated'.

To anticipate the Germanic evidence cited in the next chapter we may note a single example of the same collocation, but with lexical substitution of other roots for 'slay' (Gmc. *slahan*, 'slay' par excellence) and 'lie' (IE **legh-*), in the archaic Old English laws of Wihtræd (25);

> gif man leud of**slea** an þeofðe, **licge** buton wyrgelde
>
> If one **slay** a man (who is committing) theft, let him **lie** (dead) without wergeld.

From the point of view of diachronic poetics, Achilles' pitiless words to Lycaon **κάτθανε** καὶ Πάτροκλος 'Patroklos also died', which we discussed earlier, is a variant of underlying ***πέφαται** Πάτροκλος 'Slain is Patroklos', with the basic formula in annunciatory function. But synchronically Achilles' utterance is motivated in the passage as a continuation of the imperative in the preceding line (106), ἀλλά, φίλος, **θάνε** καὶ σύ 'Die too, my friend!' This explains the difference in tenor and tone between the diachronically formulaic, annunciatory verb in **κεῖται** Πάτροκλος/Σαρπηδών and that in Achilles' bitter words to Lycaon's corpse, which he has just flung in the river: 21.122 ἐνταυθοῖ νῦν **κεῖσο** μετ' ἰχθύσιν 'Lie there now among the fishes!' Similarly 21.184 **κεῖσ'** οὕτως 'Lie as you are!'

We can observe the same tension between the diachronic and the synchronic readings of the verb 'lie' in the passages from RV 1.32 cited above. While they parallel the Greek usage, they have a synchronic immediacy and vividness which is brought out by the present tense alternating with the narrative imperfect, and by the similes: the *ahi* 'lies like branches lopped by an axe,' 'lies like a cow with her calf.'

Such contrasts point up the interplay between synchronic text analysis—conventional literary "criticism"—and what for want of a better term I have tendentiously called diachronic and comparative "intertextuality" (chap. 27.3). They are part of what makes the study of these ancient texts worthwhile.

---

7. See Frisk, GEW s. v., Chantraine, DELG s. v. θείνω.

54

Further Indo-European comparisons and themes

In Germanic the root **ḱei-* 'lie' has been replaced by **legh-*. But the (natural enough) association of the new lexical item with the dragon-slaying formula is found in *Beowulf* as well.

At Beowulf's death the young warrior Wiglaf looks upon the tableau of the two lifeless bodies, the hero and his nemesis (2822-26):

þæt hé on eorðan geseah
þone léofestan   lífes æt ende
bléote gebǽran.   **Bona** swylce **læg**,
egeslíc eorðdraca   ealdre beréafod,
bealwe gebǽded

that he saw on the ground
the one dearest to him   at life's end
wretchedly bearing.   His **slayer** also **lay**,
terrible earth-dragon   deprived of life,
hard-pressed by ruin.

The parallelism of the two, their balance in syllabicity and semantics, is iconic to the two deaths in equipoise: hero and dragon. *Bona* and *læg* give the roots *g^{wh}*en-* and **legh-*. The phrase *ealdre beréafod* is semantically comparable to Greek ϑυμὸν ἀπηύρα discussed in chap. 49. The presence of the superlative *léofest* recalls the nexus we explored in chap. 50; see also below.

A few score lines before, the dying king had bidden Wiglaf let him see the treasure (2745-6):

nú se **wyrm ligeð**,
swefeð sáre wund,   since beréafod

Now that the **dragon lies**,
sleeps sorely wounded, deprived of treasures.

The dragon lies dead; not just wounded, he sleeps the sleep of the dead. The prominence given *swefeð* 'sleeps', line and clause-initial and alliterating, is unusual for a finite verb form in Old English verse.

In the linking of LIE (**k̂ei-*, **legh-*), SLAY/ BE SLAIN (**gʷhen-*, **tk̂en-*), and SLEEP (**su̯ep-*, **ses-*) in the context of the basic formula we may have yet another Indo-European formulaic and thematic nexus, as S. Jamison suggests to me. Compare RV 1.103.7:[1]

tád indra préva vīryàṃ cakartha
yát **sasántaṃ vájreṇā́bodhayó 'him**

That, o Indra, was the manly deed you performed,
that you "**waked**", as it were, the **sleeping serpent** with your **cudgel**.

As Jamison shows, *sasántam . . . ábodhayaḥ* in context must equal *ásvāpayaḥ* 'you put to sleep', i.e. 'slew'. She also cites RV 1.121.11 *tvám vṛtrám . . . vájreṇa siṣvapaḥ* 'you put Vṛtra to sleep with a cudgel'.

In Euripides' *Heracles* the hero sleeps after his monstrous deed—one of his *kilbiṣāni*, cf. chap. 41—, the murder in his madness of his children and his wife. The hero's sleep is narrated three times in fifty lines: by the herald, by the chorus, and by his father Amphitruon. Each is a version, in ascending complexity, of the basic formula:

1013-14 **εὕδει** δ' ὁ τλήμων **ὕπνον** οὐκ εὐδαίμονα
παῖδας **φονεύσας** καὶ δάμαρτ'

He **sleeps**, unhappy man, no happy **sleep**,
having slain children and wife.

The Chorus' first word is φόνος (1016), repeated by φόνον (1021); then when the great doors open,

1032-4 ἴδεσθε δὲ τέκνα πρὸ πατρὸς
ἄθλια **κείμενα** δυστάνου,
εὕδοντος ὕπνον δεινὸν ἐκ παίδων **φόνου**

You see the miserable children **lying** before
their wretched father, who **sleeps** a terrible **sleep**
after the **slaying** of his children.

1. Discussed in Jamison 1982:6-16.

Then at last the Chorus asks Amphitruon εὕδει; 'does he sleep?' and the latter replies,

1061-3 ναί, **εὕδει** <γ'> **ὕπνον** ἄ**υπνον** **ὀλομε-**
νον ὃς **ἔκανεν** ἄλοχον, **ἔκανε** δὲ ψαλμῶι
τέκεα **τοξήρει**

Yes, he **sleeps**, but **sleeps** the un-**sleep** of the
dead, for he **slew** his wife and **slew** his
children with the twanging **bow**.

Just as in Vedic the basic formula includes here the specification of the WEAPON. For the metrics see chap. 38.

We come finally to yet another possibly inherited thematic nexus: the linking of LIE (**k̂ei-*, **legh-*), SLAY/BE SLAIN (**g^when-*, **tk̂en-*), and FIRST (**pr̥h_3-mo-*, **pr̥h_3-to-*, etc.).

A curious passage narrated by Beowulf mentions the warrior Hondscio ("Glove"), first to be slain by Grendel (2077-9):

hé **fyrmest læg**,
gyrded cempa; him Grendel wearð
mǽrum maguþegne tó múð**bonan**

He **lay first**,
the belted warrior; Grendel became
mouth-**slayer** to him, the famous young warrior.

He lay (**legh-*) first (**pr̥h_3-mo-*) in death, his killing told by the basic formula (*-bonan*, **g^when-*). Hondscio is thus a sort of Protesilaos-figure.

Protesilaos of the speaking name was first (πρῶτος) of the host (λαός) of the Achaeans to land at Troy, and first to be killed. M. West in his speculative configuration of an 'original' *Iliad* (1988a:161) terms Protesilaos a 'critical agent,' without further comment. Compare *Il.* 2.701-2:

τὸν δ' **ἔκτανε** Δάρδανος ἀνὴρ
νηὸς ἀποθρωίσκοντα πολὺ **πρώτιστον** 'Αχαιῶν

A Dardanian man **killed** him
as he leapt from his ship, far the **first** of the Achaeans.

FIRST is by its nature a superlative, and attracts double superlative marking as here πρώτιστος (and *fyrmest*). The word in that position in the line clearly recalls the 'best of the Achaeans' discussed earlier.

The Trojan pendant is Sarpedon in *Il.* 16.558-9 quoted above (chap. 53), which provides the verb LIE in the same nexus:

κεῖται ἀνὴρ **ὃς πρῶτος** ἐσήλατο τεῖχος Ἀχαιῶν
Σαρπηδών

Low **lies** the man **who** was **first** to leap the wall of the Achaeans,
Sarpedon.

In Old English *Hondscio* "Glove" has himself a speaking name; it is curiously indexed also by *Glóf hangode* '[Grendel's] glove hung down' only 9 lines later. When we add the Old Norse warrior's name *Vǫttr* (*Skáldskaparmál*, *Ynglingasaga*), from Germanic **wantuz* (source of French *gant*), it is clear that Germanic verbal tradition of some antiquity is in play, though its meaning remains to me obscure.[2]

In any case it is tempting to see the traces of an older thematic nexus in these Greek and Germanic collocations, though here with FIRST as with SLEEP, and for that matter LIE and SLAY/BE SLAIN, the role of universality cannot be excluded. FIRST is widespread in the mythological narrative of the manly deeds of the HERO, referring to his SLAYING of the SERPENT. The locus classicus is RV 1.32.1 *vīryā̀ni . . . yā́ni cakā́ra* ***prathamā́ni*** *. . . áhann áhim* . . . 'the manly deeds . . . which he did first . . . he slew the serpent . . .' For Greek cf. Pindar, *Isth*. 6.48 θηρός, ὃν **πάμπρωτον** ἀέθλων κτεῖνά ποτ' ἐν Νεμέαι '(the skin) of the beast which as the very first of my labors I slew in Nemea'. For the force of the verb κτεῖνα compare πέφνεν in the previous line 31, also with Herakles as subject. In the examples of Hondsciō and Protesilaos FIRST has been moved from the exploit of the victor to the death of the victim, but it is equally a thematic presence in the structure.

The first line of Vergil's *Aeneid* naturally comes to mind,

Arma uirumque cano, Troiae **qui primus** ab oris

I sing of arms and the man **who first** from the shores of Troy . . .

For all that this epic is a sophisticated, crafted, 'learned' work—however moving as literature—, one can point to traditional, 'Indo-European' touches as well, like *cano* : Greek ἀείδω,[3] but also Old Irish *ar-cain Fénechus* 'Irish law sings', with the same verb **kane/o-*. The relative clause defining the Indo-European hero or his exploits has been discussed earlier (chap. 30); *qui primus* can be directly compared, mutatis mutandis, with ὃς πρῶτος, *yā́ni prathamā́ni*, and ὃν πάμπρωτον above.

Observe finally that the pregnant use of FIRST can also be documented from the third century B.C. in our earliest monument of literary Latin prose, the Columna Rostrata proudly commemorating the victories of the 'real' war hero C. Duilius over the Carthaginians in 260 B.C. (Degrassi, ILLRP 319):

enque eodem mac[istratud bene
r]em nauebos marid consol **primos** c[eset copiasque

2. Skjærvø notes that in Modern Norwegian *en vott* also means a weak, dependent person.

3. Perhaps itself influenced by Hittite *išhamiškizzi* 'I sing' (also epic-initial), of Hurrian provenience.

c]lasesque nauales **primos** ornauet pa[rauetque

And in the same command he as consul **first** performed an exploit in ships at sea, and he was the **first** to equip and train crews and fleets of fighting ships.

55

The song of victory in Greek

Those who have lost a companion lament, but the winning side exults in the victory song. This has its own poetic form in Greek: the paean (Hom. παιήων, cf. the Linear B divine name *pajawone* Παιαϝονει).[1] And we have a fragment—the incipit—of an actual paean in the text of the *Iliad* itself: a poem within a poem.[2] After having killed Hector, Achilles finishes his address to the Achaeans with the words (*Il.* 22.391-4):

νῦν δ' ἄγ' ἀείδοντες παιήονα, κοῦροι 'Αχαιῶν
νηυσὶν ἐπὶ γλαφυρῇισι νεώμεθα, τόνδε δ' ἄγωμεν.
ἠράμεθα μέγα κῦδος· ἐπέφνομεν Ἕκτορα δῖον,
ὧι Τρῶες κατὰ ἄστυ θεῶι ὣς εὐχετόωντο

But come, singing our song of victory, o sons of the Achaeans,
let us return to the hollow ships and bring this corpse.
We have won us great glory; we have slain godly Hector,
whom the Trojans would pray to in their city as to a god.

Achilles is giving not only the theme of the paean but the very words. Lines 393-4 are a direct quotation, as seen by Nagy 1979:79. Achilles is here intoning the first four lines of a paean in paroemiacs:

ἠράμεθα μέγα κῦδος·
ἐπέφνομεν Ἕκτορα δῖον,
ὧι Τρῶες κατὰ ϝάστυ
θεῶι ὣς εὐχετόωντο.

The cataphoric, discourse-initial verb in the first line as well as the verse-initial form of πεφνέμεν is characteristic of the paroemiac verse, as is the variable syllable length

1. The paean is not restricted in function to a song of victory or thanksgiving for deliverance, nor are its formal features easily and unequivocally described. See the exhaustive discussion in the important forthcoming edition, Rutherford 1994.

2. For others, in Greek and Latin, see Kassel 1981, Handley 1988, and Watkins 1989:794.

of the short line and the cadence ⏑ ⏑ – ⏓ : cf. the Rhodian song ἦλθ', ἦλθε, χελιδών 'Come, come, o swallow' (PMG 848).

This example of a poem within a poem, a "hidden verse", where the poem is the incipit of a paean, is not confined to Greek. We have a striking example in the Rigveda. In chap. 5 we had occasion to cite the obscure hymn 4.1, which in verses 13-17 narrates the cosmogonic Vala-myth: the poet-priests by remembering the thrice-seven secret names of the cows smash open with their divine word the cave of the demon Paṇis and release the imprisoned cows which are the light, the dawn's rays, the 'milk of the dawn cows'. Verse 14cd (the subject of *c* is the Aṅgirases, of *d* the mortal poet-priests):

> paśváyantrāso abhí kārám arcan
> vidánta jyótiś cakṛpánta dhībhíḥ
>
> Their cattle released, they sang the victory:
> "They found the light! They desired (it) with their thoughts!"

For *kāráḥ* 'victory, the winning stroke' see Mayrhofer EWA s.v. The verb is *ábhi arc-* 'sing to, celebrate in song'. Just as in the Homeric Greek example the verb of the paean itself comes both discourse- and sentence-initial in the two hemistichs. We may have another line of this paean, possibly the final, in the subsequent verses. The freeing of the light banished the darkness and re-established the sun in the heavens, 'looking at the straight and the crooked among men' (*ṛjú márteṣu vṛjinā́ ca páśyan* 17, itself an inherited formula). The Aṅgirases woke from the darkness and saw the heaven-sent jewel (18ab), followed by 18c which Geldner puts in quotation marks:

> víśve víśvāsu dúryāsu devā́ḥ
>
> "All the gods are in all (their) houses."

The doubly balanced and framed line, with double alliteration flanking the caesura,

> (v_i (v_{ii} || d_{ii}) d_i),

would be a fitting conclusion to the paean.

The paean is the appropriate victory-response in the dragon-slaying myth. Pythian Apollo *Puthoktónos*, killer of Python, was to be hymned with the paean by the Cretan merchants dragooned to be priests in the Homeric *Hymn to Apollo*:

(500) ἰηπαιήον' ἀείδειν

Sing the paean-cry "Hail, Healer",

(517-19) ἰηπαιήον' ἄειδον
οἷοί τε Κρητῶν παιήονες, οἷσι τε Μοῦσα
ἐν στήθεσσιν ἔθηκε θεὰ μελίγηρυν ἀοιδήν

Sing the paean-cry "Hail, Healer"
after the manner of the Cretan paean-singers and those
in whose hearts the goddess-Muse placed honey-voiced song.

Just so in the Indic dragon-slaying myth, all the gods cried the victory-cry *kārá-bhára-*[3] to Indra. RV 5.29.8:

kārám̐ ná víśve ahvanta devā́
bháram índrāya yád áhim̐ jaghā́na

All the gods cried 'Victory!' to Indra
as (one cries to a winning contestant), when he slew the serpent.

Another Greek example links the form of the paean-cry to the basic formula itself, by lexical substitution. Pindar, *Paean* 6 (Rutherford C8)[4] sets forth the death of Achilles' son Neoptolemos as a τίσις, or vengeance, of the god Apollo. Rutherford in his study suggests that the Pythoctonia-aetiology of the paean-cry (as opposed to the Homeric Hymn's Cretan aetiology) is found at least as early as Pindar's sixth *Paean*, where 'the point of the allusion would be to suggest that as an opponent of Apollo Neoptolemos is a sort of second Delphic dragon' (p. 7). This is surely correct, but the Neoptolemos-serpent equation (cf. Vergil *Aen.* 2.471) is given first and immediately by the phraseology of the basic formula itself:

112-20 **ὤ[μο]σε** γὰρ θεός,
γέ[ρον]θ' ὅ[τι] Πρίαμον
π[ρ]ὸς ἑρκεῖον **ἤναρε**
βωμὸν ἐ[πεν]θορόντα, μή νιν εὔφρον' ἐς οἶ[κ]ον
μήτ' ἐπὶ γῆρας ἱξέ-
μεν βίου· ἀμφιπόλοις δὲ
μ]υριᾶν περὶ τιμᾶν
δηρι]αζόμενον **κτάνεν**
<ἐν> τεμένεϊ φίλωι γᾶς παρ' ὀμφαλὸν εὐρύν.
<ἰὴ> ἰῆτε νῦν, μέτρα παιηό-
ν]ων ἰῆτε, νέοι.

For the god had **sworn** that because he had **killed** old Priam as he leapt toward the altar of Zeus Herkeios, he would reach neither his kindly home nor old age in life. As he quarreled with the attendants over vast prerogatives Apollo **slew** him in his own sanctuary by earth's broad navel. *iē iēte*! measures of paean-cries, *iēte*! o youths.
(tr. Rutherford)

3. Compare the similar collocation *kārínam bháram* at RV 8.65.1. Similar collocations of *bhára-* 'winning' with forms of the root *kr̥-* 'make' in the sense of 'win' suggest that *kāra-* 'victory', formerly taken as a 'song of victory', is a form of the same root.

4. See Rutherford 1991 and 1994 passim.

Here ὤμοσε is the equivalent of the sentence of a divine τίσις (**k^wei-*). Because ἤναρε 'he slew' (equivalent of **g^when-*, see chap. 36), the god ὤμοσε 'swore' and killed him (κτάνεν, again equivalent of **g^when-*). Note that both ἤναρε and κτάνεν lack an overt subject. The passage is preceded by a nominal form of the root **g^when-* (Παῖδα Θέτιος) θρασεῖ **φόνωι** πεδάσαις (86). That both verbs function in this paean as substitutes for a form of πεφνέμεν in the basic formula is in accord with Pindar's usage. Compare *Nem.* 3.46-51, where they recur in the same order, also without overt subject and likewise preceded by the nominal from φόνος,[5] in the narration of the boyhood deeds of Achilles—a theme inherited from Indo-European times:[6]

ἔπρασσεν **φόνον**,
κάπρους τ' **ἔναιρε** . . .
. . .
κτείνοντ' ἐλάφους

He would do slaughter and slay boars . . . killing deer.

The diction of the Homeric ἐπέφνομεν Ἕκτορα δῖον was lasting in Greek. The proof lies in a "real" paean (PMG 858), preserved in a fragmentary papyrus, a paean to the East Wind Euros who is invoked as 'savior of Sparta'.[7] It consists of 19 paroemiac verse lines, most gravely mutilated; but the meter is clear from lines 18-19 with their cadence ⏑ ⏑ – ⏓, and the genre from the signature refrain ἰὲ Παιὰν ἰήιε Παιάν:

τὺ δεπα
πέφαται παν[
μετάδος πω . . . ρασκ[
ἵει νυν οὖρον ἐπαγρ[
πολεμ . . . μονον. [
[
[
[
αρη[
λιαρὸν ῥηέθροις Εὐρο[
Εὖρ' ὦ σωτὴρ τᾶς Σπάρτας
κατὰ πάντα μόλοις μετὰ νίκας·
ἰὲ Παιὰν ἰήιε Παιάν.

In line 8 in verse-initial position there is **πέφαται**, alliterating with the following word, like **πέφαται** . . . Πάτροκλος, **ἐπέφνομεν** Ἕκτορα, and ***áhann áhim***.

5. Cf. as well Callimachus, *Hy.* 2.91-104, cited in chap. 38.

6. Compare the boyhood deeds of Heracles, Indra, Kṛṣṇa, Cú Chulainn, Finn, Achilles (Aichil mac Péil) in the Middle Irish version of Statius's Achilleid (ed. Ó hAodha) and even Jesus in the Old Irish Blathmac poems (ed. Carney), from the apocryphal gospel of Thomas.

7. The occasion is unknown. See the discussion in Rutherford 1994. He numbers the fragment R33 in his repertory.

The first verse of RV 6.59 gives one of the earliest paean-like instances of Vedic *han-* in the passive (*-ta-* verbal adjective):[8]

> prá nú vocā sutéṣu vāṃ
> vīryā̀ yā́ni cakrā́thuḥ
> **hatā́so** vām pitáro devā́śatrava
> índrāgnī jī́vatho yuvám
>
> I will now tell you two at the pressing of the manly deeds which you two performed. **Slain** are your fathers who have the gods as rivals; Indra and Agni, you two live.

The form is identical with the basic formula, just as in Greek. A "proleptic" paeanic line occurs in RV 6.63.10d, at the end of a classic two-verse *dānastuti* 'gift-praise', the praise by the poet of the gifts of his patrons for the poem:

> hatā́ rákṣāṁsi purudaṁsasā syuḥ
>
> Slain may the demons be, o you two of the many wondrous deeds (Indra and Agni).

Curiously, the Vedic epithet would go mechanically into Greek as a not implausible *πολυδηνέε. Such paeanic formulations are rare in Vedic mythological narrative. But we will see in chap. 56 of the following part that they are very common in the Atharvan language of charms, and both formulaically and stylistically directly comparable to the Greek paeans.

The fragmentary alliteration which we noted in the paean to Euros the East Wind as well as in the Vedic examples can be paralleled by phonetic embellishment in other examples of the same genre in Greek: a characteristic of a more "popular" literary type. A striking example, precisely because it is situated within another literary form and composed by a master, is the paean to Sleep in Sophocles' *Philoct.* 827ff.:[9]

> Ὕπν' ὀδύνας ἀδαής, Ὕπνε δ' ἀλγέων
> εὐαὴς ἡμῖν ἔλθοις, εὐαίων,
> εὐαίων, ὦναξ· ὄμμασι δ' ἀντίσχοις
> τάνδ' αἴγλαν, ἃ τέταται τανῦν.
> ἴθι ἴθι μοι, Παιών

8. Finite passive forms of *han-* are rare and used only absolutely in the Rigveda in the negative collocation *ná hanyate, ná jīyate* 'he is not slain, he is not conquered' 3.59.2, 5.54.7 etc. Where other languages oppose active and passive in the formula 'he who kills will be killed,' Vedic switches subject of active verb: see chap. 31. Passives are similarly rare in Avestan, aside from the nominal *jata-*, limited to the 3sg. aorist *jaini* (Yt 19.92-3, 3x [cited in chap. 29]) and one apparent example of pres. *janiiā̊nti* 'will be slain' (Yt. 8.61), doubtless a late nonce creation. Otherwise we find the compound middle forms *niγne*, **niγnāire, nijaγnənte* (Yt. 13.48) in passive function.

9. See Haldane 1963:53ff., Lamerre 1985, Rutherford 1994, who calls it 'far the most conspicuous παιάν in Greek tragedy'. I give the text as in Lloyd-Jones and Wilson 1990 (OCT) and Dawe 1985 (Bibl. Teub.). The meter, with somewhat different colometry and reading, is discussed by Dale 1968.

Sleep, unversed in pain, Sleep, unversed in anguish,
may you come to us blowing fair, you of the
good life, good life, lord. May you hold up
to our eyes this light of healing, which is spread
now. Come, come to me, Healer.

The three word repetitions in five lines (Ὕπνε, εὐαίων, ἴθι) are a feature of liturgical language and an inherited stylistic feature, if not a universal.[10] The rhyming εὐ**αίων** - Π**αίων** is particularly appropriate to the paean, as Haldane notes. In fact, virtually every syllable resonates with one or more others in a veritable kaleidoscope of phonic figures:

ODunas **AD**aēs hupn**E D**';
Adaēs . . . **A**lgeōn;
ad**ĀĒS** . . . eu**ĀĒS**;
alge**ŌN** . .. euai**ŌN**, euai**ŌN**, **ŌN**aks;
elth**OIS** . . . antiskh**OIS** . . . m**OI**;
ōna**KS** . . . anti**SK**hois;
t**ĀN**d, aigl**ĀN**, h**Ā** . . . ta **NŪN**;
Tand' . . . **T**e**T**a**T**ai **T**anūn;
AIglan . . . tetat**AI** . . . p**AI**ōn.

The whole is finally demarcated, bounded by a phonetic *dúnad* or closure between the first word and the last (chap. 9), which transforms these lines of the chorus from a sequence to a set:

hú**PN**
——
Paiō**N**

An adept at the genre of the paean, Sophocles here proves his skill in the poetics of another age. The poem contains 49 syllables, of which no less than 38 participate in a phonetic repetition figure of one or more of syllable onset, 'rhyme', or coda. One would have to go to Dark Age and Medieval Ireland for an equivalent expression of the "art of the syllable": see chap. 9.

10. Haldane 1963:55 n. 1, with references, to which add also Watkins 1970b. With ἴθι ἴθι compare the charm in AV 17.6,7 *úd ihy úd ihi sūrya* 'rise, rise o Sun'. Note in Greek Bacchylides 3.21 θεὸν θεόν, Euripides, *Herc.* 772 θεοὶ θεοί. The first words of the rhymed prologue to the Archaic Irish Eulogy of St. Columba, ca. 598 AD, the earliest attested vernacular literary work in Europe, are (LU 427) *Dia Dia da-rrogus re tias ina gnūis* 'God, God, let me invoke him before I go into his presence'.

VII

From myth to charm

56

From dragon to worm

1. India and Ireland

In Bacchylides 5.109-10, describing the depredations of the Calydonian boar, we find a lexical variant of the basic formula in the canonical V(erb) O(bject) word order:

> **σφάζε** τε **μῆλα**, **βροτῶν**
> **ϑ'** ὅστις εἰσάντα μόλοι
>
> He **slew** the **sheep**, **and** any **mortal** who came against him.

The collocation man-slaying, beast-slaying is itself a traditional Indo-European theme, closely associated with the basic formula. It may describe the SERPENT (**og^w^hi-*), as in Avestan (Yt. 9.11, 19.40, 92, 93, of the hero Kərəsāspa):

> yō **janaṯ ažīm** sruuarəm
> yim **aspō**.garəm **nərə**.garəm
>
> Who **slew** the **horse**-devouring,
> **man**-devouring horned **serpent**,

and in its Pahlavi formulaic descendent (Pahlavi Rivāyat, chap. 30 above):

> **až** ī srūwar bē **ōzad** ī **asp**-ōbār ī **mard**-ōbār
>
> He **slew** the **horse**-devouring, **man**-devouring horned **serpent**.

The phrase may equally well be applied to the HERO, as in the Avestan hymn to Mithra (Yt.10.101):

> hō paoiriiō gaδąm **nijaiṇti**
> **aspaēca** paiti **vīraēca**

haϑra.taršta ϑrə̊ŋhaiiete
uuaiia **aspa.vīraja**

He **smashes** first his weapon down on **horse** and **man**,
frightens both with sudden fright, the **smiter of horse and man**.

It is applied to the god or hero's WEAPON (**u̯edh-*), like the lightning bolt of the Maruts in RV 7.56.17c:

āré **gohā́ nr̥hā́ vadhó** vo astu

May your **ox-slaying, man-slaying weapon** be far away.

It should be noted that the opposition is man : beast, and that horse, ox, and sheep are only tokens of the latter. The same opposition underlies the inherited formulaic pairs Avestan *pasu vīra*, Umbrian *ueiro pequo* 'man (and) beast', and the metonymic Vedic *dvipā́d cátuṣpād*, Umbrian *dupursus peturpursus* 'two-footed, four-footed' discussed in chap. 12. The two formulas appear in the same hymn to Rudra, 1.114.1c, 10a:

yáthā śám ásad **dvipáde cátuṣpade**
. . .
āré te **goghnám utá puruṣaghnám**

That weal be for the **two-footed and the four-footed**
. . .
May your **ox- and man-killing** (weapon) be far away.

Greek μῆλον 'sheep' has its only cognate in Old Irish *míl* 'animal, beast', which would indicate that Greek μῆλον like many descendents of IE **pek̂u-* has undergone semantic specialization from an earlier more general sense. It is interesting to observe further that Bacchylides' μῆλα βροτῶν ϑ' in the older sense of 'beasts and men' may be reconstructed as an alliterative pair

$*meh_1lo$- mr̥to-,

where the phonetic figure of identity serves to index the semantic opposition, just as in ***last but not least***. Compare the quest for alliteration that led to Vedic *paśu- puruṣa-* 'beast and man' or Latin *pastores pecua* 'shepherds and flocks' (chap. 12). The collective neuter plural μῆλα, *pecua* versus the animate plurals βροτῶν, *pastores* are another index, this time grammatical, to the same opposition.

Another "intertextual" link suggests that the phrase σφάζε τε μῆλα βροτῶν ϑ' is not just a nonce creation of Bacchylides. The verb σφάζω (**sphag-i̯ō*) is confined to Greek; it has no cognates. But Klingenschmitt 1982:227 has suggested that Armenian *spananem*, aorist *spani* 'I slay, slew' may represent a blend of pre-Greco-

Armenian *_sphag_- and *_k̂þen_-, respectively Greek σφαγ- and κτεν-. Now _spananem_ is in Armenian the dragon-slaying verb par excellence: _zvišapn spananel_ 'to slay the dragon' (_višap_, from Iranian) in the folk epic David of Sassoun, passim.[1] One might want to suggest that the blend was rather *_sphag_- × *_g^when_-, the more so since the root of κτείνω, Vedic _kṣaṇoti_ 'wounds' may itself be an Indo-European rhyme-form to *_g^when_-.

We saw in chapters 53 and 55 that the basic formula of _áhann áhim_ 'he slew the serpent' and its congeners is a proclamation of victory, a paean: 'Slain are your fathers' _**hatā́so**_ _vām pitáras_, 'We have slain godlike Hector' **ἐπέφνομεν** Ἕκτορα δῖον. The most powerful force in the world view of the Indo-Europeans was the spoken word (chap. 6). If the dragon or serpent is conceived of as a monstrous sort of worm, then the mythographic formula, the paean which proclaims the death of the dragon can assure by verbal magic, by the power of the spoken word, the destruction of the worm. The verbal magic is the homeopathic, analogic magic of a charm or incantation. Such a charm using the root *_g^when_- and the basic formula is found in each of two traditions at opposite ends of the Indo-European world: India and Ireland.

The Atharvaveda contains three hymns or spells against worms which have been justly familiar in Indo-European literature ever since they were first studied and translated by Adalbert Kuhn (1864:49ff., 135ff.). We will return presently to these texts; for the moment I cite just the three verses 2.32.3-5, repeated in 5.23.10-12:

atrivád vaḥ **krimayo hanmi** kaṇvaváj jamadagnivát
agástyasya bráhmaṇā sáṃ pinaṣmy aháṃ **krímīn**
ható rā́jā **krímīṇām** utaíṣāṃ sthapátir **hatáḥ**
ható hatámātā **krímir hatá**bhrātā **hatá**svasā
hatā́so asya veśáso **hatā́saḥ** páriveśasaḥ
átho yé kṣullakā́ iva sárve té **krímayo hatā́ḥ**

Like Atri **I slay** you, **o worms**, like Kaṇva, like Jamadagni;
with the formula of Agastya I mash together the **worms**.
Slain is the king of the **worms**, also their chief is **slain**;
slain is the **worm**, with its mother **slain**, its brother **slain**,
its sister **slain**. **Slain** are its neighbors, **slain** its further
neighbors, also those that are as it were petty; all those worms
are **slain**.

Atri, Kaṇva, Jamadagni, and Agastya are legendary ṛṣi's, poet-seers. The paeanic character of this incantation is unmistakeable: 'I slay . . . , Slain is . . . ' That the triad of verses form a poetic unity appears from their repetition; note that 3a _krimayo hanmi_ and 5d _krímayo hatā́s_ make a _dúnad_, a closure or ring. One of the Indo-European words for 'worm' makes its earliest recorded appearance here;[2] it is not found in the

1. References at chap. 23.2 n. 14.
2. The manuscripts hesitate between _krími_- and _kṛ́mi_-; Whitney adopts the former in text and translation, but the latter is original.

Rigveda. But we have an exact cognate in Old Irish *cruim*, Welsh *pryf*, Lithuanian *kirmìs*: Indo-European **kʷr̥mi-s*, itself an Indo-European rhyme to **u̯r̥mi-s*, Latin *uermis*, English *worm*. The similarity relation of dragon and worm moves in both directions: Old English *wyrm* and Old Norse *ormr* both mean dragon as well as worm, as does Pahlavi *kirm*. The collocation of the roots **kʷr̥mi-/u̯r̥mi-* and **gʷhen-* belongs to the narrative of myth in Pahlavi ***kirm** ōzad* and Old Norse ***orms** ein**bani*** (see chapters 29 and 43), to the language of charm in Vedic *vaḥ **krimayo hanmi***.

It is in the language of charm that we find the basic mythographic formula in Old Irish. It is in one of the very few fragments of Old Irish preserved in an Old English manuscript (Harl. 585, late 11th cent.), in Old English context. The collection of "leechdoms and wortcunning"[3] contains a charm against worms (*wyrm gealdor*) to be sung into the ear, right or left according as male or female, of a person or animal who has swallowed a worm in water. It begins:

gono mīl orgo mīl marbu mīl

I slay the beast, I slaughter the beast, I kill the beast.

The form *gono* is our only attestation of the 1sg. present absolute of *gon(a)id*, IE **gʷhen-*; *mīl*, spelled *miil* in the body of the extremely garbled Old Irish text, which may reflect archaic Old English and/or Old Irish scribal practice (Oliver, to appear), is the only cognate of Greek μῆλον in Bacchylides' σφάζε τε μῆλα above. Old Irish *gono mīl* 'I slay the beast' and Atharvavedic *vaḥ krimayo hanmi* 'I slay you, o worms' or *ható rājā krimīṇām* 'slain is the king of the worms' continue the same cultural tradition, with the same verb. They are, we may say again (cf. chap. 35), two performances of the same text.

2. Germanic

Adalbert Kuhn's original equation (1864) involved on the one hand (pp. 135-57) the comparison of the Atharvan worm charms proper (AV 2.31, 2.32, 5.23) with a number of medieval and early modern West and North Germanic charms against worms (as a symbol of disease) described typically as white, black, or red: the poetic device common to most of these is the (perenially attractive) rhyme 'red' : 'dead' (roet : toet, roet : doet, etc.). They are thus proper to Germanic alone, and not valid comparanda for Indo-European per se.

On the other hand Kuhn noted (pp. 63-74) the Old High German (9th-cent. ms. in Munich) and Old Saxon (10th-cent. ms., in Vienna) charms contra vermes (Braune-Helm, Althochdeutsches Lesebuch[13] [Tübingen, 1958] 89):

gang uz, nesso, mit niun nessinchilinon,

3. Cockayne 1961:13.10-11 (no. 10). It has been studied by Thurneysen 1919 and Meroney 1945.

uz fonna marge in deo adra, vonna den adrun
in daz fleisk, fonna demu fleiske in daz fel,
fonna demo velle in diz tulli

Go out, worm, with nine little worms, from the marrow to the veins, from the veins to the flesh, from the flesh to the skin, from the skin to this arrow.

gang ût, nesso, mit nigon nessiklînon, ut fana
thema marge an that bên, fan theme bêne an
that flêsg, ût fan themo flêsgke an thia
hûd, ût fan thera hûd an thesa strâla

Go out, worm, with nine little worms, from the marrow to the bone, from the bone to the flesh, from the flesh to the skin, from the skin to this arrow.

Together with other medieval German charms against consumption, Kuhn compared these with Vedic hymns (RV 1.168, AV 2.33) itemizing the expulsion of *yakṣma* 'disease, consumption' from all the parts of the body enumerated, from head to foot and top to toes.

Kuhn's first and probably most famous comparison (pp. 49-63) was of the Old High German second Merseburg spell (10th cent.) and AV 4.12, 'to heal serious wounds' (Whitney). The former reads:

Phol ende Uuodan   vuoron zi holza
nu uuart demo Balderes volon   sin vuoz birenkit
thu biguol en Sinthgunt   Sunna era suister
thu biguol en Friia   Volla era suister
thu biguol en Uuodan   so he uuola conda.
sose benrenki, sose bluotrenki, sose lidirenki.
ben zi bena   **bluot zi bluoda**
lid zi geliden   sose gelimida sin

Phol and Wodan were riding to the woods, Balder's foal wrenched his foot. Sinthgunt conjured it, sister of Sunna; Frija conjured it, sister of Folla; Wodan conjured it, as well as he could. As bone-wrench, so blood-wrench, so joint-wrench. **Bone to bone, blood to blood, joint to joint**; so be they joined.

Verses 3-5 of AVŚ 4.12, which are significantly the first three of the Paippalāda (AVP 4.15), are

sáṃ te majjā́ majjñā́ bhavatu sám u te páruṣā páruḥ
sáṃ te māṁsásya vísrastaṃ sám ásthi ápi rohatu

majjā́ majjñā́ sáṃ dhīyatāṃ cármanā cárma rohatu
ásṛk (te?) asnā́[4] rohatu māṁsáṃ māṁséna rohatu
lóma lómnā sáṃ kalpayā tvacā́ sáṃ kalpayā tvácam
asthnā́ ásthi (vṛ?) rohatu chinnáṃ sáṃ dhehy oṣadhe

Let your marrow be together with marrow, and your joint together with joint. Let what of your flesh has fallen apart (be) together (with flesh); let bone grow over (with bone). Let marrow be put together with marrow, let skin grow with skin; let your blood grow with blood, let flesh grow with flesh. Fit together hair with hair, fit together skin with skin. Let your bone grow with bone; put together what is broken, o plant.[5]

Kuhn's comparisons and his claims for common inheritance, genetic filiation, have generated nearly a century and a half of controversy, ranging from the uncritical acceptance of Romanticism on the one hand or National Socialism on the other, through more cautious and informed acceptance to rejection in favor of the assumption of parallel convergence or independent creation, purely typological similarity, or finally straightforward agnosticism.[6] There is an obvious difficulty in excluding parallel convergence which inheres where the subject matter is the enumeration and articulation of the parts of the human body in various languages and cultures; consider only the American English children's litanies like *dem bones, dem bones, dem dry bones: de head bone connected to de neck bone, de neck bone* etc., scarcely of "Indo-European" date or provenience. But two new sets of textual data, the most important of which was gathered by S. Jamison, together with the theoretical framework argued for eloquently by E. Campanile, combine in my view to tip the balance of inherent plausibility in favor of a genetically inherited, Indo-European origin for the texts of this genre attested in several early Indo-European cultural traditions. To these two sets of evidence and the conclusion to be drawn from them the next chapter is devoted.

4. Reading *asnā́* with AVP 4.15.3c 'let your blood grow with blood,' and *asthnā́* with AVP 14.15.2c, with L. Alsdorf, Kleine Schriften 25-6 and Zysk 1985:74-5 and 199-200. The order is still uncertain, and the verses unsound.

5. One thinks of a plant like our wildflower *boneset* (*Eupatorium perfoliatum*), whose 'veiny, wrinkled leaves *unite basally* around the stem (perfoliate),' Peterson and McKenny 1968:46. In 17th-century England the name was given to the common comfrey (*Symphytum officinale*). The NED s. v. cites from 1670 fracturas ossium consolidat, unde et anglice a nonnullis *boneset* dicitur.

6. A nearly exhaustive survey up to the middle 60's may be found in Schmitt 1967:ch. 8. Schmitt carefully reported the critical views of Schlerath 1962, and finally considered the question undecidable. Later views in Campanile 1977:88-96 and 1990:69-71 (informed and emphatic acceptance), Zysk 1985 (hesitant acceptance; more enthusiastic 1992), and Jamison 1986 (cautious acceptance); see further below for this critical study.

57

The charms of Indo-European

S. Jamison in a 1986 study demonstrated conclusively, on the basis of a mass of documentation, that 'Vedic texts give us almost tediously ample evidence that the five terms . . . *lóman* "hair", *tvác-* "skin", *māṁsá-* "flesh", *ásthi-* "bone", and *majján-* "marrow", arranged in that particular order, are the fixed traditional expression of the make-up of the canonical beast' (172). 'The series is sometimes expanded by the insertion of additional terms or, more rarely, abbreviated . . .

HAIR	lóman[1]
SKIN	tvác
blood	ásr̥k
fat	médas-
FLESH	māṁsá
sinews	snā́van-
BONE	ásthi
joint	páruṣ-
MARROW	majján-

It is in fact, in an expanded version that we meet it first, in an AV curse . . . adding 'sinews' . . . cf. also AV 4.12 [compared by Kuhn] (173-4).' It is not found in the Rigveda because as 'a piece of codified folk wisdom' (compare the 'popular' initial of *lóman-*, not *róman-* 'hair') it was more appropriate to AVic than to RVic discourse. And most strikingly, 'this formulaic system has a good chance of being inherited from Indo-Iranian' (177) since, though lacking in the Avesta for the same reason as the Rigveda, it occurs several times in Pahlavi, in the Greater Bundahišn, which is a repository of traditional lore . . . though the series are not precisely identical to each other, or to the Vedic series, their kinship seems unmistakable (178):

Gr. Bund. 28.4	SKIN	pōst	28.22	FLESH	gōšt
	FLESH	gōšt		veins	rag

1. Jamison's capitals indicate the fivefold "most orthodox" sequence. I have slightly simplified her list, omitting Sanskrit lexical variants and the late (Aitareya Āraṇyaka) *prāṇa-*, and added *paruṣ-* from the earliest (AVŚ, AVP) attestation.

BONES	astag	fat	pīh
veins	ragān	BONES	astag
blood	xōn	MARROW	mazg
stomach	aškamb	blood	xōn
HAIR	mōy	HAIR	mōy.'

BONES and MARROW are thus common Indo-Iranian cognates both in linguistic form and in linear ordering.

The "point" of these Indic and Iranian lists, which assures their legitimate comparability and ultimate genetic kinship, is precisely their arbitrariness. They are not simply enumerations or catalogues of the parts of the human or animal body in contiguous order—no limbs are involved, n. b.—but a traditional ordered list, viewed as arbitrary and immutable, of what are the constituent parts, the make up of *paśu* (MS 3.3.3 [34:14ff.], Jamison, p. 167) or *puruṣa* (ŚB 10.2.3.5, Jamison, p. 172), from the outside in (as in Indic) or the inside out (as in Iranian). As Jamison shows, this list, slightly adjusted but in its same traditional order persisted into the period of classical Sanskrit medicine and medical law, in the doctrine of the 7 *dhātus*[2] or organic components.

We have now for the first time, in Jamison's work, an arbitrary list which is a structural set. The sequence is conceptually similar, at times virtually identical in India (where it can be observed over more than a millennium) and Iran, and therefore necessarily of at least common Indo-Iranian antiquity. As such it can serve as a solid point of departure for comparison further afield.[3]

2. To the second level of reception of the Indian medical doctrine belong the Tocharian A and B translations of the Garbhasūtra, a Buddhist medical text on the development of the embryo, texts XII (A, no. 151a1-4) and XXX (B, no. 603) in Krause-Thomas, Tocharisches Elementarbuch II, in sequential sentences of the type (B) 'In the 22nd week the marrow in the body develops'. The list in B is

mrestīwe	'marrow'
sñaura	'sinews'
mīsa	'flesh'
ewe	'inner skin'
yetse	'outer skin'
yetse takarşke	'visible skin'
y[okanma?]	'hairs'.

That of A is

ysār	'blood'
mäśśunt	'marrow'
puskāñ	'sinews'
śwāl	'flesh'
[-]	
yats	'outer skin'.
[-]	

The difference between the lists in the two Tocharian languages is striking, as is the fact that they appear to have fewer words in common in these lists than do Indic and Iranian.

3. Methodologically comparable is the ranked hierarchy in the categories of property arbitrarily attached in Old Indian law to the sanctions of false witness, in Iranian law to the classes of contract, of which the higher part in each tradition coincides in virtually every particular with the inventory of the ancient

It should be clear that mere enumerations of sequences of body-parts in the Veda, like RV 1.168, AV 2.33, compared by A. Kuhn to the Old High German and Old Saxon *nesso*-worm spells, are not apt for external comparison. These are predicated on the universals of human physiology. They always begin with the head and work down to the feet, and may or may not include internal organs as well as visible body parts. AV 2.33 and the closely corresponding RV 10.163 agree in going from head (eyes, nose, ears, chin, brain, tongue) to trunk (neck, nape, vertebras, spine, shoulders, forearms) to innards (guts, heart, lungs, bowels, rectum, navel) to legs (thighs, kneecaps, heels, toes, haunches, backside) with a summation of 'every limb, every hair, every joint'. See Zysk 1985:15-16, 105. For AV 2.33.6ab see below.

The same sort of list is found in Avestan, in V. 8.35-72 (similarly 9.15-26) describing the purification rite for someone who has come in contact with a corpse. One must pour water on the person, starting with the top of the head, to drive away the corpse-demon, *druxš yā nasuš*. The demon will then flee to the back of the head, and so on, with successive applications of 'good waters', and successive demonic retreats, till the final application to the right and left toes, at which point the demon flies off. Filliozat 1975 correctly recognized that these are surely independent of the expulsion of the yakṣmas in Vedic.

The same applies to several Hittite rituals involving the successive enumeration and apposition of the body-parts of a newborn child to those of a scapegoat who is then killed ('eyes are fitted [*ḫandān*] to eyes, . . .') or those of an ailing celebrant ('let it take the illness of his arse, . . .'). So for example in G. Beckman's birth ritual text C (StBoT 29, 1983, 44) rev. 11-16 a scapegoat is held to the newborn, and the 'eyes are fitted (*ḫandān*) to eyes', and so on to over a total of 13 body parts to 'foot'. KUB 43.53 i 1′-18′ (with a fragmentary OH/OS duplicate, transcribed in Neu, StBoT 25, 1980, no. 9) enumerates no less than 21 body parts, beginning with 'head corresponds (*dākki*) to head', finishing with 'feet' and as an afterthought 'hands'. The Middle Hittite ritual of [f]Tunnawiya CTH 760 I.1 edited by Hutter (1988), and its parallel CTH 760 I.2 edited by Beckman (1990), each contain two lists, beginning 'head is fitted (*ḫandan*) to head' and 'head will lift sickness of head', and continuing respectively to 'foot' and 'toenail'. For the three remaining body parts in each list see below. Such lists should not be utilized for comparative purposes, by elementary principles of the comparative method, and Adalbert Kuhn was wrong to do so.

On the other hand the Germanic *nesso*-worm spells in Old High German and Old Saxon, from two different languages but clearly in some sense the same text, are directly comparable to the Indic and Iranian lists of the parts of the canonical creature, and their kinship is equally unmistakable:

OHG	MARROW	marg	OSax.	MARROW	marg
	sinews	âdra		BONE	bên
	FLESH	fleisk		FLESH	flêsg
	SKIN	fel		SKIN	hûd.

Roman legal category of *res mancipi*, which require a formal ritual for their conveyance: large cattle (bovines and equines), men, and land, Skt. *go'śvapuruṣabhūmi-*. See Watkins 1987a.

They provide moreover a clear contiguity relation, an indexical link in Germanic between the pragmatic function of the basic formula—killing the WORM (*nesso*)—and the sequential formula MARROW . . . SKIN.

At this point we can introduce the Merseburg spell, with its sequence of curative juxtapositions:

BONE to bone	ben zi bena
blood to blood	bluot zi bluoda
joint to joint	lid zi geliden.

Kuhn was correct this time in comparing AV 4.12.3-5 *majjā́ majjñā́* 'MARROW with marrow' etc., not for the juxtaposition of the body parts but rather for their sequence. The same Atharvaveda in our other earliest attestation of the list, a curse in AV(Ś) 12.5.68-70 (lacking in AVP), has the sequence (from the outside in), but without the apposition of body part to body part:

lómāni asya sáṃ chindhi, tvácam asya ví veṣṭaya
māṁsā́ni asya śātaya, snā́vāni asya sáṃ vṛha
ásthīni asya pīḍaya, majjā́nam asya nír jahi

His HAIR cut up, his SKIN strip off,
his FLESH cut in pieces, his SINEWS wrench off,
his BONES distress, his MARROW smite out.

It is this sequence in AV 12.5.68-70 which makes sense out of the somewhat garbled and repetitive sequences of AV(Ś) 4.13.5-5 (AVP 4.15.1-3).

This passage in AV 12.5 has the added feature that it is framed both by an instance of the basic formula and by forms of the word for 'joint' *párvaṇ-*, the same word as *páruṣ-* 'joint' in AV 4.12.3.[4] Compare verses 66-67,

vájreṇa śatá**parvaṇā** . . . prá śíro **jahi**

With a hundred-**jointed cudgel** . . . **smite** forth (his) head,

with 70-71

majjā́ny asya nír **jahi**
. . . **párvāṇi** ví vrathaya

Smite out his marrow . . . (his) **joints** unloosen.

The two *jahi*'s form a canonical compositional ring which serves to index and demarcate the sequenced list. The passage establishes a clear indexical link, a

4. Heteroclitic **per-u̯r̥/*per-u̯on-/*per-u̯n̥-/*per-un-*, K. Hoffmann 1975:327-37.

contiguity relation between the basic formula SLAY (**g*ʷ*hen-*) ADVERSARY and the formulaic sequence MARROW . . . HAIR in an Atharvan magical charm. Arranging these four lists, the Old High German, Old Saxon, Canonical Creature, and Atharvaveda, in the same order we obtain:

OHG	*OS*	*Can. Creat.*	*AV 12.5*
MARROW	MARROW	MARROW	MARROW
		joint	
	BONE	BONE	BONE
SINEW		SINEW	SINEW
FLESH	FLESH	FLESH	FLESH
		fat	
		blood	
SKIN	SKIN	SKIN	SKIN
		HAIR	HAIR.

We noted the universal 'head to foot', 'head to toe' lists in Vedic, Avestan, and Hittite. An exception to this pattern is AV 2.33.6ab, which is the only pāda to have no correspondent in RV 10.163. The lines are:

asthíbhyas te majjábhyaḥ, snā́vabhyo dhamánibhyaḥ

From your BONES, MARROW, SINEWS, BLOOD VESSELS.

I suggest it is a real and inherited 'canonical creature' sequence incorporated into an otherwise universal enumeration. (For *asthíbhyas te majjábhyaḥ* the Paippalāda (4.15) has *hastebhyas te māṁsebhyas*, an obvious garbled phonetic echo.)

In the same way the two lists in the Hittite CTH 760 texts edited by Hutter and Beckman run from head to sole of foot or head to toenail, obvious universal enumerations. But each continues with three body parts not found in any of the other lists, one separated by a paragraph line, in the order

BONE (*ḫaštai*), SINEW (^{UZU}SA), BLOOD (*ēšḫar*),

and

SINEW (^{UZU}SA), BONE (*ḫaštiyanza*), BLOOD (*išḫananza, ēšḫananza*).

Again it is tempting to see an inherited sequence tacked on to a universal enumeration.

Again comparing the Vedic and Hittite to the Old High German second Merseburg spell we have

OHG	*AV 2.33*	*Hitt 1*	*Hitt 2*
BONE	BONE	BONE	SINEW
	MARROW		
	SINEW	SINEW	BONE
BLOOD	BLOOD VESSEL	BLOOD	BLOOD
JOINT			

Despite the single perturbation of order the correspondences are striking.

AV 12.5.66 and 71 cited above also establish a clear indexical link, a contiguity relation between the word for 'joint' *páruṣ-/párvaṇ-* in both AV passages (4.12, 12.5) attesting the formulaic sequence MARROW ... HAIR. 'Joint' *páruṣ-/párvaṇ-* is part of the sequence in AV 4.12, but outside it in AV 12.5, and absent from all later Vedic and Classical Sanskrit literature. For this reason it was not further considered by Jamison. But I would suggest we retain it as a descriptive designation for the interior endpoint of the sequence itself. Synchronically, in both AV attestations the word is adjacent or closest to MARROW in the sequence, and farthest from HAIR. And diachronically, the meaning, history and etymology of *páruṣ-/ párvaṇ-* is set forth very clearly by Hoffmann in the paper just cited. It is an old word, a derivative of the root **per-* 'come through', a suffixed verbal abstract **per-u̯r̥*, **per-u̯on-/-u̯n̥-* 'coming through'. As Hoffmann shows, the 'joint' in the sacrifical animal is 'the place you come through' in cutting. Exact cognates are Greek πεῖραρ, πείρατος (*περ-ϝr̥, *περ-ϝn̥) 'end, limit, achievement', in the common formula πείρατα γαίης 'ends of the earth', 'the place you come through to', and Hittite ^{NA_4}*peruna-* 'rock', oldest form *peru (*perur)*, *perun-* (identical with the Greek and Vedic) together with Avestan *paruuan-* (chap. 12) and Vedic *párvata-* (**per-u̯n̥-to-*) 'rocky, (rocky) mountain', 'what you come down to',[5] 'bedrock', 'rock bottom' (RV 10.108.7 *ádribudhna-*) suggested by Hoffmann as a characteristic of observable neolithic excavated, cave-like dwellings. We may have a very old word indeed.[6]

We pass now to Irish. Jamison in her original study had already compared a passage from a Modern Irish folk tale in translation, the tale of Finn mac Cumaill (Fionn mac Cumhaill) chewing his thumb to achieve wisdom. It is cited from O'Rahilly 1946:335 (with Jamison's capitalization): 'from SKIN to FLESH, from FLESH to BONE, from BONE to MARROW, from MARROW to (the inmost core).' From O'Rahilly note also the Irish (S. Kerry) *Chogain sé an órdóg ón gcroiceann go dtí an fheoil, ón bhfeoil go dtí an cnámh, ón gcnámh go dtí an smior, 's ón smior go dtí an smúsaig*. The word *smúsach*, also glossed 'marrow' or 'red marrow', O'Rahilly renders 'inmost core': it is clearly to be understood as the very center, the HEART of

5. Note the epithet in *Il.* 8.478 τὰ νείατα πείρατα . . . / γαίης καὶ πόντοιο 'the nethermost ends of the earth and the sea.'

6. For this word in the ancient formula TREE (**dru-*) and ROCK see chap. 12. Note finally the connection with the dragon-slaying myth, where the locale of the combat and victory are typically either the mountains (*párvata-*, e.g. RV 1.32.1) or a cave or hole (e.g. *Illuyankas*) or the bottom of the sea or lake (e.g. *Beowulf*, *Fergus mac Léti*).

the MARROW. Another and doubtless related word *smúas*[7] appears in the tale variant (Co. Monoghan) *nuair a chuirfeadh se i n-a bhéal í agus nuair a chognóchad se í ó fhéith go smuais* 'when he would put it (his thumb) in his mouth and would chew it from SINEW to MARROW HEART'.[8] The oldest occurrence of the sequence is in a paper manuscript of 1821 (Eg. 149) of a literary text from the Finn-cycle, *Cath Finntrágha.* It is printed by K. Meyer in his 1885 edition of this text from Rawlinson B 487, as part of a lengthy passage not found in the latter (p.62): *do chuir an órdóg ionna bhéal ⁊ cognus go cnamh í ⁊ assin go smior ⁊ assin go smúsach ⁊ do foillsígheadh eólus do . . .* 'he put his thumb in his mouth and chewed it to the BONE, and from there to the MARROW and from there to the MARROW HEART and knowledge was manifested to him . . . ' The 1821 ms. is a copy of one of 1777 (RIA 23 L 39), all of Munster origin, according to C. O'Rahilly in her edition (1962:xxvii). The passage may well be a later accretion to this text of the later 15th century, but when is uncertain; the form and sequence is invariant from that of the folktales more than a century later.

The earliest attestation of the word for the endpoint of the folk sequence is Duanaire Finn 62.63 (DF ii 266 in Murphy 1933) *ag ithe smaoíse mo lámh* 'eating the marrow of my hands'. Murphy dates the poem to the 15th century (p. 143). According to Murphy's glossary (1953:321) *smaoís* is 'a modern spoken form of *smúas*', *smaoíseach* of *smúsach.* In any case Classical Modern Irish *ithe smaoise* provides the critical verbal link between the Modern Irish folk sequence and the Old Irish phrase *teinm laeda* (*laído*).

T. F. O'Rahilly showed quite convincingly that 'we may justly see in this folk-tale formula a traditional paraphrase' of the mantic process known as *teinm laído* 'gnawing of marrow heart', by implication 'gnawing down to the marrow-heart', associated with Finn mac Cumaill since early Old Irish times.[9] This is one of 'the three arts which establish a poet in his prerogative'; *in trēide nemthigius filid*, which Finn learned in his boyhood along with *imbus for-osnai* 'divination which illumines' and *díchetal di chennaib* 'incantation from heads'. It is then that he made the lay *Cétemon* to prove his poetic skill (*éicse*).[10] We can consider established the existence in these Irish texts of the Finn cycle, both literary and oral-traditional, of the same formulaic list or sequence of body parts from the outside in, which we observe in Germanic,

---

7. Old Irish *u*-stem *smir*, Welsh *mer* 'marrow' (IE **smeru-*) is cognate with Old English *smeoru*, Old Norse *smjǫr* 'grease, fat, butter'. I would suggest that to the pair *smúas*, also attested as *smaoís*, and *smúsach*, attested also as *smúasach*, *smaoíseach* ("expressive" **smou-ss-*/ **smū-ss-*) 'marrow heart', we can compare—at the level of the root, to be sure—Greek μυ-ελός 'marrow', attested from Homer on, and hitherto without etymology.

8. From the text passages cited in the Academy's Dict. s. v. *smúas* it appears that *smir* and *smúas* were proverbial inseparable entities; *smior* and *smúsach* likewise occur together in expressions in Modern Irish. The phonetic index of the shared initial has doubtless played a role over the centuries.

9. Old Irish *teinm* is the verbal noun of the cognate of Greek τένδω 'gnaw', as in the Hesiodic passage ἀνόστεος ὃν πόδα τένδει 'the boneless one gnaws his own foot' (*Op.* 524), which I discuss in Watkins 1978a in connection with the Finn-legend. The 'boneless one' is a kenning for the penis, as I show; Finn's acquistion of mantic wisdom by gnawing his own thumb is, as I tried to suggest, perhaps too obliquely, an image of autofellatio. The point seems misunderstood in Campanile 1986 and 1990:125-7.

10. On the poem and its date see most recently Carney 1971, with earlier references. The citations are from the opening prose, printed in Murphy, Early Irish Lyrics 156. On the figure of Finn see J. Nagy 1985.

Indic, and Iranian. We can consider established also that the knowledge and wisdom acquired by Finn in the way paraphrased by the sequence is mantic and poetic in nature, and manifested in poetry (*éicse*).

The same sequence is observable elsewhere in Irish, this time in Old Irish mythological texts of a different cycle. Krause 1929:42 compared the phrase BONE to BONE, BLOOD to BLOOD, JOINT to JOINT of the Merseburg spell with a curative formula in *Cath Maige Tuired* (Gray 1982) uttered by Míach, son of the legendary physician Dían Cécht, to Núadu, king of the Túatha Dé Danann, called *Arcatlám* 'silverhand' since Dían Cécht had replaced his hand cut off in battle with one of silver:

§33[11] Boi dano Nuadu oca othrus, ⁊ do-breth lám argait foir la Dían Cécht co lúth cecha láme inte. Níba maith dano lia macc-som sin .i. la Míach. At-réracht-som don láim ⁊ as-bert

"**alt** fri **halt** di ⁊ **féith** fri **féith**"

⁊ ícsus fri teora nómada . . .

Now Nuadu was being treated, and a silver arm was put on him by Dían Cécht, with the movement of any hand in it. But his son Míach did not like that. He went up to the hand and said

"JOINT to JOINT of it, and SINEW to SINEW"

and he healed it in nine days and nights . . .

While the similarity to the apposition of the Merseburg charm is clear, two parts alone do not constitute a formulaic sequenced set. For this we must go to the next paragraph of the same text, which Krause did not quote (nor R. Schmitt):

§34. Ba holc la Dían Cécht in frepaid sin. Do-léic claidem i mullach a maic co ro-teind[12] a **tuinn** fri **féoil** a chinn. Ícsus in gillae . . . Atcomaic aithirriuch co ro-teind a **féoil** co rrodic **cnáim**. Ícsus in gillae . . . Bíssius in tress béim co ránic **srebonn** a inchinn(e). Ícsus in gillae . . . Bíssius dano in cethramad mbéim co tórba[13] a n-**inchinn** conid apud Míach ⁊ as-bert Dían Cécht nach n-ícfad liaig fadessin ont ṡlaithe-sin.

Dían Cécht did not like that cure. He heaved a sword at the top of his son's head

11. I have normalized the text, since for our purposes nothing is gained by retaining the idiosyncratic orthography of Harleian 5280.

Much has been made of this Old Irish text by Georges Dumézil and his epigones as a manifestation of Indo-European trifunctional mythology. See the introduction to the text by E. A. Gray, as well as the series of essays by her in *Éigse* 18-19, 1981-83. There is no necessary connection between the text as preserving possible traditional "mythologemes" of Indo-European date, and the same text as preserving possible traditional "stylemes" of Indo-European date. But the coincidence is not without interest.

12. The weak s-preterite in both occurrences in this text forbid emending to the attested strong reduplicated *-tethaind*. But it is surely significant that this is the same verb as in Finn's ***teinm*** *laído* 'gnawing down to the marrow-heart', and the boneless one's ὃν πόδα **τένδει** 'gnaws his own foot'.

13. *co nderba* cod.; uncertain. I prefer Gray's suggestion in her note ad loc.

> and cut his SKIN to the FLESH of the head. The lad healed it. He struck him again and cut his FLESH until he reached the BONE. The lad healed it. . . He struck it the third blow and reached the MEMBRANE of his brain. The lad healed it . . . Then he struck it the fourth blow and reached the BRAIN so that Míach died, and Dían Cécht said that no physician could heal himself of that blow.

The identical traditional sequence from the outside in is evident. The phrase JOINT to JOINT, SINEW to SINEW becomes meaningful as a comparandum first only by virtue of its contiguity in *Cath Maige Tuired* (CMT) with the five-member sequence, and the similarity of that to the five-member sequence in the Finn cycle:

CMT	SKIN (tonn)	Finn	SKIN (croicenn)
	FLESH (féoil)		FLESH (féoil)
	BONE (cnám)		BONE (cnám)
	MEMBRANE (srebonn)		MARROW (smir)
	BRAIN (inchinn)[14]		MARROW HEART (smúsach)

The reduced structure 'from SINEW to MARROW HEART' (*ó **fhéith** go smuais*) in a variant of the Finn-tale finally can be compared directly to the reduced structure in the CMT curative formula 'JOINT to JOINT of it, and SINEW to SINEW' (*alt fri halt di, ⁊ **féith** fri **féith***) by virtue of the identity of the two members. From the position of the SINEW (*féith*) as farthest from the MARROW HEART it follows that the JOINT must be closest to it, and therefore that the CMT curative formula is looking from inside out.

Pragmatically we should note that in one set (Finn) the formulaic sequence is to acquire poetic wisdom; in another (CMT §34) it is a curative verbal formula spoken by a physician-healer, again a manifestation of the doctrine of the power of the word. It is further striking that the jealousy provoked by the success of the curative formula leads to the kin-slaying (Old Irish *fingal*) of Míach by his father Dían Cécht: precisely the pragmatic domain of the basic hero/adversary-slaying formula among gods and men in the Indo-European world (Orestes, Oedipus, Hiltibrant, Cain . . .). If the basic formula itself does not occur in the passage in CMT, it is not far beneath the surface.

A direct link is found in the Middle Irish place-name tradition (*dindṡenchas*) of the river Barrow (Berba), *Metr. Dind.* 2.62. According to the oldest manuscript (LL) Dían Cécht killed Mechi the son of the Morrigain, but in order to kill a serpent in his heart, which would have destroyed all the flocks and herds of Ireland if unchecked: *Nathir . . . Aire-sin ros-marb*[15] *Dían Cécht* 'the serpent . . . therefore Dían Cécht killed it.' Killing the serpent is thus a kind of cure. The other *Dindṡenchas* manuscripts both verse and prose (§13, RC 15, 1895, 304) have instead of Dían Cécht mac Cécht, which Gwynn adopts in his later corrigenda, probably rightly, for the alliteration with *-marb*. In view of the curative function and the Túatha Dé Danann connections I would

14. The equivalence of BRAIN and MARROW on a symbolic level is amply proven by the number of languages where the same word is used for both, ranging from ancient Avestan to modern Russian.

15. The reading of M; the other mss. have *romarb*.

suggest not identifying the name as the hero Mac Cécht of the Conaire cycle but rather—perhaps garbled—as the son (*mac*) of Dían Cécht. The connexion between the basic formula (*nathir . . . ros-marb*, cf. *marbu mīl* in the Old Irish charm with which we began) and Dían Cécht was in this case sufficiently strong for the scribe of LL to introduce the name into his text, if it is indeed an error.

Having examined and analyzed the two sets of comparative evidence, the ordered lists of the constituents of the canonical creature and the arbitrary links of these lists with the mythographic basic formula in the same Indo-European traditions, we are in a position to draw the appropriate conclusion, which we may think of as the reconstruction of a proto-text.

The same contiguity relation we observed in the Atharvaveda between the basic formula SLAY (*g^{w}*hen-*) ADVERSARY and the traditional list beginning or ending with MARROW(-HEART) recurs therefore not only in Germanic but in Celtic as well: three traditions, three witnesses. These contiguity relations (vertical axis) may be mapped onto a grid with the similarity relations (horizontal axis) among the four cognate traditions showing the traditional list. The whole is a model of one aspect of the typical Indo-European charm, pragmatically the domain of the poet-healer, the professional of the spoken word. The whole is remarkably specific. Each structure point is indicated by a key word or phrase. Those basic formulas in parentheses belong to the domain of myth in their traditions rather than the derived charm, but show obvious lexical similarity. The Indo-European roots in boldface mark cognate key words.

India	*Iran*	*Ireland*	*Germanic*
ható krímis	(kirm ōzad)	gono mīl	(orms einbani)
vajreṇa jahi		nathir . . . rosmarb	nesso
***g^{w}hen-** ———	***g^{w}hen-** ———	***g^{w}hen-** ———	***g^{w}hen-**
|	|	|	|
majjā́	mazg	smúas	marg
***mosg-** ———	***mosg-**		***mosg-**

If we admit the verbal, pragmatic, and cultural-historical cognateness of the basic formula with its key word SLAY (*g^{w}*hen-*), then we must also admit the verbal, pragmatic, and cultural-historical cognateness of the traditional list with its key word MARROW (**mosg-*). And if the agreement in verbal expression requires us to reconstruct an Indo-European basic formula with *g^{w}*hen-*, then the agreement in verbal expression also requires us to reconstruct an Indo-European traditional list with **mosg-*.

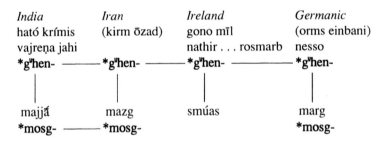

In this we can vindicate a prematurely bold claim of Adalbert Kuhn (1864:63). Kuhn had found in Jacob Grimm, *Deutsche Mythologie* 1181 a Dano-Norwegian folk healing spell parallel to the Merseburg spell, with the phrase *Jesus lagde marv i marv, been i been, kjöd i kjöd* 'Jesus put marrow in marrow, bone in bone, flesh in flesh . . . ' Danish *marv* and Vedic *majján-* alike derive from IE **mosg-*, as Kuhn pointed out, and he was moved to say, 'In *majjam majjñā, marv i marv* haben wir also den letzten rest des einstigen wortlauts der ursprünglichen segensformel erhalten.' This was dismissed—legitimately at the time—as a 'Spiel des Zufalls' by Schmitt 1967:288 n. 1670, invoking also Schlerath 1962.

As we saw earlier, Kuhn's comparison with AV 4.12.3 'marrow with marrow' was correct not for the juxtaposition of the body parts but for their sequence, and so it is here; the Dano-Norwegian sequence is precisely MARROW-BONE-FLESH, from the inside out, and as such legitimately comparable to the AV sequence beginning with MARROW. Once again Kuhn's instinct has stood the test of time.

The agreement in semantics, in linear sequence, in structural relations and in pragmatics of these sets of texts in Vedic and Pahlavi, Indic and Iran in the East, and West Germanic, Old High German and Old Saxon, together with Irish, both Early and Modern in the farthest West require the postulation of a community of origin, which we may securely date at least to the period of late Common Indo-European. The close verbal similarity of the Hittite lists, even though we have not as yet evidence for a contiguity relation with the Hittite mythographic basic formula, could argue for projecting a charm of this type even further back to Proto-Indo-European itself.

A note on the forms

The Avestan, Germanic and Slavic words for 'marrow, brain' presuppose thematic **mosgo-* (**mozgo-*). Vedic *majján-* is an *n*-stem **mosg-*(*e*)*n-*, which also underlies Church Slavonic adjectival *moždanъ* (**možgěnъ* < **mozg-en-no-*) and *moždenь* 'marrow'. For the latter see A. Vaillant, Gramm. comp. 4.459. A heteroclitic nom.-acc. to **mosg-*(*e*)*n-* would be **mosg-r̥*; with the regularly dissimilated final stop which we see in the body-parts *yákr̥t* (~ *yakn-*) 'liver' beside *ásr̥k* (~ *asn-*) 'blood' and Gk. ἀστράγ-αλος (~ Ved. *asthn-*) we would get **mosgr̥t*. Such a form is indeed found, but metathesized to *mostr̥g*; it underlies Avestan *mast*(*ə*)*rəg-an-* 'brains' (with Gershevitch 1959 ad Yt.10.72, rather than 'temples' with Bartholomae). The same form yields the Indic **mastra-* surviving in Pashai *mastrák* 'brain', as well as *mast-íṣkas* attested already in Rigveda 10; see Turner, Comp. Dict. 9926 and Mayrhofer, KEWA s. v. *mast-íṣkaḥ*.

The (tabu?) dissimilation **mosgr̥t* ⇒ **mostr̥g* which led to the creation of a stem **most-* may well be Pre-Indo-Iranian, since it appears common to the two Tocharian languages as well. Tocharian B *mrestīwe* 'marrow' shows a form transposed from **mestr-*, IE **most-r-*; it is the only form which shows the IE vocalism is unambiguously **o*, not **a*. Tocharian A *mäśśunt* is probably palatalized from *mäst-*; the *ä* must be secondary.

In view of the symbolic autofellatio of Finn's gnawing his thumb to the marrow, we might even propose seeing the same metathesis output in the etymologically obscure Latin *masturb-ārī* (from **mostr̥g*(^{u})- with the Latin *a* of *mare*, *lacus*?).[16]

The tabu metatheses we have identified can be seen in modern languages as well. While Old Prussian shows *muzgeno*, 'marrow', East Baltic has transposed **masg-en-*

16. For another recent attempt see Adams 1985, building on and modifying Hallett 1976.

(*mazg-*) to *smag-en-*: Lith. *smãgenis* (nom. pl.) 'marrow, brains', Latv. *smadzenes*. We also find secondary *e*-vocalism in Lith. *smẽgenos*, *smẽgenys*, Latv. *smedzenis* (cf. Toch. A *mäśś-*).

It is finally not to be excluded that the Irish forms in *sm-* (*smúas*, *smúsach*, *smaois*), thought differing in vocalism, might likewise owe something of their form to tabu deformations, and contaminations or blends. The *-s(-)* of these forms could reflect a metathesized *mosg-* > *mogs-*, *moks-* > *moxs-* > *moss-*; a blend **smu-* (μυ–ελός) × **moss-* = **smouss-*?

58

Indo-European medical doctrine

The comparative study of Indo-European medicine was begun by Darmesteter 1877, who noted the three types of healing in Avestan, V. 7.44, and compared them with the three types of ailment and the three types of cure practiced by the mythical physician Asklapios in Pindar, *Pyth.* 3.47-53. The Avestan set are the medicine of the knife (*karətō.baēšaza*) and the medicine of plants (*uruuarō.baēšaza*) and the medicine of formulas (*mąϑrō.baēšaza*). The last is the best, since it cures 'from the innards' (*haca uruϑβąm*).[1] The Pindaric passage is:

> τοὺς μὲν ὦν, ὅσσοι μόλον **αὐτοφύτων**
> **ἑλκέων ξυνάονες**, ἢ πολιῶι χαλκῶι μέλη **τετρωμένοι**
> ἢ χερμάδι τηλεβόλωι,
> ἢ θερινῶι πυρὶ **περθόμενοι** δέμας ἢ
> χειμῶνι, λύσαις ἄλλον ἀλλοίων ἀχέων
> ἔξαγεν, τοὺς μὲν **μαλακαῖς ἐπαοιδαῖς** ἀμφέπων,
> τοὺς δὲ **προσανέα** πί-
> νοντας, **ἢ** γυίοις περάπτων πάντοθεν
> **φάρμακα**, τοὺς δὲ **τομαῖς** ἔστασεν ὀρθούς

> They came to him with **ulcers that the flesh had grown**,
> or their limbs **mangled** with gray bronze, or bruised
> with the stone flung from afar, or the body **stormed** with
> summer fever, or chill; and he released each man and led him from
> his individual grief. Some he treated with **gentle incantations**; some
> with **healing potions** to drink, **or** he tended their limbs with **salves**
> from near and far; and some **by the knife** he set on their feet again.
> (tr. R. Lattimore, slightly altered)

1. That is, from the inside out, as in the traditional formulaic sequences we have seen. For the translation cf. Lommel 1927.

The correspondence is perfect:

karətō.baēšaza	τετρωμένοι	τομαῖς
uruuarō.baēšaza	περθόμενοι	φάρμακα
mąϑrō.baēšaza	αὐτοφύτων ἑλκέων	ἐπαοιδαῖς.

Darmesteter spoke of these as 'le Manuel de l'étudiant en médecine' in the period of Indo-European unity. The next to enter the discussion was E. Benveniste 1945 bringing the whole into the domain of G. Dumézil's Indo-European ideology of the three functions, corresponding to the three types of curative treatment. Benveniste also added to the dossier a three-fold set of ailments in a Rigvedic hymn to the Aśvins as healing divinities: 10.39.3 *andhásya cit nāsatyā kr̥śásya cid yuvā́m íd āhur bhiṣájā rutásya cit* 'they said you two, o Nāsatyas, were healers of the blind, the consumptive, and the fractured'. The correspondences or 'fit' of these to the Pindaric set of ailments is intelligible on a symbolic level, but is neither perfect nor without controversy (Dunkel, to appear). Benveniste also noted the agreement of Avestan *vīmaδ-* 'physician' and its derivative *vīmāδaiia-* 'treat' with Latin *medērī* 'treat', *medicus* 'physician', which allows the reconstruction of a medical component of the semantics of the root **med-* already in Indo-European times. Benveniste suggested 'take the appropriate measures' as the basic meaning. In this connection the name of the physician daughter of the Old Irish legendary physican Dían Cécht, Airmed (**are-medā*), probably contains the same root. Cf. OIr. *ar-midethar* 'hits the mark, succeeds, attains (truth)'.

J. Puhvel 1970 contributed a lengthy study to the problem. He regarded (improbably) the similarities between the Avestan, Vedic, and Pindaric passages as due to the diffusion of Indic Ayurvedic medical theory through the Achaemenid court via Greek physicians who served there, like Ktesias (or Herodotus' [3.129ff.] Demokedes of the speaking name). He weaves a much more complex Dumézilian tapestry, classifying healing vaguely into 'Varuṇaic' and 'Mitraic-Aryamanic' (priests), 'Rudraic' (warriors), and 'folk-medicine ("third estate")', the last including both herbs and spells. His model is unfortunately based on an expanded version of the Avestan list of V. 7.44 found in Yt. 3.6 (to Aṣ̌a vahišta), which gives the types of healers, beginning with *aṣ̌ō.baēšaza* 'who heals with truth' and *dātō.baēšaza* 'who heals with law', and then the three healers with knife (*karəta*), plant (*uruuarā*) and formula (*mąϑra*). The remainder of the passage is basically identical with V. 7.44, and gives the highest place (*baēšaziiōtəmō* 'most healing' to that of the holy formula. The Y.3.6. passage, as Geldner clearly stated in his edition ad loc., is taken from the V. 7.44 original,[2] with *aṣ̌a* and *dāta* added on.

Puhvel and Benveniste's Dumézilian attribution of different cures to different classes was criticized by Campanile 1977, who suggested that Dumézil's tripartition

2. V. 7.36-44 is a self-contained section on the law of medical practice, licensing, and fees ('If he operates on three *daēuua*-worshippers and they die, he is disqualified forever. If he operates on three *daēuua*-worshippers and they come out of it, he is qualified and can operate on Mazdā-worshippers too . . .').

of Indo-European society was not to be understood in terms of rigid castes, but only in a functional and ideological sense; tripartition involved not Indo-European society but the symbolic manner in which this society conceived of reality and reacted to it. Puhvel's views are reiterated substantially without change in his 1987 work, likewise those of Campanile in a publication of 1990.

Whether or not Puhvel, or for that matter Benveniste, would accept Campanile's premises, I find the latter's view in this respect quite compelling. Darmesteter 1877 is sufficient proof that one does not need a Dumézilian framework in order to recognize the same tripartite conceptualization of medicine in two different Indo-European societies, and to draw the conclusion indicated by the comparative method.

We can add a third member of the comparison, a three-fold concept of medicine in Old Irish, in *Cath Maige Tuired*. This was basically seen by Puhvel (1970:378-9), but the direct comparison was somewhat muddied by his ideological superstructure. The three categories in Avestan and in Pindar may be set against three successive paragraphs of CMT, which tell the 'saga' of Míach son of Dían Cécht:

§33	Míach restores Nuadu's hand by *incantation*, 'joint to joint, and sinew to sinew'	mąϑrō.baēšaza	ἐπαοιδαῖς
§34	Míach is killed by four skilled *cuts* of his father's sword, 'surgical strikes'	karətō.baēšaza	τομαῖς
§35	From Míach's grave grow 365 *herbs* corresponding to the number of his joints and sinews. His sister Airmed (IE **med-*) arranges them but Dían Cécht mixes them up to conceal their healing properties.	uruuarō.baēšaza	φάρμακα

Again the conclusion is given by the comparative method: the number and the precision of the similarities require the postulation of a common original, in this case a Common Indo-European ideology of medical practice.

59

The poet as healer

To the controversy initiated by Kuhn in 1864, centered rightly or wrongly on the Old High German second Merseburg charm, the theoretical contribution of Campanile 1977, reiterated 1990, was to recognize that magical, carminative medicine was in Indo-European culture and society a manifestation of the power of the spoken word, of which the Indo-European poet was both the custodian and the professional. 'Kuhn's old view . . . is the most likely, since it is intended not in a crudely reconstructive sense, but in the sense that all these materials represent expressions, historically differentiated, of a common tradition' (1977:93). 'Magical curative medicine, magical preventive medicine . . . are all aspects of the same reality which conceives of illness, physical or metaphysical, as controllable by the spoken word' (1977:94). 'We do not have the right to judge such textual agreements [in medical doctrine as Videvdat and Pindar, etc.] in a way different from any other similarities; we must, that is, recognize in them an element of Indo-European poetic culture, which attests how the elaboration of healing formulas is part of the competence of the poet' (1990:71). The Atharvan poet is well-aware of his place in the tradition: 'like Atri, Kaṇva, Jamadagni . . . with the formula (*bráhmaṇā*) of Agastya . . . ' (AV 2.32.2 above). Similarly the nameless composer of the second Merseburg spell displays considerable skill in handling of meter, vocabulary, and style.[1] The focus is on the rhetoric, not the cure.

We may take the three Atharvan hymns against worms (both real and as a symbol of disease) as an ideal illustration of what Campanile has rightly termed the 'total' character of Indo-European poetic culture. They are particularly apt to illustrate the interplay between poetic form—in the deployment of formulaic utterances—and the pragmatic function which the poet is called on to control. As we saw earlier, the basic technique is that of the homeopathic paean. The verbal proclamation of victory by the basic formula assures the destruction of the worm: *ható rā́ja krímīṇām* 'slain is the king of the worms'. The formula succeeds because of its truth: *satyó mántraḥ kaviśasta ŕ̥ghāvān* 'true is the powerful formula spoken by the poet', as we saw in chap. 6, with its Old Avestan cognate *haiϑīm mąϑrəm* 'true, real formula'.

But the poet has other techniques as well. Consider AV 2.31.1:

1. Schmitt 1967:289, with references.

índrasya yā́ mahī́ dṛṣát
krímer víśvasya tárhaṇī
táyā pinaṣmi sáṃ krímīn
dṛṣádā khálvāṁ̐ iva

The great millstone which is Indra's,
bruiser of every worm,
with that millstone I crush the worms
like *khalva*-grains.

Fronting the name of the divinity around the relative pronoun assures the prominence—and patronage —of Indra *ahihá* 'serpent slaying'. The verse has lexical and morphological or syntactic echoes at every pāda boundary (marked by a #): *dṛṣát* a# *dṛṣadā* #d, *krímer* #b *krímīn* c#, *táyā* #c *dṛṣadā* #d, where the two instrumental constituents *táyā* . . . *dṛṣádā* must be read "vertically", so to speak, and frame the "horizontal" verb phrase *pinaṣmi sáṃ krímīn* with inversion of normal word order. To these embellishments of sound, meaning, and word order comes a further syntactic one. The poet begins with a fine Indo-European bipartite relative sentence, with antecedent appearing both in the preposed relative clause and in the following matrix clause: 'which millstone . . .', 'with that millstone . . . ' We have a feature of Vedic formal style which recurs in the 'high' style of Hittite, of Archaic Latin, and also of Oscan: Vetter 11, Buck 4 (with plate II) *V. Aadirans V. eítiuvam paam . . . deded, eísak eítiuvad . . .* 'the money which V. A. son of V. gave . . . , with that money . . . ' showing double fronting, of the name of the donor and the money, around the relative pronoun.[2]

The second verse shows another Indo-European styleme, linked to the first verse by the echo *tárhaṇī* 1b#, *atṛham* 2a#:

dṛṣṭám adṛ́ṣṭam atṛham

I have bruised the seen (and) unseen (worm).

With this phrase compare AV 5.23.6 and 7:

út purástāt sū́rya eti, viśvádṛṣto adṛṣṭa**hā́**
dṛṣṭā́ṁś ca **ghnánn** adṛ́ṣṭāṁś ca, sárvāṁś ca pramṛṇán krímīn

Up in the east goes the sun, seen of all, **slayer** of the unseen,
slaying the seen and the unseen, and slaughtering all worms.

dṛṣṭáś ca **hanyā́tām** krímir
utā́dṛṣṭáś ca **hanyatām**

2. The handsome inscription is from Pompeii, late 2nd cent. BC. To term the construction *attractio inversa* (so Vetter) is unhistorical. The archaic-sounding construction *urbem quam statuo uestra est* (Vergil, *Aen.* 1.573) results from deletion of nominative *urbs* from the matrix clause, and fronting the accusative *urbem* around the relative pronoun in the relative clause.

Let the seen worm **be slain**
and let the unseen **be slain**

The verb *han* (*g^{u}*hen-*) and the object 'worms' signals the presence of the Indo-European basic dragon-slaying formula, which is thus linked by contiguity to the formulaic merism 'seen (and) unseen'. M. Durante showed (1958:68) that the latter phrase in the worm hymns offered an exact parallel to Latin *morbos uisos inuisosque* 'diseases seen and unseen' in Cato's prayer (chap. 12) and Umbrian *uirseto auirseto uas* 'seen (or) unseen ritual flaw'. The phrase has every right to be considered an Indo-European formula in its semantics even though lexicon and morphology differ in Vedic, Latin, and Umbrian. Note in particular its co-occurrence with another inherited formula ('two-footed, four-footed') in AV 8.8.14cd and 15cd:

dvipā́c cátuṣpād iṣṇāmi, yáthā sénām amū́ṃ **hánan**
dṛṣṭā́n ádṛṣṭān iṣṇāmi, yáthā sénām amū́ṃ **hánan**

What is **two-footed, four-footed** I dispatch, that they may **slay** yonder army; **the seen, the unseen** I dispatch, that they may **slay** yonder army.

Inherited stylemes often come in groups, which might indicate—we can only speculate—something about the way they were learned by the poet. But while 'seen and unseen' may be diachronically an inheritance in AV 2.31.2, they are synchronically only tokens of a merism *A* + *neg A* which is itself inherited, even though not all tokens of it are. The function of the merism is to designate a totality, as clearly in AV 5.23.6d (see chap. 12). The next strophe (2.31.3) shows two more tokens of this figure:

algáṇḍūn hanmi mahatā́ vadhéna
dūnā́ ádūnā arasā́ abhūvan
śiṣṭā́n áśiṣṭān ní tirāmi vācā́
yátha krímīṇāṃ nákir úcchiṣ(y)ātai

The *algaṇḍus* I slay with the great weapon;
burnt (or) unburnt they have become sapless;
those left (or) not left I draw down by my spell,
that none of the worms be left.

Neither token is likely to be inherited; the synchronic function of the figure, to mark a totality, is primary and overt. The passage and the Atharvan worm-charms as a set are paradigmatic for the interplay of the diachronic and the synchronic in Indo-European poetics.

The charms examined hitherto have attested the basic dragon-slaying formula with the serpent transposed into a worm, real or figurative. The roster would be incomplete, though, without the predictable examples where the serpent of myth has become a real live snake.

AV 7.88 consists of a single metrically irregular strophe of 12 : 10 : 14 = 36 syllables, thus equal in length to the *bṛhatī* (8 : 8 : 12 : 8) which the tradition calls it. Its art lies in repetition with variation and in the syllable plays on *ahi* 'snake' leading up to and including the basic formula itself: (*ahi*) : *-ehi*, (*ahi*) : *ari-*, (*ahi*) : *asi*, *ahi-* : *-ehi*, ***ahi-*** : ***jahi***:

> ápehy árir asy árir vā́ asi
> viṣé viṣám apṛkthā viṣám íd vā́ apṛkthāḥ
> **ā́him** evā́bhyápehi táṃ **jahi**
>
> Go away, you are the enemy, you are indeed the enemy;
> in poison you have mixed poison, poison indeed you have mixed.
> Go straight away to the **snake**, **smite** him.

We find the same phrase applied to Indra and fully amplified in a spell of counter-magic against witchcraft: AV 8.5.15 *yás tvā kṛtyā́bhir* . . . ***jíghāṁsati*** / . . . *tvám indra táṃ* ***jahi*** *vájreṇa śatáparvaṇā* 'whoever wants to slay you with witchcraft,... slay him, o Indra, with the hundred-jointed cudgel'. For the reciprocal figure cf. chap. 31.

K. Hoffmann in a masterly philological analysis (1975:562-569) has recovered in the Paippālada Atharvaveda a hymn to the peripheral but ancient Vedic storm god *Parjanya*.[3] AVP 2.70 begins with subjectless verbs, only identifying the deity in verse 2:

> 1ab apādyaud apātatanad apaskandya **vadhed ahim**
> 2ab yat parjanya(s) stanayati sarvaṃ saṃvijate jagat
> 3cd **ahīṃs** tvaṃ vidyutā **jahi** māsmākam puruṣān **vadhīḥ**
>
> He has blitzed away, has thundered away (the snake); having made it jump aside, may he **smite** the **snake** . . . When Parjanya thunders, the whole living world quakes . . . **smite** the **snakes** with your lightning, **smite** not our men.

It is not excluded that *parJAnya* . . . *JAhi* is a 'secret' phonetic figure; and the name of the god may be etymologically 'strike, beat, smite', IE **per-*, extended **per-gʷ-* (Russ. *peru*, Armen. *harkanem* 'I beat').

In Iranian we can point to the formula in a list of atonements for certain ritual offenses in V. 14.5: *baēuuarə* ***ažinąm*** *udarō.θrąsanąm auua.****janiiāṯ***, *baēuuarə* ***ažinąm*** *spakanąm*[4] *kahrpunanąm auua.****janiiāṯ*** 'he shall kill 10,000 belly-crawling snakes, he shall kill 10,000 dog-snakes, lizards.'

---

3. Cognate with Lithuanian *Perkū́nas* and Slavic *Perunъ*, as well as with Greek κέραυνος 'thunderbolt'. For the tabu deformations in these divine names see Jakobson 1985:1-32. On Parjanya, note Puhvel 1987:55: 'He is an ancient variant of the [Storm God] type, shunted to the Vedic periphery by the ascendancy of Indra.'

4. Note the only Old Iranian attestation of the word *spaka* 'dog' known to Herodotus: 1.110.1 σπάκα τὴν κύνα καλέουσι οἱ Μῆδοι 'The Persians call the bitch *spaka*'.

The basic formula of the paean—'slain is X'—can be transformed into a variety of charms. The assimilation of the mythical serpent adversary to worm or snake is a natural homeopathy, and the technique remains a song in praise of the victory. But with other adversaries the formula may be pressed into the service of blame, satire, and invective. I cite as a final example the late Rigvedic, Atharvan-like hymn 10.155, said to be a charm to drive away a witch. Verse 4 would seem to be intended to ward off all malevolent creatures of either sex, marked both by antithetical grammatical gender marking and explicit pejorative sexual identification. The latter terms are both attested only here and later quoted passages:

> yád dha prā́cīr ájaganta
> úraḥ[5] maṇḍūradhānikīḥ
> **hatā́** índrasya śátravaḥ
> sárve budbudáyāśavaḥ
>
> If you all (fem.) have gone away,
> . . . you all of the rusty pubes,
> then **slain** are Indra's rivals (masc.),
> all those with the fizzy semen.

The mock-heroic is crude but effective. Pragmatically we are a long way from the basic Indo-European mythographic formula with which we started,

HERO SLAY (*g^{u}hen-*) ADVERSARY,

but its verbal instantiation is preserved unchanged. It is yet another illustration of the perseverance of the Indo-European Word.

5. The syntactic connection of *úraḥ* ('breast') in b in unclear, and I have omitted it in translation. Purely phonetically ***ura*** . . . -***ūra***- in b serves to parallel the reduplicated ***bud-bud***- in d.

Abbreviations

Academy Dic.	1983. Dictionary of the Irish Language. Dublin: Royal Irish Academy.
AiGr.	Wackernagel, Jacob, [Debrunner, A., Renou, L. and R. Hauschild]. 1896-1964. Altindische Grammatik. Göttingen: Vandenhoeck and Ruprecht.
ANET	Pritchard, James B., ed. 1955. Ancient Near Eastern Texts Relating to the Old Testament. Princeton: University Press.
Bartholomae, Air. Wb.	Bartholomae, Christian. 1904-6. Altiranisches Wörterbuch. Berlin: de Gruyter.
Bloomfield, Vedic Concordance	Bloomfield, Maurice. 1906. A Vedic Concordance. Cambridge: Harvard University Press.
Bosworth-Toller	Bosworth, J. and T.N. Toller. 1882[-1972]. An Anglo-Saxon Dictionary. Oxford: Clarendon Press.
Buck	Buck, Carl Darling. 1973. The Greek Dialects: Grammar, Selected Inscriptions, Glossary. Chicago/London: University of Chicago Press.
CEG	Hansen, Petrus Allanus. 1983. Carmina Epigraphica Graeca Saeculorum VIII-V A. Chr. N. Berlin: de Gruyter.
Chantraine, DELG	Chantraine, Pierre. 1968[-80]. Dictionnaire étymologique de la langue grecque. Paris: Klincksieck.
CHD	Güterbock, Hans G. and Harry A. Hoffner, eds. 1980- . The Hittite Dictionary of the Oriental Institute of the University of Chicago. Chicago: Oriental Institute.

CIH	Binchy, D.A. 1978. Corpus Iuris Hibernici. Dublin: Institute for Advanced Study.
CIL	1893- . Corpus inscriptionum Latinarum. Berlin: Reimer.
CTH	1971. Catalogue des textes hittites. Paris: Klincksieck. [Premier supplement in Revue Hittite et Asianique 30 (1972) 94-133.]
Debrunner, AiGr.	*see* AiGr.
EIL	Murphy, Gerard. 1956. Early Irish Lyrics. Oxford: Clarendon Press.
Ernout	Ernout, Alfred. 1966. Recueil de textes Latins archaïques. Paris: Klincksieck.
Ernout-Meillet, DEL	Ernout, Alfred and Antoine Meillet. 1959. Dictionnaire étymologique de la langue latine. 4th edition. Paris: Klincksieck.
EWA	Mayrhofer, Manfred. 1986- . Etymologisches Wörterbuch des Altindoarischen. Heidelberg: Winter.
Forcellini	Forcellini, Aegidius. 1965. Totius Latinitatis Lexicon. Padua: Gregoriana. [Reprint of the 1805 edition.]
Frisk, GEW	Frisk, Hjalmar. 1960-72. Griechisches etymologisches Wörterbuch. Heidelberg: Winter.
Geldner	Geldner, Karl Friedrich. 1951-57. Der Rig-Veda. Aus dem Sanskrit übersetzt und mit einem laufenden Kommentar versehen. (Harvard Oriental Series 33-6.) Cambridge: Harvard University Press.
Grassmann	Grassmann, Hermann. 1964. Wörterbuch zum Rig-Veda. Wiesbaden: Harrassowitz. [Reprint of the 1872 edition.]
Grimm, *Deutsche Mythologie*	Grimm, Jakob, with introduction by Leopold Kretzenbacher. 1968. Deutsche Mythologie. Graz: Akademische Druck- und Verlagsanstalt.

HAB	Sommer, Ferdinand and Adam Falkenstein. 1938. Die hethitisch-akkadische Bilingue des Hattušili I. (Bayerische Akademie der Wissenschaften, Phil.-hist. Abteilung, Abhandlung, Neue Folge 16) Munich: Bayerische Akad. der Wiss.
Hofmann, LEW	Walde, A. and J.B. Hofmann. 1938-56. Lateinisches etymologisches Wörterbuch. Heidelberg: Winter.
ICS	Masson, Olivier. 1983. Les inscriptions chypriotes syllabiques, 2nd. ed. Paris: Klincksieck.
IEG	West, M. L. 1971-2 [1992²]. Iambi et Elegi Graeci. Oxford: Clarendon Press.
IG	1873- . Inscriptiones Graecae. Berlin: de Gruyter.
ILLRP	Degrassi, Attilio. 1957-63. Inscriptiones latinae liberae rei publicae. Firenze: La Nuova Italia.
KBo	1916- . Keilschrifttexte aus Boghazköi. Berlin: Mann.
KEWA	Mayrhofer, Manfred. 1956-80. Kurzgefaßtes etymologisches Wörterbuch des Altindischen. A Concise Etymological Sanskrit Dictionary. Heidelberg: Winter.
Kretschmer, Vaseninschr.	Kretschmer, Paul. 1969. Die griechischen Vaseninschriften ihrer Sprache nach untersucht. Hildesheim: Olms.
KUB	1921- . Keilschrifturkunden aus Boghazköi. Berlin: Mann.
Laroche	Laroche, Emmanuel. 1960. Les hiéroglyphes hittites. Paris: Centre nationale de la recherche scientifique.
Lewis and Short	Lewis, Charlton T. and Charles Short. 1879. A Latin Dictionary. Oxford: Clarendon Press.
Liddell-Scott-Jones	*see* LSJ

LSJ	Liddell, Henry George and Robert Scott. 1968. A Greek-English Lexicon. Revised and augmented throughout by Sir Henry Stuart Jones with the assistance of Roderick McKenzie. Oxford: Clarendon Press.
Monier-Williams	Monier-Williams, Sir Monier. 1899. A Sanskrit-English Dictionary. Oxford: Oxford University Press.
OLD	Glare, P. W., ed. 1968-82. Oxford Latin Dictionary. Oxford: Clarendon Press.
PMG	Page, Denys L. 1962. Poetae melici Graeci. Oxford: Clarendon Press.
PMGF	Davies, Malcolm. 1991. Poetarum melicorum Graecorum fragmenta. Oxford: Clarendon Press.
Poetae Lat. Min.	Baehrens, Emil. 1910. Poetae Latini Minores. Leipzig: Teubner.
Pokorny, IEW	Pokorny, Julius. 1959. Indogermanisches etymologisches Wörterbuch. Bern: Francke.
Puhvel, HED	Puhvel, Jaan. 1984- . Hittite Etymological Dictionary. Berlin: de Gruyter.
Renou, EVP	Renou, Louis. 1955-69. Etudes védiques et pāṇinéennes. Paris: Institut de Civilisation Indienne.
RIA Dict.	*see* Academy Dic.
Schwyzer	Schwyzer, Eduard. 1960. Dialectorum Graecarum exempla epigraphica potiora. Hildesheim: Olms.
SEG	1923- . Supplementum Epigraphicum Graecum. Leyden: Sijthoff and Noordhoff.
SLG	Page, Denys, ed. 1976. Supplementum lyricis Graecis: poetarum Lyricorum Graecorum fragmenta quae recens innotuerunt. Oxford: Clarendon Press.

StBoT	Studien zu den Boğazköy-Texten. Wiesbaden: Harrassowitz.
Thompson, Motif-index	Thompson, Stith. 1977. Motif-index of folk literature. In The Folktale. Bloomington: Indiana University Press.
Tischler	Tischler, Johann. 1977- . Hethitisches etymologisches Glossar. Innsbruck: Innsbrucker Beiträge zur Sprachwissenschaft.
Turner, Comp. Dict.	Turner, R. L. 1969. A Comparative Dictionary of the Indo-Aryan Languages. London: Oxford University Press.
Vaillant, Gramm. comp.	Vaillant, André. 1950-1977. Grammaire comparée des langues slaves. Lyon: IAC.
VKG	Pedersen, Holger. 1909-13. Vergleichende Grammatik der keltischen Sprachen. Göttingen: Vandenhoeck und Ruprecht.
de Vries	de Vries, Jan. 1961. Altnordisches Etymologisches Wörterbuch. Leiden: Brill.
Wack.-Debr.	*see* AiGr.

References

Adams, Douglas Q. 1985. Latin *Mas* and *Masturbari*. Glotta 63.241-47.

Alexiou, Margaret. 1978. Modern Greek folklore and its relation to the past. The evolution of Charos in Greek tradition. (Byzantina kai Metabyzantina, 1). Malibu: Undena.

Alsdorf, Ludwig. 1974. Kleine Schriften. Wiesbaden: Steiner.

Anderson, J.G.C. 1938. Tacitus, Germania. Oxford: University Press.

Archi, Alfonso. 1979. Auguri per il Labarna. Studia Mediterranea Piero Meriggi Dicata, ed. by O. Carruba, 27-51. Pavia: Aurora.

Armstrong, John. 1985. A glossarial index of nouns and adjectives in IGT II-IV. Proceedings of the Harvard Celtic Colloquium 5.187-410.

Arnold, E.V. 1967. Vedic Metre. Delhi: Motilal Banarsidas. [Reprint of the 1905 edition.]

Athanassakes, Apostolos. 1988. Gods, heroes, and saints against the dragon. Ancient World 17.41-63.

Axelson, Bertil. 1945. Unpoetische Wörter. Ein Beitrag zur Kenntnis der lateinischen Dichtersprache. Lund: Gleerup.

Bader, Françoise. 1971. La racine **swer-* 'veiller sur' en grec. Bulletin de la Société de Linguistique 66.139-211.

——. 1976. Un nom indo-européen de l'homme chez Homère. Revue de Philologie 50.206-12.

——. 1984. Review of Priests, Warriors, and Cattle by B. Lincoln. Bulletin de la Société de Linguistique 79:2.96-108.

——. 1985. Review of Ricostruzione linguistica e ricostruzione culturale, ed. by Franco Crevatin. Bulletin de la Société de Linguistique 80:2.104-8.

——. 1986. Review of Scritti Riccardo Ambrosini. Bulletin de la Société de Linguistique 81:2.125-35.

——. 1989. La langue des dieux, ou l'hermétisme des poètes indo-européens. Pisa: Giardini.

——. 1990a. La langue des dieux. Hermétisme et autobiographie I-II. Les Etudes Classiques 58.3-26, 221-45.

——. 1990b. Le liage, la peausserie et les poètes-chanteurs Homère et Hésiode: la racine **seh₂-* 'lier'. Bulletin de la Société de Linguistique 85.1-59.

——. 1991. Autobiographie et héritage dans la langue des dieux: d'Homère à Hésiode et Pindare. Revue des Etudes Grecques 103.383-408; 104.330-345.

——. 1993. Le narcisse, les cigales, et les sirènes ou les difficultés de la communication. Pisa: Giardini.

Bailey, Sir Harold. 1952. Six Indo-Iranian notes. 4. *nadá-*. Transactions of the Philological Society, 61-62.

Baumbach, Lydia. 1979. The Mycenean Greek vocabulary II. Glotta 49.151-190.

Bechert, Johannes. 1964. βουφονέω. Münchener Studien zur Sprachwissenschaft 17.5-17.

Bechtel, Friedrich. 1917. Die historischen Personennamen des Griechischen bis zur Kaiserzeit. Halle: Niemeyer. [Reprinted Hildesheim 1964.]

Beckman, Gary. 1982. The Anatolian myth of Illuyanka. Journal of the Ancient Near Eastern Society 14.11-25.

——. 1983. Hittite Birth Rituals. Studien zu den Boğazköy-Texten 26. Wiesbaden: Harrassowitz.

——. 1990. The Hittite "Ritual of the Ox" (CTH 760.I.2-3). Orientalia 59.34-55.

Benveniste, Emile. 1945. Symbolisme social dans les cultes gréco-italiques. Revue de l'Histoire des Religions 129.5-16.

——. 1945. La doctrine médicale des Indo-Européens. Revue de l'Histoire des Religions 130.5-12.

——. 1948. Noms d'agent et noms d'action en indo-européen. Paris: Maisonneuve.

——. 1949. Don et échange dans le vocabulaire indo-européen. L'année sociologique, 3e série, 7-20.

——. 1966. Problèmes de linguistique générale [I]. Paris: Gallimard.

——. 1968. Phraséologie poétique de l'indo-iranien. Mélanges d'indianisme à la mémoire de Louis Renou, 73-79. Paris: Boccard.

——. 1969. Le vocabulaire des institutions indo-européennes. Paris: Minuit.

——. 1970. Les valeurs économiques dans le vocabulaire indo-européen. Indo-European and Indo-Europeans, ed. by G. Cardona et al., 307-20. Philadelphia: University of Pennsylvania Press.

—— and Louis Renou. 1934. Vṛtra et Vṛϑragna. Etude de mythologie indo-iranienne. Cahiers de la Société Asiatique 3. Paris: Imprimerie Nationale.

Berg, Nils. 1978. Parergon metricum: der Ursprung des griechischen Hexameters. Münchener Studien zur Sprachwissenschaft 37.11-36.

Bergin, Osborn. 1939. The native Irish grammarian. Rhys Lecture. Proceedings of the British Academy 24.205-34.

——. 1955. Irish Grammatical Tracts 5. Metrical faults. Ériu 17 Supplement, 259-93.

——. 1970. Irish Bardic Poetry (with a foreword by D. A. Binchy compiled and edited by David Greene and Fergus Kelly). Dublin: Institute for Advanced Study.

Bernabé, A. 1986. Hetitas y Aqueos. Aspectos recientes de una vieja polemica. Estudios clásicos 28(90).134-97.

——. 1988. Un mito etiológico sobre el Tauro (CTH 16) en Nonno (*Dion.* 1.408s.). Aula Orientalis 6.5-10.

Bernadete, Seth. 1959. Translation of the Persians. In The Complete Greek Tragedies, vol. 1: Aeschylus, ed. by David Grene and Richmond Lattimore. Chicago: University of Chicago Press.

Bierbaumer, P. 1976. Der botanische Wortschatz des Altenglischen. Grazer Beiträge zur englischen Philologie 2.127-28.

Biggs, Robert D. 1993. Descent of Ištar, line 104. Nouvelles Assyriologiques Brèves et Utilitaires 1993, 74.
Binchy, Daniel A. 1940. Críth Gablach. Dublin: Institute for Advanced Study.
——. 1952. The saga of Fergus mac Léti. Ériu 16.33-48.
——. 1955. *Bretha Nemed.* Ériu 17.4-6.
——. 1966. *Bretha Déin Chécht.* Ériu 20.22-48.
——. 1972. Varia Hibernica. 1. The so-called 'rhetorics' of Irish saga. Indo-Celtica. Gedächtnisschrift für Alf Sommerfelt, ed. by H. Pilch and J. Thurow, 29-38. München: Hueber.
Bloch, Raymond. 1981. Gli Etruschi e Roma. Atti dell'Incontro di Studio in Onore di Massimo Pallottino. Roma: Bretschneider.
Bond, G.W. 1981. Euripides, Heracles. Oxford: Oxford University Press.
van den Bosch, Lourens. 1985. The Āprī hymns of the Ṛgveda and their interpretation. Indo-Iranian Journal 28.95-122, 169-89.
Boyce, Mary. 1975-82. A History of Zoroastrianism, vols. I and II. Handbuch der Orientalistik, 1. Abt., 8. Bd., 1. Abschn., Lfg. 2, Heft 2A. Leiden: Brill.
Braswell, B.K. 1980. Three linguistic notes on Pindar. Glotta 58.205-22.
Braune, Wilhelm and Karl Helm. 1958. Althochdeutsches Lesebuch. 13th edition. Tübingen: Max Niemeyer.
Breatnach, Liam. 1981. The "Caldron of Poesy". Ériu 32.45-94.
——. 1984. Canon law and secular law in early Ireland: the significance of *Bretha Nemed.* Peritia 3.439-59.
——. 1986. The ecclesiastical element in the Old Irish legal tract *Cáin Fhuithirbe.* Peritia 5.36-52.
——. 1987. Uraicecht na Ríar. The Poetic Grades in Early Irish Law. Dublin: Institute for Advanced Study.
——. 1989a. An edition of *Amra Senáin.* Sages, Saints and Storytellers. Studies in honor of J. Carney, ed. by D. Ó Corráin, L. Breatnach, and K. McCone, 7-31. Maynooth: An Sagart.
——. 1989b. The first third of *Bretha Nemed Toísech.* Ériu 40.1-40.
——. 1991. Zur Frage der "Roscada" im Irischen. Metrik und Medienwechsel–Metrics and Media, ed. by H.F.C. Tristram, 197-206. Tübingen: Narr.
Bremmer, Jan. 1982. The suodales of Poplios Valesios. Zeitschrift für Papyrologie und Epigraphik 47.133-47.
—— and N. M. Horsfall. 1987. Roman Myth and Mythography. Bulletin of the Institute of Classical Studies Supplement 52.
Brereton, Joel. 1981. The Ṛgvedic Ādityas. American Oriental Series 63. New Haven: American Oriental Society.
Brind'Amour, Pierre. 1978. L'origine des jeux seculaires. Aufstieg und Niedergang der römischen Welt: Geschichte und Kultur Roms im Spiegel der neueren Forschung, vol. 2, 1334-1417. Berlin: de Gruyter.
Brown, W. Norman. 1972. Duty as Truth in Ancient India. Proceedings of the American Philosophical Society 116.252-68.
Bryce, Trevor R. 1988. Review of Troy and the Trojan War, ed. by Machteld J. Mellink. Bibliotheca Orientalis 45.668-80.

Buecheler, Franz. 1883. Umbrica. Bonn: Cohen.
Bundy, Elroy T. 1962. Studia Pindarica. Berkeley: University of California Press. [Reprinted 1986.]
Burkert, Walter. 1966. Greek Tragedy and Sacrificial Ritual. Greek, Roman and Byzantine Studies 7.87-121.
—. 1975. Apellai und Apollon. Rheinisches Museum 118.1-21.
—. 1979. Structure and History in Greek Mythology and Ritual. Berkeley: University of California Press.
—. 1983. Homo Necans. Translated by P. Bing. Berkeley: University of California Press.
—. 1985. Greek Religion. Cambridge: Harvard University Press.
—. 1987. Ancient Mystery Cults. Cambridge: Harvard University Press.
Burrow, Thomas. 1973. The Sanskrit language. New and revised edition. London: Faber and Faber.
Caland, W. 1904-13. The Baudhāyana Śrauta Sūtra. [Reprinted New Delhi 1982.]
—. 1928. Das Śrauta Sūtra des Āpastamba. [Reprinted Wiesbaden 1969.]
Calder, William M. 1963. The inscription from Temple G at Selinus. Greek, Roman and Byzantine Studies, Monograph 4.
— and J. Stern. 1970. Pindaros und Bakchylides. Darmstadt: Wissenschaftliche Buchgesellschaft.
Campanile, Enrico. 1977. Ricerche di cultura poetica indoeuropea. Pisa: Giardini.
—. 1986. 'Ανόστεος ὃν πόδα τένδει. o-o-pe-ro-si. Festschrift E. Risch, 355-62. Berlin: de Gruyter.
—. 1987. Indogermanische Dichtersprache. Studien zum indogermanischen Wortschatz, ed. by W. Meid, 21-28. Innsbruck: Innsbrucker Beiträge zur Sprachwissenschaft.
— (ed.). 1988. Alle origini di Roma. Atti del colloquio tenuto a Pisa il 18 e 19 settembre 1987. Pisa: Giardini.
—. 1990. La ricostruzione della cultura indoeuropea. Pisa: Giardini.
—. 1993. Reflexions sur la réconstruction de la phraséologie poétique indo-européenne. Diachronica 10.1-12.
Campbell, David A. 1991. Greek Lyric III. Cambridge: Harvard University Press.
Carey, Christopher. 1981. A Commentary on Five Odes of Pindar. New York: Arno.
Carey, John. 1988. Three notes. Celtica 20.123-29.
Carini, Maria Francesca. 1982. Il rituale di fundazione KUB XXIX 1. Ipotesi intorno alla nozione etea arcaica della regalità. Athenaeum 60.483-520.
Carney, James. 1955. Studies in Irish Literature and History. Dublin: Institute of Advanced Study.
—. 1964. The Poems of Blathmac. Dublin: Irish Texts Society.
—. 1971. Three Old Irish accentual poems. Ériu 22.23-80.
—. 1981. Linking alliteration ("fidrad freccomail"). Éigse 18.251-62.
Carruba, Onofrio. 1964 [1965]. Ahhijawa e altri nomi di popoli e paesi dell' Anatolia occidentale. Athenaeum N.S. 42.269-98.
—. 1966. Die Beschwörungsritual für die Göttin Wišuriyanza. Studien zu den Boğazköy- Texten 2. Wiesbaden: Harrassowitz.

—. 1969. Die Chronologie der heth. Texte. Zeitschrift der Deutschen Morgenländischen Gesellschaft. Supplementband 1.226-249.

—. 1972. Beiträge zum Palaischen. Istanbul: Nederlands Historisch-Archeologisch Instituut in het Nabije Oosten.

Chadwick, John and Lydia Baumbach. 1963. The Mycenaean Greek vocabulary. Glotta 41.157-271.

Chantraine, Pierre. 1929. Review of Parry 1928. Revue de Philologie 3.295-300.

—. 1949. Les verbes grecs signifiant 'tuer'. Die Sprache 1.143-49.

—. 1973. Grammaire homérique I. Phonétique et morphologie. 5e tirage. Paris: Klincksieck.

Clover, Carol and John Lindow. 1985. Old Norse-Icelandic Literature. A Critical Guide. Ithaca: Cornell University Press.

Cockayne, T.O. 1961. Leechdoms, Wortcunning and Starcraft of Early England. Reprinted with an introduction by G. Singer. London: Holland.

Colli, Giorgio. 1977. La sapienza greca. Milano: Rosenberg.

Considine, Patrick. 1966. Acta Classica 9.15-25.

Cowgill, Warren. 1960. Greek *ou* and Armenian *oč'*. Language 36.347-50.

—. 1980. The etymology of Irish *guidid* and the outcome of $*g^{w}h$ in Celtic. Lautgeschichte und Etymologie, ed. by M. Mayrhofer, M. Peters and O.E. Pfeiffer, 49-78. Wiesbaden: Reichert.

Dale, A.M. 1968. The Lyric Metres of Greek Drama^{2}. Cambridge: Cambridge University Press.

Darmesteter, James. 1877. Ormazd et Ahriman. Paris: Vieweg.

—. 1878. Iranica VI. Une métaphore grammaticale de la langue indo-européenne. Mémoire de la Société de Linguistique 3.319-21.

Dandekar, Ramchandra N. 1974. The two births of Vasiṣṭha. A fresh study of Rigveda 7.33.9-14. Antiquitates Indogermanicae. Gedenkschrift Hermann Güntert, ed. by M. Mayrhofer et al., 223-32. Innsbruck: Innsbrucker Beiträge zur Sprachwissenschaft.

d'Avezac, M. 1852. Ethicus et les ouvrages cosmographiques intitules de ce nom. Paris: Inpreimerie nationale.

Davies, Malcolm. 1991. Poetarum Melicorum Graecorum Fragmenta. Oxford: Oxford University Press.

Debrunner, Albert. 1917. Griechische Wortbildungslehre. Heidelberg: Winter.

De Lamberterie, Charles. 1978. Armeniaca I-VIII: études lexicales. Bulletin de la Société de Linguistique 73.243-85.

—. 1981. Mythe et langue en Arménie. La geste de Vahagn. Thèse, Paris.

Delbrück, Berthold. 1865. Zeitschrift für Völkerpsychologie und Sprachwissenschaft 3.266-99.

Denniston, J.D. 1966. The Greek Particles. Corrected reprint of the 2nd edition. Oxford: Clarendon Press.

— and Denys Page. 1957. Aeschylus: Agamemnon. Oxford: Clarendon Press.

Detienne, Marcel. 1973. Les maîtres de vérité dans la Grèce archaïque. 2e édition. Paris: Maspero.

—. 1986. L'Apollo meurtrier et les crimes de sang. Quaderni Urbinati di Cultura

Classica 22.7-27.
—— and Jean-Pierre Vernant. 1978. Les ruses de l'intelligence. 2nd edition. Paris: Gallimard.
Dhabhar, B.N. 1913. The Pahlavi Rivâyat accompanying the Dâdistân-î Dînîk. Bombay: K.R. Cama Oriental Institute.
Diakonoff, Igor M. 1985. Hurro-Urartean borrowings in Old Armenian. Journal of the American Oriental Society 105.597-603.
——. 1986. Hurro-Urartean as an Eastern Caucasian Language. München: Kitzinger.
Dillon, Myles. 1947. The Hindu Act of Truth in Celtic Tradition. Modern Philology 44.137-40.
Dobbie, Elliot van Kirk. 1942. The Anglo-Saxon Poetic Records VI: The Anglo-Saxon Minor Poems. New York: Columbia University Press.
Dover, Kenneth J. (ed.). 1980. Ancient Greek Literature. Oxford: Oxford University Press.
Dowsett, Charles. 1986. Little Satana's Wedding Breakfast. Armenian Studies in Memoriam Haïg Berbérian, ed. by D. Kouymjian. Lisbon: Calouste Gulbenkian Foundation.
Dressler, Wolfgang. 1968. Studien zur verbalen Pluralität. Österreichische Akademie der Wissenschaften, Phil.-hist. Klasse, Sitzungsberichte 259,1.
——. 1969. Eine textsyntaktische Regel der indogermanischen Wortstellung. Zeitschrift für Vergleichende Sprachforschung 83.1-25.
Dronke, Peter. 1994. Verse with prose from Petronius to Dante. The art and scope of the mixed form. Cambridge: Harvard University Press.
Duchesne-Guillemin, Jacques. 1937. Gr. ἱερός – Skr. *iṣirá-*. Mélanges E. Boisacq I, 333-38.
Dumézil, Georges. 1959a. Notes sur le bestiaire de l'Edda et du R̥gveda. Mélanges de linguistique et de philologie Ferdinand Mossé in memoriam, 104-12. Paris: Didier.
——. 1959b. Les dieux des Germains. Paris: Gallimard.
——. 1966. La religion romaine archaïque. Paris: Payot.
Dunkel, George. Forthcoming. The three malfunctions of the Dumézilian theory. Lecture, Haverford, 1991.
Durante, Marcello. 1958. Prosa ritmica, alliterazione e accento nelle lingue dell'Italia antica. Ricerche Linguistiche 4.61-98.
——. 1960. Ricerche sulla preistoria della lingua poetica greca. La terminologia relativa alla creazione poetica. Atti dell'Accademia Nazionale dei Lincei. Anno 358, Serie ottava. Rendiconti. Classe di Scienze morali, storiche e filologiche 15.231-49.
——. 1962. Ricerche sulla preistoria della lingua poetica greca. L'epiteto. Atti dell'Accademia Nazionale dei Lincei. Anno 359. Serie ottava. Rendiconti. Classe di Scienze morali, storiche e filologiche 17.25-43.
——. 1970. Studi sulla preistoria della tradizione poetica greca. Parte I. Incunabula Graeca 50. Roma: Ateneo.
——. 1976. Studi sulla preistorica della tradizione poetica greca. Parte II. Incunabula Graeca 64. Roma: Ateneo.

Durham, Edith. 1987. High Albania. Boston: Beacon. [Reprint of the 1909 edition.]
Edwards, Anthony T. 1988. ΚΛΕΟΣ ΑΦΘΙΤΟΝ and oral theory. Classical Quarterly 38.25-30.
Eggeling, J. 1882-1900. The Satapatha-brâhmana according to the text of the Mâdhyandina school. Oxford: Clarendon Press. [Reprinted Delhi 1978.]
Eichner, Heiner. 1973. Die Etymologie von heth. *meḫur*. Münchener Studien zur Sprachwissenschaft 31.53-107.
——. 1983. Etymologische Beiträge zum Lykischen der Trilingue vom Letoon bei Xanthos. Orientalia 52.48-66.
——. 1988-90 [1992]. Pikenische Pietas: Das Zeugnis des südpikenischen Cippus von Castignano; Ein Heldendenkmal der Sabiner mit trochäischem Epigramm eines pikenischen Plautus des fünften Jahrhunderts v. Chr.; Reklameiamben aus Roms Königszeit (Erster Teil). Die Sprache 34.195-238.
——. 1993. Probleme von Vers und Metrum in epichorischer Dichtung Altkleinasiens. Österreichische Akademie der Wissenschaften, Phil.-hist. Klasse, Denkschriften 238. Bd., 97-169.
Evans, Jonathan D. 1987. The Dragon. In Mythical and Fabulous Creatures. A Source Book and Research Guide, ed. by Malcolm South, 27-58. New York: Greenwood Press.
Falk, Harry. 1986. Bruderschaft und Würfelspiel. Freiburg: Hedwig Falk.
Feydit, Frédéric (tr.) 1964. David de Sassoun, Epopée en vers. Paris: Gallimard.
Fehling, Detlev. 1969. Die Wiederholungsfiguren und ihr Gebrauch bei den Griechen vor Gorgias. Berlin: de Gruyter.
Filliozat, Jean. 1975. La doctrine classique de la médecine indienne; ses orgines et ses parallèles grecs. 2nd edition. Paris: Ecole Française d'Extrême Orient.
Finkelberg, Margalit. 1986. Is ΚΛΕΟΣ ΑΦΘΙΤΟΝ a Homeric formula? Classical Quarterly 36.1-5.
Finnegan, Ruth. 1970. Oral Literature in Africa. Oxford: Clarendon Press.
——. 1977. Oral Poetry: Its Nature, Significance and Social Context. Cambridge: Cambridge University Press.
Floyd, Edwin D. 1980. ΚΛΕΟΣ ΑΦΘΙΤΟΝ: an Indo-European perspective on Early Greek. Glotta 58.133-57.
Foley, John Miles (ed.). 1981. Oral Traditional Literature. A Festschrift for Albert Bates Lord. Columbus: Slavica.
——. 1985. Oral-Formulaic Theory and Research: An Introduction and Annotated Bibliography. New York: Garland.
—— (ed.). 1986. Oral Tradition in Literature: Interpretation in Context. Columbia: University of Missouri Press.
—— (ed.). 1987. Comparative Research on Oral Traditions: A Memorial for Milman Parry. Columbus: Slavica.
——. 1988. The Theory of Oral Composition: History and Methodology. Bloomington: Indiana University Press.
Fontenrose, Joseph. 1980. Python. Berkeley: University of California Press. [Paperback reprint of 1959 edition.]
Forssman, Bernhard. 1965. περ' ἰγνύσι hy. Merc. 152. Zeitschrift für Vergleichende

Sprachforschung 79.28-31.
——. 1966. Untersuchungen zur Sprache Pindars. Wiesbaden: Harrassowitz.
Fox, Leonard. 1989. Kanuni i Lekë Dukagjinit. The Code of Lek Dukagjini. Albanian Text Collected and Arranged by Sh. Gjeçov. Translated by L. Fox. New York: Gjonlekaj.
Fraenkel, Eduard. 1925. Zum Texte römischer Juristen XXIV. Hermes 60.440-43. [Reprinted in Kleine Beiträge zur klassischen Philologie, 2. Bd., 442-45. Roma: Edizioni di Storia e Letteratura.]
Fraser, P.M. and E. Mathews. 1987. A Lexicon of Greek Personal Names. Oxford: Oxford University Press.
Gagé, Jean. 1932. Recherches sur les jeux séculaires. Revue des Etudes Latines 10.441-57.
Gamkrelidze, Tamaz V. and Vjačeslav V. Ivanov. 1984. Indoevropejskij Jazyk i Indoevropejcy. Tbilisi: Izdatel'stvo Tbilisskogo Universiteta.
Garbe, R. 1882-1902. The Śrauta Sūtra of Apastamba. [Reprinted New Delhi 1983.]
Garrett, Andrew and Leslie Kurke. Forthcoming. Pudenda Hethitica Harvardiana. Harvard Studies in Classical Philology 95.
Geib, R. 1975. Die Formel *áyus prá tṛ* im Ṛg-Veda. Indo-Iranian Journal 16.269-83.
Geldner, Karl F. 1886-95. Avesta, die heiligen Bücher der Parsen. Stuttgart: Kohlhammer.
Gercenberg [Hertzenberg], Leonid G. 1972. Morfologičeskaja struktura slova v drevnix indoiranskix jazykax. Leningrad: Nauka.
Gernet, Louis. 1982a. Anthropologie de la Grèce ancienne. Paris: Flammarion.
——. 1982b. Droit et pré-droit en grèce ancienne. Droit et institutions en grèce antique. Paris: Flammarion.
Gershevitch, Ilya. 1959. The Avestan Hymn to Mithra. Cambridge: Cambridge University Press.
——. 1969. Amber at Persepolis. Studia Classica et Orientalia A. Pagliaro Oblata II, 167-251. Roma: Herder.
Gerstein, M.R. 1974. Germanic *Warg:* the Outlaw as Werewolf. Myth in Indo-European Antiquity, ed. by G.J. Larson, 131-56. Berkeley: University of California Press.
Giacomelli, Gabriella. 1963. La lingua falisca. Firenze: Olschki.
Gildersleeve, Basil. 1885. Pindar. Olympian and Pythian Odes. New York: American Book Company.
Gimbutas, Marija. 1974. An archaeologist's view of PIE* in 1975. Journal of Indo-European Studies 2.289-307.
Gippert, Jost. 1986. Zur Metrik der Gathas. Die Sprache 32.257-75.
Goldhill, Simon. 1987. The great city Dionysia and civic ideology. Journal of Hellenic Studies 107.58-76.
——. 1990. Expanded version of Goldhill 1987 in Nothing to do with Dionysus? Athenian Drama in its Social Context, ed. by J.J. Winkler and F. Zeitlin, 97-129. Princeton: Princeton University Press.
Gordon, Edmund I. 1967. Hittite ^{D}KASKAL.KUR. Journal of Cuneiform Studies 21.70-88.

Gordon, E.V. 1949. An Introduction to Old Norse. Oxford: Oxford University Press. [Reprint of 1927 edition.]
Götze, Albrecht. 1929. Die Pestgebete des Muršiliš. Kleinasiatische Forschungen 1.161-251.
Gray, Elizabeth (ed.). 1982. Cath Maige Tuired, The Second Battle of Mag Tuired. Dublin: Irish Texts Society.
Greene, David. 1977. Archaic Irish. Indogermanisch und Keltisch, ed. by R. Ködderitsch and K.H. Schmidt, 11-33. Wiesbaden: Harrassowitz.
Greene, David and Frank O'Connor. 1967. A Golden Treasury of Irish poetry A.D. 600-1200. London: Macmillan.
Greppin, John. 1991. Some effects of the Hurro-Urartean people and their languages upon the earliest Armenians. Journal of the American Oriental Society 111.720-30.
Güntert, Hermann. 1914. Über die ahurischen und daēvischen Ausdrücke im Avesta. Sitzungsberichte der Heidelberger Akademie der Wissenschaften, Bd. 5, Nr. 11.
——. 1921. Von der Sprache der Götter und Geister. Halle: Niemeyer.
Gurney, Oliver. 1979. The symbolism of "9" in Babylonian and Hittite literature. Journal of the Department of English (University of Calcutta) 14.27-31.
Gusmani, Roberto. 1986. Lydisches Wörterbuch. 3. Ergänzungsheft. Heidelberg: Winter.
Güterbock, Hans Gustav. 1952. The Song of Ullikummi. Revised text of the Hittite version of a Hurrian myth. New Haven: American Schools of Oriental Research. [=Journal of Cuneiform Studies 5.135-161, 6.8-42.]
——. 1956. Notes on Luvian Studies. Orientalia 25.113-40.
——. 1964. A view of Hittite literature. Journal of the American Oriental Society 84.107-14.
——. 1986. Troy in Hittite texts? Wilusa, Ahhiyawa, and Hittite history. Troy and the Trojan War, ed. by Machteld J. Mellink, 33-44. Bryn Mawr: University Press.
Hainsworth, Bryan. 1993. The Iliad: A Commentary. Vol. 3. General editor G.S. Kirk. Cambridge: Cambridge University Press.
——, [J.B.]. 1968. The Flexibility of the Homeric Formula. Oxford: Oxford University Press.
Hajnal, Ivo. 1994. Studien zum mykenischen Kasussystem. Berlin: de Gruyter. [1992 Diss. Zürich.]
Haldane, J.A. 1963. A paean in the Philoctetes. Classical Quarterly 13.53-56.
Hale, Mark. 1987. Notes on Wackernagel's law in the language of the Rigveda. Studies in Memory of Warren Cowgill (1929-1985), ed. by C. Watkins, 38-50. Berlin: de Gruyter.
——. Forthcoming. Wackernagel's Law. Phonological and syntactic factors determining clitic distribution in the language of the Rigveda. Cambridge: Cambridge University Press.
Hallett, Judith. 1976. Masturbator, Mascarpio. Glotta 54.292-307.
Hamilton, J.N. 1970. Phonetic texts of the Irish of North Mayo. Zeitschrift für Celtische Philologie 31.125-60.

Hamp, Eric P. 1961. Albanian *be, besë*. Zeitschrift für Vergleichende Sprachforschung 77.252-53.

—. 1985. An archaic poetic statement. Živa Antika 35.85-86.

Handley, Eric P. 1988. Hidden verses. Vir Bonus Discendi Peritus (BICS Supplement 51), 166-74. London: University of London Press.

Hansen, Peter H. 1983. Carmina Epigraphica Graeca. Berlin: de Gruyter.

Harris, Joseph. 1985. Die altenglische Heldendichtung. Neues Handbuch der Literaturwissenschaft, Bd. 6. Europäisches Frühmittelalter, ed. by K. von See, 238-46. Wiesbaden: Aula.

Haslam, Michael. 1978. The versification of the new Stesichorus (P.Lille 76abc). Greek, Roman and Byzantine Studies 19.29-58.

Hasluck, Margaret. 1954. The Unwritten Law in Albania. Cambridge: Cambridge University Press.

Haudry, Jean. 1985. Les Indo-Européens. 2nd edition. Paris: Presses Universitaires de France.

Henrichs, Albert. 1993. "Why should I dance?": ritual self-referentiality in the choral odes of Greek tragedy. unpublished ms.

Herren, Michael. 1991. Hibernolateinische und irische Verskunst mit besonderer Berücksichtigung des Siebensilblers. Metrik und Medienwechsel–Metrics and Media, ed. by H.F.C. Tristram, 173-188. Tübingen: Narr.

Heubeck, Alfred. 1955. Mythologische Vorstellungen des alten Orients im archaischen Griechentum. Gymnasium 508-25.

—. 1957. Weitere Bemerkungen zu den griechischen Personennamen auf den Linear-B-Tafeln. Beiträge zur Namenforschung 8.275-85.

—, Stephanie West and J.B. Hainsworth. 1988. A Commentary on Homer's Odyssey. Oxford: Clarendon Press.

Hiersche, Rolf. 1966. Zur Sappho 2.9 D^2. κὰμ μὲν γλῶσσα ἔαγε 'die Zunge ist gebrochen'. Glotta 44.1-5.

Hillebrandt, A. 1927-29. Vedische Mythologie. 2nd edition. 2 vols. Breslau. [Reprinted Hildesheim 1965.]

Hoffmann, Karl. 1967. Der Injunktiv im Veda. Heidelberg: Winter.

—. 1975. Aufsätze zur Indoiranistik. Wiesbaden: Reichert.

—. 1992. Aufsätze zur Indoiranistik. Bd. 3. Wiesbaden: Reichert.

Hoffner, Harry A., Jr. 1968. A Hittite epic about merchants. Journal of Cuneiform Studies 22.34-45.

—. 1988a. The Song of Silver. Documentum Asiae Minoris Antiquae, ed. by E. Neu and C. Werner, 143-66. Wiesbaden: Harrassowitz.

—. 1988b. A scene in the Realm of the Dead. A Scientific Humanist: Studies in Memory of Abraham Sachs, ed. by E. Leichty, M. D. Ellis, and P. Gerardi, 191-99. Philadelphia: University Museum.

—. 1990. Hittite Myths, tr. by H.A. Hoffner, ed. by G. Beckman. Society of Biblical Literature. Writings from the Ancient World, ed. by Burke O. Long. Atlanta: Scholars Press.

Hope Simpson, R. and J.F. Lazenby. 1970. The Catalogue of Ships in Homer's Iliad. Oxford: Oxford University Press.

van den Hout, Theo P.J. 1991. A Tale of Tiššaruli(ya): A Dramatic Interlude in the Hittite KI.LAM Festival. Journal of Near Eastern Studies 50.193-202.
Huld, Martin E. 1984. Basic Albanian Etymologies. Columbus: Slavica.
Humbach, Helmut. 1959. Aussage plus negierte Gegenaussage. Münchener Studien zur Sprachwissenschaft 14.23-33.
—, P.O. Skjærvø and J. Elfenbein. 1991. The Gāthās of Zarathushtra and the Other Old Avestan Texts. Heidelberg: Winter.
Hutter, Manfred. 1988. Behexung, Entsühnung und Heilung: Das Ritual der Tunnawiya für ein Königspaar aus mittelhethitischer Zeit (KBo XXI 1–KUB IX 34–KBo XXI 6). Orbus Biblicus et Orientalis 82. Freiburg/Schweiz: Universitätsverlag/Göttingen: Vandenhoeck & Ruprecht.
Huxley, George. 1960. Achaeans and Hittites. Oxford: Blackwell.
Insler, Stanley. 1967. Studies about the Sanskrit root *ar/r̥*. Indogermanische Forschungen 72.251-58.
—. 1975. The Gāthās of Zarathustra. Leiden-Teheran-Liège: Brill.
Ivanov, Vjačeslav V. and Vladimir N. Toporov. 1965. Slavjanskie jazykovye modelirujuščie semiotičeskie sistemy. Moskva: Nauka.
—. 1970. Le mythe indo-européen du dieu de l'orage poursuivant le serpent: réconstruction du schéma. Echanges et communications. Mélanges C. Lévi-Strauss. Paris-The Hague: Mouton.
—. 1974. Issledovanija v oblasti slavjanskix drevnostej. Moskva: Nauka.
Jakobson, Roman. 1952. Studies in Comparative Slavic Metrics. Oxford Slavonic Papers 3.21-66. [Reprinted in Jakobson's Selected Writings IV, 414-63. The Hague: Mouton.]
—. 1971. Selected Writings II: Word and Language. The Hague: Mouton.
—. 1979. Selected Writings V. The Hague: Mouton.
—. 1985. Selected Writings VII: Contributions to Comparative Mythology. The Hague: Mouton.
—. 1987. Language in Literature. Cambridge: Harvard University Press.
Jamison, Stephanie. 1979a. The case of the agent in Indo-European. Die Sprache 15.129-43.
—. 1979b. Remarks on the expression of agency with the passive in Vedic and Indo-European. Zeitschrift für Vergleichende Sprachforschung 93.196-219.
—. 1982. 'Sleep' in Vedic and Indo-European. Zeitschrift für Vergleichende Sprachforschung 96.6-16.
—. 1986. Brāhmaṇa syllable counting, Vedic *tvác* 'skin', and the Sanskrit expression for the canonical creature. Indo-Iranian Journal 29.161-81.
—. 1988. The quantity of the outcome of vocalized laryngeals in Indic. Die Laryngaltheorie, ed. by A. Bammesberger, 213-26. Heidelberg: Winter.
—. 1991. The Ravenous Hyenas and the Wounded Sun. Myth and Ritual in Ancient India. Ithaca: Cornell University Press.
—. 1994. Draupadī on the walls of Troy: *Iliad* 3 from an Indic perspective. Classical Antiquity 13.5-16.
—. Forthcoming. Sacrificed Wife/Sacrificer's Wife. Women, ritual, and hospitality in ancient India. Oxford: Oxford University Press.

Janko, Richard. 1984. Forgetfulness in the golden tablets of Memory. Classical Quarterly 34.89-100.

——. 1992. The Iliad: A Commentary. Vol. 4. General editor G.S. Kirk. Cambridge: Cambridge University Press.

Jasanoff, Jay H. 1978. Stative and Middle in Indo-European. Innsbruck: Innsbrucker Beiträge zur Sprachwissenschaft.

Jeffery, Lillian H. 1990. The Local Scripts of Archaic Greece. Revised edition, with a supplement by A.W. Johnston. Oxford: Clarendon Press.

—— and A. Morpurgo Davies. 1970. ΠΟΙΝΙΚΑΣΤΑΣ and ΠΟΙΝΙΚΑΖΕΝ. Kadmos 9.118-54.

Jonsson, Lars. 1993. Birds of Europe. Princeton: Princeton University Press.

Joseph, Lionel S. and Jared S. Klein. 1981. A new restoration in the Faliscan Ceres-inscription, with notes on Latin *molere* and its Italic cognates. Harvard Studies in Classical Philology 85.293-300.

Kammenhuber, Annelies. 1964-65. Die hethitische Vorstellung von Seele und Leib. Zeitschrift für Assyriologie NF 22.150-212, 23.177-223.

Kassel, Rudolf. 1981. Dichterspiele. Zeitschrift für Papyrologie und Epigraphik 42.11-20.

Katz, Joshua T. 1994. Αὐτάρ, ἀτάρ, and the meaning of the particle ταρ. Ms., to appear.

Keith, A.B. 1914. The Veda of the Black Yajus School, entitled Taittiriya sanhita. (Harvard Oriental Series 18-19.) Cambridge: Harvard University Press. [Reprinted Delhi 1967.]

——. 1920. Rigveda Brahmanas: the Aitareya and Kauṣītaki Brāhmaṇas of the Rigveda. Harvard Oriental Series 25. Cambridge: Harvard University Press.

Kellens, Jean. 1974. Les noms-racines de l'Avesta. Wiesbaden: Reichert.

——. 1984. Le verbe avestique. Wiesbaden: Reichert.

——. 1991a. Zoroastre et l'Avesta ancien. Travaux de l'Institut d'Etudes Iraniennes de l'Université de la Sorbonne Nouvelle, 14. Louvain-Paris: Peeters.

——. 1991b. L'avestique de 1972 à 1990. Kratylos 36.1-31.

——, and Eric Pirart. 1988-91. Les textes vieil-avestiques I-III. Wiesbaden: Reichert.

Kellerman, Galina. 1978. The King and the Sun-God in the Old Hittite Period. Tel Aviv 5.199-207.

Kelly, Fergus. 1973. A poem in praise of Columb Cille. Ériu 24.1-34.

——. 1975. Tiughraind Bhécáin. Ériu 26.66-98.

——. 1976. Audacht Morainn. Dublin: Institute for Advanced Study.

——. 1986. An Old Irish text on court procedure. Peritia 5.74-106.

Kiparsky, Paul. 1976. Oral poetry: some linguistic and typological considerations. In Stolz-Shannon 1976, 73-106.

Kirk, G.S. 1985. The Iliad: A Commentary. Vol. 1. General editor G.S. Kirk. Cambridge: Cambridge University Press.

Klaeber, Fredrick. 1950. Beowulf. 3rd edition. Lexington: Heath.

Klingenschmitt, Gert. 1982. Das altarmenische Verbum. Wiesbaden: Reichert.

Krapp, George P. and Elliot van Kirk Dobbie. 1936. The Anglo-Saxon Poetic Records III: The Exeter Book. New York: Columbia University Press.

Krause, Wolfgang. 1929. Die Kelten. Tübingen: Mohr.
—. 1930. Die Kenning als typische Stilfigur der germanischen und keltischen Dichtersprache. Halle (Saale): Niemeyer.
— and Werner Thomas. 1960-64. Tocharisches Elementarbuch. Heidelberg: Winter.
Kuhn, Adalbert. 1853a. Ueber das alte *s* und einige damit verbundene lautentwicklungen. Zeitschrift für Vergleichende Sprachforschung 2.260-75.
—. 1853b. Ueber die durch nasale erweiterte verbalstämme. Zeitschrift für Vergleichende Sprachforschung 2.455-71.
—. 1864. Indische und germanische sagensprüche. Zeitschrift für Vergleichende Sprachforschung 13.49-74, 113-17.
Kurke, Leslie. 1989. Pouring prayers: a formula of IE sacral poetry? Journal of Indo-European Studies 17.113-25.
Lamerre, W. 1985. L'ode au Sommeil. Antiquité Classique 54.158-79.
Laroche, Emmanuel. 1959. Dictionnaire de la langue louvite. Paris: Maisonneuve.
—. 1975. Reviews of KUB 44-46 and KBo 22. Revue Hittite et Asianique 33.63-71.
Latacz, Joachim. 1979. Homer: Tradition und Neuerung. Darmstadt: Wissenschaftliche Buchgesellschaft.
Latte, Kurt. 1960. Römische Religionsgeschichte. München: Beck.
Lattimore, Richmond. 1951. The Iliad of Homer. Chicago: University of Chicago Press.
—. 1960. Greek Lyrics. 2nd edition. Chicago: University of Chicago Press.
Lazard, Gilbert. 1984. La métrique de l'Avesta. Orientalia (Acta Iranica, 9), 285-300. Leiden: Brill.
Lazzeroni, Ricardo. 1971. Su alcuni deverbali greci e sanscriti. Studi e Saggi di Linguistica 11.40-50.
—. 1988. Sopravvivenze latine di ideologia indoeuropea. In Campanile (ed.) 1988, 17-26.
Lehmann, Winfred P. 1986. A Gothic Etymological Dictionary. Leiden: Brill.
— and Helen-Jo Jakusz Hewitt (eds.) 1991. Language Typology 1988. Typological Models in Reconstruction. Amsterdam: Benjamins.
Lejeune, Michel. 1953. A propos de trois inscriptions italiques. Revue des Etudes Anciennes 54.340-42.
—. 1972. Phonétique du grec ancien et du mycénien. Paris: Klincksieck.
—. 1974. Manuel de la langue venète. Heidelberg: Winter.
Leo, Friedrich. 1913. Geschichte der römischen Literatur. Berlin: Weidmann.
Lerza, Paola. 1982. Stesicoro. Genova: Melangolo.
Leskien, August. 1891. Die Bildung der Nomina im Litauischen. Königliche Sächsische Gesellschaft der Wissenschaften Leipzig, Phil.-hist. Klasse, Abhandlungen 12.151-618.
Lesky, Albin. 1950. Hethitische Texte und griechischer Mythos. Anzeiger der Österreichischen Akademie der Wissenschaften, 237-60. [Reprinted in Lesky's Gesammelte Schriften, 356-71.]
—. 1963. Geschichte der griechischen Literatur. Bern: Franke.

Leumann, Manu. 1950. Homerische Wörter. Basel: Reinhardt.
Lévi, Sylvain. 1890. Le théatre indien. Paris: Emile Bouillon.
——. 1898. La doctrine du sacrifice dans les Brāhmaṇas. Paris: Presses Universitaires de France. [Reprinted 1966.]
Levin, Beth and Malka Rappaport. 1988. Nonevent *-er* nominals: a probe into argument structure. Linguistics 26.1067-83.
Littleton, C. Scott. 1982. The New Comparative Mythology. 3rd edition. Berkeley: University of California Press.
Lloyd-Jones, Hugh. 1959. The end of the *Seven against Thebes*. Classical Quarterly N.S. 9.80-115.
——. 1985. Pindar and the after-life. Fondation Hardt. Entretiens 31.245-83. Geneva: Vandœuvres.
Lommel, Hermann. 1927. Die Yäšt's des Awesta. Göttingen-Leipzig: Vandenhoeck & Ruprecht.
Lord, Albert Bates. 1960. The Singer of Tales. Cambridge: Harvard University Press.
——. 1991. Epic Song and Oral Tradition. Ithaca: Cornell University Press.
Lüders, Heinrich. 1951-59. Varuṇa I-II. Göttingen: Vandenhoeck & Ruprecht.
Lühr, Rosemarie. 1982. Studien zur Sprache des Hildebrandliedes. Regensburger Beiträge zur deutschen Sprach- und Literaturwissenschaft 22. Frankfurt-am-Main: Lang.
Luppe, W. 1989. Zu den neuen Goldblättern aus Thessalien. Zeitschrift für Papyrologie und Epigraphik 76.13-14.
MacCana, Proinsias. 1970. Celtic Mythology. London: Hamlyn.
MacDowell, D.M. 1978. The Law in Classical Athens. Ithaca: Cornell University Press.
Malul, Meir. 1993. Eating and drinking (one's) refuse. Nouvelles Assyriologiques Brèves et Utilitaires 1993, 99.
Marazzi, Massimiliano. 1982. "Costruiamo la reggia, 'fondiamo' la regalità": note intorno ad un rituale antico-ittita (CTH 414). Vicino Oriente 5.117-69.
Marinetti, Anna. 1985. Le iscrizioni sudpicene. I. Testi. Florence: Olschki.
Marquardt, J. 1938. Die altenglische Kenning. Schriften der Königsberger Gelehrten Gesellschaft.
Martinet, André. 1972. Des labio-vélares aux labiales dans les dialectes indo-européens. Indo-Celtica. Gedächtnisschrift A. Sommerfelt, ed. by H. Pilch, 89-93. München: Hueber.
Mauss, M. 1924. Essai sur le don. Année Sociologique, Nouvelle Série I.
Mayrhofer, Manfred. 1966. Die Indo-Arier im Alten Vorderasien. Wiesbaden: Harrassowitz.
——. 1974. Die Arier im Vorderen Orient - ein Mythos? Sitzungsberichte der Österreichischer Akademie der Wissenschaften 294,3.
Mazon, Paul. 1931-68. Eschyle (Budé). Paris: Belles Lettres.
McCone, Kim. 1986. Hund, Wolf und Krieger bei den Indogermanen. Studien zum indogermanischen Wortschatz, ed. by W. Meid, 265-70. Innsbruck: Innsbrucker Beiträge zur Sprachwissenschaft.
——. 1990. Pagan past and Christian present. Maynooth: An Sagart.

McManus, Damian. 1983. A chronology of the Latin loan-words in Early Irish. Ériu 34.21-72.
—. 1988. Irish letter names and their kennings. Ériu 39.127-68.
—. 1991. A Guide to Ogam. Maynooth Monographs 4. Maynooth: An Sagart.
Meid, Wolfgang. 1978. Dichter und Dichterkunst in indogermanischer Zeit. Innsbruck: Innsbrucker Beiträge zur Sprachwissenschaft, Vorträge.
—. 1984. Bemerkungen zum indogermanischen Wortschatz des Germanischen. Das Germanische und die Rekonstruktion der indogermanischen Grundsprache, ed. by J. Untermann and B. Brogyanyi, 91-112. Amsterdam: Benjamins.
Meillet, Antoine. 1897. De la partie commune des pādas de 11 et 12 syllabes dans le maṇḍala III du Ṛgveda. Journal Asiatique, 9e série, 10.266-300.
—. 1923. Les origines indo-européennes des mètres grecs. Paris: Presses Universitaires de France.
—. 1925. La méthode comparative en linguistique historique. Paris: Champion. [Reprinted 1954.]
—. 1926. Gr. οἰστός. Festschrift für P. Kretschmer. Beiträge zur griechischen und lateinischen Sprachforschung, 140-1. Vienna: Verlag für Jugend und Volk.
—. 1929. Review of Milman Parry 1928a and b. Bulletin de la Société de Linguistique 29.100-2.
—. 1937. Introduction à l'étude comparative des langues indo-européennes. 8th edition. Paris: Hachette.
—. 1948. Aperçu d'une histoire de la langue grecque. 6th ed. Paris: Hachette.
Meiser, Gerhard. 1986. Lautgeschichte der umbrischen Sprache. Innsbruck: Innsbrucker Beiträge zur Sprachwissenschaft.
Meister, Karl. 1921. Die homerische Kunstsprache. Leipzig: Preisschriften der Jablonowskischen Gesellschaft, 48.
Melchert, H. Craig. 1977. Ablative and Instrumental in Hittite. Harvard dissertation.
—. 1979. Three Hittite etymologies. Zeitschrift für Vergleichende Sprachforschung 93.262-71.
—. 1984a. Studies in Hittite Historical Phonology. Zeitschrift für Vergleichende Sprachforschung Beiheft. Göttingen: Vandenhoeck & Ruprecht.
—. 1984b. Notes on Palaic. Zeitschrift für Vergleichende Sprachforschung 97.23-43.
—. 1988. Word-final *-r* in Hittite. A Linguistic Happening in Memory of Ben Schwarz, ed. by Yoël L. Arbeitman, 215-34. Louvain-la-Neuve: Peeters.
—. 1993a. Lycian Lexicon. 2nd edition. Chapel Hill.
—. 1993b. Cuneiform Luvian Lexicon. Chapel Hill.
Merkelbach, Reinhold. 1961. Aeneas in Cumae. Museum Helveticum 18.83-99.
—. 1989. Zwei neue orphisch-dionysische Totenpässe. Zeitschrift für Papyrologie und Epigraphik 76.15-6.
Meroney, Howard. 1944. The nine herbs. Modern Language Notes 59.157-60.
—. 1945. Irish in the Old English Charms. Speculum 20.172-82.
von Mess, A. 1901. Der Typhonmythus bei Pindar und Aeschylus. Rheinisches Museum 56.167-74.
Mikasa, H.R.H. Takahito (ed.). 1988. Essays on Anatolian Studies in the second

millennium B.C. Bulletin of the Middle Eastern Culture Center in Japan 3.
Momigliano, Arnaldo. 1963. An interim report on the origins of Rome. Journal of Roman Studies 53.95-121.
Morandi, A. 1982. Epigrafia Italica. Roma: Ateneo.
Moreschini, Adriana Quattordio. 1985. 'Αργεϊφόντης: proposta di interpretazione. Scritti in onore di Riccardo Ambrosini, 183-92. Pisa: Giardini.
Morpurgo Davies, Anna. 1987. 'To put' and 'to stand' in the Luvian languages. Studies in Memory of Warren Cowgill (1929-1985), ed. by C. Watkins, 205-28. Berlin: de Gruyter.
—. 1988a. Meillet, Greek and the Aperçu. Antoine Meillet et la linguistique de son temps (Histoire, épistémologie, langage, tome 10, fascicule II), 237-52.
—. 1988b. Mycenean and Greek Language. Linear B: A 1984 Survey (Bibliothèque des Cahiers de l'Institut de Linguistique de Louvain, 26), 75-125. Louvain-la-Neuve: Peeters.
Motta, Filippo. 1985. Un frammento di Filarco relativo ai Galati. Scritti in onore di Riccardo Ambrosini, 147-57. Pisa: Giardini.
Much, Rudolf. 1959. Die Germania des Tacitus. Heidelberg: Winter.
Murphy, Gerard (ed.). 1926. Duanaire Finn I-II. Dublin: Irish Texts Society.
—. 1952. *Baile Chuind* and the date of Cín Dromma Snechta. Ériu 16.145-51.
— (ed.). 1953. Duanaire Finn III. Dublin: Irish Texts Society.
—. 1961. Early Irish Metrics. Oxford: Oxford University Press.
Nagy, Gregory. 1974. Comparative Studies in Greek and Indic Meter. Cambridge: Harvard University Press.
—. 1979. The Best of the Achaeans. Concepts of the Hero in Archaic Greek Society. Baltimore: Johns Hopkins University Press.
—. 1990a. Pindar's Homer. Baltimore: Johns Hopkins University Press.
—. 1990b. Greek Mythology and Poetics. Ithaca: Cornell University Press.
Nagy, Joseph Falaky. 1985. The Wisdom of the Outlaw. Berkeley: University of California Press.
Narten, Johanna. 1960. Das vedische Verbum *math*. Indo-Iranian Journal 4.121-35.
—. 1982. Die Aməṣ̌a Spəṇtas im Avesta. Wiesbaden: Harrassowitz.
—. 1986. Der Yasna Haptaŋhāiti. Wiesbaden: Reichert.
Neu, Erich. 1974. Der Anitta-Text. Studien zu den Boğazköy-Texten 18. Wiesbaden: Harrassowitz.
—. 1980a. Die hethitischen Verben des Kaufens und Verkaufens. Die Welt des Orients 11.76-89.
—. 1980b. Althethitische Texte in Umschrift. Studien zu den Boğazköy-Texten 25. Wiesbaden: Harrassowitz.
—. 1988. Varia Hurritica. Sprachliche Beobachtungen an der hurr.-heth. Bilingue aus Hattuša. Documentum Asiae Minoris Antiquae, Festschrift H. Otten, 235-254. Wiesbaden: Harrassowitz.
— and Heinrich Otten. 1972. Hethitisch "Mann", "Mannheit". Indogermanische Forschungen 77.181-90.
Neumann, Günter. 1979. Τέλφουσα. Zeitschrift für Vergleichende Sprachforschung 93.85-89.

Neve, Peter and Heinrich Otten. 1939. Ausgrabungen in Boğazköy-Hattuša 1988. Deutsches Archäologisches Institut, Archäologischer Anzeiger 3.271-337.
Norden, Eduard. 1939. Aus altrömischen Priesterbüchern. Lund: Gleerup.
——. 1958. Die antike Kunstprosa. Darmstadt: Wissenschaftliche Buchgesellschaft. [Reprint of the 1898 edition.]
——. 1966. Agnostos Theos. Darmstadt: Wissenschaftliche Buchgesellschaft. [Reprint of the 1913 eidtion.]
Nyberg, H.S. 1933. La légende de Keresāspa. Oriental Studies in honour of C.E. Pavry. Oxford: Oxford University Press.
——. 1964-74. Manual of Pahlavi. Wiesbaden: Harrassowitz.
Obbink, Dirk. 1992. Poetry and performance in the Orphic gold leaves. Paper presented to the American Philological Association, New Orleans, 29 December 1992.
Oertel, Hanns. 1898. Contributions from the Jaiminīya-Brāhmaṇa to the history of the Brāhmaṇa literature. Indrasya kilbiṣāni. Journal of the American Oriental Society 19.118-25.
——. 1937. Zur altindischen Ausdrucksverstärkung satyasya satyam. Sitzungsberichte der Bayerischen Akademie der Wissenschaften, Phil.-hist. Klasse, Abhandlungen 5.
Oettinger, Norbert. 1976. Die Militärischen Eide der Hethiter. Studien zu den Boğazköy-Texten 22. Wiesbaden: Harrassowitz.
——. 1979. Die Stammbildung des hethitischen Verbums. Nürnberg: Carl.
——. 1982. Reste von *e*-Hochstufe im Formans hethitischer *n*-Stämme einschließlich des '*umma*' Suffixes. Investigationes Philologicae et Comparativae. Gedenkschrift für H. Kronasser, ed. by E. Neu, 162-77. Wiesbaden: Harrassowitz.
O'Flaherty, Wendy Doniger. 1980. Women, Androgynes, and Other Mythical Beasts. Chicago: University of Chicago Press.
Ó hAodha, Donnchadh. 1981. The Middle Irish version of Statius' Achilleid. Proceedings of the Royal Irish Academy 79 C 4.
——. 1991. The first Middle Irish Metrical Tract. Metrik und Medienwechsel–Metrics and Media, ed. by H.F.C. Tristram. Tübingen: Narr.
Oldenberg, Hermann. 1917. Die Religion des Veda. Stuttgart: Magnus.
Oliver, Lisi. 1995. The Language of the Early English Laws. Harvard dissertation.
O'Meara, John J. 1949. Giraldus Cambrensis. The First Recension of the Topographia Hiberniae. Proceedings of the Royal Irish Academy 52 C 4.
——. 1982. Giraldus Cambrensis. The History and Topography of Ireland. Dublin: Dolmen/Humanities Press.
Opland, Jeff. 1983. Xhosa Oral Poetry: Aspects of a Black South African Tradition. Cambridge: Cambridge University Press.
O'Rahilly, C. (ed.). 1962. Cath Finntrágha. Dublin: Institute for Advanced Study.
O'Rahilly, T.F. 1946. Early Irish History and Mythology. Dublin: Institute for Advanced Study.
Osthoff, Hermann. 1878. Das Verbum in der Nominalkomposition. Jena.
Otten, Heinrich. 1958. Hethitische Totenrituale. Deutsche Akademie der Wissenschaften zu Berlin. Institut für Orientforschung 37. Berlin: Akademie-

Verlag.
——. 1963. Eine ätiologische Erzählung von der Überquerung des Taurus. Zeitschrift für Assyriologie 55.156-73.
——. 1988. Die Bronzetafel aus Boğazköy. Studien zu den Boğazköy-Texten Beiheft 1. Wiesbaden: Harrassowitz.
—— and V. Souček. 1969. Ein althethitisches Ritual für das Königspaar. Studien zu den Boğazköy-Texten 8. Wiesbaden: Harrassowitz.
van Otterlo, W.A.A. 1944. Untersuchung über Begriff, Anwendung und Entstehung der griechischen Ringkomposition. Mededelingen der Koninklijke Nederlandsche Akademie van Wetenschappen, Afd. Letterkunde, N.R. 7:3.
——. 1948. De Ringcompositie als Opbouwprincipe in de epische Gedichten van Homerus. Verhandelingen der Koninklijke Nederlandsche Akademie van Wetenschappen, Afdeeling Letterkunde, N.R. 51:1.
Özgüç, Tahsin. 1988. İnandıktepe. Ankara: Türk Tarih Kuruma Basımevi.
Page, Denis L. 1959. History and the Homeric Iliad. Berkeley: University of California Press.
——. 1962. Poetae Melici Graeci. Oxford: Oxford University Press.
——. 1972. Supplementum Lyricis Graecis. Oxford: Oxford University Press.
——. 1973. Stesichorus: The *Geryoneïs*. Journal of Hellenic Studies 93.138-154.
Pagliaro, Antonino. 1961. Ἱερός in Omero e la nozione di 'sacro' in Grecia. Saggi di critica semantica, 110-40. Messina/Firenze: d'Anna. [Reprint of the 1953 edition.]
Pallottino, Massimo. 1991. A History of the Earliest Italy. Translated by M. Ryle and K. Sopin. Ann Arbor: University of Michigan Press.
Parry, Adam. 1971. The Making of Homeric Verse. Oxford: Clarendon Press.
Parry, Milman. 1928a. Les formules et la métrique d'Homère. Paris: Belles Lettres.
——. 1928b. L'epithète traditionelle dans Homère. Paris: Belles Lettres.
——. 1930. Studies in the epic technique of oral verse-making. I. Homer and Homeric style. Harvard Studies in Classical Philology 41.73-147. [Reprinted in Adam Parry 1971.]
Parsons, Peter. 1977. The Lille 'Stesichorus'. Zeitschrift für Papyrologie und Epigraphik 26.7-36.
Pasquali, Giorgio. 1936. Preistoria della poesia romana. Firenze: Sansoni.
Pavese, Carlo O. 1966. XPHMATA, XPHMAT' ANHP ed il motivo della literalità nella seconda Istmica di Pindaro. Quaderni Urbinati di Cultura Classica 2.103-42.
——. 1968. Semantematica della poesia corale greca. Belfagor 22.389-430.
Pelliccia, Hayden. 1985. 'Hymnal' tenses, the gnomic aorist, and the Proto-Greek injunctive. Yale University dissertation.
Peters, Martin. 1980. Untersuchungen zur Vertretung der indogermanischen Laryngale im Griechischen. Vienna: Verlag der Österreichischen Akademie der Wissenschaften.
——. 1986. Zur Frage einer 'achäischen' Phase des griechischen Epos. o-o-pe-ro-si. Festschrift E. Risch, 303-19. Berlin: de Gruyter.
——. 1989. Sprachliche Studien zum Frühgriechischen. Habilitationsschrift, Vienna.
Petersen, Roger Tory and Margaret McKenny. 1968. A Field Guide to Wildflowers.

Boston: Houghton Mifflin.
——et al. 1983. A Field Guide to the Birds of Britain and Europe. London: Collins.
Pfeiffer, Rudolf. 1959. Vom Schlaf der Erde und der Tiere. Hermes 87.1-6.
Pickard-Cambridge, A.W. and T.B.L. Webster. 1962. Dithyramb, Tragedy and Comedy. 2nd edition. Oxford: Clarendon Press.
Pighi, Giovanni B. 1965. De Ludis Saecularibus Populi Romani Quiritium. Amsterdam: Schippers. [Reprint of the 1941 edition.]
Pisani, Vittore. 1964. Le lingue dell'Italia antica oltre il Latino. 2nd edition. Torino: Rosenberg and Seller.
Poccetti, Paolo. 1979. Nuovi documenti italici a complemento del Manuale di E. Vetter. Pisa: Giardini.
Porzig, Walter. 1930. Illuyankas und Typhoeus. Kleinasiatische Forschungen 1.379-86.
Pott, August Friedrich. 1857. Etymologische spähne. Zeitschrift für Vergleichende Sprachforschung 6.95-142.
Poultney, James W. 1959. The Bronze Tables of Iguvium. American Philological Association Monograph 18.
Pritchard, James B. 1955. Ancient Near Eastern Texts relating to the Old Testament. Princeton: University Press.
Puech, Aimé. 1958-62. Pindare (Budé). 4th ed. Paris: Belles Lettres.
Puhvel, Jaan. 1970. Mythological reflections of Indo-European medicine. Indo-European and Indo-Europeans, ed. by G. Cardona, H. Hoenigswald, and A. Senn, 369-82. Philadelphia: University of Pennsylvania Press.
——. 1987. Comparative Mythology. Baltimore: Johns Hopkins University Press.
——. 1991. Homer and Hittite. Innsbruck: Innsbrucker Beiträge zur Sprachwissenschaft, Vorträge 47.
Race, William H. 1982. The Classical Priamel from Homer to Boethius. Leiden: Brill.
——. 1987. Pindaric encomium and Isokrates' Evagoras. Transactions of the American Philological Association 117.131-55.
Radke, Gerhard. 1965. Die Götter Altitaliens. Münster: Aschendorf.
Reichelt, Hans. 1967. Awestisches Elementarbuch. Darmstadt: Wissenschaftliche Buchgesellschaft. [Reprint of the 1904 edition.]
——. 1968. Avesta Reader. Berlin: de Gruyter. [Reprint of the 1911 edition.]
Renou, Louis. 1952. Grammaire de la langue védique. Lyon: IAC.
Risch, Ernst. 1979. Zur altlateinischen Gebetssprache. Incontri Linguistici 5.43-53.
——. 1987. Die älteste Zeugnisse für κλέος ἄφθιτον. Zeitschrift für Vergleichende Sprachforschung 100.3-11.
Rix, Helmut. 1990. Review of Studies in Memory of Warren Cowgill (1929-1985), ed. by C. Watkins. Kratylos 35.41-8.
Ruijgh, C.J. 1967. Etudes sur la grammaire et le vocabulaire du grec mycénien. Amsterdam: Hakkert.
——. 1985. Problèmes de philologie mycénienne. Minos, n.s. 19.105-67.
Russell, James R. 1986-87. Some Iranian images of kingship in the Armenian Artaxiad Epic. Revue des Etudes Arméniennes 20.253-70.
——. 1987. Zoroastrianism in Armenia. Harvard Iranian Series 5. Cambridge:

Harvard University Press.

——. 1991. Dragons in Armenia: Some Observations. Journal of Armenian Studies 5.3-12.

——. 1993. A Zoroastrian *mantra*. Lecture, Hebrew University, Jerusalem, 25 January 1993.

Rutherford, Ian. 1991. Neoptolemus and the paean-cry: an echo of a sacred aetiology in Pindar. Zeitschrift für Papyrologie und Epigraphik 88.1-10.

——. Forthcoming. Pindar's Paeanes. Oxford: Oxford University Press.

Sanjana, D.P. 1896. The Kârnâmê î Artakhshîr î Pâpakân. Bombay: Education Society.

Santucci, James A. 1976. An outline of Vedic Literature. Missoula, Montana: Society for Biblical Literature.

Sasunc'i Davit'. [1961] Hayakan Žołovrdakan Epos. Erevan: Haypethrat.

de Saussure, Ferdinand. 1878. Mémoire sur le système primitif des voyelles en indo-européen. Recueil des publications scientifiques de F. de Saussure. Geneva: Droz.

Schibli, Hermann S. 1990. Pherekydes of Syros. Oxford: Clarendon Press.

Schleicher, August. 1852. Die Formenlehre der kirchenslawischen Sprache, erklärend und vergleichend dargestellt. Bonn.

Schlerath, Bernfried. 1962. Zu den Merseburger Zaubersprüchen. II. Fachtagung für Indogermanische und Allgemeine Sprachwissenschaft (Innsbrucker Beiträge zur Kulturgeschichte Sonderheft 15), 139-49. Innsbruck.

——. 1968. Awesta-Wörterbuch. Vorarbeiten II. Wiesbaden: Harrassowitz.

——. 1974. Gedanke, Wort und Werk im Veda und im Awesta. Antiquitates Indogermanicae. Gedenkschrift Hermann Güntert, 201-22. Innsbruck: Innsbrucker Beiträge zur Sprachwissenschaft.

——. 1992. [Response.] Proceedings of the XXXII International Congress for Asian and North African Studies (Zeitschrift der Deutschen Morgenländischen Gesellschaft Supplement 9), ed. by A. Wetzler and E. Hammerschmidt, 391-3.

Schmidt, Hanns-Peter. 1958. Vedisch *vratá* und awestisch *urvaϑa*. Hamburg: Cram, de Gruyter und Co.

——. 1964. Die Kobra im Ṛgveda. Zeitschrift für Vergleichende Sprachforschung 78.296-304.

Schmidt, Karl Horst. 1985. Die indogermanischen Grundlagen des altarmenischen Verbums. Zeitschrift für Vergleichende Sprachforschung 98.214-37.

Schmitt, Rüdiger. 1961. Nektar. Zeitschrift für Vergleichende Sprachforschung 77.88.

——. 1967. Dichtung und Dichtersprache in indogermanischer Zeit. Wiesbaden: Harrassowitz.

—— (ed.). 1968. Indogermanische Dichtersprache. Wege der Forschung 165. Darmstadt: Wissenschaftliche Buchgesellschaft.

——. 1973. Indogermanische Dichtersprache und Namengebung. Innsbruck: Innsbrucker Beiträge zur Sprachwissenschaft.

Schönfeld, Moritz. 1911. Wörterbuch der altgermanischen Personen- und Völkernamen. Heidelberg: Winter. [Reprinted Darmstadt 1965.]

Schramm, G. 1957. Namenschatz und Dichtersprache. Studien zu den zweigliedrigen Personennamen der Germanen. Zeitschrift für Vergleichende Sprachforschung Ergänzungsheft 15. Göttingen: Vandenhoeck & Ruprecht.

Schröder, F.R. 1927. Ein altirischer Krönungsritus und das idg. Rossopfer. Zeitschrift für Celtische Philologie 16.10-12.

von Schroeder, L. 1881-86. Mâitrâyaṇî-saṃhitâ. [Reprinted Wiesbaden 1972.]

—. 1900-10. Kāṭhaka: Die Saṃhitā der Kāṭhaka-Śākhā. Leipzig: Brockhaus. [Reprinted Wiesbaden 1970-72.]

von Schuler, Einar. 1957. Hethitische Dienstanweisungen für höhere Hof- und Staatsbeamte. Graz (Selbstverlag des Herausgebers).

Schulze, Wilhelm. 1933. Kleine Schriften. Göttingen: Vandenhoeck & Ruprecht. [2nd edition 1966.]

Schürch, Peter. 1971. Zur Wortresponsion bei Pindar. Europäische Hochschulschriften, Series 15, Vol. 2. Bern and Frankfurt: H. Lang and Cie.

Schwartz, Martin. 1986. Coded sound patterns, acrostichs, and anagrams in Zoroaster's oral poetry. Studia Grammatica Iranica. Festschrift H. Humbach, ed. by R. Schmitt and P.O. Skjærvø. München: Kitzinger.

—. 1990. Hospitalities and formalities (√*WAZ*, √*BRAZ*). Iranica Varia: Papers in honor of Profesor E. Yarshater (Acta Iranica, 30). Leiden: Brill.

Schwyzer, Eduardus. 1960. Dialectarum graecarum exempla epigraphica potiora. Hildesheim: Olms. [Reprint of the 1923 edition.]

—, [Eduard]. 1968. Griechische Grammatik. München: Beck.

Seaford, Richard. 1984. Euripides, Cyclops. Oxford: Clarendon Press.

Seebold, Elmar. 1967. Die Vertretung idg. *$g^{u}h$ im Germanischen. Zeitschrift für Vergleichende Sprachforschung 81.104-33.

—. 1980. Etymologie und Lautgeschichte. Lautgeschichte und Etymologie, ed. by M. Mayrhofer, M. Peters, and O.E. Pfeiffer, 435-84. Wiesbaden: Reichert.

Segal, Charles. 1990. Dionysus and the Gold Tablets from Pelinna. Greek, Roman and Byzantine Studies 31.411-19.

Siebert, Frank T. 1967. The original home of the Proto-Algonquian people. Contributions to Anthropology: Linguistics I (National Museum of Canada, Bulletin 214). Ottawa: Department of the Secretary of State.

Siecke, Ernst. 1907. Drachenkämpfe. Untersuchungen zur indogermanischen Sagenkunde. Leipzig.

Silverstein, Michael. 1979. Parallelism in ritual speech. Parasession, Chicago Linguistic Society.

de Simone, Carlo. 1988. Gli imprestiti etruschi nel latino arcaico. In Campanile 1988:27-42.

Singer, Charles. 1920. Early English Magic and Medicine. Proceedings of the British Academy 9. London: Oxford University Press.

Solmsen, Friedrich. 1949. Hesiod and Aeschylus. Ithaca: Cornell University Press.

Sommer, Ferdinand. 1922. Hethitisches 2. Boghazköi-Studien 7.

— and Adam Falkenstein. 1938. Die hethitisch-akkadische Bilingue des Ḫattušili I (Labarna II). Abhandlungen der Bayerischen Akademie der Wissenschaften, Phil.-hist. Abt., N.F. 16.

Soysal, Oğuz. 1987. Puḫanu's tale. Hethitica 7.173-253.

——. 1989. Der Apfel möge die Zähne nehmen! Orientalia 58.171-92.

Starke, Frank. 1980. Appendix. Keilschrift-luwisch *manā-*[tti] 'sehen', *mammanna-*[i] 'schauen'. Kadmos 19.143-48.

——. 1985. Die Keilschrift-luwischen Texte in Umschrift. Studien zu den Boğazköy-Texten 30. Wiesbaden: Harrassowitz.

——. 1990. Untersuchung zur Stammbildung des keilschrift-luwischen Nomens. Studien zu den Boğazköy-Texten 31. Wiesbaden: Harrassowitz.

Starobinsky, Jean. 1971. Les mots sous les mots. Les anagrammes de Ferdinand de Saussure. Paris: Gallimard.

Stevens, P.T. 1971. Euripides, Andromache. Oxford: Oxford University Press.

Stolz, Benjamin A. and Richard S. Shannon (eds.) 1976. Oral Literature and the Formula. Ann Arbor: University of Michigan Press.

Ström, A.V. 1967. Indogermanisches in der Völuspa. Numen 14.186-87.

Szemerényi, Oswald. 1987. Scripta Minora. Innsbruck: Innsbrucker Beiträge zur Sprachwissenschaft.

Taylor, Lily Ross. 1934. New light on the history of the secular games. American Journal of Philology 55.101-20.

——. 1970. Secular Games. The Oxford Classical Dictionary, ed. by N.G.L. Hammond and H.H. Scullard, 969-70. Oxford: Clarendon.

Thieme, Paul. 1929. Das Plusquamperfectum im Veda. Göttingen: Vandenhoeck & Ruprecht.

——. 1952. Studien zur indogermanischen Wortkunde und Religionsgeschichte. Berichte über die Verhandlungen der Sächsischen Akademie der Wissenschaften zu Leipzig. Phil.-hist. Kl. 98:5. Berlin: Akademie-Verlag.

——. 1953. Die Heimat der indogermanischen Gemeinsprache. Akademie der Wissenschaften und der Literatur. Abhandlungen der Geistes- und sozialwissenschaftlichen Klasse, Nr. 11. Mainz/Wiesbaden.

——. 1965. Īśopaniṣad (=Vājasaneyi-Saṁhitā 40) 1-14. Journal of the American Oriental Society 85.96.

——. 1972. "Sprachmalerei". Zeitschrift für Vergleichende Sprachforschung 86.64-81.

——. 1975. The concept of Mitra in Aryan belief. Mithraic Studies, ed. by I.R. Hinnells, 21-39. Manchester: Manchester University Press.

——. 1984. Kleine Schriften. Wiesbaden: Steiner.

Thomson, Robert W. 1981. Moses Khorenats'i. History of the Armenians. Delmar, New York: Caravan.

Thuilier, J.P. 1985. Les jeux athlétiques dans la civilisation étrusque. Rome: Ecole Française de Rome.

Thurneysen, Rudolf. 1891. Mittelirishe Verslehren. Irische Texte 3.1-182.

——. 1919. Grammatisches und Etymologisches. 6. Ir. *marbu* 'ich töte'. Zeitschrift für Celtische Philologie 13.106.

——. 1921. Die irischen Helden- und Königssagen bis zum 17. Jahrhundert. Halle: Niemeyer.

——. 1932. Colmán mac Lénéni und Senchán Torpéisc. Zeitschrift für Celtische

Philologie 19.193-209.
——. 1946. A Grammar of Old Irish. Translated by D.A. Binchy and Osborn Bergin. Dublin: Institute for Advanced Study.
—— et al. 1936. Studies in Early Irish Law. Dublin: Institute for Advanced Study.
Tichy, Eva. 1980. Zum Kasusgebrauch bei Kausativa transitiver Verben. Die Sprache 26.1-18.
——. 1981. Hom. ἀνδροτῆτα und die Vorgeschichte des daktylischen Hexameters. Glotta 59.28-67.
Tolkien, J.R.R. 1938. Beowulf: The Monsters and the Critics. Proceedings of the British Academy (1936), 245-95.
Toporov, Vladimir Nikolaevič. 1974. ΠΥΘΩΝ, Ahi Budhnya, Badnjak i dr. Ètimologija 1974. Moskva: Nauka.
——. 1975-. Prusskij Jazyk. Slovar' 1-5. Moskva: Nauka.
——. 1981. Die Ursprünge der indoeuropäischen Poetik. Poetica 13.189-251.
Tsantsanoglou, K. and G.M. Parássoglou. Two gold lamellae from Thessaly. Hellenica 38.3-16.
Vendryes, Joseph. 1959. Lexique étymologique de l'irlandais ancien. A. Dublin/ Paris: Institute for Advanced Study/CNRS.
Vermeule, Emily T. 1979. Aspects of Death in early Greek art and poetry. Berkeley: University of California Press.
Vernant, Jean-Pierre and Pierre Vidal-Naquet. 1988. Myth and tragedy in Ancient Greece. Translated by Janet Lloyd. New York: Zone.
Vetter, Emil. 1953. Handbuch der italischen Dialekte. Heidelberg: Winter.
——. 1957. Zum sechsten Buch Varros *De lingua Latina*. Vjesnik za Arheologiju i Historiju Dalmatinsku (Mélanges Abramić), 56-59. 76-80.
——. 1958. Zum Text von Varros Schrift über die lateinische Sprache. Rheinisches Museum 101.257-85, 289-323.
Vian, Francis. 1960. Le mythe de Typhée et le problème de ses origines orientales. Eléments orientaux dans la religion grecque ancienne, 17-37. Paris: Presses Universitaires de France.
Vine, Brent. 1988. Greek ἕπω and Indo-European **sep-*. Indogermanische Forschungen 93.52-61.
Visser, Edzard. 1988. Formulae or single words? Würzburger Jahrbuch für die Altertumswissenschaft N.F. 14.21-37.
Wackernagel, Jakob. 1953. Kleine Schriften. Göttingen: Vandenhoeck & Ruprecht.
Wagenvoort, Henryk. 1956. Studies in Roman literature, culture, and religion. Leiden: Brill.
Walcot, Peter. 1966. Hesiod and the Near East. Cardiff: University of Wales Press.
Wathelet, Paul. 1970. Les traits éoliens dans la langue de l'épopée grecque. Roma: Ateneo.
Watkins, Calvert. 1961. Indo-European origins of a Celtic metre. Poetics/Poetyka/ Poetika 1.99-117.
——. 1963a. Preliminaries to a historical and comparative analysis of the syntax of the Old Irish verb. Celtica 6.1-49. [Reprinted in Watkins 1994:3-51.]
——. 1963b. Indo-European Metrics and Archaic Irish Verse. Celtica 6.194-249.

[Reprinted in Watkins 1994:349-404.]

——. 1967. Latin *sōns*. Studies in honor of G.S. Lane, 186-94. Chapel Hill: University of North Carolina Press. [Reprinted in Watkins 1994:405-13.]

——. 1969a. Indogermanische Grammatik III/1: Formenlehre. Heidelberg: Winter.

——. 1969b. A Latin-Hittite Etymology. Language 45.235-42. [Reprinted in Watkins 1994:414-21.]

——. 1970a. Language of gods and language of men: remarks on some Indo-European meta-linguistic traditions. Myth and Law among the Indo-Europeans, ed. by J. Puhvel, 1-17. Berkeley: University of California Press. [Reprinted in Watkins 1994:456-72.]

——. 1970b. Studies in Indo-European legal language, institutions, and mythology. Indo-European and Indo-Europeans, ed. by G. Cardona et al., 321-54. Philadelphia: University of Pennsylvania Press. [Reprinted in Watkins 1994:422-55.]

——. 1973. An Indo-European agricultural term: Lat. *ador,* Hitt. *ḫat-*. Harvard Studies in Classical Philology 77.187-93. [Reprinted in Watkins 1994:473-79.]

——. 1975a. Latin *iouiste* et le vocabulaire religieux indo-européen. Mélanges Emile Benveniste, de. by M. Dj. Moïnfar, 527-34. Paris: Société de Linguistique. [Reprinted in Watkins 1994:505-12.]

——. 1975b. Some Indo-European verb phrases and their transformations. Münchener Studien zur Sprachwissenschaft 33.89-109. [Reprinted in Watkins 1994:189-209.]

——. 1975c. Latin *ador,* Hittite *ḫat-* again: addenda to Harvard Studies in Classical Philology 77, 1973. 187-193. Harvard Studies in Classical Philology 79.181-87. [Reprinted in Watkins 1994:480-86.]

——. 1975d. La désignation indo-européenne du 'tabou'. Langues, discours, société. Pour E. Benveniste, ed. by J.C. Millner et al., 208-14. Paris: Editions du Seuil. [Reprinted in Watkins 1994:513-19.]

——. 1975e. La famille indo-européenne de grec ὄρχις: linguistique, poétique et mythologie. Bulletin de la Société Linguistique 70.11-26. [Reprinted in Watkins 1994:520-35.]

——. 1976a. Observations on the "Nestor's Cup" inscription. Harvard Studies in Classical Philology 80.25-40. [Reprinted in Watkins 1994:544-59.]

——. 1976b. The etymology of Irish *dúan*. Celtica 11.270-77. [Reprinted in Watkins 1994:536-43.]

——. 1976c. Towards Proto-Indo-European syntax: problems and pseudo-problems. Papers from the Parassession on Diachronic Syntax, 305-26. Chicago: Linguistic Society. [Reprinted in Watkins 1994:242-63.]

——. 1976d. Syntax and metrics in the Dipylon vase inscription. Studies in Greek, Italic, and Indo-European Linguistics, offered to Leonard R. Palmer on the occasion of his 70th birthday, ed. by A. Morpurgo Davies and W. Meid, 431-41. Innsbruck: Innsbrucker Beiträge zur Sprachwissenschaft. [Reprinted in Watkins 1994:231-41.]

——. 1977. A propos de μῆνις. Bulletin de la Société de Linguistique 72.187-209. [Reprinted in Watkins 1994:565-87.]

——. 1978a. ἀνόστεος ὃν πόδα τένδει. Etrennes de septantaine offertes à M. Lejeune.

Paris: Klincksieck. [Reprinted in Watkins 1994:588-92.]

—. 1978b. "Let us now praise famous grains". Proceedings of the American Philosophical Society 122.9-17. [Reprinted in Watkins 1994:593-601.]

—. 1978c. On confession in Slavic and Indo-European. Studies in Honor of Horace G. Lunt, ed. by E. Scatton et al. (Folia Slavica, 2), 340-59. [Reprinted in Watkins 1994:602-21.]

—. 1978d. A Palaic carmen. Linguistic and literary studies in honor of Archibald A. Hill, 3.305-14. The Hague: Mouton.

—. 1979a. NAM.RA GUD UDU in Hittite: Indo-European poetic language and the folk taxonomy of wealth. Hethitisch und Indogermanisch, ed. by E. Neu and W. Meid, 269-87. Innsbruck: Innsbrucker Beiträge zur Sprachwissenschaft. [Reprinted in Watkins 1994:644-62.]

—. 1979b. *Is tre ḟír flathemon*: Marginalia to *Audacht Morainn*. Ériu 30.181-98. [Reprinted in Watkins 1994:626-43.]

—. 1981. Language, Culture, or History? Papers from the Parasession on Language and Behavior, Chicago Linguistic Society, 238-48. [Reprinted in Watkins 1994:663-73.]

—. 1982. Aspects of Indo-European poetics. The Indo-Europeans in the Fourth and Third Millennia, ed. by E. Polome (Linguistica Extraneana, Studia 14), 104-20. Ann Arbor: Karoma. [Reprinted in Watkins 1994:674-90.]

—. 1983. 'Blind' in Celtic and Romance. Ériu 34.113-16. [Reprinted in Watkins 1994:691-94.]

—. 1985a. Indo-European $*k^{u}e$ 'and' in Hittite. Sprachwissenschaftliche Forschungen. Festschrift für J. Knobloch, ed. by H.M. Ölberg and G. Schmidt, 491-97. Innsbruck: Innsbrucker Beiträge zur Kulturwissenschaft. [Reprinted in Watkins 1994:300-6.]

—. 1985b. The American Heritage Dictionary of Indo-European Roots. Revised ed. Boston: Houghton Mifflin.

—. 1986a. The Language of the Trojans. Troy and the Trojan War, ed. by Machteld J. Mellink, 45-62. Bryn Mawr: Bryn Mawr University Press. [Reprinted in Watkins 1994:700-17.]

—. 1986b. The Name of Meleager. o-o-pe-ro-si: Festschrift für Ernst Risch zum 75. Geburtstag, ed. by A. Etter, 320-28. Berlin: de Gruyter.

—. 1986c [1988]. The Indo-European background of a Luvian ritual. Die Sprache 32:324-33.

—. 1987a. 'In the interstices of procedure': Indo-European legal language and comparative law. Studien zum Indogermanischen Wortschatz, ed. by W. Meid, 305-14. Innsbruck: Innsbrucker Beiträge zur Sprachwissenschaft. [Reprinted in Watkins 1994:718-27.]

—. 1987b. Linguistic and archeological light on some Homeric formulas. Studies in Honor of Marija Gimbutas, ed. by S. Skomal and E.C. Polomé, 286-98. Washington: Journal of Indo-European Studies Monograph Series. [Reprinted in Watkins 1994:728-40.]

—. 1987c. How to kill a dragon in Indo-European. Studies in memory of Warren Cowgill (1929-1985), ed. by C. Watkins, 270-99. Berlin: de Gruyter.

——. 1987d. Two Anatolian forms: Palaic *aškummāuwa*, Cuneiform Luvian *wa-a-ar-ša*. Festschrift for Henry Hoenigswald on the Occasion of his 70th Birthday, ed. by G. Cardona and N. Zide, 399-404. Tübingen: Narr. [Reprinted in Watkins 1994:309-14.]

——. 1987e. Questions linguistiques palaïtes et louvites cunéiformes. Hethitica 8.423-26.

——. 1989. New parameters in historical linguistics, philology, and culture history. Language 65.783-99. [Reprinted in Watkins 1994:315-31.]

——. 1990. Some Celtic phrasal echoes. Celtic Language, Celtic Culture. Festschrift for Eric P. Hamp, ed. by A. Matonis and D. Melia, 47-56. Van Nuys: Ford and Bailie. [Reprinted in Watkins 1994:741-50.]

——. 1991. A Celtic-Latin-Hittite etymology. Lingering over Words: Studies in Ancient Near Eastern Literature in honor of William L. Moran, ed. by Tz. Abusch, J. Huehnergard, and P. Steinkeller (Harvard Semitic Studies 37), 451-53. Atlanta: Scholars Press. [Reprinted in Watkins 1994:751-53.]

——. 1992a. Culture history and historical linguistics. Oxford International Encyclopedia of Linguistics, ed. by William Bright, 1.318-22. Oxford/New York: Oxford University Press.

——. 1992b. Stylistic reconstruction. Oxford International Encyclopedia of Linguistics, ed. by William Bright, 4.86-89. New York: Oxford University Press.

——. 1993. Another thorny problem. Linguistica XXXIII. Bojan Čop septuagenario in honorem oblata. Ljubljana.

——. 1994. Selected Writings. Innsbrucker Beiträge zur Sprachwissenschaft 80. Innsbruck.

Weber, A. 1852. The Vâjasaneyi-sanhitâ in the Mâdhyandina- and the Kâṇva-çâkhâ with the commentary of Mahîdhara. Berlin: Drümmler. [Reprinted Chowkhamba 1972.]

——. 1855. The Çatapathabrâhmaṇa in the Mâdhyandina-çâkhâ with extracts from the commentaries of Sâyaṇa, Harisvâmin, and Dvivedaganga. Berlin: Drümmler. [Reprinted Chowkhamba 1964.]

——. 1871-72. Indische Studien 11-12. Leipzig: Brockhaus.

Weiss, Michael. 1993. Studies in Italic nominal morphology. Cornell University dissertation.

——. 1994. Erotica: On the prehistory of Greek desire. Paper presented to the 13th East Coast Indo-European Conference, University of Texas, Austin.

West, Martin. 1966. Hesiod, Theogony. Oxford: Clarendon Press.

——. 1973. Greek poetry 2000-700 B.C. Glotta 51.161-87.

——. 1978. Hesiod, Works and Days. Oxford: Clarendon Press.

——. 1982. Greek Metre. Oxford: Clarendon Press.

——. 1988a. The rise of the Greek epic. Journal of Hellenic Studies 108.151-72.

——. 1988b. Hesiod. Theogony and Works and Days. Oxford: Oxford University Press.

Westphal, Rudolf. 1860. Zur vergleichenden metrik der indogermanischen völker. Zeitschrift für Vergleichende Sprachforschung 9.437-58.

Whitney, William Dwight. 1905. Atharva-veda Saṁhitā. Revised and edited by C.

R. Lanman. (Harvard Oriental Series 7-8.) Cambridge: Harvard University Press.

Winnington-Ingram, R.P. 1985. The origins of tragedy. The Cambridge History of Classical Literature, vol. 1: Greek Literature, ed. by P.E. Easterling and B. Knox, 258-63. Cambridge: Cambridge University Press.

Woodbury, Leonard. 1968. Pindar and the mercenary Muse: *Isthmian* 2.1-13. Transactions of the American Philological Association 99.527-42.

Wünsch, R. 1916. Hymnos. Pauly-Wissowa, Real-Encyclopädie 17.141-83.

Zuntz, Günther. 1971. Persephone. Oxford: Oxford University Press.

Zysk, Kenneth G. 1985. Religious Healing in the Veda. Transactions of the American Philosophical Society 75, part 7.

——. 1992. Reflections on an Indo-European Healing Tradition. Studies in Honor of Edgar C. Polomé (Journal of Indo-European Studies Monograph 9), 2.321-36.

Index of names and subjects

Index of passages

Index of words

Indo-Iranian

Sanskrit (unless otherwise specified)

Germanic